MW00777674

Bill Hefley and Wendy Murphy (Eds.)

Service Science: Research and Innovations
in the Service Economy

For other titles published in this series, go to
www.springer.com/series/8080

Paul P. Maglio · Cheryl A. Kieliszewski ·
James C. Spohrer
Editors

Handbook of Service Science

Foreword by
Carl J. Schramm and William J. Baumol

 Springer

Editors

Dr. Paul P. Maglio
IBM Research – Almaden
650 Harry Road
San Jose CA 95120-6099
pmaglio@us.ibm.com

Dr. Cheryl A. Kieliszewski
IBM Research – Almaden
650 Harry Road
San Jose CA 95120-6099
USA
cher@us.ibm.com

Dr. James C. Spohrer
IBM Research – Almaden
650 Harry Road
San Jose CA 95120-6099
USA
spohrer@us.ibm.com

Series Editors:

Bill Hefley
Katz Graduate School of Business &
College of Business Administration
University of Pittsburgh
Mervis Hall
Pittsburgh, PA 15260 USA
wehefley@katz.pitt.edu

Wendy Murphy
IBM c/o
1954 Rocky Cove Lane
Denton, NC 27239 USA
wendym@us.ibm.com

ISSN 1865-4924   e-ISSN 1865-4932
ISBN 978-1-4419-1627-3   e-ISBN 978-1-4419-1628-0
DOI 10.1007/978-1-4419-1628-0
Springer New York Dordrecht Heidelberg London

Library of Congress Control Number: 2010924288

© Springer Science+Business Media, LLC 2010
All rights reserved. This work may not be translated or copied in whole or in part without the written permission of the publisher (Springer Science+Business Media, LLC, 233 Spring Street, New York, NY 10013, USA), except for brief excerpts in connection with reviews or scholarly analysis. Use in connection with any form of information storage and retrieval, electronic adaptation, computer software, or by similar or dissimilar methodology now known or hereafter developed is forbidden.
The use in this publication of trade names, trademarks, service marks, and similar terms, even if they are not identified as such, is not to be taken as an expression of opinion as to whether or not they are subject to proprietary rights.

Printed on acid-free paper

Springer is part of Springer Science+Business Media (www.springer.com)

Table of Contents

Part 1: Context: Origins

Part 2: Context: Theory

Part 3: Research and Practice: Design

Part 4: Research and Practice: Operations

Part 5: Research and Practice: Delivery

Part 6: Research and Practice: Innovation

Part 7: Future

Foreword

Carl J. Schramm

Ewing Marion Kauffman Foundation

William J. Baumol

Berkley Center for Entrepreneurial Studies

New York University

The transformation of the American economy over the last twenty to thirty years has frequently been characterized as the rise of the service economy. In the conventional telling, the United States moved from being primarily an agricultural nation in the nineteenth century, to having an industrial and manufacturing economy through much of the twentieth century, to finally becoming a service economy at the outset of the twenty-first century. Services now account for approximately 80 percent of economic activity, while agriculture has fallen to roughly one or two percent, with manufacturing making up the remainder.

This narrative is alternately told in positive and negative light. Those with a sanguine outlook on the U.S. economy see this as an upward progression, moving more and more people off the farm and out of factories and into more fulfilling, Maslovian hierarchy-oriented jobs. Accordingly, we have finally reached the cusp of achieving the vision long ago laid down by John Maynard Keynes, in which everyone enjoys more fun, leisure, and altogether more pleasure (Keynes, 1930). More nostalgic and pessimistic observers interpret the transition to a service economy as social and economic degeneration, an empty world in which we do little more than perform menial tasks and services for each other. To strengthen our national character and chart a brighter future, we must once again become a manufacturing-based economy—making things, in this dour view, is the *sine qua non* of economic promise.

Neither of these narratives holds much truth. In the first case, it is inaccurate to suppose that there is some far-off utopia of leisure to which we are inexorably advancing. The benefits of economic growth, to be sure, are real and substantial, but they are different from what is often presumed (or expected) to be the case. So we expect that a service economy brings increasing amounts of leisure—yet it turns out that people actually like to work, and thus the division of hours between work and leisure changes little. Likewise, nostalgia for a manufacturing economy is badly misinformed. Work today is generally safer and in many cases more cognitively-demanding than in the industrial economy of fifty or one hundred years ago.

We are not, contrary to semi-popular belief, a nation of burger-flippers and store-front greeters. And, such conflation of manufacturing and economic health is often based on the American experience in the immediate postwar decades—a time of rapid economic expansion, of course, but also a period during which nearly half of the American population was excluded from mainstream economic participation. In any case, even when manufacturing represented its highest historical share of economic output, it was matched by services—manufacturing has never accounted for a greater share of the economy than services.

So what does a service economy mean? Economic models of growth have in recent years determined that knowledge, human capital (education and skills), and innovation now play a larger role in propelling the economy than they did in previous eras. Yet these elements have always been important to economic growth to one degree or another—what's different today is that the entire structure of the U.S. and world economies is changing. As one of us has written, "Ahistoric models that do not distinguish one type of economic system from another are, to say the least, handicapped" (Baumol, 2002).

Whereas the United States could once be characterized as a system of "bureaucratic capitalism," we now stand firmly within an era of "entrepreneurial capitalism" (Baumol, Litan, & Schramm, 2007). As the name implies, the founding and growth of new firms, entrepreneurship, has become immensely more important to our society and economy than it once was. This transformation, moreover, is intimately bound up with the rising share of services in the economy and, more importantly, the changing character of services. And it is this change that the emerging discipline of service science seeks to study and facilitate. We live not only in a world of services but also in a world of ever-expanding possibilities and networks of activities. Indeed, networks and entrepreneurship are perhaps the twin hallmarks of this new and highly innovative service economy.

It is no longer accurate to think of our economy as solely defined by services—the array of innovations and business types is so vast as to defy any attempt at general categorization. As Jim Spohrer, the founding Director of IBM's Service Research efforts which began at the Almaden Research Center and who is one of the godfathers of service science, points out, our economy and society today are dominated by complex networks of service systems—overlapping systems that ceaselessly interact and create value. If we persist in thinking in terms of a manufacturing and services dichotomy and of which one we should have more or less, we will miss the changing nature of the economy and the urgent need for greater understanding of these *service system networks*. The increasing complexity and interactive capability of these networks mean we need to explore the expansive possibilities for service innovation and integration across different types of service systems. Failure to understand can have deleterious consequences.

Take the current recession and the global financial crisis that helped precipitate it: a common theme in the autopsy literature is that the global financial system suffered from a number of vulnerabilities that could have been prevented and, in some cases, were anticipated. A deeper understanding of the nature of service system networks may not have helped forestall the crisis, but could have lessened the impact. As it is, the financial crisis will likely act as a spur to the field of service science.

Service science is, therefore, clearly of the utmost importance for critical, short-run phenomena, such as economic fluctuations. But it is also of comparable importance for the long-run performance of the economy. Indeed, the process of innovation is itself a service, with invention obviously serving as a critical input to production processes. Inventions are created by humans—not by machines and, therefore, clearly qualify as a service. Moreover, the entrepreneurial activity that ensures the effective utilization of innovations is also a service. Without these inventions, our societies would still be condemned to yield no more than the primitive living standards of the seventeenth century and earlier.

This book, and the illumination it casts on the role of service system networks in the economy, is badly needed. Discussions of the economy's production processes in economics textbooks still tend to focus on manufacturing and agriculture. But there is every reason to believe that analysis of the workings of the service sector offers an indispensable key to understanding the economic issues of today. This sector is of the utmost importance for the future of the economy and the well-being of society.

This Handbook, then, comes at a time when the insights it offers are of constantly growing significance for both the short- and long-run health of the global economy—the continuing recession deserves a full exploration, and may in fact serve as a hinge point in the continuing transformation of economic activity. We welcome the continuing efforts of Jim, Paul, Cheryl, and service scientists everywhere as they work at the highest pursuit of scientific enterprise: understanding.

References

Baumol, W. J. (2002). Services as leaders and the leader of the services. In Jean Gadrey &Faiz Gallouj (eds.), *Productivity, Innovation and Knowledge in Services*. Edward Elgar.

Baumol, W. J., Litan, R. & Schramm, C. J. (2007). *Good Capitalism, Bad Capitalism and the Economics of Growth and Prosperity*. Yale University Press.

Keynes, J. M. (1930/1963). Economic Possibilities for our Grandchildren. In J. M. Keynes, *Essays in Persuasion*, pp. 358-373. Norton.

Preface

We are students of service. Our education began just a few years ago, after IBM acquired Price Waterhouse Coopers Consulting and IBM Research focused squarely on IBM's service businesses for the first time (Horn, 2005). As it turned out, we had a lot to learn. And we still do. This volume represents only the most recent leg on our educational journey. It will not be the last.

Service Science, also known as *Service Science, Management, Engineering, and Design (SSMED)*, aims to be a new, interdisciplinary approach to study, improve, create, and innovate in service (Spohrer & Maglio, 2008, 2010). Though various approaches to service go back a long time (see for instance, Delaunay & Gadrey, 1992; Fisk, Brown, & Bitner, 1993; Smith, Karwan & Markland, 2007), Service Science is relatively new (Chesbrough, 2005). But already, a number of journal special issues and edited volumes collecting papers on it have already begun to appear (e.g., Hefley & Murphy, 2008; Spohrer & Riecken, 2006). In fact, when we first conceived of this volume, our idea was to take some articles from a special issue of the *IBM Systems Journal* that we had guest edited (Maglio, Spohrer , Seidman, & Ritsko, 2008), reprint some classic papers (to name just two, Shostack, 1977; Heskett, Jones, Loveman, Sasser, & Schlesinger, 1994), and invite a few new contributions to create a volume that marked a moment in the development of Service Science. Our publisher, Springer, liked the idea that we wanted to create an edited volume on Service Science, but they envisioned something more comprehensive. In the end, they convinced us to put together a *Handbook of Service Science* containing all original contributions in a much larger volume that would definitively mark the history, practice, and possibilities of Service Science. Well, we certainly have a much larger volume than we originally set out to produce – whether it is definitive remains to be seen.

Our approach to putting together the *Handbook* was simple: Create a list of as many important papers and books in service that we could think of, select thirty or forty, and invite the authors to write an essay related to, updating, or going beyond their original work. Simple. Actually, it was pretty simple. And it worked. We are truly gratified that so many service pioneers and other distinguished scholars agreed to contribute, and we are truly thrilled with what has been produced. We hope you are too.

We thank everyone who helped and encouraged us to put this volume together, including Bill Hefley and Wendy Murphy, co-editors of the Service Science series at Springer, Melissa Fearon and Jennifer Maurer, our contacts at Springer, Josephine Cheng, Mark Dean, Jai Menon, and Robert Morris, our bosses at IBM, Carl Schramm and William Baumol, who wrote the foreword, and of course all the contributors, whose extraordinary work we are lucky enough to showcase here.

PPM, CAK, JCS
San Jose, California
September 1, 2009

References

Chesbrough, H. (2005). Toward a science of services. *Harvard Business Review, 83*, 16-17.

Delaunay, J. & Gadrey, J. (1992). *Services in economic thought*. Boston: Kluwer.

Fisk, R. P., Brown, S. W., & Bitner, M. (1993). Tracking the evolution of the services marketing literature. *Journal of Retailing, 69*, 61 – 103.

Hefley, B. & Murphy, W. (2008). *Service Science, Management and Engineering: Education for the 21st Century*. Springer, New York.

Heskett, J. L., Jones, T. O., Loveman, G. W. , Sasser, W. E. J., & Schlesinger, L. A. (1994). Putting the Service-Profit Chain to Work. *Harvard Business Review, 72*(2), 164-174.

Horn, P. (2005). The new discipline of services science. *Business Week,* Jan 21, 2005.

Maglio, P. P., Spohrer, J., Seidman, D. I, & Ritsko, J. J. (2008). Special Issue on SSME. *IBM Systems Journal, 47.*

Shostack, G. L. (1977). Breaking free from product marketing. *Journal of Marketing, 41*, 73 – 80.

Smith, J. S., Karwan, K. R., & Markland, R. E. (2007). A note on the growth of research in service operations management. *Production and Operations Management,* 16(6), 780-790.

Spohrer, J. & Maglio, P. P. (2008). The emergence of service science: Toward systematic service innovations to accelerate co-creation of value. *Production and Operations Management, 17*(3), 1-9.

Spohrer, J. & Maglio, P. P. (2010). Service science: Toward a smarter planet. In W. Karwowski & G. Salvendy (Eds.), *Introduction to service engineering*. New York: Wiley & Sons.

Spohrer, J. & Riecken, D. (2006). Special Issue on Services Science, *Communications of the ACM,* 49(7).

Contributors

Melissa Archpru Akaka is a Doctoral Student in Marketing at the Shidler College of Business at the University of Hawaii at Manoa. Her research interests include value and value co-creation as well as cultural and international issues. Prior to her graduate and doctoral studies, Ms. Akaka worked in the travel industry and the not-for-profit sector. She has an M.B.A. and a B.B.A. in marketing, both from the University of Hawaii at Manoa.

John H. Bailey is a Senior User Experience Architect at CA, Inc., where he creates leading-edge user experiences for the management of information technology. Previously, John was a research scientist at the IBM Almaden Research Center where he did research on service systems, specializing in human factors in information technology service engagement and delivery. He has also been the Lead User Experience Architect for IBM WebSphere Application Server and a manager for user-centered design. Prior to working at IBM, John was a Research Fellow with The Consortium of Universities of the Washington Metropolitan Area, conducting research in simulation, training, and virtual reality at the US Army Research Institute. He has published in the areas of virtual reality, human-computer interaction, automation, simulation and training, systems administration, and service systems. John has a Ph.D. in Human Factors Psychology from the University of Central Florida.

Guruduth Banavar is the Director of IBM's India Research Laboratory (IRL) and the Chief Technologist of IBM India/South Asia. He holds a Ph.D. in Computer Science from the University of Utah and has been a researcher and leader at IBM's Thomas J. Watson Research Center in New York. His broad technical interests and contributions have been in Service Science, Pervasive Computing, Distributed Systems, and Programming Models.

Rahul C. Basole is a research scientist in the Tennenbaum Institute at the Georgia Institute of Technology. His research focuses on technology, innovation, and information management in extended enterprises and business ecosystems with a particular emphasis on converging industries such as telecommunications, biotechnology, healthcare, and global manufacturing. Dr. Basole has published extensively in leading engineering, management, and computer science journals and is editor of Enterprise Mobility: Technologies, Applications, and Strategies (IOS, 2008). Dr. Basole is a member of the Institute for Operations Research and Management Science (INFORMS), the Association for Information Systems (AIS), and the Decision Sciences Institute (DSI).

William J. Baumol is professor of economics and Academic Director of the Berkley Center for Entrepreneurial Studies at New York University, and professor emeritus at Princeton University. Professor Baumol has written some 500 articles and 40 professional books, including *Performing Arts: The Economic Dilemma, Contestable Markets and the Theory of Industry Structure, The Free-Market Innovation Machine,* and *Good Capitalism Bad Capitalism.*

He holds eleven honorary degrees, is a past president of the American Economic Association, and has been elected to three of the United States' leading honorific societies, including the National Academy of Science, as well as to the world's oldest honorary academic society in Italy, the Accademia Nazionale dei Lincei.

Mary Jo Bitner is the PetSmart Chair in Services Leadership and Academic Director of the Center for Services Leadership in the W. P. Carey School of Business, Arizona State University. She has been actively involved in service research her entire career and has focused her research on customer satisfaction with services, customer-employee interactions, and the infusion of technology into service encounters.

Gaurav Bhalla is President of Knowledge Kinetics, a company focusing on customer-driven innovation and value co-creation. He was formerly the Global Innovation Director at Kantar-TNS, and has also held management positions at Nestle, Richardson Vicks and Burke.

Jeanette Blomberg is a research staff member at the IBM Almaden Research Center. Prior to assuming her current position, Dr. Blomberg was a founding member of the pioneering Work Practice and Technology group at the Xerox Palo Alto Research Center (PARC), Director of Experience Modeling Research at Sapient Corporation, and industry-affiliated professor at the Blekinge Institute of Technology in Sweden. Since joining IBM Research she has led projects focused on interactions among IT service providers and their clients, collaboration practices among globally distributed sales teams, the place of stories in corporate imaginaries, and new approaches to work-based learning. Her research explores issues in social aspects of technology production and use, ethnographically-informed organizational interventions, participatory design, case-based prototyping, and service innovation. Dr. Blomberg is an active member of the Participatory Design community, having served as Program Co-Chair twice, and she sits on a number of advisory boards including the Foresight panel of the IT University of Copenhagen, the Program in Design Anthropology at Wayne State University, and the Ethnographic Praxis in Industry Conference (EPIC). Jeanette received her Ph.D. in Anthropology from the University of California, Davis and before embarking on her career in high tech she was a lecturer in cultural anthropology and sociolinguistics at UC Davis.

David E. Bowen, PhD Michigan State University, is the G. Robert & Katherine Herberger Chair in Global Management at Thunderbird. His work centers on organizational behavior and human resource management in services, as well as the role of a "global mindset" in global leadership effectiveness. Recently, he received the "2008 Christopher Lovelock Career Contributions to the Services Discipline Award" from the American Marketing Association; the best paper award at the 10th International Research Seminar in Services Management, France, 2008; and the award for best article in 2007 in Academy of Management Perspectives. He is on the editorial review boards of the Journal of Service Research and the Journal of Service Management.

John R. Bryson is Professor of Enterprise and Economic Geography and Head of the Society, Economy and Environment research group, University of Birmingham. He is Vice-President of the European Association for Research on Services (www.RESER.net). His research interests include the growth of advanced services and more recently service activities and high-added value manufacturing. He is editor of the book series on Services, Economy and Innovation published by Edward Elgar and is also European Editor of Regional Science Policy and Practice. His books include *Service Worlds: People, Organizations and Technologies* (Routledge, 2004), *The Handbook of Service Industries* (Edward Elgar, 2008) and *Industrial Design, Competition and Globalization* (Palgrave Macmillan, 2009).

Richard B. Chase, Professor Emeritus of Operations Management at the Marshall School of Business, University of Southern California, is the originator of the customer contact theory for service processes, with articles on the subject in Management Science and Operations Research, and the Harvard Business Review. His most recent HBR paper is "Want to Perfect Your Company's Service? Use Behavioral Science" (with Sriram Dasu). He is also coauthor with Robert Jacobs of *Operations & Supply Management,* 12th edition. He was honored in the January 2009 issue of POMS for his contributions to service operations management.

Eng K. Chew is a professor of business/IT in University of Technology Sydney. He is a former Chief Information Officer of SingTel Optus, Australia. He has two decades of telecommunications industry experience. He received BEE and PhD (EE) from Melbourne and Sydney Universities, Australia, respectively.

Henry Chesbrough is Executive Director of the Center for Open Innovation at the Haas School of Business at UC Berkeley. His research focuses on managing technology and innovation. His 2003 book, *Open Innovation,* articulates a new paradigm for organizing and managing R&D. An academic version of open innovation, *Open Innovation: Researching a New Paradigm,* with Wim Vanhaverbeke and Joel West, was published in 2006. His most recent book, *Open Business Models,* extends his analysis of innovation to business models, intellectual property management, and markets for innovation. He is a member of the Editorial Board of Research Policy and the California Management Review.

Daniel Connors is a research staff member in the Business Analytics and Mathematical Science Department at IBM Research, Yorktown Heights, New York. Daniel holds B.S.E., M.S. and Ph. D. degrees in Electrical Engineering. His research interests include modeling, simulation, optimization and design of business processes and design of decision support tools for manufacturing, supply chain logistics and workforce analytics.

Peter W. Daniels is Professor of Geography and Deputy Pro-Vice-Chancellor, University of Birmingham. He has held a number of fellowships and visiting posts at universities in Australia, the United States, Hong Kong, and Italy. A past-President of the European Research Network on Services and Space (RESER), his research interests include the growth of advanced services and their role in urban and economic development. He has published numerous journal papers and books on the on the rise of service industries, especially advanced services, in the economies of the UK, Europe, North America and the Asia-Pacific and their role in globalization and international trade.

Andrew Davies is a Reader in the Innovation and Entrepreneurship Group, Imperial College Business School, Imperial College London. He is a co-director of the EPSRC Innovation Studies Centre and theme leader of research on innovation in project business. He is author of *The Business of Projects: Managing Innovation in Complex Products and Systems*, Cambridge University Press (2005), co-authored with Michael Hobday, and *The Business of Systems Integration,* Oxford University Press (2003, 2005), co-edited with Andrea Prencipe and Michael Hobday. He is an Associate Editor of Industrial and Corporate Change.

Faridah Djellal is a Professor of economics at Tours University (France) and a member of CLERSE-CNRS and GERCIE. Her research fields are innovation and technology in services, geography of services, employment in services. She has published articles in several journals, including Urban Studies, International Journal of Urban Research, Research Policy, Revue Française de Gestion, Revue d'économie industrielle. She is the author or editor of several books including (with Faïz Gallouj) *Measuring and improving productivity in services: issues, strategies and challenges* (Edward Elgar 2008), and *The Handbook of Innovation and Services* (Edward Elgar, 2009).

Bo Edvardsson is the Director of the Service Research Center (CTF) at the University of Karlstad, Sweden, and the editor of Journal of Service Management. He is the author, co-author or editor of 17 books, for instance *Customer Involvement in Service and business development,* Imperial College Press, London (2007) and *Values-Based Service for Sustainable Business: Lessons from IKEA,* Routledge, London (2009). He has published 80 articles in scholarly journals. He is a fellow at Hanken School of Economics in Finland, Center for Service Leadership at W.P. Carey School of Business. Arizona State University (ASU) USA and National Tsing Hua University Taiwan. His current research interest lies in the field of new service development, service innovation and dynamics in customer relationships.

Raymond P. Fisk (B.S., M.B.A., and Ph.D. from Arizona State University) is Professor and Chair of the Department of Marketing, at Texas State University-San Marcos. He has published in the Journal of Marketing, Journal of Retailing, Journal of the Academy of Marketing Science, Journal of Service Research, European Journal of Marketing, Service Industries Journal, International Journal of Service Industry Management, Journal of Health Care Marketing, Journal of Marketing Education, Marketing Education Review and others. He has published five books: *Interactive Services Marketing, 3rd Ed., Services Marketing Self-Portraits: Introspections, Reflections and Glimpses from the Experts, Marketing Theory: Distinguished Contributions, AIRWAYS:*

A Marketing Simulation, and Services Marketing: An Annotated Bibliography. He is Past President of the American Marketing Association's Academic Council. He received the Career Contributions to the Services Discipline Award from the AMA Services Marketing Special Interest Group.

Faïz Gallouj is Professor of Economics at Lille University (France) and member of CLERSE CNRS. He is the Director of two master programmes specialised in services and in innovation economics. His main current field of research is innovation and performance in the service sector. He is the author or editor of a dozen books on innovation and performance in services including recently: (with Faridah Djellal) *Measuring and improving productivity in services* (Edward Elgar 2008), and *The Handbook of Innovation and Services* (Edward Elgar, 2009). Faïz Gallouj is also the Editor of the french journal « Economies et Sociétés » (Services Economics and Management Series).

Susanne Glissman has more than ten years experience in business process management, business design, information management, and application development. As research scientist at IBM's Almaden Service Research Center, she combines her knowledge in these areas to advance business architecture and enterprise architecture concepts. Susanne holds a Diploma in Wirtschaftsinformatik (equivalent to a dual BS & MS in Economics & Computer Science) from the University of Paderborn, Germany. She received her PhD in 2009 from the University of St. Gallen, Switzerland. During her PhD program, Susanne also worked as visiting scholar at the Stanford Artificial Intelligence Lab.

Robert J. Glushko is an Adjunct Full Professor in the School of Information at the University of California, Berkeley. He received a PhD in Cognitive Psychology at UCSD in 1979, and a MS in Software Engineering from the Wang Institute in 1985. He has ten years of experience working in corporate R&D, about ten years as an entrepreneur as the founder or co-founder of three companies, and just under ten years as an academic.

Michael E. Gorman is a Professor in the Department of Science, Technology & Society at the University of Virginia, where he teaches courses on ethics, invention, discovery and communication. His research interests include experimental simulations of science, described in his book *Simulating Science* (Indiana University Press, 1992) and ethics, invention and discovery, described in his book *Transforming Nature* (Kluwer Academic Press, 1998). With support from the National Science Foundation, he created a graduate concentration in Systems Engineering in which students create case-studies involving ethical and policy issues; these studies are described in Gorman, M.E., M.M. Mehalik, and P.H. Werhane, *Ethical and environmental challenges to engineering* (2000, Englewood Cliffs, NJ: Prentice-Hall). He has edited a volume on *Scientific and Technological Thinking* (Lawrence Erlbaum Associates, 2005). His current research is in the kind of interdisciplinary trading zones that will be needed to achieve technological and social progress, especially in service science, nanotechnology and the environment; cutting edge work on these topics will appear in his edited volume, Trading zones and interactional expertise: Creating new kinds of collaboration (MIT Press, forthcoming).

Michael J. Gregory is Head of the Manufacturing and Management Division of the University Engineering Department and of the Institute for Manufacturing (IfM) at University of Cambridge since 1998. At the IfM, Gregory links science, engineering, management and economics and integrating education, research and practice and has over 230 staff and research students and a 100 undergraduate and Masters students. Mike's work links industry and government and he has published in the areas of manufacturing strategy, technology management, international manufacturing and manufacturing policy. He chairs the UK Manufacturing Professors Forum and is a member of the UK Government's Ministerial Advisory Group on Manufacturing.

Dwayne D. Gremler is currently Professor of Marketing at Bowling Green State University in Ohio, and previously he worked for ten years as a software engineer. His research is concerned with customer loyalty in service businesses, customer-employee interactions in service delivery, service guarantees, servicescapes, and word-of-mouth communication.

Stephen J. Grove (B.A, M.A, Texas Christian University; Ph.D., Oklahoma State University) is a Professor of Marketing at Clemson University. He has published in the Journal of Retailing, Journal of the Academy of Marketing Science, Journal of Service Research, Journal of Public Policy and Marketing, Journal of Macromarketing, Journal of Business Research, Journal of Personal Selling and Sales Management, Journal of Advertising, The Service Industries Journal, European Journal of Marketing, Journal of Services Marketing, Managing Service Quality, Marketing Management and others. He is co-author of the text, *Interactive Services Marketing, 3rd Ed.* and the book, *Services Marketing Self- Portraits: Introspections, Reflections and Glimpses from the Experts.* He has also twice served as Chair of the American Marketing Association's Services Marketing Special Interest Group (SERVSIG) and as a member of the AMA's Academic Council.

Gerhard Gudergan is Head of Department Service Management of FIR at RWTH Aachen University. Research areas covered are service engineering, lean services and community management.

Evert Gummesson is Professor of Marketing and Management at the Stockholm University School of Business, Sweden. His research interests embrace service, relationship and many-to-many marketing, and qualitative methodology.

Anders Gustafsson is a professor of business administration in the Service Research Center at Karlstad University, Sweden. Dr. Gustafsson is an author of nine books including: *Competing in a Service Economy: How to Create a Competitive Advantage through Service Development and Innovation* (Jossey-Bass, 2003), *Improving Customer Satisfaction, Loyalty and Profit: An Integrated Measurement and Management System* (Jossey-Bass, 2000), *Conjoint Measurement - Methods and Applications* (Springer, 2007 4th edition). In addition, Dr. Gustafsson has published over 100 academic articles, book chapters and industry reports. He has published articles in journals such as Journal of Marketing, Journal of Economic Psychology and Journal of Service Research.

Alan Hartman is the Service Science focal point for the IBM India Research Laboratory. He holds a Ph. D. from the University of Newcastle, Australia, and an M. Sc. from the Israel Institute of Technology, both in Mathematics. He has worked in the IBM Research Division at the Haifa and India Research Laboratories since 1983. He has also held visiting appointments at the University of Toronto and Telstra Research Laboratories. His research interests include Service Science, Software Engineering, Hardware Verification, and Mathematical Optimization.

James L. Heskett is Baker Foundation Professor Emeritus at the Harvard Business School, having joined the faculty there after completing his Ph.D. at Stanford University and teaching at The Ohio State University. He served as President of Logistics Systems, Inc. His teaching has spanned the subjects of marketing, logistics, service management and general management. He is the author of the books, *Business Logistics* (1962), *Marketing* (1976), *Managing in the Service Economy* (1986) and co-author of *Service Breakthroughs* (1990), *Corporate Culture and Performance* (1992), *The Service Profit Chain* (1997), and *The Ownership Quotient* (2008), among others. He has served as a consultant to many companies, is a director of Limited Brands, and has served on more than a dozen other for-profit and not-for-profit boards of directors.

Kazuyoshi Hidaka is a manager at the Tokyo Research Laboratory, IBM Japan, Ltd. He completed a graduate course in energy science at the Graduate School of Tokyo Institute of Technology in March 1984, and obtained a dissertation doctorate in science from Waseda University's Graduate School in March 1996. He has worked for IBM Japan Tokyo Research Laboratory since 1984. Following an assignment to IBM's Watson Research Center in the U.S., he returned to the Tokyo Research Laboratory and is now in charge of on-demand business services research. He is affiliated Fellow of National Institute of Science and Technology Policy. Board member of Japanese Society for Industrial and Applied Mathematics. Member of Information Processing Society of Japan, and a member of The Operations Research Society of Japan.

Barbara Jones is a Research Fellow and member of the European Work and Employment Research Centre. Her current research interests are methods of capturing new skills and emerging occupations in distributed environments including developing methods for handling the fusion of disparate bodies of legacy tacit knowledge in the convergence of occupations driven by technological change.

Uday Karmarkar is the LA Times Chair Professor of Technology and Strategy at the UCLA Anderson School of Management. He founded and directs the UCLA BIT Global Research Network, which has 20 partner institutions in 16 countries, studying information-intensive industries. He has a B.Tech from IITB, a Ph.D. from MIT Sloan School and was on the faculties of the GSB,

University of Chicago and the Simon School, Rochester. His research interests include the information economy, information-intensive industries, technology management and operations strategy. He has published over 75 papers and articles, and conducted projects and studies for more than 50 firms and organizations in the United States and Asia. Dr. Karmarkar is an Honorary Institute Fellow and a Distinguished Alumnus of IITB, Mumbai.

Cheryl A. Kieliszewski is a research scientist at the IBM Almaden Research Center and manages a team focused on business intelligence and analytics technologies. Her research work has focused on understanding the impact of work practices on technological and organizational design to improve the human-system relationship in addition to research in human-computer interface design and specification. She has been with IBM since November 2000, having worked in both the Research Division and Systems and Technology Division. Cheryl has over 10 years of research and applied human factors engineering experience investigating human behavior, expectations and the implications for technology design and implementation on the end user. She has published in the areas of transportation and driver error, human-computer interaction, systems administration, service systems and service science. Cheryl received her Ph.D. from Virginia Tech in Industrial and Systems Engineering with an emphasis in Human Factors Engineering.

Per Kristensson is Associate Professor in Psychology at the Service Research Center (CTF) and the Department of Psychology at Karlstad University, Sweden. He has a PhD in Psychology from Gothenburg University and a Licentiate Degree from Luleå Technical University. Dr Kristensson has published over 30 articles in leading journals and peer-reviewed conference proceedings. His research mainly concerns topics as consumer behaviour, management of technology and cognitive psychology. In respect to user involvement he has published articles in Journal of Product Innovation Management, Journal of Service Research, Creativity and Innovation Management and Journal of Services Marketing to name but a few.

Robert F. Lusch is the Lisle & Roslyn Payne Professor of Marketing in the Eller College of Management at the University of Arizona. His research is in the areas of the service-dominant logic of marketing, competitive strategy and marketing channels. Professor Lusch has served as Editor of the Journal of Marketing and is the author of 125 scholarly articles and 18 books. On two occasions the American Marketing Association recognized him with the AMA/Maynard Award for Theoretical Contributions to Marketing and the Academy of Marketing Science awarded him the Distinguished Marketing Educator Award. Professor Lusch has served as Chairperson of the American Marketing Association.

Linda Macaulay is Professor of System Design and Director of the Centre for Service Research at Manchester Business School and is twice holder of the prestigious IBM Faculty Award 2004 and 2006 for work on e-business patterns. Her background is in Mathematics and Computation and her interests are in designing systems to meet the needs of users and other stakeholders. She plays a leading role in the Service Science agenda in the UK through www.ssmenetuk.org.

Paul P. Maglio is senior manager of Service Systems Research at the IBM Almaden Research Center in San Jose, California. His group encompasses social, cognitive, computer and business sciences, and aims at creating a foundation for research in how people work together and with technology to create value. He holds a bachelor's degree in computer science and engineering from MIT and a Ph.D. in cognitive science from the University of California at San Diego, and he is currently an Associate Adjunct Professor at the University of California, Merced, where he teaches Service Science.

Richard Metters is Associate Professor at the Goizueta Business School, Emory University. His research interests include the role of national culture in service work, service sector inventory, and revenue management.

Ian Miles is Professor of Technological Innovation and Social Change, and co-Director of the Centre for Service Research. Much of his work on technological innovation has concerned new Information Technologies, and he has been particularly interested in service industries as users and sources of innovation. Apart from analyses of services in general, Miles is particularly associated with Knowledge-Intensive Business Services (KIBS), pioneering research into these industries. His research covers both managerial and policy dimensions of these issues, and uses tools such as case studies and survey analysis.

Aleksandra (Saška) Mojsilović is a member of the Business Analytics and Mathematical Science Department at IBM Research, Yorktown Heights, New York. Aleksandra holds PhD in Electrical Engineering. Her research interests include signal processing and mathematical modeling. Aleksandra is the author of over 50 publications and holds eleven patents. She received a number of awards for her work including the 2001 IEEE Young Author Best Paper Award, 2002 European Conference on Computer Vision Best Paper Award, 2004 IBM Market Intelligence Award and 2007 IBM Outstanding Technical Achievement Award. Aleksandra currently serves as an Associate Editor for the IEEE Signal Processing Magazine.

Claire Moxham is a Lecturer in the Decision Sciences and Operations Management Group at Manchester Business School. Her areas of expertise include performance measurement, process improvement, and the application of 'industrial' management techniques to the public and voluntary sectors.

Rogelio Oliva is Associate Professor of Information and Operations Management at the Mays Business School in Texas A&M University and Adjunct Professor at the MIT Zaragoza Logistics Program.

Lakshmish Ramaswamy is an assistant professor in the Computer Science department at the University of Georgia. He obtained the Ph.D. degree in computer science from Georgia Tech in 2005. Dr. Ramaswamy was a visiting scientist at IBM India Research Labs in 2008. He is the recipient of the best paper award of WWW-2004 and the 2005 Pat Goldberg Memorial best paper award. His research interests include Internet-scale distributed systems, service science, and anti-spam systems.

Guang-Jie Ren recently completed the doctoral program at the Institute for Manufacturing, part of the Department of Engineering, University of Cambridge, and started as a researcher in IBM Almaden's Service Research group in 2009. He has been honoured with an Overseas Research Studentship and Raymond and Helen Kwok Scholarship from the Cambridge Overseas Trust. Born in Shanghai and of the same age as China's reform, he has been fortunate to witness the dramatic changes around that nation and globally. Trained as an industrial engineer in operations management, his research examines the trend of service business development in manufacturing industries (servicisation phenomenon).

William B. Rouse is the Executive Director of the Tennenbaum Institute at the Georgia Institute of Technology. He is also a professor in the College of Computing and School of Industrial and Systems Engineering. Dr. Rouse has written hundreds of articles and books, including most recently *People and Organizations* (Wiley, 2007), *Essential Challenges of Strategic Management* (Wiley, 2001) and the award-winning *Don't Jump to Solutions* (Jossey-Bass, 1998). He is editor of *Enterprise Transformation* (Wiley, 2006), co-editor of *Organizational Simulation* (Wiley, 2005), and co-editor of the best-selling *Handbook of Systems Engineering and Management* (Wiley, 2009). Dr. Rouse is a member of the National Academy of Engineering, as well as a fellow of four professional societies - Institute of Electrical and Electronics Engineers (IEEE), the International Council on Systems Engineering (INCOSE), the Institute for Operations Research and Management Science (INFORMS), and the Human Factors and Ergonomics Society (HFES).

Roland T. Rust is Distinguished University Professor and David Bruce Smith Chair in Marketing at the Robert H. Smith School of Business, University of Maryland, where he serves as Executive Director and of two research centers: the Center for Excellence in Service, and the Center for Complexity in Business. Professor Rust is the founder of both the Journal of Service Research and the annual Frontiers in Service Conference.

Scott E. Sampson is the James M. Passey Professor of Business Management at Brigham Young University where he teaches Service Management and Supply Chain Management in BYU's top-tier MBA and undergraduate business programs. His research involves service paradigms, service design, and service quality measurement. He has published articles in Management Science, Operations Research, and other top journals, and a textbook on the *Unified Service Theory* (UST). He has received multiple best paper awards, including the "Most Influential Service Operations Paper Award" for a 2006 article on the UST. Scott received his MBA and PhD degrees from the University of Virginia.

Pamela Samuelson is the Richard M. Sherman Distinguished Professor of Law and Information at the University of California at Berkeley. She is a Director of the Berkeley Center for Law and Technology and has been a Contributing Editor to Communications of the ACM since 1990.

Jorge Sanz has held multiple positions in academia, research and also in industry working with global responsibilities in different countries. He has been with IBM Almaden Research, San Jose, California in 1984-1993; he was Director of Systems Integration & New Technologies, IBM, 1993-1995; Director for Alliances in Telecommunications and Media, IBM, 1996-1998 and Strategy Manager for IBM Telecom in Latin America, 1998-2000. Dr. Sanz was also an entrepreneur by holding positions in Medcenter Solutions, a start-up, where he worked as a COO establishing the operations, defining healthcare solutions, and M&As in 2000-2001. He was also President of the University of St. Andrews, Argentina, in 2001-2002 and held different professor appointments at the University of Illinois at Urbana-Champaign, in 1993-1994 and in 1981-1983. Dr. Sanz is a Fellow Member of IEEE since 1991, has several published books and more than one hundred reviewed papers in journals and international conferences. Since 2003, he has been working as a manager and doing services research on business modeling, business architecture, industry evolution, and business performance at the IBM Almaden Research Center.

Earl W. Sasser, Jr. is a Baker Foundation Professor at Harvard Business School and has been a member of the faculty there since 1969. Sasser developed the School's first course on the management of service operations in 1972. Sasser has co-authored a number of books in the field of service management including *Service Breakthroughs: Changing the Rules of the Game, Management of Service Operations, The Service Management Course, The Service Profit Chain and The Value Profit Chain*. His most recent book, *The Ownership Quotient: Putting the Service Profit Chain to Work for Unbeatable Competitive Advantage* (with Professor James L. Heskett and Joe Wheeler), was published by the Harvard Business School Press in 2008. Sasser has written or co-written ten articles for the Harvard Business Review, including *"Putting the Service Profit Chain to Work," "Zero Defections: Quality Comes to Services" and "Why Satisfied Customer Defect."* Professor Sasser serves as a consultant to a number of companies in North America, Asia and Europe.

Benjamin Schneider is Senior Research Fellow at Valtera and Professor Emeritus (University of Maryland). Ben's interests concern service quality, organizational climate and culture, staffing issues, and the role of manager personality in organizations. He has published 140 journal articles and book chapters, as well as nine books, the most recent being (with W. H. Macey, K. M. Barbera, and S. A. Young), *Employee engagement: Tools for analysis, practice and competitive advantage* (Wiley-Blackwell, 2009). Ben has won numerous awards for his scientific contributions. Beyond his academic work Ben has consulted on service quality issues with numerous companies including Chase-Manhattan Bank, Citicorp, IBM, Allstate, American Express, Giant Eagle, Microsoft and Toyota.

Carl J. Schramm, President and CEO of the Ewing Marion Kauffman Foundation since 2002, is one of the world's most recognized thought leaders on fostering and advancing entrepreneurship. Trained both as an economist and lawyer, Schramm began his career on the faculty of Johns Hopkins University. An active entrepreneur, Schramm was a cofounder of HCIA, Inc. and Patient Choice Health Care. Besides many leading academic journals, Schramm's work has appeared in Foreign Affairs and The Wall Street Journal. He is the author of *The Entrepreneurial Imperative* and a second book *Good Capitalism, Bad Capitalism* with Will Baumol and Robert Litan, which is available in seven languages.

James C. Spohrer, Director of IBM Global University Programs since 2009, established IBM's first Service Research group at the Almaden Research Center in Silicon Valley in 2002. He led his group to attain IBM awards for modeling customers and mapping global service systems including performance measures, costing and pricing of complex, inter-organizational service projects, analytics and information service innovations, process improvement methods, innovation foresight methods, to name a few. Working with service research pioneers from many academic disciplines, Jim advocates for Service Science, Management, Engineering, and Design (SSMED) as an integrative framework for global competency development, economic development, and advancement of science.

John D. Sterman is the Jay W. Forrester Professor of Management at the MIT Sloan School of Management and Director of MIT's System Dynamics Group.

Stephen L. Vargo is a Shidler Distinguished Professor of Marketing at the University of Hawai'i at Manoa. His primary areas of research are marketing theory and thought and consumers' evaluative reference scales. He has had articles published in the Journal of Marketing, the Journal of the Academy of Marketing Science, the Journal of Service Research, and other major marketing journals and serves on six editorial review boards, including the Journal of Marketing, Journal of the Academy of Marketing Science, and the Journal of Service Research. Professor Vargo has been awarded the Best Article of the Year Award by the Australia and New Zealand Marketing Academy and the Harold H. Maynard Award by the American Marketing Association for "significant contribution to marketing theory and thought."

Lars Witell is associate professor at the Service Research Center (CTF) at Karlstad University, Sweden. He is also an associate professor in quality and service development at the department of Management and Engineering at Linköping University, Sweden. He conducts research on service innovation, customer co-creation and service transition in manufacturing companies. He has written approximately 30 book chapters and papers in scientific journals, such as Journal of Service Management, Quality Management Journal, Managing Service Quality and International Journal on Technology Management as well as in the popular press, such as Wall Street Journal.

Valarie A. Zeithaml is the David S. Van Pelt Family Distinguished Professor of Marketing and an award-winning teacher and researcher at the University of North Carolina. For her work in services marketing, Dr. Zeithaml received the 2009 AMA Irwin/McGraw-Hill Distinguished Marketing Educator Award and the 2008 Paul Converse Award, both granted for significant lifetime contributions to the marketing discipline.

Anatoly Zherebtsov, Senior Consultant XJ Technologies Company Ltd., received his MSc in Mathematics & Computer Science from Novosibirsk State University, Russia in 2004. Anatoly has been employed by XJ Technologies since 2004. Anatoly has participated in several simulation-based projects in the areas of rail transportation, supply chain management, warehouse modeling, IT infrastructure modeling, business process modeling, and asset management. Anatoly is currently involved in management and development within European Integrated Project MODELPLEX.

Introduction

Why a Handbook?

Paul P. Maglio

IBM Research-Almaden, San Jose, California, USA

Cheryl A. Kieliszewski

IBM Research-Almaden, San Jose, California, USA

James C. Spohrer

IBM Research-Almaden, San Jose, California, USA

Why a handbook? We can answer that question with a question: What does a service scientist need to know? This volume presents multidisciplinary perspectives on the nature of service, on research and practice in service, and on the future of research in service. It aims to be a kind of reference, a collection of papers by leading thinkers and researchers from across the spectrum of service research – the collected basics for a budding service scientist.

Service science is the study of value cocreation

Service science is an interdisciplinary approach to study, improve, create, and innovate in service (Spohrer & Maglio, 2008, 2010). We think of service as value cocreation – broadly speaking, as useful change that results from communication, planning, or other purposeful and knowledge-intensive interactions between distinct entities, such as individuals or firms (Spohrer & Maglio, 2010). And so we think of service science as the systematic search for principles and approaches that can help understand and improve all kinds of value cocreation (Spohrer & Maglio, 2010).

P.P. Maglio et al. (eds.), *Handbook of Service Science*, Service Science: Research and Innovations in the Service Economy, DOI 10.1007/978-1-4419-1628-0_1,
© Springer Science+Business Media, LLC 2010

To start, there are many kinds of value cocreation. There are many ways to divide up the expertise, labor, and risk associated with diverse human activities. Traditional service sector activities include transportation, retail, healthcare, entertainment, professional services, information technology services, banking, and insurance, to name just a few (see also US Census Bureau, 2007). One firm provides a service, such as banking, and a customer benefits by being able to securely store and access funds. The bank cannot exist without the funds customers store and the customer cannot have the convenience of access through various mechanisms (checking, automatic tellers, bank branches) without the capabilities the bank provides. Value is cocreated by the interaction of the two. A broader view supposes that all economic activity depends on value cocreation between different entities, and more specifically, that all economic activity is fundamentally an exchange of service for service (see, for instance, Vargo, Maglio, & Akaka, 2008, and the chapter by Vargo, Lusch, and Akaka in this volume). The key point is that different entities bring different capabilities and resources to bear and value results from interaction of resources and capabilities.

There are many different theories and methods that might be useful in the search for principles and approaches to understand and improve value cocreation. Disciplines that have focused on service include marketing, operations, industrial engineering, information systems, computer science, and economics, to name just a few. Marketing has long held that certain kinds of service activities need to be characterized and sold differently from goods (see, e.g., Shostack, 1977), and operations and industrial engineering have long understood that service processes need to be constructed differently from goods production processes (e.g., Levitt, 1972) and particularly in the context of specific technologies (e.g., Mills & Moberg, 1982). Modern computer science focuses on web services and service-oriented computing (e.g., Marks & Bell, 2006; Zhang, 2007), which aim to transform the way programs and applications are built from small components. Economics has long distinguished tangible goods from intangible services (e.g., Smith, 1776/2000; see also Delaunay & Gadrey, 1992).

It is ambitious – and perhaps a little silly – to suppose there might be a single science that can cover all of service, a science that combines theories and methods from such a wide range of existing disciplines and applies them to such a wide range of value-cocreation phenomena. At the very least, service science is already enhancing the conversation among different people and different disciplines focused on service (see also, Rust, 2004; Hefley & Murphy, 2008; IfM & IBM, 2008; Spohrer & Riecken, 2006). Some commonalities are already evident, and some progress is already being made. For example, we see Vargo and Lusch's (2004) service-dominant logic as one of the corner stones of service science (Maglio & Spohrer, 2008). Its primary definition is that service is the application of competences for the benefit of another entity, and its primary tenet is that all economic activity is an exchange of service for service. Drawn to its logical conclusion, this effectively flips the usual "goods-dominant" worldview on its head and takes service to be the primary category. According to service-dominant logic, rather than service being a kind of inferior, intangible good, goods themselves embody the tangible aspects of service competence and obscure the true nature of the underlying service for service exchange. Such a profound shift in worldview is difficult to make, and not everyone agrees with it (e.g., Achrol & Kotler, 2006; Levy, 2006). More importantly, it is not always easy to get it right, and we admit to being inconsistent in how we have viewed service over the last few years (see the chapter by Vargo, Lusch, and Akaka in this volume). But we are coming around.

Another potential fundamental of service science is the service system (Maglio, Srinivasan, Kreulen, & Spohrer, 2006; Maglio & Spohrer, 2008; Maglio, Vargo, Caswell, & Spohrer, 2009; Spohrer, Maglio, Gruhl, & Bailey, 2007). This idea of service emerging out of systems of interacting components goes back much further than our use of it, of course: Some have focused on service systems for optimizing waiting and queuing processes (e.g., Riordan, 1962), some for the interaction among parts of a production process that includes firms and customers together (Chase, 1978), and some for the larger constellation of stakeholders (including suppliers, competitors, customers, and others) that together conspire in the generation of mutual value (Normann, 1984). For us, the key point is that value cocreation emerges from the interaction of many parts – and it can be formalized, analyzed, and designed despite its complexity.

Structure of the book

No organization is perfect. No matter what structure we choose, something will seem out of place. With that in mind, the book is organized in three main parts: Context, Research and Practice, and Future. We outline each in turn.

The first part is Context. It sets the stage for what's to come, introducing many of the basic concepts about service that will recur throughout. It is organized in two parts, Origins and Theory. Origins celebrates some of the seminal and pioneering work in service research with updates to several classics. Richard Chase reviews his seminal Harvard Business Review article (Chase, 1978) in "Revisiting 'Where Does the Customer Fit in a Service Operation?' Background and Future Development of Contact Theory;" Chase's customer contact theory remains important and influential, and here he reviews and places it in the modern service context. James Heskett and Earl Sasser update their seminal Harvard Business Review article (Heskett, Jones, Loveman, Sasser, & Schlesinger, 1994) on the service profit chain in "The Service Profit Chain: From Satisfaction to Ownership," incorporating new research findings and new concepts that have followed from it. Benjamin Schneider and David Bowen recap their popular book (Schneider & Bowen, 1995) in "Winning the Service Game: Revisiting the Rules by Which *People* Co-Create Value," demonstrating that the key to service is people, front-stage, backstage, client-side, and everywhere. Roland Rust and Gaurav Bhalla provide an overview of critical notions of customer equity and customer lifetime value in "Customer Equity: Driving the Value of the Firm by Driving the Value of Customers," focusing squarely on the revenue side – the customers – rather than the cost side – the operations (see also Rust, Zeithaml & Lemon, 2000).   John Bryson and Peter Daniels set a broad service context in "Service Worlds: The 'Services Duality' and the rise of the 'Manuservice' economy" by summarizing a bit of their book (Bryson, Daniels, & Warf, 2004), and then taking it further, arguing that service might not be its own category, but is blended with manufacturing and so we have to understand it at a much finer grain.

The section on Theory lays out several different but related approaches to weaving a comprehensive approach or theory of service. Scott Sampson follows the tradition of Chase by emphasizing the role of the customer in service operations to create a powerful framework for understanding service in "The Unified Service Theory: A Paradigm for Service Science" (see also Sampson and Froehle, 2006). Stephen Vargo, Robert Lusch, and Michelle Akaka connect the influential service-dominant logic (e.g., Vargo & Lusch, 2004) to the foundation of service science in "Advancing Service Science with Service-dominant Logic: Clarifications and Conceptual Development". Finally, James Spohrer and Paul Maglio develop concepts and theory around service systems in "Toward a Science of Service Systems: Value and Symbols" (see also Maglio, Vargo, Caswell, & Spohrer, 2009; Spohrer & Maglio, 2009).

The second part is Research and Practice. It emphasizes empirical data and practical experience through the study and implementation of real-world services. It is broken into four sections: Design, Operations, Delivery, and Innovation. The section on Design takes the perspective of the service itself, considering mainly issues in effective service creation and development. In "Technology's Critical Impact on the Gaps Model of Service Quality, "Mary Jo Bitner, Valerie Zeithaml, and Dwayne Gremler review and update the now standard gaps model of service quality (see also Parasuraman, Berry & Zeithaml, 1990), particularly in the context of modern service technology. In "Seven Contexts for Service System Design," Robert Glushko develops a kind of taxonomy for service design that aims to bridge front-stage and back stage concerns across a variety of service situations (see also Glushko & Tabas, 2009). In "Business Architecture for the Design of Enterprise Service Systems," Susanne Glissmann and Jorge Sanz describe the fundamentals behind business architecture, particularly from the perspective of business services. In "People, Activities, and Information in Highly Collaborative Knowledge-based Service Systems," Cheryl Kieliszewski, John Bailey, and Jeanette Blomberg discuss their research and insights into service work practices and their implications for service system design.

The section on Operations reviews a variety of work related to management and engineering of service systems. In "The Neglect of Service Science in the Operations Management Field," Richard Metters expounds on the need for education and research in service by educators and researchers in operations in his personal essay (see also Metters and Marucheck, 2007). In "Death Spirals and Virtuous Cycles: Human Resource Dynamics in Knowledge-Based Services,"

Rogelio Oliva and John Sterman explain their system dynamics modeling approach to understanding the relation between human aspects of work and business aspects of service performance and quality (see also Oliva & Sterman, 2001). In "Service Science – A Reflection from Telecommunications Service Perspective," Eng Chew provides a case study in the application of service science ideas to telecom services, demonstrating both applicability and potential insight into process, innovation, and value. In "Service Engineering – Interdisciplinary and Multiperspective Framework to New Solution Design," Gerhard Gudergan explains the concepts and background of several approaches to service engineering.

The section on Delivery takes the perspective of implementation, focusing mainly on how service delivery actually works. In "The Industrialization of Information Intensive Services," Uday Karmarkar extends and updates his Harvard Business Review article (Karmarkar, 2004) on how industrialization of information services works, along with its social and business implications. In "Workforce Analytics for the Services Economy," Aleksandra Mojsilović and Daniel Connors show how optimization-based approaches to workforce management are critical to modern large-scale service delivery. In "Understanding Complex Product and Service Delivery Systems," William Rouse and Rahul Basole extend their article in the IBM Systems Journal (Basole & Rouse, 2008) showing how service value can be viewed as network flows through the use of many specific industry examples. In "A Formal Model of Service Delivery," Guruduth Banavar, Alan Hartman, Lakshmish Ramaswamy, and Anatoly Zherebtsov develop a formal model of service delivery that takes account of front-stage and backstage processes together in a way that enables analysis and reasoning about design.

The section on Innovation pulls together a variety of perspectives on the nature and processes of new service development and service improvement. In "Service Innovation," Ian Miles provides a broad review of service innovation studies, and starts to place them in a modern service context (see also Miles, 2008). In "Innovation in Services and Entrepreneurship: Beyond Industrialist and Technologist Concepts of Sustainable Development," Faridah Djellal and Faïz Gallouj discuss how models of sustainability and innovation do not take account of services, and show how a service perspective has a lot to offer. In "Service Innovation and Customer Co-development," Bo Edvardsson, Anders Gustafsson, Per Kristensson and Lars Witell apply service-dominant logic to understand the role of the customer in service innovation. In "Advancing Services Innovation: Five Key Concepts," Henry Chesbrough and Andrew Davies develop a novel model of service innovation based squarely on the notion of value cocreation. In "What Effects do Legal Rules have on Service Innovation?" Pamela Samuelson provides a concise history and context of intellectual property, contract, and tort law related to services, particularly digital information services and software, and suggests where the legal landscape may be heading and draws out implications for service innovation.

The third part of the book is Future. It focuses on the problems and prospects for building a truly interdisciplinary service science. Evert Gummesson gives a very personal account of the context of service, its history as a field, and the prospects for true integration of disciplines in "The Future of Service is Long Overdue."

Raymond Fisk and Stephen Grove provide their own historical perspective on the study of service, and how various strands of research (disciplines) might or might not come together in "The Evolution and Future of Service: Building and Broadening a Multidisciplinary Field" (see also Fisk, Brown, & Bitner, 1993). Michael Gorman characterizes service science as a kind of trading zone that brokers knowledge between different areas in "Normative Scenarios and Their Role in Service Science Trading Zones." James Spohrer, Guangjie Ren, and Michael Gregory review and update the recent "Cambridge Report" (IfM & IBM, 2008), defining key terms for Service Science and showing global progress toward the vision of service innovation roadmaps for all nations in "The Cambridge-IBM SSME White Paper Revisited." Kazuyoshi Hidaka describes service research and educational activities in "service science, Management, and Engineering in Japan." Linda Macaulay, Claire Moxham, Barbara Jones, and Ian Miles connect specific skills and service science education needs in "Innovation and Skills: Future Service Science Education."

In the end, of course, it is not clear there is – or there will be – a single, unified service science. But it is clear there is progress. There are common elements and themes, and common concerns and approaches that converge on the central real-world phenomena of value cocreation. A dialog has emerged among many proponents who aspire to a deeper scientific foundation for their views on service, one that attempts to define key terms and to incorporate them into fundamental insights and principles. We hope this collection has furthered that dialog and has captured much of what every service scientist should know.

References

Achrol, R. & Kotler, P. (2006). The service-dominant logic for marketing: A critique, in Robert F. Lusch and Stephen L. Vargo (Eds.), *The Service-Dominant Logic of Marketing: Dialog, Debate, and Directions,*. Armonk, New York: M.E. Sharpe, 320-333.

Basole, R. C., & Rouse, W. B. (2008). Complexity of Service Value Networks: Conceptualization and Empirical Investigation. *IBM Systems Journal*, 47(1), 53-70.

Bryson, J. R., Daniels, P. W., & Warf, B. (2004). *Service worlds: People, organisations, and technologies.* New York: Routledge/Taylor & Francis

Chase, R. B. (1978). Where does the customer fit in a service operation? *Harvard Business Review*, 56, 137 – 142.

Delaunay, J. & Gadrey, J. (1992). *Services in economic thought.* Boston: Kluwer.

Fisk, R. P., Brown, S. W., & Bitner, M. (1993). Tracking the evolution of the services marketing literature. *Journal of Retailing*, 69, 61 – 103.

Gluhsko, R. J. & Tabas, L. (2009). Designing Service Systems by Bridging the "Front Stage" and "Back Stage." *Information Systems and E-Business Management*, 7.

Hefley, B. & Murphy, W. (2008). *Service Science, Management and Engineering: Education for the 21st Century.* Springer, New York.

Heskett, J. L., Jones, T. O., Loveman, G. O., Sasser, W. E., Schlesinger, L. A. (1994). Putting the service profit chain to work. *Harvard Business Review*, 72, 164 – 174.

IfM & IBM. (2008). *Succeeding through Service Innovation: A Service Perspective for Education, Research, Business and Government.* Cambridge, UK: University of Cambridge Institute for Manufacturing. ISBN: 978-1-902546-65-0

Karmarkar, U. (2004). Will you survive the services revolution? *Harvard Business Review*, 82, 100 – 107.

Levitt, T., (1972). Production-line approach to services. *Harvard Business Review*, September-October, 41-52.

Levy, S. J. (2006). How new, how dominant?, in Robert F. Lusch and Stephen L. Vargo (Eds.), *The Service-Dominant Logic of Marketing: Dialog, Debate, and Directions.* Armonk, New York: M.E. Sharpe, 57-64

Maglio, P. P. & Spohrer, J. (2008). Fundamentals of service science. *Journal of the Academy of Marketing Science*, 36, 18-20.

Maglio, P. P., Srinivasan, S., Kreulen, J. T., Spohrer, J. (2006). Service systems, service scientists, SSME, and innovation. *Communications of the ACM*, 49(7), 81-85.

Maglio, P. P., Vargo, S. L., Caswell, N. & Spohrer, J. (2009). The service system is the basic abstraction of service science. *Information Systems and e-business Management*, 7.

Marks, E. A., & Bell, M. (2006). *Service-Oriented Architecture: A Planning and Implementation Guide for Business and Technology.* Wiley. Hoboken, NJ.

Metters, R., & Marucheck, A. (2007) Service Management - Academic Issues and Scholarly Reflections from Operations Management Researchers, *Decision Sciences*, 38, 195-214.

Miles, I. (2008). Patterns of innovation in service industries. *IBM Systems Journal*, 47, 115-128

Mills, P. K. & Moberg, D. J. (1982). Perspectives on the technology of service operations. *Academy of Management Review*, 7, 467-478.

Normann, R. (1984). *Service Management: Strategy and Leadership in the Service Business.* New York: Wiley and Sons.

Oliva, R. & Sterman, J. D. (2001). Cutting corners and working overtime: Quality erosion in the service industry. *Management Science*, 47, 894 – 914.

Parasuraman A., Berry, L. L. & Zeithaml, V. A. (1990). *Understanding Measuring and Improving Service Quality: Findings from a Multiphase Research Program.* The Free Press.

Riordan, J. (1962). *Stochastic Service Systems.* New York: Wiley.

Rust, R. T. (2004). A call for a wider range of service research. *Journal of Service Research*, 6.

Rust, R. T., Zeithaml, V. A., & Lemon, K. N. (2000). *Driving Customer Equity.* New York: The Free Press.

Sampson, S. & Froehle, C. M. (2006). Foundations and implications of a proposed unified services theory. *Production and Operations Management*, 15, 329 – 343.

Schneider B. & Bowen, D. E. (1995). *Winning the Service Game.* Boston, MA: Harvard Business School Press.

Shostack, G. L. (1977). Breaking free from product marketing. *Journal of Marketing*, 41, 73-80.

Smith, A. (1776/2000). The Wealth of Nations. New York: The Modern Library.

Spohrer, J. & Maglio, P. P. (2008). The emergence of service science: Toward systematic service innovations to accelerate co-creation of value. *Production and Operations Management*, 17, 1-9.

Spohrer, J. & Maglio, P. P. (2010). Service science: Toward a smarter planet. In W. Karwowski & G. Salvendy (Eds.), *Introduction to service engineering.* New York: Wiley & Sons.

Spohrer, J., Maglio, P. P., Bailey, J. & Gruhl, D. (2007). Steps toward a science of service systems. *Computer*, 40, 71-77.

Spohrer, J. & Riecken, D. (2006). Special Issue on Services Science, *Communications of the ACM*, 49(7).

US Census Bureau (2007). North American Industry Classification System (NAICS). US Department of Commerce Publication PB2007100002. Available at http://www.ntis.gov/products/naics.aspx.

Vargo, S. L. & Lusch, R. F. (2004). Evolving to a new dominant logic for marketing. *Journal of Marketing*, 68, 1 – 17.

Vargo, S. L., Maglio, P. P., and Akaka, M. A. (2008). On value and value co-creation: A service systems and service logic perspective. *European Management Journal*, 26(3), 145-152.

Zhang, L. J. (2007). *Modern Technologies in Web Services Research*. IGI Publishing. Hershey, PA.

Part 1
Context: Origins

Revisiting "Where Does the Customer Fit in a Service Operation?"

Background and Future Development of Contact Theory

Richard B. Chase

Marshall School of Business
University of Southern California

In 1978 I asserted that a "rational approach to the rationalization" of services requires first of all a classification system that sets one service activity system apart from another (Chase 1978). The classification I developed came about from an effort to derive a business classification scheme and was predicated on the extent of customer contact with the service system and its personnel during the service delivery process. Based upon open systems theory, I proposed that the less direct contact the customer has with the service system, the greater the potential of the system to operate at peak efficiency. And, conversely, where the direct customer contact is high, the less potential exists to achieve high levels of efficiency. In this chapter I will review the contact approach as it was discussed in the article and offer some suggestions for its future development.

Classifying Manufacturing and Service Systems

The customer contact approach came about from an effort to derive a classification system that explicitly captured the role and impact of the customer as opposed to things, which is the basis of most product classifications. The standard approach to manufacturing system classification in 1978 and even today is the product process matrix proposed by Hayes and Wheelwright (1979). This uses the self evident terms of unit, batch, and mass production to specify how process efficiency varies with volume. Service systems, by contrast, are generally classified according to the service they provide, as delineated in the North American Industry Classification System (NAICS) code. This classification, though useful in presenting aggregate economic data for comparative purposes, does not deal with the

P.P. Maglio et al. (eds.), *Handbook of Service Science*, Service Science: Research and Innovations in the Service Economy, DOI 10.1007/978-1-4419-1628-0_2,
© Springer Science+Business Media, LLC 2010

production activities by which the service is carried out. It is possible, of course, to describe certain service systems using manufacturing terms, but such terms, as in the case of the NAICS code, are insufficient for diagnosing and thinking about how to improve the systems without one additional piece of information. That piece—which I believe operationally distinguishes one service system from another in terms of what they can and cannot achieve in the way of efficiency— is the extent of customer contact in the creation of the service. Extent of contact may be roughly defined as the percentage of time the customer must be in the system relative to the total time it takes to serve him. Generally, the greater the percentage of contact time between the service system and the customer, the greater the degree of interaction between the two during the production process.

From this conceptualization, it follows that service systems with high customer contact are more difficult to control and more difficult to rationalize than those with low customer contact. In high-contact systems, such as those listed in Figure 1, the customer can affect the time of demand, the exact nature of the service, and the quality of service since he or she tends to become involved in the process itself. In low-contact systems, by definition, customer interaction with the system is infrequent or of short duration and hence has little impact on the system during the production process.

As a side comment, service managers have always recognized that the back office (i.e., processes out of customer view) and the front office (i.e., processes involving customer contact) are different in the demands they make on operations. However, the specific implications of these demands were not made clear in the production and operations literature in the 1970s, which historically focused on the back office. Three writings, one by an executive, one by a marketing scholar, and one by an organization theorist were very useful in thinking about the issue. John Reed, CEO of City Bank captured the spirit of this distinction in a 1970's article in Bankers Magazine titled, "Sure It's a Bank but I think of it as a Factory," in which he talked about how production management could be readily applied to the processing of checks in the back office. Harvard marketing professor Ted Levitt pointed out that all services have a service front stage and a manufacturing like back stage component (Levitt 1976). James D. Thompson, a professor of business administration and sociology at Indiana University pointed out that from an open systems theory perspective, "customers or clients intrude to make difficult standardized activities required by [high volume long-linked] technology." From these writings I inferred that the front office is inherently at least, less efficient than the back office. An additional design perspective provided by Thompson's work is that a low-contact system has the capability of decoupling operations and sealing off the "technical core" from the environment, while a high-contact system does not. As he notes, "The technical core must be able to operate as if the market will absorb the single kind of product at a continuous rate, and as if inputs flowed continuously at a steady rate with specified quality." (Thompson 1967).

Pure services (typically high contact)	Mixed services (typically medium contact)	Quasi-manufacturing (typically low contact)

Entertainment centers
Health centers
Hotels
Public transportation
Retail establishments
Schools
Personal services
Jails
	"Branch" offices of:
	    financial institutions
	    government
	    computer firms
	    law firms
	    ad agencies
	    real estate firms
	Park service
	Police and fire
	Janitorial services
	Moving companies
	Repair shops
		"Home" offices of:
		    financial institu-
		tions
		    government
		    computer firms
		    law firms
		    ad agencies
		    real estate firms
		Wholesale
		Postal service
		Mail order services
		News syndicates

← higher contact   lower contact →
Increasing freedom to design efficient production procedures →

Figure 1. Classification of various service systems by extent of required customer contact in the creation of the service product

Effects of High Contact on Design Decisions

An important feature of the contact perspective is that the customer's presence affects virtually every operating decision of the service firm: The following are a few examples:

- *Facility location*: high contact operations are typically nearer to customers than low contact operations.
- *Facility layout:* high contact operations need to accommodate customer's physical and psychological needs, instead of just enhancing production.
- *Product design:* high contact operations must include the environment of the service and hence has fewer attributes than low contact operations.
- *Process design:* high contact operation processes have a direct immediate effect on the customer while in low contact systems the customer is not directly involved in the process.
- *Worker skills*: high contact workers comprise a major part of the service product and must be able to interact with the public, while low contact workers need only technical skills.
- *Quality control:* high contact quality standards are often in the eye of the beholder and hence variable, while low contact quality standards are generally measureable and hence fixed.

- *Capacity planning:* high contact capacity levels must be set to match to peak demand to avoid lost sales, while low contact operations can set capacity at some average demand level.

The managerial implications of these differences are as follows: First, unless the system operates on an appointments-only basis, it is only by happenstance that the capacity of a high-contact system will match the demand on that system at any given time. The manager of a supermarket, branch bank, or entertainment facility can predict only statistically the number of people that will be in line demanding service at, say, two o'clock on Tuesday afternoon. Hence employing the correct number of servers (neither too many nor too few) must also depend on probability. Low-contact systems, on the other hand, have the potential to exactly match supply and demand for their services since the work to be done (e.g., forms to be completed, credit ratings analyzed, or household goods shipped) can be carried out following a resource-oriented schedule permitting a direct equivalency between producer and product.

Second, by definition, the required skills of the work force in high-contact systems are characterized by a significant public relations component. Any interaction with the customer makes the direct worker in fact part of the product and therefore his attitude can affect the customer's view of the service provided. Obviously, you want to have "people - people" in high contact positions.

Third, high-contact systems are at the mercy of time far more than low-contact systems. Batching of orders for purposes of efficient production scheduling is rarely possible in high-contact operations since a few minutes' delay or a violation of the law of the queue (first come, first served) has an immediate effect on the customer. Indeed, "unfair" preferential treatment in a line at a box office often gives rise to some of the darker human emotions which are rarely evoked when such machinations are carried out by a ticket agent operating behind the scenes.

Questions for analyzing current contact strategy

Applying the foregoing concepts for analyzing a company's current contact strategy entails answering several questions:

- *What is your current contact mix?* Is it a pure service, mixed service, or quasi- manufacturing? What percentage of your business activity in terms of labor hours is devoted to direct customer contact? A good indication of where a production system falls along the contact continuum can be obtained by using the industrial engineering techniques of work sampling and system mapping.

- *Can you realign your operations to reduce unnecessary direct customer service?* Can tasks performed in the presence of the customer be shifted to the back office? Can you divide your labor force into high-contact and no-contact areas? Can you set up plants within plants to permit development of unique organizational structures for a narrower set of tasks for each subunit of the service organization?
- *Can you take advantage of the efficiencies offered by low-contact operations?* In particular, can you apply the OM concepts of batch scheduling, inventory control, work measurement, and simplification to back-office operations? Can you now use the latest technologies in assembling, packaging, cooking, testing, and so on, to support front- office operations?
- *Are your job designs and compensation procedures geared to your present structure?* Are you appropriately allocating contact and no-contact tasks? Have you matched your compensation system to the nature of the service system — for example, high-contact systems based on time and low-contact systems on output? Are you using cost or profit centers where these two measures are subject to control by the on-site manager?
- *Can you enhance the customer contact you do provide?* With all nonessential customer-contact duties shifted, can you speed up operations, by adding part-time, more narrowly skilled workers at peak hours, keep longer business hours, or add personal touches to the contacts you do have? As Sesser and Pettway (1976) note: "Although bank tellers, chambermaids, and short-order cooks may have little in common, they are all at the forefront of their employers' public images." If the low-contact portion of a worker's job can be shifted to a different work force, then the opportunity exists to focus that worker's efforts on critical interpersonal relations aspects.
- *Can you relocate parts of your service operations to lower your facility costs?* Can you shift back-room operations to lower rent districts, limit your contact facilities to small drop-off facilities such as film development boxes made famous by Fotomat in the 1970's, or get out of the contact facilities business entirely through of vending machines or jobbers?

Applying the concept

Going through the process of answering these policy questions should trigger other questions about the service organization's operation and mission. In particular, it should lead management to question whether its strength lies in high contact or low contact, and it should encourage reflection on what constitutes an optimal balance between the two types of operations relative to resource allocation and market emphasis. Also, the process should lead to an analysis of the organization structure that is required to effectively administer the individual departments as well as the overall organization of the service business. For example, it is quite probable that separate managements and internally differentiated structures will be in order if tight coordination between high-contact and low-contact units is not necessary. Where tight coordination is necessary, particular attention must be paid to boundary-spanning activities of both labor and management to assure a smooth exchange of material and information among departments.

Author's comments, 2008: Future development of contact theory and service classifications

Self-service technologies and telecommunications are two areas where contact theory needs additional refinement, or perhaps reconceptualization. Self-service always presented bit of a problem since one could have high customer contact and high efficiency. However, the fact that sales opportunity is low at the ATM or do-it -yourself car wash (the examples I was thinking of when I wrote the 1978 article) seemed like a minor point which did not invalidate the general argument. Today, though, self-service is far more pervasive, as evidenced for example, by self checkout in the supermarket, airport check-in, and blood pressure measuring devices at the drug store. Such technologies can enable customers to be more efficient producers benefiting themselves as well as the service organization. Of equal significance to the evolution of customer contact is how remote contact as manifested via the internet affects sales opportunities and production efficiency. To get a better grasp of this requires extending the classification scheme to account not just for a customer's remote interactions with a business, but for his or her interaction with other remote customers as well. As suggested by Sampson (2008), we have three categories: (1) *Pure virtual customer contact* where companies such as eBay and SecondLife enable customers to interact with one another in an open environment. (2) *Mixed virtual and actual customer contact* where, for example, customers interact with one-another in a server-moderated environment such as product discussion groups, YouTube, and WikiPedia, and (3) *Technology enhanced customer contact* where a consultant from a service provider takes remote control of a customer's computer to solve operating problems at the customer's desk.

In addition to knowledge about virtual encounters, significant progress in classification also calls a better understanding of customer psychology as it plays out in a service interaction. For example, based upon a review of the psychology literature, Chase and Dasu (2001) found extensive support for having an encounter end on a high note. Thus, a classification categorization might be based upon the difficulty of achieving a positive finish for various encounter structures. A simple example of the issue is whether a server should convey good news first or bad news first. In a call center, it may be best to give the bad news that a shipment will be delayed to get to the point right away, whereas when a doctor has bad news to convey, it might be best to build up to it gradually.

In conclusion, we have recently seen the introduction of two theories of services. One is "Service Dominant Logic," for marketing (Vargo and Lusch 2004), and the other is the "Unified Services Theory," which has an operations management orientation (Sampson and Froehle 2006). Reviews of these theories are found elsewhere in this volume. Such theory development is welcome and needed, but I would suggest that a key measure of the utility of these theories or any other theory for service engineering is how they can be used to create *operationally useful* classification systems. For example, any theory that puts all business processes in one category, such as calling everything a "service," will probably be of little managerial value. Three capabilities of useful classification systems are: (a) they enable service engineers to design interactions with the same rigor industrial engineers design physical processes, (b) they guide economic tradeoffs by managers, and (c) they facilitate service innovation.

References

Chase, R. B. 1978. Where Does the Customer Fit in a Service Operation? *Harvard Business Review*, 56 (6), November-December, pp.137-142.

Chase, R.B. and Dasu, S. 2001. Want to Perfect Your Company's Service? Use Behavioral Science. *Harvard Business Review*, 79 (6), June, pp.78-85.

Hayes, R. H. and Wheelwright, S.C., 1979. The Dynamics of Process-Product Life Cycles. *Harvard Business Review*, 57, (2), March-April, pp. 127 – 136.

Levitt, T. 1976. The Industrialization of Service. *Harvard Business Review* 56, (5). September-October, pp. 63-71

Sampson, S. E. 2008. Personal Communication.

Sampson, S. E., and Froehle, C.M., 2006. Foundations and Implications of a Proposed Unified Services Theory. *Production and Operations Management* 15(2), Summer, pp. 329-343.

Sasser, W. E. and Pettway, S. 1974. Case of Big Mac's Pay Plans, *Harvard Business Review* 54, (6), November-December, pp 30 - 36.

Thompson, J. D. 1967. *Organizations in Action* (New York: McGraw-Hill), p. 20.

Vargo, S. L. and Lusch, R. F. 2004. Evolving to a New Dominant Logic for Marketing. *Journal of Marketing*, 68, 1 – 17.

The Service Profit Chain

From Satisfaction to Ownership

James L. Heskett

Harvard Business School

W. Earl Sasser, Jr.

Harvard Business School

Prior to the establishment of the first formal courses in service management in the early 1970s, little research had been carried out to examine the properties of service activities that distinguished them from more-extensively examined activities of manufacturing organizations. While the traditional techniques of manufacturing management were invaluable to service managers, it was quickly discovered that service managers had to contend with a set of problems that the traditional tools could not solve.

There were few measures and no conceptual frameworks to guide early researchers. What became very obvious was that an integrative, cross-functional approach was needed. It was out of that need that frameworks such as the service profit chain and its "sister," the strategic service vision, arose. Both were intended to guide and shape best practice as well as research. That intent is being realized through a growing body of research and idea dissemination. As the research progresses, new measures of service effectiveness have emerged. What began as an exploration of customer and employee satisfaction has progressed to an examination of customer and employee commitment (or engagement) and, ultimately, "ownership" as better predictors of growth, profitability, or overall organizational success.

P.P. Maglio et al. (eds.), *Handbook of Service Science*, Service Science: Research and Innovations in the Service Economy, DOI 10.1007/978-1-4419-1628-0_3,
© Springer Science+Business Media, LLC 2010

The Service Profit Chain

The service profit chain posits, simply, that profit (in a for-profit organization) and growth (or other measures of success in for-profit or not-for-profit organizations) results from customer loyalty generated by customer satisfaction, which is a function of value delivered to customers. Value for customers in turn results from employee loyalty and productivity, a function of employee satisfaction, which is directly related to the internal quality (or value) created for employees (Heskett, Jones, Loveman, Sasser, and Schlesinger, 1994). The relationships are causal, not correlative. Management intervention intended to enhance profit and growth begins internally with employees. The relationships hold for operating units of a multi-unit organization as well as entire organizations. They are equally applicable to the service arms of manufacturing companies as well as not-for-profit organizations.

These relationships have been the focus of researchers since they were first suggested. Examinations of various aspects of these relationships were carried out beginning in the late 1970s to the mid-1980s (Schneider and Bowen, 1985; Parkington and Schneider, 1979; Heskett, 1986). Some of this was reported by contributors (including Shostack and Johnson and Seymour) to a path-breaking symposium on "the service encounter," in 1985 (Czepiel l, Soloman, and Surprenant, 1985). Elements of what later came to be known as the service profit chain were first portrayed as a "self-reinforcing service cycle" (Heskett, Sasser, and Hart, 1990) and later acquired the name that has characterized them since (Heskett, Sasser, Schlesinger, Loveman, and Jones, 1994). More recently, in the emerging service science literature, the self-reinforcing nature of service as win-win or value-cocreation interactions among service system entities has been highlighted (Spohrer, Maglio, Bailey, and Gruhl, 2007; Spohrer and Maglio, in press).

The early research on service profit chain relationships was largely case based, consisting of data obtained from individual organizations that demonstrated a correlation between elements of the chain. Studies that measured causal relationships in the entire chain followed. These included Anthony Rucci's examination of time lags in the effects between employee satisfaction, customer satisfaction, and store level revenue in a large retailing company (Rucci, 1997) and David Maister's (2001) measurement of causal relationships in the entire chain in his study of several thousand employees of 139 offices in 29 professional service firms, concluding that financial performance and what he termed "quality and client relationships" were driven by employee satisfaction.

Service profit chain elements are executed through what has come to be known as an operating strategy. But to what end? The answer lies in the context provided by another set of concepts, known collectively as the strategic service vision.

The Strategic Service Vision

The strategic service vision is a systematic way of thinking about strategy in a service firm. It consists of a target market (emphasizing the need for market *focus*), a service concept (basically a business definition centered around *results*— not products or services—provided for customers, positioned against results desired by customers and results offered by competitors), the operating strategy (designed to *leverage* value for customers over costs incurred in creating the value through organization, controls, policies, and practices related to the service profit chain), and support systems (created to achieve *excellence* in the capability provided to frontline service providers). It argues for a comprehensive and internally-consistent approach to the design and execution of successful service offerings. The framework applies to both internal customers (employees as well as other internal departments) as well as customers more traditionally thought of as external to the organization.

This set of concepts was evolving at the same time as those associated with the service profit chain. Related conceptual frameworks had been put forth by several authors (see, for example, Sasser, Olsen, and Wyckoff, 1978; and Normann, 1984). They were expanded by Heskett (1986). The strategic service vision clearly relies on and relates to a number of long-examined concepts from marketing (target market focus), operations (process design), human resources (organization theory), and management control (balanced scorecard measurement and reporting) reflecting the fact that service management lies at the intersection of these business functions and disciplines.

If the service profit chain is essentially a systematic way of thinking about an operating strategy embedded in the strategic service vision, two other related concepts provide linkages between employees, customers, and financial performance as well. They are: (1) customer and employee value equations and (2) what has come to be known as the "mirror effect."

Value Equations

Two links in the service profit chain relate to value both external (for customers) and internal (for employees) to the firm, suggesting the need for definitions of value. As a result, value equations have been formulated based on what customers and employees tell us about what they value most in their purchases and relationships or jobs, respectively. Elements of the equations are the most important of a larger number of factors and are intended to provide a basis for guiding both the planning and execution of strategies for meeting customer and employee needs.

Specifically, the customer value equation posits that:

Value to Customers = (Results + Quality of the Customer Experience)/(Price + Access Costs)

As noted early on (Sasser, Olsen and Wyckoff, 1978): "The service level is the consumer's perception of the quality of the service. It is a complex bundle of explicit and implicit attributes that attempts to satisfy the needs of a consumer.... The consumer explicitly or implicitly ranks service offerings on the basis of service level and price."

The customer value equation assumes that customers seek to buy or rent results (Christensen and Raynor, 2003; Levitt, 1960), not products or services, while engaging in a positive experience, taking into account both the explicit price and implicit costs of obtaining the results, including the ease of doing business with an organization and its people (access costs). Unfortunately, managers often think only of their products ("we sell hamburgers") rather than in terms of a total bundle of results that the consumer purchases. A fast-food restaurant that merely sells "hamburgers" can also have slow, surly personnel, dirty and unattractive facilities and few return customers.

Similarly, employee surveys have shown generally that they especially value, in varying orders of importance: (1) the quality (fairness) of a boss's decisions regarding people, (2) opportunities for personal development (more important in recent years), (3) the degree to which work is recognized, (4) the quality of one's associates on the job, (5) the capability and latitude granted to solve problems for customers, and (6) reasonable compensation (Schlesinger and Zornitsky, 1991)

From this work, we can formulate an employee value equation as follows:

Value to Employees = (Capability to Deliver Results + Quality of Work Experience)/(1/Total Income + "Job Access Costs")

In this case, many of the factors influencing employee satisfaction relate to the latitude provided for solving customers' problems as well as the quality of the workplace. But they are tempered by both compensation and job access costs such as the degree of job continuity and ease of maintaining work/life balance.

One reason that these value equations deserve attention is the level of interest in something that has come to be known as the "mirror effect."

The "Mirror Effect"

Data gathered from various multi-unit organizations under many conditions (even at country management levels) have demonstrated correlations between customer and employee satisfaction as well as strong inverse relationships between customer satisfaction and employee turnover rates in the service profit chain (Schneider and Bowen, 1985, 1993, and 1995; Schlesinger and Heskett, 1991). Further, these behaviors are linked to financial performance.   The thesis holds that this knowledge, characterized as a "mirror effect," can, for example, be used as the basis for internal best practice exchange in helping poor performing units learn from those with better performance in a multi-unit organization.

Valid questions have been raised, however, about the validity of comparing units with different characteristics in examining the "mirror effect." For example, several studies have concluded that the nature of the service provided (or the kind of value sought by the customer) affects the strength of the relationship between employee and customer satisfaction (Bowen and Lawler, 1992). Other factors affecting the strength of the relationship may be store or unit size, the degree of emphasis on profit and growth in certain stores, service standards set by competitors to which customers have been exposed, and the degree to which the service encounter is mediated by technology. This argues for carefully constructed samples of units to be examined as well as close attention to the nature of the measures used (Silvestro and Cross, 2000; Loveman, 1998).

Based on research to date, it is safe to conclude that the service profit chain and related conceptual frameworks will be regarded as hypotheses for some time to come. They were set forth to articulate relationships capable of measurement in a field, service management, that had had little systematic attention. As such, they tempt examination. Since they were first articulated, many studies have examined one or more aspects of the relationships embodied in these concepts. While most of the studies have confirmed many aspects of the initial hypotheses, some of the hypotheses have fared better than others. In the process, added conceptual development and measurement has taken place, further enriching the field.

Where We Stand Today: From Satisfaction to Ownership

In its simplest form, the service profit chain is about developing an environment in which highly capable, engaged employees, acting as owners, interact with customers to create customer value far superior to that offered by the competition. As a result, these customers remain as customers [Retention], they buy more [Related Sales], they tell others about their positive customer experience [Referrals] and they make suggestions for enhancing the customer experience by suggesting new products or services and process improvements [Research and Development] These four "R's" of customer behavior fuel long term profitability and growth. Employees working in such an environment mirror these behaviors with high retention rates, strong motivation to improve the quality of their work life by recruiting others to work with them, and efforts to make suggestions on how to make things better.

More recent work on these ideas has moved service profit chain concepts forward, offering new measures that have increased the appeal of the concepts to practicing managers. This, in turn, has yielded a more systematic body of data that promises to provide benchmarks against which the performance of individual operating units and entire organizations can be measured. Further, it has led to the exploration of a "hierarchy" of employee and customer attitudes and behaviors, including: satisfaction (an attitude), loyalty (a behavior), commitment (an attitude), and ownership (an attitude characterized by certain behaviors).

Research to date suggests stronger relationships between financial measures and behaviors than between financial measures and attitudes. The research has progressed from the early examination of the impact of satisfaction on performance to more recent work on the effects of ownership.

Satisfaction

Consider, for example, the measurement of customer attitude. For years, attention has centered on measures of customer satisfaction with products or services. While isolated measures of satisfaction have served little purpose, trend measurement has proved useful in assessing an organization's relationship with its customers.

To the extent that satisfaction influences loyalty, customer satisfaction may be linked as well to future performance. However, studies of relationships between customer satisfaction and financial performance have not, under some conditions, validated the relationship (Silvestro and Cross, 2000). Similar results have been obtained in efforts to compare employee satisfaction with financial performance (Keiningham, Aksoy, Daly, Perrier, and Solom, 2006). This raises questions as to whether an attitude such as customer satisfaction leads directly to behaviors (for example, customer loyalty) that have more direct relationships with financial performance. It has prompted work to find measures with stronger linkages to financial performance. One such measure is the net promoter score.

Net Promoter Score

One problem disrupting the relationship between customer satisfaction and profit is the way in which the profit is earned. This thesis posits that some profits are earned at the expense of customer relationships (bad profits) while others result from strong relationships (good profits) (Reichheld, 2006). In an effort to provide a measure that produces a stronger linkage between customer attitude and profit, Reichheld and his associates developed a measure of what some have called customer commitment or engagement. It is the Net Promoter Score, based on responses to the question, "How willing would you be to recommend (this company, experience, product, or service) to a friend?" The net score is obtained by subtracting those very willing to do so from those not so willing to do so.

Whether or not relationships between customer commitment and financial measures are stronger than for customer satisfaction measures is a matter of debate. One problem is that both measure customer attitude as opposed to a behavior such as loyalty, thereby running the risk of a disconnect between what customers say they will do and what they actually do. Nevertheless, the net promoter score has made accessible to management an understandable measure that is relatively simple and easy to administer. It has become widely enough used that it may provide benchmarks against which a single organization's performance can be measured. And it is provoking a new wave of research to examine its effectiveness, efforts that will call added attention to these concepts. (See, for example, Keiningham, Cooil, Andreassen, Aksoy, 2007).

Ownership

Unease with the emphasis on measuring attitudes vs. behaviors, combined with new technologies for the exchange of ideas, has led to the exploration of the implications of "ownership" behaviors among customers and employees (Graf, 2007; Heskett, Sasser, and Wheeler, 2008; Cook, 2008). Ownership among customers is characterized by the frequency and value of actual referrals of new customers as well as constructive criticism involving suggestions for improving existing products and services as well as proposals for new ones. Employees exhibit ownership by referring new talent to their organizations and offering suggestions for improving such things as processes, products, or services.

The hypothesis that a customer/owner is worth many times that of a more casual, often price-sensitive, customer has been born out by research which incorporates the value of both customer referrals and suggestions for product, service, or process improvements in lifetime value estimates. To date, employee lifetime value has been less well documented than that for customers.

Early work on these ideas suggests that, in many industries, a business may produce outstanding results if it is able to engage relatively small numbers of customers as owners. It also suggests that relationships with good customers improve by engaging them in ownership activities on behalf of the organization. This generally requires high proportions of employees acting as owners, further emphasizing the need for employee satisfaction and engagement.

Ownership measures have more direct relationships to financial outcomes than do those related to attitude (satisfaction) or intent (willingness to promote). On the other hand, they require the measurement of customer and employee behaviors, in part based on what customers and employees themselves claim they have done in a recent time period. The accuracy of these kinds of measures requires further examination. However, in one recent study, strong relationships were established between customer profitability and the level of ownership behaviors among both customers and the employees serving them in a situation in which net promoter scores were not good predictors of either customer ownership or profitability (Heskett, Sasser, and Wheeler, 2008). All of this suggests that there is much more work to be done in examining service profit chain relationships at each level of the employee and customer "hierarchy" of attitudes and behaviors.

Challenges for the Future

Challenges for the future exploration of the service profit chain take several forms, including measurement, validation, and application.

Measurement

Most of the studies of service profit chain relationships to date rely on large amounts of data required to examine even a portion of the chain. This may require that researchers relinquish control over the collection of at least a portion of the data needed, relying to some degree on already-existing data in organizations under study. Because managers often collect data for purposes other than research, it can raise questions ranging from relevance to accuracy.

One way of studying cause and effect in the chain is through the vehicle of the longitudinal study. Longitudinal studies carried out in a single organization require unusual access to an organization and its management as well as consistency of measurement over relatively long periods of time. As a result, factor analyses of opinions regarding retrospective or prospective behaviors may be used more frequently to study the phenomena. These are always subject to the criticism of the validity of relationships between what people say they have done or will do and actual behaviors. It will require added efforts to validate such opinion-based data, perhaps through selective sampling of actual behaviors and their comparisons with survey responses.

Of greater concern is the lack of comparability among studies carried out in different organizations. Ideally, those interested in carrying out this kind of research would establish some category "definitions" with recommended methods for collecting such data. Presumably, these would even include suggested wordings of questions to be employed in the data gathering. This would require leadership of the kind provided by an association or other academic organization.

Links in the chain related to value require more attention. While efforts have been made to define value equations for both customers and employees, as presented earlier, these involve notional measures. For example, how do we measure and compare such things as results, quality of experience, and access costs for research purposes? Presumably, this is best done by asking customers or employees to quantify them. But it will require even clearer definitions of exactly what we mean by each of these terms.

Further work on the impact of customers and employees as "owners" in the chain, and the extent to which their behaviors mirror each other, will require more fully-developed measures of the lifetime value of customers and especially that of employees. The latter will have to take into account not only the impact of employee turnover on recruiting and training costs, but also those associated with productivity, attendant customer behaviors, and the benefits to the organization of psychic ownership.

Validation

Many studies that examine service profit chain hypotheses have been conducted to date. They can be characterized as partial vs. holistic, single-company vs. industry or multi-industry, "snap shot" vs. longitudinal, and firm wide vs. unit level in nature.

Studies of selected linkages in the service profit chain have generally been supportive of the hypotheses (Lau, 2000; Hallowell, 1996). As noted earlier, the small number of comprehensive examinations of the chain have tended to produce what might be considered as "weak links" at certain points (Silvestro and Cross, 2000), suggesting that under certain conditions, one or more sets of relationships may have limited relevance to financial outcomes. Alternatively, this may suggest the need for benchmarking results against those of comparable organizations in the same business to filter the impact of externalities on the data.

Issues of validation range from conditions under which service profit chain data is collected to the admission or exclusion of certain pieces of data. Again, the challenge of validation is different in studies involving a snapshot of a number of operating units at one point in time as opposed to longitudinal research. For example, externalities such as time lags between management actions and effects on employee and customer satisfaction, loyalty, engagement, and ownership may produce strong relationships between certain measures and weak ones between others. Unless the data is lagged or collected over a period of time (Rucci, 1997), the effect of time is lost.

Performance within multi-unit organizations varies greatly from unit to unit. This is true even for the best-performing organizations. For example, one study found no significant relationship between employee satisfaction and store performance until the data was examined by size of store (Keiningham, Aksoy, Daly, Perrier, and Solom, 2006). To date, studies that have compared only the best and worst performing units—excluding those in the middle of the performance spectrum on service profit chain measures—have produced the most statistically significant contrasts on all dimensions.

Attitudes and behaviors of customer-facing employees quite likely have strong influence on customer attitudes and behaviors. When their data is comingled with that of their superiors not in contact with customers, it may dilute the findings.

Application

Ironically, management acceptance and application of service profit chain relationships have outpaced their validation by researchers. That may be due to both the intuitive attractiveness of the conceptual framework, the communication of the concepts from academe to practitioners through consultants, and the positive "word of mouth" that certain applications have received. Whatever the explanation, firms from Australia to France have built their strategies around the ideas, judging from narratives which in some cases have even been presented in company annual reports.

Widespread application presents both an opportunity and an obligation for academic research. It means that there is ample availability of data waiting to be examined. But it is quite possible that some management action is based on mistaken assumptions, perhaps resulting from misleading or poorly-collected data, creating an obligation to extend current research to provide better guidance to practitioners considering the organized application of service profit chain concepts. This will require: (1) better definitions of terms used to describe service profit chain elements, perhaps even an ontology and epistemology of service phenomena as called for in the emerging service science literature; (2) recommended methods of collecting and organizing data; (3) standardized as well as new approaches to analysis; and (4) widespread sharing of results among both researchers and practitioners. It is work that is waiting to be done.

References

Bowen, David E., and Edward E. Lawler III, "The empowerment of service workers: what, why, how and when," *Sloan Management Review*, Vol. 33, No. 3 (1992), pp. 31-39.

Christensen, Clayton M., and Michael E. Raynor, *The Innovator's Solution: Creating and Sustaining Successful Growth* (Boston: HBS Press, 2003), at p. 74.

Cook, Scott, "The Contribution Revolution: Letting Volunteers Build Your Business," *Harvard Business Review*, October, 2008, pp. 60-69.

Czepiel, John A., Michael R. Soloman, and Carol F. Surprenant, eds., *The Service Encounter* (Lexington, MA: D. C. Heath & Company, 1985).

Graf, Albert, "Changing roles of customers: consequences for HRM," *International Journal of Service Industry Management*, Vol. 18, No. 5., 2007.

Hallowell, Roger, "The relationships of customer satisfaction, customer loyalty, and profitability: an empirical study," *International Journal of Service Industry Management*, Vol. 7, No. 4, (1996), pp. 27-42.

Heskett, James L., *Managing in the Service Economy* (Boston: HBS Press, 1986).

Heskett, James L., W. Earl Sasser, Jr., and Christopher W. L. Hart, *Service Breakthroughs: Changing the Rules of the Game* (New York: The Free Press, 1990), pp. 12-13.

Heskett, James L., Thomas O. Jones, Gary W. Loveman, W. Earl Sasser, Jr., and Leonard A. Schlesinger, "Putting the Service Profit Chain to Work," *Harvard Business Review*, March-April, 1994, pp. 164-174.

Heskett, James L., W. Earl Sasser, Jr., and Joe Wheeler, *The Ownership Quotient* (Boston: Harvard Business Press, 2008)

Johnson, Eugene M., and Daniel T. Seymour, "The Impact of Cross Selling on the Service Encounter in Retail Banking," in John A. Czepiel, Michael R. Soloman, and Carol F. Surprenant, eds., *The Service Encounter* (Lexington, MA: D. C. Heath & Company, 1985), pp. 225-239.

Keiningham, Timothy L., Lerzan Aksoy, Robert M. Daly, Kathy Perrier, and Antoine Solom, "Reexamining the link between employee satisfaction and store performance in a retail environment," *International Journal of Service Industry Management*, Vol. 17., No. 1, 2006, pp. 51-57.

Keiningham, Timothy L., Bruce Cooil, Tor Wallin Andreassen, and Lerzan Aksoy, "A Longitudinal Examination of Net Promoter and Firm Revenue Growth," *Journal of Marketing*, Vol. 71, July, 2007, pp. 39-51.

Lau, R. S. M., "Quality of work life and performance: an ad hoc investigation of two key elements in the service profit chain model," *International Journal of Service Industry Management*, Vol. 11, No. 5, 2000, pp. 422-437.

Levitt, Theodore, "Marketing Myopia," *Harvard Business Review*, July-August, 1960, at p. 45.

Loveman, Gary W., "Employee satisfaction, customer loyalty, and financial performance: an empirical examination of the service profit chain in retail banking." *Journal of Service Research*, Vol. 1, No. 1, August, 1998, pp. 18-31.

Maister, David, *Practice What You Preach: What Managers Must Do To Create A High Achievement Culture* (New York: The Free Press, 2001), pp. 77-84.

Normann, Richard, *Service Management: Strategy and Leadership in Service Businesses* (Chichester, England: John Wiley & Sons, 1984).

Parkington, J. J., and B. Schneider, "Some Correlates of Experienced Job Stress: A Boundary Role Study," *Academy of Management Journal*, vol. 22, 1979, pp. 270-281.

Reichheld, Fred, *The Ultimate Question: Driving Good Profits and True Growth*, (Boston: HBS Press, 2006)

Rucci, Anthony, presentation at 25th Anniversary Conference, New York Human Resources Institute, February, 1997.

Sasser, W. Earl Jr., R. Paul Olsen, and D. Daryl Wyckoff, *Management of Service Operations* (Boston: Allyn and Bacon, 1978), pp. 8-21.

Schlesinger, Leonard A., and Jeffrey Zornitsky, "Job Satisfaction, Service Capability, and Customer Satisfaction: An Examination of Linkages and Management Implications," *Human Resource Planning*, Vol. 145, No. 2 (1991), pp. 141-149.

Schlesinger, Leonard A., and James L. Heskett, "Breaking the cycle of failure in services," *Sloan Management Review*, Vol. 32, No. 3 (1991), pp. 17-28.

Schneider, Benjamin, and David E. Bowen, "New Services Design, Development and Implementation and the Employee," in William W. George and Claudia E. Marshall, eds., *Developing New Services* (Chicago: American Marketing Association, 1985), pp. 82-101.

Schneider, Benjamin, and David E. Bowen, "Human Resources management Is Critical," *Organizational Dynamics*, 1993, pp. 39-52.

Schneider, Benjamin, and David E. Bowen, *Winning the Service Game* (Boston: HBS Press, 1995).

Shostack, G. Lynn, "Planning the Service Encounter," in John A. Czepiel, Michael R. Soloman, and Carol F. Surprenant, eds., *The Service Encounter* (Lexington, MA: D. C. Heath & Company, 1985), pp. 243-253.

Silvestro, Rhian, and Stuart Cross, "Applying the service profit chain in a retail environment: Challenging the 'Satisfaction mirror'", *International Journal of Service Industry Management*, Vol. 11, No. 3, 2000, pp. 244-268.

Spohrer, Jim, Paul P. Maglio, John Bailey, and Dan Gruhl, Steps toward a science of service systems. Computer, 40, (2007), 71-77.

Spohrer, Jim and Paul P. Maglio, Service science: Toward a smarter planet. To appear in W. Karwowski & G. Salvendy, eds., *Introduction to service engineering*, (in press).

Winning the Service Game

Revisiting the Rules by Which *People* Co-Create Value

Benjamin Schneider

Valtera Corporation and University of Maryland, La Jolla, CA, USA

David E. Bowen

Thunderbird School of Global Management, Glendale, AZ, USA

The chapter presents a summary and extension of our book, *Winning the Service Game*, published in 1995 by Harvard Business School Press (Schneider & Bowen, 1995). We summarize the "rules of the game" we had presented there concerning the production and delivery primarily of consumer services and note several advances in thinking since we wrote the book. We emphasize that people (customers, employees, and managers) still are a prominent key to success in service and that this should be fully recognized in the increasingly technical sophistication of service science. The foundation of this thesis is the idea that promoting service excellence and innovation requires an understanding of the co-creation of value by and for people. Further, that such co-creation is most likely to effectively occur when an appropriate psycho-social context is created for people as they produce, deliver and experience a service process. Such a context is the result of understanding the complexities of the people who are a central component of the service delivery system.

© Benjamin Schneider and David E. Bowen. Used by permission. Summary and update of *Winning the Service Game* published by the Harvard Business School Press (1995) and copyrighted © 1995 by Benjamin Schneider and David E. Bowen.

P.P. Maglio et al. (eds.), *Handbook of Service Science*, Service Science: Research and Innovations in the Service Economy, DOI 10.1007/978-1-4419-1628-0_4.

Introduction

Consumer services are frequently delivered by people to people and the people who deliver them work with and for other people; people are a big part of consumer service delivery and they are the focus of our work. People played a large role in our book, *Winning the Service Game* (Schneider & Bowen, 1995) but over time we have become even more focused on the people part of service. That is, as the new field of service science proceeds, the emphasis appears to be on winning via linear programming, operations management, engineering solutions, information technology, economies of scale, and mathematical formulae. These foci provide a potential tactical advantage with regard to efficiency in the design of service delivery systems to mass markets and to businesses but they tend to ignore the social psychology of consumer service delivery contexts and the relationships among the people (customers, employees, and managers) involved.

Executives are continuously seeking ways to simplify complex problems and consumer service delivery is a complex problem. It is complex precisely because it involves people interacting with each other in a social psychological context and the paradox of the technical and engineering emphases in service science is that it tends to ignore this social psychology. And when people are mentioned it is typically with regard to their skills and knowledge and the ways those integrate with other systems parameters: "Creating and delivering a service requires the use of some collection of assets, whether capital assets such as information technology infrastructure, consumable assets such as service parts and materials, labor assets such as skilled employees, or intangible assets such as an individual's skills or an organization's proprietary data or processes" (Dietrich & Harrison, 2006).

This kind of narrow focus on "labor as skills" reminded us of the recent research in England (Birdie et al., 2008) where the impact of operations management and human resources management practices on company productivity were examined. The authors looked at 22 years worth of data from 308 companies that had implemented HR practices (empowerment, extensive training, and teamwork) and/or operations management initiatives (total quality management, just-in-time manufacturing, advanced manufacturing technology, and supply-chain partnering). The results were striking, and we quote: "[W]e found performance benefits from empowerment and extensive training, with the adoption of teamwork serving to enhance both. In contrast, none of the operational practices were directly related to productivity…" (Birdie et al., 2008, p. 468).

On Avoiding the Commoditization of Service

We are not here to claim that operations management- and engineering-based principles are ineffective in service organizations. Indeed, services operations management, *together* with services marketing and services human resource management, is essential to service management effectiveness. That has been the fundamental conclusion of the field of services management that long-preceded service science. Winning the service game requires the two-fold appreciation that: (a) operational practices can help organizations operate both more efficiently and more effectively but (b) if everyone is doing the same thing there is not competitive advantage to it. Thus, the results of the British study summarized reveal that there is no relationship across the companies between the adoption of operational procedures and success—there is no competitive advantage. Does this mean the organizations have not improved their efficiency and effectiveness? No; all it means is that the adoption of these techniques has not improved their competitive advantage. Additionally, we maintain that the more technical and operational implementations of service science are more easily copied by competitors than those that reside in dealing with the complexities of people, the interactions among them, and the values of the larger organization in which they reside. Thus we claim that ignoring the social psychology of the various parties to service delivery and the setting in which they interact is dangerous to the long-term health of service organizations because that is what can yield *sustainable* competitive advantage. It is dangerous to ignore people in consumer services because, first, the customers are people and ignoring their psychology, especially when customization is important, makes all service delivery alike. Second, ignoring people, makes those who deliver service to customers also a commodity and to be treated as such by management. The recent debacle at Circuit City, where long-term sales and service employees were fired because their salaries were commensurate with their skills and experience, is a good case in point. That is, within six months of these firings Circuit City declared bankruptcy because sales had dropped precipitously with customers complaining about the lack of knowledge of the sales people. Third, people *are* the organizations in which they work. It is always surprising to us how management can think of their organizations as somehow separate from the people who work in and manage them when an organization is nothing without the people who are there. One of us has coined the term and written about "The People Make the Place" (Schneider, 1987). And we have become increasingly concerned with the idea that if the place in which people work does not create an appropriate service climate or culture for them then they will fail to focus on serving customers, customers will be dissatisfied and not return and long-term profits and market value will suffer (Schneider, Macey, Lee & Young, 2009b).

Are we overstating the case, the case being that service science has tended to downplay the importance of people and the social systems in which they behave? Consider the following quote about the importance of people by Spohrer et al. (2007, p. 75) as they define service science:

> "Three types of key resources make up all service. [1] **People.** The more they're needed and the longer it takes to educate them or get them to competent performance, the more expensive human resources typically become. For example, each profession has only a limited number of people, and training more people with those professional skills takes time and educational investment. So scaling a service system that depends on human resources might require seeking out labor from another less expensive geography,

repurposing and retraining people from another industry sector, or identifying demographic segments yet to join the labor force."

In our estimation this does not portray people in the complexity marketing and human resources scientists have defined them. That complexity includes their talents, of course, but also their motivations, their attitudes, the nature of the service climate and culture in which they interact, and indeed the technical systems they use in creating value for each other and the organizations of which they are a part (Lovelock & Wirtz, 2004).

Our chapter can be viewed then as a service science cautionary tale, on several fronts. First is to guard against the new discipline of service science paying less attention to the role of people, and the inter-related disciplines of social psychology, organizational behavior and industrial-organizational psychology, than it does to the role of more technical approaches, and the disciplines that relate to them. To the credit of Jim Spohrer and others who have defined the field of service science, people issues are occasionally afforded attention in the stated definition of service science. Yet, the human resource/people piece does seem to be addressed with a narrow focus on skills and talent and the literature on the importance of context (organizational climate and organizational culture) is not explored at all.

Second is to be mindful of the factors that may lead to an under-emphasis on people in service science. For example, service science emerged primarily in a B2B business context. That context can invite an emphasis on economies of scale and the techniques that yield them that obscures and may even try to smooth over the uniqueness, contributions and expectations of people. Finally, we caution to keep in mind the endgame of service science—service innovation. In our estimation the true wellspring of innovation will remain as the minds and hearts of engaged customers, employees, and managers—people—committed to ongoing improvement in the co-creation of value.

In sum, the issue is not whether the new field designation of service science is a bad one but where the new designation is headed. For example, the new web-based journal *Service Science* (2009) has produced its first issue and articles are about automated optimal control, hyper-networks, computational thinking, and network transformation services. Spohrer (2009) in his editorial comment says the right things about interdependencies but the first issue of the new journal is narrow in its focus on B2B issues and information technology systems. The field of Economics has become increasingly behavioral—people-oriented—in the last decade or so; is the field of Service Science taking Service Management *less* behavioral? So, we raise here a cautionary flag.

In what follows, we elaborate on these points as we summarize the key issues raised in the 1995 book, as we were asked to do for this volume. Readers will see that the book in many ways addressed the issues just outlined but did so in less direct ways than we just did and will do so in what follows. We do the summary by chapter so interested readers can obtain an appropriate "feel" for both the structure and the content of the book. In the book we had 53 "rules of the service game" which we repeat at the beginning of each chapter summary as they form a useful outline for what follows. These rules were developed largely with the B2C sector in mind, but they have considerable relevance for many B2B service relationships, as well. Service effectiveness in both settings requires knowing the rules by which to attract and retain the right mix of customers, employees, and managers within a psycho-social context that offers a value proposition to all three stakeholders. Many of our "rules" draw upon fundamental principles of individual and organizational psychology that can help inform management about how to manage people and their organizational contexts in *both* B2C and B2B settings.

Finally, we imagine that many of these rules from 1995 may sound like dated common sense here in 2009. Now if only common sense was common practice! We would even suggest that perhaps winning the service game is as much about getting better at executing the science we already know, as it is about generating new science.

Chapter 1: Building a Winning Service Organization by Mastering the Rules of the Game

The central point in Chapter 1 was that the rules of the service game are different from the rules of the manufacturing game. Service organizations in the extreme deliver to customers an experience rather than a tangible good so it is the delivery that counts since that is what creates the experience. If service organizations need to think differently about how they operate then managers need to think differently about what their organization is and how it behaves. Service organizations must function differently because customers are as much a part of the organization as the employees, including management.

We advocated a way of viewing service organizations in our 1995 book that aligns well with the recent service science perspective on service systems as dynamic, functionally-integrated combinations of resources. We indicated that the goal is the development of a seamless service system and we (Schneider & Bowen, 1995, pp. 2 and 8) offered:

> "...a unique view of service organizations---one that treats a service business as comprised of three tiers: a customer tier, a boundary tier, and a coordination tier. This three-tiered model stands in sharp contrast to traditional functional ways of slicing up organizations—like into marketing, human resources, and operations management. ....It is, instead, a book on how to strategically and holistically manage the hundreds of things that must be done well across three tiers to win the service game. ...the three-tiered view of service firms, based on permeable tiers, not grounded in functions—can yield seamlessness in service delivery. By seamlessness, we mean that service, in all of its dimensions and characteristics, is delivered without a hitch."

The customer tier we conceptualized in terms of expectations for quality and needs, with an emphasis on customer needs for security, esteem and justice. The boundary tier we conceptualized as everything with which customers come in contact when interacting with a service delivery firm including the people, the equipment/technology, and the physical space. In addition, that which supports the boundary tier—the "back office" and the equipment and technology designers—are also part of this tier because they link directly to customers through service delivery employees. In our framework, the designers of systems and procedures are critical to the creation of a service climate because employees must use them to serve customers and customers experience the degree to which those systems serve them or the organization.

The coordination tier was labeled "coordination" rather than "management" to emphasize again a service perspective of weaving together the various parties and elements of service, not controlling or managing them, per se. The point is that in service delivery, since it is an experience being created for customers, it cannot be managed as it unfolds. So, compared to a manufacturing environment where the production process can be stopped to make corrections, in service delivery once the process begins it unfolds as a whole without intervention. The role of management, like the conductor of an orchestra, is to coordinate all of the elements required for excellence to emerge.

We emphasized the idea that the goal of the coordination tier is the creation of a service climate or culture such that all functions and subsystems in the firm—marketing, operations, finance, human resources—see service quality as the raison d'etre of their function and of the entire organization. This focus on service climate was based on early research in bank branches that had shown that when employees at the boundary tier view their organization as one that has a positive service climate the *customers* they serve report receiving higher service quality (Schneider, 1980).

Figure 1 shows the results from the first study that revealed this relationship between employee reports and customer reports. In other words, when employees report their company really emphasizes service quality in all they do then the customers with whom they interact report positive service quality experiences.

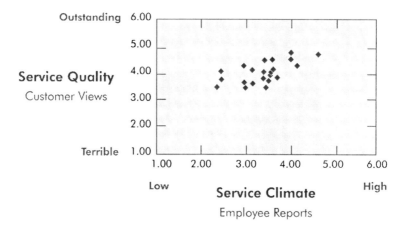

Figure 1. Relationship Between Employee Service Climate Perceptions and Customer Perceptions of Service Quality in Retail Bank Branches

There are now dozens of studies in the published academic literature that report similar results (Dean, 2004; Schneider & White, 2004) and this kind of research has come to be called "linkage research" (Wiley, 1996). The research has been carried out with samples of hotels, branch banks, auto dealerships, insurance agencies and regions, supermarkets, and so forth, wherever and whenever organizations have multiple outlets that serve customers. There is now also research at the firm level of analysis that reveals service employee perceptions of service climate relate directly to firm customer satisfaction and indirectly to financial and market performance for diverse service industry firms (airlines, telecommunications, retail, financials, and so forth; Schneider, et al., 2009b).

The point is that companies, and units within companies, that promote service quality in all they do across their subsystems create an environment for employees in which they are *engaged* in serving customers—and where customers respond with positive appraisals. Of course, what is important about those positive appraisals is that they lead to customer satisfaction, loyalty, retention, and sales and ultimately to positive financial and market performance (Anderson, Fornell, & Mazvancheryl, 2004; Gruca & Rego, 2005).

The chapter summaries that follow first present the rules and then a summary of the major points for that chapter, followed by extensions and more recent thinking as appropriate.

Customer Tier-Chapter 2: Meeting Customer Expectations

1. Manage the intangible
2. Really watch out for "habituated" expectations
3. Identify customers' two-tiered expectations
4. Analyze the complex "quality psychology" of *your* customers
5. Plan for recovery from systems failures
6. Know who really knows your customers
7. Monitor quality for improvement, not for data
8. Focus or falter in the marketplace

Services tend to be less tangible than goods so it is very important for management to understand that *how* the service is delivered is at least as important as *what* is delivered. That is, if you think about a restaurant, there is the food itself that is delivered and then there is *how* the food is delivered. Understanding what market niche a company wishes to occupy and exploit is all about understanding customer expectations for both what is delivered and how it is delivered. The problem with intangibles is that expectations for them are less clear than are expectations for tangibles; again, intangibles are experiences and tangibles can be touched and felt and used.

The reason why it is important for a business to know *its* customers' expectations is because they are the relevant market. We proposed in the chapter that the keys to competitive advantage with regard to customer expectations are to know the following:

- Firm-specific customers' expectations
- Firm-specific customers' evaluations of service quality
- Firm-specific customers' evaluations of the firm's major competitors' service quality

The point we made is that a firm must do better than its major competitors to be competitive; perfection is not the goal but being superior to the competition is.

Customers are not necessarily aware of their expectations until something happens to violate those expectations. We called people's everyday expectations of which they are unaware "habituated expectations." Such expectations exist subconsciously and only come to awareness when violated. For example, when we enter a room we flick on the light switch and subconsciously expect the light to go on. Only when it does not go on do we understand we carry that expectation. In fact, the more reliable a service is over time the more customers' expectations become habituated. But understand that a service can be unreliably *superior* as well as inferior; positive changes in service delivery can raise to consciousness the excellence with which a service has been delivered.

Service researchers and practitioners are quite familiar with inferior reliability in service delivery and deal with it under the label "recovery" as in "we need to recover from that screw-up." When customer expectations are violated firms must recover to at least achieve where they were prior to the error. Recovery must be instantaneous and it must be extraordinary for it to be memorable; almost half of the reports on dissatisfying service experiences are for poor recovery to a service delivery failure (Tax & Brown, 2000). Recovery is very difficult because it involves the coordination of all parties involved (Michel, Bowen, & Johnston, 2009).

There has been some debate about whether service recovery can yield positive consequences for organizations that do it well; this notion is called the service recovery paradox. In other words, should a company make an error just to show how terrific it really is and thereby enhance customer satisfaction and loyalty? While there is occasional research that reveals the potential for improvements in customer satisfaction and loyalty following excellent recovery (DeWitt, Nguyen, & Marshall, 2008), the overwhelming evidence suggests this is not the usual case and it is especially damaging if following recovery the service is poor (Michel & Meuter, 2008).

What is interesting about customer expectations is that they contain two elements, one having to do with the *content* of the expectation and the other having to do with the *form*. So, people who go to a Quality 8 motel have expectations for the reliability and responsiveness of the service they will receive and so do those who go to the Ritz-Carlton. But the form of those expectations will differ greatly because people have different expectations as a function of the market niche in which they are "playing the game." And the same people at different times and for different reasons play both games and they bring to those games different expectations for what constitutes good service. Companies must know the expectations of their customers so they can focus on them; if they do not focus on a particular niche or segment they will falter because no organization can serve all market segments effectively (Davidow & Uttal, 1989).

Finally we were and continue to be strong believers in monitoring customer perceptions of service quality, especially with regard to the content and form appropriate for a given company. But we are only in favor of such monitoring if the data are used to make improvements. And the key to making improvements in service delivery resides in the employees who serve them; more on this later.

Customer Tier-Chapter 3: Respecting Customer Needs

    9. Recognize that quality starts with needs
  10. Recognize that violating a need means losing a customer
  11. Respect customers' needs for security
  12. Respect customers' needs for esteem
  13. Respect customers' needs for justice

Customer satisfaction has implicitly and frequently explicitly been built on a "met expectations" model. In our book we introduced the idea that customer needs provided an additional (not an alternative, but an additional) focus for understanding customer satisfaction. We noted that expectations are frequently *sub*-conscious but that needs are frequently *un*conscious and that needs reflect larger psychological issues of relevance to people—like identity issues (self-esteem), how safe I feel (security), and how fairly I think I am treated by the world (justice). Indeed we noted that violation of needs could produce stronger negative reactions than violation of expectations might produce. In a later paper (Schneider & Bowen, 1999) we developed these ideas further in explicating the role of need gratification and need violation in understanding customer delight and outrage, more extreme forms of satisfaction and dissatisfaction.

The major point we made with regard to needs is that they are more fundamental than expectations. They are more about customers as people rather than customers as customers; *all* companies must respect customer needs because they are fundamental to life and human existence. So, the variability that exists for knowing your customers' expectations so you can focus on them is not as relevant when it comes to needs because all people share these needs and the issue is how well systems are designed to meet and/or exceed them.

The three needs on which we focused were the needs for:

- *Security*: The need to feel secure and unthreatened by physical, psychological or economic harm.
- *Esteem*: the need to have one's self-esteem maintained and enhanced.

- *Justice*: the need to be fairly and justly treated.

The security need is very relevant for that entire class of services included in health care (including ambulance services) and government services like police and firefighting. In addition, the entire financial services industry, from insurance to banking and investing, is directly concerned with meeting people's needs for security. At the time of this writing, for example, the financial services industry in the U.S. was in melt-down with the Dow Jones Industrial Average having shrunk almost 50 percent in the space of 8 months; people were scared, especially retirees, because their security was threatened. As an interesting side note we speculate that the extreme downturn in the financial services world occurred when Secretary of the Treasuring Henry Paulson allowed Lehman Brothers to fail. We think this sent a message to people that *any bank* could fail and that their security was definitely threatened. Without belaboring the issue too much we can say that many facets of people's worlds send the message that they can feel secure:

- Signs on elevators in hotels as to how to behave in case of fire.
- Instructions by cabin attendants on airplane flights.
- Drills on how to abandon ship if necessary on cruises.

People scoff outwardly at these but their repetition sends the consistent message that it is okay to feel secure. Less obvious is the message sent by inattention to cleanliness, torn carpets, chipped paint, dirty tableware, and so forth in restaurants and elsewhere; the message is "unsafe." This is perhaps best summed up at Disneyland where the phrase "Unclean equals unsafe" is the mantra (Stratton, 1991).

The need for esteem is violated every time customers are made to feel stupid through poor signage, being blamed for errors even if the firm made the error, and being treated as a child rather than an adult. And this extends to every service encounter where the customer is required to co-produce his or her service: ATMs, ordering a meal at McDonalds, working with a business consultant, explaining to a physician how they feel, and so forth. In other words, every time a customer must behave as part of the service experience (when they must "co-produce value") their self-esteem has the potential to come under attack. This means that services must be designed so they at a minimum facilitate the service encounter to maintain people's self esteem and in the best case enhance people's feeling of self-esteem by making it possible for customers to perform their co-creation roles competently and effectively.

In the chapter we paid particular attention to poor signage, especially for newcomers to a new service establishment. Old-timers navigate easily and this is seen as the norm by the bank or hospital or supermarket but what about those who are new? We understand that firms like Costco, which has NO SIGNS to where different items are, want people to wander so they see all of what is available but they should at least make a map available for those who want one instead of setting things up to irritate new customers and make them feel stupid as they wander aimlessly around. This also applies to providing sufficient directions for users to navigate a company website.

Our second pet peeve is failure of service delivery people to recognize the presence of a customer by making eye contact and nodding to indicate they are aware of the customer. Our identities are important to us and we like to feel important but to not even have our presence acknowledged is a dissatisfying experience striking at the core of our esteem.

Finally on esteem there are the race, gender and age issues in customer service that requires attention by firms. We note in the chapter how badly, for example, women who go to get their car repaired feel they are treated. Thus, *USA Today* (1994) reported the following data:

- 57 percent of women feel that auto mechanics don't show women the same respect as men.
- 35 percent of women feel mechanics treat them like idiots.
- 33 percent of women feel mechanics make them feel uncomfortable about what they don't know.

Similar issues emerge for minorities in encountering majority establishments where research (Butz & Deitch, 2005) reveals:

- Denial of an apartment rental when it is clear the apartments are available.
- Denial of a job when the job is open and they clearly qualify.

Finally, age becomes an increasingly important focus for service organizations of all kinds, not just the various kinds of long term care residential living facilities that are being created by Marriott and Hyatt among others. Age is important because we are an aging population that we can all count on, older people have more wealth and, most importantly, the self-esteem of the aged is more tenuous than is true for younger people. That is, as eye sight, hearing, and physical robustness all begin to decline the aging population does what it can to retain its esteem. But soda bottles that no longer can be gripped to be opened (forget about the tabs on soda cans), suitcases than can no longer be lifted into overhead racks on airplanes, and frequently non-working escalators requiring the walking of steps all contribute to feelings of a loss of esteem. Firms just must do a better job of being sensitive to such issues, and they can do this by consulting with their aging customers—and their aging employees.

The need for justice for us focused on the need for distributive, procedural and interactional justice. There are three bases for making judgments about fair treatment, equity being the one most people think of first. Equity has to do with the following: Are my outcomes (e.g., a pay raise) in the same proportion to my inputs (e.g., in the form of effort and performance) as are other's outcomes in relationship to their inputs. For customers equity is probably less relevant than are need and equality as a basis for judging fairness. Need here refers to the question: Am I getting what I need regardless of what others are getting. And equality here refers to the question: Am I getting the same as everyone else is getting. All three, equity, need, and equality enter into people's calculations of justice, with the latter two most relevant in consumer services.

Perhaps the most common issue that concerns justice for customers is "the wait." People can feel unfairly treated whenever they have to wait—for the reservation at the restaurant, on hold with the call center, at the physician's office and at the post office. "The wait" invokes issues of justice so managing wait times in ways that feel fair to customers needs to be studied in your situation.

A second common issue emerges when customers feel that an implicit or even explicit agreement with the service facility has not been met with satisfaction. This issue invokes what academics call a violation of a "psychological contract" (Rousseau, 1990). The psychological contract is what two parties to a relationship each feels they are due from the relationship. The problem with psychological contracts is that they are rarely made explicit—that is why they are called psychological contracts—and they are thus easily violated. Firms need to try and track the psychological contracts their customers have with them and violations of them so they can plan to not violate them in the future.

Finally, and related to the psychological contract, the issue of recovery we mentioned earlier enters into the question of fair treatment as well because people have implicit expectations of how a business should react to recovery-relevant circumstances. Here too service businesses need to track the kinds of recovery demands they confront and head them off so they do not reappear. Of course service businesses cannot anticipate all of the circumstances under which they will need to recover so they should have principles in place to deal with events requiring recovery (Tax & Brown, 2000). For example, service employees might be given empowerment to make immediate restitution up to a given level—like Ritz-Carlton does for its "ladies and gentlemen serving ladies and gentlemen;" more on empowerment for employees later.

In summary, customers' fundamental needs have not been much attended to in services marketing research or practice yet even this cursory exploration of them makes it clear that there are fundamental psychological issues that customers bring to the service setting. Firms would do well to heed the warning to think not just about customer expectations but to think about their customers' needs too. Such awareness and concern can lead to tactics and strategies for targeted segments of the population—women, the aged, minorities—whereby such groups can feel secure, have their esteem maintained and perhaps enhanced, and feel fairly treated. Such tactics acknowledge that customers are people first with people's needs even when they are customers.

What it is important for readers to grasp is that this chapter on customer needs and the prior chapter on customer expectations are central to service businesses being able to create the satisfaction and loyalty they require for sustainable competitive advantage. To implicitly wish these away with hyper-networks or automated optimal control has the potential for customer alienation. Of course, used as ways of meeting a specific firm's customers' expectations and needs these forms of information technology can become an aid in creating potential market differentiation but the firm has to know its customers intimately and well to make those decisions.

Customer Tier-Chapter 4: Utilizing Customer Talents

> 14. Clarify the customers' co-production role
> 15. Improve customer ability through selection and training
> 16. Motivate customers to participate
> 17. Conduct customer performance appraisals
> 18. Watch for clues that customers could do more
> 19. Rely on customers as substitutes for leadership
> 20. Draw on customers as *co-designers* of the service delivery system

This chapter was about thinking of customers as co-producers rather than customers as mere recipients. So, rather than thinking of customers as masters to be served, we thought of customers as relationships in which the pursuit of common good was the goal. This perspective on customers has been adopted in the new field of service science, at least verbally. That is various papers outlining a theory of service science have made it clear that a goal of service science is to involve customers in the co-creation of value (Gadrey, 2002; Sampson & Froehle, 2003; Spohrer et al., 2006; Tien and Berg, 2003). But further reading in these papers yields the impression that the clear focus for now is on the conceptualization and execution of a service system to meet presumed customer requirements rather than the involvement of those customers and their skills and knowledge in the co-creation of value.

In retrospect, this chapter can be viewed as having foreshadowed customer co-creation of value as one of the central tenets of the "service-dominant (S-D) logic" of marketing (Vargo & Lusch, 2004). In S-D logic, value emerges only during the consumption experience and can not be embedded in manufacturing and the output itself. The customer is always the co-creator of value, together with employees and other resources of the organization. Service is a relational process in which value is created for and *with* the customer.

We conceptualized three co-production roles customers can serve:

- The human resources role—as another source of the production of services; as partial employees.
- Substitutes for leadership—as a source of direction to service employees.
- Organizational consultants—as partners in the design of effective service delivery systems.

In the human resources role we built on the work of Lovelock and Young (1979) who wrote the early and detailed comprehensive description of how to

"Look to your customers to increase productivity." What we added was the idea of actually treating customers as human resources who needed to be carefully selected, well-trained, highly motivated and carefully appraised—and helped when they failed to do their job! On the issue of selecting customers we saw this as a variant on the idea of market segmentation. We suggested, as we noted earlier, that service firms must clearly define their market and in doing so consider the role they want customers to play in productivity. By including such tactics in choosing their market niche firms can identify the attributes of customers they wish to serve and include such attributes in marketing and advertising schemes.

We were particularly concerned about the training of customers because, as we indicated earlier, customers do not like to feel stupid—and they do if they do not know what to do and/or how to do it. People still do not use self check-in kiosks at the airport because they fear not being able to do it correctly; they need training and there should be a special kiosk line for those who want to get trained though we have never seen one. And customers are frequently unaware of ways they could be personally more productive that would enhance both their and their service firms' competence. For example, customers could be periodically encouraged to review the various service agreements they have to ensure they are getting the best deal from their phone and/or cable contracts, their various insurance policies, and so forth. Being encouraged by one's existing company, with explicit information about what to look for, could well serve to enhance customer loyalty as well as save the company the time that calls to the call center would involve for call center employees to do this kind of review. And involving customers via sharing information and other tactics can facilitate their sharing ideas for new services development and innovations in service delivery, more broadly.

With regard to the idea of customers as substitutes for leadership, this was meant to make explicit the fact that service employees pay attention to customer demands—and some research indicates they pay more attention to customer demands than they do to their formal leaders (Bowen, 1983). Of course customers can be making demands the firm does not want employees responding to either positively or negatively. So, how can customers be useful substitutes for leadership? They can be trained in ways that make them useful both for the company and themselves.

Customers should be used as consultants to the organization. In the B2B sector this is frequently the case but in consumer services this is less frequently used as a tactic for enhancing the service delivery systems of the firm. We encouraged the development of consumer panels to assist in the design of delivery systems so that they serve customers as well as the organization. What we meant here was that firms design service systems to provide them the data they need and want and these frequently overwhelm what customers need and want. For example, to cash a check at a teller stand is enormously time-consuming because the bank requires so many operations by the teller; ditto for opening an account at the bank. Involving customers intimately in the design of such systems would perhaps make them more useful to both parties for the long term relationship both parties desire.

Finally, an implicit motivation for us titling the chapter "Utilizing customer talents" was the idea that people desire to be and feel competent—by this we refer back to the earlier discussion of the need for self-esteem. It follows that companies that do the best job at making their customers be and feel competent will likely reap the joint rewards of improved overall productivity and customer loyalty. But it does not come free because companies have to invest in designing ways to select their customers appropriately, train them, monitor their behaviors to seek ways to improve it and educate their work force in how to work effectively with customers.

Boundary Tier-Chapter 5: Managing Personal Contact Through Hiring and Training

21. Reduce the high stress faced by boundary workers in serving both management and customers.
22. Hire people for *your* jobs in *your* business
23. Deepen the applicant pool to increase employee quality
24. Hire based on how people *behave* in the hiring process
25. Hire the right personality types (rigorously)
26. Manage both staff quality and staff levels
27. Know that informal training = learning the culture
28. Reinforce formal training's two key benefits back on the job

This chapter was the first of three concerning the boundary tier—the tier of the service firm that interacts most directly with the firm's customers. The second chapter was about reward systems and the third was about those features of the boundary between the service firm and customers that are physical, tangible and relatively fixed.

We paid great attention to the attributes of the people who deliver service, especially via who gets hired (selection) and how they learn to be competent (training). In particular we emphasized the importance of hiring and training that is relevant for the jobs of a specific company—we are not strong believers in off-the-shelf hiring and training unless they have been shown to be relevant for a firm's specific jobs and values. We believe this for two important reasons:

Hiring and training using off-the-shelf procedures makes employees a commodity because it says to both them and you that they are no different from those hired and trained by other firms with similar jobs. Such practice sends the wrong message to employees.

Hiring using unproven practices for jobs in a company will likely not yield the best possible people for a firm and, in addition, such procedures can lead to law suits if they are found to be discriminatory. Firms thus gain two advantages from hiring practices designed specifically for them: more productive people through legally defensible practices (Ployhart, Schneider, & Schmitt, 2006).

We set the stage for explication of the issues involved in hiring and training by noting the importance of understanding that the hiring and training is for people who work at the boundary of the organization and, thus, are susceptible to a variety of potentially conflicting demands on them. In short, boundary workers can experience high levels of stress in their work when they try to simultaneously meet the demands of customers and management (and also professional norms for positions such as nursing). Especially when management sends conflicting messages about what service workers should be doing—e.g., provide excellent service but make sure you don't spend too much time with each customer—it is imperative that the workers hired and put on the job be competent and knowledgeable and have the kind of personality orientation to be able to deal with such conflicts and the demands of these complex jobs. One tactic, of course, is for management to try to reduce such conflicts by clearly stating how they want service to be delivered and then by visibly rewarding and supporting such behavior.

The foundation of all hiring and training is the job analysis that identifies the knowledge and skills/abilities required for effective performance of *specific* jobs and the personality to deal with the kinds of relationships with customers required by *those* jobs and the conflicts inherent in specific kinds of service work. Job analysis is a formal process and is not something done by some manager sitting down and writing a job description. Job analysis that specifies in detail the knowledge, skills/abilities and personality required to do the job is the basis for effective hiring and training (Goldstein & Ford, 2002).

We should mention here a perspective on knowledge and skills/abilities required for effective service performance that comes from service science, not our book. Service science proposes that "T-shaped" professionals are the type of people needed for effective service systems. T-shaped people are "… those who are deep problem solvers with expert thinking skills in their home discipline but also have complex communication skills to interact with specialists from a wide range of disciplines and functional areas" (Succeeding through service innovation, White Paper, 2008; p. 19). Obviously this is an important perspective but not for the kind of customer service on which we focus here.

The popular press would have us believe that it is personality that makes for effective performance in customer service jobs—and it is true that personality is important—but the fact is that skills/ability are even more fundamental to job performance, especially soon after entry to the new job (Ployhart et al., 2006). We also presented a definite bias for selection based on watching people behave in simulations of the job rather than just relying on tests or interviews. Simulations at the management level are called assessment centers (Ployhart et al., 2006) but we strongly believe that simulations for service work can be very useful because firms get to see people behave in situations that can mimic real world situations including nasty customers, conflicts in what to do under recovery circumstances, and so forth. Firms can design or have designed such simulations so that they are specifically relevant for a specific firm and its jobs.

Two last points on selection deserve repeating here:

1. Firm hiring is only as good as the applicant pool from which the firm can make choices. Companies with positive service quality reputations have larger applicant pools because people's identities are wrapped up in where they work and a firm known for its positive characteristics yields positive feelings for those who work there— and for people who are seeking work.

2. No company we have ever worked with has employees who feel the staffing levels are what they should be; in every company employees feel short-handed by management. So, the issue is by how much are they short-handed? The staffing levels of service organizations are particularly vulnerable to cost-cutting because it is hard to calculate the specific contributions made by each worker to the profitability of the firm. We worked with one company where they fired the receptionist because they were not "productive" so the receptionist job fell to those who were "productive." Guess what, productivity went down!

Our major emphasis in the chapter was on selection because who a company hires provides the foundation for what that company will look like to (a) itself and (b) its customers. Nevertheless all the excellent hiring decisions in the world will not produce an excellent service work force if the training and coordination of those people is also not excellent and if the context in which people work does not strongly promote service excellence. With regard to training we made three specific points:

1. Training includes socialization to the new job and the new work place. Because people model what they see others doing and get impressions of the new work place from what other people say is important it is critical to put newcomers in situations where they get to model and chat with the kinds of people who best represent what the organization wants customers to experience (Louis, 1990).

2. Much classroom training is wasted because when trainees go back to the job what they learn in training is not reinforced there. Newcomers who return from training are told some variation of the following: "Forget what they just taught you in the classroom; we'll show you how it is really done."

3. Training that is not based on a job analysis of the complete job will focus on the easily identifiable skills, especially technical skills (e.g., computer skills), and ignore the interpersonal issues that are associated with service work. This is a big mistake because even if people are hired with the right personality, they still need help in learning the specifics of how to be helpful to custom-

ers on the job, knowing how to deal with complaining and abusive customers and so forth. As we noted earlier, the payoffs in productivity for companies appear to be well worth the investments made in it. This is true not only for the direct performance/productivity outcomes but also because service employees' own self-esteem is enhanced when they feel competent to deal with the many variables, both technical and interpersonal, associated with these jobs. Training is another thing companies can do that benefits the company, the customer, and the employees, too (Goldstein & Ford, 2002).

We placed great emphasis on who companies hire and how they initiate them through socialization and training to the new job and company because it is who companies hire and how they treat them as newcomers that customers experience. That is, newcomers are the foundation of service delivery because in most companies it is newcomers who staff the front lines, including the phones, and have immediate contact with customers. All the great systems in the world won't compensate for poor decisions on who to hire and incomplete or even inappropriate training. Simultaneously if employees are not surrounded by a climate of service excellence all of their skills will be for naught.

Boundary Tier-Chapter 6: Managing Personal Contact Through Reward Systems

29. Capitalize on the given that employees are motivated
30. Make certain that all rewards pass the seven tests of effectiveness
31. Diversify the reward system
32. Honor employee psychological contracts to enhance service quality for customers

There are several fundamental issues underlying this chapter and they can be succinctly summarized as follows:

- Employees are motivated to do their jobs well and to serve customers well; the job of management is to create the conditions that foster and release that motivation and not to "motivate them."
- Managers and executives think about rewards primarily in terms of money; they need to broaden their concepts of rewards to include goal accomplishment and PR (praise and recognition) as well.
- Money as a reward tends to fail the seven basic tests associated with any reward system (Kerr, 1975; Lawler, 2003) and these are summarized as follows:

1. *Availability*: The reward must be available in abundance and easily distributed; money is a zero sum game and difficult to administer.
2. *Flexibility*: The reward must be flexible in to whom you give it and for what reasons; money is inflexible in the amounts that can be given to people across different salary levels.
3. *Reversibility*: Once given, the reward should not be permanent; salary and merit increases are permanent and bonuses are assumed to be repeated.
4. *Performance Contingency*: Pay levels are so tightly tied to tenure and position that there is little room for it to be used based on performance contingency unless pay is based on an incentive system. Worse, pay tied to performance yields the outcome of only the performance that will obtain the pay because nothing else matters.
5. *Visibility*: The reward must be visible to all since rewards are used as a basis for judgments of fairness; pay is not visible.
6. *Timeliness*: Rewards to be effective must follow closely in time the performance for which they are made; annual pay increases and bonuses are not timely.
7. *Durability*: The reward should have an effect that lasts beyond the immediate delivery of it; pay tends to be absorbed by the recipient with little attention paid to it after it is obtained.

Pay as the key reward strategy of an organization sends the message to employees that they are viewed by management as seeking it and nothing more from work. The research shows that people seek more from work than pay even though they come to work for pay—indeed pay is a good way to get people to come to work but not the best way or the only way to get them to perform at high levels. For performance other diverse tactics are effective: jobs designed that are challenging and meaningful; goals that are internalized, accepted, and specific with accompanying feedback and recognition on performance; and rewards given that are seen as fair both in terms of the amount given (fairness through equity) and the bases for the decisions to give them (fairness through procedures).

The New Rules of Engagement

We began this original chapter defining motivation in terms of three elements: the energy, the direction, and the persistence of behavior. In recent years these have come to be subsumed under the topic of employee engagement. Employee engagement according to Macey and Schneider (2008) has two components: *feelings* of engagement and *behavioral* engagement. The feelings of engagement connote feelings of absorption, attachment and enthusiasm; engagement behaviors involve persistence, proactivity, and extra-ordinary action, i.e. discretionary effort above and beyond formally-specified job requirements that can provide a firm a human resource-based competitive edge. The Macey and Schneider conceptualization follows the logic with which we opened this chapter and the chapter on rewards in the book: Management must create appropriate conditions for employees to be engaged, which is their natural inclination. For engagement, the model is that people who feel fairly treated (in all ways, not just financially), develop trust in their management (immediate as well as corporate) and this trust permits them to feel psychologically safe, and to then feel and be engaged (Macey et al., 2009).

Recent research utilizing a new measure of employee engagement reveals statistically significant relationships across companies between employees' feelings of being engaged at work in what they do and ROA, profitability, and market value (as indexed by the Tobin (1969) q, an index that compares market value to the costs of asset replacement); these results are shown in Figure 2 (Schneider, Macey, Barbera, & Martin, 2009a).

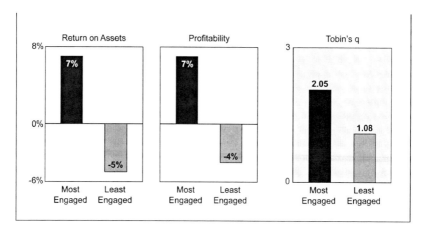

Figure 2. Relationship of Employee Engagement to Financial and Market Outcomes for 65 firms. Shown are the results when the top and bottom 25% of firms on employee engagement are examined with regard to ROA (Return on Assets), Profitability, and Tobin's q (see text for an explanation of Tobin's q)

What is particularly interesting about the work on employee engagement is that internal analyses of data gathered to help in fully understanding the construct reveal that the drivers of employee engagement are different from the drivers of employee satisfaction. The drivers of engagement are the issues we raised in the original book: fair treatment, jobs that are challenging, praise and recognition and so forth while the drivers of satisfaction have to do with benefits packages, compensation and other forms of financial security. This is interesting because at the local level managers have control over fair treatment, recognition and jobs but no control over the drivers of satisfaction!

In summary, it is even clearer to us now than it was when we drafted the original book 15 years ago that rewards at work must take many forms and these rewards must acknowledge people as being motivated to do well in their work. Further it is management's responsibility to create the right work conditions to release—or engage—that motivation. When management understands this logic then employees will experience their work world as supportive of their motivations to do well, customers will experience the service they receive as being of high quality, and the companies themselves will profit.

Boundary Tier-Chapter 7: Managing Nonpersonal Contact With a Personal Touch

33. Avoid the human resources trap
34. Manage the service tangibles - customer psychology link
35. Do not advertise service quality; deliver it
36. Manage the core service as if your business depended on it
37. Protect your core service with your service bundles
38. Create one seamless face of personal and nonpersonal contact with customers

Many businesses fail to consider in detail the many "touch points" they have with customers. This is a serious error especially in service businesses because the more intangible the service the more customers look for tangible indicators of how good the service is. Lawyers understand this well and so they design their offices with fine wood paneling and leather-bound chairs and books to connote quality. Theater and symphony owners understand this so they design beautiful interiors to the theaters and concert halls with great presence of red velvet to connote excellence and quality. Do supermarkets understand this when they permit potholes in the parking lot, chipped paint inside the store, dirty and non-functioning shopping carts? Do airlines understand this when they have dirty seats for passengers, coffee-stained tray tables, and disgusting baggage carousels?

We could of course belabor the point with other examples (and we do in the book) but here we simply note that a smiling and competent service delivery person will have trouble compensating for all of the nonpersonal defects customers must put up with in many service firms. That is, while to this point we have heavily emphasized the people logic we think is imperative, it is important to understand that people are not *the* key to excellence and customer satisfaction but *a* key; this is what we meant by not falling into the human resources trap. Firms that get service quality right have excellence in all facets of the service system: the core service itself (food quality in a restaurant), the equipment and machinery used to deliver the service (computers and information technology at the bank), the facilities encountered by customers (the theater for plays), the ambience or "tone" of the facility (the piano at Nordstrom), and so forth (cf. Bitner, 2000). In other words, excellent service firms create a "bundle" of experiences for customers and ensure that the core service itself is as fine as it can be since that is ostensibly the reason for the visit to the firm in the first place.

It is critical to note that while we have separated out various elements of the service bundle experience for explicit consideration here, customers do not experience the elements so much as they experience the bundle. Customers do not say consciously to themselves "Oh look at that chipped paint," or "Why is there a tear in the carpet" or "This advertisement is really disgusting." What customers do is literally package or bundle their experiences into an overall impression of the firm and this is what they carry in their heads. For this reason it is very important for firms to understand that everything with which the customer comes in contact must be presented to them in a seamless way because to them it is all sewn together; when there is a fray in the stitching anywhere it affects the quality perceptions of the entire garment.

Coordination Tier-Chapter 8: Designing a Customer-Focused Service System

39. Adopt a "service logic" across all functions
40. Balance the competing logics of different degrees of customer contact
41. Ensure a match between Operations Management's service delivery focus and the strategic focus of the business
42. Curb marketing's customer focus—unless it fits your market segment
43. Decide whether you really need a marketing department to be marketing oriented
44. Adopt the three keys to a market-oriented company
45. "Servicize" the HRM function
46. Invest (more) in R&D for the development of information and human technology
47. Diagnose your service logic with internal service audits and service mapping

This chapter could have been called "All those forces operating behind the boundary with which the customer comes in contact." So, it discusses in some detail the inter-related roles of Human Resources Management (HRM), Marketing, and Operations Management and how they influence what the (a) employees who deliver service experience and (b) what the customers in turn experience. In short, this chapter, and the *coordination* tier, overall, emphasized the cross-functional and interdisciplinary imperatives of service practice and scholarship with rules that figure prominently in today's service science and service-dominant logic.

The fundamental message of the chapter is the importance of these functions adopting a service logic in all they do. A "service logic" describes how and why a unified service system works. It is a set of organizing principles which govern the service experiences of customers and employees (Kingman-Brundage, George, & Bowen, 1995). This means, for example, if HRM does not train employees in how to be courteous, fair, and responsive but only trains them on technical issues (e.g., information technology) then the service they deliver to customers will not have a human touch. Or, consider the role of Marketing with a service logic: Marketing that advertises new products/services prior to the time employees have been trained to deliver them does not have a service logic. Or, consider the issue for OM: if OM sees its main function as moving customers in and out of the service facility as quickly as possible then the quality of the service delivered from a customer's standpoint may suffer. As we said in the book, if all restaurants were cafeterias this would maximize efficiency but at what costs?

It should be clear that these three central functions of a service system must act in concert if the results of their actions are to be optimal from the standpoint of delivery and customer satisfaction. One example of how this fails was just provided: advertising products/services prior to training. This could, of course be expanded to include advertising them prior to the systems for their delivery being in place. Or, HRM may fail to keep OM informed about the quality of the applicant pool for new employees and then OM designs systems and procedures beyond the capacity of employees to do the delivery of them. Or management may decree that customer service center calls can never last more than 30 seconds to increase efficiency, save costs—and perhaps kill customer service quality.

Basically, these three functions have different "logics" that determine their approaches and, the problem is, they are frequently in conflict with each other. Marketing wants things done quickly to obtain competitive advantage, OM wants to keep the customer out of production as much as possible and make everything efficient, and HRM takes forever to get things done right—employee attitude surveys, new selection and appraisal programs, and training. We frequently hear the following question about HRM: How come HRM has never learned to be service-oriented? About Marketing we hear: How come Marketing can't do some internal marketing to get everyone on the same page? And for OM we hear: How come operations can't make information technology systems employees can easily and efficiently use to serve customers?

One potential resolution to the differing logics of OM and Marketing is to consider amount of customer contact and participation in production. Where customer contact is high then efficiency cannot be the primary goal of OM — *unless* the organization is exceptionally skilled at managing customers as co-producers so that their involvement is not a source of uncontrollable variance and expense. Also, when the marketing strategy is differentiation in the market then OM efficiency goals must be supplanted by an emphasis on quality rather than efficiency and cost leadership. Concerning Marketing, when differentiation is the strategy then it must be internally as well as externally focused because service delivery quality depends so much on everyone understanding and being committed to the most positive customer experience.

HRM also has conflicts with Marketing's desire to offer customers many options to lure them in and keep them as customers. What HRM fears is that too many options require many different kinds of competencies—requiring different kinds of people be selected, different kinds of training be available, and so forth. When marketing is clear about the market segment of strategic interest then some of these tensions disappear because the offerings are more focused or targeted. Indeed, we noted that when the strategic segment is clear then a Marketing department may not be necessary with marketing being accomplished throughout the organization with the result being a market- or customer-oriented *firm* (Shah et al., 2006). The three keys to a market- or customer-oriented firm we listed were these:

1. Make marketing a line function.
2. Take internal marketing as seriously as external marketing.
3. Monitor indexes of both customer and employee satisfaction and how they relate to each other.

A key to decreasing some of these tensions is to have an internal audit of the way the three functions work together. Organizations seem to seek input from customers on how well they are doing in serving them but the internal audit, asking how functions serve each other is not very prominent—but should be. Such an audit produces an inventory that the different functions can share and discuss and try to work in ways that maximize the seamlessness of delivery from the customers' standpoint—after all it is service to customers that is the key to competitive advantage. Such audits produce information about the market segment being targeted, the contributions each function makes to focusing on the customer, the way service quality is going to be defined and each function's contributions to that definition, and explicit consultation with customers to validate the perspective developed. The service audit is then used to assess how well the firm is doing and a "service map" explicitly defining the steps in the service delivery sequence and each functions' role(s) in it can then be prepared as the defining document for delivery.

Coordination Tier-Chapter 9: Creating a Service Culture

48. Manage through culture, not managers
49. Avoid cultural schizophrenia
50. Use employees as sources of external market research
51. Empower your employees—the right way
52. Recognize that managing any one aspect of service in isolation will compromise seamlessness

53. Persist in coordinating a service culture

Symphony orchestras are a useful metaphor for what we wanted to accomplish in the book and make explicit in this chapter. The orchestra is a good metaphor for several reasons:

1. Orchestras have conductors who serve to coordinate the many different parts that need to be played to have the seamlessness required for excellence. It is the conductor's vision that all must adopt for excellence to emerge.
2. The parts being played by different musicians are NOT the same but it is from their exquisite individual excellence *and* exquisite coordination that something seamless and excellent emerges. One often hears that people must be "On the same page" but this is not useful. People need to be playing the notes they need to be playing and sensitive to the notes others play and the job of the conductor is to keep them functioning seamlessly together.
3. Conductors can't play each part or even monitor each and every player. Once the baton comes down for the piece to begin there is no stopping the unfolding of the piece. The players must know their own part and play it well without each and every note they play being managed; players must be empowered—and coordinated.

This chapter was all about how the seemingly disparate elements involved in service delivery to customers can be coordinated through a culture based on a service logic shared by the players.

Figure 3 shows the numerous layers at which culture in organizations functions (Schneider & Bowen, 1995, p. 239). There we see that at the deepest levels of the psychology of people in an organization reside the values, meanings and assumptions that hopefully they share. Then there are the routines and behaviors that get played out in different functions in the organization that impact eventually the behaviors employees reveal directly to customer with whom they interact. It is the core values, meanings, and assumptions that management is responsible for espousing—and in a service organization these concern the way people will be cared for and served regardless of whether those people are employees or customers. Then their behavior must be coordinated.

Who does the coordination? In our perspective it is a team of line managers, not staff managers, who must be responsible for this coordination. They must take responsibility for owning what the core values are and ensuring their implementation through the staff functions from which they require support so that the appropriate customer-centric service culture can be established. As in Chapter 8, the responsibilities of the different functions differ and it is the job of the line management coordination team that must ensure all players are playing the same piece—that the appropriate customer-centric culture is created.

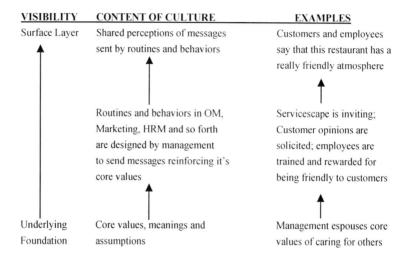

VISIBILITY	CONTENT OF CULTURE	EXAMPLES
Surface Layer	Shared perceptions of messages sent by routines and behaviors	Customers and employees say that this restaurant has a really friendly atmosphere
	Routines and behaviors in OM, Marketing, HRM and so forth are designed by management to send messages reinforcing it's core values	Servicescape is inviting; Customer opinions are solicited; employees are trained and rewarded for being friendly to customers
Underlying Foundation	Core values, meanings and assumptions	Management espouses core values of caring for others

Figure 3. The service culture

We used the term "appropriate customer-centric culture" purposely just now. This means that not all service cultures must be the same to be competitively successful. This means that some service organizations will choose to be cost leaders while others will be quality leaders. The key to success is not the strategy chosen—the piece to be played, if you will—but carrying out the strategy more effectively than the competition. This also means, then, that not all employees in all strategies are equally empowered since in cost leadership and low contact, employee empowerment is less required than in a high quality and high contact world. Indeed there is recent research that shows that in low contact and highly tangible service facilities, it is less useful to have a positive service quality culture than when the service is high on *in*tangibility and characterized by high customer contact (Mayer, Ehrhart, & Schneider, 2009). So, the service culture you create must be appropriate for your strategy; not all cultures should be created equal but they should be created to win *your* service game.

Winning Service Remains a "Game Between Persons"

We will close this chapter the same way we began our book in 1995—by thinking of service in terms of the metaphor of a "game." Our choice years back was framed by Daniel Bell's (1973) prescient book, *The Coming of Post-Industrial Society,* in which he used the metaphor of a game to describe the transformation in the nature of work and organizations over the years. First, there was a "game against nature" in which skills of brawn and energy were needed for work such as farming and fishing. Then, with the advent of the industrial revolution, came the "game against fabricated nature." Now the game was between man and machine.

New forms of organization and new skills were necessary to coordinate the efforts of labor segmented by function and level. Particularly in the areas of management science and marketing, models of organization and delivery became quite sophisticated.

Then, in the 1970s, the nature of post-industrial work became what Bell expressed as a "game between persons"—between professional and client; clerk and customer. This game was very knowledge-based and required not just technical skills, but interpersonal skills such as empathy. A theme of this chapter is that even today, even with the advent of the new service science, service and the cocreation of value is still very much a game between persons. And if engineering, linear programming, operations and the like are *over*-emphasized then we run the risk of treating service as a game against fabricated nature.

One of the wonderful contributions of service science is to strongly advocate an integrated, systems perspective for designing the rules by which people play the service game. A summary thought as to how to apply that systems perspective is to answer three questions used to surface a "service logic" from its underlying separate logics (Kingman-Brundage, George, & Bowen, 1995):

Customer Logic—"What is the customer trying to do, and why?"
Employee Logic—"What are employees trying to do, and why?"
Technical Logic—"How are service outcomes produced, and why?"

The new service science can help design the principles and techniques by which the answers to these questions are surfaced and integrated to the benefit of all stakeholders. And certainly many of these principles will need to be highly technical and sophisticated. Yet, again, we should remain mindful of the people basics, many of which are covered by the seemingly simple rules we outlined here having to do with people and the contexts in which they function. Not all of service science has to be rocket science.

References

Anderson, E. W., Fornell, C. C., & Mazvancheryl, S. K. (2004). Customer satisfaction and shareholder value. *Journal of Marketing, 68*, 172-185.

Bell, D. (1973). *The coming of post-industrial society: A venture in social forecasting.* New York: Basic Books.

Birdie, K., Clegg, C., Patterson, M., Robinson, A., Stride, C. B., Wall, T. D., & Wood, S. J. (2008). The impact of human resource and operational management practices on company productivity: A longitudinal study. *Personnel Psychology, 61*, 467-501.

Bitner, M. J. (2000). The servicescape. In T. A. Swartz & D. Iacobucci (Eds.), *Handbook of services marketing and management* (pp. 37-5). Thousand Oaks, CA: Sage.

Bitner, M. J., Booms, B. H., & Tetreault, M. S. (1990). The service encounter: Diagnosing favorable and unfavorable incidents. *Journal of Marketing, 54*, 71-84.

Bowen, D. E. (1983). *Customers as substitutes for leadership.* Ph. D. Dissertation, East Lansing, MI: Michigan State University.

Brief, A. P., Butz, R. M., & Deitch, E. A. (2005). Organizations as reflections of their environments: The case of race composition. In R. L. Dipboye & A. Colella (Eds.), *Discrimination at Work: The psychological and organizational bases* (pp. 119-248). San Francisco: Jossey-Bass.

Davidow, W. H., & Uttal, B. (1989). Service companies: Focus or falter. *Harvard Business Review, 67,* 77-85.

Dean, A. (2004). Links between organisational and customer variables in service delivery: Evidence, contradictions, and challenges. *International Journal of Service Industry Management, 15,* 332-350.

DeWitt, T., Nguyen, D. T., & Marshall, R. (2008). Exploring customer loyalty following service recovery: The mediating effects of trust and emotions. *Journal of Service Research, 10,* 269-281.

Gadrey, J. (2002). The misuse of productivity concepts in services: Lessons from a comparison between France and the United States. In J. Gadrey & F. Gallouj (Eds.), *Productivity, innovation and knowledge in services: New economic and socioeconomic approaches.* Edward Elgar Publishing.

Goldstein, I., & Ford, J. K. (2002). *Training in organizations* (4th Edition). Wadsworth.

Gruca, T. C., & Rego, L. L. (2005). Customer satisfaction, cash flow, and shareholder value. *Journal of Marketing, 69,* 115-130.

Kerr, S. (1975). On the folly of rewarding A while hoping for B. *Academy of Management Journal, 18,* 769-783.

Kingman-Brundage, J., George, W. R., & Bowen, D. E. (1995). Service logic: Achieving service system integration. *International Journal of Service Industry Management, 6,* 20-39.

Lawler, E. E., III (2003). Reward practices and performance management system effectiveness. *Organizational Dynamics, 32,* 396-404.

Louis, M. (1990). Acculturation in the work place: Newcomers as lay ethnographers. In, Schneider, B. (Ed.), *Organizational climate and culture* (pp. 85-129). San Francisco: Jossey-Bass.

Lovelock, C. & Wirtz, J. (2004). *Services marketing: People, technology, strategy, 5th ed.* Upper Saddle River, NJ: Pearson/Prentice-Hall.

Macey, W. H., & Schneider, B. (2008). The meaning of employee engagement. *Industrial and Organizational Psychology: Perspectives on Science and Practice, 1,* 3-30.

Macey, W. H., Schneider, B., Barbera, K., & Young, S. A. (2009). *Employee engagement: Tools for analysis, practice, and competitive advantage.* London: Wiley/Blackwell.

Mayer, D. M., Ehrhart, M. G., & Schneider, B. (2009). Service attribute boundary conditions of the service climate – customer satisfaction link. *Academy of Management Journal, 52,* 1034-1050.

Michel, S., Bowen, D. E., & Johnston, R. (2009). Why service recovery fails: Tensions among customer, employee, and process perspectives. *Journal of Service Management, 20,* 253-273.

Michel, S. & Meuter, M. L. (2008). The service recovery paradox: True but overrated? *International Journal of Service Industry Management, 19,* 441-457.

Ployhart, R. E., Schneider, B., & Schmitt, N. (2006). *Staffing organizations: Contemporary practice and research.* Lawrence Erlbaum Associates.

Rousseau, D. M. (1990). *Psychological contracts in organizations: Understanding written and unwritten agreements.* Thousand Oaks, CA: Sage.

Sampson, S. E. & Froehle, C. M. (2006). Foundations and implications of a proposed unified services theory. *Production and Operations Management,* 329-343.

Schneider, B. (1980). The service organization: Climate is crucial. *Organizational Dynamics, 9,* 52-65.

Schneider, B. (1987). The people make the place. *Personnel Psychology, 40,* 437-453.

Schneider, B. & Bowen, D. E. (1995). *Winning the service game.* Boston: Harvard Business School Press.

Schneider, B., & Bowen, D. E. (1999). Understanding customer delight and outrage. *Sloan Management Review, 41,* 35-46.

Schneider, B., Macey, W. H., Barbera, K. M., & Martin, N. (2009a). Driving customer satisfaction. *People and Strategy*, *32*, 22-27

Schneider, B., Macey, W. H., Lee, W., &Young, S. A. (2009b). Organizational service climate drivers of the American Customer Satisfaction Index (ACSI) and financial and market performance. *Journal of Service Research, 12*, 3-14.

Schneider, B., & White, S. S. (2004). *Service quality: Research perspectives.* Thousand Oaks, CA: Sage.

Service Science (2009). Volume 1, Issue 1.

Shah, D., Rust, R. T., Parasuraman, A., Staelin, R. A., & Day, G. S. (2006). The path to customer centricity. *Journal of Service Research, 9*, 113-124.

Spohrer, J. (2009). *Editorial Column:* Welcome to our declaration of interdependence. *Service Science, 1*, i-ii.

Spohrer, J., Maglio, P. P. Bailey, J. & Gruhl, D. (2007). Steps toward a science of service systems. *IEEE Transactions, 40*, 71-77.

Stratton, B. (1991). How Disneyland works. *Quality Progress, 24*, 19.

Succeeding through service innovation: A service perspective for education, research, business, and government (2008). White Paper, University of Cambridge Institute for Manufacturing and IBM. Cambridge, UK: Cambridge Institute for Manufacturing.

Tax, S. S., & Brown, S. W. (2000). Service recovery: Research insights and practice. In T. A. Swartz & D Iacobucci (Eds.), *Handbook of services ma. keting and management* (pp. 271-286). Thousand Oaks, CA: Sage.

Tien, J. M. & Berg, D. (2003). A case for service systems engineering. *Journal of Systems Science and Systems Engineering, 12*, 13-38.

Tobin, J. (1969). A general equilibrium approach to monetary theory. *Journal of Money, Credit, and Banking, 1*, 15-29.

USA Today (1994). USA snapshots: Lady you need a new engine. *USA Today*, January 7, p. 1.

Vargo, S. L. & Lusch, R. L. (2004). Evolving to a new dominant logic for marketing. *Journal of Marketing, 68*, 1-17.

Wiley, J. W. (1996). Linking survey results to customer satisfaction and business performance. In A. I. Kraut (Ed.), *Organizational surveys: Tools for assessment and change* (pp. 330-359). San Francisco: Jossey-Bass.

Customer Equity

Driving the Value of the Firm by Increasing the Value of Customers

Roland T. Rust

Department of Marketing

Robert H. Smith School of Business

University of Maryland, College Park, Maryland, USA

Gaurav Bhalla

Knowledge Kinetics, Reston, Virginia, USA

From the standpoint of the firm, service science involves two areas of study—1) how to reduce costs through greater efficiency and productivity, and 2) how to increase revenues by providing better service to customers. We focus on the second area of study, which to date has been underrepresented in the recent service science literature. Better service to customers results in greater revenues, higher profits, and a higher customer lifetime value. Customer equity, the sum of the customer lifetime values across the current and future customers of the firm, is thus the logical metric for evaluating the success of revenue expansion efforts. We summarize research findings that show that customer equity is a good proxy for the stock market value of the firm, and explain why this should be the case. We also outline the key drivers of customer equity and suggest how firms can use customer equity to evaluate the return on investment (or projected return on investment) from strategic expenditures.

P.P. Maglio et al. (eds.), *Handbook of Service Science*, Service Science: Research and Innovations in the Service Economy, DOI 10.1007/978-1-4419-1628-0_5,
© Springer Science+Business Media, LLC 2010

Introduction

It may be argued that the success of any business (whether in the service sector or not) is reliant on providing service to customers (Chase 1978, Vargo and Lusch 2004). Thus, for a business, service science means improving service to increase profitability and ultimately the value of the firm (Karmarkar 2004). One aspect of service science is methods for enhancing productivity and efficiency (e.g., Fitzsimmons and Fitzsimmons 2007). That aspect has received considerable attention because cost reductions immediately transfer to the bottom line. We will concentrate instead on the second aspect of service science, which is to increase revenues by attracting and retaining customers.

We will show that the customer equity of the firm (Rust et al. 2000), the expected discounted profit streams obtained from the firm's customers, is an excellent proxy for the market value of the firm. One might say that the market value of the firm, as derived from the stock price times the number of shares, and the customer equity of the firm, as measured from the firm's customers, are two sides of the same coin. Put another way, increasing the firm's customer equity is essentially equivalent to increasing the market value of the firm. If the firm can figure out how to drive its customer equity, it will have the machinery necessary for driving its market value.

With that in mind, we describe methods of identifying the key drivers of customer equity, how to focus strategy on those drivers, and how to project and/or measure the return on investment of expenditures focused on those drivers. This provides a company with a roadmap of how to drive the firm's market capitalization and stock price, from the customers' side. It facilitates the accountability of strategic expenditures intended to drive revenue through customer attraction and retention, and permits them to be evaluated on the same basis as cost-based investments (e.g., investment in new cost-cutting technology or the implementation of more efficient systems or management practices).

The remainder of this chapter is organized as follows: the next section provides an introduction to customer lifetime value and customer equity, the following section discusses the relationship between customer equity and the firm's market capitalization, the section after that describes how to build statistical models to determine the impact of the drivers of customer equity, the next to last section discusses strategic and implementation issues, and the final section presents conclusions.

Customer Lifetime Value and Customer Equity

Without a customer there is no business! What could be more obvious than that? Yet, merely because something is obvious doesn't mean it's easy to act on.

In most companies, decision making systems, performance measurement metrics, and operating strategies still revolve around products and brands. A customer is a source of revenue, someone you transact business with; rarely an organizing and operating principle for the entire company.

While the general sentiment that customers are important and need to be acquired and cultivated has been in existence for the better part of a century, thinking related to the value of a customer to a company, what a company does to increase the value of the customer, and the relationship between the value of customers to the company and the financial value of the firm, are of more recent vintage.

In the last decade, strategic thinkers have been very active in urging companies to change the way they think about customers. Companies are being urged to think about customers, not merely as a source of transactions, but as a potential source of enduring relationships; as assets that can help create long term value for a company. The customers as assets notion is appealing both emotionally and intellectually; customers are the primary source of future earnings for a company.

Customer Lifetime Value (CLV)

To transition to the "customers as assets" way of thinking, companies need to embrace the concept of CLV. Simply stated, CLV is a relative measure of how valuable a specific customer is to a company, for the duration of time over which this customer does business with the company. It is important to point out that lifetime does not refer to the life of the customer, but to the time period over which he/she actively does business with a company.

More formally, CLV is the net present value of a customer's contribution stream over the life of his/her purchase relationship with the company. Net present value of a customer's contribution stream is preferred over the net present value of profits, as assignment of many fixed costs is arbitrary in the computation of profitability (Berger and Nasr 1998).

CLV has a rich and established history in the academic world (e.g., Dwyer 1989; Berger and Nasr 1998; Reinartz and Kumar 2000). In the commercial world, direct and database marketing professionals have been using CLV models for several years to help with more effective segmentation and targeting of customers and prospects. However in the past CLV thinking and adoption was hindered due to the effort and complexity of data availability, data gathering, and data analysis. More recently, Gupta and Lehmann (2005) have presented a much simpler approach to CLV computation. They recommend calculating CLV using the formula:

$$CLV = m(r/1+i-r)$$

where

> m = contribution margin from a customer per period (e.g., per year, per quarter, etc.)

> r = retention rate, expressed in decimals or as a percentage (e.g., .8 or 80%)

> i = discount rate, also expressed in decimals or as a percentage (e.g., .1 or 10%)

Application of the above formula for computing CLV requires the following assumptions:

- Contributions remain constant for the entire life of a customer with a company
- Retention rates stay constant over time, and
- CLV is estimated over an infinite horizon

Gupta and Lehmann also suggest modifications to the formula when contribution and retention rates change (grow or decline), and for finite time horizons.

Key features, characteristics, and assumptions underlying CLV thinking are presented below:

- CLV thinking assumes that a company keeps track of customer level data; who the customer is, how much (s)he spends with the company, the number of times each customer is engaged, the vehicles through which they are engaged, the cost of each engagement, etc.
- Implicit in CLV is consideration of the competitive set as earnings from customers are contingent on brand choice
- Accordingly, different customers will have different value for the com-pany, as they are likely to differ in terms of amount spent, brand choice, and duration of contact with a company
- Since CLV computes net present value of contribution per customer, cur-rent and near term earnings are valued more than earnings that occur in later time periods.

Customer Equity (CE)

Unlike CLV, which is an individual-specific measure, CE is an aggregate measure. When we aggregate the customer lifetime values of a firm's individual customers, the result is the "customer equity" of the firm. Customer equity is therefore the sum of the customer lifetime values of the firm's current and future customers. Customer equity can be computed at any level of aggregation – total market, market segment, or sub-segment. Clearly it is in the firm's best interests to increase its CE over time, in the most cost-effective way, i.e., with the minimum amount of effort. How best to achieve this goal is an important question and will be addressed in a following section.

Embracing CLV and CE has significant implications for how a company thinks about customers, strategy, marketing and growth.

- The value of the customer asset base can be measured through CE, either at the level of the total market or at the level of a segment.
- As the key forward-looking customer metric related to the value of the firm, customer equity should be an integral part of financial reporting (Wiesel, Skiera and Villanueva 2008).
- The goal of all revenue expansion activities should be to grow a firm's CE.
- The relative value of all strategic expenditures can be measured and assessed in terms of CE outcomes.   Strategic expenditures can be regarded as investments and an ROI can be computed for them, where the returns are the gains in CE.
- Strategic budget decisions, whether new investments or reallocations can now be evaluated in terms of their net impact on CE (e.g., Rust, Lemon and Zeithaml 2004; Hanssens, Thorpe and Finkbeiner 2008).

CE also has other macro implications, most notably as they are linked to shaping marketing strategy and serving as a proxy for the value of a firm. Additionally, a company operating with a CE mindset will have to organize itself differently. The second half of this chapter will discuss these issues and implications in greater detail.

Customer Equity – A New Performance Metric

Continental Airlines is one of large mainstream airlines in the US. In late 1994, Continental had lost an average $960 million per year for the previous four years. Customers were annoyed by the way the airline was being operated—unreliable, dirty, and frequently losing passenger baggage. The Department of Transportation ranked Continental last on the list based on its on-time airline rankings. By March 1995, Continental had moved from last to first in the on-time rankings. In 2000, Continental Airlines was ranked number one in customer satisfaction by J. D. Power and Associates—an unprecedented recovery! The biggest underlying success factor was Continental's ability to win back customer satisfaction. There was no doubt that Continental had a winning customer management formula, but was the formula profitable? What about the cost of satisfying the customers? Between 2001 and 2005, Continental Airlines reported an average net loss of about $200 million per year.

The underlying theme of this example is that for metrics to be useful to management, they need to address multiple outcomes, such as sales, satisfaction, growth, and profitability, in both the short and long run. Brad Anderson, the CEO of Best Buy echoed a similar sentiment in a Dec. 2008 interview with Fortune, when he suggested that the term Black Friday, be changed to Red Friday! Typically, the Friday after the Thanksgiving holiday in USA is a very heavy shopping day. The goal of most retailers is to rack up high volumes of sales. In most cases though, the sales are generated through deep discounting, causing stores to lose money; hence Anderson's request for a change of label from Black Friday to Red Friday, to draw attention to the losses incurred by Best Buy and other retailers.

CLV and CE are a new family of performance metrics with the following characteristics:

- Since they are focused on contribution, they balance both the revenue and cost components.
- Unlike customer satisfaction and market share, which are based on historical performance, CLV and CE are forward looking metrics, since they focus on net present value of future contributions.
- CLV and CE provide a true apples-to-apples comparison and can be used to evaluate the attractiveness of a diverse set of marketing investments, ranging from digital advertising to call center responsiveness.

It is not surprising therefore that the early adopters of these metrics are very bullish in their ability to bring more accountability to evaluating marketing's contribution to the economic success of a company.

In a special Harvard Business Review edition, Managing for the Long-Term, Lodish and Mela (2007) declare that companies become so entranced in their ability to price and sell in real time, that they neglect investments in their brands' long-term health. Like with Continental and customer satisfaction, it is easy to buy short-run gains in market share. Over the long-run the company may not have any cash left to buy share, as was the case with General Motors. It is impossible to buy CE, thereby making it a more reliable indicator of a company's long-term health.

Customer Equity and Market Capitalization

One of the most remarkable and important features of customer equity is that it is a customer-related proxy for the value of the firm. This is true both from a theoretical standpoint and (increasingly) from an empirical standpoint as well. The close relationship between customer equity and market capitalization means that the firm can figure out how to drive its market cap (and stock price) by improving drivers of customer equity.

The Value of the Firm

From finance theory, the value of the firm is no more than the sum of its discounted cash flows. At any point in time we do not know exactly what those are, because that would involve predicting all future cash transactions, which is a practical impossibility. However the customer equity framework enables us to build a pretty good proxy for future cash flows. This is because the most important of the firm's cash inflows are likely to be its revenues from customers—revenues are the primary source of income for almost every company. If we ad-just those inflows by the direct cost of obtaining that revenue (e.g., the cost of providing the service to the customer), then we have left the contribution. Looking at that over time we have the discounted contribution stream for each customer, which is the customer lifetime value (CLV). Summing that across the cur-rent and future customers of the firm yields the firm's customer equity (CE). Thus we can see that from a theoretical standpoint the customer equity of the firm should be an excellent proxy for the value of the firm, its market capitalization. Normalizing market cap by the number of shares outstanding, we can see that customer equity also provides an excellent proxy for the firm's stock price.

Examples and Evidence

Rust, Lemon and Zeithaml (2004) studied the customer equity of firms in the airline industry, and did a detailed customer equity analysis for American Air-lines, based on a survey of domestic customers. That analysis indicated a total customer equity in 1999 (the date of data collection) of $7.3 billion. Because that analysis was based on a limited domestic sample and ignored profits from international customers or other non-flight sources of income, the correspondence with American's market cap ($9.7 billion) was quite good.

Gupta, Lehmann and Stuart (2004) analyzed five companies, estimating their customer equity on the basis of attraction and retention statistics, combined with market growth patterns, and compared the customer equity to the firms' market-cap. They found that for three of the five firms studied (Ameritrade, Capital One, and E*Trade) there was a good correspondence between customer equity and market cap. The two outliers were Amazon.com and eBay, both of which had much higher market cap than the customer equity would indicate was justified.

Kumar and Shah (2009) provided the most convincing comparison to date. They performed a field experiment with two Fortune 1000 companies (a B2C firm and a B2B firm) in which they implemented marketing efforts intended to increase customer lifetime value and customer equity. They then monitored how changes in customer equity related to changes in market cap over time. They found that they could predict stock price over time, based on shifts in customer equity, to within a 12%-13% prediction band. As customer equity went up, the stock price tended to go up, and when customer equity went down the stock price went down.

Across all of these studies, it is clear that customer equity is a very good proxy for market cap, and that shifting customer equity actually can shift market cap and stock price. This provides a lever, from the customer side, to manage the value of the firm.

Modeling and Driving Customer Equity

Given that customer equity is central to the value of the firm, the manage-rial issue becomes how to drive customer equity, how to track progress, how to determine statistically the key drivers of customer equity, and how to evaluate re-turn on investment based on customer equity.

The Drivers of Customer Equity

It is useful to classify the drivers of customer equity into three main drivers that are important for every company (Rust, Zeithaml and Lemon 2000). Researchers have shown that customer perceptions of these three drivers can significantly predict future sales, even if we control for the level of current sales (Vogel, Evanschitzky and Ramaseshan 2008). The first driver is Value Equity, which can be thought of as the rational or objective driver. We like to think of it as reflecting "the customer's head." Value equity includes such things as perceived quality, price paid, and convenience.

The second driver is Brand Equity, which can be thought of as a subjective or emotional driver. We like to think of it as reflecting "the customer's heart." Brand equity includes such things as brand image, brand awareness, corporate responsibility, and other intangibles.

The third driver is Relationship Equity (originally called "retention equity"), which can be thought of as the switching costs that make it difficult for the customer to leave the brand. We like to think of it as being "the glue that binds the customer to the firm." Relationship equity includes such things as the customer's knowledge of the company, the company's knowledge of the customer, personal ties, frequent customer programs, and the like.

Driving Value Equity

The best ways to drive value equity are to either increase what the customer gets (e.g., improve quality) or decrease what the customer gives up (e.g., lower price) (Zeithaml 1988). Value equity tends to be more important in business-to-business settings, and less important in scenarios in which quality and price are roughly comparable across competitors. One important factor driving value equity is convenience. A significant advantage in convenience (e.g., a bank with an ATM machine nearby) can offset disadvantages in quality and/or price.

Driving Brand Equity

Brand equity has been the darling of the marketing world for the last 20 years, and it is vitally important to driving customer equity. At the same time, it is important to realize that brand equity is not everything. For example, a brand with excellent brand equity but poor value may still be unsuccessful. Traditional advertising still plays a large role in driving brand equity, but social media are playing a larger role over time. Brand equity is most important in situations involving low involvement and impulse buying. For example, brand equity is particularly central in consumer packaged goods. Brand equity can be built by a wide range of activities, such as increasing brand awareness (through advertising and word-of-mouth), building emotional connections between customers and the brand (e.g., using brand communications to connect with the customer's lifestyle), and carefully choosing brand partners (e.g., Disney and McDonald's promoting a new Disney movie).

Driving Relationship Equity

Relationship equity is the customer equity driver that is increasing fastest in importance, as the firm's ability to obtain, store and analyze information about customers increases because of advances in technology. Relationship services, such as financial services, communication (e.g., Internet, telephone, cable TV), and professional services, find relationship equity to be central. Any company that can build a database involving the relationships with its customers has a tremendous opportunity to drive relationship equity through customer relationship management (CRM) efforts. Because business-to-business typically has these characteristics, along with personal relationships (e.g., key account managers or sales people), B2B often finds relationship equity to be a very important driver of customer equity.

Modeling Customer Equity

From a practical business standpoint, there are two main approaches to modeling customer equity (Rust, Lemon and Zeithaml 2006). The traditional approach, albeit a limited one, is to consider only the actions of the firm that are directly addressable to individual customers, and to model the purchase behavior and customer lifetime value of those customers as a function of the firm's actions (e.g., Kumar and Reinartz 2005). The broader and more general approach (Rust, Lemon and Zeithaml 2004) is to evaluate all of the main drivers of customer equity at once, based on customer perceptions. This approach requires only a sample of the customers in the market and does not require a longitudinal database. We will focus on the latter approach here.

The survey approach (see Rust, Lemon and Narayandas, 2005 for more details) involves collecting information, similar to that collected in a customer satisfaction survey, on the drivers of customer equity. For example there may be several value equity drivers measured, several brand equity drivers, and several relationship equity drivers. The drivers are chosen such that they map to specific expenditure categories that the firm can choose between. Along with rating data on the drivers, typically obtained on an interval rating scale, such as a 1-10 scale, the survey also obtains frequency of purchase information, volume of purchase in-formation, most recent brand purchased (or share of wallet), and purchase intention probabilities. The latter are carefully calibrated using market share data to remove any possible response bias.

The statistical details of analyzing the survey data are beyond the scope of this chapter, but can be found elsewhere (Rust, Lemon and Zeithaml 2004). In essence the statistical model includes a) a choice model to evaluate probability of purchase, 2) a Markov chain model to project brand choices over time for each customer, and 3) a customer lifetime value model to project each customer's customer lifetime value (this requires additional information from the firm, including discount rate and time horizon). The customer equity of the firm is then calculated as the average customer lifetime value times the number of customers.

It is worth noting that a firm's share of customer equity is a more pertinent measure of firm health than market share. This is because market share is current-focused and customer equity is forward-looking. That is, a declining firm may have a good market share but poor customer equity (e.g., think of General Motors in the 1980's). Also customer equity is based on profit, rather than just sales.

Return on Investment

The model described in the previous section facilitates the calculation of return on investment, from any customer-facing expenditure. Let us suppose, for example, that the firm spends $500 million (in net present value) to improve its service quality rating by .2 on a 5-point scale. The model in the previous section can be used to estimate the increase in customer equity. The return on investment is then (change in customer equity – expenditure) / expenditure. The model can also be used in a "what if" way, to explore the ROI that would result from prospective expenditures. Details may be found elsewhere (Rust, Lemon and Zeithaml 2004; Rust, Lemon and Narayandas, D 2005). This approach has been used by many companies worldwide across many different industries.

Implementation Issues

CE and Corporate Strategy

In this section our primary objective is to help the reader understand how CE can be used to help a company make strategic choices that are beneficial to its long-term profitability. Michael Porter said it best, that all strategy is about investment and allocation of resources. But how does a company decide which investments and/or resource allocation decisions make most long-term economic sense? Especially if the investment decisions happen to be as diverse as improving service quality, adding retail hours, and adding product features.

CE is a concrete decision support tool that allows a company to compare the value of disparate marketing investments, effectively allowing it to compare apples to oranges. Following the general approach described previously, the firm performs the following steps:

- Determines the key drivers of value equity, brand equity and relationship equity in its business
- Surveys the customers in the market
- Builds a statistical model of driver impact and CLV

- Ranks the drivers in terms of their importance, i.e., their ability to influence CE
- Run simulations to project changes in CE and resulting ROI from predicted changes in perceptions of CE drivers
- Choose the strategic expenditures with the best projected return
- Implement strategic expenditures
- Estimate ROI that was achieved by the expenditures

Figure 1 provides the framework for using CE to guide marketing invest-ment and resource allocation decisions. The goal of any marketing investment should be to improve company performance and hence customer perceptions on at least one CE driver. The ROI metric signals the relative attractiveness of the increase in CE to the amount of expenditure.

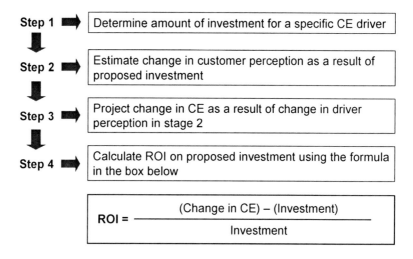

Figure 1. A Framework for Evaluating Strategic Investments
Using the Customer Equity Metric

The framework can be applied to answer a variety of investment questions. Discussion of a few key scenarios follows to illustrate how the above frame-work can help allocate scarce marketing resources more effectively.

Scenario 1 – Are we spending too much? While it is true that the goal of any marketing investment should be to improve company performance and hence customer perceptions on at least one CE driver, it is equally true that these improvements are not likely to be linear. Take the case of advertising. Initially, increases in advertising expenditures are likely to improve awareness and customer preference. However, subsequent increases in expenditure are less likely to generate the same gains in awareness and preference.

The ROI indicator can give us a strong clue of whether companies are spending too much in trying to improve perceptions on a specific CE driver. In plain English, companies are likely to be spending too much if expenditure increases do not produce commensurate increases in CE, or if the ROI indicator is flat or declining for increasing levels of marketing expenditure.

Scenario 2 – Are we spending enough to make a difference? Consider a mid-tier cell phone handset provider, such as LG. Let's assume that the company has a $100 million marketing budget, of which $20 million have been earmarked for building Relationship Equity. Of this amount, say $ 5 million has been set allocated for training in-store representatives. Past marketing research has shown that in-store reps are a major force in converting fence sitters, i.e., consumers with weak brand preferences, who are willing to buy a lesser known brand if they can be convinced on its product merits and relative value.

The key question is whether $5 million is enough? Returning to our framework, we can see that a $5 million investment will make a difference only if it can influence an improvement in the relationship equity of in-store reps for LG. If it can't then the company is not spending enough.

Often for budgetary reasons, companies can only afford to spend a cer-tain amount to improve specific drivers of CE, such as demonstration models, sales rep knowledge, ease of use, etc. However, this may not be enough, as it does not pass the ROI test. Investments constrained by budgetary factors may produce negligible gains in CE. The company may have gained psychological comfort knowing it invested in a specific driver of CE, but that psychological comfort did not result in long-term economic gains, as the amount spent was not enough, as it did not result in a positive incremental ROI.

Scenario 3 – Shifting resources between investments. Here again, we can apply the proposed framework. If the reallocation is more effective, it should result in a higher ROI. Take the case of a bank. Let's assume that the bank wants to influence the key CE driver – Regis Bank is convenient to bank at. Let's also assume that up until now Regis Bank has mainly relied on drive-through banking to influence the perception of convenience. However, management is wondering whether longer lobby hours would be more effective than more drive-through lanes in influencing the perception of convenience (a key driver of CE). Application of the ROI framework can help management deter-mine what would be more effective, additional drive-through lanes, or longer lobby hours.

Scenario 4 – Are we paying too much for an acquisition? Growth is important for all companies. However, organic growth is not always easy to come by and companies often rely on mergers and acquisitions to generate revenue growth, achieve cost reduction, or both. In 2008, despite the overall M&A market falling by 33% due to bearish economic and credit conditions, there were plenty of large scale acquisitions. A few of the top 10 acquisitions in 2008 are listed below:

- Philip Morris International acquired rival Rothmans Inc., in 2008 for 2 billion Canadian dollars

- InBev purchased US-based beer producer Anheuser-Busch, for 60.4 billion dollars
- Verizon Wireless purchased Alltel for 28.1 billion dollars, thus becoming the biggest Internet provider in United States, overtaking AT&T
- Drug company Novartis AG bought 77% stake in Alcon from Nestle in 2008, paying roughly 27.7 billion dollars
- US-based Mars Inc. purchased the world's biggest chewing gum producer Wm Wrigley, Jr. Co. for 23.2 billion dollars

Given that billions of dollars exchange hands in an acquisition, a logical question is how do companies value candidates for acquisition? How does Verizon Wireless determine that 28.1 billion dollars for Alltel is approximately the right price? How can Verizon be reasonably sure that it did not overpay for the acquisition? Most of the current valuation techniques are more art than science, and vary extensively from one acquisition situation to an-other. Is there a better way?

We believe that CE is the better way. All other things being equal, a company is overpaying for an acquisition when it pays more than the overall value of the acquired company. The real issue then becomes assessing accurately the overall value of the company being acquired. In a previous section of this chapter we demonstrated that CE is an excellent proxy for the overall value of the company. This suggests that the total future value of all actual and potential customers (the firm's customer equity) should form the upper bound for the amount an acquiring company should pay. From a customer point-of-view that's what an acquisition is – the purchase of all actual and potential customers of the company being acquired.

A CE-based system for valuing an acquisition would work in the following way:

- Estimate the total number of customers being acquired through the acquisition
- Using CLV and CE principles, estimate the total value of these customers to the company
- If tangible assets (other than customers) also being acquired, add the value of these assets to the customer value
- This combined value of customer assets and tangible assets should theoretically represent a fair price for the company being acquired.

CE and Organization

The adoption of CE as a performance metric and a strategic tool to allocate scarce and competing resources can be successful only if accompanied by significant and fundamental changes in organization structure. At the heart of the CLV-CE philosophy is a single dominant logic – a company must have complete and holistic understanding of the value of individual customers or market segments. Management mind-sets that focus and organize around products, product lines, technologies, or costs, clearly are unable to provide this customer perspective, as they deal with markets as if they were homogenous aggregates.

So what are the key features of a customer-focused organization and how does it differ from one focused on maximizing product sales and/or on minimizing costs? Before describing key features of a customer-focused organization, it may be helpful to share a few case studies. We can then draw on the case studies to highlight the key features and themes.

IBM. For the longest time IBM perceived itself to be a technology company selling software, hardware, and technical services to its various customers. It was only natural then that IBM should have organized itself around product lines, like PCs, servers, software, and technical/support services.

Following several performance setbacks, IBM under Louis Gerstner, realizing that its customers were looking to IBM for business solutions and not just component sales, reorganized itself using a front-back hybrid design. The front-end was focused on customer needs, offering comprehensive business solutions, not just components. The back end comprised of the original product units, who now became suppliers to the front-end solution sellers.

First USA and Capital One. Historically, First USA transacted its business with little differentiation across its customers. This approach was consistent with its corporate structure, which was organized around products or functions. The company's customer acquisition strategy was based on luring customers from other credit card companies and using affinity partners. The company did not make an investment in archiving customer data. Therefore, it lacked the ability to compute individual customer profitability. Employees were mandated to try to retain all customers irrespective of whether they appeared as good or bad prospects in the long run.

By contrast, Capital One's primary focus is customers. The company conducts business by micro-segmenting its customer base so that each customer can be individually serviced in consonance with the customer's value potential. Furthermore, Capital One set up a customer data warehouse that has an unmatched ability to mine any customer's information in a matter of seconds. For instance, when a customer calls, computers instantly access the full history of the customer and cross-reference it with millions of other customers. If a valuable customer calls to cancel a credit card, the call-routing system automatically rattles out three attractive counter-offers that the customer service representative can use to negotiate. In a nutshell, each customer is treated differently. Capital One's deep commitment to knowing its customer is evident from the fact that in 2000, Capital One ran 45,000 tests on product variants, procedural changes, and customer interactions.

Best Buy.   Notwithstanding the current adverse retail climate, Best Buy has been an intelligent and successful electronics retailer for several years. Based on observation and customer inputs, Best Buy realized that a TV is not just a TV, and that approaching every customer with the same sales pitch may be efficient, but may not meet the needs of the customer.

So, in 2006, the store created five customer group personas with different needs and interests:

- Buzz (active, younger male)
- Barry (affluent professional male)
- Jill (busy suburban mom)
- Ray (family man who wants practical technology)
- BB4B (small employers). Sales people were trained to ask questions that would diagnose customer needs and encouraged to customize their sales pitch accordingly.

Furthermore, store layout and product assortments were altered in various stores to better meet the needs of the store's dominant customer persona. For example, the Barry stores have leather couches and popcorn to drive home theater sales, and the Buzz stores have large video game islands with plasma TVs.

While the case studies are not identical, they do have some common features.

- First, all companies that are customer-focused are dedicated to increasing the total range and volume of transactions with their customers and/or market segments. They do this by developing an organization structure around customers/segments.   The allegiance of the customer-facing portion of the organization is to the total set of customer needs, not to any element of the company's product portfolio.
- The customer-facing group assumes responsibility for optimizing the sum total of the customer's experience with the company – all activities related to products, services, and relationship management are worked through this organization.
- Clearly, this requires specialization and specialists – in the nature of the customer's business and business issues. For example, over and above the systems expertise, IBM client facing personnel are likely to have an additional specialization in Retail, Technology, or Finance.
- The activity of these specialists is often coordinated with the help of customer departments. Some companies, like Hershey, Oracle, Samsung, and Sears have gone one step further and invested in creating the

position of Chief Customer Officer to coordinate the activities of the various customer departments.

- In addition to purely structural arrangements, like the ones described above, customer focused organizations invest in creating customer data-bases, that allow the company to measure and monitor discreet product and service transactions at the customer/segment level.
- They also invest in developing accounting and financial processes that al-low them to monitor costs and revenues at the level of custom-ers/segments thereby enabling the computation of CLV and CE at the customer/segment level.

Undoubtedly, there would be other organizational alignments that would also occur, such as rewards and recognition. Unfortunately, discussion of all is-sues is beyond the scope of this section. The major purpose here was to draw attention to how organizations that choose CE and CLV to drive their financial and marketing performance relate to customers differently than companies that choose other per-formance metrics, such as market share and revenue growth.

Conclusions

Firms are increasingly realizing that their financial health is based on the value of their customer base. Customer equity, the sum of the lifetime values of the firm's current and future customers, is the best measure of the value of the firm's customers and is a good proxy for the total value of the firm. An increasing num-ber of leading firms are adopting methods for measuring and analyzing customer equity, using them to make their marketing efforts financially accountable.

Customer equity gives firms a customer-focused way of evaluating the value of the firm, and, more important, a way to increase the value of the firm by address-ing customer-facing issues. Customer equity has been shown to map well to mar-ket capitalization, and changes in customer equity likewise correspond to changes in market cap. Modeling customer equity can be done by any firm, even those that do not have extensive customer databases. Customer equity modeling can identify the key drivers that drive customer equity (and therefore market cap), can project the ROI of expenditures designed to improve customer equity, and can evaluate the ROI of expenditures that have been actually made.

References

Berger, Paul D. and Nada L. Nasr (1998), "Customer Lifetime Value: Marketing Models and Applications," Journal of Interactive Marketing, 12 (1), 18-30.

Chase, R.B. (1978), "Where Does the Customer Fit in a Service Operation?" Harvard Business Review, 56 (6), 137-142.

Dwyer, F. Robert (1989), "Customer Lifetime Valuation to Support Marketing Decision Making," Journal of Direct Marketing, 3 (4), 8-15.

Fitzsimmons, J.A. and M.J. Fitzsimmons (2007), Service Management: Operations, Strategy, Information Technology. Sixth edition, McGraw-Hill Irwin, New York, NY.

Gupta, Sunil, Donald R. Lehmann and Jennifer A. Stuart (2004), "Valuing Customers," Journal of Marketing Research, 41 (February), 7-18.

Hanssens, Dominique M., Daniel Thorpe and Carl Finkbeiner (2008), "Marketing When Customer Equity Matters," Harvard Business Review, 86 (May), 117-123.

Karmarkar, Uday (2004), "Will You Survive the Services Revolution?" Harvard Business Review, 82 (6), 100-107.

Kumar, V. and Werner Reinartz (2005), Customer Relationship Management: A Database Approach, New York: John Wiley & Sons.

Kumar, V. and Denish Shah (2009), "Expanding the Role of Marketing: From Customer Equity to Market Capitalization," Journal of Marketing, forthcoming.

Lodish, Leonard M. and Carl F. Mela (2007), "If Brands Are Built Over Years, Why Are They Managed Over Quarters," Harvard Business Review, 85 (July/August), 104-112.

Reinartz, Werner and V. Kumar (2000), "On the Profitability of Long-Life Customers in a Non-Contractual Setting: An Empirical Investigation and Implications for Marketing," Journal of Marketing, 64 (4), 17-35.

Rust, Roland T., Katherine N. Lemon and Das Narayandas (2005), Customer Equity Management, Upper Saddle River, NJ: Pearson Prentice-Hall.

Rust, Roland T., Katherine N. Lemon and Valarie A. Zeithaml (2004), "Return on Marketing: Using Customer Equity to Focus Marketing Strategy," Journal of Marketing, 68 (January), 109-127.

Rust, Roland T., Katherine N. Lemon and Valarie A. Zeithaml (2006), "Measuring Customer Equity and Calculating Marketing ROI," in Rajiv Grover and Marco Vriens, Eds. Handbook of Marketing Research, Thousand Oaks, CA: Sage, 588-601.

Rust, Roland T., Valarie A. Zeithaml and Katherine N. Lemon (2000), Driving Customer Equity, New York: The Free Press.

Vargo, S.L. and R.F. Lusch (2004), "Evolving to a New Dominant Logic for Marketing," Journal of Marketing, 68, 1-17.

Vogel, Verena, Heiner Evanschitzky and B. Ramaseshan (2008), "Customer Equity Drivers and Future Sales," Journal of Marketing, 72 (November), 98-108.

Wiesel, Thorsten, Bernd Skiera and Julian Villanueva (2008), "Customer Equity: An Integral Part of Financial Reporting," Journal of Marketing, 72 (March), 1-14.

Zeithaml, Valarie A. (1988), "Consumer Perceptions of Price, Quality and Value: A Means-End Model and Synthesis of Evidence," Journal of Marketing, 52 (3), 2-22.

Service Worlds

The 'Services Duality' and the Rise of the 'Manuservice' Economy

John R. Bryson

School of Geography, Earth and Environmental Sciences

The University of Birmingham, UK

Peter W. Daniels

School of Geography, Earth and Environmental Sciences

The University of Birmingham, UK

In this chapter ideas originally presented in *Service Worlds* (2004) are elaborated and developed into a more nuanced understanding of the complex symbiotic relationships that exist between manufacturing and service functions. Economic geographers have researched service industries, employment and functions going back to the early 1980s but they, and service researchers in other disciplines, have ignored manufacturing companies for too long on the grounds that there is something distinctive about the service relationship. Many manufacturing firms have been transformed into service firms; firms that create and provide product and service bundles. This realization coincides with the movement to construct a new discipline of service science and is a welcome opportunity to engage with that debate. It is timely to develop a multi-disciplinary, service-informed understanding of the manufacturing sector that highlights the service aspects of manufacturing and simultaneously reveals the difficulties of classifying activities as either services or manufacturing. Ultimately, we must move beyond the traditional bipolar division of the economy and begin to focus on value creation and production processes. This involves a shift towards understanding the ways in which manufacturing and service functions are combined to create value in the evolving Service World or, perhaps, in the new *manuservice* economy.

P.P. Maglio et al. (eds.), *Handbook of Service Science*, Service Science: Research and Innovations in the Service Economy, DOI 10.1007/978-1-4419-1628-0_6,
© Springer Science+Business Media, LLC 2010

Introduction

During 2003 we put the finishing touches to a book manuscript that was published in 2004 as *Service Worlds: People, Organization, Technologies* (Bryson, et al., 2004). In the book proposal that was reviewed by the publisher in 2000 we suggested that continual change and evolution is one of the primary features of both a capitalist economy and of organizations. Then, as now, change was being driven by technological innovation and by the introduction of new forms of organization, management and work with the transformation of employment away from manufacturing to service activities one of the key outcomes. We cautioned, however, that this should not be equated with a shift of capitalism from a manufacturing to a service economy; rather, there was an on-going transformation of capitalism in the form of a continual evolution of the division of labor. This was stimulating the creation of a wide variety of new, often less tangible, support functions that fed into the manufacturing production process and that were increasingly driving the production process. These less tangible aspects of the production process are playing a more important role in the design, production and sale of products. From our position as economic geographers, a new perspective on the economy was needed in which service industries were amongst *the* key players. *Service Worlds* offers an analysis of this transformation of the economy and the production process but with a particular focus on the broad category of producer services and especially business and professional services.

The original book proposal specified five aims:

1. To consolidate current thinking about the relationships between services, manufacturing, society and space.
2. To provide a user-friendly account of the diversity of theoretical perspectives for understanding the new economic geography of advanced capitalist economies.
3. To inform these theoretical perspectives through a series of detailed firm and employee case studies.
4. To provide a geographical account of the development of service/manufacturing industries (employment, occupations, organizations) and their changing role in the production system.
5. To highlight and examine the significance of the increased blurring of the distinction between service and manufacturing functions in the processes of production and consumption.

For the purpose of this chapter we will elaborate on the ideas that we began to explore under the rubric of the fifth aim (above). *Service Worlds* made a number of important contributions that were intended to inform a more nuanced understanding of the complex symbiotic relationships that exist between manufacturing and service functions. It is worth stressing at this point that *Service Worlds* is but one component of a tradition of research by economic geographers that has explored service industries, employment and functions going back to the early 1980s (see for example Davies, 1972; Beyers, 1983; Daniels, 1983a&b, 1985a&b, Beyers, et al., 1985; Kellerman, 1985; Marshall, 1982). Some of this work predates the discovery of services in disciplines like marketing, business studies, or sociology, although it was also undoubtedly informed in part by some important early contributions by economists that were notable for analyses of the significance of services from an aspatial perspective (see for example Stigler, 1956; Fuchs, 1968, 1969; Stanback, 1979; Stanback, et al., 1981). It also predates the movement to construct a new discipline of service science (Chesbrough, 2005; Chesbrough and Spohrer, 2006; Ganz, 2006; Spohrer, 2008; Spohrer and Maglio, 2008). Many, if not all, of the contributions made by economic geographers to the debate on the rise and role of services in the modern economy have, regrettably perhaps, been largely overlooked in the service science debate (for a review see Bryson, et al., 2004; Bryson and Daniels, 2007).

The movement to create a service science discipline embraces the development of a transdisciplinary research agenda. Thus:

> 'Service Science is about integration, optimization and sustainability. This includes innovation and application of best practices . . . Service Science aims to provide a clear and common understanding of service system complexity. We have pieces today, but existing knowledge is not integrated into a unified whole. Service Science provides motivation, methods and skills for integration' (IfM and IBM, 2008: 7).

This research agenda is interesting when placed in the context of the discipline of geography and the sub-discipline of economic geography that has always followed a transdisciplinary research agenda in so far as the subject draws upon and contributes to many different academic debates. Perhaps this is one of the reasons why so many geographers were amongst the first social scientists to discover the world of services. The contribution that economic geographers have made to the emergence of service science has recently been acknowledged by Spohrer and Maglio (2008:6) who have suggested that: 'Bryson, Daniels and Warf (2005) may have the beginning of a deep theory that might underlie a service science in their recent book, *Service Worlds*.'

As economic geographers it is therefore useful to have the opportunity to elucidate and develop some of our ideas regarding services as part of this collection and to explore how some of the ideas that led to the development of *Service Worlds* could usefully be embraced by service science. However, we do not propose to provide a summary of the arguments that we assembled in *Service Worlds* but to develop and elaborate one of its central tenets. This concerns the significance of the increased blurring of the distinction between services and manufacturing functions in the production and consumption process which, it is suggested, can be captured using a new conceptual framework: 'the services duality' and the 'manuservice' economy. The services duality is a term that we have developed that highlights the fact that services play two important roles in the co-production of value. First, they are combined within the production processes of both goods and services as intermediate inputs that contribute directly and indirectly to the co-production of value. Second, value is created through services that are embedded directly in other products or services or attached to them in complex ways. This is to acknowledge the commercial importance of service bundles that are co-produced in diverse and evolving relationships between service creators and consumers. This duality is really a distinction between production-related services and product-related services. It is important to be clear on our terminology. In this argument production refers to processes that can create services or products or service/product combinations and the term product refers to a physical good, a service or a hybrid that blends goods and services together (Bryson, 2009b&c; Bryson and Taylor, 2010). These terms are intended to capture the essence of the on-going blurring of the categories of manufacturing and services that continues apace. They are also intended to alert the service science community to the valuable conceptual and empirical contributions that have been made by economic geographers to understanding the contributions services make to production processes (Beyers, et al., 1985; Bryson 1997; Daniels and Bryson, 2002; Bryson, 2009b&c).

What do we mean by 'Service Worlds'? The term is intended to highlight the integral importance of service activities to the production process; tangible or intangible, goods or service. We argued that Service Worlds are complex, constantly evolving, heterogeneous, and that their existence is also long-established (Bryson, 2008a). Services are:

> '. . . as old as capitalism and have played a central role in its development. Service Worlds are not just about knowledge and information-rich activities performed by a highly paid elite workforce, but also include a growing cohort of poorly paid manual service workers who function as an essential support for those in well-paid work. A Service World is also one in which there is a direct, even dialectical, relationship between service production and consumption. They frequently take place simultaneously so that any attempt to isolate production from consumption or consumption from production becomes meaningless; it is too much of an over-simplification of the economic. This contradicts the consumption or material cultures 'turn' in the social sciences that increasingly isolates the consumption moment from its production moment. In the Service World the distinction between services and manufacturing is at best misleading and at the worst a fundamental distortion of the way in which the production system operates. It is a World in which large multinational firms, professional partnerships; small and medium-sized firms as well as sole practitioners are all integral to the production process. It is also a World that incorporates shop workers, care workers; in other words the multitude of low-paid supporting service workers. At one level the Service World is about the enhanced importance of knowledge in the production process, but this is only one of its most visible parts in that there are additional dimensions, such as the legal systems and institutional structures that are used to regulate and control the evolving production system. For example, the intellectual value of physical products is regulated and protected by industrial patents, but patents cannot protect most service knowledge; a new global legal architecture needs to be developed.' (Bryson, et al., 2004: 4).

An important contribution to the complexity that is Service Worlds can be attributed to the wider process of production by which value is created through blending together manufacturing and service functions. However, perhaps the incorporation of the word 'service' in the title of *Service Worlds* gave too much emphasis to the role performed by services in the wider process of production. In hindsight it may have been more accurate to write about Production Worlds (of which services were a part) but that would possibly have been less interesting than Service Worlds?

Service Worlds began by observing that over the last thirty years developed market economies have been transformed into service economies (Fuchs, 1968; Gershuny, 1978; Bearse and Karasek, 1981; Gershuny and Miles, 1983; Castells, 1989; Daniels, 1993; Bryson, 1996, 1997; Bryson, et al., 2004; Bryson and Daniels, 2007; Rubalcaba, 2007). This has involved a shift towards service employment and to a lesser extent service outputs and exports (Bryson, 2008a). The development of service-led economies or post-industrial societies (Bell, 1973) has been associated with a growth in low-paid service employment, for example in retailing and tourism and leisure services, but also growth in relatively high-paid business and professional services occupations or those activities that provide intermediate inputs into the production process (Greenfield, 1966; Illeris, 1989; Bryson, 1997; Bryson, et al., 2004; Rubalcaba and Kox, 2007). An important academic literature has begun to provide a theoretical overview for understanding the growth in service occupations and activities (Bryson, et al., 2004; Bryson and Daniels, 2007; Webster, 2002). Much of this literature has concentrated on understanding the growth and role of business and professional services (Rubalcaba and Kox, 2007), on service innovation (Gallouj, 2002), and on service productivity (Gadrey and Gallouj, 2002; Van Ark, et al., 2002; Djellal and Gallouj, 2008). The focus has been on services in their own right at the expense of attention to the interrelationships and interdependencies that exist between services and manufacturing. The latter has been transformed in ways that embrace services and it is this transformation that is explored in this chapter.

Services in manufacturing: closing the gap

Service-type functions have assumed a more critical role in processes of production as well as in the division of labor. Service functions now comprise 70-80 per cent of the 'production costs' of most manufacturing companies. There has been an increase in service related occupations within the manufacturing sector and especially in the group of 'other professionals' that includes occupations such as business, finance and legal professionals (Pilat and Wölfl, 2005: 12). In some countries over 50% of manufacturing workers are engaged in service-related occupations (Pilat and Wölfl, 2005: 36). The growth in this category of service-related occupations within manufacturing companies suggests that there is merit in seeking to develop a complex and sequential definition of manufacturing that highlights the different phases at which service functions are incorporated into the manufacturing process. It is possible to identify five stages where services come into play:

Before manufacturing (financing, research), *During manufacturing* (finance, quality control, safety), *Selling* (logistics, distribution networks), *During products and systems utilization* (maintenance, leasing, insurance, after-sales servicing, repairs), *After products and systems utilization* (recycling, waste management) (Giarini, 1997, 2002). This service-inclusive definition of manufacturing draws clear attention to the interdependencies that exist between manufacturing and service functions. If accurate, it provokes questions about the merits of continuing to segment analyses of the contemporary economy into broadly discrete manufacturing and services sectors.

Part of the rationale for doing so is that it has long been argued that services deserve separate treatment. In a seminal paper Hill (1977) explores the distinctiveness and the attributes that distinguish services from manufacturing (Holmstrom, 1985; Illeris, 1989). This sense of the distinctiveness has been reinforced by studies of service innovation and productivity and efforts to classify certain economic activities as services for statistical and other purposes. At best, the latter has been a frustrating task confronted by an ever-changing portfolio of new economic activities stimulated by the diversification and diffusion of information and communications technology. Thus, the 'official data sources . . . tend to give more detail on old-established rather than newer forms of economic activity' (Marshall and Wood, 1995: 27). In relation to the collection of official statistics in the UK, for example, manufacturing categories have consistently outnumbered service categories by the order of two to one. It is little wonder that this has led to the proposition that 'the notion of a *separate* 'service sector' is an arbitrary outcome of classification procedures designed for other purposes: it represents a 'chaotic conception' (Sayer, 1984: 126). The problem endures (see for example US Census Bureau, 1993). But does it matter? Is it now a moot point whether efforts to produce industrial or occupational classifications that are services-specific (see, for example Marshall and Wood, 1995) are worth pursuing? This is especially the case if, as already noted, services are now so heavily embedded within all corners of the economy.

Meanwhile, debates on the attributes of service activities in the advanced economies are moving on. Research is increasingly engaged in attempting to understand the operation of particular service activities or service processes, for example the research into the experience economy (Pine and Gilmore, 1999) or the research that is informing the debates about service innovation (Gallouji, 2002; Department of Trade and Industry, 2007). Nevertheless, the presumption of a distinction between service and manufacturing activities continues to underpin much of this work. There is no doubt that this distinction has been extremely valuable as a conceptual tool. But the variety and depth of the interdependencies that now exist between manufacturing and services suggests that further research and theoretical development that may lead to revision of this conceptual dichotomy is required. While this is a difficult task, current classifications are constructed looking backwards rather than forwards (Bryson, 2009a); a debate over the ways in which service and manufacturing processes are being combined in complex ways to create competitive advantage and new business models is urgently required. Many manufacturing firms have been transformed into service firms and, conversely, many service firms are becoming more like manufacturing firms whose outputs are mass produced service products rather than customized service experiences (Bryson, 2007). This is an interesting issue in that a mass produced service product might appear to the consumer to be a customized product. The nub of the problem, then, is that academics and policy makers are constrained by existing well established terminologies. It is a simple exercise to segment an economy into manufacturing and service firms but much more difficult to position manufacturing firms that no longer manufacture in the conventional sense or manufacturing firms that derive most of their profit from the sale of services.

As a prelude to our argument we begin with a brief reflection on the way in which language and measurement or classification shapes interpretations of economic structures. The ways in which structural economic shifts involving manufacturing and services have been represented are then outlined. The scope for a more integrated approach is then explored by juxtaposing evidence that service relationships impart a distinctiveness that justifies separate treatment with arguments for long-standing manufacturing-service relationships. While there may be merit in both lines of reasoning, we suggest that in any event the way in which economies have worked, and especially the businesses within them, during the 1990s and at the start of the new millennium have distorted the distinction between the two sectors, or between a product and a service. The chapter is concluded with the suggestion that the rather artificial division between manufacturing and services is not sustainable and should be replaced by a focus on production, projects and tasks.

Language and measurement problems: constraints and enablers

The social and natural sciences are enabled and constrained by the structure and content of the language they deploy as well as by the ideologies which lie explicitly or implicitly behind different interpretations of the economy (Martin, 1994: 39). The social world is created, sustained and changed through talk and via language. The same is true of academic disciplines. To Mangham (1986: 82): '[o]organizations . . . are constituted by active, willful individuals talking to each other . . . It is through words that [managers] appeal, persuade, request, coax, cozen, assign, declare, debate, agree, insult, confer, teach, advise, complain, irritate, anger, correct, socialize, recruit, threaten, promise, praise, ridicule, condemn'. This argument holds true if the word 'organization' in this sentence is replaced with 'economic geographers' or 'economists'. Social scientists are also constrained and enabled by the classifications that are used to collect and structure the analysis of empirical data. Social scientists, like artists, engage with 'objective reality' in the same way, but via language and through concepts and ideologies constructed upon a particular language. Thus, a social scientist's understanding of 'reality' is conditioned and controlled by their language. The dominance of a language based around production and manufacturing in the social sciences denied the importance of service activities for many years, whilst in recent years service researchers have been perhaps equally guilty with respect to manufacturing.

Language is never neutral; it comes with culturally and country specific meanings. This means that the terms that are used to describe and classify industry may have different meanings in each country. It is important never to assume that a term used in Spain to describe a service occupation has the same meaning in another national context. Winch highlights this problems in a comparative analysis of the construction industry, noting that there exists:

> '. . . extensive variation in the configuration [of the construction industry]. Construction business systems have evolved over very long periods, and display well-rooted rigidities, with the balance between the actors in the system hard fought and hard won. . . [for example] the French *architecte* has a much more constrained and limited role in the construction process than the British architect; the German *Architekt* has a state-derived role in obtaining building permits which the British counterpart does not, and so on. In the case of some actors such as the German *Prufstatiker*, the British quantity surveyor, and the French *bureau de contróle*, there is simply no close comparator in other systems' (Winch, 2000: 95).

These structural differences in the organization of production systems are often hidden by the use of terms that appear to act as simple signpost descriptors to occupational activities.

This argument is relevant to economies and to research on services in particular. An absence of a name leads to a process or a thing being ignored or remaining invisible to the academic gaze and vice versa; the existence of a label may lead to distortions as academics focus on understanding that which has been named and labeled and at the same time overlook developments in the structure of economic systems or production processes. The existence of concepts such as 'service functions' and 'service occupations', for example, draws attention towards service activities and away from manufacturing. This promotes bifurcation of the economy and has encouraged the development of separate discourses centered on manufacturing and on services. Thus, some researchers have interpreted the shift away from manufacturing to service employment as the demise of the manufacturing part of the economy (Bacon and Eltis, 1976). Others have argued that 'manufacturing matters' (see for example Cohen and Zysman, 1987). Both positions can be perceived as polar opposites driven by an emphasis on *either* a service- *or* a manufacturing-biased discourse.

The words 'manufacturing' and 'services' are not neutral terms but come with past associations. Classical political economists like Adam Smith equated the category of 'service work' with *unproductive labor* or labor that does not add 'to the value of the subject upon which it is bestowed' (Smith, 1776 [1977]: 429-30). He developed a simple bipolar classification of labor based upon the concepts of 'productive and 'unproductive' labor and argued that a whole range of service activities are essentially unproductive. It is worth noting that when Smith refers to service work he is describing the activities performed by civil servants and 'menial servants' and says of the latter group that their 'services generally perish in the very instant of their performance, and seldom leave any trace or value behind them for which an equal quantity of service could be afterwards be procured' (Smith, 1776 [1977]: 430). This division between 'productive' and 'unproductive' labor is outdated and very much an eighteenth- and nineteenth-century conceptualization of the economy. Nevertheless, academics and policy-makers still understand the economy by sub-dividing it into categories and the danger exists that policy makers become fixated on one or two sub-categories, for example the creative class (Florida, 2002; Bryson 2007) or the new economy (Daniels, et al., 2006).

If the language of 'services' and 'manufacturing' is put to one side there is scope for a rethinking of the economic system towards the processes of production, consumption and circulation (PCC). The emphasis on PCC could be the start of a new project that attempts to explore the space economy of commodity production and consumption. The twist in the argument is to integrate the emphasis in the service discourse on relationships (between people) (Hochschild, 1983; Bryson, 2007) with the manufacturing discourse. The aim should be to produce a unified discourse in which services and manufacturing no longer matter when they are isolated from each other, but both matter when they are conceptualized as one integrated production system. Thus, production is also consumption and consumption is also production (see Marx, 1973: 90) and, in the same way, services and manufactured goods provide services. In terms of our argument, manufacturing is also service driven and services are also manufacturing driven. The two sectors of the economy become one discourse of production and consumption and of consumption and production.

There is invariably a time lag between alterations in economic structures or in the measurement of economic activities and the creation of suitable terminology. The on-going structural realignment being experienced by economies makes it impossible for governments to ensure that their national economic statistics are an adequate reflection of economic activity. This has always been the case. For example, the United Kingdom (UK) *Standard Industrial Classification of Economic Activity* (SIC) is a measure of economic activity, but essentially it is a backward looking measure; the SIC cannot be constantly amended to take into consideration on-going developments in the division of labor or as functions are created and firms are established that deliver new types of products and services that do not fit with the existing SIC. The UK's SIC has a long history of periodic change as it attempts to mirror the current structure of the economy; it was first introduced in 1948 and the classification was revised in 1958, 1968, 1980, 1992 and 1997.

Just as the UK and other countries were revising their SICs it became apparent during the late 1980s that something rather interesting was happening in both the British and American economies; the rapid and unexpected growth of a heterogeneous group of activities that came to be labeled as business services (Greenfield,

1966; Bryson, 1996, 1997; Bryson, et al., 2004; Rubalcaba and Kox, 2007). Most national SICs are less than helpful for monitoring this development; they have always provided an excellent tool for measuring manufacturing industries but until relatively recently failed to capture the diversity of the service-side of the economy (Blackstone, 1997). Thus, initially social scientists examining the growth of business services had to rely on SIC 8395 ('other business services not elsewhere specified') as the primary measure for business services. The number of employees in SIC 8395 in the UK doubled in only six years, from 156,000 in 1981 to 316,000 in 1987 and it included a heterogeneous set of activities such as management consultants, market research and public relations consultants, document copying, duplicating and tabulating services and other services 'primarily engaged in providing services to other enterprises' such as employment agencies, security services, debt collection, press agencies, freelance journalists, translators and typing services (Bryson, et al., 1993). Meanwhile, the European Union's NACE classification, for example, categorizes most business services under the residual category 'Other Business Services' (NACE 74) while perhaps the most proactive and comprehensive categorization is incorporated in the North American Industry Classification System (NAICS 2007).

From Manufacturing to Services to 'Manuservices'

Efforts to match official classifications of economic activity with rapidly evolving production activities will no doubt continue against the backdrop of ongoing uncertainty about how to accommodate services. In the meantime and after 'three centuries of economic thought on services, which were also three centuries of service growth' (Delaunay and Gadrey, 1992) it is possible to identify three conceptual positions. First, the debate over the development of a service economy is false or at worst misleading as all that is occurring is the development of an extended division of labor (Walker, 1985). This represents a production-centered view of society that is grounded in, or informed by, Marxist theory. Second, there are conceptualizations that place service functions centre stage in any analysis and even go as far as arguing that '[f]ar from being derivative or parasitical, the service sector is a vital force in stimulating and facilitating economic growth' (Riddle, 1986: 22; see also Daniels, 1983a). The 'basic function of the manufacturing sector is to provide the equipment (assets) and supplies for the extractive industries, for other manufacturing processes, for commercial service producers, and for self-service' and the 'service sector is, in truth, the facilitative milieu in which other productive activities become possible' (Riddle, 1986: 25-26). In a similar vein, services are the vehicle by which new technology is introduced into the goods production process and, as such, are increasingly the dynamic forces driving the production of goods (Grubel and Walker, 1989). Third, there are approaches that question the distinction that is made between services and manufacturing functions (Daniels and Bryson, 2002; Bryson, 2009b) and this is the perspective that is developed here. This is not a new argument; it can be traced back to Ochel and Wegner who noted that the:

'...distinction between goods and services (word processor versus software) may sometimes become increasingly archaic and irrelevant, because the integration of different types of production is growing and the traditional distinction is masking the fundamental changes which are actually emerging from modern technologies, new patterns of demand and social behavior' (Ochel and Wegner, 1987, 11).

Later, Reich maintained that the:

'...distinction that used to be drawn between 'goods' and 'services' is meaningless, because so much of the value provided by the successful enterprise .... entails services: the specialized research, engineering, and design services necessary to solve problems; the specialized sales, marketing and consulting services necessary to solve problems; and the specialized strategic, financial, and management services for brokering the first two. Every high value enterprise is in the business of brokering such services' (Reich, 1992: 85).

These and similar insights were ignored until this century when the distinction between manufacturing and service functions began to receive much more attention (Daniels and Bryson, 2002; Howells. 2002; Gallouj, 2002; Pilat and Wölfl, 2005). However, this has not included consideration of the efficacy of the generic terms 'manufacturing sector' and 'service sector' (see for example, Bryson and Daniels, 1998b). Indeed, the word 'service' and 'manufacturing' (or 'secondary' and 'tertiary') may be restraining our understanding of contemporary economic processes.

It is not difficult to find advocates of the view that the growth of services as a distinct category is not so much a 'physiological' stage in economic development, as a 'pathological' aberration in this process (Galbraith, 1967; Bacon and Eltis, 1976; Reubens, 1981; Cohen and Zysman, 1987). In the United Kingdom the media, as well as trade associations, still propound the view that a strong economy has to have a developed and productive manufacturing base (Lyons, 1998). James Dyson has recently posed the following question:

'So why does Britain need a manufacturing industry in this supposed age of the service economy? My answer is simple. We have no choice. Only one in **seven** British jobs is in manufacturing, yet they generate nearly **two-thirds** of exports. Manufacturing creates the wealth and spending power that feed the service industry' (Dyson, 2004: 5, emphasis in the original).

Dyson is not calling for a return to a manufacturing-dominated economy, but for an appreciation that manufacturing involves a set of manufacturing and service functions. Thus, 'manufacturing companies and entrepreneurs need to have their ideas **here** [UK]. Do the engineering here. Develop the technology **here**. Oversee the production from **here**. Plan the marketing and organize the selling from **here**' (Dyson, 2004: 10, emphasis in the original). All these are service functions, but they are manufacturing-related service functions.

It is now difficult to identify a manufactured good that does not incorporate one or more service inputs or is embedded in a set of service relationships. At a very basic level, decisions about whether to manufacture a good, and in what quantity, are informed by market research and design assessments, while sophisticated advertising creates demand for the good. Conversely, many service activities, spanning specialist medical treatment to worldwide parcel delivery, would be impossible without the availability of manufactured goods.

Somewhat overlooked in the context of the manufacture and sale of products is the emphasis placed on performance, display and experience (Crang, 1994; Rapport, 1998; Pine and Gilmore, 1999; Sundbo and Darmer, 2008). Customers can experience the manufacturing process by exploring the visitor centers of multinational companies such as Cadbury Schweppes, Ford, Volkswagen, or the Boeing Company. They can also visit shops operated by 'manufacturing' companies, for example Apple's on-line application store or one of Apple's retail stores. Customers are entertained at exhibitions that promote sales of, for example, cars or boats. Similarly, glossy car brochures and sophisticated websites are a form of remote performance aimed at persuading potential customers that the company has the reputation, experience and knowledge to provide a vehicle that is safe, efficient, and reliable and value for money. The fact that manufacturing incorporates so many service elements suggests that in many instances they can be described as *'manuservice'* production systems, or hybrid manufacturing systems (Bryson, 2009b) that compete through blending manufacturing and service functions. It might even be the case that the service economy is being replaced by a *'manuservice economy'*, but perhaps this is a step too far?

Evidence for the existence of manuservice production systems certainly exists (Pilat and Wölfl, 2005; Bryson, 2009b). In-depth interviews with more than 60 SMEs in the UK provides some of the evidence (Bryson and Daniels, 1998a). The uncertain boundary between the sectors is illustrated by, first, a company that began life producing and selling software and has now moved into the production of hardware, but via a subcontractor. Second, a company which began life as a manufacturer of machine tools which has converted itself to a service company which just designs tools, handles the client relationships and subcontracts the production of the tool/machine, and then installs the equipment for the client. This company is now considering making a return to manufacturing. A third company specializes in the design (a service) and the manufacture of products for the optical industry.

Such evidence indicates that 'discrete' service and manufacturing companies are being replaced, or at least transformed into manuservice companies. The manufacturing process is becoming increasingly a service process. There are a number of reasons why this is happening. The competition in the field of manufactured products demands that a company's client base is utilized as fully as possible. By including service-driven relationships profits can be more reliably sustained. At the same time, manufactured products are simultaneously more complicated, reliable and have longer life expectancy. Service relationships help to compensate for this, as well as enabling firms to foster long-term client relationships that may translate into further transactions. Finally, manufacturing firms are traditionally less concerned with the relationship marketing that allows service companies to build on initial sales either in the form of later sales or feedback from clients that is used for product innovation which might subsequently lead to further sales to the same set of clients. With manufacturing companies now more explicitly incorporating service company client relationships into their relationships with consumers, the breakdown of the distinction between the manufactured and service component of a product becomes more obvious.

Therefore, to identify a distinction between the manufacturing and the service sector requires an answer to the question: 'when does the manufacturing process stop and the service function commence?' In our view, this is an increasingly meaningless question. This can be illustrated using the example of the UK where there has been a recent call for the development of an 'extended' definition of manufacturing (BERR, 2008) which blurs or blends manufacturing and service functions together and highlights the importance of service inputs, for example design, in the production process (Rusten and Bryson, 2007; Rusten, et al., 2007). Thus, it has been argued that:

> '…manufacturing has evolved but our understanding of it has not, manufacturing firms turn ideas into products and services. In today's globally competitive landscape manufacturers are inventors, innovators, global supply chain managers and service providers. What was once seen just as production is now production, research, design, and service provision.' (Livesey, 2006: 1).

This policy-led debate is critical of 'traditional' definitions of manufacturing (DTI, 2004; BERR, 2008) and it is refreshing that government departments are willing to consider alternative definitions. These alternative conceptualisations of economic activity are becoming increasingly sophisticated. Thus, the United Kingdom's most recent manufacturing strategy acknowledges that:

> 'What is new about the current phase of globalisation is the increasingly global location of the production of intermediate goods such as components and parts production. This separation has included not only the physical component parts of products, but the accompanying knowledge intensive services, such as R&D, inventory management, quality control, and other professional and technical services' (BERR, 2008: 15).

This is a clear indication that the British Government now acknowledges that service functions are intertwined with manufacturing processes and that each function may have its own distinctive geography in the global economy (Bryson, 2008a).

The 'Service Duality': Production- and product-related services

The challenge is how to develop conceptual frameworks that begin to take into consideration the new, extended definition for manufacturing; a definition that blends manufacturing and service functions together (Bryson 2009b&c; Bryson and Taylor, 2010). We argue that there are two possible avenues that are worth exploring. The first of these is predicated on an acceptance that manufacturing and service functions have become increasingly difficult to separate and that in some cases, as we have already suggested, it might be useful to begin to blend the words 'manufacturing' and 'services' together to form, for example, a concept of the *manuservice economy* or *manuservice business models*. Perhaps the service science community would prefer to reverse the concept and to begin to develop an analysis of the *servicemanu* economy. This is, however, somewhat of a play on words that may be conceptually interesting, but is rather difficult to implement empirically. It is perhaps worth noting that in a recent face-to-face interview with a law firm the product delivery process was described by a senior partner using the word 'manufacturing'; the company's lawyers 'manufacture' drafts and documents.

The second avenue involves further exploration of what we term the 'services duality' framework. In some respects this suggestion is influenced by the *Innovation Value Chain* (IVC) approach that has been recently proposed by Hansen and Birkinshaw (2007) as a general framework within which firms' innovation activities can be considered. In the IVC approach innovation is conceptualized as a three stage sequential process that involves knowledge investment, innovation process capability and value creation capability (Hansen and Birkinshaw, 2007: 122). This is a very structured and phased approach towards understanding innovation within firms. Our 'services duality' idea recognizes that services are entwined within production processes, but at many different stages. It is important to note, for example, that knowledge-intensive business services (KIBS) provide production-related inputs into the activities of their clients (Rubalcaba-Bermejo, 1999), but that such services are also being increasingly created by client companies and placed into products or sold to support products and/or services. An example would be a company that can provide training courses for individuals and firms that purchase their products.

The concept of a services duality highlights the importance of both the activities of KIBS (production-related services) and services that are developed to support products, or in other words product-related services. This is to argue for a sequential analysis of the role that services play within the process of production as intermediate inputs and combined with products for final consumption. It is a duality because the approach distinguishes between *production-related services* (intermediate inputs) and *product-related services* (servicing, software, training, provision of content, finance packages, etc) (Figure 1). It seems to be the case that considerable academic research has gone into exploring the economics and operational dynamics of production-related services (Rubalcaba-Bermejo, 1999; Rubalcaba and Kox, 2007) but product-related services have been largely overlooked. This duality approach therefore provides a conceptual tool for operationalizing the extended definition of manufacturing. A more detailed elaboration of the services duality has been provided elsewhere; the following section provides a brief overview of what it involves (Bryson, 2008b&c, 2009b).

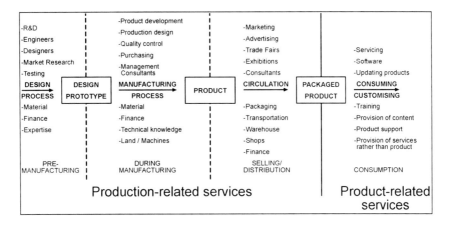

Figure 1. The Services Duality: Production- and Product-Related Services

Holistic Production and the Services Duality: a Projects and Tasks approach

The concept of an *extended division of labor* is widely used as a way of conceptualizing economic change (Walker, 1985; Bryson et al., 2004; Bryson and Rusten, 2005, 2006; Bryson, 2008a). In essence it is based on dividing production processes into their component parts, but we have argued that this is becoming much more difficult as services and manufacturing products and processes become more intertwined in line with the notion of services duality. We have suggested that one way of resolving this problem is to think in terms of a new language for describing and theorizing the manufacture of both goods and services (Daniels and Bryson, 2002). This may, however, be overstating what is required and it may, in fact, be sufficient to return to an older language based around understanding the creation of value in production systems.

If social scientists need to reconceptualize the production process we would pose the following question: what are the principles that should underpin the development of a simple theory of production that takes account of the services duality? The first principle is that many services are increasingly the product of a complex manufacturing process and can be engineered or manufactured (service) products (Fähnrich and Meiren, 2007; Bryson, 2007) that are not that dissimilar to the products engineered and created in factories. The primary difference here is that employees are more visible in the service production process than in the manufacturing production process. Goffman (1984) has argued that people perform 'roles' (sister/brother, son/daughter, parent, teacher, management consultant, etc) and that these take place in *back* and *front regions*. A 'role' is the outcome of interactions that take place between back and front regions, but in most cases the consumer is only aware of what is occurring in the front region (Goffman, 1984: 109-140). Goffman explains that front regions are places where performances are given, whilst back regions are places that are 'relative to a given performance, where the impression fostered by the performance is knowingly contradicted as a matter of course' (Goffman, 1984: 114). In the back region the performance may be created, illusions and impressions will be openly constructed, and props and equipment stored.

It would seem that the service literature has largely concentrated on understanding the front regions of service production systems (Hochschild, 1983; Teboul, 2006; Bitner et al., 2008) at the expense of an exploration of back regions. 'Facing' services tend to be consumed and partially produced in front regions but are also partially planned, designed and delivered in back regions. The shift towards the manufacture of services is therefore a shift towards a blending of front and back regions for the production and consumption of services. In much the same way, the development of hybrid products is partly about enhancing the visibility of a product's front region. Older manufacturing systems were based upon workers who were largely invisible to consumers as they were positioned in back regions. Today, manufacturing workers are becoming more visible and this process is partly being driven by corporate social responsibility, the Internet, television and partly by the enhanced service components that are contained within, and wrapped around, manufactured products.

The second principle is the seamless blending of manufacturing and service functions within production processes and within products. Two blending moments can be identified. The first blending moment is a process that is invisible to consumers but which results in output that is visible. In this instance the expertise-content required to produce products is increasing with a related requirement for greater quantities of expert/service labor to be incorporated into products. This first moment involves production-related services. The second blending moment reflects the way in which actual products are changing so that they become either service-enhanced or service-driven. *Service-enhanced products* are those in which a conventional product or process has been redesigned to take advantage of new forms of expertise. A *service-driven product* is one in which the service element of the product may be more important than the actual physical product. In this case a company may decide to outsource the manufacturing component of its activities as most of the value and consumer visibility may be based on the service expertise or content elements of the product.

The initial two principles, that services can be engineered or manufactured and that they can be seamlessly blended within processes and products, provide the rationale for the third and final principle. This is the crucial importance of treating the production process holistically since its increasing complexity means that we must begin to identify and conceptualize the interrelationships that occur between the different elements (manufacturing and service operations) that come together to create value. This 'coming together' can occur within the same company or can be part of a co-ordinated value chain of independent companies that are managed by one organization or even an individual to create a product (physical product, service, hybrid product). A value chain is a collection of companies – suppliers, financers, manufacturers and distributors – that are brought together, sometimes consciously and sometimes unconsciously, to create and sell a completed product. The concept of a value or a commodity chain (Gereffi, 2001; Gereffi, et al., 2005) provides a methodological tool for analyzing and understanding how groups of people or firms come together in front and back regions to create products and value.

It is difficult to begin to develop a conceptual framework by focusing on the totality of production systems. The intention is to understand the complete value creation system, but in order to reach this end point it is essential to begin to subdivide the production process. Given this, it is possible to argue that, rather than focusing on the attributes of a holistic production process, it may be more fruitful to focus our analyses on production projects. This is an approach to understanding the production of value through the manufacture of products (physical products, services, hybrid products). An effort is made to avoid using words that are established metaphors by developing instead a layered approach to understanding value creation. The first layer is a focus on production rather than manufacturing or services. There are obvious problems with the word 'production' as it is closely associated with physical products, but it is also associated with the production of service experiences such as, for example, films and theatrical events. This first layer begins with a *product, an economic sector* or *a firm* and involves trying to identify and understand the ways in which value is created. This involves understanding value creation in production systems that incorporate the service duality. The focus is on value creation for manufactured hybrid products (product-related services) and the geographies of such value creation.

The second layer focuses on *tasks*. Every product is the orchestrated outcome of a range of tasks (manufacturing processes and production- and product-related services), each of which contributes to costs as well as to profits. The creation of value in a production process requires the bringing together of a range of different tasks, each of which may have its own geography. Some tasks may be mechanized or computerized and some will also require face-to-face contact, either within a production unit or between producers and consumers. Yet other tasks can be provided within a firm and some can be outsourced or be delivered by foreign providers. Whatever is required from the tasks, the outcome is a product via a production process that blends or bundles separate but related tasks together (manufacturing and service functions) that are undertaken in different locations and at different times.

While this may be a methodological rather than a theoretical approach to understanding value creation, it foregrounds it, along with the production process, ahead of any focus on manufacturing or service activities. It highlights the interactions that occur in an economy to produce wealth and does so by developing a holistic approach to identifying and conceptualizing value creation. It does not assume that services are different and distinctive to manufacturing processes but assumes that services are produced or manufactured to create added value or wealth.

It is also important to stress that the *Production Project/Task* (PPT) approach to understanding the economy is not driven by geography; it does not fetishise or foreground spatial relationships or global relationships. A global production networks approach can lead to an overemphasis on global relationships at the expense of an underestimation of the importance of other forms of geographic relationship. This is not to say that a PPT approach cannot be inherently spatial or even global; it only need be so when geographical relationships play a central role in value creation. Firms create value by blending different ways of delivering tasks that are required for the same production project. Such tasks can be developed by the firm or they can be outsourced to local firms, foreign subsidiaries or third party suppliers. Thus, firms engaged in a production project are joined together by various forms of backward and forward linkages that include contract-based market-mediated transactions, dependent relationships in a heavily controlled 'supply chain', complete vertical integration, and cooperative relationships. A fully functioning industrial district, for example, will encapsulate all of these.

While a PPT approach may be conceptually appealing, we do need to be cognizant of at least two difficulties arising from the question of how to determine the boundaries of a production project. In a PPT methodology these boundaries must be determined by the time and resources available to the research team and by the limits attached to the difficulty of obtaining information. The first difficulty is that a firm is not the same thing as a production project; many firms will consist of combinations of different degrees of involvement with different production projects and tasks. This means that a PPT approach might mean that the researcher would have to begin to simultaneously unravel many different production projects. The PPT approach is not a firm-based approach, rather it is an approach predicated upon the identification of value creation through the development and management of production projects and tasks. By themselves firms do not create value; value is created via projects and tasks.

The second difficulty is that the PPT approach requires that consideration is given to the affiliated or supporting infrastructure that is positioned behind a production project or task. It is important to consider equipment producers, information/expertise providers, banking and financial institutions, education systems, transportation systems and ICT. These and other supporting infrastructures are the outputs of other production projects which means that each project may be part of an extremely complex array of intermeshing production projects. Some of these projects, however, will be more or less important to the PPT case under investigation. There are clearly opportunities for further detailed research designed to identify ways of surmounting these operational difficulties with the implementation of a PPT approach.

Measurement and the Services Duality

An exploration of the services duality requires the application of both quantitative and qualitative methodologies (Crum and Gudgin, 1977; Pilat and Wölfl, 2005). Much research has been undertaken into exploring production-related services, but difficulties still exist regarding an understanding of the impact of intermediate inputs on the activities of client firms (Bryson, et al., 1999a&b). Qualitative research is required to explore these impacts and is also required to explore the creation and delivery of product-related services (Bryson, 2009b). This qualitative research stage is an essential step towards achieving modifications to some of the existing national surveys of economic activity.

Existing datasets can be used to explore the services duality and three types are especially important. First, input-output tables can be analyzed to identify the broad pattern of output and employment flows between industries. They enable the analysis of the direct and indirect effects of an alteration in demand in one sector on the outputs (employment and output) of another sector. These tables reflect the existing industrial classifications that are in use and hide the internal structure of industries. Thus input-output tables can tell us nothing about the mix of functions that exist inside a company. Second, occupational data, for example the British Labor Force Survey, can be used to explore the distribution of job categories within an industry. Such datasets can thus be used to explore the changing employment structure of industrial groups and can be used to highlight service activities that are performed inside manufacturing firms. Third, firm or micro-level data is required to explore the services duality in considerable depth. Micro-level studies are expensive, but the shift that is occurring towards production- and product-related services suggests that, in the near future, detailed sectoral studies will need to be undertaken in order to be able to explore the ways in which firms incorporate services into their business models.

Measuring the integration of service functions into the value chains of manufacturing firms is a difficult challenge, but it is one that economists and others must begin to explore. At the moment, no one dataset is available and multiple datasets must be analyzed in order to identify and explore the relationships that occur between manufacturing and service functions.

Conclusion

In *Service Worlds* we concluded by highlighting the dangers of making simple overgeneralizations and argued that:

> '...we jettison, or leave behind, many of the dichotomies that have characterized
> economic and social analysis of services in general: production/consumption,
> manufacturing/services, global/local, economic/cultural and work/leisure. There is no
> need for us to slavishly follow artificial bifurcations of either/or when the complexity of

services, and of economic and social life in general, merits using both' (Bryson, et al., 2004: 244-245).

This call for the reader to understand services in this way was really an appeal to service researchers to be aware of the ways in which the language deployed by social scientists influences the ways in which they interpret the world. In the same way our text, written mainly during 2003, could be used as a call for the establishment of a discipline of service science in which 'research needs to be organized around the object of research – in this case services – and not within the bounds of established academic traditions' (Ganz, 2007: 234). We admit to taking a cautious approach to the call to establish a discipline of service science. Perhaps, our caution comes from our disciplinary position; as economic geographers engagement with other disciplines and academic debates is accepted as good practice. Unlike our colleagues based in management and marketing there are no restrictions imposed upon us regarding where we can publish; geographers are not constrained by the journal lists and rankings that determine the publication strategies of colleagues based in business schools. This means that our analyses of the developing service economy and society has never been constrained by our disciplinary background. In these terms it would be possible to argue that, for quite some time, economic geographers have organized their research on services around the object of study and they have never been bounded by established academic traditions.

We agree, therefore, that the call to formulate a 'service science' research agenda must be treated seriously, but also with some caution. As academics based in a discipline with a long tradition of transdisciplinary research we are concerned that the object of enquiry should be the value or wealth creation process. In many instances the starting place for this analysis will of course be services, but it is important to acknowledge that in many instances other production forms (manufacturing, etc) will be as important, perhaps even more important, than the service element. There is still a possibility that analysts might become too fixated on the service elements of production processes, simultaneously forgetting that value creation occurs by blending service and manufacturing functions together or by integrating goods into service systems and services into production systems that are designed to create value.

By our language(s) we are known and through our language(s) we know the world. Words, definitions, and concepts force the researcher to think about specific questions and issues and to conceptualize the world in a particular way. We suggest that the terms 'manufacturing' and 'services' have been useful for charting structural shifts in employment (see for example Daniels and Bryson, 2002). However, they are now an impediment to the way in which social scientists think about the structure and operation of both the economy and economic organizations. It is time to change the language(s) and the theory and to begin to look at the world through a different set of language filters and conceptual frameworks. This is a very big task but with a significant payback if we are to formulate new and realistic conceptualizations of our social, cultural and economic milieu as we move through the twentieth-first century. It is important to note that this involves a set of conceptual, as well as methodological, alternatives to the way that research is undertaken.

The dynamic nature of the manufacturing/service interface seems to make the artificial division of these two economic sectors unsustainable. If this is the case, then it seems realistic to suggest that social scientists have to reconsider the boundaries that they place around economic activities. Although the economy may know no boundaries, observers will have a bounded understanding because that is the way in which they work. The implication of some of the changes outlined in this chapter is that the distinction between service and manufacturing activities is even less clear than it may already have been in the past. Assuming that it is still important this has the effect of hampering the way in which economic geographers conceptualize economic activities. By extension, a reconceptualization of the way in which social scientists specify boundaries between economic activities is now required

Service/manufacturing terminology needs to be replaced by an appreciation of the services duality and the complex ways in which service and manufacturing functions are combined to create and realize value. This is an approach that emphases the shift that has occurred towards the creation of manuservice production processes and products and perhaps even to the development of a manuservice economy. Production systems are increasingly founded upon complex combinations of manufacturing and service knowledge. The production of products and services should be conceptualized as a process that consists of a complex and evolving blending of manufacturing and service processes or perhaps more correctly production processes. It is impossible to manufacture without services and services cannot be created or delivered without manufactured products (Bryson, et al., 2008).

For too long service researchers have ignored manufacturing companies on the grounds that there is something special about the service relationship. Perhaps it is time to forget about this distinction? It is time to develop a service-informed understanding of the manufacturing sector. This would highlight the service aspects of manufacturing and at the same time reveal the difficulties of continuing to classify activities as either services or manufacturing. Ultimately, we must move beyond the bipolar division of the economy into manufacturing and services activities and begin to focus on value creation and production processes. This is to shift the focus away from manufacturing and service industries towards understanding the ways in which manufacturing and service functions are combined to create value in the evolving Service World or, perhaps, in the new manuservice economy.

References

Bacon, R. and Eltis, W. (1976). *Britain's economic problems: too few producers*. London: Macmillan.

Bearse, P. J. and Karasek, R. A. (1981). *Services: the new economy*. Totowa: Allenheld and Osmun.

Bell, D. (1973). *The coming of post-industrial society: a venture in social forecasting*. New York: Basic Books.

Beyers, W. B. (1983). Services and industrial systems, paper presented at the Annual Meeting of the Association of American Geographers, Denver, CO, 24027 April.

Beyers, W. B., Alvine, M. J. and Johnson, E. K. (1985). *The service economy: export of services in the central Puget Sound region*. Seattle: Central Puget Sound Development District.

Bitner, M. J., Ostrom, A. & Morgan, F. (2008). Service blueprinting: A practical technique for service innovation, *California Management Review*, 50, 66 – 94.

Business, Enterprise and Regulatory Reform (BERR) (2008). *Manufacturing: new challenges, new opportunities*. London: UK Department of Business, Enterprise and Regulatory Reform.

Blackstone, B. (1997). Measuring the elusive service sector, *CSI Reports: The Service Economy*, 11, 12-13, 19.

Bryson, J.R. (1996). Small business service firms and the 1990s recession in the United Kingdom: Implications for local economic development, *Local Economy Journal*, 11, 221-236.

Bryson, J.R. (1997). Business Service Firms, Service Space and the Management of Change, *Entrepreneurship and Regional Development*, 9, 93-111.

Bryson, J.R. (2007). A 'second' global shift? the offshoring or global sourcing of corporate services and the rise of distanciated emotional labour, *Geografiska Annaler* 89B (S1), 31-43.

Bryson, J.R. (2008a). Service economies, spatial divisions of expertise and the second global shift, in Daniels, P.W. *et al. Human geography: issues for the 21st century.* (pp. 339-337). Harlow: Prentice Hall.

Bryson, J.R. (2008b). Value Chains or Commodity Chains as Production Projects and Tasks: Towards A Simple Theory of Production, Spath, D.; Ganz, W. (Eds.) *Die zukunft der dienstleistungswirtschaft - trends und chancen heute erkennen* (pp. 264-287). Munich: Carl Hanser Verlag.

Bryson, J.R. (2008c). Wertschöpfungs-und Warenketten als Produktionsprojekte und Aufgaben: Auf dem Weg zu einer einfachen Produktionstheorie, in Spath, D.; Ganz, W. (Eds.), *Die zukunft der dienstleistungswirtschaft: trends und chancen heute erkennen* (pp. 261-286). Munich: Carl Hanser Verlag.

Bryson, J.R. (2009a). Economic geography: business services, in Kitchin, R. & Thrift, N. (eds.) *International encyclopedia of human geography.* London: Elsevier.

Bryson, J.R. (2009b). *Hybrid manufacturing systems and hybrid products: services, production and industrialization*. Aachen: University of Aachen, in press.

Bryson, J.R. (2009c). Service innovation and manufacturing innovation: bundling and blending services and products in hybrid production systems to produce hybrid products, in Gallouj F. (Ed), *Handbook on innovation in services*. Cheltenham: Edward Elgar, in press.

Bryson, J. R. and Daniels, P. W. (1998b). Understanding the rise and role of service activities and employment in the global economy: an introduction to the academic literature, Bryson J. R. and Daniels P. W. (eds.) *Service industries in the global economy: volume 1, service theories and service employment*. Cheltenham: Edward Elgar.

Bryson, J.R., Daniels, P.W. and Ingram, D.R. (1999a). Evaluating the impact of business link on the performance and profitability of SMEs in the United Kingdom, *Policy Studies*, 20(2), 95-105.

Bryson, J.R., Daniels, P.W. and Ingram, D.R. (1999b). Methodological problems and economic geography: the case of business services, *The Service Industries Journal*, 19(4), 1-17.

Bryson, J R, Daniels, P W and Warf, B (2004). *Service worlds: people, organizations, technology.* London: Routledge.

Bryson, J.R. and Daniels, P.W. (eds.) (2007). *The handbook of service industries in the global economy,* Cheltenham: Edward Elgar.

Bryson, J.R., Keeble, D. and Wood, P. (1993). The creation, location and growth of small business service firms in the United Kingdom, *The Service Industries Journal* 13(2), 118-131.

Bryson, J.R. and Rusten, G. (2005). Spatial divisions of expertise: knowledge intensive business service firms and regional development in Norway, *The Services Industries Journal,* 25(8), 959-977.

Bryson, J.R. and Rusten, G. (2006). Spatial divisions of expertise and transnational 'service' firms: aerospace and management consultancy, in Harrington', J.W. and Daniels, P.W. (Eds) *Knowledge-based services, internationalization and regional development* (pp. 79-100). Aldershot: Ashgate.

Bryson, J.R .and Taylor, M. (2010). Competitiveness by design and inimitability through service: understanding the dynamics of firm-based competition in the West Midlands Jewellery and Lock Industries, *The Service Industries Journal,* 30(4), in press.

Bryson, J.R., Taylor, M. and Cooper, R. (2008). Competing by design, specialization and customization: manufacturing locks in the West Midlands (UK), *Geografiska Annaler: Series B, Human Geography,* 90(2), 173-186.

Castells, M. (1989). *The informational city.* Oxford: Blackwell.

Chesbrough, H. (2005). Toward a science of services, Harvard *Business Review,* 83, 16-17.

Chesbrough, H. and J. Spohrer (2006). A research manifesto for services science. *Communications of the ACM,* 49(7), 35-40.

Cohen, S. S. and Zysman, J. (1987). *Manufacturing matters: the myth of the post-industrial economy.* New York: Basic Books.

Crang, P. (1994). It's showtime: on the workplace geographies of display in a restaurant in South East England, *Environment and Planning D: Society and Space,* 12, 675-794.

Crum, R. E. and Gudgin, G. (1977). *Non-production activities in UK manufacturing.* Regional Policy Series 95, No.3, Brussels: Commission of the European Communities.

Daniels, P. W. (1983a). Service industries: supporting role or centre stage?, *Area,* 15, 301-309.

Daniels, P. W. (1983b). Business services in British provincial cities: location and control, *Environment and Planning A,* 15, 1101-1120.

Daniels, P. W. (1993). *Service industries in the world economy.* Oxford: Blackwell.

Daniels, P.W. and Bryson, J.R. (2002). Manufacturing services and servicing manufacturing: changing forms of production in advanced capitalist economies, *Urban Studies,* 39(5-6), 977-991.

Daniels, P. W., Leyshon, A., Bradshaw, M. J. and Beaverstock, J. V. (eds.) (2006). *Geographies of the new economy: critical reflections.* London: Routledge.

Davies, R. L. (1972). The location of service activity, in Chisholm, M and Rodgers, B (eds.) *Studies in human geography.* London: Heinemann.

Delaunay, J. C. and Gadrey, J. (1992). *Services in economic thought: three centuries of debate.* Dordrecht: Kluwer.

Department of Trade and Industry (2004). *Competing in the global economy: the manufacturing strategy two years on.* London: Department of Trade and Industry.

Department of Trade and Industry (2007). *Innovation in services.* London: Department of Trade and Industry.

Djellal, F. and Gallouj, F. (2008). *Measuring and improving productivity in services: issues, strategies and challenges.* Cheltenham: Edward Elgar.

Dyson, J. (2004). Engineering the differences, *The Richard Dimbleby Lecture,* BBC, broadcast on 8th December, transcript available at http://news.bbc.co.uk/1/s hared/bsp/hi/pdfs/dyson_10_12_04.pdf, accessed 10th January 2009.

Fahnrich, K.P. and Meiren, T. (2007). Service engineering: state of the art and future trends, in Spath, D. and Fähnrich, K.P. (Eds) *Advances in services innovations* (pp. 3-16). Springer: Berlin.

Florida, R. (2002). *The rise of the creative class and how it's transforming work, leisure, community, and everyday life*. Basic Books. New York.

Fuchs, V. R. (1968). *The service economy*. New York: Columbia University Press.

Fuchs, V. R. (1969). *Production and productivity in the service industries*. New York: National Bureau of Economic Research.

Galbraith, J. K. (1967). *The new industrial state*. New York: Signet Books.

Gallouj, F. (2002). *Innovation in the service economy: the new wealth of nations*. Edward Elgar, Cheltenham.

Ganz, W. (2006). Strengthening the services sector-need for action and research, in Spath D. and Fähnrich K.P (Eds), *Advances in services innovations* (pp. 223-256). Springer: Berlin.

Gereffi G. (2001). Shifting governance structures in global commodity chains, with special reference to the internet, American *Behavioural Scientist*, 44, 1616–1637.

Gereffi G., Humphrey J., Sturgeon T. (2005). The governance of global value chains, *Review of International Political Economy*, 12, 78–104.

Gershuny, J. (1978). *After industrial society?: the emerging self-service economy*. London: Macmillan.

Gershuny, J. and Miles, I. (1983). *The new service economy*. London: Pinter.

Giarini, O. (1997). Notes on economics, globalization and insurance, *Information Letter 152*, Geneva: Geneva Association (mimeo).

Giarini, O. (2002). The globalization of services in economic theory and economic practice: some conceptual issues, in Cuadrado, J.R., Rubalcaba, L. and Bryson, J.R. (eds) *Trading services in the global economy* (pp. 58-77). Cheltenham: Edward Elgar.

Goffman, E. (1984). *The presentation of self in everyday life*. Harmondsworth: Penguin..

Greenfield, H. I. (1966). *Manpower and the growth and producer services*. New York: Columbia University Press.

Grubel, H. G. and Walker, M. A. (1989). *Service industry growth: causes and effects*. Vancouver: Fraser Institute.

Hansen, M.T. and Birkinshaw, J. (2007). The innovation value chain, *Harvard Business Review*: 85(6), 121-130.

Hill, T. P. (1977). On goods and services, *Review of Income and Wealth*, 23, 315-333.

Hochschild, A.R. (1983). *The managed heart*. London: University of California Press.

Holmstrom, B. (1985). The provision of services in a market economy, in Inman, R. (Ed), *Managing the services economy: prospects and problems* (pp. 183-213). Cambridge: Cambridge University Press.

Howells, J. (2002). Innovation, consumption and services: encapsulation and the combinational role of services, Paper presented at the 12th International RESER Conference, 26-27 Sept, 2002, Manchester.

IfM and IBM (2008). Succeeding *through service innovation: A service perspective for education, research, business and government*. Cambridge, UK: University of Cambridge Institute for Manufacturing.

Illeris, S. (1989). *Services and regions in Europe*. Aldershot: Gower.

Kellerman, A. (1985). The evolution of service economies: a geographical perspective, *Professional Geographer*, 37, 133-143.

Livesey, F. (2006). *Defining high value manufacturing*. Cambridge, UK: University of Cambridge Institute for Manufacturing.

Lyons, R. (1998). Britain needs taskforce to rescue manufacturing, *Sunday Times*, 13 September.

Mangham, I.L. (1986). *Power and performance in organizations*: Blackwell: Oxford.

Marshall, J. N. (1982). Linkages between manufacturing industry and business services, *Environment and Planning A*, 14, 1523-1540.

Marshall, J. N. and Wood, P. A. (1995). *Services and space: key aspects of urban and regional development.* Harlow: Longman.

Martin, R. (1994). Economic theory and human geography, in D. Gregory, R. Martin and G. E. Smith (eds.) *Human geography: society, space and social* science (pp. 21-53). London: Macmillan.

Marx, K. (1973). *Grundrisse*. Harmondsworth: Penguin.

Ochel, W. and Wegner, M. (1987). *Service economies in Europe: opportunities for growth.* London: Pinter.

Pilat, D. and Wölfl, A. (2005). M*easuring the interaction between manufacturing and services.* Statistical Analysis of Science, Technology and Industry, STI Working Paper 2005/5, Paris: OECD.

Pine, J. and Gilmore, J. (1999). *The experience economy.* Harvard Business School Press, Boston.

Rapport, N. (1998). Hard Sell: Commercial performance and the narration of the self, in Hughes-Freeland, F. (Ed) *Ritual, performance, media* (pp. 177-194). London: Routledge.

Reich, R. (1992). *The work of nations.* New York: First Vintage Books.

Reubens, E. P. (1981). The services and productivity, *Challenge*, 24, 59-63.

Riddle, D. I. (1986). *Service-led growth: the role of the service sector in world development.* New York: Praeger.

Rubalcaba-Bermejo, L. (1999). *Business services in European industry: growth, employment and competitiveness.* Luxembourg: Office for Official Publications of the European Communities.

Rubalcaba, L. (2007). *The new service economy: challenges and policy implications for Europe,* Cheltenham: Edward Elgar.

Rubalcaba, L. and Kox, H. (2007). *Business services in European economic growth.* Basingstoke: Palgrave.

Rusten, G., Bryson, J.R. and Aarflot, U. (2007). Places through product and products through places: industrial design and spatial symbols as sources of competitiveness, *Norwegian Journal of Geography*, 61(3), 133-144.

Rusten, G. and Bryson J.R. (2007). The production and consumption of industrial design expertise by small and medium-sized firms: some evidence from Norway, *Geografiska Annaler*, 89(1), 75-87.

Sayer, A. (1984). *Methods in social science.* London: Hutchinson.

Smith, A. (1977 [1776]). *The wealth of nations.* Penguin Books, Harmondworth.

Spohrer, J, Maglio, P. P., Bailey, J. Gruhl, D. (2007). Toward a science of service systems, *Computer*, 40(1), 71-77.

Spohrer, J. and Maglio, P.P. (2008). The emergence of service science: towards systematic service innovations to accelerate co-creation of value, *Production and Operations Management*, 17(3), 1-9.

Stanback, T. M .(1979). *Understanding the service economy: employment, productivity, location.* Baltimore, Md.: Johns Hopkins University Press.

Stanback, T. M., Bearse, P. J., Noyelle, T. J. and Karasek, R. A. (1981). *Services: the new economy.* Totowa, NJ: Allanheld, Osmun.

Stigler, G. J. (1956). *Trends in employment in the service industries.* Baltimore. Md: Johns Hopkins University Press.

Sundbo, J. and Darmer, P. (eds.) (2008). *Creating experiences in the experience economy.* Edward Elgar: Cheltenham.

Teboul, J. (2006). *Service is front stage: positioning services for value advantage.* London: INSEAD Business Press.

US Census Bureau (1993). Services classifications. *Issues Paper No 6*, Washington DC: Economic Classification Policy Committee.

Van Ark, B, Inklaar, R. and McGuckin, R.H. (2002). Changing Gear: Productivity, ICT and Service Industries: Europe and the United States. *Research Memorandum GD-60*, Groningen: University of Groningen, Groningen Growth and Development Centre.

Walker, R. (1985). Is there a service economy?: the changing capitalist division of labor, *Science and Society*, 49(1), 42-83.

Webster, F. (2002). *Theories of the information society*. London: Routledge.

Winch, G. (2000). Construction business systems in the European Union, *Building Research and Information*, 28, 88-97.

Part 2
Context: Theory

The Unified Service Theory

A Paradigm for Service Science

Scott E. Sampson

Marriott School of Management

Brigham Young University, Provo, Utah, USA

This chapter discusses a Unified Service Theory (UST) that has been set forth as a foundational paradigm for Service Operations, Service Management, and now Service Science. The fundamental purpose of the UST is to unify the various phenomena we call "services" (i.e., service processes) in a way that demonstrates both how they are distinct from non-services and how they share common managerial principles. The UST prescribes boundaries for Service Science and reveals a gamut of service topics of interest to designers, managers, and researchers. Although the UST has its origins from a business operations perspective, it draws a common thread between the various perspectives pertaining to service.

The Need for Paradigms

All sciences, including Service Science, are founded on paradigms. A paradigm is "a philosophical and theoretical framework of a scientific school or discipline within which theories, laws, and generalizations and the experiments performed in support of them are formulated" (Merriam-Webster 2008).

For example, physics has a paradigm of quantum mechanics, which proposes that discrete particles possess measurable attributes and exhibit predictable behavior. Quantum mechanics replaced traditional Newtonian mechanics as a foundational paradigm of physics; Newtonian mechanics was found to adequately explain some phenomena but to be inconsistent with others.

This chapter is dedicated to the late and great Christopher Lovelock. Few have contributed more to service management thought than Christopher, and he epitomized the ideal of interdisciplinary collegiality.

P.P. Maglio et al. (eds.), *Handbook of Service Science*, Service Science: Research and Innovations in the Service Economy, DOI 10.1007/978-1-4419-1628-0_7,
© Springer Science+Business Media, LLC 2010

Paradigms provide reasonable scope to fields of study. Some physicists have attempted to devise a "theory of everything" that encompasses all known phenomena (at least all known phenomena pertaining to physics). Although such hypergeneralizations are intellectually appealing, rarely do such ideas develop beyond the stage of imagination.

There have been a number of common paradigms associated with the study of services[1]. These paradigms have attempted to answer this fundamental question: If one is studying services, what exactly is being studied? For example, in business it is common to express a service paradigm in terms of "goods versus services," which implies that services are different from goods. If so, the question then becomes how they differ, and if those differences impact how they should be designed and managed.

Some have argued that services, i.e. service processes, apply knowledge and skills to provide benefits to others, and recognize that physical goods are also embodiments of knowledge and skills that provide benefits to others. The conclusion some have espoused is that since goods are service providers then everything is a service. (e.g., Gummesson 1995, p. 150; Vargo and Lusch 2004b, p. 334) That conclusion would lead one to believe that the study of service is the study of everything. Such a broad paradigm provides little discriminatory value in terms of revealing unique managerial insights. Advancement of a Service Science hinges on a belief that service is somehow distinctive and that services possess managerial differences from non-services.

Interestingly, some of the long-held paradigms of service management have been recently refuted – particularly by leading researchers in services marketing and service operations (Nie and Kellogg 1999, p. 351; Grove, Fisk, and John 2003, p. 133; Vargo and Lusch 2004b, p. 334; Edvardsson, Gustafsson, and Roos 2005, p. 115). The researchers have issued a resounding call for new service paradigms. A few new paradigms have been proposed, and in some cases old paradigms have been revived for reconsideration (Lovelock and Gummesson 2004; Vargo and Lusch 2004a).[2]

---

[1] Throughout this chapter the term "services" is used to mean "service processes" or "processes which are each characterized as a service." Unfortunately, in some fields the term "services" has acquired an undesirable connotation of "intangible products," and some have proposed banning the use of the plural term "services" altogether (Vargo and Lusch 2008b). Herein the plural term "services" is used for grammatical convenience in referring to multiple service processes, and is not intended to be a digressive reference to intangible products. A risk of abandoning the plurality of "services" is trivializing the vast variety of "service" manifestations. Note that the singular term "service" has specific meanings in contexts such as the military, religion, horse breeding, and so forth, so even that singular term requires some contextual understanding.

[2] Vargo and Lusch have claimed that their version of Service-Dominant Logic is neither a theory nor a paradigm, but rather a mindset (Vargo and Lusch 2008a, p. 9). They argue that it does not have a "worldview" status, but then suggest that it is "a foundation for a general theory of marketing," and "a basis for reorienting theories of society and economic science." They also describe it as an "alternative to the traditional goods-centered paradigm...." We therefore treat Service-Dominant Logic as a paradigm, or something comparable to a paradigm.

A well-crafted paradigm can provide great benefits to the formation of a science and to those who are contributors and students of the science. Thomas Kuhn, one of the leading scientific philosophers of the past century, describes paradigms as assumptions shared by members of a given discipline (1970). By knowing these assumptions, participants from various backgrounds can more easily come together within the common foundation.

Paradigms are also useful because they direct the activities within the science. As stated by Lovelock and Gummesson, "A paradigm shapes the formulation of theoretical generalizations, focuses data gathering, and influences the selection of research procedures and projects" (2004, p. 21). A truly useful paradigm will also have practical implications, such as leading to significant managerial insights.

In summary, a "good" Service Science paradigm will need to provide reasonable scope, encapsulate common assumptions, and help identify advancement activities. At a minimum, a Service Science paradigm should help those studying services decide what a service is and how services are distinct from "non-services."

Unification around an Elephant

Establishing a Service Science paradigm is particularly difficult given the diversity of perspectives that are becoming involved. Individuals come from many different disciplines that generally have their own long-standing paradigms. Thus, an additional goal of a Service Science paradigm should be accommodating the integration and/or interaction of various perspectives (IfM and IBM 2008, p. 10). This implies attaining some degree of unification of the various service perspectives.

Service Science is somewhat unique in that its formation was instigated primarily by applied researchers from industry (IBM) instead of basic researchers coming from academia[3]. There has been significant and rapid success in building bridges between academia and industry in this effort. The practitioners expressed great interest in drawing upon the decades of research in service-related topics, and the service academics were glad to have an interested audience for their research as well as conference sponsorship and funding opportunities.

It has been pleasant to see the great cooperation that emerged between practitioners from different and similar industries. Modern economies are founded on gaining and protecting competitive advantages coming from knowledge and innovation, yet the companies involved have seemed eager to share ideas for the common good.

---

[3] Arguably, Computer Science had a similar history, with strong motivation coming from industry, particularly IBM.

The bigger ecumenical challenge is reconciling differing perspectives within academia. Academic disciplines have a tradition of being insular. Part of this stems from the preconception that when someone becomes a true expert in a given field, it becomes ever more difficult for those with common knowledge to communicate with them. An unfortunate side effect of this is that without interaction among experts in different fields the experts tend to overestimate the vastness of their knowledge and become blind to their biases.

If anyone doubts the unfortunate reality of this academic isolationism, simply ask any university professor who is about to retire how many times during his or her career that he or she had academic discussions or collaborations with professors "across the street" in other colleges, or even two floors down in another department within the college. Do business school professors really know what takes place in information science schools or design schools or engineering schools or law schools? Probably not.

Indeed, bringing academics together in a Service Science is like the proverbial six blind men encountering an elephant. Each man describes the elephant differently—as being like a pillar, a rope, a giant fan, etc.—depending on what part of the elephant they encounter. The blind men do not realize that they are only understanding part of the picture.

The ecumenical task is even more difficult given the penalties assessed for cross-functional research. Occasionally one hears at academic conferences or university meetings a call for more cross-functional research, but it is invariably couched, either explicitly or implicitly, in a restriction to those who have no impending need for getting tenure or promotion! Even those who have received all of the standard promotions available from the academy are subject to disincentives for cross-functional research – such as getting beaten up by journal reviewers for not upholding the specific biases of a journal's discipline.

This bias blindness exists in industry as well. People in healthcare speak healthcare lingo. People in auto manufacturing speak auto manufacturing. People in software engineering speak software engineering. People in garbage collection speak garbage collection.

A prominent illustration of industry-speak is how different industries talk about "service." In healthcare, service relates to ideas of "bedside manner." In auto manufacturing, service pertains to repairing defective products. In software engineering, service pertains to loosely coupled software interfaces – so-called "Service Oriented Architecture" (SOA). And in garbage collection, service seems to have something to do with whether or not they pick up your empty garbage can if it falls over during emptying, instead of just leaving it lying in the street.

The unification objective of the Unified Service Theory is to provide a basis for unification within Service Science on multiple dimensions. One is to identify the commonality between service that occurs within seemingly disparate industries – to reveal the common service basis for healthcare, auto repair, SOA, garbage collection, etc. Another is to provide a common foundation for Service Science that various disparate disciplines can relate to and identify with. Much of the strength of the unification will come from not only demonstrating commonalities within the Service Science umbrella, but also emphasizing how markedly different service manifestations are from non-service manifestations.

The Unified Service Theory[4]

In presenting the Unified Service Theory, I do not claim to be exempt from the propensity for disciplinary bias. My background is in service operation management, and by habit I take a production and operations perspective. This implies that I view the world as series of production processes – each converting some inputs into some outputs with the intent of producing value in terms of need-filling potential.

There are three conditions that hopefully can help mitigate the effects of disciplinary bias. The first is what seems to be my attention deficit disorder that has enabled me to wander among various disciplines over the years. Although my graduate training and professorial position is in business management and operations, my undergraduate degree is in human resource development, I have consulted in computer technology for many years, my hobby is legal work (IP), and I own a small engineering firm. My current interest is molecular biology and DNA, which is manifest in my more recent theories of service systems (Sampson, Menor, and Bone 2010).

The second is the fact that my recitation of the Unified Service Theory (UST) is not original, but is simply a packaging and presentation of ideas that great thinkers in other areas taught many years ago. The UST may sit on an interesting precipice between those who discount it as being outside of their discipline's traditional paradigm on one side, and those who think their discipline came up with it years before on the other side. I cite a number of the prior allusions to the UST below. Doubtless there are others who formulated UST concepts many years ago, but that I cannot acknowledge because I have not been able to find their published recitations. I offer a blanket acknowledgement and wish to give them full credit for their valuable contributions.

Third, by acknowledging the bias I wonder if the bias might be somehow lessened. I would hypothesize that the most biased individuals tend to be those who think they have no biases. Nevertheless, I am sure I must have an operations management bias.

Arguably, the central principle of the operations management discipline is the I/O model: inputs are transformed into outputs through production processes, as depicted in Figure 1. Operations management people believe that this is universal—all processes can be described in terms of the I/O model. The model applies

---

[4] In previous recitations this theory has been called The Unified Services Theory, meaning a theory which unifies otherwise distinctive service processes. It is hoped that using the singular term "Service" will portray similar meaning.

to service processes just as well as non-service processes, but the UST premise is that the application to service processes is universally distinct from the application to non-service processes.

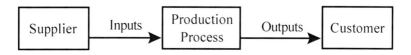

Figure 1. Traditional I/O Model

Traditional business perspectives on service focus on what service providers provide to customers. People refer to "service delivery" of "service products" which makes one think of service as being something customers *get* from service providers. Many researchers, including me, emphasize that services are really processes—that *service* is something service providers *do* more than *give*. Such services (i.e., service processes) may not involve tangible components, but usually do. Operations management people would contend that everything is a process, service or otherwise. But again, we are cautious about considering any perspectives that claim that everything is the same.

The UST is unusual in that at the elemental level it is *not* founded in what service providers provide, or even the processes they use to deliver the service. Instead, the UST is based on the distinction of *what customers provide to the service provider* and to the service process. It is succinctly stated as follows:

The Unified Service Theory: Services are production processes wherein each customer supplies one or more input components for that customer's unit of production. With non-service processes, groups of customers may contribute ideas to the design of the product, but individual customers' only participation is to select, pay for, and consume the output. All considerations unique to service are founded in this distinction.

The UST asserts that the universally distinguishing feature of services is the involvement of customers in production processes by involving process inputs that are controlled and supplied by customers (Spohrer and Maglio 2008). In Riddle's (1986) words, "services are activities that produce changes in persons or the goods they possess." Or, restating Lovelock (1983), customer inputs include customers' selves, their belongings, and/or their information. Customers are therefore suppliers to service processes, as depicted in Figure 2. This *customer-supplier service paradigm* (the UST) holds that customer inputs are a necessary and sufficient condition for a service process to be a service process, and the lack of customer inputs characterizes all non-service processes (Sampson 2000). The UST has broad managerial significance: processes that involve customer inputs possess management concerns similar to one another, but involve different concerns from processes not dependent upon customer inputs (Sampson, Menor, and Bone 2010).

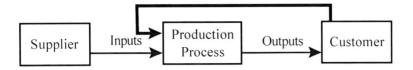

Figure 2. Service I/O Model

In order to understand the UST service paradigm, a few definitions are in order: inputs, customers, and production processes...

Inputs (i.e., input components) are things (tangible or intangible resources) that come into a process and are used by the process to produce some benefit. In this context we refer to *inputs* as components for *specific* units of production, not payments *after* production and not "customer input" in the sense of general feedback or ideas about the process or outcome.

Customers are individuals or entities that determine if the organization shall be compensated (or rewarded) for production, which customers may be consumers (beneficiaries) or may just be decision makers. For example, college students buy textbooks but it is the instructors who decide whether to use a given textbook in a course.

Production processes are sequences of steps that provide value propositions and therefore warrant compensation. Organizations may have other processes that simply *prepare* for production, such as maintaining equipment, that do not directly warrant compensation but are nevertheless necessary. Details and examples of these three essential concepts are described in the article by Sampson and Froehle (2006).

Clarification through a Process Paradigm

As mentioned, the concept of services being reliant upon customer inputs is not new, but has been cited in passing in research literature and other publications (Silvestro, *et al.* 1992, p. 66; Bitner, *et al.* 1997, p. 195; Wright 1999, p. 5; Lovelock 2001, p. 37; Chervonnaya 2003, p. 335; Fitzsimmons and Fitzsimmons 2004, p. 21; Zeithaml, Bitner, and Gremler 2006, p. 393). However, the central, defining power of the concept has not been widely recognized. One reason for this might be that various researchers tend to categorize firms or industries, not individual processes within firms (Wemmerlöv 1990, p. 24).

The paradigm shift provided by the customer-supplier service paradigm (the UST) is this: Customer inputs are the defining feature of service *as long as we identify the customer (relative to the service provider) and specify the process being analyzed.* The paradigm is a process perspective—all businesses, "service businesses" or otherwise, are composed of processes that transform inputs into outputs. The customer-supplier paradigm proposes that the one core factor which distinguishes traditional make-to-stock manufacturing[5] processes from service processes is not the occurrence of processes nor the nature of process outputs (which may be tangible or intangible), but the distinct nature of process inputs. The nature of the acts differ, as does the nature of the output, but that is primarily due to the nature of the inputs—customer inputs lead to processes and outputs that are distinct in character from those devoid of customer inputs (Sampson, Menor, and Bone 2010).

Consider the example given by Rathmell in his 1966 article titled "What is Meant by Services?" Rathmell follows the phrase "a good is a thing and a service is an act" with the statement, "If a product is purchased, it is a good; but if it is rented or leased, the rentee or lessee acquires a service" (pp. 33–34). The UST perspective would say that a product is a good (i.e., a thing) regardless of whether it is purchased or rented (Hill 1977, p. 320). Customers observe the goods rental process, but rarely observe the goods manufacturing processes. If a manufacturing process does not involve customer inputs yet the rental process does, then the rental process, as a service process, will in all likelihood be less efficient than the manufacturing process, will be subject to greater variability, will experience lower utilization, and so forth. Service processes and outputs are fundamentally different from non-service processes and outputs due to the dependence upon customer inputs.

Therefore, one part of the existing confusion over terms comes from comparing service *processes* (acts) to manufacturing *outputs* (goods). The process of home construction is an act, whether it is building large quantities of tract homes for future sales or building a one-of-a-kind custom home for a meticulous client. The outputs of car manufacturing, car sales, car repair, and car rental are all cars. The distinguishing question of the UST is, "What are the customer input components to the given process?" Those processes without customer inputs are very different from those involving customer inputs, and the degree and nature of customer inputs provide further insights.

Another form of confusion comes from studying complex aggregations of service and non-service processes, such as companies or industries. Attempting to classify an entire company or industry as either "service" or "non-service" can lead to confusion. Even defining a particular line of business can become convoluted. One might ask, "Is a restaurant a service?" A restaurant is a business comprised of a wide variety of processes. You need to indicate which restaurant process you are considering in order to identify if it is a service process. The process of a chef designing new food offerings is not normally dependent upon customer inputs (other than a consideration of general customer opinions) and is not a service process—unless it is outsourced, in which case the restaurant is the customer of the outsource provider (Hill 1977, p. 320). The same is similar for the supply-procurement process. Seating customers and taking customer orders requires

---

[5] The UST classifies traditional make-to-stock manufacturing a non-service when it is accomplished without inputs from customers. Custom manufacturing requires at least an information input from customers, therefore would be categorized as a service. For more explanation, see (Sampson and Froehle 2006, p. 336) or (Sampson 2001, p. 142).

customer inputs, and is a service process. Preparing food for customers is a "back-office" service process, as is preparing the check. Restaurants involve goods, and involve both service and non-service processes.

Service Systems and Supply Chains

The other important key to comprehending the UST is realizing that rarely do processes occur in isolation. Rather, processes exist in systems and supply chains, wherein each process feeds other processes. The field of operations management approached a renaissance in recent years with the realization that analyzing and managing a given process without consideration for "upstream" supplier processes or "downstream" customer processes leads to suboptimal decisions. The field (or sub-field or meta-field) of Supply Chain Management is primarily concerned with understanding interactions between such interrelated processes.

The concept of supply chains originates from the manufacturing context. It is based on the idea that outputs from a given production process (see Figure 1) become inputs to other production processes. Supply chains are examples of systems, which include various types of interacting entities.

As Ellram, Tate, and Billington point out, the representation of services in Supply Chain Management literature is sparse and inadequate (2004). Some writers claim that supply chain concepts are relevant to manufacturing and service, but then proceed to focus on manufacturing examples–a manifestation of traditional operations management bias. The service examples tend to be appendages to manufacturing supply chains, such as retail. Some services have major goods components, and thus benefit from approaches such as supplier certification and selection, synchronous production, and supplier integration. It is not at all clear how to apply such approaches to services that do not have major goods components.

The UST sheds light on service supply chains by showing how they involve customers both as suppliers of inputs and consumers of outputs (Sampson, 2001, p. 135). Such supply chains are not conveniently linear, but are bidirectional (Sampson 2000). The most effective supply chain management for services will involve understanding the function, capabilities, and disposition of customers as suppliers. Just as manufacturing supply chains benefit when suppliers operate in harmony with the given firm, so service firms (i.e., firms replete with service processes) benefit when customer-suppliers act in harmony with the firm.

Similarly, the UST suggests that *service systems* be defined as configurations of entities in which a given entity is a provider of resource components and simultaneously or subsequently the beneficiary of the processed components. This captures the idea of services being entities that process other entities (or process their belongings/information). A non-service system is conversely a configuration of entities such that in a given interaction the individual entities are either providers of input resource components or beneficiaries of the improved output components, but not both. Note that most productive systems are hybrids in that they contain both service configurations and non-service configurations—and that each configuration type should be managed accordingly.

Also note that contrary to some views, most activities in modern economic systems are *not* the exchange of service for service, but rather the exchange of service for a generic resource (money) which can later be exchanged for service as necessary. This "indirect exchange" of service is the foundation of productive economies.

Service systems, as with supply chains, contain many interactions between various entities, some of which are service interactions and some of which are non-service interactions. It is important to remember that the UST is a process paradigm: it is a given process or interaction within a system that exhibits or does not exhibit the service characteristic.

Customer Intensity and Coproduction

A concept that is a companion to the UST is *customer intensity*, which recognizes that input components provided by customers can impact the production process to different degrees. In a basic sense, customer intensity is the degree with which variation in customer input components causes variation in the production process. Variation in production processes often translates into increased costs and usually causes increased complexity. Input components coming from customers can vary in many ways, including the timing of their provision, the condition of the inputs, the degree to which the inputs need to be improved, and whether/how the customer inputs include a labor element (i.e., customer effort).

Labor inputs coming from customers are often called "coproduction." Customer coproduction is not a necessary condition for a service, but it is a sufficient condition (since effort qualifies as an input component). Coproduction can be a significant cause of customer intensity, since coproducing customers vary in skill and in willingness to comply with procedures specified by the service provider. Service providers may attempt to reduce customer intensity, and thus reduce the cost effects, by training customers and providing them with structured automation. This is easier said than done, since customers lack the incentives and economies of scale (e.g., experience-curve effects) of non-customer labor.

The UST as a useful paradigm

The one significant change to the UST since it was first introduced in 1998 was replacing "nearly all" with simply "all" in reference to "managerial themes unique to services [being] founded in the customer-input distinction" (Sampson 2001, p. 16). A motivation for this change is that a counter-example has yet to surface. Perhaps an easier justification is to consider the UST as a normative theory, which renders it a tautology. Nevertheless, it is an extremely useful tautology for various reasons.

First, the UST provides a reasonable scope to Service Management and Service Science. The UST says that services are not everything, but simply those productive interactions that involve customers as suppliers of component inputs.

Second, the UST justifies the study of seemingly disparate service business under a unified science. For example, although lawn care and dentistry fill very different customer needs, they both involve processing customer input components and therefore both experience numerous managerial issues that are implied by that condition. Some of those issues will be discussed the subsequent sections of this chapter, and others can be found in publications by Sampson (2001) and Sampson and Froehle (2006).

Third, the UST has the potential to integrate and connect the perspectives of a wide variety of disciplines contributing to Service Science. The integrating element is differentiating on customer input components. As we have seen, the application to business operations is the following:

- **Business operations** are processes that transform input components to produce more valued output products.

    - *Service operations* are processes involving input components that come from each individual customer. Service operations management is largely about managing customer influences on the ability to produce.
    - *Non-service operations* are processes that are performed independent from customers. Non-service operations have few time and space constraints on production, at least relative to typical service operations.

This UST perspective can be applied in any number of other disciplinary paradigms. Here are examples for other business disciplines.

- **Business marketing** is the process or technique of promoting, selling, and distributing a product or service (to customers) (Merriam-Webster 2008).

    - *Service marketing* is marketing in which the customer is *engaged* in the production process by virtue of providing component inputs. This implies that we are promoting, selling, and distributing an interaction experience.
    - *Non-service marketing* is marketing in which the customer is buffered (in time and space) from production, instead focusing on promoting, selling, and distributing the output of production.

- **Human Resource Management (HRM)** is the function within an organization that focuses on recruitment of, management of, and providing *direction* for the people who work in the organization.[6]

---

[6] http://humanresources.about.com/od/glossaryh/f/hr_management.htm

- *Service HRM* is HRM in which customers work in the organization, by providing either labor or other component inputs. The distinctive challenge is accommodating variation in customer efforts, contributions, and interactions with employees, which customer variations can be difficult to direct and control.
- *Non-service HRM* is HRM in which the labor in the organization is comprised of non-customers (employees), who are more susceptible to direction than customer labor.

Here are a few examples of the UST applied to engineering.

- **Software architecture** is the structure or structures of the system, which comprise software components, the externally visible properties of those components, and the relationships between them. (Wikipedia)

  - *Service-oriented software architecture* is software architecture in which the customers (routines calling externally visible procedures) provide inputs to routines in terms of loosely-coupled process requirement requests.
  - *Non-service oriented software architecture* is software architecture in which calling routines (customers) are expected to conform to predefined application program interfaces (APIs).

- **New Product Development (NPD)** is the complete process of bringing a new product or service to the market. (Wikipedia)

  - *Service NPD* (aka *New Service Development*) is NPD in which the product involves a process that is contingent upon customer input components, therefore must consider the uncertainties surrounding customer influence on the production process. This customer intensity usually warrants increased robustness in process design.
  - *Non-service NPD* is NPD in which the product will subsequently be produced independent of customers, thus allowing tight specification of product attributes.

Fourth, the UST is a useful paradigm because it encapsulates and explains the wide variety of perspectives on service discussed in the extant literature. For example, one popular perspective on service from the marketing literature is and has been the so-called IHIP, which is that services are characterized (defined) by four attributes: Intangibility, Heterogeneity, Inseparability, and Perishability. Lovelock and Gummesson (2004) described how IHIP have been commonly accepted as *the* paradigm for services, but they also point out flaws in IHIP. Others have likewise refuted IHIP. Grove, Fisk, and John surveyed a panel of service experts and found some inclination to drop IHIP and to "eliminate the goods versus services distinction altogether" (2003, p. 113). Vargo and Lusch (2004b) argue that IHIP characteristics "(a) do not distinguish services from goods, (b) only have meaning from a manufacturing perspective, and (c) imply inappropriate normative strategies" (p. 324). Edvardsson, Gustafsson, and Roos (2005) assert that "We could conclude that the IHIP characteristics should not be used in the future as generic service characteristics," which they follow by a declaration that "service characteristics [i.e., IHIP] are outdated: therefore, when are we going to stop using them when teaching?" (p. 115).

Might I suggest that the reason IHIP is popular yet refutable is because IHIP is an inadequate paradigm for service marketing or Service science in general. As an alternate paradigm, the UST can be used to explain both the popularity of IHIP and the misperceptions of IHIP. In the next section we will explore this application of the UST.

UST and IHIP

As just mentioned, Lovelock and Gummesson (2004) reviewed service management literature and showed that IHIP was the incumbent paradigm. Within the broader field of marketing, they highlight the widespread tendency among authors of introductory marketing management texts to use IHIP as the basis for identifying services. Lovelock and Gummesson describe the development of each characteristic and show how each fails as a definitive characteristic across businesses commonly held to be services.

The UST states that "All managerial themes unique to services are founded in [the customer input] distinction." That means that if a characteristic is unique to service processes, that characteristic will be explained by the reliance on customer inputs. Correspondingly, if a characteristic is not explained by customer inputs, then it is not a characteristic that is unique to service. Let us consider each of the IHIP characteristics in this regard.

IHIP #1: Intangibility

The most prevalent misconception coming from IHIP is the assertion that services are defined by intangibility (Lovelock and Gummesson 2004, p. 25). Various researchers have also refuted that assertion and concluded that it is without merit (Laroche, Bergeron, and Goutaland 2001; Vargo and Lusch 2004b). The UST both supports that conclusion and provides a possible explanation for the confusion. Some customer inputs are intangible, such as customer minds (e.g., in education) and customer information (e.g., in tax accounting). But many customer inputs are tangible, including customers themselves (e.g., as a patient or passenger) and their belongings (e.g., yard for landscaping, clothes for tailoring, documents for shredding services, etc.).

How is it conceivable that individuals can so easily ignore the tangible nature of most services? One possible explanation is that when customers provide the primary tangible inputs to the process, those inputs may not be perceived as being an integral part of the product (Sampson, 2001, p. 100). Consider dentistry as an example. Dentistry is considered by some to be an intangible service. Patients leave dental offices having been acted upon, but with no physical product except perhaps a new toothbrush and a floss sampler. Yet, such a view ignores a highly tangible output of the process: the patients' cleaned and repaired teeth. Even though the teeth were provided by customers as process inputs, they are tangible nonetheless. If a factory produces false teeth from ceramic material, those teeth are certainly considered tangible, but no more tangible than the cleaned and repaired teeth which emerge from dentists' work. When we consider the tangibility of customer inputs we see that the apparition of intangibility of service largely dissolves.

This is not to imply that highly intangible services do not exist. The UST provides for intangible customer input components such as customer information. Such inputs can be manipulated in purely intangible ways and delivered back to the customer in an intangible form. Lovelock and Gummesson (2004) cite examples of Internet-based services in banking, insurance, news, research, etc. (p. 26). They note how the emergence of Internet-based services "sharpens our recognition of just how much physical tangibility exists in most other services" (p. 27).

Further, there are numerous examples of intangible products that are not services. One example is prepackaged software, such as operating systems produced by Microsoft. Even though the software is delivered on physical disks, the software product itself is an intangible set of codes and information. Microsoft's production of operating systems is not a service process, since it does not involve any customer inputs. Customers merely select, pay for, and consume the output, and occasionally provide general feedback about product features.

IHIP #2: Heterogeneity

The term heterogeneity has been used to describe service in different ways such as variability in service providers and their operations, as well as variability in the execution of a given service process (Lovelock and Gummesson 2004, p. 25). Morris and Johnston (1987) identify two causes of service variability: variability in service resources and variability in customer inputs. The UST argues that the variability in customer inputs is the one that is unique to service (Sampson 2001, p. 108). The UST argues that the reason heterogeneity is attributed to service in IHIP is due to heterogeneity of customer inputs. Other sources of heterogeneity are not unique to service.

Indeed, variability in non-customer inputs such as employed labor occurs both in service and in manufacturing. Non-services, such as make-to-stock manufacturing processes, can put systems in place to limit the impacts of labor variability.

With services, employee labor that interacts with customers is particularly subject to interpersonal interaction variability, which is likely to be attributed more to the variability of customers (who change from one transaction to the next) than variability of employees (who change less during a work shift).

IHIP #3: Inseparability

Inseparability is the characteristic in which production and consumption are temporally linked. The characteristic is also called "simultaneous production and consumption," or simply "simultaneity," implying that service consumption occurs at (or near) the same time as service production (Fitzsimmons and Fitzsimmons 2004, p. 23).

The UST explains inseparability by customer inputs being essential to service processes, implying that the service production process cannot be accomplished without those essential inputs. The presentation of customer inputs generally corresponds to the presentation of demand, which is motivated by a desire to consume the service. In theory, a customer could provide inputs for future demand, allowing the service provider to produce in advance of demand. In reality, customers typically do not provide inputs until they are ready to demand the service.

Although services cannot typically produce without customer demand, the "consumption" process of receiving benefits from the service might occur during or after production. In some cases the extraction of benefits does not happen during production, implying that production and value-extracting consumption do not occur simultaneously. For example, a man may have his tuxedo dry cleaned in anticipation of the next time he wears it, which may be months in the future. Demand for dry cleaning occurs before the process, but arguably, consumption may not occur until some time later.

Perhaps a more accurate depiction of inseparability is that production is tied to demand, which, as implied by the UST, is that demand precedes production (Sampson 2001, p. 52). Service providers have processes that prepare for production without customer demand and inputs, but cannot actually produce in a revenue-generating sense without customer inputs.

IHIP #4: Perishability

The perishibility element of IHIP has been described in two major ways. The first pertains to the perishability of the service process output, which is not generalizable, and can be easily refuted (Sampson 2001, p. 82). We have already described how service output can be consumed at a time well after services are produced. Furthermore, that output might be consumed over a great deal of time, with little or no diminishment of the output. One would hope that education services fit in that category—that students extract the benefit of the knowledge output for many years after completing an education program. Some surgical procedures, such as hip replacement, produce an output that lasts longer than the lifetime of the patient.

Indeed, some service output is more durable than typical manufacturing goods. We see that other services have output that is extremely perishable, such as massage services where the relaxation effect may wear off in mere hours. Manufacturing also produces products that are highly perishable, such as foodstuffs. Perishable output is a poor differentiator between services and non-services (Lovelock and Gummesson 2004, p. 30; Vargo and Lusch 2004b, p. 331).

The second manifestation of service "perishability" is the accurate observation that service capacity is perishable (Sampson 2001, p. 60). More precisely, it is that service capacity without corresponding demand is lost forever (Fitzsimmons and Fitzsimmons 2004, p. 24). Conversely, manufacturing capacity without corresponding demand is not lost forever, but can be easily employed producing for future demand. Services do not have that luxury, due to the production requirement of customer inputs (Sampson 2001, p. 52, 310). A hotel example will be given below.

The perishable capacity concept has major implications for capacity planning and utilization. It may be true that both services and non-services are concerned about utilization, but the management context is quite different.

A bed manufacturer can achieve a target of near-100% utilization of production capacity during both high-demand and low-demand seasons. During periods of low demand the manufacturer produces beds to inventory, and during high demand sells from inventory and from production. This makes it possible to design plant capacity to meet average demand across the seasonal cycle. If a bed manufacturer desires to produce to full capacity at times of low demand, typically the only constraints are needs for maintenance, repair, and changeover (assuming other process inputs are readily available and that inventory holding costs are tolerable). Demand is not a capacity utilization constraint (although Just-In-Time production might be desirable for cost reasons). Uncertainty or expectations of reduced demand can lead to decisions for lower utilization of capacity, but that reduction is a decision, and not a constraint.

The hotel manager faces a very different problem of capacity management. If demand is seasonal (which it usually is), the hotel will have lower utilization during slow times and perhaps have excess demand during busy times. If the times of excess demand have more customers than available rooms then the result will likely be lost sales. It would be nice if the vacant room capacity during slow times could be used to produce "hotel stays" for customers during busy times, but such cannot happen unless the customer inputs (selves and belongings) are shifted to the slow times. The hotel capacity during slow times is perishable, and cannot be utilized to meet future demand. The hotel can *prepare* for future demand, such as by cleaning rooms, training staff, and other tasks that are not contingent upon customer-self inputs (thus defined as "non-service" tasks). But such preparation has limits, and falls short of actually satisfying future demand in a productive (e.g., revenue generating) way. Therefore, just-in-time *production* for the hotel manager is inadvertent, and not a cost-based decision (Sampson, 2001, p. 310–312). What the manager does need to decide is how to plan capacity given the inevitable times of low utilization, and perhaps decide about providing incentives for customers to shift their inputs (and demand) from high-demand periods to low-demand periods.

The bottom line is that even though service output may or may not be perishable, the service capacity is perishable in that without corresponding demand and customer inputs that capacity is lost. This is an important implication of the UST.

IHIP as Symptoms

Although it is easy to reject IHIP as the defining elements of service, we need not go so far as to discard them as useless. The UST explains the IHIP phenomena and shows that IHIP represents *symptoms of services* which, when understood correctly, provide insight about service processes (Sampson 2001, p. 49). Understanding the UST increases the practical value of IHIP. Just as studying the symptoms of an illness benefits from understanding the cause of the illness, so also does understanding the symptoms of services benefit from understanding the defining core of service processes (i.e., reliance upon customer inputs).

Other UST Implications

Lovelock and Gummesson (2004) described various issues besides IHIP which relate to service management and which should be encompassed in a service paradigm. In this section we will review some of those issues and show that the service reliance on customer input components—which is the crux of UST—leads to useful managerial insights.

1. Service inventory

The service output perishability fallacy is related to a misconception that service output cannot be inventoried (Lovelock and Gummesson, 2004, p. 29). Manufacturers produce components or end items which are stored for future production and consumption. Service processes can produce output for future consumption, as long as customers have provided the requisite inputs prior to production. But, since providing customer inputs is typically equated with demand, there is usually little justification for the service provider keeping service production in storage for future needs. In other words, it is not that it is impossible to keep service output in inventory, but it is impractical to do so (Sampson, 2001, p. 90).

There is an aspect of "inventory management" which is both relevant and important for services, which comes from the UST focus on customer inputs. In one sense, inventory represents a delay between the timing of production and demand. For manufacturing, inventory "fills the time gap" between production and demand. With services, demand precedes production due to the reliance on customer inputs. If customer inputs arrive well in advance of production—for example, in a case of insufficient capacity—then those inputs might wait in "inventory." Such customer-input inventory is often called a waiting line or a queue (Fitzsimmons and Fitzsimmons 2004, p. 428; Lovelock and Gummesson 2004, p. 30).

Customer inventories, or queues, are like manufacturing inventories in that both are caused by a timing difference between production and demand. However, customer inventories typically have much higher holding costs, measured in minutes instead of months. The holding costs are incurred directly by the customers (Sampson, 2001, p. 318) and indirectly by the service provider (e.g., lost sales). The holding costs for manufacturing inventories are incurred directly by the producer and indirectly by the customers (e.g., higher prices).

2. Pseudo-services

The previous section on intangibility gave prepackaged software production as an example of a *pseudo-service*, which is a non-service process that has a significant intangible element and thus is sometimes mistaken for a service process even though it does not rely on customer inputs (Sampson 2001, p. 154). Lovelock and Gummesson (2004, p.31) give other examples of processes we would call pseudo-services:

- Entertainment delivered through prerecorded and edited means
- News or religion services broadcast by radio or TV
- Prerecorded self-study educational services
- Other intellectual property, such as software

It is possible for entertainment, religious services, and education to be delivered as services. However, if they are "prerecorded" (recorded before the customer experiences them) then the recording process does not depend upon customer inputs (assuming the customer is defined as the viewer). Consider the example of motion picture production. The production process involves producers, directors, writers, grips, set designers, actors and actresses, and other personnel turning intangible ideas into an intangible video representation. Movie producers generally produce movies with no inputs from customers, and few of the typical characteristics of service apply to movie production processes. In many regards, the movie production process is more akin to manufacturing processes than it is to service processes. Movie producers add value by assembling content into a viewable product.

Live entertainment, conversely, is a service, in that the artists on the stage cannot produce in a value-adding and revenue-generating sense without the input of customer minds and attention. It is interesting to note that live theater "service product" might be considered quite tangible (facilities, props, actors) whereas the non-service movie-production product (recorded image) might be considered intangible. Service entertainment may be more tangible than "manufactured" entertainment.

One other example of a pseudo-service is electricity generation (Schmenner 1995, p. 1). Some people think of electricity generation as "electric service," but it is not a service according to the UST. Electricity generation, as with other energy production processes, generally occurs without any inputs from customers. The difference between electricity production and the production of other energy types, such as gasoline, is that it is presently extremely expensive to store electricity for any period of time. It would take an enormous number of batteries to store the electricity needed to power even a small city. A few characteristics of service are observed in electricity generation (primarily simultaneity), not because electricity generation is a customer-input–dependent service, but because it is costly to store electricity.

3. Customer evaluation of services

Lovelock and Gummesson (Lovelock and Gummesson 2004, p. 27) refer to and question Zeithaml's (1981) and Nelson's (1974) classifications of service or good product features based on how easy they are to evaluate prior to purchase. The concept is that company offerings may possess three types of attributes:

- Search qualities, which can be precisely assessed by customers prior to purchase,
- Experience qualities, which cannot be precisely assessed prior to purchase but can be assessed through consumption,
- Credence qualities, which cannot be precisely assessed even after purchase and consumption (thus requiring customers to rely on experts for assessment).

These three qualities supposedly lie on a continuum from easy to difficult to evaluate. The point is that search properties tend to dominate for goods, whereas experience (and credence) properties tend to dominate for services (Zeithaml

1981).[7] This distinction is based on an assumption of mental intangibility, in that services are supposedly more difficult to define, formulate, and understand (Lovelock and Gummesson 2004, p. 26).

Lovelock and Gummesson point out that there is no basis for belief that mental intangibility will persist after repeated experience with a service (2004, p. 27). However, it is easier to justify the significance of mental intangibility when considering potential customers with no prior experience with the given service provider. The UST says that customer inputs are central to service production and not to non-service production such as manufacturing goods to stock. A potential customer can review the published features of a manufactured good and be quite confident that the good they will receive will be as described. Even better, a friend can objectively describe the good to the potential customer with confidence that the good will have the same characteristics for the potential customer, even if the potential customer does not share an appreciation for those characteristics.

Services involve customer inputs that can be very unique from one customer to the next. Therefore, if a friend objectively tells a potential customer about his experience with a service provider, there is no guarantee that the potential new customer, who provides different inputs, will have the same experience (Sampson, 2001, p. 282). A hypothetical example is shopping at a home improvement store. A friend says "I like Home Depot because when I go there they always have the answers to my gardening questions." The potential new customer goes to Home Depot and discovers that they do not have answers for her questions—perhaps because she is more experienced at gardening and thus asks more difficult questions than her friend. The "has answers" quality does not have a discrete and consistent manifestation, but varies based on the inputs (and experience) of individual customers.

Both manufactured goods and services experience variance in customers' subjective evaluations of outputs; an item may be valued by one customer and not valued by another. Where manufactured goods and services differ is in the objective assessments of production and outputs, due to the absence or presence of stochastic customer inputs. Objective assessment of manufacturing output can be reliability communicated, which is the essence of search qualities.

4. Ownership and customer competition

Lovelock and Gummesson proposed *nonownership* as an alternate paradigm for studying services, but, unlike the UST, they "make no claim that the proposed new paradigm offers a panacea with necessarily general properties" (Lovelock &

---

[7] Note that this discussion refers to the traditional market perspective that companies sell goods and/or services. Recall that the UST perspective does not consider goods and services to be two distinct things, since tangible items (goods) are often involved in processes that have customer-component inputs (services).

Gummesson, 2004, p. 34). A nonownership perspective on service was presented by Judd in 1964, but for some reason it never attained the prominence of IHIP (Lovelock and Gummesson 2004, p. 23). Judd himself acknowledged that the nonownership definition has "the defect of any definition by exclusion in that, from the definition itself, nothing can be learned about what are the essential characteristics of a service" (Judd 1964, p. 59), which may or may not be true. Judd looked instead to some future development of a positive definition of service.

The UST, as a positive definition, reveals important issues about ownership in services. Applied to service, the ownership concept means that customers own their inputs prior to production, and usually own their inputs after production. Customers may also come to own physical items attached during production. The production facility and production equipment are typically owned by the service provider, before, during, and after production, which is not wholly different from manufacturing, where the plant and equipment are owned by the manufacturer. The significant difference regarding ownership is that with services a component of the output was previously owned by the customer.

Another perspective of ownership is also interesting to study: with many services, the customer has the alternative of purchasing necessary equipment and producing the service himself or herself (Bitner, *et al.* 1997, p. 198). For example, a Chinese restaurant customer can purchase a wok and cook at home, an investment broker customer can purchase investment analysis software and self-invest, and an airline customer can purchase a motor home for vacation travel. In these cases the customer can replace a service provider with a combination of owned manufactured goods and self-service (Sampson 2001, p. 148).

This alternative leads to the significant phenomenon in which customers are themselves the chief competitors for many services (Sampson 2001, p. 202–205). Service providers sometimes need to convince do-it-yourself customers that they would be better off using the service provider. For some services, such as reconstructive surgery, the convincing is easy. For other services, such as personal tax accounting, the convincing may be much more difficult. Customers have the advantage of owning and controlling their inputs, and may have the advantage of increased levels of customization (getting it exactly how they want it). Service providers, on the other hand, usually have advantages of economies of scale and expertise.

This customer-as-competitor issue is mostly distinct to services, and rarely seen in manufacturing. Manufacturers are connected into supply chains and are so efficient that self-production is not a reasonable option for most customers, such as end consumers. Only NASA would be willing to spend the tens of thousands of dollars to design and produce one screwdriver, whereas the rest of us are content with simply purchasing one at a hardware store. A few manufacturers, such as strawberry jam producers, compete with people willing to make and bottle their own blend of jam. But such examples are not very common in this day and age.

5. Manufacturing service appliances

The customer-as-competitor issue has implications for manufacturing strategy. Lovelock and Gummesson (p. 35) assert that manufactured goods can form the basis for service delivery, as just discussed. Vargo and Lusch (2004b) are a bit bolder in their assertion that physical goods are "merely the distribution vehicle...for service provision." (p. 330). They refer to such goods as "appliances" which only create value when they are used to serve customer needs. Vargo and Lusch correspondingly reject the notion that value creation can occur in factories (2004b, p. 331,333); plant managers may disagree (but it is a semantic issue).

The UST posits that service processes add value to customer inputs. Manufactured goods are "service providers" in that they can be used by self-serving customers or service businesses to add value to customer inputs. In this sense, manufacturers become "service-provider providers"—providing products that provide service (Sampson 2001, p. 148). This concept has major implications for the provision of manufactured goods; manufacturers do not serve customers directly, but serve them indirectly through their products. The goods-products are thus representative agents of the manufacturer.

The "service-provider provider" concept implies that manufacturers would be wise to consider the service processes that will occur with their products. One example of this is the simplification of user instructions accompanying various consumer goods such as digital cameras, computers, and microwave ovens. There was a time when such items came with complex operating instructions—a great burden to all but the most disciplined consumers. The rest of us rely heavily on the single-sheet "getting started" instructions that may be the only instruction that we ever read.

Lovelock and Gummesson (2004) discussed other managerial considerations of service, such as pricing (p. 35), in which the UST also provides valuable insights (Sampson 2001, p. 297). Space does not allow further elaboration, so the reader is referred to other recitations (Sampson 2000; Sampson 2001; Sampson and Froehle 2006; Sampson 2010).

Service Innovation

One area not discussed by Lovelock and Gummeson, but which deserves the penultimate comment, is the tremendous value of the UST in directing service innovation efforts. We previously mentioned how the UST distinguishes New Service Development (NSD) from New Product Development. The key to successful NSD is understanding the impact of customer components on service processes. Customers can assume many roles in service processes, including supplier, labor, specification provider, quality inspector, and sometimes the customer is the product. The UST prescribes that valuable and effective service innovations will be found by looking for ways to enhance customers' roles in service processes. This often involves providing new tools or procedures for customers, or making a process more robust to variation in customer-provided components.

For example, personal investment services have experienced numerous innovative transformations in recent years. There was a time when most investors visited a stock broker, provided personal information and financial objectives (i.e., customer as supplier), then left it to the broker to identify suitable investments. Innovative investment services such as Charles Schwab started providing customers with information about different investments that allowed customers to do their own research (i.e., customer as labor). Subsequent innovations include tools that allow customers to track the performance of investments (customer as quality inspector), and even allow customers to initiate investment transactions immediately (minimizing customer as inventory waiting for transactions to occur). The innovative evolution of personal investment services demonstrates how service innovation tends to focus on enhancing customer roles of supplying inputs, labor, etc.

Chapter Summary

The UST formalizes a concept that other researchers have alluded to for many years. Lovelock and Gummesson state, "without customers who require service at a specific time, either to themselves or their possessions, there can be no output at most service organizations" (2004, p. 30). The UST proposes that this concept be recognized as definitional, perhaps restated as, "without customers who require service at a specific time, providing themselves and/or their possessions as input components, there can be no production and output coming from service processes" (which emphasizes the production process perspective).

Further, the UST demotes IHIP characteristics from being definitional to simply being symptoms of service. Two major implications are (1) that IHIP characteristics may occur in non-service processes by reasons other than the reliance on customer inputs, and (2) that the occurrence of IHIP characteristics changes as the nature of customer inputs change. Generally, as customer inputs increase in intensity, so also do the IHIP characteristics.

Also, comparing "goods" with "services" is a confusing correlation. It is clearer and more useful to compare service processes (which involve customer inputs) with non-service processes (which do not involve customer inputs). Making this distinction leads to numerous managerial insights pertaining to inventory management, customer competition, service pricing, and so forth.

This chapter primarily focused on applying the UST paradigm to business management contexts. However, the UST has application to a wide variety of service systems. For example, the UST has been applied to software architecture

(Sampson 2010). As a re-framing of traditional issues, the UST provides a useful paradigm on which to build Service Science.

References

Bitner, M. J., W. T. Faranda, A. R. Hubbert, V. A. Zeithaml. 1997. Customer contributions and roles in service delivery. *International Journal of Service Industry Management* **8**(3) 193.
Chervonnaya, O. 2003. Customer role and skill trajectories in services. *International Journal of Service Industry Management* **14**(3) 347-363.
Edvardsson, B., A. Gustafsson, I. Roos. 2005. Service portraits in service research: a critical review. *International Journal of Service Industry Management* **16**(1) 107-121.
Ellram, L. M., W. L. Tate, C. Billington. 2004. Understanding and Managing the Services Supply Chain. *Journal of Supply Chain Management* **40**(4) 17-32.
Fitzsimmons, J. A., M. J. Fitzsimmons, 2004. *Service Management: Operations, Strategy, and Information Technology*, 4th Edition, Irwin / McGraw-Hill, New York.
Grove, S. J., R. P. Fisk, J. John. 2003. The future of services marketing: Forecasts from ten services experts. *The Journal of Services Marketing* **17**(2/3) 107.
Gummesson, E., 1995. Relationship marketing: Its role in the service economy. *Understanding Services Management*, W. J. Glynn and J. G. Barnes, eds., John Wiley & Sons, New York, 244-268.
Hill, T. P. 1977. On Goods and Services. *Review of Income & Wealth* **23**(4) 315-338.
IfM and IBM, 2008. Succeeding through Service Innovation: A Service Perspective for Education, Research, Business and Government. University of Cambridge Institute for Manufacturing, Cambridge, United Kingdom.
Judd, R. C. 1964. The case for redefining services. *Journal of Marketing* **28**(1) 58.
Kuhn, T. S., 1970. *The Structure of Scientific Revolutions*, 2nd Edition, University of Chicago Press, Chicago.
Laroche, M., J. Bergeron, C. Goutaland. 2001. A three-dimensional scale of intangibility. *Journal of Service Research* **4**(1) 26.
Lovelock, C. 1983. Classifying Services to Gain Strategic Marketing Insights. *Journal of Marketing* **47**(3) 9-20.
Lovelock, C., 2001. *Services Marketing*, 4th Edition, Prentice Hall, Englewood Cliffs: New Jersey.
Lovelock, C., E. Gummesson. 2004. Whither Services Marketing? In Search of a New Paradigm and Fresh Perspectives. *Journal of Service Research* **7**(1) 20-41.
Merriam-Webster, 2008. Online dictionary. (website: http://www.m-w.com)
Morris, B., R. Johnston. 1987. Dealing with Inherent Variability: The Differences Between Manufacturing and Service? *International Journal of Operations & Production Management* **7**(4) 13.
Nelson, P. 1974. Advertising as Information. *Journal of the Political Economy* **82**(4) 729.
Nie, W., D. L. Kellogg. 1999. How Professors of Operations Management View Service Operations? *Production and Operations Management* **8**(3) 339-355.
Riddle, D. I., 1986. *Service-Led Growth: The role of the service sector in world development*, Praeger Publishers, New York.
Sampson, S. E. 2000. Customer-supplier duality and bidirectional supply chains in service organizations. *International Journal of Service Industry Management* **11**(4) 348-364.
Sampson, S. E., 2001. *Understanding Service Businesses: Applying principles of the Unified Services Theory*, 2nd Edition, John Wiley & Sons, New York.

Sampson, S. E., 2010. A Unified Services Theory. *Introduction to Service Engineering*, G. Salvendy and W. Karwowski, eds., John Wiley & Sons, Hoboken, New Jersey, 31‐47.

Sampson, S. E., C. M. Froehle. 2006. Foundations and Implications of a Proposed Unified Services Theory. *Production and Operations Management* **15**(2) 329-343.

Sampson, S. E., L. J. Menor, S. A. Bone, 2010. Why We Need a Service Logic? *Journal of Applied Management and Entrepreneurship* **15** (3).

Schmenner, R. W., 1995. *Service Operations Management*, Prentice Hall, Englewood Cliffs, NJ.

Silvestro, R., L. Fitzgerald, R. Johnston, C. Voss. 1992. Towards a Classification of Service Processes. *International Journal of Service Industry Management* **3**(3) 62.

Spohrer, J., P. P. Maglio. 2008. The Emergence of Service Science: Toward Systematic Service Innovations to Accelerate Co-Creation of Value. *Production and Operations Management* **17**(3) 238-246.

Vargo, S. L., R. F. Lusch. 2004a. Evolving to a New Dominant Logic for Marketing. *Journal of Marketing* **68**(1) 1.

Vargo, S. L., R. F. Lusch. 2004b. The Four Service Marketing Myths: Remnants of a Goods-Based, Manufacturing Model. *Journal of Service Research* **6**(4) 324.

Vargo, S. L., R. F. Lusch. 2008a. Service-dominant logic: continuing the evolution. *Academy of Marketing Science. Journal* **36**(1) 1.

Vargo, S. L., R. F. Lusch. 2008b. Why "service"? *Journal of the Academy of Marketing Science* **36**(1) 25-38.

Wemmerlöv, U. 1990. A taxonomy for service processes and its implications for system design. *International Journal of Service Industry Management* **1**(3) 13-27.

Wright, J. N., 1999. *The Management of Service Operations*, Cassell, London.

Zeithaml, V. A., 1981. How Consumer Evaluation Processes Differ Between Goods and Services. *Marketing in Services*, J. H. Donnelly and W. R. George, eds., American Marketing Association, Chicago, 186-190.

Zeithaml, V. A., M. J. Bitner, D. D. Gremler, 2006. *Services Marketing: Integrating Customer Focus Across the Firm*, Fourth Edition, McGraw-Hill/Irwin, New York.

Advancing Service Science with Service-Dominant Logic

Clarifications and Conceptual Development

Stephen L. Vargo

Shidler College of Business

University of Hawaii, Honolulu, USA

Robert F. Lusch

Eller College of Management

University of Arizona, Tucson, USA

Melissa Archpru Akaka

Shidler College of Business

University of Hawaii, Honolulu, USA

Service Science is an interdisciplinary effort to understand how service systems interact and co-create value. Service-dominant (S-D) logic is an alternative perspective to the traditional, goods-dominant (G-D) logic paradigm, which has been recognized as a potential theoretical foundation on which a science of service can be developed. While there are efforts to support and develop an S-D-logic-grounded service science, the paradigmatic power of G-D logic remains strong. This is evidenced by several recurring misconceptions about S-D logic and its application in service science. This chapter aims to guide the advancement of an S-D-logic-grounded service science by clarifying several misconstruals associated with S-D logic and moving forward with the formalization of key concepts associated with S-D logic and service science.

This chapter draws heavily on previous writings of the authors, especially Lusch and Vargo (2008); Lusch et al. (2008); Vargo and Akaka (2009); Vargo and Lusch (2006); Vargo et al. (2010).

P.P. Maglio et al. (eds.), *Handbook of Service Science*, Service Science: Research and Innovations in the Service Economy, DOI 10.1007/978-1-4419-1628-0_8,
© Springer Science+Business Media, LLC 2010

Introduction

The emergence of service science and its study of service systems – dynamic value-creating configurations made up of people, organizations and technology (Spohrer et al., 2007) – stems from the need to understand intangible, dynamic and evolutionary aspects of exchange. Service-dominant (S-D) logic (Vargo and Lusch, 2004) has been recognized as a potential philosophical foundation from which a science of service, and the investigation of service systems, can be built (Maglio and Spohrer, 2008). S-D logic is based on the premise that service, the application of competences for the benefit of another, is the fundamental basis of exchange. According to Maglio and Spohrer (2008, p. 19), S-D logic may provide the "right perspective, vocabulary, and assumptions on which to build a theory of service systems, their configurations, and their modes of interaction." This alternative perspective to the traditional, goods-centered logic focuses on concepts such as value co-creation, operant resources, and phenomenological value. It describes and explores the processes that take place when value is created in a mutually reciprocal manner, through systems of exchange.

Although S-D logic has been suggested as the theoretical foundation for service science (Maglio and Spohrer, 2008), the stronghold of the traditional, goods-dominant (G-D) logic paradigm remains. The paradigmatic power of G-D logic can be found in commonly used concepts such as value-added, profit maximization and transactions. This goods-centered language establishes a lexicon that has led to misinterpretations, and, thus, misrepresentations of an S-D-logic-grounded science of service (Vargo and Akaka, 2009). Focusing the study of exchange on units of output (tangible and intangible) and the divide between consumers and producers hinders the conceptual shift from goods- to service-dominant logic, even in the context of service science and service systems.

The purposes of this chapter are to (1) present S-D logic as a theoretical foundation for service science, (2) highlight and clarify some of the predominant misconstruals associated with S-D logic, and (3) describe and discuss S-D-logic-related concepts with the aim of advancing service science through the formalization of the language with which service science, grounded in S-D logic, can be investigated. The common misconstruals highlighted and clarified in this chapter relate to (1) the S-D logic meaning of "service," (2) service as the basis of all exchange, and (3) the nature of value (co)creation among service systems. As mentioned, these misinterpretations of S-D logic are largely driven by the continued influence of the G-D logic paradigm, particularly its separation of producers and consumers and its identification of goods and services as different types of exchange output.

The clarification of S-D logic's foundational premises points toward several core constructs related to service science and the study of service systems. These constructs include service, value, system, interaction and resources and can be viewed and described from both the G-D logic and S-D logic perspectives. However, the concepts emphasized within G-D logic differ dramatically from those used within an S-D logic view (e.g., transaction vs. relationship) and the transition from goods- to service-dominant logic can be difficult.

To achieve the purposes of this chapter, we first contrast G-D logic and S-D logic as alternatives for service science and provide support for S-D logic as a theoretical foundation for service science. We then clarify several misconstruals associated with S-D logic, specifically those mentioned above. The influence of the G-D logic lexicon is explained and we discuss how its paradigmatic power may be reflected in, and potentially limit, the current development of service science. We outline the core constructs for studying service systems and compare and contrast G-D-logic- and S-D-logic-related concepts associated with each. The S-D-logic-related concepts are described and elaborated to aid in the formalization of the language needed for advancing the study of service science from an S-D logic view. Finally, the implications of an S-D logic founded service science are presented and discussed.

Alternative Logics for Service Science

Service science is an interdisciplinary field that "combines organization and human understanding with business and technological understanding to categorize and explain the many types of service systems that exist as well as how service systems interact and evolve to co-create value" (Maglio and Spohrer, 2008, p. 18). Service systems are "value co-creation configurations of people, technology, value propositions connecting internal and external service systems and shared information" (p. 18). Service systems are considered the basic unit of analysis in service science. These dynamic network structures are conceptualized as "open system[s] (1) capable of improving the state of another system through sharing or applying its resources…and (2) capable of improving its own state by acquiring external resources" (Spohrer et al., 2008).

Service systems establish an abstract phenomenon capable of being analyzed within a variety of disciplines and industries (Spohrer et al., 2008). They are continuously interconnected with other service systems and range in size from an individual person to a world-wide exchange system (e.g., the global economy). Maglio and Spohrer (2008, p. 18) explain:

> The smallest service system centers on an individual as he or she interacts with others, and the largest service system comprises the global economy. Cities, city departments, businesses, business departments, nations, and government agencies are all service systems. Every service system is both a provider and client of service that is connected by value propositions in value chains, value networks or value creating systems (Normann, 2001).

The normative function of a service system is to connect people, technology and information through value propositions with the aim of co-creating value for all service systems participating in the exchange of resources.

The challenge with developing a science of service is the lack of cohesiveness in research related to service (Chesbrough and Spohrer, 2006; Edvardsson et al., 2005). The study of service has largely been conducted within individual business-related disciplines, such as management, operations, marketing and IT (Bitner and Brown, 2006), as well as in engineering and computer science schools (Chesbrough and Spohrer, 2006), with little integration or cross fertilization of ideas. Moreover, the concept of service has been studied using different meanings and, thus, has been operationalized in different ways (Edvardsson et al., 2005). Service science aims to integrate these seemingly disparate areas of research by focusing on service as the central phenomena of interest (IfM and IBM, 2007).

G-D logic and S-D logic establish two alternative theoretical frameworks for service science and the study of service systems. The traditional, G-D logic provides a view of economic exchange and value creation that focuses on the production and distribution of tangible goods and considers services as special types of goods with undesirable qualities (e.g., intangible, perishable products) or add-ons to tangible products (e.g., post-sale service). Alternatively, S-D logic focuses on value creation as a process that necessarily includes the participation, in varying degrees, of all parties involved. This perspective considers service – the application of skills for the benefit of another – in its own right, rather than in relation to goods. S-D logic argues that service is central to value creation and economic exchange. Although goods are still seen as important, they are considered as vehicles for (indirect) service provision.

Goods-Dominant Logic

The traditional, G-D logic view of economic exchange, concentrates on manufacturing and distribution activities and considers value to be created by the firm and destroyed (consumed) by customers (see Vargo and Lusch, 2004). In G-D logic, tangible output is ideal as it can be produced away from the customer, standardized and inventoried until sold. Intangible output (i.e.,"service") is considered less desirable because of qualities that make it difficult to standardize (heterogeneity), produce away from customers (inseparability), and store or inventory (perishability) (Zeithaml et al., 1985). The normative goal in G-D logic is to maximize operational efficiency and reduce firm costs in order to increase financial profits.

G-D logic is grounded in the work of Smith (1776) and the development of economic philosophy and science that followed. Smith's work initially acknowledged labor as the source of "real value" and emphasized the importance of the division of labor in creating value in society. He explained that real value was measured in terms of the labor required to achieve a benefit, or "value-in-use." Although his political views highlighted the importance of the division of labor and how it contributes to the creation of real value, value-in-use, Smith's work was ultimately guided by his normative goal of increasing national wealth for England. This effort took place in the context of the 18th century, an era in which limitations on the transfer of information made the exchange of tangible goods, embedded with knowledge and skills, ideal. Thus, Smith focused his efforts on more measurable, – what he called "nominal," – sources of value, particularly tangible, exportable resources and the price paid for them in the market – "value-in-exchange."

Smith's emphasis on nominal value, value-in-exchange, was intensified by the advancement of the Industrial Revolution and the desire of economic philosophers' to develop economics into a legitimate Newtonian science. Thus, economic science was developed through models that focused on the production and distribution of tangible products, embedded with utility and exchanged for money. This goods-centered paradigm developed over the years and became the dominant paradigm for economics and other business-related disciplines (see Vargo and Morgan, 2005), including management, marketing, information technology, etc.

Within G-D logic, value is considered to be created by the firm through production and value-added activities such as distribution and sales. In early studies related to economic exchange, the dominance of this goods-centered orientation left the concept of service largely ignored. As attention grew towards intangible aspects of exchange, service became known as an add-on to the tangible core good or a type of product that did not fit well with goods-based models of exchange. Services were eventually identified as different from goods based on their "unique" characteristics of intangibility, heterogeneity, inseparability and perishability (Zeithaml et al., 1985). Generally, this conceptualization of service emphasizes undesirable qualities in service "products" that make them difficult to study with goods-based models of exchange.

The G-D logic perspective views recent economic activity as shifting from goods to services. This stems from an increasing number of market offerings that cannot be categorized as goods (e.g., are not tangible and standardized) and therefore are considered services. G-D logic implies that goods are the ideal form of exchange, because they can be standardized and stored, and that the models developed for investigating exchange must be adapted to study the less-desirable exchange of services. Using this goods-centered paradigm as the theoretical foundation for service science suggests that the development of the discipline is focused on a particular, inferior type of exchange phenomena. Alternatively, S-D logic provides a perspective that considers service as the underlying driver of the economy and concentrates on intangible and dynamic aspects of all exchange.

Service-Dominant Logic

S-D logic establishes an alternative perspective for investigating exchange, which focuses on service – the application of competences for the benefit of another – as the central process for value creation and treats goods as a vehicle for service provision (Vargo and Lusch, 2004). This service-centered view is consistent with Smith's initial discussion of real value and value-in-use. S-D logic proposes that market exchange is the process of parties using their specialized knowledge and skills for the benefit of other parties. In other words, exchange is driven by reciprocal and mutually beneficial service provision.

S-D logic is rooted in ten foundational premises (FPs) that establish a dynamic, service-centered framework for exploring exchange-related phenomena. The FPs are presented in Table 1 and discussed below as they relate to service science and the study of service systems.

Table 1. Foundational Premises of Service-Dominant Logic
(adapted from Vargo and Lusch, 2008)

-	Premise	Explanation/Justification
FP1	Service is the fundamental basis of exchange.	The application of operant resources (knowledge and skills), "service," is the basis for all exchange. Service is exchanged for service.
FP2	Indirect exchange masks the fundamental basis of exchange.	Goods, money, and institutions mask the service-for-service nature of exchange.
FP3	Goods are distribution mechanisms for service provision.	Goods (both durable and non-durable) derive their value through use – the service they provide.
FP4	Operant resources are the fundamental source of competitive advantage.	The comparative ability to cause desired change drives competition.
FP5	All economies are service economies.	Service (singular) is only now becoming more apparent with increased specialization and outsourcing.
FP6	The customer is always a co-creator of value.	Implies value creation is interactional.
FP7	The enterprise cannot deliver value, but only offer value propositions.	The firm can offer its applied resources and collaboratively (interactively) create value following acceptance, but cannot create/deliver value alone.
FP8	A service-centered view is inherently customer oriented and relational.	Service is customer-determined and co-created; thus, it is inherently customer oriented and relational.
FP9	All economic and social actors are resource integrators.	Implies the context of value creation is in networks of networks (resource-integrators).
FP10	Value is always uniquely and phenomenological determined by the beneficiary.	Value is idiosyncratic, experiential, contextual, and meaning laden.

S-D logic's most basic premise – that service is the basis of all exchange (FP1) – suggests that service is always exchanged for service, and, thus, all economies are service economies (FP5). With its consideration of service as the basis of exchange, S-D logic indicates that the apparent shift in the economy is not one from goods to services, but rather it is a shift from focusing on tangible and static to intangible and dynamic resources (FP4). S-D logic establishes the primacy of *operant resources* (those that act upon other resources to create benefit), such as competences, over *operand resources* (those resources which must be acted on to be beneficial), such as natural resources, goods and money (Constantin and Lusch,

1995; Vargo and Lusch, 2004). That is, within S-D logic, operant resources (e.g., knowledge and skills) are the underlying source of value and drivers of value creation. In addition, S-D logic argues that value-creating resources are not limited to the firm; customers, suppliers, and other stakeholders (e.g., government or society as a whole) also constitute operant resources and contribute to value creation.

While S-D logic views service as the central driver of the economy, it also recognizes that the direct service-for-service exchange is often masked by a web of interconnected intermediaries associated with exchange (FP2). Market complexities such as goods, money and organizations add to the dynamics of exchange among service systems (Figure 1). As these intermediaries contribute to the complexity of the market, they maintain important roles in the facilitation of exchange (FP3). Additionally, as specialization in the market increases, and many firms turn to outsourcing alternatives, service systems become increasingly complex and direct service-for-service exchange is often difficult to trace.

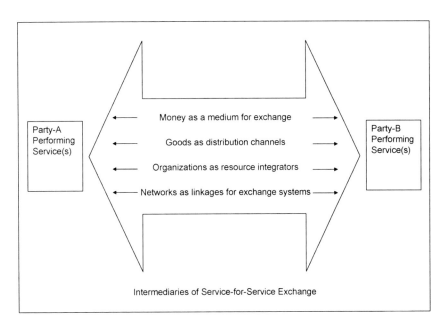

Figure 1. Service(s) Exchanged for Services (adapted from Vargo et al., 2010)

S-D logic's FP6 and FP7 emphasize the customer's role in the process of value creation. These FPs argue that value is always co-created in a process that requires the active participation of the firm, its customers and other stakeholders. More specifically, S-D logic argues that firms cannot create and deliver value; they can only propose value (FP7) and provide service as an input to the realization of value by the service beneficiary, usually the customer. In other words, value is not created until the beneficiary of a service (e.g., customer) integrates and applies the resources of a particular service provider (e.g., firm) with other resources. The service provider's resources are integrated in the context of the beneficiary's access to private and public and resources, as well as resources from other service providers. This resource-integration process (FP9) occurs within and among service systems as resources are exchanged to create value for all participating service systems. Thus, the co-creation of value among service systems incorporates the integration and application of resources from service providers (e.g, firms), by service beneficiaries (e.g., customers) but, because value is always based on the context and perspective, it is always derived and determined by the beneficiary (FP10).

Clarifications of S-D logic in Service Science

While S-D logic has been suggested as a theoretical foundation for service science (Maglio and Spohrer, 2008), the development of the discipline has also been influenced by the assumptions of G-D logic. For example, whereas S-D logic argues that service is the basis of all exchange and that all economies are service economies, much of the literature regarding the development of service science suggests that the importance of the discipline stems from the evolution to a new "service economy" and the growth of the "service sector" (e.g., Spohrer et al., 2007). This acknowledgement of a growing service economy stems from the goods vs. service distinction established in G-D logic. Also, it is common to find reference to "services" science (plural – emphasizing intangible units of output) rather than "service" science (singular – emphasizing a process of value creation), although the latter is the common reference used by the discipline's primary originators (e.g., Maglio and Spohrer, 2008). The development of service science has clearly drawn attention toward intangible and dynamic aspects of exchange, including those in which S-D logic is grounded. However, the distinction between goods and services continues to underlie the development of service science, and, thus, evidence of the G-D logic paradigm remains.

The influence of G-D logic is noticeable in the language used to describe and investigate phenomena associated with economic exchange, including that related to service systems and service science. The deeply seeded roots of the G-D logic lexicon have created difficulties for the communication and development of S-D logic and, not surprisingly, have influenced the development of service science in its attempts to use S-D logic as a theoretical foundation. Thus, understandably, the pervasiveness of the G-D logic lexicon contributes to much of the misinterpretation of S-D logic and its theoretical foundation for service science. A number of misperceptions related to the language associated with S-D logic have been identified, such as the concepts of "service" versus "services" and "co-creation" versus "co-production" (Lusch and Vargo, 2006; Vargo and Lusch, 2006; Vargo and Lusch, 2008; Vargo et al., 2010). More specifically, evidence of G-D logic's paradigmatic power can be found in the misconceptions related to several fundamental principles of S-D logic and service science: (1) the S-D logic meaning of service, (2) service as the basis of all exchange, and (3) the nature of value (co)creation among service systems.

The S-D Logic Meaning of Service

The distinction between goods and services as alternative types of products reflects a central aspect of the G-D logic orientation. This separation is specifically questioned by S-D logic and its argument that service is the basis of all exchange. As noted, whereas in G-D logic services are viewed as an intangible (inferior to goods) unit of output, in S-D logic service is considered a process of applying resources for the benefit of another and the underlying basis of exchange. This difference in the meaning of service is crucial for the implementation of an S-D logic foundation of service science. Ironically, the term service, from the S-D logic view, also suggests that there are no "services" (an intangible type of output that differs from goods) in S-D logic, except as the term is occasionally used to refer to various processes – never intangible output internally created by the firm.

Service, defined as a process in which one applies resources to benefit another, is not a new or novel concept (Lusch and Vargo, 2006). It falls in line with the perspective of a number of scholars who argue for service as central to value creation and exchange (e.g., Bastiat, 1860; Gummesson, 1995; Gronroos, 2000). The shift from defining service as a unit of output to a process of applying one's resources for the benefit of another emphasizes intangible and dynamic (operant) resources in exchange. Importantly, the S-D logic meaning of service suggests that service is not only recently gaining in importance. Rather, "it is only from the perspective of a model that includes the fundamental assumption that exchange is driven by goods (G-D logic) that the importance of service is just now becoming apparent and that the economy is perceived to be transitioning from goods focused to service focused" (Vargo and Lusch, 2006, p. 45), as discussed in the following section.

Service as the Basis of All Exchange

The shift from a goods- to service-dominant meaning of service requires the understanding of service as a transcending concept to goods. In other words, S-D logic does not consider service as a substitute for goods. Rather than replacing goods with services or a goods logic with a services logic, S-D logic makes service and service logic superordinate to goods and goods logic in terms of classification as well as function. This transcendence of service establishes a relationship in which G-D logic is nested within S-D logic. This nested relationship implies that the theoretical and conceptual components of G-D logic are relevant, but are not as deep or broad in scope as those of S-D logic. Thus, S-D logic broadens the conceptual lens from which service-related phenomena can be studied.

The transcendence of service as the basis of all economic exchange implies that the increased attention toward service(s) because of a growing "services economy," or the emergence of a "services revolution" (e.g., that a major portion of economic activity in developing countries is in "services") is, ironically, based on the influence of the G-D logic paradigm. Contrary to this popular perspective of the new or emerging services economy, service provision is not just now becoming abundant, nor is it recently gaining importance. The recognition of a new or emergent services economy centers on the distinction between goods and services as alternative forms (tangible versus intangible) of products, which is based on the G-D logic view and its meaning of services.

S-D logic and its meaning of service suggest that service is always exchanged for service and, thus, there is not so much of a service revolution as there is a service realization or a revelation in service-centered thinking. This foundational understanding of service is essential if a "service system" is to be an inclusive (of value-creating activities) term and thus service science is to be inclusive of all phenomena involved in the mutual creation of value through service provision. Without this inclusivity, almost by definition, service science becomes a science of the exception – a science of somewhat inferior products. On the other hand, from an S-D logic view, in which service is central to exchange, service systems are made up of all "types" of exchange or more accurately, all processes associated with exchange. These processes include, but are not limited to, activities such as farming, manufacturing, distribution and delivery. In addition, service systems are found in *all* industries, from automotive to IT to retailing.

Although S-D logic suggests that service has always been the basis of exchange, there is, arguably, one revelation that is making the nature of service provision more apparent – the information revolution (Rust and Thompson, 2006). That is, the increase in specialization that has drawn attention toward intangible and dynamic aspects of exchange appears to be driven by exponential increases in knowledge and the ability to exchange information (i.e., operant resources) in a relatively pure, "liquefied" or "dematerialized" (Norman, 2001) form – that is without being transported by people and/or matter – through digitization. Advances in the capability of separating information from matter have furthered specialization as it relates to the division of labor and have increased the scope of the market (e.g., global) from which resources can be attained (e.g., outsourced). Thus, while service has not increased in importance in recent years, the service-nature of exchange has gained attention due to increasing complexities in the market and the decreasing necessity of tangible objects in exchange.

Nature of Value (Co)Creation among Service Systems

Generally, two broad conceptualizations of value have been discussed with regard to economic exchange: "value-in-exchange" and "value-in-use" (see Vargo et al., 2008). Although traditional market-related research focuses on value-in-exchange, more recently, attention has been refocused on value-in-use, to some extent indirectly, through service- and systems-related (i.e., B2B) research. The increasing emphasis on value-in-use suggests that value is being co-created with and determined by customers, rather than produced and distributed by the firm. This notion of value co-creation has been developed by Prahalad and Ramaswamy (2000) and others (see Normann and Ramirez, 1993) and adopted and elaborated in S-D logic.

Likewise, service science has adopted value co-creation as one of the key components of service systems. However, in some cases it is discussed from the perspective of a production orientation, focused on value-added and value-in-exchange. As such, this production-orientation of value co-creation suggests at least a residual adherence to the G-D logic notion of *making "services."* Arguably, this position is often reflected in the study of phenomena related to "service-oriented architecture," "servitization," "service operations," "service factories," etc., all of which have been associated with service science, even if not fundamental to it. Perhaps more contentiously, the production-orientation of value co-creation is possibly reflected in, if not driven by, the "management" and "engineering" specifications of the extended title of service science – "service science management and engineering" (SSME).

This observation is not intended as a criticism of either management or engineering or their ties to service science. Rather, it simply suggests that these disciplines, as traditionally understood, tend to concentrate on design specifications and operational processes within the firm rather than viewing the scope of the broader value co-creation space. This focus on the firm and its operational efficiency is generally in line with the main issues related to G-D logic. Moreover, the emphasis of value co-creation beyond the activities of the firm does not suggest that production and manufacturing and related activities are not important in the value-creation process. Rather the discussion of the difference between co-creation and co-production is intended to highlight the role of co-production within the supoerordinate process of value co-creation.

S-D logic's conceptualization of value co-creation extends beyond the customer's involvement in the production, design customization or assembly processes (Vargo et al., 2008). The term "co-production" was used in the original article presenting S-D logic as an alternative to the G-D logic paradigm (Vargo and Lusch, 2004). However, since then, Lusch and Vargo (2006; see also Vargo and Lusch, 2006; 2008), have used the term "co-creation of value" to convey the customer's (and others') collaborative role in value creation. "Co-production" has since been used in S-D logic to describe the customer's (and others') participation in the development of a firm's offering (e.g., design, self-service). Based on these conceptualizations, the customer's role in *co-production is optional*, whereas his/her role in value creation is not; *value is always co-created*.

Advancing Service Science with S-D Logic Language

It has been suggested that S-D logic provides the appropriate theoretical framework and language for discussing and studying service science and service systems (Maglio and Spohrer, 2008). However, the misconstruals associated with S-D logic, discussed above, clearly indicate that the goods-centered lexicon reflects more than just words available to discuss economic exchange and service science; it reflects the underlying paradigm for thinking about and understanding commerce, the market and exchange in general. This has presented problems for discussing and describing S-D logic's counter-paradigmatic view of service science and, more specifically, service systems.

The use of S-D logic friendly concepts such as value co-creation and operant resources indicates that service science is moving toward a more service-centered foundation. However, the paradigmatic power of the G-D logic lexicon described above continues to limit the vocabulary available for discussing S-D logic and service science. If the language of S-D logic is to establish the foundation and aid in the advancement of service science as suggested (Maglio and Spohrer, 2008), the concepts currently used to discuss S-D logic and related phenomena must be formalized and developed. In an effort to develop the appropriate vocabulary for discussing service science from an S-D logic view, the comparison of G-D logic and S-D logic concepts have been made (Lusch and Vargo 2008; Lusch et al., 2008). These concepts represent several key constructs that can be used in the study of social and economic exchange among service systems. These constructs are (1) service, (2) value, (3) system, (4) interaction, and (5) resources. Table 2 presents these constructs and compares and contrasts their associated G-D logic and S-D logic concepts. To move forward with developing the language needed to describe and investigate service systems, the S-D logic concepts are described and elaborated below.

Table 2. Contrasting G-D Logic and S-D Logic Concepts (adapted from Lusch and Vargo, 2008; Lusch et al., 2008)

Core Constructs	G-D Logic Concepts	S-D Logic Concepts
Service	Goods & Services	Serving & Experiencing
	Transaction	Relationship & Collaboration
Value	Value-added	Value Co-creation
	Value-in-Exchange	Value-in-Context
	Price	Value Proposing
System	Supply Chain	Value-creation Network
	Asymmetric Information	Symmetric Information Flows
Interaction	Promotion/Propaganda	Open Source Communication
	Maximizing Behavior	Learning via Exchange
Resources	Operand Resources	Operant Resources
	Resource Acquisition	Resourcing

Service

Arguably, the most critical distinction between the language associated with G-D logic and that of S-D logic is found in the disparate meanings of the term service. The misperceptions and misinterpretations of S-D logic that stem from the conceptualization of "service" lead to the misunderstanding of much of the phenomena described within the S-D logic framework. As mentioned, most of the issues surrounding the term service seem to be tied to the fact that in G-D logic the term "services" (plural) is usually intended to refer to (intangible) units of output, whereas in S-D logic the term "service" (singular) refers to a process of doing something for or with another entity. Some have raised concerns that the term service has too much baggage (e.g., Lehmann, 2006), while others have suggested that the S-D logic definition of service is "novel" or "inconsistent" in relation to the conventional meaning of service (e.g., Achrol and Kotler, 2006; Levy, 2006). Still others argue that "service" is the wrong word choice, which creates a false dichotomy between goods and service (e.g., Brodie et al., 2006). Vargo and Lusch (2006) have acknowledged the baggage associated with the term "services." However, for reasons discussed above, they argue that the term "service" is precisely correct, if not essential to understanding exchange.

The S-D logic meaning of service, shifts the focus of exchange from transactions to relationships. With this conceptual shift, service is the common denominator of mutually beneficial exchange relationships and goods are considered service-provision mechanisms. In other words, with service as the underlying basis of exchange, the exchange of goods becomes a special case of indirect service provision. Thus, the false dichotomy between goods and service(s) (Brodie et al., 2006) is not created by S-D logic, but rather is rooted in G-D logic thinking and is, arguably, resolved in S-D logic (Lusch and Vargo, 2006).

Serving and Experiencing

S-D logic focuses on the interaction among service systems. The significance of that interaction is not found in the transfer of ownership of output (as in G-D logic), but in the interaction itself. The focus of S-D logic is in serving the needs of one or more service systems (e.g., customers) (Lusch et al., 2008). In other words, S-D logic centers on *service – the process of providing benefit (in conjunction with other service systems) –* rather than services – intangible goods – and the manufacturing and distribution of units of output. S-D logic's emphasis on service as a collaborative process necessarily includes the service beneficiary (e.g., customer) in the process of serving. As a part of the serving process, the customer is required to partake in *experiencing – determining value from a phenomenological and contextual standpoint –* the service. From this perspective, market interactions are more generally concerned with customer solutions and experiences rather than ownership.

Relationships and Collaboration

At the heart of the G-D logic view of resource exchange is the notion of a discrete transaction taking place between a producer (creator of value) and a consumer (destroyer of value). However, this producer/consumer dichotomy is inconsistent with the service-for-service exchange and the process of value co-creation that has been identified as a key driver of exchange in service systems (Maglio and Spohrer, 2008). Importantly, the S-D logic notion that service is always exchanged for service implies interdependence and reciprocity – that is, all parties are simultaneously both "producers" and "consumers" of value.

This reciprocal and mutually beneficial service-for-service exchange implies relationship. In S-D logic, however, relationships are viewed as more than merely repeat patronage. A service-centered perspective of exchange relationships among service systems highlights the interdependence of each service system, based on the specialization and the division of labor among systems. As specialization increases, so does the interdependence among systems. As service systems become increasingly interdependent, relationships emerge and the potential for collective action or collaboration increases. Thus, if the advancement of service science is guided by S-D logic it must consider relational aspects of customers and society at large.

Value

In addition to the confusion regarding value co-creation and co-production, the G-D logic lexicon sometimes constrains perceptions of value, as it relates to S-D logic. Some have suggested that the conceptualization of value associated with S-D logic represents only "functional" benefits (e.g., Prahalad, 2004; Shembri, 2006). However, Vargo and Lusch (2006) explained that this apparent focus on utilitarian value is a reflection of the influence of the G-D logic lexicon rather than a limitation of S-D logic.

S-D logic's emphasis on phenomenological and experiential value was clarified with the addition of FP10 – value is always uniquely and phenomenologically determined by the beneficiary (Vargo and Lusch, 2008). In line with S-D logic's perspective of value, in service science value has been defined as "improvement in a system, as judged by the system or the system's ability to fit an environment" (Spohrer et al., 2008). This understanding of value, based on context and perspective, has been used as a framework for the exploration of value creation in service systems (Vargo et al., 2008). It establishes a foundation for discussing and studying service systems using S-D logic-related concepts such as value co-creation, value-in-context, and value proposition.

Value Co-creation

It is clear that value co-creation is one of the core concepts for investigating exchange among service systems from an S-D logic view. In service systems, value co-creation is the purpose and driver of interaction, relationship development and exchange (Spohrer et al., 2008). According to Spohrer et al. (2008), service systems engage in three main activities to co-create value: (1) proposing value, (2) accepting a proposal, and (3) realizing the proposal. Thus, at least two service systems must engage in both applying and integrating resources in order for service to be realized and for value co-creation to occur.

Although S-D logic is inherently customer-centric – that is, the beneficiary is considered the determiner of value – value co-creation does not focus solely on the beneficiary. This perspective would neglect to recognize the benefits the firm receives from an exchange. Value co-creation implies that value created through exchange is based on the mutually beneficial relationships among service systems and each system makes a decision for whether or not the result of the exchange is valuable, based on context and experience.

In addition, value co-creation is not limited to the activities or resources of any individual exchange occurrence. Value is ultimately derived through the assimilation of existing and new knowledge and other resources and is influenced by the context of the environment as well as the resources of interconnected service systems. The investigation of service systems from an S-D logic grounded framework establishes a dynamic system of transferring, applying and generating operant resources (e.g., knowledge). Within the mindset of a service-for-service exchange, the force, or purpose, of exchange rests in each system's desire to better its own circumstance and/or to provide benefits for others – ultimately the creation of value. The conditions that create value for service systems through exchange depend on the availability of resources and configuration of the system(s).

Value-in-Context

S-D logic's redirection of the focal point of value creation, away from a firm's output (and value-in-exchange) and towards the value uniquely derived and determined by an individual service system (e.g., customer – i.e., value-in-use), emphasizes a phenomenological and experiential conceptualization of value that has most recently been recognized in S-D logic as "value-in-context" (see Vargo et al., 2008). Value-in-context emphasizes the importance of time and place dimensions and network relationships as critical variables in the creation and determination of value.

Focusing on phenomenologically determined value implies that the context of value creation is as important to the creation of value as the competences of the participating parties. Although environmental resources, such as social, ecological and governmental surroundings, are traditionally considered exogenous to value creation, the contextual nature of co-created value suggests otherwise. Although it is not possible to control all aspects of the environment, this does not mean that these resources are not integrated in the process of value creation. In fact, resources such as time, weather and laws, which are often considered exogenous and uncontrollable by individuals and organizations, are often integrated – if not relied on – in the value creation process by all service systems (e.g., customers, firms, families, countries).

Value Proposing

Maglio and Spohrer (2008) explain that value propositions connect internal and external service systems within value chains, value networks or value-creating systems. The concept of value proposing recognizes that value is composed of benefits and costs that unfold as a service beneficiary (e.g., customer) integrates the service-provider resources. Often, this process takes place over time. In other words, the trade off of benefits versus costs is discovered in the customer's personal realization of the value proposition, rather than prior to, or at the time of, the transaction (payment or commitment to pay) or value-in-exchange. Essentially, firms do not produce and/or deliver value; they can only propose value and, if the proposition is accepted, then, with the participation of the customer, co-create value. For competitive advantage, these value propositions should be more compelling than those of competitor service providers (Vargo and Lusch, 2004).

System

According to Spohrer et al. (2008), "a system is a configuration of resources including at least one operant resource, in which the properties and behavior of the configuration is more than the properties and behavior of the individual resources." The study of systems inherently incorporates the exploration of networks and the relationships and resources that establish links within and among them. The study of system structures and network configurations provides a dynamic framework for examining complex processes of exchange.

S-D logic's notion of resource integration implies that value creation takes place in networks of relationships and resources (value-creation networks). This service-centered perspective embraces the idea that value creation is a process of integrating, applying and transforming resources, which requires multiple actors and implies networks. In addition, all systems contributing to value creation are considered both service providers and service beneficiaries. This mutually beneficial relationship of service-for-service exchange establishes a balanced, symmetric framework, essentially the opposite of G-D logic's asymmetrical framework, which separates firms as producers (value creators) and customers as consumers (value destroyers).

Value-creation Network

Given the foundation of G-D logic and its ties to manufacturing and the Industrial Revolution, it is understandable that the traditional conceptualization of value creation is based on a linear supply chain. Within this model, supply chains are often characterized in terms of physical gaps (e.g., geographical distances) between producers and consumer (see Lusch et al., 2010). To close these gaps, intermediaries, such as wholesalers and retailers, emerged and contributed to the output of the firm through a seemingly vertical process and structure. While the supply chain was envisioned as something physical, the real source of wealth and value was in the knowledge and information (operant resources) embedded in tangible materials (raw materials and finished goods) and was used by the intermediaries to close the gaps highlighted above.

As mentioned, it is increasingly possible to separate or "liquefy" (Normann, 2001) information apart from goods. Thus, without information being embedded in a tangible product, most supply-chain concepts are inadequate. The liquification of information changes the location and nature of work as well as the connectivity of resources. In other words, as information is liquefied, the place where value is created and the work associated with its creation change as well as the medium through which the resources travel (e.g., mailing a letter versus sending an email). As the ability to liquefy information increases exponentially, opportunities arise in which firms can concentrate on specific competences and outsource or look to others for complementary competences.

From an S-D logic view, the "venue" of value creation in service systems takes place in the value configurations – interactions among social and economic actors – and thus, value is created within and among service systems, at various levels of aggregation (Vargo and Lusch, 2008). This network framework for value creation requires reconceptualizing the supply chain in terms of a dynamic system of resources – service system – which represents the connection of distinct (mostly operant) resources. Because networks are not limited to linear, vertical or horizontal arrangements and are arranged in an infinite number of ways, their configurations can become a major source of innovation and competitive advantage. That is, the network perspective inherent to S-D logic and service systems suggests new opportunities for configuring all the resources that are necessary to solve a given problem at a given time and place – what Normann (2001) labels "density creation." In S-D logic, value networks or what have been increasingly referred to as service ecosystems are "spontaneously sensing and responding spatial and temporal structure of largely loosely proposing social and economic actors through institutions and technology, to (1) co-produce service offerings, (2) exchange service offerings, and (3) co-create value" (Lusch et al., 2010).

Symmetric Information

Spohrer et al. (2008) define economic exchange as "the voluntary, reciprocal use of resources for mutual value creation by two or more interacting systems."

This focus on the symmetric exchange of information and resources implies that (1) firms should not mislead customers, employees or other stakeholders by withholding critical information or manipulating communications and (2) all exchange partners are equally important in the process of value creation (Lusch et al., 2008).

Along the same vein, S-D logic suggests that actors involved in an exchange are relational and thus openly share relevant information. This is different from suggesting the actors give up intellectual property, which is quite a different discussion. The symmetric flow of information is not equivalent to the granting of property rights or sharing of property rights in intellectual property.

In the global service system, information symmetry is essential for driving out organizations and leaders that are not trustworthy. In S-D logic, organized service systems (e.g., firms and government entities) promote the symmetric flow of information and communication both externally (e.g., across firms and customers) and internally (e.g., within the firm). Additionally, the symmetric treatment of trading partners means that all parties in an exchange should be treated as equals. This perspective fosters interaction among social and economic actors, which involves collaborative communication as well as learning through exchange.

Interaction

As noted, G-D logic is developed from a deterministic equilibrium-based Newtonian model of science. Alternatively, S-D logic's service-for-service, interdependent and interactive model implies dynamic, non-equilibrium and non-deterministic relationships and models of exchange. Thus, just as Newtonian models of science have been subordinated by more dynamic, relational, and emergent models, such as relativity, quantum theory and complexity theory, so too should an S-D-logic-founded science of service. That is, theories and models developed for service science, within an S-D logic mindset, should focus on interactive and dynamic aspects of exchange, such as collaborative communication among service systems and the learning that takes place via exchange.

Collaborative Communication

S-D logic's symmetric framework and focus on value co-creation suggest that the interaction between and among service systems should be characterized by collaborative communication among multiple parties, rather than unidirectional messages from one party to another. In service systems, collaborative communication is founded on trust, learning and compromise. This notion of collaborative communication is not limited to the relationship between firms and customers, but also includes the interaction among employees and other relevant stakeholders (e.g., shareholders, society) that may be involved with or affected by service exchange.

With collaborative communication among service systems, customers, as well as employees and other stakeholders, are considered as partners or key collaborators in value creation rather than "consumers" or destroyers of value. This treatment of customers, employees and other stakeholders as participating in open and active communications with firms highlights S-D logic's primacy of operant resources. The interactions among multiple service systems do not occur on a one-to-one or dyadic basis, but rather a "many-to-many" (Gummesson, 2005) conversation takes place with regard to value creation in exchange. In large part, this multiple-party conversation has become increasingly possible, or at least more evident, because the Internet has established a public resource through which communities of customers and other stakeholders can engage in dialogue with or without the active participation of the firm.

Learning via Exchange

Dynamic interaction and open communication among service systems provides a mechanism for learning via the exchange process. As mentioned, the S-D logic mindset refocuses the purpose of exchange from the acquisition of tangible, operand resources to the integration, application and generation of intangible, operant resources. Just as value in a service system is judged by the relative improvement of the system (Spohrer et al., 2008), in S-D logic, social and economic actors exchange with other actors in order to improve their existing conditions, generally by improving the conditions of others (Lusch et al., 2007). The service-for-service foundation of S-D logic establishes the basic hypothesis that, if an actor takes a certain action (engages in exchange) and changes (improves its circumstance), then it will be better off. However, the improvement of wellbeing for any service system (from an individual to the global service system) is a process that requires feedback and learning.

For the firm, one of the most critical metrics of feedback, which contributes to learning, is based on financial assessments of the firm. That is, financial feedback (e.g., revenue and/or profit) allow entities to learn how they are doing in helping to create value in the market. Thus, although S-D logic places a strong emphasis on value-in-use and value-in-context, it does not ignore value-in-exchange. While S-D logic argues that value-in-exchange could not exist independent of value-in-use, it recognizes the importance of value-in-exchange as feedback to the firm and an intermediary of service provision.

Resources

It is clear that the study of resources plays a key role in understanding S-D logic and the relationships within and among service systems. At the heart of service systems is the transfer and sharing of resources. Four categories of resources have been identified and examined: (1) resources with rights, (2) resources as property, (3) physical entities, and (4) socially constructed entities (Maglio and Spohrer, 2008). Maglio and Spohrer (2008, p. 19) explain that "[e]ntities within service systems exchange competence along at least four dimensions: information-sharing, work-sharing, risk-sharing, and goods-sharing." They suggest that the key to understanding the exchange of resources within service systems is found in the distribution of competences, such as knowledge and skills, among service systems and understanding the value propositions that connect such systems.

Resource-advantage (R-A) theory (Hunt and Morgan, 1995) is a resource-based view of the firm and market competition (Penrose, 1959) that has been recognized as one of the fundamental conceptualizations tied to the emergence of S-D logic. R-A theory posits that heterogeneous, imperfectly mobile resources meet hetero-geneous demands in the market. This theory implies that substantial variation exists among firm resources, as well as customer needs, and proposes resource-based comparative advantages. While R-A theory provides a theoretical foundation for exploring resources related to the firm, S-D logic expands the focus of resources beyond the firm, to systems of service exchange or service systems (Lusch and Vargo, 2006). S-D logic focuses on the operant resources of customers, employees and the environment and considers them endogenous, rather than exogenous, to the value-creation process. Thus, the competences of customers, employees and other stakeholders are key components of competitive advantage (Lusch et al., 2007). Moreover, the S-D logic consideration of resources treats both operant and operand resources as inputs in the value-creation process. In other words, the creation and determination of value depend on the process of "resourcing" (Lusch et al., 2008) which converts a potential resource into a specific benefit and involves (1) resource creation, (2) resource integration, and (3) resistance removal.

Operant Resources

One of the most critical differences between S-D logic and G-D logic, along-side the difference between their meanings of service, is the distinction between operand and operant resources (Constantin and Lusch, 1994; Vargo and Lusch, 2004). Operand resources have been identified as those resources which need to be acted upon (e.g., goods), while operant resources are those that are able act upon other operand (and operant) resources (e.g., knowledge and skills). Operant resources are generally intangible and invisible, dynamic and infinite. This means that although the resources cannot be produced and distributed per se, they can evolve, transform and multiply. Because operant resources are producers of effects, they enable humans with their ingenuity to increase the value of natural resources and generate new operant resources (new ideas and knowledge). Almost by definition, G-D logic is centered on operand, tangible resources, while S-D logic makes operant, intangible resources primary in exchange.

S-D logic, and its emphasis on value co-creation, considers customers, employees and other stakeholders as operant resources, those which act upon other resources to co-create value. Thus, the ability to compete in the market is a function of both individual and collective (organizational) knowledge, and a firm's ability to contribute to value creation in the market also relies on the resources of customers and other external stakeholders (e.g., government entities). S-D logic's primacy of operant resources does not diminish the importance of operand resources in value creation, but it emphasizes the idea that operand resources only become valuable via the application of operant resources.

Resourcing

According to S-D logic, value creation only occurs when a potential resource (usually operant) is applied and contributes to a specific benefit. This activity has been termed "resourcing" (Lusch et al., 2008) and includes the creation and integration of resources and the removal of resistances. The first aspect of resourcing, the creation of resources, either operant or operand, always involves the application of an operant resource. Human ingenuity has led to the development of countless resources, both operand and operant, and continues to drive the evolution of the market as well as society.

The second aspect, resource integration, is a basic function of all service systems (e.g., firms, families and nations). At the firm level, organizations are considered resource integrators, as are departments held within the firm. Essentially, organizations transform employee-level, microspecialized competences (knowledge and skills) as well as other internal and external (e.g., market-acquired) resources into service provisioning.

The third aspect of resourcing, the removal of resource resistances, removes barriers that can prevent resources from being useful. The removal of resistances (e.g., lobbying for new laws) is a process that involves not only firms or service providers, but also involves the effort of customers, users or beneficiaries. In fact, often times the barrier to resource creation stems from customer resistances. These resistances are generally due to negative attitudes that individuals or groups of individuals hold against a particular firm or industry that prevents businesses from making their resources available in the market. It is through this process of resourcing that the resources of one service system can contribute to the co-creation of value between that and other systems.

Implications for Service Science

Building a true science of service requires solid theoretical foundations and the development of core constructs and concepts. This is no easy task. The advancement of service science becomes particularly difficult when faced with the challenge of applying an alternative logic to the traditional, goods-centered paradigm. The paradigmatic grip of the G-D logic lexicon makes it hard to break away from traditional understandings of concepts such as service and value.

The clarification of S-D logic above addressed the issues related to the S-D logic meaning of service, service as the basis of all exchange, and the nature of value co-creation among service systems. From these clarifications it is evident that service, the act of doing something for and with another party, can be done directly or indirectly (e.g., through a good). Thus, in an S-D-logic grounded understanding of service science there are no "services" (intangible units of output), there is only the service provision that occurs among service systems. Moreover, although attention towards intangible aspects of exchange has increased in recent years, there is no new service economy. Importantly, from the S-D logic view, economic activity has always been driven by service-for-service exchange and the process of value co-creation – the collaborative effort among service systems to create value for others and for themselves.

Based on the need for the clarification of S-D logic concepts, it is clear that the pervasiveness of the G-D logic paradigm remains strong. The importance of distinguishing G-D logic concepts from S-D logic concepts is that the vocabulary used to describe phenomena within each directs academics and practitioners down vastly different paths with regard to understanding economic exchange. G-D logic terms, such as transaction, value-added and price, point toward asymmetrical processes of value creation and tangible aspects of exchange. Alternatively, S-D logic vocabulary, such as relationship, value co-creation and value-in-use, highlight dynamic and reciprocal phenomena associated with exchange.

The clarification of S-D logic, particularly as a foundation for service science, is done here to draw attention toward the influence of the dominant goods-centered paradigm. In order for S-D logic to contribute to and potentially guide the advancement of service science, misinterpretations of its foundational premises need to be reevaluated. Moreover, for S-D logic to aid in the future advancement of service science the language used to discuss S-D logic and service science must be more clearly defined and agreed upon.

The use of S-D logic friendly terms in the discussion of service science indicates that the transition to a service-centered science of service has begun. This move is also evidenced by the subtle but powerful switch from calling the discipline services science (the original title) to service science. However, formalization of the terms and further development of the concepts associated with S-D logic and service science is needed. Several core constructs of S-D logic and service science and their related concepts were presented here. We suggest that this collection of key concepts may help to establish a framework from which theory development and testing can be furthered and service-centered models of exchange explored.

References

Achrol, R. and Kotler, P. (2006). The Service-Dominant Logic for Marketing: A Critique. In R. F. Lusch and S. L. Vargo (Eds.) *The Service-Dominant Logic of Marketing: Dialog, Debate, and Directions*, (320-333). Armonk, New York: M.E. Sharpe.

Bastiat, F. (1860). *Harmonies of Political Economy* (Patrick S. Sterling, Trans.). London: J. Murray.

Bitner, M. J. and Brown, S. W. (2006). The Evolution and Discovery of Services Science in Business Schools. Communications of the ACM, 49(7), 73-78.

Brodie, R. J., Pels, J and Saren, M. (2006). From Goods- Toward Service-Centered Marketing: Dangerous Dichotomy or an Emerging Dominant Logic? In R. F. Lusch and S. L. Vargo (Eds.) *The Service-Dominant Logic of Marketing: Dialog, Debate, and Directions*, (307-319). Armonk, New York: M.E. Sharpe.

Chesbrough, H. and Spohrer, J. (2006). A Research Manifesto for Services Science. *Communications of the ACM*, 49(7), 35-40.

Constantin, J. A. and Lusch, R. F. (1994). *Understanding Resource Management*. Oxford, OH: The Planning Forum.

Edvardsson, B., Gustafsson, A. and Roos, I. (2005). Service Portraits in Service Research: A Critical Review. International Journal of Service Industry Management. 16(1), 107-121.

Gronroos, C. (2000). *Service Management and Marketing: A Customer Relationship Management Approach*. West Sussex, UK: John Wiley and Sons.

Gummesson, E. (1995). Relationship Marketing: Its Role in the Service Economy. In W. J. Glynn and J. G. Barnes, (Eds). *Understanding Services Management*, (244-268). New York: John Wiley & Sons.

Gummesson, E. (2006). Many-to-Many Marketing as Grand Theory. In R. F. Lusch and S. L. Vargo (Eds.) *The Service-Dominant Logic of Marketing: Dialog, Debate, and Directions* (339-353). Armonk, New York: M.E. Sharpe.

Hunt, S. and Morgan, R. M. (1995). The Comparative Advantage Theory of Competition. *Journal of Marketing*, 59(April), 1-15.

IfM and IBM. (2007) *Succeeding through Service Innovation: A Discussion Paper*. Cambridge, United Kingdom: University of Cambridge Institute for Manufacturing. ISBN: 978-1-902546-59-8.

Lehmann, D. R. (2006). More Dominant Logics for Marketing: Productivity and Growth. In R. F. Lusch and S. L. Vargo (Eds.) *The Service-Dominant Logic of Marketing: Dialog, Debate, and Directions* (296-301). Armonk, New York: M.E. Sharpe.

Levy, S. J. (2006). How New, How Dominant? In R. F. Lusch and S. L. Vargo (Eds.) *The Service-Dominant Logic of Marketing: Dialog, Debate, and Directions* (57-64). Armonk, New York: M.E. Sharpe.

Lusch, R. F. and Vargo, S. L. (Eds.) (2006). *The Service-Dominant Logic of Marketing: Dialog, Debate, and Directions*. Armonk, New York: M.E. Sharpe.

Lusch, R. F. and Vargo, S. L. (2008). The Service-Dominant Mindset. In B. Hefley and W. Murphy, (Eds.) *Service Science, Management and Engineering Education for the 21ˢᵗ Century*. New York: Springer.

Lusch, R. F.,Vargo, S. L., and O'Brien, M. (2007). Competing through service: Insights from service-dominant logic *Journal of Retailing*, 83(1), 5-18.

Lusch, R. L.,Vargo, S. L., and Tanniru, M. (2010). Service, Value Networks, and Learning. *Journal of the Academy of Marketing Science.* (in press and available through SpringerLink).

Lusch, R. F.,Vargo, S. L., and Wessels, G. (2008). Toward a Conceptual Foundation for Service Science: Contributions from Service-Dominant Logic. *IBM Systems Journal* 47(1) 5-14.

Maglio, P. P. and Spohrer, J. (2008). Fundamentals of Service Science. *Journal of the Academy of Marketing Science,* 36(1), 18-20.

Normann, R. (2001). *Reframing Business: When the Map Changes the Landscape*. New York, NY: John Wiley & Sons.

Normann, R. and Ramirez, R. (1993). From Value Chain to Value Constellation: Designing Interactive Strategy. *Harvard Business Review*, 71(July-August), 65-77.

Penrose, E. (1959). *The Theory of the Growth of the Firm*. New York: John Wiley.

Prahalad, C.K. (2004). The Cocreation of Value. *Journal of Marketing*, 68(January), 23.

Prahalad, C.K. and Ramaswamy V. (2000). Co-opting Customer Competence. *Harvard Business Review,* 78(January/February), 79-87.

Rust, R. and Thompson D. V. (2006). How Does Marketing Strategy Change in a Service-Based World?: Implications and Directions for Research. In R. F. Lusch and S. L. Vargo (Eds.) *The Service-Dominant Logic of Marketing: Dialog, Debate, and Directions*, (381-392). Armonk, New York: M.E. Sharpe.

Shembri, S. (2006). Rationalizing Service Logic, or Understanding a Service Experience?. *Marketing Theory.* 6(3), 381-92.

Smith, A. (1776), *An Inquiry into the Nature and Causes of the Wealth of Nations.* London: W. Strahan and T. Cadell.

Spohrer, J., Maglio, P. P., Bailey, J. and Gruhl, D. (2007). Steps Toward a Science of Service Systems. *Computer,* 40, 71-77.

Spohrer, J., Vargo, S., Caswell, N. and Maglio, P. (2008). The Service System is the Basic Abstraction of Service Science. *41st Annual HICSS Conference Proceedings.*

Vargo, S. L. and Akaka, M. A. (2009). Service-Dominant Logic as a Foundation for Service Science:Clarifications. *Service Science,* 1(1), 32-41.

Vargo, S. L. and Lusch, R. F. (2004). Evolving to a New Dominant Logic for Marketing. *Journal of Marketing,* 68(1), 1-17.

Vargo, S. L. and Lusch, R. F. (2006). Service-Dominant Logic:What It Is, What It Is Not, What It Might Be. In R. F. Lusch and S. L. Vargo (Eds.) *The Service-Dominant Logic of Marketing: Dialog, Debate, and Directions,* (43-56). Armonk, New York: M.E. Sharpe.

Vargo, S. L. and Lusch, R. F. (2008). Service-Dominant Logic:C ontinuing the Evolution. *Journal of the Academy of Marketing Science,* 36(1), 1-10.

Vargo, S. L., Lusch, R. F. Akaka, M. A. and He, Y. (2010). The Service-Dominant Logic of Marketing: A Review and Assessment. *Review of Marketing Research,* 6, 125-167.

Vargo, S. L. and Morgan, F. W. (2005). Services in Society and Academic Thought:An Historical Analysis. *Journal of Macromarketing,* 25(1), 42-53.

Vargo, S. L., Maglio, P and Akaka, M. A. (2008). On Value and Value Co-creation:A Service Systems and Service Logic Perspective. *European Management Journal,* 26, 145-152.

Zeithaml,V. A., Parasuraman, A. and Berry, L. L. (1985). Problems and Strategies in Services Marketing. *Journal of Marketing,* 49(Spring), 33-46.

Toward a Science of Service Systems

Value and Symbols

James C. Spohrer

    IBM Research-Almaden

Paul P. Maglio

    IBM Research-Almaden

Economics has accumulated a great body of knowledge about *value*. Building on economics and other disciplines, service science is an emerging transdiscipline. It is the study of value-cocreation phenomena (Spohrer & Maglio, 2010). Value cocreation occurs in the real-world ecology of diverse types of service system entities (e.g., people, families, universities, businesses, and nations). These entities use symbols to reason about the value of knowledge. Like mathematics (quantity relationship proofs) and computer science (efficient representations and algorithms), service science must ultimately embody a set of proven techniques for processing symbols, allowing us to model the world better and to take better actions. In addition, the emergence of service science promises to accelerate the creation of T-shaped Science, Technology, Engineering, and Math (STEM) professionals who are highly adaptive innovators that combine deep problem solving skills in one area with broad communication skills across many areas. This paper casts service science as a transdiscipline based on symbolic processes that adaptively compute the value of interactions among systems.

Introduction: Value and Symbols

Economics, more than any other single scientific discipline, has studied value. For example, economic practice has studied the historical and regional variations in prices of things and of labor. Supply and demand matter. Many price variations can only be understood in terms of national legal and political practices. Within business and family structures, certain activities seem to operate outside the normal price system. Written and unwritten laws and policies matter. For example, the costs of government, health care, education, insurance, electricity,

P.P. Maglio et al. (eds.), *Handbook of Service Science*, Service Science: Research and Innovations in the Service Economy, DOI 10.1007/978-1-4419-1628-0_9,
© Springer Science+Business Media, LLC 2010

communications, transportation, energy, food, water, tobacco, alcohol – really everything – can vary tremendously across social-organizational entities, regions, and time periods. Events and their outcomes matter. For example, positive events, including discovery of natural resources, new uses for materials, new scientific knowledge, technological and business model innovations, or other new reasons for optimism can ignite major growth of jobs and wealth. And negative events, including natural disasters, wars, inflation, depressions, discovery of hazards, and many other factors can wreck havoc on networks of interconnected systems. All this interdependence suggests that rather than resulting from the actions of a single agent or entity, value is necessarily cocreated as a result of interactions of multiple entities. Value cocreation is the primary object of study service science (Spohrer & Maglio, 2010).

Service science aims to improve our ability to create service innovations systematically and reliably. Economists traditionally define the service sector to include government, education, medical and healthcare, banking and insurance, business consulting, information technology services, retail and wholesale, tourism and hospitality, entertainment, transportation and logistics, and legal among others.[1] By the traditional method of economic segmentation, the service sector accounts for most of the world's economic activity (Wolfl, 2005), but is the least studied and least understood part of the economy (Triplett & Bosworth, 2004). Innovation in service is not approached as systematically as innovation in agriculture and manufacturing, which have experienced large productivity and quality gains (Chesbrough & Spohrer, 2006). To remedy this, service science aims to provide theory and practice around service innovation.

In this paper, we argue that the concepts of *value cocreation* and *service system entities* are fundamental to service science. In particular, we define *service as value cocreation phenomena that arise among interacting service system entities* (Maglio & Spohrer, 2010). Division-of-labor is a well-known value-cocreation mechanism. A service system entity is a system that includes one or more people and any number of technologies that adaptively computes and adjusts to the changing value of knowledge. The history of service innovations can be summarized concisely as the evolving repertoire of value-cocreation mechanisms used by service system entities.

Mathematics supports reasoning about what is possible or impossible to know about quantity relationships on the basis of formal logic. Computer science provides estimates of the cost of computing, given specific physical computer architectures and energy costs (e.g., space and time complexity). Computer science depends deeply on both mathematics and physics; as Newell and Simon (1976) argued, the *physical symbol system* is the fundamental abstraction of computer science (see also Newell, 1980). A physical symbol system is a real-world entity that uses symbols to shape its future behavior. Symbols are encoded

[1] "Development of NAICS" (http://www.census.gov/epcd/www/naicsdev.htm). The North American Industrial Classification System (NAICS), which replaced Standard Industrial Classification (SIC), consists of 20 sectors of which 16 are service related (US Bureau of Census, 2007).

physically, for instance, in transistors, books, neurons, or other materials. Symbols guide both internal behavior and mediate interactions with other entities. Physical symbol systems provide a link between mathematics and physics (Pattee, 2001). Physical symbol systems are fundamental to service science as well: simply put, *service system entities are physical symbol systems*. Without effective symbolic reasoning about value – what we call *processes of valuing* – systematic service innovation would be more akin to evolution than engineering. Of course, value is much more than just symbolic processes of valuing.

To most people, value is how much something is worth – the price another is willing to pay. A price is a value signal squeezed into a short sequence of symbols, an indication of currency and amount (e.g., $5.60, €3.99). Exchange rates and prices are of practical importance. Paying the price creates desired change – it can change who owns something or has access rights to resources. There are many contexts, perspectives, and ways to reason about changes in the world, and ways to create and prevent those changes (von Mises, 1998).

However, value is more than a price or a short sequence of symbols. For example, we all value relationships with other people, and would find it impossible – even socially unacceptable – to reduce the value of a relationship to a price. What is the value of a relationship? Of someone's sense of identity or reputation? Of the way a beautiful sunset makes us feel? Even when we cannot easily or responsibly reduce this sense of valuing something to a price, we still can and often do use symbols to reason about and communicate with others about our *processes of valuing* – if just to say the word "priceless."

In this paper, we introduce our perspective on service science. First, we summarize some of the background literature: what have service research pioneers accomplished, what myths persist and why, how do existing disciplines conceptualize service, and how has service science been emerging most recently?. Second, we describe different types of service systems and the dimensions used to analyze those systems. Third, we discuss the foundations of symbolic processes of valuing. We highlight the evolution of new types of service system entities and the value-cocreation mechanisms that sustain them, focusing specifically on symbol manipulation processes for determining value. Our thesis is that *symbol manipulation is increasingly important as a mechanism for value cocreation*. Finally, we discuss the implications of viewing service systems as entities capable of reasoning about the value of knowledge.

Background: A Complex History

Scholars from economics, marketing, operations, management, engineering, and more – have focused on service over the last two hundred years. We describe a tiny sampling of their works here (summarized in Table 1; for more history, see Berry & Parasuraman, 1993; Brown, Fisk & Bitner, 1994; Vargo & Lusch, 2004a; Gummesson, 2007).

Table 1. Pioneers of service research

What is...	Proposals	References
service?	Non-productive labor	Smith
service?	Competence exchange	Bastiat
optimal exchange?	Comparative advantage	Ricardo
cause of service growth?	Lagging productivity	Clark
result of service growth?	Productivity stagnation	Baumol
model of service systems?	Queuing theory; Systems dynamics; Two-part production system	Riordon; Fitzsimmons; Oliva & Sterman; Mandelbaum; Mills & Moberg
result of service growth?	More tech industrialization	Levitt; Quinn; Zysman
service marketing?	IHIP, 6P's	Judd; Shostack; Berry; Brown; Gronroos, Gummesson
service quality?	GAPS; Linkage; SERVQUAL	Zeithaml & Bitner; Schneider & Bowen; Parasuraman
optimal learning?	Exploration & Exploitation	March
optimal investing?	Profit-chain; Customer equity	Heskett, Sasser, Schlesinger; Rust
service operations?	Customer Contact; Unified Theory; Offering Continuum; Waiting and Queues; Front/Back-Stage	Levitt; Chase; Maister; Larson; Davis; Johnston; Teboul; Sampson; Roth & Menor
B2B service?	Professional relationships	Maister; Bolton; Christopher
service design?	Theater; Hyperreality	Grove & Fisk; Pine & Gilmore; Edvardsson
service innovation?	Customer-focus	Gustafsson & Johnson; Miles; Gadrey & Gallouj; Van Ark, Broersma& Den Hertog; Tidd & Hull
result of service growth?	More innovation	Baumol; Tien & Berg; Gutek
lean techniques?	Lean solutions	Womack & Jones
service?	Rental; perspective on value creation through the lens of the customer	Lovelock & Gummesson; Edvardsson, Gustafsson & Roos
service?	Application of competence; offering	Vargo & Lusch; Gummesson

What is service? Smith (1776/1904) used an example to introduce the distinction between productive and unproductive labor – an instance of service illustrated unproductive labor. According to Smith, the wealth of nations depends on maximizing productive labor and minimizing unproductive labor. Nations that aspire to greater wealth should shift the competencies of their people to activities with the highest profit margins, and ensure those people have the best technology and organizational infrastructure to support them. That is productive labor. Though elsewhere, Smith acknowledged the value and even the necessity of a great many service activities, the damage was done. To this day, service research struggles with the burden of the misconception that service activities are unproductive and ought to be minimized. Creating research-driven service innovation capabilities is an overdue priority for nations and businesses (Baumol, 2002; IfM & IBM, 2008; UK Royal Society, 2009).

What is service? What is optimal exchange? Later political economists provided insights into the nature of value cocreation and exchange. Bastiat (1850/1979) realized that human competence, which he called service, was the foundation for all exchange, even the exchange of material products for money. The best way to understand value was to study service exchange and understand direct and indirect human efforts to apply knowledge for the benefit of others. Ricardo (1817/2004) realized that the optimal performance of productive activities was relative to the range of competencies and opportunities for interactions. Thus, being "relatively less bad at performing a task" can be the basis for value cocreation in a population with diverse competences and needs. Taken together, Bastiat and Ricardo's findings set the stage for a deep appreciation of knowledge-driven value-cocreation interactions between entities. In the short run, advantage may go to those with either superior competences or superior comparative advantages. In the long run, advantage may go to entities that can learn fastest. When it comes to value cocreation, knowledge is king – primarily knowledge of how to do things (competencies) and knowledge of others (their relative competencies and needs), and secondarily knowledge to create new competencies and relationships.

Why service growth? Clark (1940/1957) provided a first mapping of national competences – their relative strengths in agriculture, manufacturing, and service. Developed nations were using technology to dramatically improve productivity (competences) related to agricultural and manufactured goods. As their populations grew, a relatively larger percentage of the population was finding its comparative advantage in other areas of the economy, broadly labeled the service sector. Competences inside family groups were beginning to be externalized as productivity grew in agriculture and manufacturing. He hypothesized that national labor pools would shift to areas of economic activity with lagging productivity growth rates. Nations compete by increasing productivity and shifting labor to areas of comparative advantage.

What is the ultimate result of service growth? As Clark predicted, because the US was leading the world in agricultural and manufacturing productivity growth, export markets saturated, and workers in those two areas shrank to less than fifty percent. Baumol explained why the salaries associated with jobs that did not experience large productivity increases also rose (Baumol & Bowen, 1966). "Baumol's Cost Disease," not unlike Smith's unproductive labor example, became the source of a misconception that large service sectors were bad.

How have service systems been modeled? Mathematical and computer models of service systems mark a turning point in the scientific study of service. One of the first characteristics of service systems to be modeled was the stochastic nature of the capacity limits under variable demand. Riordan (1962) used queuing theory to analyze telephone switching networks to develop a theory of stochastic service systems. Queuing theory is used to analyze other types of service systems, ranging from ambulance emergency response to call centers (e.g., Fitzsimmons & Fitzsimmons, 2007; Mandelbaum and Zeltyn, 2008). Mills and Moberg (1982) used a two-component model of service systems with a technical component akin to a manufacturing core that could be sealed off and standardized, but with a customer interface component required to deal with uncertainty and variability of diverse customers. Oliva and Sterman (2001) developed a systems dynamics approach to model the erosion of quality in service businesses when hiring lags behind demand spikes (see also Oliva & Sterman, this volume).

How will technology influence the evolution of service productivity? Levitt (1976) introduced the concept of industrialization of service via technology. Quinn and Paquette (1990) showed that technology would provide the service sector with a path to continuous productivity improvements, and that standardized technology-based service components would provide an architecture for new service development. Zysman (2006) referred to the algorith mic revolution, which puts service productivity on an ICT-based improvement curve.

How is service marketing different? Economists measured the growth of the service sector and the concerns about productivity stagnation. Meanwhile, academics in business schools took note and outlined managerial implications. Marketing was first. Judd (1964) argued for a better definition of services. A market transaction that does not transfer ownership has three main categories: rented goods services, improvement of owned goods services, and non-goods services. Shostack (1977) argued that service marketing should break free of product marketing. Shostack's writings and speeches helped condense some of the thoughts in the air at the time, suggesting that services were intangible, heterogeneous, inseparable, and perishable (the IHIP characteristics),[2] and that marketing should take account of 6 P's – Product, Price, Place, Promotion, People, and Process. In Europe, Gronroos (1977) and Gummensson (1977) were also

---

[2] "Philosophical contributions from three centuries provided a set of 'characteristics' of services that have now been claimed to distinguish them from goods. The most famous are intangibility, heterogeneity, inseparability and perishability, now known as the IHIPs. In Scotland, Adam Smith (1723-1790) discussed perishability of services; in France, Jean-Baptiste Say (1767-1832) introduced intangibility (immateriality) and inseparability; and in England Joan Robinson (1903-1983) brought in heterogeneity. Services seem then to have been dropped from the economics agenda, but the interest was revived in management and marketing. The earliest marketing references for these characteristics appeared in the beginning of the 1960s" (Gummesson, 2007).

making the case. Berry and Parasuraman (1993) and Brown, Fisk, and Bitner (1994) documented the rise of service marketing.

How is service quality different?   Service marketing brought a focus to improving service quality. SERVQUAL (Parasuraman, Zeithhaml & Berry, 1985), the GAPS Model (Zeithaml, Bitner, Gremler, 2006), and the Linkage Model (Schneider & Bowen, 1993) provided multiple angles on service quality. The human element – both customers and employees – is prominent in all three (see also Schneider & Bowen, this volume; Bitner, Zeithaml & Gremler, this volume).

What is optimal learning? Like optimal exchange, optimal learning is an important foundation for a science of service systems – the ability to change competences and relationships.   March (1991) introduced the notions of exploration and exploitation in organizational learning. If an environment is changing rapidly, an entity capable of learning (e.g., individual or organization) risks extinction if it does not adapt. The entity ought to invest resources in exploration to maintain its fit (competences and relationships). If the environment is very stable, an entity may do well simply exploiting existing behavioral patterns (competences and relationships). An optimal learning rate is a function of the environmental change rate. Exploration attempts to innovate with no guarantee of success. Menor, Tatikonda, and Sampson (2002) examined new service development in the context of exploitation and exploration.

What is optimal investing? Heskett, Sasser, and Schlesinger (1997) described the service-profit chain, demonstrating a direct and strong relationship between profit, growth, customer loyalty, customer satisfaction, the value of goods and services delivered to customers, as well as employee capabilities, satisfaction, loyalty, and productivity (see also Heskett and Sasser in this volume). Rust, Zeithhaml, and Lemon (2000) suggested investing with a keen sense of "total customer lifetime value" allows a firm to make bold and successful strategies pay off (see also Rust & Bhalla, this volume).

What are service operations? About the same time that service marketing was taking root in business schools, service operations was also taking root. Levitt (1972) advocated a production-line approach to service – as well as the notion of front and back stage operations, later developed further by Teboul (2006). Chase (1981) advanced a customer-contact theory to estimate the potential for improving service productivity in service systems.   The greater a provider's need for customer contact and the more diverse the customers, the less opportunity for standardization and productivity improvements (see also Chase, this volume). Johnston (1989) even proposed that the customer be viewed as an employee, in need of training to improve productivity and quality. Going beyond mathematical models of service, Maister (1985) explored the psychology of waiting in queues. Larson (1987) examined the implications for social justice.   Davis (1991) examined queues, and the way customer interaction in service processes can lead to trade-offs that managers of service operations must make in service system design. Roth and Menor (2003) distinguished the unique methods and research agenda of service operations management that combines quantitative and qualitative models. Sampson and Froehle (2006) proposed a unified service theory to understand processes with customer input (see also Sampson, this volume).

What is B2B service? The majority of service research has explored business-to-consumer (B2C) interactions and processes. Business-to-business (B2B) service was explored by Maister (1993) in the context of professional service firms. Bolton, Smith, and Wagner (2003) further explored factors that strike the right balance in successful relationships in complex B2B contexts. Christopher, Payne, and Ballantyne (1991) provided a broad perspective on the practice of relationship marketing. The nature of complex network relationships is an important topic in B2B service (Gummesson, 2007; Vargo, 2009). Building off traditional supply chain management, the notions of service value chain management and globally integrated enterprise are emerging priorities (Palmisano, 2006).

What is service design? Grove and Fisk (1992) conceived the service experience as theater, and service design as akin to staging a production. Pine and Gilmore (1999) described an experience economy in which service providers compete on the design of customer experiences. Edvardsson, Enquist, and Johnston (2005) explored the future of service design, envisioning hyperreality simulations to provide customers with a "try before you buy" capability.

What is service innovation? The increasing importance of service innovation has been well documented in recent years (Gadrey & Gallouj, 2002; Van Ark, Broersma, den Hertog, 2003; Tidd & Hull, 2003; Gustafsson & Johnson, 2003; Miles, 2006, 2008; Spath & Fähnrich, 2007). Though many sophisticated service innovation models have been developed and contrasted with product and process innovation models, one common denominator comes through – service innovation is necessarily customer-focused. Customers change and service innovation must keep up to reduce customer costs while working to increase customer value. Customer competences (as in self-service models) and relationships (access to other experts or customers) constantly change (see also Miles, this volume).

How are lean techniques being applied to service? Womack and Jones (2005) observed that consumption is often hard work for the consumer and is unpaid work to boot. The principles expressed in the voice of the customer are "Solve my problem completely. Don't waste my time. Provide exactly what I want. Deliver value where I want it. Supply value when I want it. Reduce the number of decisions I must make to solve my problems."

What is the ultimate result of service growth? Baumol (2002) developed a new sector productivity model. As long as the research sector ("the queen of the service sector") enjoys even a small increase in productivity over time, all other sectors that depend on scientific research (which today is almost all sectors) can realize continuous productivity gains from innovation. Baumol's disease was cured (Triplett & Bosworth, 2003). Tien and Berg (2007) developed a calculus for service innovation that links productivity gains to increasing knowledge about customers. Technology-enabled mass customization will make all sectors more like custom service (e.g., shoes and clothing personalized, medicines and foods personalized, etc.). However, Gutek (1995) warned that a shift from personal relationships to high productivity impersonal interactions may have unintended consequences.

What is service? Lovelock and Gummesson (2004) exposed the problems with IHIP and other models, and proposed a rental or resource access model of value cocreation. Edvardsson, Gustafsson, and Roos (2005) reexamined the problems with existing definitions and suggested that service is best conceptualized as a perspective on value creation through the lens of the customer. Gummesson (2007) suggested that from a provider perspective, the word "offerings" can replace both "goods" and "services", and along with Vargo and Lusch (2004), noted that "service" (in the singular) is the core concept underlying both "goods" and "services". A provider offers a value proposition (the offering) to the customer, but value *actualization* occurs in a separate customer process. Thus value is the outcome of cocreation interactions between providers (with offerings) and customers (with actualizations). Gummesson advocated going beyond the customer-provider dyad to consider, complex adaptive networks of customer-provider entities and their diverse offerings and actualizations (see also Gummesson, this volume).

What is service? Vargo and Lusch (2004) turned the page on the early days of service research, in which goods and services were contrasted, by introducing *service-dominant logic* (see also Vargo, Lusch & Akaka, this volume). As mentioned, most people had considered services to be an inferior form of goods, but one that was unfortunately growing like an unsightly weed on developed economies, stagnating needed productivity growth, interfering with efforts to remain globally competitive, causing wage inflation, and lowering the quality of jobs and thereby quality of life in developed nations. Service-dominant logic, like Bastiat (1850/1979), viewed service-for-service exchange as the fundamental driver of the economy, and goods-dominant logic as hiding the fundamental nature of exchange. Vargo and Lusch (2004) suggested defining service as a type of process, specifically the process of one or more entities applying competences (knowledge, resources) for the benefit of another. The service-dominant logic view established a foundation on which to build a science of service system entities and their value-cocreation interactions (Spohrer & Maglio, 2010).

Myth Busting

Unfortunately, myths or misconceptions about service persist. In this section, we bust them (see Table 2 for summary).

Table 2. Persistent myths about service

Myth	Reality	Reference(s)
Productivity is stagnant in service sector	Augmenting human and organizational performance with technology innovations, making hidden information accessible, or incentive alignment strategies are three of many ways to increases service sector performance	Baumol
Service sector jobs are low skill and low wage	Service sector leads in the creation of new high skill and high pay jobs	Herzenberg, Alic, Wial; Levy & Murnane
Service sector is all labor, and little technology	Service sector is extremely knowledge and technology intensive	Royal Society Report
STEM (Science Technology Engineering and Math) graduates cannot find good jobs in the service sector	Service sector hires most STEM graduates in developed economies to improve and innovate service	Royal Society Report
Service quality is subjective and resists systematic improvement	Service quality can be scientifically studied and improved; Intimately, connected to accurate service productivity measurement	Schneider & Bowen; Gadrey & Gallouj
Service sector is too diverse to be studied systematically	There are just four broad types of service based on resource types; Service transforms entities or their property	Spohrer & Maglio; Hill

Productivity is stagnant in the service sector. Baumol (2002) put to rest this myth. His revised sector model showed that *scientific research productivity* is the key, along with new tools of science – from better computers to better gene sequencing equipment. Of course, national economic statistics validate just this reality (Triplett & Bosworth, 2003). Scientific advances include: augmenting human and organizational performance with technology (e.g., bar code scanners at retail check out, self service retail check out), making hidden information accessible and incentive alignment strategies (e.g., electricity rate schedules visible at time of use on appliances). So why does this myth persist? Perhaps most people's view of the service sector is of waitresses, chamber maids, retail clerks, and trash collectors. Because these jobs do not seem to be changing much, people over generalize. This is likely to change in the coming decades. For example, robotic trash vehicles are already working in prototypes.

Service sector jobs are low skill and low wage jobs. Herzenberg, Alic, and Wial (2000) showed high skill and high wage jobs are growing fastest in the service sector. A comprehensive view of the full range of service sector jobs includes professional, scientific, technical jobs. Levy and Murnane (2004) also demonstrated that computers and other types of information and communications technologies (ICT) create demand for more expert thinking and complex communications skills in the workplace. So why does the myth persist? With so few jobs today in agriculture and manufacturing sectors, perhaps people are romanticizing old types of jobs. Or perhaps if one is a professor, an executive, a doctor, or politician, it is hard to recognize one is in a service sector job. This is likely to change as knowledge-intensive service activities increase and people begin to associate knowledge workers with the predominant service sector jobs.

Service sector is all labor and little technology. The UK Royal Society (2009) provided a clear account of the transformative nature of technology in major service innovations. From internet-based to smart phone-based businesses and from financial services to health care, many aspects of life are becoming instrumented, interconnected, and intelligent to support improved quality of service. Technology allows new service offerings to scale up faster and reach more customers in less time. So why does the myth persist? Perhaps the growth in public sector jobs, government, public safety, healthcare, and education is what is top of mind for most people. We see the number of teachers, police officers, fire fighters, nurses, or public service agents increasing or stable, and do not see the increasing use of technology needed to perform these jobs well.

Science, Technology, Engineering, and Math (STEM) graduates cannot find good jobs in the service sector. The UK Royal Society (2009) report confirmed that 82% of STEM graduates in the UK found jobs in the service sector, and most contribute to continuous innovation there. So why does the myth persist? Many of the routine everyday service sector jobs that most of us are likely to encounter (waitress, retail clerk, etc.) do not require college degrees. Professionals simply do not see themselves as service sector workers.

Service quality is subjective and resists systematic improvement. Schneider and Bowen (1993) and Gadrey and Gallouj (2002) provided evidence that service quality can be the focus of scientific investigations and improvement. In fact, service quality and service productivity are often intimately linked, as when Automatic Teller Machines (ATM) were introduced and quickly revolutionized what most people do when they visit a bank – they interact with an ATM, when and where they want. So why does the myth persist? One reason is that people's expectations of quality are continually rising.

Service sector is too diverse to be studied systematically. Hill's (1977) view of service was transformation of an entity or its possessions (economic transactions that do not change ownership). Spohrer and Maglio (2010) suggested that just four types of resources are transformed.   So why does the myth persist? Perhaps the relatively primitive way in which new service systems and value propositions are designed provides part of the answer. Methodologies for creating value propositions are becoming more sophisticated (Anderson, Kumar, & Narus, 2007). When a computer-aided design (CAD) tool exists to create new designs from building blocks systematically, this myth will begin to fad.

Many Disciplines, Many Views of Service

A wide range of academic disciplines have developed views of service. This is one indication that service science, as an emerging transdiscipline, can ultimately make a contribution to many other disciplines (see Table 3 for a summary).

Table 3. Disciplinary views of "service"

Discipline	Focus	References
Economics	Service is a distinct type of exchange, a category for counting output, jobs, businesses, exports, etc.; A service is a change in the condition of a person or a good belonging to some economic entity, brought about as a result of some other economic entity	Triplett; Hill
Marketing	Service is a distinct type of exchange, delivered by a distinct type of process, often characterized by customized human interactions ("moments of truth"); Service is the application of competence for the benefit of another	Shostack; Bitner & Brown; Carlzon; Vargo & Lusch
Operations	Service is a distinct type of production process, characterized by dependence on customer inputs	Chase; Sampson
Industrial & Systems Engineering	Service systems and networks present a distinct type of engineering problem, characterized by customer variability (including processing times and queues)	Riordan; Mandelbaum
Operations Research	Service systems and networks present a distinct modeling and optimization problems, characterized by dynamic and stochastic capacity and demand	Thomas & Griffin; Dietrich & Harrison
Computer Science	Service is an abstraction for network-accessible capabilities with unique discovery, composition, and modeling challenges	Zhang; Seth; Endrei

Information Systems	Service systems can be improved using properly managed information system Service systems are work systems	Rai & Sambamurthy; Alter
Social Sciences	Service systems are related to socio-technical systems, as well as systems engineering models of enterprises	Rouse & Baba
Behavioral Sciences	Service is an experience, shaped by many factors including waiting in queues and customer expectations	Chase & Dasu; Maister

Economics. As exemplified in Triplett and Bosworth's (2004) analysis, service can be viewed as a distinct type of exchange, a category for counting and analyzing jobs, businesses, exports, as well as inputs and outputs (productivity). Unsatisfied with a negative definition of service as an exchange that does not involve transfer of physical goods, Hill (1977) proposed that a service is a change in the condition of a person, or a good belonging to some economic entity, brought about as a result of some other economic entity, with the approval of the first person or economic entity. From a service science perspective, Hill's definition begins to place emphasis on *interaction* of economic entities.

Economists measure and count entities and their exchanges. Money-for-things-type exchanges make sense when counting in the agriculture and manufacturing sectors. Money-for-labor-promises-etc-type exchanges make sense when counting in the service sector. Economists measure that a smaller percentage of the total exchanges are of the money-for-things type. Thus, from the traditional economics perspective, the growth of the service sector results. Measurement can get complicated because of exceptions (e.g., restaurant and retail are service providers that transfer ownership of goods), diverse types of entities (e.g., people, businesses, and nations), and aggregation methods (e.g., sectors, markets). In an age of increased outsourcing, economists noticed that when a manufacturing firm outsources parts of its business (e.g., product design) – even though the same people may be doing the same work, but now part of a new separate entity – the statistics shift to count the jobs and revenue in the service sector rather than as part of the manufacturing sector. Understandably, this creates some amount of cognitive dissonance, and the sense that perhaps the growth of the service sector is more illusion than reality, especially when sectoral counting is so sensitive to insourcing and outsourcing decisions of businesses (Triplett & Bosworth, 2003).

Bastiat (1850/1977) and Vargo and Lusch (2004) note that "things" result from skilled labor (harvesting or manufacturing requires the application of knowledge), and so argue that "service" is more fundamental than things. They claim the basis of all economic exchange is *service for service exchange*, which was much clearer before mass production and money, when the barter of custom-made offerings was the norm. The first foundational proposition of service dominant logic is that service is the fundamental basis of exchange.

As society enters the age of wikinomics (Tapscott & Williams, 2006), exchange of money for labor is not always present. Clark (1940/1957) noted the reverse trend that value created inside families was shifting to external markets that involved paying others for family-related service (e.g., child care, eating out). Service system entities are complex and dynamic (insourcing and outsourcing), and the nature of value cocreation itself is often linked to identity and reputation (wikinomics, peer production).

Marketing. Marketing as a function in business firms provides customer insights, both for existing customers and potential future customers. These insights are used by other functions (strategy, communications, production, and delivery) to improve decision making. Service is a distinct type of exchange (Judd 1964; Shostack 1977), delivered by a distinct type of process (Bitner & Brown 2006), often characterized by customized human interactions or "moments of truth" with customers (Carlzon 1987). Service is the application of competence for the benefit of another (Vargo & Lusch, 2004).

Operations. Service is a process, characterized by dependence on customer inputs (Chase 1981; Sampson & Froehle 2006). The customer input can range from a little to a lot. For example, citizens of a society confer tacit agreement to comply with laws and standard operating procedures – a sometimes small individual input, though in aggregate necessary to the proper functioning of society. At the other end of the spectrum, a person working with a doctor may be required to provide not only his or her body for surgery, but also required to eat, exercise, and make necessary financial arrangements to receive service. Self-service procedures that make use of a provider's infrastructure may require even more serious effort and customer inputs. Complex business to business (B2B) or business to government (B2G) service offerings may require hundreds or even thousands of people to interact.

Industrial and Systems Engineering. Service systems and networks present a distinct type of engineering problem characterized by customer variability (Riordan 1962; Mandelbaum & Zeltyn, 2008). By making simplifying assumptions, modeling entities as stochastic service systems becomes possible. These types of models provide needed formalisms for engineers to build simulation models of service networks, and measure performance under diverse operating assumptions and constraints. Engineers build computer-aided design tools to manage service component libraries (Sanz, Nyak & Becker, 2006).

Operations Research. Service systems and networks present a distinct type of modeling and optimization problem (Thomas & Griffin, 1996; Dietrich & Harrison, 2006). Often real-time sensors allow analytics and statistical learning methods to be applied to continuously adapt and tune performance of models. Statistical control theory, game theory, and mechanism design theory may also be used to increase the sophistication of the mathematical models to address dynamic environments, human psychology, and other factors.

Computer Science. Service is an abstraction for network-accessible capabilities with unique discovery, composition, and modeling challenges (Zhang, 2007; Sheth et. al, 2006; Endrei et. al, 2004). Computer science can be used to create software components to automate service, as well as to improve self-service. When these components are network accessible and composable, web services can allow re-use of simple building blocks. In addition, computer science approaches to modeling business and societal enterprises (with service-oriented architectures) as well as use-case models can enable new service design, and planning of work transformation or enterprise transformation projects. Service-oriented architecture (SOA) refers to networks of loosely coupled, communicating service components.

Information Systems. Information systems are service systems; service systems are work systems (Rai & Sambamurthy, 2006; Checkland & Howell, 1998/2005; Alter, 2008). If improving the performance of a service system is a priority, then that system will likely become instrumented, interconnected, and intelligent (partial algorithmic control) using information systems. Information systems create both an engineering challenge and a management challenge, as they require technology upgrades and on-going investment. The system must work as designed from functional, regulatory, and business model perspectives.

Social Sciences. Service systems are closely related to socio-technical systems and systems engineering models of enterprises (Rouse & Baba, 2006). Social systems are broader than service systems, and include social insects for example. Advanced socio-technical systems, on the other hand, are nearly isomorphic with the concept of service systems, as they require symbolic processes of valuing. Service science borrows from the social sciences, but with the premise that symbolic value-cocreation mechanisms explain change. Informal service system entities (language), formal service system entities (writing), and globally integrated formal service system entities (digitization) are three evolutionary stages (Spohrer & Maglio, 2010). At each stage, value cocreation potential increases through better use of symbol processing in people and technology, allowing improved coordination. Another relative of service science is coordination theory. Coordination theory draws from computer science, organization theory, operations research, economics, linguistics, and psychology. Coordination is the process of managing dependencies among activities (Malone & Crowston, 1994).

Behavioral Sciences. Service experience is shaped by factors, including waiting in queues and customer expectations (Maister, 1985; Chase & Dasu, 2001). Psychology matters because people are the primary source of variability in service design. Individual differences are a source of variability that designers struggle to accommodate. Nevertheless, in some ways, people are both predictably rational and predictably irrational. Behavioral sciences, including experimental economics, have useful results to improve value-cocreation mechanism design (Ariely, 2008).

Emergence of Service Science

Recently, a new science of modern service, which aims to tie together disciplinary views in a theoretically coherent and practically important way, has begun to emerge (see Table 4 for a small sampling). Of course, this whole volume is a testament to the emergence of service science and the integration challenge.

Table 4. Some recent thought related to service science

What is ...?	Proposals	References
service?	Value creation systems; co-production; value constellations	Normann & Ramirez; Normann; Wright
a science of service?	Involves technology to improve productivity and quality for B2B	IBM
proper perspective on service?	Service-Dominant Logic	Vargo & Lusch
Why under-studied?	Too many myths, too few facts	Chesbrough & Spohrer
Why now?	Economic importance; physical, information, social progression in science	Maglio, Kreulen, Srinivasan & Spohrer
a service system?	Dynamic resource configurations	Spohrer, Maglio, Bailey & Gruhl
work evolution in service?	Z-model	Spohrer & Maglio
needed to make progress?	National service innovation roadmaps reports	IfM & IBM
complexity of service networks?	Direct and indirect actors	Basole & Rouse
progress in education?	SSME and related programs	Hefley & Murphy
service entity interaction?	ISPAR	Maglio, Vargo, Caswell & Spohrer
value?	value in use	Vargo, Maglio, Akaka
needed discipline integration architecture?	Time, stakeholder/measures, resources/access-rights	Spohrer & Kwan
service system learning?	Run-Transform-Innovate	Spohrer & Maglio
service system scaling?	Digitally Connected Scaling	Hsu
the problem with local optimization?	Does not lead to global optimization	Ricketts
service system design?	Transformative technologies	Glushko; UK Royal Society
response to disasters?	Humanitarian service science	Haselkorn
response to globalization?	Intercultural service systems	Medina-Borja

What is service?   The essence of service is value creation (Normann & Ramirez, 1993; Normann, 2001).   Networked entities alternately liquefy and solidify access to resources in new higher density constellations that create more value.   Wright (2000) described human history as "evolving better *non-zero sum games*" – games that do not simply shift value (i.e., win-lose) but create more than they consume (i.e., win-win or value cocreation) – the intended meaning of Smith's "productive labor."

Could there be a science of service?   IBM (2004) reported on a workshop in which academics explored the possibility of collaborating on building a science of modern service.   The conclusion was positive, with a recognition that foundations had been put in place by pioneers from multiple academic disciplines.   However, much work remained, especially in the area of business-to-business (B2B) service. Creating a science of service would require shifting, aligning, and integrating knowledge from existing areas, as well as creating new tools and knowledge that organizations might consider proprietary.   Science is the agreed upon methods and standards of rigor used by a community to develop a body of knowledge that accounts for observable phenomenon with conceptual frameworks, models, theories, and laws that can be both empirically tested and applied within a world view or paradigm (Kuhn, 1962).   Getting a unified community to agree on what service science is, and what its top research challenge should be, was acknowledged to be non-trivial.

What would be a proper perspective or worldview on which to base a science of service?   Vargo and Lusch (2004) captured the debate that was taking place in many businesses, especially manufacturing firms with rapidly growing service revenues.   A growing realization was that goods-dominant logic (GDL) and service-dominant-logic (SDL) made different assumptions about creating and measuring *value*. SDL established a worldview for thinking about service that stands in sharp contrast to GDL, which guides most people's thinking about value and economic exchange today (Vargo & Lusch, 2004, 2008).   SDL defines service as the application of competence (knowledge) for the benefit of another.   SDL's first foundational proposition is that all human economic exchange is service-for-service exchange.   Goods can only be harvested or manufactured through the application of competence.   Most people see the value in the goods, rather than appreciating the true source, the application of competence.

Why has service been understudied?   Chesbrough and Spohrer (2006) argued that given the economic importance of the service sector, as well as two decades of US National Academy of Engineering Reports (2003) confirming this, that the area remains understudied.   In spite of evidence, the persistence of myths and conceptual confusions, with no unified service science community to refute them, has been at the root problem.   In fact, disciplinary approaches to service might be working at cross purposes, maintaining the conceptual confusions and causing policy makers and government funding agencies to be justifiably cautious. Chesbrough and Spohrer's proposed service science research manifesto was a starting point to unify researchers on a set of research challenges, and begin to overcome the myths with demonstrable progress.   They also pointed to the emergence of computer science, over fifty years earlier, which despite many challenges and delays, was ultimately established as a new discipline. Significant progress was made once researchers and practitioners aligned around a common research agenda. For service science, they suggested a research agenda with a focus on provider-customer interactions and provider-customer knowledge-sharing enabled by ICT advances.

Why now? If the economic statistics argument were the main driver, service science might have emerged at least two decades earlier, when National Academy reports were advocating more service research and technology to industrialize service components (Guile & Quinn, 1988). Maglio et. al. (2006) went beyond the normal economic statistics, arguing that in the 1800's the study of physical work (steam engines) matured into a science, in the 1900's computational work (computers), and the 2000's societal work (digital networks) would likely mature into a science. Hsu (2009) argued that digitally connected scaling creates the opportunity for modern service science. Statistics suggest the need, and digital networks create the opportunity for value cocreation mechanisms to become more widespread and more instrumented for scientific study (Berners-Lee et al, 2006; Foster, 2005).

What is a service system entity? Service is value-cocreation, that is, beneficial changes that result from communication, planning, or other purposeful interactions between distinct entities (Spohrer & Maglio, 2010). For our purposes, an entity capable of intentional value-cocreation interactions can be viewed as a service system entity (Spohrer, Maglio, Gruhl & Bailey, 2007; Maglio, Vargo, Caswell & Spohrer, 2009). They can be thought of as dynamic configurations of resources that include one or more persons, and evolve complex structure and interaction patterns (Spohrer & Maglio, 2010). A service ecology is a population of such entities that, as a whole, are better off working together than working alone (Vargo, Maglio & Akaka, 2008; Spohrer & Maglio, 2010). So our object of study is value-cocreation mechanisms, our basic abstraction is the service system entity, and our ultimate goal is to develop methods and theories that can be used to explain and improve our service ecology (Spohrer & Maglio, 2010).

What is the nature of work evolution in service? Spohrer and Maglio (2008) proposed a Z-model of work evolution for maturing service offerings. First, an offering is delivered by people, often highly skilled and specialized. Second, people using technology tools deliver the offering.   Third, standardization and migration to the lowest cost labor geography occurs.   Fourth, an automated component becomes a building block for higher value offerings. For example, (a) customer technical support calls for a start up may be handled by the director of engineering, (b) later, employees with a Frequently Asked Questions (FAQ) tool may answer the calls, (c) still later, an employee of a call center outsourcing business may answer, and (d) finally, an automated speech recognition system may be used (self service).   The customer technical support example helps illustrate the way a service system may adapt to the changing value of knowledge in the system: value-add knowledge in people, shared information, organizations, and technology.

What is needed to make progress? IfM and IBM (2008) called for nations to create *service innovation roadmaps* to accelerate investment in service research and education, specifically, for a doubling of investment before 2015. As reported in Spohrer, Ren and Gregory (this volume) nations are using such roadmaps to guide investment on a shared agenda to accelerate service innovation.

What is the relative complexity of different service networks for different industries? Basole and Rouse (2007; see also Rouse & Basole in this volume) provided a framework for modeling and calculating a measure of the complexity of different configurations and structures of service networks. Certain configurations allow innovations to spread rapidly and other configurations hinder the spread of innovations to customers. In general, public sector networks have higher complexity and lower rates of innovation spreading than private sector networks.

What progress is occurring in educating students to be prepared for a productive life in a modern service economy? Hefley and Murphy (2008) collected papers and perspectives from one of the largest events ever to focus on education for a 21st century service economy. Progress in the separate discipline silos, alignment (consensus on core concepts) and integration (common models and tools) were discussed.

How do service system entities interact? Not all interactions result in value cocreation. Maglio, Vargo, Caswell, and Spohrer (2009) presented the Interact-Service-Propose-Agree-Realize (ISPAR) model of entity interactions. Of the ten possible outcomes described, less than fifty percent result in value cocreation. However, the others may contribute value by accelerating learning curves and improving resilience.

What is value? Vargo, Maglio, and Akaka (2008) provided a service science and service-dominant logic perspective on value and value cocreation. They argued that value is fundamentally derived and determined in use – the integration and application of resources in a specific context – rather than in exchange – embedded in firm output and captured by price. The current paper builds on these ideas by introducing the concept of *processes of valuing* as one way in which entities can estimate potential for value-in-use.

What is an architectural framework for discipline alignment and integration? Spohrer and Kwan (2008) and Spohrer and Maglio (2010) provided an architecture to integrate disparate disciplines into a service science transdiscipline. The architecture links disciplines to a time dimension (past, present, and future), stakeholder and measures dimensions (customer, quality; provide, productivity; authority, compliance; competitor, sustainable innovation), and resource and access rights dimensions (people, privileged access; technology, owned-outright; organizations, leased-contracted; shared information, shared access).

What is service system learning? Building on March's (1991) exploration and exploitation model of organizational learning systems, Spohrer and Maglio (2010) developed a run-transform-innovate model of service system learning. Run-transform-innovate is terminology borrowed from IBM's CIO office, and represents best practice decision making when investing for organizational change (Sanford, 2006). Run is budget for operate and maintain. Transform is budget to copy best practices. Innovate is budget to invent new best practices. Innovate is often the riskiest, but also has the most potential for reward.

What is service system scaling? Hsu (2009) presented a theory of digitally connected scaling. Franchising is a scaling model that was used in the past. Digitally connected scaling overcomes limitations of franchising and other scaling models that require providers to establish local operations in geographies.

What is the problem with local optimization? Ricketts (2007) presented a central challenge in service system and network optimization, namely local optimization does not often lead to global optimization. In fact, local optimization is likely to increase the demand on the most bottlenecked component. Ricketts showed how to apply the Theory of Constraints to professional service businesses that depend on human knowledge and skills. This work is an excellent example of reworking a manufacturing-oriented methodology to become relevant for service businesses.

What is service system design? Glushko's framework (this volume) provides a approach to information-intensive service system design (see also Glushko & Tabas, 2009). The focus is on the information required and the responsibility of the providers and customers. The result is substitutable and combinable building blocks of service systems for different service contexts. Increasingly service design depends on STEM graduates because of the growing sophistication of service systems (UK Royal Society, 2009).

What is a service science response to disasters? Haselkorn (2008) developed the area of humanitarian service science. When a disaster occurs, such as a hurricane or earthquake, thousands of lives can plunged into turmoil and chaos. Every basic service is disrupted and quality of life suffers. How to increase the speed of rebuilding is an important area of research. Haselkorn's work demonstrates the importance of using simulation technology to plan and prepare for disasters, and accelerate rebuilding. This is an emerging frontier in engineering research that explores how to effectively design, evaluate, and predict the behavior of market-based service systems extended into non-profit areas.

What is a service science response to globalization? Medina-Borja (2008) developed the area of intercultural service science. Service delivery varies from New Delhi to New York. Whenever the provider and customer are of different cultures anomalies may arise. Outcomes are influenced by the cultural and social background of those involved. Intercultural service science will be an increasingly important source of insights to inform service system design in the next decade.

We could have chosen from hundreds of other recent publications on service systems, service networks, and service science. A more comprehensive survey is needed to do justice to the explosion of thinking in this emerging area. Nevertheless, this snapshot shows the growing importance of this area.

Complex Dimensions of Service Systems

There is a great variety of service systems – value cocreation arrangements among distinct entities.   As mentioned, a service system entity is a value-cocreation configuration of people, technology, other internal and external service system entities, and shared information (Spohrer & Maglio, 2010). This recursive definition highlights that fact that they have internal structure and external structure in which value is cocreated directly or indirectly with other service system entities. Individuals, families, firms, nations, and economies are all instances of service system entities. In this section, we describe just a few kinds of service system entities and their value-cocreation relationships to demonstrate some of the complexity inherent in understanding, improving, and innovating in service systems in the real world (see Table 5 for a summary).

Table 5. Examples of service system entities and their dimensions

Entities	Dimensions	References
Universities	People, organizations, information	Maglio, Kreulen, Srinivasan & Spohrer; Spohrer, Maglio, Bailey & Gruhl
IT service providers	People, technology, organizations, business	Blomberg; Pinhanez; Maglio, Kreulen, Srinivasan & Spohrer; Spohrer, Maglio, Bailey & Gruhl
Contact centers	People, technology, information	Cheng, Krishna, Boyette, & Bethea; Maglio, Kreulen, Srinivasan & Spohrer
Banking services	People, processes, information, organizations, business	Alter; Oliva & Sterman
Internal process transformations	Organizations, processes, technology, business	Krishna, Bailey & Lelescu,

Universities. Universities are service system entities (Maglio et al, 2006; Spohrer et al, 2007). They aim to transform student knowledge. Typically, the cost is not borne by students alone; rather, universities are supported by a number of sources, including individual, corporate, non-profit, and government sponsors. Although potentially beneficial to everyone involved, this economic arrangement results in a service equation that is much more complex than that of a single, unambiguous service client.   Rather than managing a single value-cocreation relationship, universities manage relationships among multiple clients and partners, who may or may not know or care about the others.   Expectations and results vary.   The student is likely to judge quality on qualitative measures, whereas a corporate or government supporter might rely more on collective quantitative measures, such as standardized performance measures and number of graduates.

IT service providers. An IT service provider offers to take over the operation and maintenance of client's IT investments, and to do it better and cheaper than the client–IT outsourcing (see also Maglio et al, 2006; Spohrer et al, 2007). The provider aims to improve the efficiency of client IT operations, reducing cost over time by applying unique skills, experience, and capabilities. The size and nature of outsourcing service arrangements vary from multi-billion dollar mega-deals, in which the service provider takes over all IT investments of a large company, to smaller deals in which the provider agrees to just take over a single functional area, such as help-desk operations or web-server operations. The structure of the deal is captured in a contract. Contractual service level agreements (SLAs) are the metrics that match client business objectives to quantifiable performance indicators. IT outsourcing SLAs often include commitments by the provider to perform some activity within an agreed to amount of time (e.g., resolve high severity IT-related problems in less than 60 minutes), or to maintain some minimal level of service availability (e.g., no more than 120 number of minutes down-time per unit month). Though SLAs are conventional and useful, achieving SLAs is just one measure of client satisfaction, and serve mainly as a starting point for a long-term relationship between provider and client (Blomberg, 2008). The client often has substantial responsibilities even after the contract is signed, for instance alerting the provider to problems, providing information when appropriate, and even maintaining machines that might be physically located at the client site (Pinhanez, 2008). As service system entities, IT service providers depend on people, technology, and organizations both internally and externally, and engage in formal business relationships with clients and partners.

Contact centers. Contact centers staff the phones for an enterprise, handling contacts from customers such as order-taking, complaint-handling, or problem-resolving (Maglio et al, 2006). Most view contact centers as cost centers to be controlled or reduced. From a service provider's perspective, the model is simple: stop incoming calls when possible; if the call must be taken, minimize time to resolve it; if the problem cannot be resolved by phone, dispatch service at the lowest cost. Stakeholders include the client that has outsourced customer contact; the service provider; call takers; individual accounts; schedulers; ecosystem of business partners; and quality managers. Each stakeholder has distinct goals. For instance, the client wants reliable service provided in a cost-effective and high-quality way, and the service provider wants to increase revenue, reduce cost, and maximize profit. Analysis of stakeholders, their pain points, and their measurements reveal the interrelatedness of the system components internally and externally. By taking an end-to-end view, focusing on transforming the system by introducing appropriate processes, metrics, technology, and tools to work in concert across stakeholders, transformation can be accomplished as a combination of process changes, organizational changes, technology changes, and tool changes (Cheng et al, 2007). For example, if one area of high cost is call volume routed from Level 1 (basic, inexpensive call takers) to Level 3 (highly skilled, expensive call takers), several corrective actions may be taken. The problems that flow to Level 3 can be better understood and Level 1 call takers can be trained in those problem areas. Better tools for employees and self-service for end users can also be introduced. In the end, coordinating people, technology, and information across the system is the only sensible approach for improving performance of complex contact centers.

Banking services. We can consider bank loan approval as a kind of service system entity that requires customers to interact with bank documents and personnel (Alter, 2008). Stakeholders include the applicant, loan officer, credit analysts, loan committee, risk managers, and more. Processes include filling out forms, sharing documents, approval processes, and explanation of results, among many others. More precisely, requests may arrive by phone (inquiries), mail (customer requests and communications with branches), and daily computer-generated reports identifying problematic accounts that require immediate action, such as overdrafts, and missing payments (Oliva & Sterman, 2001). For most requests, either a letter or a phone conversation with the customer results. The organizational incentives and lines of communication within the bank must be appropriately aligned or else performance will suffer (Oliva & Sterman, 2001).

Internal process transformation. Process transformation in any large enterprise can be difficult, as it requires transformation in social, technical, and organizational systems at once (Sanford, 2006). For instance, deploying a new technology to replace a web-based ordering system required alignment of stakeholders including the CIO's office, the team responsible for web ordering, the team developing the new technology, client organizations, and more (Krishna, Bailey & Lelescu, 2007). Different stakeholders have different incentives. A change that looks appropriate to one stakeholder (e.g., for cost reasons) might seem inappropriate to another (e.g., harder to use or integrate into existing systems).

Making Progress: Structures and Mechanisms Coevolving

Abstractly, service science studies entities, interactions, and outcomes. The entities are dynamic configurations of resources. When the entities interact to cocreate value, they access resources in a coordinated and purposeful manner. Consistent value cocreation outcomes are not accidents – they depend on sophisticated structures and mechanisms. More concretely, over the course of human history, the structures and mechanisms that give rise to value cocreation both change and remain the same. Division of labor (mechanism) within families or kin groups (structure) existed thousands of generations ago, and today division of labor within businesses and nations is still visible. Yet many modern value cocreation mechanisms (and their associated structures) also exist – such as compound interest (banks), installment payment plans (retail stores and credit card companies), and granting patents (nations).

In this section, we connect service-oriented structures and mechanisms to reasoning with symbols about the knowledge of value (and value of knowledge). To achieve this connection, we revisit the concept of *physical symbol systems*, and show that service systems are in fact physical symbol systems.

Physical Symbol Systems

Simon (1996) suggested that sciences of the human-made ("artificial") world ought to complement sciences of the natural world. The human-made world contains two primary types of artifacts: physical artifacts such as a car, and symbolic artifacts such as the Pythagorean Theorem. Both are outcomes of human creativity, one tangible, the other intangible. Further thought reveals two secondary types of artifacts: organizational entities such as the United States, and professional entities such as jazz musicians. Of course, it is no accident that these four types of artifacts correspond to the four types of resources in service science (Spohrer & Maglio, 2010): A car or any other technology or part of the environment is physical and has no legal rights; the Pythagorean Theorem or any other shared information is not physical and has no rights; the United States or any other formal organization is not physical and has legal rights; a jazz musician, a person, is physical and has rights. We view service science as one of Simon's *sciences of the artificial.*

Simon (1996) observed that the growing hierarchical complexity of the artificial world was not unlike that found in the biological world. Hierarchical complexity means that common building blocks can be found repeatedly, thus demonstrating that complex things are built from simpler things, if one can just understand the mechanisms that prefer certain combinations over others. For biology, Darwin's (1872) theory of evolution proposed the mechanism of natural selection to explain the way that essentially random processes could give rise to the diversity and complexity of species. Kaufman (1995) proposed autocatalysis as an additional mechanism to explain the chemical foundations of certain biological processes in networks that underlie the complexity and diversity of biological species. Mechanisms are part of the explanations for how complex structures arise – *mechanisms and structures coevolve.*

Simon (1996) saw a profound and essential difference between the two types of complex systems, natural and artificial. Unlike the biological world, artifacts in the human-made world are designed with a purpose: cars for transportation, Pythagorean Theorem to solve construction problems, the United States to form a more perfect union, and jazz musicians for entertainment. Human-made artifacts serve a purpose. Symbols and symbolic reasoning are used to make and improve artifacts. Humans are unique in the quantity and quality of symbol use, a truly symbolic species (Deacon, 1997).

Newell and Simon (1976) posited that physical symbol systems are necessary and sufficient for intelligent behavior of systems in the real world. Symbols can be generated in an arbitrary way (interpretation), put into correspondence with items in the world (designation), and support accumulation of new knowledge (learning). Broadly speaking, a physical symbol system is a real-world entity that uses symbols to shape its future behavior. The symbols must be encoded in physical substances. The symbols must be used to guide both internal behavior and mediate interactions with the environment.

Service systems are physical symbol systems that compute the changing value of knowledge in the global service system ecology. Structures and mechanisms are coevolving based on knowledge of how best to use symbols to calculate value. This does not mean that symbols are the only way to calculate value; we suggest only that the concept of value includes symbolic reasoning (along with much more). Nevertheless, structures and mechanisms are coevolving in a highly constrained manner because of increasing use of symbolic reasoning in processes of valuing, that is, in the algorithms people use to calculate value. For example, if our algorithm for calculating value is "benefits minus costs," then the coevolution of structures and mechanisms for value is shaped by "benefits minus costs." Of course, the constraints also include real world selection pressures and autocatalytic properties of value cocreation phenomena. If our algorithm for calculating value is flawed, reality will eventually show through. So if mortgaged-backed securities in fact are not spreading and reducing risks, but instead are concentrating and increasing risk in a few institutions, then the bubble will burst and our understanding of the value of that knowledge will begin to be adjusted. The bottom line is simply to understand that structures and mechanisms are coevolving, and service science should help explain both history (how did we get here?) and possible futures (where are we going?).

History: How did we get here?

The coevolution of structures and mechanisms is part of every science, and begins with physics (particles and forces) and proceeds forward. Chemistry (molecules and forces) and biology (life forms and processes) arise next in the sequence. One view of biology is in terms of three levels of structures (uni-cell, multi-cell, and neural-social).

Service science can also be viewed in terms of three levels of entity structures (informal, formal, and globally-integrated-formal). Because structures and mechanisms coevolve, informal entities begin when spoken language (cognitive technology) and tools (physical technology) in family or kinship group structures support division of labor and coordinated interactions at a level that separates humans from their primate ancestors (Deacon, 1997). Formal service system entities begin when written laws, money, and agriculture in early towns and cities support division of labor and coordinated interactions that separates urban dwellers (and those connected into extensive supply chains) from hunter-gathers living directly off the land (Seabright, 2005). Trusting strangers and mechanisms for validating identity and reputations of entities becomes increasingly important, when one is in frequent contact with strangers in roles, rather than well-known kin in roles. Next, globally integrated formal service system entities begin when the internet and smart phones in early on-line communities and social networking structures allow division of labor and coordinated interactions to expand into blended virtual and augmented-reality worlds for IT-augmented humans and enterprises (Engelbart, 1962, 1980; Spohrer, 1999; Spohrer & Engelbart, 2004; Palmisano, 2006).

Friedman (2008) provided a recent evolutionary account of humans changing to address the fundamental social dilemma: what is good for the individual is not always what is good for the group. Morals are a group's shared understanding of what is right and wrong, and how people are supposed to behave, especially when opportunities for cooperation present themselves. What biologists call mutualism, economists call mutual benefit – and its existence is not easy to explain.

Only within the last fifty years did *kinship selection* (the so called "selfish gene") arise as an explanation. Simply put, the more closely related two people are, the more logical it is to suppose that what benefits a kin in fact benefits the individual. So if people behave according to a "kinship enhanced" value equation, genes are more likely to accrue benefits and survive, even if an individual sacrifices some benefits or incurs some additional costs. Assume that an individual is likely to perform an action if the likely benefits (B) minus the likely costs (C) are greater than zero (B-C>0). The kinship-enhanced value equation that promotes the survival of the family genes is simply (rB-C>0), where r is the degree of relatedness of the individuals. For an individual or an identical twin, r=1.0. For an immediate family member (mother, father, sibling), r = 0.5 because half the genes are in common. Uncles and aunts share a quarter of their genes with nieces and nephews, so r=0.25. The survival of the family genes is improved with this kinship-enhanced value equation.

But what about cooperating with those who are not related? That is, when the one who benefits (recipient) does not have a significant number of genes in common with the individual who incurs the cost of helping. Only within the last forty years has an explanation arisen that piggy-backs on top of the kinship-enhanced value equation. The mechanism is known as *reciprocity*, and involves the social norm that maintains one's reputation as a useful identity in a group. Reciprocity says that it is important to reciprocate and return gifts of roughly the same value or slightly more value after a not-too-long period. The "reciprocity enhanced" value equation is simply (dB-C>0), where d plays a role similar to r and can vary between 0 and 1. Specifically, d=q/(1+i)t, where q is the probability the favor will be returned (0 to 1) based on the reputation of the individual, i is an applicable interest rate (for weighing alternative investments of time, effort, etc.), and t is the time delay (0 to infinity). Assuming that recipient has a good reputation as a reciprocator, and the cost is relatively low, then whether the recipient helps, the genes are likely to have an increased chance of survival through cooperating with others. As in the evolutionary accounts of Wright (2000), Seabright (2005), and many others, Friedman's (2008) account highlights that mutual benefits and learning better ways to play win-win, benefit-benefit, or non-zero-sum games – what we call value cocreation – is central.

Future: Where are we going?

Locally, structures and mechanisms coevolve to improve repeatable value-cocreation outcomes. Whole segments of the economy change based on new knowledge that has an impact on entities' value equations and processes of valuing. For example, energy from wood, then coal, then oil or natural gas is a progression that has been influenced by reasoning about the value of new extraction and distribution knowledge.

So where are we going? How are the processes of valuing being changed by new knowledge about service systems operating in the areas of healthcare, insurance, education, government, and others? Or based on new knowledge in academic disciplines, such as engineering, economics, operations research, mechanism design, management of information systems, industrial and systems engineering, economics and law, and many others? How is new knowledge about failures changing things? As incentives in certain areas become more and more high powered to accelerate change even more rapidly, what safeguards are being put in place to ensure that risks are appropriately bounded?

Two ends of the spectrum seem especially poised for change: (a) people and education, and (b) planet and investment. We will examine each in turn.

People and Education. People are the fundamental building blocks of service systems, and they need to become better prepared by education and lifelong-learning experiences to live with and contribute to STEM-driven accelerating change. Figure 1 shows the range of systems and disciplines that 21st century professionals in general, and service scientists in particular, will likely need to know about in their job roles (Spohrer, Golinelli, Piciocchi & Bassano, in preparation; Spohrer & Maglio, 2010). The list of systems includes the major types for which people are customers. The list of disciplines includes those associated with the major dimensions of service systems.

The average person born in the later years of the US baby boom held 10.8 jobs from age 18 to age 42 (BLS, 2008). For individuals in modern society, relatively frequent job-role changes seem to be the norm. Preparing students for this type of challenging job-change environment is not easy. The days in which an engineer could find a stable career in one manufacturing business are gone (Smerdon, 1996). Today, life-long learning is needed to prepare engineers for a series of customer engagements or service projects, either as part of a consulting firm or as a specialist for hire (UK Royal Society, 2009).

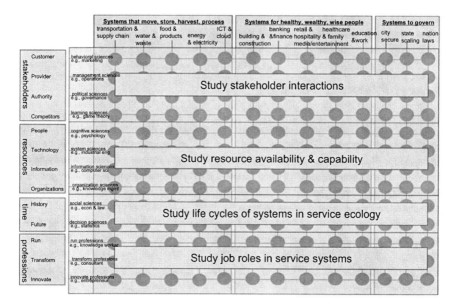

Figure 1. Service science: systems (13) and disciplines (10) or professions (3)

Figure 2 schematically shows what a T-shaped professional looks like with deep problem solving skills in one discipline and one system, as well as broad communication skills across many disciplines and systems (Donofrio, Sanchez & Spohrer, 2009; Donofrio & Spohrer, in preparation). The evidence that supports the need for more T-shaped professionals at the national level is beginning to appear. Using thirty years of economic data related to job descriptions, Levy and Murnane (2004) examined how computers create and enhance some jobs, while they eliminate and redistribute other jobs, resulting in a clear trend in U.S. occupational structure with most job growth in higher-end, high-skilled occupations, and most job elimination in the lower-end, low-skilled occupations. Their recommendation is to recognize this division and to prepare the population for the high-wage and high-skilled jobs that are rapidly growing in number – jobs that use computers and require extensive problem solving (depth) and interpersonal communication (breadth).

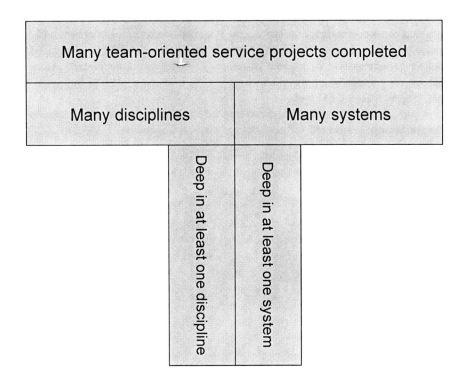

Figure 2. T-shaped professional: Deep and broad

Planet and Investment. Planet Earth needs an investment strategy that – like Moore's law for computing – leads to continuous and sustainable improvements in quality of life. Figure 3 depicts our world (largest circle) made up of many nations (next largest circles), states of regions (next smaller circles), and cities (next smaller circles) with universities (smallest circles) at their centers. In our view, each of these is a type of service system entity. The planet is getting smarter as more systems are becoming instrumented (sensors), interconnected (communications), and intelligent (algorithms help make decisions). For example, smarter cities will include many smarter subsystems, including transportation. Smarter transportation can be safer and more efficient in part because of more sensors in and around the roads as well as in cars and other vehicles that are wirelessly interconnected and can communicate about road hazards and congestions, as well as provide drivers with useful navigation and intelligent decision-making tools (IBM, 2009; see also Korsten & Sieder, 2010).

Each governing authority of each service system entity has a resource allocation decision to make – how many resources to allocate to run, transform, or innovate. As nations, states, and cities validate innovations, other nations, states, or cities that are ready can copy those best practices to improve their own operations. Becoming more systematic about these investments should lead to accelerating value cocreation, as more of the world's service systems benefit from applying proven knowledge to make their systems smarter. These efforts will be accelerated even further by the development of a computer-aided design (CAD) tool for service system design and engineering. Nearly all human-made systems that are on continuous improvement trajectories, from computers to buildings to cars, benefit from a CAD tool.

In sum, there are strong indications that improvements in coevolving structure and mechanism are poised for accelerating change (Singularity University, 2009; Spohrer & Engelbart, 2004).

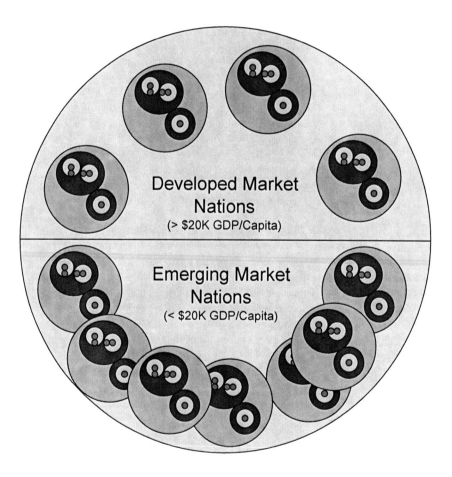

Figure 3. Planet Earth as a system of nested service systems

Conclusion

Natural sciences explain the origin and evolution of natural things. Artificial sciences explain artificial things – things designed by humans to serve a human purpose. Value cocreation is a human purpose. Service science is value cocreation science, and studies service system entity structures and their interaction mechanisms. Service science as a specialization of systems science attempts to integrate elements of many disciplines and systems around the theme of value cocreation (Spohrer & Maglio, 2010).

People accumulate knowledge of means (mechanisms) and ends (structural purposes). When means fail, we prop them back up or replace them with more reliable ones over time. People accumulate knowledge of means and ends that involve all the types of enduring resources that can be part of a service system entity: physical and non-physical resources, and resources with rights and without rights.

Change happens for a reason. Mechanisms underlie all events and all change. Scientists work to identify and validate symbolic representations of mechanisms. If change is predictable, it is because the mechanisms are well-established and stable. From a service science perspective, the social world (value cocreation mechanisms) arose from the physical world (physical mechanism) when people (the first service system entities) began to trust service (value cocreation) mechanisms (e.g., division of labor) the way they trust physical mechanisms (e.g., the sun will rise tomorrow). A sunrise does not require trust to operate, but division of labor does. Money stops working when we stop trusting in its value (Collins & Kusch, 1998; Friedman 2008).

Service science seeks to be a science based on reliable mechanisms, just as natural science is based on reliable mechanisms. From a human perspective, sometimes natural mechanisms fail to act reliably. This may be because assumptions are invalid, or other mechanisms are at work (e.g., a plane fails to fall from the sky because of Bernoulli's principle). The same is true of service (value cocreation) mechanisms. If assumptions are invalid or other mechanisms are at work, predictions may not be reliable. For example, when a computer program does not operate as predicted, it is because of invalid assumptions or other mechanisms at work. Science works to discover mechanisms, and to expose invalid assumptions and other mechanisms at work.

Here, we argued that service (value cocreation) and service systems are appropriate objects of study, and that a science of service can provide a foundation for creating lasting improvements to service systems. We sketched answers to a few basic questions about service, service system entity structure, and value cocreation mechanisms.

What is service? Service is value cocreation. Service phenomena occur when entities interact according to agreed to mechanisms that (normatively) result in value cocreation outcomes (win-win or benefit-benefit interactions).

What is a service system entity? A service system entity is a dynamic configuration of resources that can agree to grant access rights to its resources as a means (mechanism) to realize value cocreation ends (structural change outcomes) from its interactions with others.   Types of service system entity structures include: people, businesses, not-for-profit organizations, universities, cities, states, nations, and non-government organizations.   Our world is a diverse (multiple populations) ecology of interacting service systems.   Service systems adapt to the changing knowledge of value (and value of knowledge) in the ecology.   Service systems have run, transform, and innovate mechanisms to improve value cocreation interactions. They increasingly use symbols to represent, to reason and communicate about, and to implement value cocreation mechanisms.   Symbolic reasoning is used to improve the reliability of the mechanisms, and recover more rapidly from failures.

What is a value cocreation mechanism?   Mechanisms change the world (i.e., change structures, both physical and symbolic).   Value cocreation mechanisms are either value-proposition-based or governance-mechanisms-based interactions that can create change.   Value propositions are agreements between service system entities to share or exchange access to resources in order to change the world to their mutual benefit.   Because all interactions are not value-proposition-based and not all value-proposition-based interactions do not realize value-cocreation according to plan, authorities can resolve disputes (using coercion, if necessary) to change the world in prescribed or novel ways.

What is service science?   Service science is the study of service system entity structures and value cocreation mechanisms.   Service science or Service Science, Management, Engineering, and Design (SSMED) aims to understand and catalog these structures and mechanisms.   This understanding can be applied to advance our ability to design, improve, and scale service systems for practical business and societal purposes (quality, productivity, compliance, and sustainable innovation). Service science is a transdisciplinary undertaking and many academic disciplines have knowledge and methods to contribute, and practitioners working with real-world systems can contribute too.

In this chapter, we have set out the context and background, and pointed toward one possible direction for service science, namely a focus on symbolic approaches to understanding service system entity structures and value cocreation mechanisms.   But nothing is settled.   And much work remains to be done.

References

Alter, S. (2008). Service system fundamentals: Work system, value chain, and life cycle. *IBM Systems Journal*, 47, 71–85.
Anderson, J. C., Kumar, N. & Narus, J. A. (2007). *Value Merchants: Demonstrating and Documenting Superior Value in Business Markets*. Harvard Business School Press. Cambridge, MA.

Ariely, D. (2008). *Predictably Irrational: The Hidden Forces That Shape Our Decisions*. Harper Collins. New York, NY.

Ark, B. van, Broersma, L. & den Hertog, P. (2003). Services Innovation, Performance and Policy: A Review. Research Series No. 6, Strategy, Research & International Co-operation Department, Ministry of Economic Affairs, The Hague.

Basole, R. C. & Rouse, W. B. (2008). Complexity of service value networks: Conceptualization and empirical investigation. *IBM Systems Journal*, 47(1), 53-70.

Bastiat, F. (1850/1979). *Economic Harmonies. The Foundation for Economics Education*. Irvington-on-Hudson, NY.

Baumol, W. J. (2002). Services as leaders and the leader of the services, in J. Gadrey and F. Gallouj (eds.) *Productivity, Innovation and Knowledge in Services: New Economic & Socio-Economic Approaches*. Edward Elgar, Cheltenham, U.K., pp. 147-163.

Baumol, W. J. & Bowen, W. G. (1966). *Performing Arts: The Economic Dilemma*. New York: The Twentieth Century Fund.

Berners-Lee, T., Hall, W., Hendler, J., Shadbolt, N. & Weitzner, D. (2006). Creating a science of the web, *Science* 313 (August 2006), 769-771.

Berry, L. L. & Parasuraman, A. (1993). Building a new academic field-the case of services marketing. *Journal of Retailing*. 69(1), 13-60

Bitner M. J. and Brown, S. W. (2006). The evolution and discovery of services science in business schools. *Communications of the ACM*, 49(7),. 73–78.

BLS (2008). Number of jobs held, labor market activity, and earnings growth among the youngest baby boomers: Results from a longitudinal survey. US Bureau of Labor Statistics. USDL 08-0860. URL: http://www.bls.gov/news.release/pdf/nlsoy.pdf

Blomberg, J. (2008). Negotiating meaning of shared information in service system encounters. *European Management Journal*, 26, 213–222.

Bolton, R. N., Smith, A. K. & Wagner, J. (2003) Striking the right balance: Designing service to enhance business-to-business relationships. *Journal of Service Research*, 5(4), 271-291.

Brown, S. W., Fisk, R. P., Bitner, M. J. (1994). The development and emergence of services marketing thought. *International Journal of Service Industry Management*. 5(1), 21-48.

Carlzon, J. (1987). *Moments of Truth*. Cambridge, MA: Ballinger.

Chase, R. B. (1981). The customer contact approach to services: Theoretical bases and practical extensions. *Operations Research*, 29(4), 698-706.

Chase, R. B. & Dasu, S. (2001). Want to perfect your company's service? Use behavioral science. *Harvard Business Review*, 79(6), 78-84.

Checkland, P. & Holwell, S. (1998/2005). *Information, Systems, and Information Systems: Making Sense of the Field*. Wiley. Chichester, UK.

Cheng, I., Krishna, V., Boyette, N. & Bethea, J. (2007). Towards and agile service system for a global call center. *BPSC 2007*: 125–137

Chesbrough, H. & Spohrer, J. (2006). A research manifesto for services science. *Communications of the ACM*, 49(7), 35-40.

Christopher, M., Payne, A. & Ballantyne, D. (1991). *Relationship Marketing: Bringing Quality, Customer Service and Marketing Together*. Butterworth-Heinemann, Oxford.

Clark, C. (1940/1957). *Conditions of Economic Progress*. Third Edition. Macmillan. New York, NY.

Collins, H. & Kusch, M. (1998). *The shape of actions*. MIT Press. Cambridge, MA.

Darwin, C. (1872). *The Origin Of Species*. London, John Murray.

Deacon, T. W. (1997). *The Symbolic Species: The Co-Evolution of Language and the Brain*. Norton. New York, NY.

Davis, M. M. (1991). How long should a customer wait for service? *Decision Sciences*, 22(2), 421-434.

Dietrich, B. & Harrison, T. (2006). Serving the services industry. *OR/MS Today*, 33(3) (June).

Donofrio, N., Sanchez, C. & Spohrer, J. (2009). Collaborative innovation and service systems: Implications for institutions and disciplines, in D. Grasso (ed.) *Holistic Engineering*.

Donofrio, N. & Spohrer, J. (In Preparation). Research-driven medical education and practice: A case for T-shaped professionals.

Endrei, M., Ang, J., Arsanjani, A., Chua, S., Comte, P., Krogdahl, P., Luo, M. & Newling, N. (2004). *Patterns: Service-Oriented Architecture and Web Services*. IBM Red Books.

Edvardsson, B., Enquist, B., Johnston, R. (2005). Cocreating customer value through hyperreality in the prepurchase service experience. *Journal of Service Research*, 8(2), 149-161.

Edvardsson, B., Gustafsson, A. & Roos, I. (2005). Service portraits in service research: a critical. *International Journal of Service Industry Management*, 16(1), 107-121.

Engelbart, D. C. (1962). Augmenting Human Intellect: A Conceptual Framework. Summary Report AFOSR-3223 under Contract AF 49(638)-1024, SRI Project 3578 for Air Force Office of Scientific Research, Stanford Research Institute, Menlo Park, Ca., October 1962.

Engelbart, D. C. (1980). Evolving the organization of the future: A point of view, *Proceedings of the Stanford International Symposium on Office Automation*, March 23-25, 1980.

Fitzsimmons, J. A. & Fitzsimmons, M. J. (2007). *Service management: Operations, Strategy, Information Technology*. Sixth edition, McGraw-Hill Irwin, New York, NY.

Foster, I. (2005). Service-oriented science. *Science*, 308, 814-817.

Friedman, D. (2008). *Morals and markets: An evolutionary account of the modern world*. Palgrave Macmillan. New York. NY.

Gadrey, J. & Gallouj, F. (2002). *Productivity, Innovation and Knowledge in Services: New Economic & Socio-Economic Approaches*. Edward Elgar Cheltenham, U.K.

Glushko, R. J. & Tabas, L. (2009). Designing service systems by bridging the "front stage" and "back stage." *Information Systems and E-Business Management*, 7

Grove, S. J. & Fisk, R. P. (1992). The service experience as theater. *Advances in Consumer Research*, 19, 455-61.

Gronross, C. (1977). A service-oriented approach to marketing of services. *European Journal of Marketing*. 8, 588-601.

Guile, B. R. & Quinn, J. B. (1988). *Managing Innovation: Cases from the Services Industry*. National Academy Press, Washington, DC.

Gummesson, E. (1977). *The marketing and purchasing of professional services*. Stockholm: Marketing Technology Center.

Gummesson, E. (2007). Exit Services marketing – Enter service marketing. *Journal of Consumer Behaviour*, 6(2), 113-141.

Gustafsson, A. & Johnson, M. D. (2003). *Competing in a Service Economy: How to Create Competitive Advantage Through Service Development and Innovation*. Wiley/Jossey-Bass. San Francisco, CA.

Gutek, B. (1995). *The Dynamics of Service : Reflections on the Changing Nature of Customer/Provider Interactions*. San Francisco, Calif : Jossey-Bass, 1995.

Haselkorn, M. (2008). Towards a Research Program in Humanitarian Service Science and Engineering. In *Proceedings of the 5th International ISCRAM Conference*, Washington D.C., USA.

Hefley, B. & Murphy, W. (2008). *Service Science, Management and Engineering: Education for the 21st Century*. Springer, New York.

Herzenberg, S., Alic, J., & Wial, H. (1998). *New Rules for a New Economy: Employment and Opportunity in Postindustrial America*. Ithaca, NY: Cornell University ILR Press.

Heskett, J., Sasser, W. E., Jr., & Schlesinger, L. (1997). *The Service Profit Chain: How Leading Companies Link Profit and Growth to Loyalty, Satisfaction, and Value*. New York: Free Press.

Hill, T. P. (1977). On goods and services. *Review of Income and Wealth*. 23(4), 314–339.

Hsu, C. (2009). *Service Science: Design for Scaling and Transformation*. World Scientific and Imperial College Press, Singapore.

IBM (2004). Services science: A new academic discipline. Report, http://domino.research.ibm.com/comm/www_fs.nsf/ images/fsr/$FILE/summit_report.pdf

IBM (2009). Smarter Planet Initiative. URL: http://www.ibm.com/think

IfM & IBM (2008). *Succeeding through Service Innovation: A Service Perspective for Education, Research, Business and Government.* Cambridge, UK: University of Cambridge Institute for Manufacturing. ISBN: 978-1-902546-65-0

Johnston, R. (1989). The customer as employee. *International Journal of Operations & Production,* 9(5), 15-23.

Judd, R. C. (1964). The case for redefining services. *Journal of Marketing,* 28(1), 58-59.

Kauffman, S. (1995). *At Home in the Universe: The Search for Laws of Complexity.* Oxford: Oxford University Press.

Korsten, P. & Seider, C. (2010). The world's US$4 trillion challenge: Using a system-of-systems approach to build a smarter planet. IBM Institute for Business Value.

Krishna, V., Bailey, J. & Lelescu, A. (2007). Intelligent document gateway - A service system analysis. *IEEE SCC 2007,* 636–643

Kuhn, T. S. (1962). *The Structure of Scientific Revolutions.* Chicago: University of Chicago Press.

Larson, R. C. (1987). Perspectives on queues: Social justice and the psychology of queueing. *Operations Research,* 35(6), 895–905.

Levitt, T. (1972). Production-line approach to service. *Harvard Business Review,* Sept. - Oct, 41-52.

Levitt, T. (1976). The industrialization of service. *Harvard Business Review,* 54(5), 63-74.

Levy, F, & Murnane, R. J. (2004). T*he New Division of Labor: How Computers Are Creating the Next Job Market.* Princeton University Press.

Lovelock, C. & Gummesson, E. (2004). Whither services marketing? In search of a new paradigm and fresh perspectives. *Journal of Service Research,* 7(1), 20-41.

Maglio, P. P. & Spohrer, J. (2008). Fundamentals of service science. *Journal of the Academy of Marketing Science,* 36, 18-20.

Maglio, P. P., Srinivasan, S., Kreulen, J. T. & Spohrer, J. (2006). Service systems, service scientists, SSME, and innovation. *Communications of the ACM,* 49(7), 81-85.

Maglio, P. P., Vargo, S. L., Caswell, N. & Spohrer, J. (2009). The service system is the basic abstraction of service science. *Information Systems and e-business Management,* 7.

Maister, D. H. (1985), The psychology of waiting lines, in J. D. Czepiel, M. R. Solomon, & C. F. Surprenant, (eds.) *The Service Encounter,* pp. 113–123. Lexington, MA: Lexington Books.

Maister, D. H. (1993). *Managing the Professional Service Firm.* Simon & Schuster. New York, NY.

Malone, T. W. & Crowston, K. (1994). The interdisciplinary study of coordination, *ACM Computing Surveys,* 26(1), 87-119.

Mandelbaum, A. & Zeltyn, S. (2008). Service engineering of call centers: Research, teaching, and practice. In B. Hefley & W. Murphy (eds.) *Service Science, Management, and Engineering: Education for the 21st Century.* Springer. New York, NY.

March, J. G. (1991). Exploration and exploitation in organizational learning. *Organization Science,* 2(1), 71-87.

Medina-Borja, A. (2008). Models of intercultural service systems: Scholarly discussion for building a research agenda. Workshop website: http://ininweb.uprm.edu/isser/nsfworkshop/index.htm

Menor L. J., Tatikonda, M. V. & Sampson, S. E. (2002). New service development: Areas for exploitation and exploration. *Journal of Operations Management,* 20(2), 135-157.

Miles, I. (2006). Innovation in services. In J Fagerberg, D. C. Mowery & R. R. Nelson (eds.) *The Oxford Handbook of Innovation.* Oxford University Press. Oxford, UK.

Miles, I. (2008). Patterns of innovation in service industries. *IBM Systems Journal,* 47(1), 115-128

Mills,P. K. & Moberg, D. J. (1982). Perspectives on the technology of service operations. *Academy of Management Review,* 7(3), 467-478.

Newell, A. (1980). Physical symbol systems. *Cognitive Science,* 4(2), 135-183.

Newell, A. & Simon, H. A. (1976). Computer science as empirical inquiry: symbols and search. *Communications of the ACM*, 19, 113-126.

Normann, R. (2001). *Reframing Business: When the Map Changes the Landscape.* Wiley, Chichester, New Sussex

Normann, R. & Ramirez, R. (1993). From value chain to value constellation: Designing interactive strategy. *Harvard Business Review*, 71(4), 65–77.

Oliva, R. & Sterman, J. D. (2001). Cutting corners and working overtime: Quality erosion in the service industry. *Management Science*, 47(7), 894-914.

Palmisano, S. J. (2006). The globally integrated enterprise. *Foreign Affairs*, 85(3), 127–136.

Parasuraman, A., Zeithaml, V. A. & Berry, L. L. (1985). A conceptual model of service quality and its implications for future research. *Journal of Marketing*, 49(4), 41-50.

Pattee, H. H. (2001). The physics of symbols: bridging the epistemic cut. *Biosystems*, 60, 5-21.

Pine, B. J. & Gilmore, J. H. (1999). *The Experience Economy: Work is Theatre and Every Business a Stage.* Harvard Business School Press. Boston, MA.

Pinhanez, C. (2008). Service systems as customer-intensive systems and its implications for service science and engineering. *HICSS 2008.*

Quinn, J. B. & Paquette, P. C. (1990). Technology in service: creating organizational revolutions. *Sloan Management Review*, 67-78.

Rai, A. & Sambamurthy, V. (2006). Editorial notes: The growth of interest in services management: opportunities for information system scholars. *Information Systems Research*, 17(4), 327-331.

Ricardo, D. (1817/2004). *The Principles of Political Economy and Taxation.* Dover Publications. Mineola, NY.

Ricketts J. A. (2007). *Reaching the Goal: How Managers Improve a Services Business Using Goldratt's Theory of Constraints.* IBM Press.

Riordan, J. (1962). *Stochastic Service Systems.* Wiley, New York, NY.

Roth, A. V. & Menor, L. J. (2003). Insights into service operations management: A research agenda. *POMS*, 12(2), 145-164.

Rouse, W. B. & Baba, M. L. (2006). Enterprise transformation. *Communications of the ACM*, 49(7), 67-72.

Rust, R. T., Zeithaml, V. A. & Lemon, K. N. (2000). *Driving Customer Equity: How Customer Lifetime Value is Reshaping Corporate Strategy.* Free Press.

Sampson, S. E. & Froehle, C. M. (2006). Foundations and implications of a proposed unified services theory. *Production and Operations Management*, 15(2), 329-343.

Sanford, L. S. (2006). *Let go to grow: Escaping the commodity trap.* Prentice Hall. New York, NY.

Sanz, J. L., Nayak, N., & Becker, V. (2006). Business services as a new operational model for enterprises and ecosystems. The 8th IEEE International Conference on E-Commerce Technology and The 3rd IEEE International Conference on Enterprise Computing, E-commerce, and E-services (CEC/EEE'06).

Schneider, B. & Bowen, D. E. (1993). The service organization: Human resources management is crucial. *Organizational Dynamics*, 21(4), 39-52.

Seabright, P. (2005). *The Company of Strangers: A Natural History of Economic Life.* Princeton University. Princeton, NJ.

Sheth, A., Verma, K. & Gomadam, K. (2006). Semantics to energize the full services spectrum. *Communications of the ACM*, 49(7), 55–61.

Shostack, G. L. (1977). Breaking free from product marketing. *Journal of Marketing*, 41(2), 73-80.

Simon, H. A. (1996). *Sciences of the Artificial.* 3rd Edition. MIT Press, Cambridge, MA.

Singularity University (2009). Preparing humanity for accelerating technological change. URL: http://singularityu.org.

Smerdon E. T. (1996). Lifelong Learning for Engineers: Riding the Whirlwind. The Bridge, National Academy of Engineering, 26(1/2).

Smith, A. (1776/1904). *An Inquiry into the Nature and Causes of the Wealth of Nations.* W. Strahan and T. Cadell, London, U.K.

Spath, D. & Fähnrich, K. P. (2007). *Advances in Services Innovations.* Springer.

Spohrer, J. (1999). Information in places. *IBM Systems Journal*, 38(4), 602–628.

Spohrer, J. C. & Engelbart, D. C. (2004). Converging technologies for enhancing human performance: Science and business perspectives. *Annals of the New York Academy of Sciences*, 1013, 50–82.

Spohrer, J., Golinelli, G. M., Picocchi, P. & Bassano, C. (In Prepartion). An integrated SS-VSA analysis of changing jobs. *Journal of Service Scienc.*

Spohrer, J. & Kwan, S. K. (2009). Service science, management, engineering, and design (SSMED): an emerging discipline – outline & references. *International Journal of Information Systems in the Service Sector*, 1(3).

Spohrer, J. & Maglio, P. P. (2008). The emergence of service science: Toward systematic service innovations to accelerate co-creation of value. *Production and Operations Management*, 17, 1-9.

Spohrer, J. & Maglio, P. P. (2010). Service science: Toward a smarter planet. In W. Karwowski & G. Salvendy (Eds.), *Introduction to service engineering.* Wiley & Sons. New York.

Spohrer, J., Maglio, P. P., Bailey, J. & Gruhl, D. (2007). Steps toward a science of service systems. *Computer*, 40, 71-77.

Tapscott, D. & Williams, A. D. (2006). *Wikinomics: How Mass Collaboration Changes Everything.* Portfolio/Penguin. New York, NY.

Teboul, J. (2006). *Service Is Front Stage: Positioning Services for Value Advantage.* INSEAD Business Press, Palgrave MacMillan.

Thomas, D. J. & Griffin, P. M. (1996). Co-ordinated supply chain management. European *Journal of Operational Research*, 94(3), 1–15.

Tidd, J. & Hull, F. M. (2003). *Service innovation: organizational responses to technological opportunities and market imperatives.* World Scientific Publishing Company.

Tien, J. M. & Berg, D. (2007). A calculus for services innovation. *Journal of Systems Science and Engineering*, 16(2), 129-165.

Triplett, J. E. & Bosworth, B. P. (2004). *Productivity in the U.S. Services Sector: New Sources of Economic Growth.* The Brookings Institute. Washington, DC.

Triplett, J. E. & Bosworth, B. P. (2003). Productivity measurement issues in services industries: 'Baumol's Disease' has been cured. *Economic Policy Review, Federal Reserve Bank of New York*. 9(3), 23-26.

UK Royal Society (2009). *Hidden wealth: the contribution of science to service sector innovation.* RS Policy document 09/09. RS1496.

US Bureau of Census (2007). *North American Industry Classification System (NAICS).* US Department of Commerce Publication PB2007100002. Available at http://www.ntis.gov/products/naics.aspx.

U.S. National Academy of Engineering (2003). *The Impact of Academic Research on Industrial Performance.*

Vargo, S. L. (2009). Toward a transcending conceptualization of relationship: a service-dominant logic perspective. *The Journal of Business and Industrial Marketing*, 24(5-6), 373-379.

Vargo, S. L. & Lusch, R. F. (2004). Evolving to a new dominant logic for marketing. *Journal of Marketing*, 68, 1-17.

Vargo, S. L. & Lusch, R. F. (2008). Service-dominant logic: continuing the evolution. *Journal of the Academy of Marketing Science.* 36(1) 1-10.

Vargo, S. L., Maglio, P. P., & Akaka, M. A. (2008). On value and value co-creation: A service systems and service logic perspective. *European Management Journal,* 26(3), 145-152.

Von Mises, L. (1998). Human Action: A Treatise on Economics. Scholars Edition, Ludwing Von Mises Institute.

Wolfl, A. (2005). *The Service Economy in OECD Countries.* Working Paper, Directorate for Science, Technology and Industry http://www.cepii.fr/anglaisgraph/pagepers/wolfl.htm.

Womack, J. P. & Jones, D. T. (2005). *Lean Solutions: How Companies and Customers Can Create Value and Wealth Together.* Free Press. New York, NY.

Wright, R. (2000). *Non-Zero: The Logic of Human Destiny.* Vintage/Random House. New York, NY.

Zhang, L. J. (2007). *Modern Technologies in Web Services Research.* IGI Publishing. Hershey, PA.

Zeithaml, V. A., Bitner, M. J. & Gremler, D. (2006). *Services Marketing: Integrating Customer Focus across the Firm.* Fourth edition. McGraw-Hill.

Zysman, J. (2006). The 4th service transformation: The algorithmic revolution. *Communications of the ACM*, 49(7).

Part 3
Research and Practice: Design

Technology's Impact on the Gaps Model of Service Quality

Mary Jo Bitner

W. P. Carey School of Business
Arizona State University

Valarie A. Zeithaml

Kenan-Flagler School of Business
University of North Carolina

Dwayne D. Gremler

College of Business Administration
Bowling Green State University

This chapter presents a foundational framework for service science – the Gaps Model of Service Quality. For over two decades the model has been used across industries and worldwide to help companies formulate strategies to deliver quality service, to integrate customer focus across functions, and to provide a foundation for service as a competitive strategy. It was developed at a time when most services were delivered interpersonally and in real time without the advantages (and sometimes disadvantages) of technology infusion. In the intervening years, technology has profoundly changed the nature of service(s) and at the same time it has influenced strategies for closing each of the service quality gaps. Thus, this chapter has a dual purpose: to provide a general overview of the Gaps Model of Service Quality and to demonstrate how key aspects of the model have changed and evolved due to advances in technologies. We begin with background on the Gaps Model and a discussion of the role of technology and services in general. We then discuss strategies for closing each gap in the model and illustrate the influence of technologies on these fundamental management strategies.

P.P. Maglio et al. (eds.), *Handbook of Service Science*, Service Science: Research and Innovations in the Service Economy, DOI 10.1007/978-1-4419-1628-0_10,
© Springer Science+Business Media, LLC 2010

Introduction

Few would argue with the fact that services dominate the economies of the world's most advanced nations. In the U.S., services represent over eighty percent of our GDP and labor force. Further, it is apparent that services are increasing as an economic force in countries such as China, India, and other fast-growing and developing nations (Bitner and Brown, 2008). The growth of service(s) is a relentless, global phenomenon that is shaping the world's economies and profoundly affecting people's lives. Yet, despite the economic domination of services, there is relatively little formal focus within companies, governments, and universities on service excellence, service research, and service innovation compared to the focus on tangible goods and technologies (see IfM and IBM, 2007). Within this context of unabated growth of service economies, academics and business practitioners have pointed to the need for tools, techniques, frameworks, and metrics to support excellence and innovation in services across industries. While some already exist, many more are still to be developed. These tools and frameworks will be integral foundations for service science.

This chapter presents and expands one such framework – the Gaps Model of Service Quality - that has provided a strategic foundation for organizations that wish to deliver service excellence to their customers. The Gaps Model was first introduced in 1985 (Parasuraman et al., 1985; Zeithaml et al., 1990). For nearly twenty-five years it has been used across industries and worldwide to help companies formulate strategies to deliver quality service, to integrate customer focus across firm functions, and to provide a strong foundation for service excellence as a competitive strategy.

We believe that the Gaps Model of Service Quality can be a strong foundation for service science going forward. Thus, this chapter has a dual purpose: to provide a general overview of the Gaps Model of Service Quality and to demonstrate how key aspects of the model have changed and evolved due to advances in technologies. We begin with background on the Gaps Model and a discussion of the role of technology and services in general. We then discuss strategies for closing each gap in the model and illustrate the influence of technologies on these fundamental strategies.

Gaps Model of Service Quality

The Gaps Model provides an integrated framework for managing service quality and customer-driven service innovation. In the years since the model's introduction, service quality, service innovation, and customer focus have all become increasing important as competitive strategies for organizations—thus foundational, integrative frameworks have more relevance across more industries than ever. A hallmark of the model is that it captures the cross-functionality inherent in service management. Although the authors are marketing academics and the original publications appeared in marketing journals, their work has been widely cited and used across academic disciplines and implemented in different functions within organizations. The model draws heavily from logic, theories and strategies in operations, human resources, marketing, and increasingly from information systems.

Another hallmark of the model is its anchoring on the customer and integration of the customer throughout all gaps within the model. Every gap and every strategy used to close the gaps in the model retains a focus on the customer at its core. The primary goal of the model is to meet or exceed customer expectations, and strategies used to achieve that objective (whether operations, human resource, or technology-based) are ultimately anchored on the customer.

So what exactly is the Gaps Model of Service Quality? Figure 1 illustrates the full model based on the original as it appeared in the *Journal of Marketing* (Parasuraman et al., 1985) and Figure 2 describes the gaps in words. The centerpiece of the model is the Customer Gap – the gap between customer expectations and perceptions of the service as it is actually delivered. The ultimate goal is to close this gap by meeting or exceeding customer expectations. The other four gaps in the model are known as the "provider gaps" and each represents a potential cause behind a firm's failure to meet customer expectations: not listening to customers (Gap 1); failing to design services that meet expectations (Gap 2); performance and service delivery failures (Gap 3); and not communicating service promises accurately (Gap 4). At its most basic level, the logic of the model suggests that the Customer Gap is a function of any one or all of four provider gaps. The early publications enumerate the complex reasons that lie behind each of these basic Gaps. Later publications and our text (Zeithaml et al., 2009) have further elaborated on the gaps by delineating specific strategies for closing each of them. In later sections of this chapter we will expand briefly on key strategies used to close each of the gaps.

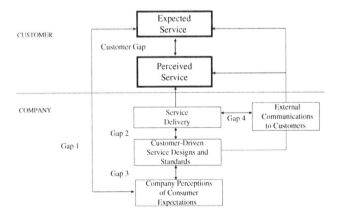

Figure 1. Gaps Model of Service Quality

- **Customer Gap**
  - the difference between customer expectations and perceptions
- **Gap 1: The Listening Gap**
  - not knowing what customers expect
- **Gap 2: The Design and Standards Gap**
  - not having the right service designs and standards
- **Gap 3: The Service Performance Gap**
  - not delivering to service standards
- **Gap 4: The Communication Gap**
  - not matching performance to promises

Figure 2. Gaps Model of Service Quality in Words

In the years since it was introduced, the Gaps Model has proved to be adaptable in meeting changes in the global business environment. For example, when the model was first introduced, few technology or manufacturing companies considered themselves to be service businesses; therefore, the message of the model was directed primarily at traditional service businesses. Today, many progressive companies in the technology and manufacturing sectors also see themselves as service businesses and the model is used in these contexts as well. Another major change in the intervening years has been the rapid development of technologies that have affected how services are communicated, designed, and delivered, as well as the types of innovative services now available to customers. An early distinction of services was the fact that they could not be provided remotely; that is, service was a local function provided in the intimate setting of a provider-customer relationship. Technology has relaxed this fundamental interpersonal, real-time requirement, resulting in increasing accessibility and globalization of services that can now be delivered and consumed anytime, anywhere. Many of these changes were not anticipated or reflected in the initial development of the Gaps Model.

Technology and Services[1]

Technology, in particular information technology, has influenced the nature of services themselves, how they are delivered, and the practice of service innovation and service management. Here we overview just a few of these basic changes and trends by identifying some key themes. We will weave these general themes re-

---

[1] This section is based on information in *Services Marketing: Integrating Customers Across the Firm,* 5th edition, 2009, by Valarie Zeithaml, Mary Jo Bitner, and Dwayne Gremler, pp. 14-19.

lated to technology and service throughout our discussion of the individual service quality gaps and strategies to close them.

Inspiring Service Innovation

Technology has been a basic force behind many service innovations now taken for granted, such as automated voice mail, interactive voice response systems, Internet-based services, and various smart services—for example the "connected car," smart meters for monitoring energy consumption, and remote health monitoring services. Internet-based companies like Amazon, e-Bay, and Second Life have sprung up, offering radically new services for consumers. And, established companies have developed brand new services based on information technology. For example, the *Wall Street Journal* offers an interactive edition that allows customers to organize the newspaper's content to suit their individual preferences and needs. Advances in information technology are also making it possible for entire suites of services including phone, Internet, video, photography, and e-mail to be available through one device such as the iPhone and similar products.

Providing Options for Service Delivery

Technology is also providing new opportunities for delivering existing services in more accessible, convenient, and productive ways. Technology facilitates basic customer service functions (bill paying, answering questions, checking account records, tracking orders), purchase transactions (both retail and business-to-business), and learning or information seeking. Over the past few decades, companies have moved from face-to-face service to telephone-based service to widespread use of interactive voice response systems to Internet-based customer service and now to wireless service. Technology also facilitates transactions by offering a direct vehicle for making purchases and conducting businesses. Finally, technology provides an easy way for customers to learn, do research, and collaborate with each other. Access to information has never been easier. For example, more than 20,000 websites currently offer health-related information, resulting in consumers having increasing involvement in their health decisions and care.

Enabling Customers and Employees

Technology enables both customers and employees to be more effective and productive in receiving and providing service. Through self-service technologies, customers can now serve themselves more effectively. Via online banking, for example, customers can access their accounts, check balances, apply for loans, and take care of just about any banking need they might have—all without the assistance of the bank's employees. These online banking services are just one example of the types of self-service technologies that are proliferating across industries. For employees, technology can provide tremendous support in making them more effective and efficient in delivering service. Customer relationship management, sales support, and product information software are broad categories of technology-based information that can aid frontline employees in providing better service. These types of software also allow employees to customize and co-create services to fit customer needs.

Expanding Global Reach

Technology also results in the potential for reaching out to customers around the globe in ways not possible when, in the not-so-distant past, services were limited to local provision. The Internet itself knows no boundaries, and therefore information, customer service, and transactions can move across countries and across continents, reaching any customer who has access to the Web. Technology also allows employees of international companies to stay in touch easily—to share information and serve on virtual work teams together, thus allowing employees to work remotely and services to be provided by global workers.

The Dark Side of Service and Technology

Lest we come across as exceedingly positive on the role of technology and service, we should acknowledge some clear constraints, paradoxes, and potential negative outcomes as well (Mick and Fournier, 1998; Bitner, 2001). Legitimate customer concerns over privacy and confidentiality raise issues for firms as they seek to learn about and interact with their customers online. Nor are all customers equally interested in using technology as a means of interacting with companies. These types of concerns are what have stymied and precluded many efforts to advance technology applications in the healthcare industry. Research on "technology readiness" suggests that some customers are simply not interested in or ready to use technology (Parasuraman and Colby, 2001). Employees can also be reluctant to accept and integrate technology into their work lives for a variety of reasons, including job insecurity and reluctance to embrace change. With technology there is also less human contact which many believe is detrimental purely from a quality of life and human relationships perspective. Finally, from a company perspective, the payback in technology investments is often uncertain and the need to balance technology and human touch in developing relationships with customers can be challenging. Technology-delivered service is not always the best answer.

Reflecting on the themes briefly outlined above, it is obvious that technology has had a profound and sometimes paradoxical influence on service(s). New models and frameworks will be needed to accommodate, predict, and control these widespread technology changes. It is also clear that well established engineering, design, and management frameworks may need to be adapted to reflect these influences. In the next sections we will focus on the impact of technology on one established framework – the Gaps Model of Service Quality.

Technology's Impact on Individual Service Gap Strategies

The remainder of this chapter will bring together the Gaps Model of Service Quality (see Figure 1) and technology by focusing on each gap in the model and expanding on how the strategies to close it have been influenced by technology. We will weave the technology themes identified above into strategies related to the gaps, illustrating how service management strategy has been influenced – and will continue to be influenced – by technology.

Customer Gap

The Customer Gap is the centerpiece of the Gaps Model. It represents the difference between customer expectations and perceptions of service performance. The model suggests that closing this gap by matching or exceeding customer expectations will result in the achievement of service quality from the customer's perspective. In the years since the introduction of the model, there has been significant focus on both customer expectations and perceptions in terms of conceptualizing these constructs (Zeithaml et al., 1993; Rust and Oliver, 2000), developing measures for them (Parasuraman et al., 1988; Brady and Cronin, 2001), and studying their effects (Boulding et al., 1993).

A prominent stream of research focuses on understanding the dimensions of service quality beginning with the identification of five key dimensions; their measures have become known as SERVQUAL (Parasuraman et al., 1988). The five dimensions of service quality (reliability, responsiveness, assurance, empathy and tangibles) and the SERVQUAL measure have been applied in and adapted to many industry settings. Related streams of research have developed in parallel to study service encounters (Bitner et al., 1990; Arnould and Price, 1993; Verhoef et al., 2004), customer satisfaction (Oliver, 1997; Fornell et al., 2006), customer loyalty (Heskett et al. 1997), and their relationships with service quality (Zeithaml et al., 1996; Rust et al., 2002). None of these now prominent streams of research existed prior to the 1980s, and all continue to spawn research today.

The original focus of the Customer Gap was on expectations and perceptions of services delivered by employees in person, via phone, or in some cases via mail.

The original SERVQUAL measures, as well as conceptual models of expectation formation and service encounters, were all based in interpersonal services. Some of the early managerial and research issues identified within this gap related to how customers learn about services and form expectations for "intangibles" that they cannot see or try prior to purchase. Other research and managerial challenges focused on how customers form judgments of service quality and satisfaction during "moments of truth" represented by an interaction with an employee.

Technology's Influence on the Customer Gap

Over the last two decades, technology advances have significantly influenced the Customer Gap. First, the nature of services themselves have changed. Now, many services are *not* delivered in person by employees, but rather are delivered via technology in the form of self-service or technology-assisted service. For example, consider just one industry – the personal photography industry. Not long ago, personal photos were taken by individuals, the film was processed by a service provider, and additional prints could be ordered and shared among friends and family. Putting together albums of photos and sharing photos with others was a labor-intensive process, often involving significant time, expense, and linking together of many different service providers. Now, individuals use digital cameras to take as many photos as they wish and they can print, manage, and share their photos online. This is just one small example of the proliferation of self-service technologies that have changed consumers' lives. How customers form expectations, choose to adopt, and evaluate these self-service technologies are subjects of contemporary research (Meuter et al., 2005).

Self-service through technology automatically puts customers in a co-production role, changing the nature of service delivery dramatically. This shift results in customers having expectations and perceptions related to their own abilities and performance that will influence their overall assessment of service excellence beyond what the employee or service provider may do. In addition to altering how services are delivered, technology advances have resulted in new services that could not have been imagined even a decade ago. What customers expect from these new, innovative, technology-driven services does not necessarily fit the mold of early models of service expectations (Parasuraman et al., 2005).

Technology has also dramatically changed how customers learn about services. Customers' ability to search the web and view photos of service locations, compare prices, and even experience services through virtual tours has changed the amount and type of information customers have prior to purchasing services. The availability of this information directly influences their expectations and ability to compare and judge services. In earlier days, customers found it difficult to gather this type of information and did not have the ability to compare services as easily as they could tangible goods that were displayed side-by-side in a retail store. To some extent the Internet now provides this same type of comparability for services.

While word-of-mouth communication has always been critical for learning about and forming expectations for service providers, technology has changed the nature of word-of-mouth communication. Web sites now include customer recommendations, glowing praise, and horror stories for just about any type of service imaginable (Ward and Ostrom, 2006). And, groups have formed online for people who are interested in particular service categories to exchange information. Many companies even sponsor these types of interactive websites themselves in order to involve customers in helping each other.

Technology has significantly impacted how customers learn about, form their expectations of, and judge services. Given these changes, it is clear that companies face new challenges as well in understanding these new expectations and designing and delivering services to meet them. In the next sections, we examine each of the provider gaps in the model, first by reviewing basic strategies for closing each one and then analyzing the effects of technology on these strategies.

Provider Gap 1: The Listening Gap

Provider Gap 1, the Listening Gap, is the difference between customer expectations of service and company understanding of those expectations. A primary cause in many firms for not meeting customers' expectations is that the firm lacks accurate understanding of exactly what those expectations are. Many reasons exist for managers not being aware of what customers expect: They may not interact directly with customers, they may be unwilling to ask about expectations, or they may be unprepared to address them. Closing the Listening Gap requires that management or empowered employees acquire accurate information about customers' expectations. Customer expectations must be assessed accurately before new services are developed, and they must be tracked after the services are introduced.

Figure 3 summarizes several key strategies for closing Gap 1. Each of these strategies is covered in greater detail elsewhere and each is backed by research and practical applications (Zeithaml et al., 2009). The first strategy is to listen to customers in multiple ways through customer research and employee upward communication. When the Gaps Model was conceived, emphasis was on traditional marketing research methods (surveys, focus groups, and complaint handling) along with methods uniquely useful in service situations such as SERVQUAL surveys, mystery shopping, and critical incidents analysis. The second strategy is to build relationships by understanding and meeting customer needs over time. In firms where customers and companies have interpersonal contact, this means anything from learning customers' names (as in a local bank) to understanding business-to-business customers' clients, changing needs, and industries. Relationship marketing is a term used to distinguish these activities from transaction-focused efforts, but relationship marketing is typically an interpersonal activity, carried out through contact people on the front lines of the service firm. The final pivotal strategy for closing Gap 1 involves knowing and acting on what customers expect when they experience a service failure. The importance of meeting customer expectations following a failure is well studied and documented (Tax et al., 1998).

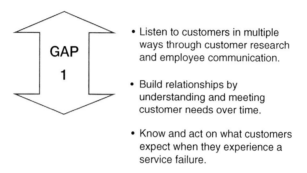

Figure 3. Strategies for Closing the Listening Gap

Technology's Influence on Provider Gap 1

The primary way technology has influenced Gap 1 is in allowing firms to know their customers in new ways. Among the most powerful facilitators of these influences are marketing research conducted on the Internet (improving ways to listen to customers) and technology-powered customer relationship management, or CRM (facilitating relationship-building with thousands, even millions, of customers through database marketing).

One of the most intriguing technological innovations is Internet or online customer research, replacing traditional comment cards and intrusive telephone calls with cyber surveys that are challenging and even fun for consumers. The application is growing rapidly, with annual spending on online research expected to reach $26 billion by 2010 (Li and Von Boskirk, 2005). The reasons are obvious— internet research has many benefits to marketers including more willing respondents, speed of collecting and analyzing data; equivalent or better data quality; and the ability to target hard-to-reach populations such as high-income consumers, those who fit a particular lifestyle or interest profile, and business-to-business markets. Internet research also offers the opportunity to use multimedia to present video and audio to give respondents the true sense of a service being researched. Finally, there need be no interviewers--and therefore no interviewer errors or bias that occur when the interviewer is in a bad mood, tired, impatient, or not objective. Internet research is also less expensive than traditional research—in fact it is 10 to 80 percent less expensive than other approaches. The Internet eliminates postage, phone, labor, and printing costs that are typical with other survey approaches. Respondents also seem to complete Web-based surveys in half the time it would take an interviewer to conduct the survey, perhaps contributing to the reduced need for incentives.

Building relationships by understanding and meeting customer needs over time is also facilitated by technology. Customer relationship management (CRM) is an important and powerful form of relationship-building that was virtually impossible prior to advances in technology-based CRM software and systems. At its best, CRM studies customers one by one to develop profiles of their individual needs, behaviors, and responses to marketing. This approach allows a company to get very close—even intimate with—thousands of customers and to tailor services uniquely to individuals. Two of the most innovative examples of database marketing include Hallmark Gold Crown and Harrah's Entertainment.

Hallmark's database, capable of recognizing customers in all Hallmark retail stores, tracks purchases, contacts, and communications so that it learns what each customer individually values about the relationship with the company. This information includes what core product or benefit has the most value to the customer and what differentiates Hallmark from its competition. The mechanism by which the company tracks this information is a Gold Crown Card that customers use to accumulate points for purchases. They receive personalized point statements, newsletters, reward certificates, and individualized news of products and events at local stores. The top 10 percent of customers—who buy more cards and ornaments than others—get special amenities such as longer bonus periods and their own private priority toll-free number, as well as very targeted communication about the specific products they value.

Another example of a technology-based relationship management approach is in the gambling industry where it has long been recognized that certain customers are better than others and that encouraging the "high rollers" to spend time in one's casinos is a worthwhile and profitable strategy. One of the main ways casinos encourage increased patronage is "comping"—giving free drinks, hotel rooms, limousines, and sometimes chips to top customers. The strategy has been limited in most casinos to customers who could be identified and followed, making the approach spotty and missing many potential repeat patrons. Harrah's Entertainment, which owns and operates 26 gambling casinos in places such as Las Vegas and Atlantic City, found a more systematic way to extend the practice to a wider group of customers (Loveman, 2003). Harrah's developed a customer relationship management system called the Total Rewards program, a loyalty program that tracks the names and addresses of repeat visitors along with what slot machines they play, how long they play, and how much money they gamble. The company's approach uses a Total Rewards card that any customer can obtain—often with the incentive of covering their slot losses for half an hour up to $100. To earn points toward drinks, rooms, and other benefits, customers allow their cards to be swiped on the casino floor to monitor the sums gambled and time spent at slot machines and card tables.

While the benefits to companies of using these types of CRM systems are clear, there is also the potential for misuse if these systems are applied in ways that take advantage of customers or intrude on their privacy. Maintaining the right balance between gathering and using customer information to build desirable relationships (for both firms and customers) and misusing information or invading customer privacy in unwanted ways is an ongoing challenge that technology in and of itself cannot solve.

Gap 2 – The Design and Standards Gap

Closing Gap 1 through research and effective management of customer relationships is necessary, but not sufficient, for achieving service excellence. Even when a company has a thorough and ongoing understanding of its customers' expectations, it is still very possible, in fact quite easy, to fail to deliver quality service. Gap 2, the design and standards gap is the next step toward ensuring against such failure. This gap focuses on translating expectations into actual service designs and developing standards to measure service operations against customer expectations.

Figure 4 summarizes several key strategies for closing Gap 2. As with Gap 1, each of these strategies is covered in greater detail elsewhere (Zeithaml et al., 2009). The first strategy is to employ well-defined new service development and innovation practices for designing services. Some have referred to this as formalization of a "services R&D" practice. While standardized new product development processes and R&D are common in technology and manufacturing, they are still quite rare in services (for a major exception, we note the investment of the IBM Corporation in service innovation research through its global research labs). A formalized process typically involves a series of steps beginning with strategy formulation and idea generation and ending with full-scale implementation (Cooper and Edgett, 1999; Edvardsson et al., 2000). Because of the nature of services (their process orientation, intangibility, co-creation by customers), it is more challenging to engage in these typical steps that are so well established in other industries. However, it is clear that following a process, engaging customers along the way, and carefully planning and prototyping the complexities of service implementation are all critically important in ensuring service designs that meet customer expectations (Henard and Szymanski, 2001).

A second strategy for closing Gap 2 relates to understanding the total customer experience and designing all elements of that experience in ways that meet or exceed customer expectations. This involves considering everything that occurs from the moment the customer engages the service through the entire length of the service experience. Common elements of the service experience that need to be designed include customer-facing processes, the physical space where the service is delivered ("servicescape"), and the interactions between service employees and customers. Viewing these operational elements from the customer's perspective and designing them to be consistent with expectations, or to reinforce a desired service image, are critical to closing Gap 2. Because of the special challenges inherent in designing services, techniques such as service blueprinting have evolved to aid in the design process (Bitner et al., 2008).

A third strategy for closing Gap 2 involves measuring service operations via customer-defined standards. When service standards are absent or when the standards in place do not reflect customers' expectations, quality of service as perceived by customers is likely to suffer. Too often services are measured based on traditional, internal measures of success which may not be reflective of customer needs and expectations.

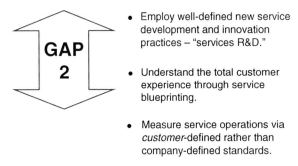

Figure 4. Strategies for Closing the Design and Standards Gap

Technology's Impact on Gap 2

The focus of the Design and Standards Gap has primarily been on designing interpersonal services and real-time operational processes to meet customer expectations. The variability inherent in interpersonal services makes designing them and standardizing them quite difficult. While the challenges inherent in designing interpersonal, real-time, face-to-face services have not disappeared, there is now increasing focus on technology-enabled services and technology-enabled processes to close Gap 2. Increasingly, customer expectations can be met through technology-enabled and highly-standardized services provided on the web. For example, consider book sales and services (just one of its many product lines) provided online by Amazon. Through its sophisticated technology infrastructure, the company is able to provide standardized ordering, payment, tracking, and recommendation services at the individual consumer level. Attempting to provide this level of service in a traditional book sales context to masses of people would likely be very idiosyncratic, probably not very consistent, and quite costly if it were done at the level Amazon performs online.

Technology has also facilitated the development of new services to meet customer needs and expectations. For example, eBay's network of buyers and sellers has created an entire service industry that provides income for individuals and small businesses and an outlet for over-production of products. In another realm, IBM and Caterpillar's real-time smart-service monitoring systems for their equipment represent innovative and efficient services that have changed the nature of repair, maintenance, and basic customer service in those industries. In health-care, the ability to monitor patient conditions remotely and to train physicians in simulated surgical techniques via video technology are just two additional exam-ples of technology-based services that meet customer expectations in very new and innovative ways.

Technology has also influenced the actual *process* of service innovation, allevi-ating some of the traditional barriers to designing new services. Some of the most challenging steps in new service development have always been the basic concept development and prototype testing steps. Now technology can be used to develop visual prototypes and virtual experiences for testing service concepts. It can also be used to engage customers more effectively in the design process by allowing them to interact in real time with the service, offering immediate feedback that can be fed into the next iteration of the service design. Service blueprinting, which started as an entirely manual process, has been automated by companies to pro-vide "living blueprints" accessible to key parties online (Bitner et al., 2008). Automated blueprints can also easily convey varying levels of detail buried a click or two behind basic steps in the blueprint. With technological advances such blueprints can now include photos or other images of physical evidence, as well as video clips that depict service processes, customer actions, or the servicescape.

Measuring service operations based on customer expectations is also much more efficient today due to technology. Tracking customer feedback and measur-ing internal operations can be done more easily and frequently through the use of web-based feedback systems and internal databases. Technology also allows easy documentation and communication of employee, team, and organizational per-formance related to standards, thus making these customer-driven standards more accessible and visible.

Gap 3 – The Service Performance Gap

Although a company may have closed both the Listening Gap (Gap 1) and the Service Design and Standards Gap (Gap 2), it may still fall short of providing ser-vice that meets customers' expectations if it is unable to deliver service in the way the service was designed. Gap 3, the Service Performance Gap, must also be closed to make sure there is no discrepancy between customer-driven service de-sign and standards and actual service delivery. Even when guidelines exist for performing service well and treating customers correctly, high-quality service per-formance is not a certainty.

The key strategies for closing Gap 3 are depicted in Figure 5. As with the other gaps and related figures, each of these strategies is covered in greater detail else-where (Zeithaml et al., 2009). The first strategy is to align the firm's human resource strategies around delivering service excellence. In particular, in order to deliver service as it was designed a firm needs to ensure that employees are willing and able to deliver quality services and that they are motivated to perform in customer-oriented, service-minded ways (Barber and Strack, 2005). In creating such a workforce, an organization must hire the right people, develop those people to deliver service quality, and retain the best people. To effectively deliver service quality, considerable attention should be focused on recruiting and hiring the right service personnel (Berry and Parasuraman, 1991). Service employees need two complementary capacities: service competencies—the skills and knowledge necessary to do the job—and service inclination—an interest in doing service-related work (Schneider and Schechter, 1991). Once the right people are in place, to provide quality service they need to be developed through ongoing training in the necessary technical skills and in interactive skills. An organization that hires the right people and trains and develops them to deliver service quality must also work to retain them. If a company wants the strongest service performers to stay with the organization, it must reward and promote them. Organizations use a variety of rewards to retain the best employees; traditional approaches such as higher pay, promotions, and one-time monetary awards or prizes are often linked to service performance.

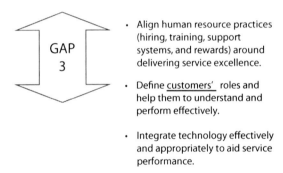

Figure 5. Strategies for Closing the Service Performance Gap

For many services, customers are participants in service production and co-creators of value (Vargo and Lusch, 2004) and, therefore, play a key role in the service delivery process. That is, customers themselves can influence whether the service meets customer-defined specifications and can potentially contribute to the widening of Gap 3. Thus, a second strategy for closing Gap 3 is to define customers' roles and assist them in understanding and performing their roles effectively. Sometimes customers contribute to Gap 3 because they lack understanding of their roles and exactly what they are to in a given situation or because they are unwilling or unable to perform for some reason. To reduce this gap the organization needs to clearly define and communicate what the customer's role entails—in essence the customer's "job description" (Schneider and Bowen, 1995). Once the customer's role is clearly defined, the firm needs to help facilitate that role. In a sense, the customer is a "partial employee" of the organization, and strategies for managing customer behavior in service production and delivery can mimic to some degree the efforts aimed at service employees discussed in the previous paragraph.

A third strategy for closing Gap 3 involves integrating technology effectively and appropriately to aid service performance. For service workers (and customers) to be efficient and effective in performing their jobs, technology that facilitates their efforts is often required. Technology can help employees to be more effective and efficient in serving customers. For example, at its Jacksonville, Florida, location Mayo Clinic invested $18 million over the past decade in computer system technology, with a large portion of the emphasis on electronic medical records. The many systems required for patient care, including pharmacy systems, laboratory systems, and monitoring systems, are now interconnected. Mayo Clinic's technology automatically notifies physicians, pharmacists, nurses, and others in the hospital when a particular treatment needs to be performed and monitors dosage amounts (Berry and Seltman, 2007). Technology can also help customers become more educated and involved in co-creating service. As an example, one company, iPrint, has created technology to allow home-office and small-business customers to perform commercial print services for themselves. Customers with little or no knowledge of graphic design are provided detailed step-by-step instructions to educate themselves and can easily create their own designs for a wide range of products from the convenience of their own offices.

Technology's Impact on Gap 3

When the Gaps Model was first conceptualized, the focus of the Service Performance Gap was primarily on the role that service *participants*—namely, employees and customers—play in the delivery of services and the interpersonal interactions required. While the issues inherent in providing an environment that facilitates service performance of employees and customers are still present, there is now an increased focus on how technology can empower and enable each group to close Gap 3. The influx of technology has enabled employees in a myriad of new ways and has created opportunities for customers to become more involved in co-creating, and even adding value to, their service experience. Technology has also made it possible for some services to be produced entirely by the customer without any contact with the firm's employees.

Technological advances have allowed customer-contact employees to become more efficient and effective in serving customers. For example, today's technology allows Symantec customer service representatives to have several online "chats" with many customers simultaneously. In attempting to resolve customer problems or answer their questions regarding the company's software products (e.g., Norton Internet Security), technological tools allow an employee to remotely connect to a customer's computer to fix a problem. Such capability allows employees to resolve problems much faster (increasing employee efficiency) and generally creates a more satisfying customer experience (increasing employee effectiveness). Thus, many firms today often explore ways that technology can be used to empower employees and close the service performance gap.

Technology has also empowered customers. Through technology customers can be more involved in co-creating and even adding value to their service experience. For several years airlines have provided the means through technology for passengers to "check-in" online, in advance of arriving at the terminal, and print their own boarding passes. Northwest Airlines (now Delta) has taken this one step further; customers can now use a smart phone, such as a Blackberry device, to receive an electronic boarding pass. The customer's device receives an electronic image that can be scanned by security at the airport, thus not only eliminating the need to wait in line to receive a boarding pass but also the requirement to carry any document. Although more of the responsibility during the check-in process has shifted to customers, most appreciate the reduced time spent waiting in lines and the freedom of not having to carry paper documents—and see this technology as adding value to their service experience.

Self-service technologies—services produced entirely by the customer without any direct involvement or interaction with the firm's employees—have also changed the way companies think about closing Gap 3 (Meuter et al., 2005). These technologies have proliferated as companies see the potential cost savings and efficiencies that can be achieved, potential sales growth, increased customer satisfaction, and competitive advantage. From the beginning, Netflix's business model was to use technology to provide customers with a way to receive DVDs at their home without stepping out the front door; this endeavor proved to be so successful that Blockbuster subsequently countered with a "Total Access" offering that also provided home delivery of DVDs. Paytrust, a company that receives bills and presents them online to customers for payment, allows customers several payment options—all without requiring any interactions with employees. Medical websites allow patients access to information about particular diseases, drugs and drug interactions, and specific doctors and hospitals; in this case technology enables patients to make more informed health-care decisions. As these examples illustrate, such technological advances have facilitated customer participation in service delivery—changing the way that Gap 3 is conceptualized and the thinking on how it can be closed.

Gap 4 – The Communication Gap

Even when a firm has done everything suggested by the other three gaps to ensure service quality, there can still be a failure to meet customer expectations if communications about the service do not match with what is delivered. Thus, the final provider gap in the model that must be closed is the Communication Gap, or Gap 4. This gap focuses on the difference between service delivery and what is communicated externally to customers through advertising, pricing, and other forms of tangible communications.

Figure 6 captures several key strategies for closing Gap 4. Each of these strategies is discussed in greater detail elsewhere (Zeithaml et al., 2009). The first strategy revolves around integrated services marketing communication that ensures that everything and everyone that sends a message or signal about the service does so in a manner that is consistent with what customers expect and what is actually delivered. The challenge with this strategy is that there are a myriad of communication channels and modes that send messages to customers—more today than every before—including traditional websites, personal sales, direct mail, print media, blogs, virtual communities, cell-phone advertising, etc. Beyond these types of channels which are also available to goods-producing firms, service customers receive additional communication from servicescapes, customer service representatives, and everyday service encounters with company employees. Ensuring that all of these channels communicate effectively and consistently is a daunting task, yet one that is essential to an integrated communication strategy.

GAP 4

- Employ integrated services marketing communication strategies around everything and everyone that sends a message or signal to the customer.

- Manage customer expectations effectively throughout the experience.

- Develop mechanisms for internal communication to avoid over-promising and ensure successful delivery.

Figure 6. Strategies for Closing the Communication Gap

A second key strategy for closing the Communication Gap is to manage customer expectations effectively throughout the service experience. Many services (for example many B2B services and consumer membership services) take place over an extended time frame that might mean a few hours, days, weeks, or even years. These types of extended service experiences often change over time, varying from the original service promise as a result of business realities (for either the provider or the customer) that change the nature of the service, customer needs that change over time, and financial pressures that may cause increases in pricing or adjustments to the service contract. Thus, it is critical that communications to the customer also change and evolve through time to ensure that expectations and service performance match. This might mean managing customer expectations relative to new business realities, often in the form of managing expectations downwards when a service previously provided is discontinued or when prices for similar services must be increased.

A final strategy for closing Gap 4 is to develop mechanisms for internal communication so that the customer hears consistent messages before the sale and during service delivery. A common cause for Gap 4 is overpromising on the part of sales and marketing. While a certain amount of promotion is needed in many cases to gain a sale, excessive promotional activity can be detrimental when it exceeds the ability of the delivery organization to keep the promises made. Customers gained in the short term from making excessive promises can be lost just as quickly through a failure to deliver. A number of internal communication strategies can help avoid the latter problem. These types of strategies including effective vertical communication that keeps employees informed of corporate strategy and marketing messages so that they communicate accurately. Selling the brand inside the company also helps employees to see its value and to be realistic about what can and should be promised to customers (Mitchell, 2002). Horizontal communication across marketing, operations, and service design teams can also help to align promises with service delivery capabilities.

Technology's Impact on Gap 4

As with the other gaps, the early focus of Gap 4 was on traditional channels of communication, including interpersonal communication (sales and real-time communication during service delivery), tangible symbols of the service (servicescape, pricing, and other physical evidence), and service advertising. All of these traditional communication channels have been affected by technology infusion. One prominent effect across all forms of communication has been the dynamic capabilities of technologies that allow quick changes in communication (via electronic updates and adjustments), dynamic pricing, and customized communication strategies for targeted segments of customers.

In addition, there are a number of new channels that service firms can use for communicating with their customers including blogs, targeted e-mails, customer communities, and employee chat with customers. The number of channels and modes of communication that must be integrated effectively has exploded, exacerbating the challenge of providing consistent messages across all of them. These new channels are not simply options that service firms can consider – more and more they are becoming *expected* by customers as means of communication.

Virtual service experiences portrayed online provide another avenue for communicating about services that was not available when the Gaps Model was first developed. In fact, in the past, one of the challenges for service firms seeking to communicate what they offer was the inability to effectively communicate an experience or true visual image of the service process. It was believed that the intangibility and process-orientation of services were characteristics that made it very difficult to effectively communicate the service offering to customers prior to purchase. While communicating an experience is still a challenge, virtual online experiences provide an avenue to at least approximate more closely what the customer can expect. These virtual experiences can provide customers with a view of the physical environment, the steps in the service process, and some idea of the service employees or technologies involved. Comparing virtual experiences across providers may also help customers to do "comparison shopping" for services—something virtually impossible only a decade ago.

Online brand communities and easy/quick mass communication via the Internet are new channels that, whether provider or customer-controlled, can influence customer expectations for service firms. While it is well known that word-of-mouth communication has always been especially important for services (whether B2B or B2C), these new avenues of peer-to-peer and customer-to-customer communication make word-of-mouth an even more important influence in setting expectations for services today.

The relative inability for customers to compare prices for services (as compared to goods) is another of the basic tenets that traditionally distinguished goods from services marketing. This fundamental pricing challenge is also changing due to the influx of technology that allows customers to comparison shop online by moving between websites and checking out photos and virtual experiences that give them cues to the value and relative price they would expect to pay.

An overriding challenge for service firms in the age of easy, quick, and accessible communication for customers via the Internet is the relative ease with which superior service, beautiful photos, and wonderful employees can be portrayed online (just as it has always been with advertising); yet, it is extremely challenging to ensure that these online "experiences" match with actual service delivery. While the channels and opportunities to communicate with customers have proliferated, effective integrated communication is more than ever a continuing challenge for service firms.

Conclusion

This chapter had two purposes: (1) to provide a brief overview of a well-established service marketing and management framework, the Gaps Model of Service Quality, and (2) to illustrate the impact of information technology on strategies associated with closing each of the gaps. We covered some of the basic strategies associated with closing each gap in the model and also provided examples of how technology advances and innovations have influenced these strategies. Our experience with the model tells us that it is fundamental to service science in its basic premises and that its associated strategies remain essential to managing effective and profitable service businesses today, just as they were when the model was first developed. It is also apparent that the model is adaptable to the changing business environment given its extended use and longevity. New technologies and service innovations have been and can continue to be incorporated into the model, resulting in better understanding of the gaps and new strategies for closing the gaps.

We believe the Gaps Model should be one of the fundamental frameworks for service science going forward. Its primary contributions are its cross-functionality from a business perspective, its incorporation of theories, ideas, and frameworks from multiple academic disciplines, and its keen focus on the customer. While service science will benefit from new theories and frameworks coming out of engineering, operations, computer science, and management, it is our belief that there are fundamental principles that currently exist that should be carried forward as part of the core of service science. The Gaps Model of Service Quality is, we believe, one of those core knowledge areas.

References

Arnould, E. J. and Price, L. L. (1993), "River Magic: Extraordinary Experience and the Extended Service Encounter," *Journal of Consumer Research*, 20 (June), 24-45.

Barber, F. and Strack, R. (2005), "The Surprising Economics of a 'People Business'," *Harvard Business Review*, 83 (June), 80–91.

Berry, L. L. and Parasuraman, A. (1991), *Marketing Services*. New York: The Free Press.

Berry, L. L. and Seltman, K. D. (2007), "Building a Strong Services Brand: Lessons from Mayo Clinic," *Business Horizons*, 50 (May–June), 199–209.

Bitner, M. J. (2001), "Service and Technology: Opportunities and Paradoxes," *Managing Service Quality*, 11 (6), 375-379.

Bitner, M. J. and Brown S. W. (2008), "The Service Imperative," *Business Horizons 50th Anniversary Issue*, 51 (January-February), 39-47.

Bitner, M. J., Booms, B. H. and Tetreault, M. S. (1990), "The Service Encounter: Diagnosing Favorable and Unfavorable Incidents," *Journal of Marketing*, 54 (January), 71-84.

Bitner, M. J., Ostrom, A. L. and Morgan, F. N. (2008), "Service Blueprinting: A Practical Technique for Service Innovation," *California Management Review*, Spring 2008, 66-94.

Boulding, W., Kalra, A., Staelin, R. and Zeithaml, V. A. (1993), "A Dynamic Process Model of Service Quality: From Expectations to Behavioral Intentions," *Journal of Marketing Research*, 30 (Winter), 7-27.

Brady, M. K. and Cronin, J. J., Jr., "Some New Thoughts on Conceptualizing Perceived Service Quality: A Hierarchical Approach," *Journal of Marketing*, 65 (July), 34-49.

Cooper, R. G. and Edgett, S. J. (1999), *Product Development for the Service Sector*, Cambridge, MA: Perseus Books.

Edvardsson, B., Gustafsson, A, Johnson, M. D. and Sanden, B. (2000), *New Service Development and Innovation in the New Economy*, Lund, Sweden: Studentlitteratur AB.

Fornell, C., Mithas, S., Morgeson, F. V. III, and Krishnan, M. S. (2006), "Customer Satisfaction and Stock Prices: High Returns, Low Risk," *Journal of Marketing*, 70 (January) 3-14.

Henard, D. H. and Szymanski, D. M. (2001), "Why Some New Products Are More Successful than Others," *Journal of Marketing*, 28 (August), 362-375.

Heskett, J. L., Sasser, W. E., Jr. and Schlesinger, L. A. (1997), *The Service-Profit Chain*, New York: The Free Press.

IfM and IBM (2007), *Succeeding Through Service Innovation: A Discussion Paper*, Cambridge, United Kingdom: University of Cambridge Institute for Manufacturing.

Li, C. and Van Boskirk, S. (2005), "U.S. Online Marketing Forecast: 2005-2010," forrester.com, May 2.

Loveman, G. (2003), "Diamonds in the Data Mine," *Harvard Business Review*, 81 (May), 109-112.

Meuter, M. L., Bitner, M. J., Ostrom, A. L. and Brown, S. W. (2005), "Choosing among Alternative Service Delivery Modes: An Investigation of Customer Trial of Self-Service Technologies," *Journal of Marketing*, 69 (April), 61–83.

Mick, D. G. and Fournier, S. (2001), "Paradoxes of Technology: Consumer Cognizance, Emotions, and Coping Strategies," *Journal of Consumer Research*, 25 (September), 123-47.

Oliver, R. L. (1997), *Satisfaction: A Behavioral Perspective on the Consumer*, New York: McGraw-Hill.

Parasuraman, A. and Colby, C. L. (2001), *Techno-Ready Marketing: How and Why Your Customers Adopt Technology*, New York: The Free Press.

Parasuraman, A, Zeithaml, V. A. and Berry, L. L. (1985)," A Conceptual Model of Service Quality and Its Implications for Future Research," *Journal of Marketing*, 49 (4), 41-50.

Parasuraman A., Zeithaml, V. A. and Berry, L. L. (1988), "SERVQUAL: A Multiple-Item Scale for Measuring Consumer Perceptions of Service Quality," *Journal of Retailing*, 64 (Spring), 12-40.

Parasuraman, A., Zeithaml, V. A. and Malhotra, A. (2005), "E-S-QUAL: A Multiple-Item Scale for Assessing Electronic Service Quality," *Journal of Service Research*, 7 (February), 213-233.

Rust, R.T. and Oliver, R. L. (2000), "Should We Delight the Customer?" *Journal of the Academy of Marketing Science*, 28 (Winter), 86-94.

Rust, R. T., Moorman, C. and Dickson, P. R. (2002), "Getting a Return on Quality: Revenue Expansion, Cost Reduction, or Both?" *Journal of Marketing*, 66 (October), 7-24.

Schneider, B. and Bowen, D. E. (1995), *Winning the Service Game*. Boston: Harvard Business School Press.

Schneider, B. and Schechter, D. (1991), "Development of a Personnel Selection System for Service Jobs," in *Service Quality: Multidisciplinary and Multinational Perspectives*, S. W. Brown, E. Gummesson, B. Edvardsson, and B. Gustavsson, eds. Lexington, MA: Lexington Books, 217–236.

Tax, S., Brown S. and Chandrashekaran, M. (1998), "Customer Evaluations of Service Complaint Experiences: Implications for Relationship Marketing," *Journal of Marketing*, 62 (April), 60-76.

Vargo, S. L. and Lusch, R. F. (2004), "Evolving to a New Dominant Logic for Marketing," *Journal of Marketing*, 68 (January), 1–17.

Verhoef, P. C., Antonides, G. and de Hoog, A. N. (2004), "Service Encounters as a Sequence of Events: The Importance of Peak Experiences," *Journal of Service Research*, 7 (August), 53-64.

Ward, J. C. and Ostrom, A. L. (2006), "Complaining to the Masses: The Role of Protest Framing in Customer-Created Complaint Web Sites," *Journal of Consumer Research*, 33 (September), 220-230.

Zeithaml, V. A., Berry, L. L. and Parasuraman, A. (1993), "The Nature and Determinants of Customer Expectations of Service," *Journal of the Academy of Marketing Science*, 21 (Winter), 1-12.

Zeithaml, V. A., Berry, L. L. and Parasuraman, A. (1996), "The Behavioral Consequences of Service Quality," *Journal of Marketing*, 60 (April), 31-46.

Zeithaml, V. A., Bitner, M. J. and Gremler, D. D. (2009), *Services Marketing: Integrating Customer Focus Across the Firm*, 5th edition, New York: McGraw-Hill.

Zeithaml, V. A., Parasuraman, A. and Berry, L. L. (1990), *Delivering Quality Service: Balancing Customer Perceptions and Expectations*, New York: The Free Press.

Seven Contexts for Service System Design

Robert J. Glushko

University of California, Berkeley

Many of the most complex service systems being built and imagined today combine person-to-person encounters, technology-enhanced encounters, self-service, computational services, multi-channel, multi-device, and location-based and context-aware services. This paper examines the characteristic concerns and methods for these seven different design contexts to propose a unifying view that spans them, especially when the service-system is "information-intensive." A focus on the information required to perform the service, how the responsibility to provide this information is divided between the service provider and service consumer, and the patterns that govern information exchange yields a more abstract description of service encounters and outcomes. This makes it easier to see the systematic relationships among the contexts that can be exploited as design parameters or patterns, such as the substitutability of stored or contextual information for person-to-person interactions. A case study for the design of a "smart multi-channel bookstore" illustrates the use of the different design contexts as building blocks for service systems.

Introduction

"Service" once only implied face-to-face interactions between two people, one offering the service and the other receiving it. Today service domains and interactions are vastly more complex. "Service systems" combine and integrate the value created in different design contexts like person-to-person encounters, technology enabled self-service, computational services, multi-channel, multi-device, and location-based and context-aware services (Maglio, et al., 2006; Spohrer, et al., 2007). Most service designers are familiar with some of these contexts, and each context has a research and practitioner literature that highlights their characteristic design concerns and methods. But few service designers are familiar with all of them, and because the design concerns and methods in one context can seem incompatible with those in others, there is relatively little work that analyzes design concerns and methods that span multiple contexts.

P.P. Maglio et al. (eds.), *Handbook of Service Science*, Service Science: Research and Innovations in the Service Economy, DOI 10.1007/978-1-4419-1628-0_11,
© Springer Science+Business Media, LLC 2010

This paper argues that for the substantial subset of service systems that can be described as "information-intensive," it is desirable to take a more abstract view of service contexts that highlights what person-to-person, self-service, and automated or computational services have in common rather than emphasizing their differences. The view reveals the intrinsic design challenges that derive from the nature of the information required to perform a service, and emphasizes the design choices that allocate the responsibility to provide this information between the service provider and service consumer. Taken together, the information requirements and the division of labor for satisfying them determine the nature and intensity of the interactions in the service system. This more abstract approach that applies to all contexts overcomes many of the limitations of design approaches that focus more narrowly on the distinctive concerns of each context.

Why seven contexts rather than five or nine? Like every classification system, this design framework is somewhat arbitrary, but the proposals in this paper don't depend on it being the best or the only way to analyze and organize design challenges and methods. The paper demonstrates that these seven contexts are conceptually coherent building blocks that enable the incremental design of many different kinds of service systems. Furthermore, an informal analysis of service systems in numerous domains suggests that these seven contexts are sufficient to describe those that currently exist as well as many that are likely to be developed.

Information-intensive services, defined in the second section, are those in which information processing or information exchange, rather than physical or interpersonal actions, account for the greatest proportion of the co-created value (Apte and Mason, 1995). The third section describes seven different service design contexts and recasts many of their typical design concerns and methods in terms of the information required to perform the service (sometimes called the "service interface"), and how the responsibility to provide this information is divided between the service provider and service consumer. The fourth section shows how this abstract description of services makes the different service contexts into substitutable and combinable building blocks of service systems and suggests some unifying design concepts and methods that apply to all of them.

The fifth section illustrates these new design concepts and methods using the design of a "smart multi-channel bookstore" service system that combines service components from many of the design contexts. Value propositions and information flows will be described from the contrasting points of view of customers, front and back stage bookstore employees, and the bookstore manager that taken together yield a holistic perspective on the service system.

"Information-Intensive" Services

Apte and his collaborators analyzed services in terms of the proportions of physical actions, interpersonal actions, and information actions "that involve the manipulation of symbols." (Apte and Mason, 1995; Apte and Goh, 2004, Apte and

Karmakar, 2007).   Information-intensive services are those in which the information actions are responsible for the greatest proportion of value created by the service system.   The most information-intensive ones are those with few or no requirements for physical and personal interactions, or where personal interactions are narrowly focused on the information exchange needed to make decisions and apply other information.   Examples include accounting, data entry and transcription, translation, insurance underwriting and claims processing, legal and professional services, customer support, and computer programming.   In these service domains documents, databases, software applications, or other explicit repositories or sources of information are ubiquitous and essential to meeting the goals of the service consumer or customer.

The recognition that services vary according to both the *absolute* and the *relative* proportions of physical, interpersonal, and information actions is a critical insight.   The most information-intensive services are entirely information-based, with no physical or interpersonal interactions required to carry them out, and can be readily automated as information systems, web services, or computational agents.

Other information-intensive services also involve essential personal or physical interactions, including traditional classroom education, emergency and surgical healthcare, logistics, sales, consulting, and personnel resources administration. Furthermore, service types that are dominated by physical or interpersonal actions, such as physical therapy, massage, restaurant dining, and entertainment – and which are thus "experience-intensive" -- usually require information exchanges to specify and co-produce the service.

Seven Contexts for Service Design

The following sections introduce seven contexts for service design.

- The "person-to-person" (Context 1), "self-service" (Context 3), and "multi-channel" (Context 4) ones are canonical in service design.
- Context 2, "technology-enhanced person-to-person" service, is introduced here to highlight the design issues that emerge in contexts that are transitional or intermediate between "pure" person-to-person service encounters and self-service ones.
- Context 5, "services on multiple devices or platforms," combines and specializes many of the design concerns for the "self-service" and "multi-channel" contexts, but it raises additional ones that make it necessary to treat it separately.
- Context 6, called "back-stage intensive" or "computational" here, is a subset of what are often called "machine to machine" or "computer to computer" services, but these labels are less precise than needed when additional contexts are introduced.

- Context 7, "location-based and context-aware services," combines and specializes design concerns from "self-service," "multi-channel," and "back stage" contexts (3, 5, and 6), but likewise raises new ones.

Each context is introduced with a scenario from a bookstore service setting, and each successive scenario builds on the previous ones to define a progressively more complex service system.

Person to person service encounters (Context 1)

The independent local bookstore exemplifies the person-to-person service setting with empowered frontline service employees, because such stores only survive if they provide highly personalized and empathetic service. Bookstore employees are motivated to recognize customers; greet them by name; remember their favorite subjects, authors, prior purchases, and spending budget – and use all of this information to recommend new books. If the customer is a new one, the bookstore employee asks about preferences, suggests some books and uses the customer's feedback to refine the employee's model of the customer, and perhaps gives a personalized tour of the bookstore.

Levitt's (1972) classic statement that "discretion (on the part of service employees) is the enemy of order, standardization and quality" might be true of highly routinized person-to-person transactional services. We are all too familiar with the bureaucratic inflexibility of service providers like the department of motor vehicles where we fill out a form, submit it to a service employee, and have an experience that is never personalized. We all also know from our own experiences that people would prefer services "their way." Mills and Moberg (1982) valiantly attempted to systematize techniques for "sealing off the technical core of service operations" to enable distinct levels of service flexibility on a continuum from "full" to "restricted" service. But they and other service design and operations researchers ultimately acknowledged the inherent tension between the goal of achieving standardization and efficiency for service providers and that of satisfying the often variable demands and preferences of service customers.

A way forward emerged with more nuanced analysis of service value creation in terms of "value" or "profit" chains in the "service production system" (Heskett, et al., 1977; Mills and Moberg, 1982) and the utility of recognizing an architectural boundary between "front office" or "front stage" services and those in the "back office" or "back stage" (Glushko and Tabas, 2009; Teboul 2006). Service operations of the former variety involve interactions with the customer, while those of the latter variety contribute to the former while remaining inaccessible or invisible to the customer.   When services are designed with a "line of visibility" separating the front and back stages in place, frontline service employees can be empowered with the discretion to adapt the service in the front stage when necessary to satisfy customers (Kelley, 1993; Lashley, 1995; Frei, 2006) in any way that doesn't jeopardize the efficient operation of the back stage.

A premise that guides the design of person-to-person services is that the quality of the service is determined in the front stage encounter between the frontline service provider and the customer (Zeithaml, et al., 1998; Bitner, et al., 2000).   It naturally follows that the typical design techniques for person-to-person services are ethnographic and participatory, immersing the designer in the customer's context to observe, participate with, and interview the customer to understand his goals and behavior (Beyer and Holtzblatt, 1998).   These methods yield a customer-focused service that emphasizes the touch points that he experiences in his interactions with the service provider.

For example, the service blueprinting technique (Bitner, et al., 2008) characterizes person-to-person services as "dynamic, unfolding over time through a sequence or constellation of events or steps... that produce value for the customer." Similarly, Benford, et al., (2009) portray the sequence of touch points as a "trajectory of interaction," Dubberly and Evenson (2008) describe it as the "customer journey" or "experience cycle, Davis and Dunn (2002) call it the "brand touchpoint wheel," and Meyer and Schwager (2007) call it the "customer corridor."

Blueprinting advocates suggest that every touch point should also be associated with tangible evidence that demonstrates or signals that the service is being delivered or co-created.   Person-to-person services that require substantial physical interactions have a great deal of intrinsic tangibility; clean and pressed clothes are clear evidence that a dry cleaning service was performed as expected. The physician's white coat and similar characteristic uniforms for other service providers tangibly reinforce quality expectations.

Many services are associated with information artifacts as tangible evidence, such as the service provider's business license hanging in the office, or invoices, receipts, warranties or diplomas given to the customer when the service is completed. For the most information-intensive services, the creation or processing of information is the sole intrinsic evidence of a service, so most of them are essentially invisible, and secondary information like transactional logs can be used to give them some persistence. This invisibility of information-intensive services no doubt contributes to the bias evident in most blueprints toward front stage services that more visibly produce customer value.

Technology enhanced person-to-person service encounters (Context 2)

A customer walks into the independent local bookstore where he's bought books for years, but the longtime employee who knows him well isn't there, and the customer doesn't recognize the new clerk behind the counter. But after the customer introduces himself, the new clerk looks him up in the bookstore's computerized bookstore management application. In an instant the new clerk sees the customer's transactional history of prior purchases, along with notes about his reading tastes written by the longtime employee. The new clerk is now able to recommend some new books that have just arrived.

After information technology became readily available to businesses and service providers, service design concepts and methods were devised to handle "technology infusion" in service encounters (Bitner, et al., 2000). General purpose information technology like database systems, as well as specialized applications for catalog, order, and customer relationship management make service operations more efficient and reliable. In addition, information management technology has increasingly been used to further empower the frontline employee with the information needed to provide personalized and satisfying customer experiences. Such technology ensures that that the information available to all frontline employees is more accurate, complete, consistent and accessible than the tacit personal memories of any of them taken individually.

Nevertheless, just because some information technology has the potential to yield more consistent, reliable, and timely service, design choices must be made about whether and where to introduce it into the service system. Technology can be used solely by the frontline employee to enhance his capabilities, or by both the frontline employee and the customer to more directly enhance their interaction. Fitzsimmons and Fitzsimmons (2006) distinguish these two cases as "technology-assisted" and "technology-facilitated" encounters. But the most important choice is whether the technology should be used to replace the frontline employee entirely, leaving a self-service encounter.

For example, fancy restaurants will employ a sommelier to make suggestions (person-to-person context), but the sommelier might sneak a peek at the "Wine Snob" (WineSnob 2009) application on his PDA to refresh his memory about wines and food pairings before he heads out to the dining room (technology assisted context). And while the sommelier would never reveal to the customer that he has relied on Wine Snob to make a recommendation, in service domains like architecture or technology consulting it is easy to imagine the service provider and customer jointly using technological aids (technology-facilitated context).

A restaurant customer might launch the Wine Snob on his PDA, and might ask the sommelier for a confirmation or second opinion. This last scenario, in which the customer provides his own ad hoc technology to enhance a service encounter, is increasingly common but not easy to systematize because by definition it was not expected by the service provider (if it had been expected, the encounter would be a "technology-facilitated" one). Perhaps "customer technology improvised" is an appropriate category for this type of technology-enhanced service encounter. And of course, the customer might access the "Wine Snob" application from his home computer before heading out to dinner (self-service context).

In addition to improving operational efficiency, technology can be used to adapt a service to satisfy a specific customer or persona by personalizing it. The degree to which a person-to-person service can be personalized is limited by the extent to which the frontline employee is able to interact with the customer to obtain information about the customer's requirements and preferences (Brohman, et al., 2003; Kolesar, et al., 1998). Likewise, personalization depends on the customer's willingness or ability to provide the information. In some situations, this is limited by concerns that the service provider can't be trusted to maintain it in a private and secure manner. Finally, even if the customer provides the information, personalization is constrained by how much of it is maintained by the service provider in an accessible and technology-supported format.

Advances in information and communications technologies have enabled information-intensive activities that create information to be separated in space and time from other processes or services that use it. This is the principle that enables the "outsourcing" of services and 24x7 global customer support (Apte and Mason, 1995, Blinder, 2007). More generally, technology-enabled service disaggregation has transformed vertically integrated and centralized firms into more virtual and network-like forms that function as compositions of collaborating services that can be located almost anywhere in the world, from Boston to Berlin to Bangalore (Palmisano, 2006).

Self-service (Context 3)

When a customer logs in to identify himself on Amazon.com or similar Internet bookseller site, the generic catalog is replaced with a personalized one that reflects his shopping history and interests explicitly expressed in search queries, abandoned shopping carts and wish lists. But unlike the physical bookstore, where following the customer around would be obtrusive, the self-service context enables the easy capture of implicit preferences and interests based on the customer's browsing history. And while an experienced and insightful bookstore employee makes recommendations by reflecting on the purchases and preferences of customers he deems similar, Amazon.com and other Internet retailers employ very sophisticated recommendation services that aggregate and analyze millions of transactions and queries (Shafer, et al., 2001), while also making dynamic adjustments to catalog content and pricing based on the customer's real-time browsing behavior.

A more fundamental change in service design than introducing technology to assist a human service provider is to use technology to transform person-to-person services into self-service ones. This eliminates the frontline employee and moves back the line of visibility between the front and back stage, giving the customer access to information that was previously visible only to the frontline employee.

A more subtle way to understand the impact of introducing technology in a service encounter is that it changes the proportions of physical, interpersonal, and information actions. From this perspective, these proportions are design parameters that can be systematically adjusted by technologies that enable the different types of actions to substitute for each other. Stored information and interpersonal interactions can often replace each other; there is no need to ask a customer to supply personal or preference information that the provider already knows from previous interactions or has obtained from data brokers.

An increasingly common design pattern for technology-enhanced person-to-person services and self-service is for the provider to support the creation and aggregation of preference information or other content from the users or customers of a service. Contributing to this "community content" (Armstrong and Hegel, 2000), "collective intelligence" (Segaran, 2007), or "crowdsourcing" (Howe, 2008) is partly self-serving because it enhances the quality of future service encounters for the contributors, as when customers rate restaurants, hotels, or other service establishments and subsequently choose only highly-rated ones. But it is often an act of generosity or altruism because many people contribute far more information or effort than pure self-interest would justify, even though they know that service will also be enhanced for those who don't contribute at all.

The ergonomics of ATM and telephone keyboards, buttons, and other hardware interaction mechanisms were the foremost design concerns of self-service technology until personal computers emerged around 1980. PCs had enough local processing capability to enable graphical software user interfaces with a greatly expanded interaction repertoire. Techniques for designing, prototyping, and evaluating software user interfaces then developed rapidly and continue to evolve along with new technology platforms for self-service applications (Grudin, 1990).

The most important of these new platforms by far was the World Wide Web, which became mainstream in the mid 1990s and continues to grow at a staggering pace. Any business or organization that provides information or carries out transactions with customers now has a web site, and the usability of these sites is the dominant design concern. "Usability" has numerous definitions but at their intersection are the goals of making applications easy to learn, efficient and engaging to use, and effective in providing functions or information that satisfies user requirements. Some usability problems with user interfaces can be detected and remedied by qualitative techniques like heuristic evaluation by experts and user "walk-throughs" with prototypes (Nielsen, 1994). However, more sophisticated analysis and measurement techniques are required to understand and overcome performance and quality of service problems, especially in service systems where the user interface is a composite application or "mash-up" that presents and integrates information from applications and sources that can be running anywhere in a global service network (Edmunds, et al., 2007; Wiggins, 2007).

Because a competitor or alternate supplier is often "just a click away," the usability and quality of service in a self-service application or web site is an important concern for designers. Most usability specialists would agree with the claim that "the success of online services is largely determined by the customer experience via the web site interface" (Massey, et al., 2008).

However, an emphasis on the usability of the front stage's appearance and behavior can sometimes inadvertently de-emphasize the invisible actions in the back stage of the service system. This isn't a critical oversight for simple transactional online services in which the customer can request and quickly receive the desired service or information. But in more complex service systems that involve substantial processing of information or physical fulfillment, the back stage services have much more to do. For example, submitting an online application for employment or university admission, or ordering from an online store, initiates many actions and information flows that won't complete for days or even months. In such service systems, a narrow focus on usability of the self-service interface as a measure of service quality is seriously incomplete. An online shopping site must be usable, and many seemingly small design details can matter a lot, but the customer's ultimate satisfaction depends far more on whether what he ordered arrives when it was promised. A front-stage experience with acceptable usability is necessary, but it is insufficient and might even be counterproductive if it sets unrealistic expectations about the ultimate outcome of the service system operation. What matters far more is the effective and efficient operation of the back stage services, a service system design challenge that is discussed in an upcoming section.

Multi-channel Services (Context 4)

> A customer gets a recommendation for a new book in an online bookstore but wants it the same day. Can he reserve it online for pickup the same day in the neighborhood bookstore store? When he arrives at the store, should the bookstore employees know what other books he looked online but didn't purchase so they can offer them at a discount? When the customer next visits the online store, are purchases he made in the neighborhood bookstore reflected in his purchase history and recommendations there?

As the Web matured as a platform for online commerce and information services, upstart firms like Amazon.com with no physical presence became competitive threats to incumbents like Barnes and Noble. For these "brick and mortar" firms, creating a web channel and finding the right mix of "bricks and clicks" was an urgent and critical strategic decision, and the concept of "multi-channel services" as a distinct service design context emerged (Gulati and Garino, 2000). The Web channel also inspired the vision of "E-government" services that would radically improve service delivery to citizens and let them avoid inefficient face-to-face encounters in government offices (Osborne and Gaebler, 1993; Gronlund, 2002).

When a service provider becomes truly multi-channel by adding an Internet channel to its existing person-to-person or self-service operations, much more is involved than just adding a self-service channel like ATMs or a telephone touch-tone or IVR user interface. These self-service technologies often support only the small subset of services that can be completed in a short transaction or information request, so the self-service channel is not a full substitute for the person-to-person service.

A web channel, however, can offer many of the same services as the physical channel along with additional personalization. This greater capability and opportunity raises fundamental business model concerns about channel conflict, sales cannibalization, customer segmentation, marketing, branding, and cross-selling (Iqbal, et al., 2003; Falk, et al., 2007). The service customer's experiences and expectations about functionality and quality are synthesized from every encounter across all channels, making the predictability of interactions important (Sousa and Voss, 2006). However, cross-channel predictability is constrained by differences in channel capability, and if those didn't exist, there would be no point in having multiple channels!

Consumers go online to do product research and to learn where to buy things or find service providers. Consumers might shop for particular brands, but they don't always buy them from the same retailer. Multi-channel retailers, on the other hand, want customers to treat their different channels as complements or substitutes for each other, because this will increase sales and strengthen loyalty (Tedeschi, 2007; Bendoly, et al., 2005; Neslin, et al., 2006). So many firms offer a "ship to store" or "local pickup" service that allows a customer to purchase or re-serve a product in the online channel but obtain faster delivery from the physical channel. Likewise, a "return to store" policy allows a purchase made and fulfilled from the online channel to be returned to the neighborhood store if it turns out to be unwanted or unsuitable. These services are simple to describe, but not easy to implement, because the ideal supply chains for online and physical channels are different (Metters and Walton, 2007).

What this all means is that the key strategy and design decisions for multichannel services concern the allocation of services to one or more channels and the manner in which the channels fit together. These decisions ultimately are implemented in terms of the content, direction, and reciprocity of information exchange between the channels. Making these decisions and communicating the resulting design to customers requires design concepts and notations that depict a unified cross-channel view of the service system. A promising new approach here is an extension of the service blueprinting technique to use a "service interface link" symbol to interconnect the separate blueprints for different channels at the points where the process of service delivery moves from one channel to another (Patricio, et al., 2008).

Services on Multiple Devices or Platforms (Context 5)

> An online bookstore can offer many services and a richer user experience to users on the home computers, but it wants to enable them to browse for books using their mobile phones. How should the catalog content and user interface be designed for multiple platforms?

Most people also use one or more other devices other than personal computers to obtain information services. In fact, many times more people in the world use mobile phones than personal computers, and many use PDAs or other devices. These devices differ on multiple dimensions – computing power, memory capacity, portability, display size and resolution, voice recognition and synthesis capability, network bandwidth, GPS capability, and so on. These capabilities are not always correlated and bundled into devices in the same combinations. Some devices are optimized for different services, applications and information types. Other devices strive with mixed success to be hybrid gadgets that combine a phone, camera, email, music player, game console, personal information manager, and computer applications platform.

The proliferation of devices and network alternatives is a challenge for service system designers. If a service provider's intended customers use different or multiple devices, the service must be designed to work on all of them. This task might be considered an extension of the self-service design problem to multiple channels. Because the devices and networks have different capabilities, this task is also analogous to service personalization, although the service is being adapted to the device and only indirectly to its user.

Many mobile phones and PDAs support limited web browsers, which gives people the expectation that they can use them to access services originally designed for browsers on personal computers. After all, they can check webmail, read blogs, weather and news, and conduct searches from their work and home offices; why not do that while commuting on a bus or train? Many business applications for sales and customer management are inherently more valuable when they can be accessed by employees at customer sites and not just in their office locations.

People don't expect their service experiences to be identical on PCs, phones, and PDAs, but they expect them all to be satisfactory and to exhibit some degree of consistency or predictability. Unfortunately, "consistency" and "predictability" are often difficult to define (Grudin, 1989; Richter, et al., 2006). Even when these goals can be specified in design terms, the differences among devices influence the user interface for obtaining the service, the user interface through which it is delivered, the informational content of the service, and the latency of service delivery (Lumsden, 2008). Furthermore, the same device or application might operate in both "always connected" and "occasionally connected" modes, which imposes the challenges of synchronizing information flows and switching transparently between local data storage and network service (Hill, et al., 2004).

Because of the complexity of these design problems, there is little consensus about the best approach for designing services to run on multiple devices or platforms. The earliest web browsers on mobile phones and PDAs weren't very capable, so many web sites and services employed a design philosophy that could be called "dumbing down" or "graceful degradation" (Florins and Vanderdonck, 2004). Sites and services designed for the most capable platform or device were adapted to other devices by applying transformations that systematically changed the user interface for more constrained devices. For example, web pages would be reformatted to fit small screen displays and eliminate navigation and selection controls that no longer worked well. For information in non-text formats, reduced display capabilities required reductions in content fidelity and resolution, and media compression and transcoding might be necessary, sometimes even dynamically (Shanableh and Ghanbari, 2000; Zhang, 2007).

Nevertheless, design approaches for multi-platform or multi-device services that try to make the design problem scalable by applying systematic or automated transformations to a single "mother of all designs" can fail to take advantage of specialized functionality on supposedly lesser devices. For example, while phones have vastly less conventional processing power than desktop computers, they can have sophisticated audio processing capability, integrated cameras, text messaging, GPS functions, and acceleration or orientation sensors.

So an alternative to "device family" or "model-based" design is "native" design. This approach defines and implements the user experience and interface for each device to take maximal advantage of its capabilities. A telephone-based application that was originally designed to use a standard touch-tone keypad would also visually display the menu choices on mobile phones with a display screen. Devices without keyboards, or with very small ones, would rely on voice input. Mobile phones equipped with cameras and QR-code (2-dimensional barcode) detection systems can take photos of the codes on objects or in advertisements and retrieve related web pages (Rohs and Gfeller, 2004). Devices with sophisticated audio processing capabilities can even use music as inputs, as does the Shazam service, which identifies a song from a recorded snippet (Shazam, 2009).

The Apple iPhone exemplifies the optimization of applications to specific devices; as of 2009, more than 50,000 applications exist for it, and most have been built exclusively for it (Apple, 2009; Tedeschi, 2009).

"Back stage-intensive" or "computational" services (Context 6)

When a customer in the local bookstore chooses a book (or accepts a recommendation for one), pays for the book with a credit card, and leaves the store with it, the customer's service encounter to purchase a book is complete.

The customer's experience in the online bookstore seems superficially equivalent to the one in the local bookstore. He chooses a book (or accepts a recommendation), enters his credit card number and address into the shopping cart form, and with a couple of mouse clicks completes the check-out process.

But even though the online encounter has completed with what is apparently a satisfactory result, most of the work to fulfill the customer's book purchase has not yet begun. Fulfillment involves invisible physical actions by warehouse, shipping, and delivery personnel, and each action presents an opportunity for service failure. The wrong book can be picked from the warehouse, or it can be lost, damaged, or delayed in delivery because of a human error, traffic congestion, bad weather, or a host of other factors.

These back stage fulfillment services are interconnected and coordinated by information exchanges among the online retailer and other businesses. The customer's expectations about the service outcome – in this case, the delivery of the book as promised – can be managed by providing him with information about the progress or state of these services. For example, the customer can be emailed the shipment tracking number from the delivery service. The customer's order of the book might have been prompted by a message from the "just published" alerting service that notifies customers when new books by their favorite authors are available. Furthermore, this "just published" service was triggered by another back stage event when the package of new books was scanned on arrival at the warehouse.

Many online retailers are virtual firms that don't own any product inventory. Their catalogs contain the goods that they can reliably obtain from distributors. The "storefront" is a self-service front stage that collects the order information and then passes it on to back stage service providers that process credit card payments, operate the warehouses, deliver packages, and so on (see Glushko and McGrath, Section 1.1, 2005). Taken together, this pattern of physical processes and information exchanges defines a type of service system known as "drop shipment."

Some of these back stage services involved in drop shipment, such as those that check inventory, verify credit, and process payments, are "pure" information services and are typically carried out entirely by automated services without any human involvement or physical actions. Of course not every back stage service can be completely automated, and shipment tracking, credit card fraud detection, customer support, and other processes in the drop shipment service system expose user interfaces to different sorts of people who need to handle exceptional or error situations. However, to the extent that a service system relies on complex back stage choreographies of information flows and the physical actions they direct, the front stage services and interfaces contribute proportionally less to the overall service outcome and user experience.

In these "back stage-intensive" or computational design contexts, it is more important to apply the design concepts and methods for "document engineering" (Glushko and McGrath, 2005) or "service-oriented architecture" (SOA) (Erl, 2004). These design perspectives view the service system abstractly as a set of cooperating services that interact by exchanging information through well-defined interfaces that specify the inputs and outputs of each service. The efficiency of this information exchange depends on how much the services agree on the meaning and encoding of the information they send and receive.

This more abstract modeling philosophy of document engineering and SOA contrasts sharply with traditional service blueprinting and other front stage or "customer-centric" approaches in some important ways. First, it de-emphasizes the differences among person-to-person, self-service, and automated or computational services, because this makes it easier to treat them as substitutable (Glushko and Tabas, 2009). This assumption of potential equivalence is well-supported by modeling notations like sequence and activity diagrams (Pilone and Pitman, 2005) that take a "bird's eye" or top-down perspective that doesn't automatically make the human customer the focus of the process model.

In addition, two distinctive document engineering methods extend the basic SOA philosophy in service system design. The first is that document engineering assumes that in information-intensive industries, documents and other sources of structured information better embody the functional and interface specifications for services than anything else. This assumption might seem tautological, but it merely restates the contrast noted earlier between information-intensive and experience-intensive services. In the former, documents and other information sources are ubiquitous and intrinsic to the goals and activities of the stakeholders and actors, so information is the most important thing to analyze. Even if document implementation or management technology changes over time, the logical model of a document can endure far longer that the tenures of the specific people who produce and use the documents.

In contrast, in experience-intensive service contexts, the interpersonal interactions between the human participants are the most important things for designers to study. Nevertheless, experiential service domains often have documents playing essential roles; for example, it would be difficult to understand a restaurant service system without analyzing menus and following customer orders from the dining room to the kitchen.

The second key method of document engineering is its alignment with the idea of industry reference models or best practices, which it uses as design patterns that define normative or idealized services, their choreography, and the information exchanges needed to request and perform them.

Location-based and Context-aware Services (Context 7)

> A customer is browsing the shelves in his neighborhood bookstore when he receives a text message on his cell phone. The message directs him to the shelf where he can locate a book that he had recently viewed in the online website of the bookstore. He locates the book, takes a photo of its bar code with the cell phone camera, and launches a price check application. He learns that the book is available at a lower price in a competitor's bookstore a half mile away that will be open for another 45 minutes. The map application on his phone shows him the best route to the other store, and he buys the book there instead.

Many new and even some not-so-new technologies have inspired another domain of service design for location-based and context-aware services. "Location" is the most obvious context attribute, but not the only one. In a widely-cited paper, Dey, et al., (2001) defined context as "any information that characterizes a situation related to the interactions between users, applications, and the surrounding environment." The environment consists of places, people, and things, and for each entity there are four categories of context information: location, identity, status (or activity), and time. This open-ended definition is bounded only by the variety and capabilities of the sensors by which context information can be acquired from the environment (Sohraby, et al., 2007).

RFID chips, essentially bar codes with built-in radio transponders, enable location tracking and context sensing to be automated. RFID receivers can be built into store shelves, loading docks, parking lots, toll booths, to detect when some RFID-tagged object is at some meaningful location. RFID tags can be made "smarter" by having them record and transmit information from sensors that detect temperature, humidity, acceleration, and even biological contamination (Want, 2006; Allmendinger and Lombreglia, 2005).

The Global Positioning System was developed as a strategic military capability but it is far more important to most people for its commercial applications. GPS navigation systems provide directions, dispatch emergency responders to vehicles (OnStar, 2009), and combined GPS and RFID devices enable vastly more efficient inventory management in global supply chains (Baars, et al., 2008).

But the most ubiquitous and day-to-day use of GPS technology in information-intensive services is in mobile phones. After the 2001 terrorist attacks, governments worldwide mandated location tracking of mobile phones. Initially, telecom carriers used tower triangulation techniques to do this, so no location information was available in the phone itself. More recent phones have built-in GPS, so the phone can now tell other applications where it is, not just the government! Of course, phones both send and receive information, so once the phone reveals location or contextual information, applications can send location-based services to it (Rao and Minakakis, 2003; Trimi and Sheng, 2008). Location is so intrinsic to mobile services that user interfaces that integrate or "mash up" information into maps have rapidly supplanted text-oriented techniques for presenting choices or search results (Programmable Web, 2009; Raper, et al., 2007).

From the perspective of service design, once again the key principle is that information replaces interaction. There is no need to ask a customer to supply location, time, or other contextual information that the provider has obtained or inferred from a back stage service or sensor. Likewise, there is no value in providing information to the customer that isn't relevant to his location or context. For example, the results for a phone browser query for "coffee" in Seattle should filter out any coffee shops in Berkeley. Likewise, a user searching for "next bus" would ideally receive just that part of the local bus timetable that specifies the schedule for his location in the next few minutes.

The limiting factor on context-aware services might well be the willingness of people to allow service providers to use information about their current or previous contexts.

Design Concepts and Methods for Information-Intensive Service Systems

Each of the 7 design contexts has characteristic design concerns and methods, highlighted in Table 1.

Table 1. The Seven Design Contexts: Concepts, Concerns, and Methods

DESIGN CONTEXT	CONCEPTS AND CONCERNS	METHODS
1. Person-to-person	Empowerment, touch points, line of visibility	Ethnography, blueprinting, personas
2. Technology enhanced p2p	Personalization	Customer modeling and segmentation, CRM
3. Self-service	Ergonomics, usability	Iterative prototyping, heuristic evaluation, customer analytics
4. Multi-channel	Complementarity, reciprocity, integration	Process modeling
5. Multiple platforms and devices	Consistency, scaleability	Capability modeling, model-based interfaces, graceful degradation
6. Back stage, computational	Information and process standards, choreography	Use cases, data and document modeling, service oriented architecture, design patterns
7. Location-based and context-aware	Sensor technology	Managing identify and privacy

At first glance, these different design concerns and methods may seem incompatible, making it easy to understand why there has been little research or practical work in service design that spans more than a few contexts. But as described in the previous sections, there are systematic relationships among the contexts that can be exploited as design parameters or patterns. Furthermore, a more abstract look at the seven contexts suggests the unifying design concept that services and service encounters can be viewed as information exchanges. The abstraction enables the contexts to function as building blocks that follow design patterns for the incremental evolution of many different kinds of information-intensive service systems.

The Relationships Among the Seven Contexts

Figure 1 depicts the seven service design contexts to show their derivational and compositional relationships. It is inspired by and extends Figure 5.1 on page 106 of Fitzsimmons and Fitzsimmons (2004).

The Seven Service Design Contexts

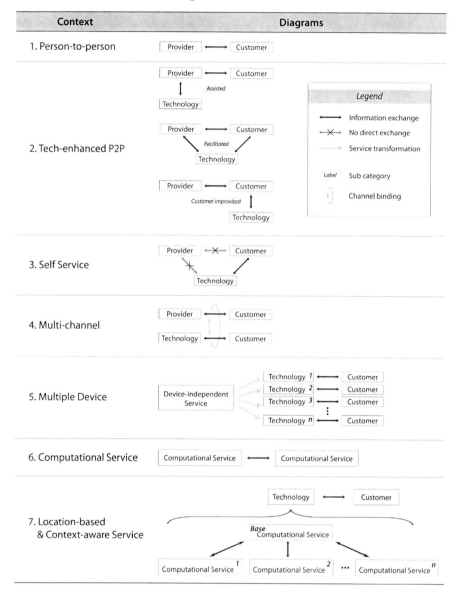

Figure 1. The Seven Design Contexts: Derivational and Compositional Relationships

- Contexts 1, 2, and 3 span a continuum of service designs that progressively incorporate technology to make services more transactional and less relational

- Multi-channel service systems (Context 4) combine person-to-person encounters and self-service by integrating information flows between them

- Multi-device services (Context 5) are self-services that run the same or appropriately transformed service on more than one device or technology platform

- Computational services (or "machine-to-machine" or "back stage" services) (Context 6) do not expose a service interface to human actors

- Computational services that transmit location, time, or other contextual information inferred from a back stage service or sensor enable location-based and context-aware services for people (Context 7)

Services and Service Encounters as Information Exchanges

Every service encounter consists of two actors: a service provider and a service consumer (Glushko and Tabas, 2009; MacKenzie, et al., 2006). "Actor" is used here in an abstract sense to include both human and computational entities, just as it is in use cases and other system modeling methods (Cockburn, 2000); services that are one-to-many can be modeled as sets of pairwise ones. The interactions between the two actors take place through an interface that describes what the service does and how it is requested. This service interface is always explicit with computational actors, where well-defined inputs and outputs are a prerequisite for the infusion of computation or automation, and where the interaction is intrinsically and exclusively an exchange of information (see the section titled "Back stage-intensive" or "computational" services in this paper; Erl, 2004; Glushko and McGrath, 2005). In contrast, the service interface is often implicit and underspecified in person-to-person encounters, and information exchange is only a part of what goes on.

Analyzing person-to-person service encounters as information exchanges might seem to ignore the essence of highly experiential service. Nevertheless, even for experiential services, it is almost always necessary for the two actors in a service encounter to engage in some amount of information exchange to identify requirements or expectations, to clarify their roles, or assess the status or quality of the service delivery.

Emphasizing the information exchange aspect of service encounters makes it easier to design and understand service systems that combine multiple design contexts because it treats them as complementary or substitutable components rather than antagonistic alternatives. It might not matter if the actor performing a translation or calculation service is a human or a computer, and the abstraction of information exchange hides the implementation. Similarly, while there is an important social dimension in service systems that use community content or crowdsourcing to enhance service quality, the aggregation of preference information or content is the underlying mechanism.

Contexts as Building Blocks for Service Systems

The numerical order of the contexts defines a typical design trajectory for service systems, as was demonstrated by the progressive complexity of the service system implied by the seven bookstore scenarios that accompanied the presentation of Contexts 1-7 in the third major section of this paper.

Contexts 1, 2, and 3 span a continuum of service designs that progressively incorporate technology to make services more transactional, with improved consistency, reliability, timeliness, and personalization. More abstract characterization of the service encounter facilitates the technological augmentation of the service provider or the substitution of a computational actor for him.

But these systematic changes in the character of the service system can reduce its experiential and relational quality. As a result, many service systems integrate person-to-person encounters and self-service (Context 4) to satisfy the types of customers who prefer the former and to provide services that create additional value through the exchange of information between channels. Banking and catalog shopping are two other categories of service that have followed this pattern of service system evolution.

Delivering some services on multiple devices or platforms (Context 5) and with location-based and context-awareness capabilities (Context 7, e.g., through sensors in mobile phones) are natural and even inevitable technology-enabled expansions of the scope of a service system. These contexts have become essential parts of service systems that run supply and distribution chains, deliver medical care, manage energy or facilities, or operate other information-intensive enterprise or inter-enterprise processes or systems of equipment (Context 6).

Instead of starting with a person-to-person service (Context 1) and adding technology contexts to it, an alternative evolutionary trajectory for service systems begins with a Context 6 back stage or computational service. Many enterprise applications, transactional systems, or sensors associated with objects or equipment generate information that is important to effective business operations but which might not initially be exposed in customer-facing interfaces. Making this information available for self-service access (Context 3) via the telephone, personal computer, or other device (Context 5) can create substantial new value, often enough to justify a secondary customer support channel to handle exception or error cases (Context 4). Self-service package tracking is an extremely successful example of this pattern where a customer-facing service was created to exploit latent value from invisible back stage services.

In a more complex example, a service system for residential energy efficiency could evolve incrementally by externalizing the information captured and created by embedded controllers and appliances (Context 6), initially giving consumers more visibility into and control of energy use with "smart" thermostats and control panels (Context 3), and then later allowing remote control access from other locations and devices (Context 5). Connecting the home system to the utility grid could enable appliances to control themselves in response to real-time energy pricing based on aggregate system demand (Context 7).

Points of View in a Service System

If complex service systems are assembled from different service contexts that share the unifying principle of information exchange, then the creation of value in the service system can be described in terms of the content and choreography of information flows within and between the contexts and their component services. The actor or service at the end of an information flow, often the stereotypical "end user" or "customer," is usually designated as the focal point of the service system, especially when the service system contains a person-to-person context. Service design techniques like blueprints or storyboards emphasize this customer-centric point of view.

Nevertheless, this point of view is arbitrary, and often many of the actors or services in a service system could be alternative or secondary points of view. What is a supply chain from one perspective is a demand chain from another. In an educational service system the conventional focus is on the teacher-student service encounter, but it is also essential to design the teacher-parent encounter. In a hospital, it is easy to default to the patient as the focal point of view, but in a teaching hospital, much of the service system is designed to educate medical students, and patients can in many ways be considered as service providers to them.

It is useful to consider multiple points of view when designing a service system, but it is essential to select one as primary. The choice shapes the priority of design requirements, constraints, and information sources; suggests relevant design patterns; identifies the front and back stages; and has profound implications for the creation and capture of value. For example, consider the restaurant service system, defined from the customer's point of view, with the front stage in the dining room and the back stage in the kitchen. Almost the same facility could be used as a cooking school, but in that service system the customers are the student cooks, the front stage is the kitchen, and the people eating the food in the dining room are back stage feedback to the cooks.

Design Case Study: "Smart Multi-channel Bookstore"

A service system for a "smart multi-channel bookstore" called "Bookland" was recently designed as a course project by a team of graduate students at the University of California, Berkeley (Blong, et al., 2008). The team – Devin Blong, Jonathan Breitbart, Julian Couhoult, and Jessica Santana – assumed the role of consultants to a large chain bookstore that also has a web retail site. Their goals were to improve customer satisfaction, increase sales, improve the efficiency of store operations, and enable the company to gather more useful marketing information. The Bookland service system is similar in many ways to the hypothetical service system implied in the presentation of the seven contexts in the third section of this paper, but the presentation here will emphasize more of the aspects of the service system that operate in the physical bookstore.

The consulting team's strategy was to build a "smart multi-channel" service system that better integrates the online and offline customer experiences, that uses RFID technology to enhance operational and customer services, and that incorporates the requirements of a broader range of stakeholders beyond the bookstore customer. Their design explicitly provides services that target both frontline and back stage bookstore employees and the bookstore manager.

Information Flow in the Bookland Service System

The operation of the Bookland service system can be described in terms of the flow of information between the different actors and contexts it contains. The key components of Bookland, highlighting the information exchanges and touchpoints where the contexts interconnect, are as follows:

- A loyalty / membership program that customers can join in either channel; the customer's membership number is the primary data key that links online and offline identities and information. Customers are issued a RFID-enabled "smart card" that they can use to sign in at self-service kiosks and customer service desks.
- A customer profile built from information about customer behavior and transactions in both the online and physical channels; used by back stage personalization and marketing services that operate in both channels.
- Book identity information encoded in RFID tags, used to track book locations and enable "finding" services for customers and "reshelving" and other inventory management services for employees.
- Customer service desks where technology-enhanced person-to-person bookstore services are provided.
- Self-service kiosks in the bookstores where customers can search for books, receive recommendations and promotions, and print out shopping

lists and store maps that show the location of selected and recommended items.

- Bookstore management "dashboards" used by employees and managers to provide customer service and perform scheduled and event-driven operational services involving RFID-tagged books.
- A "store map" composite application framework that can depict book location information in two different ways: to guide customers to find books in their normal locations, and to guide employees to find misplaced "zombie" books so that they can be returned to their normal locations.

The information flow through all of these contexts is shown in Figure 2, which schematically combines a floor plan for a physical bookstore with the online one and some of the important information sources and services. The tight integration and recurrent information flows between the two channels highlights the multichannel essence of the Bookland service system.

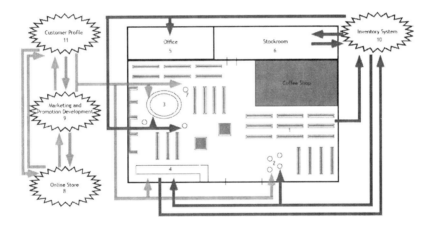

Figure 2. Information Flows in the "Bookland" Service System

1. **Bookshelves.** Each book (or item) is tagged with an RFID chip. When items are moved from the shelf, their location can be tracked anywhere in the store.
2. **Self-Service Kiosks.** Kiosks are located near the bookstore entrance (#2 in Figure 2) and throughout the store (#7), where customers can wave/swipe their membership cards or type in their customer ID to log in. These kiosks display personalized welcome pages and tailored promotions (See Figure 3). They also provide search and browsing functions and display real-time inventory and

location information on a store map. Customers can scan any item in the store at a kiosk to obtain additional information, such as customer and editorial reviews and related items, at which time the book is added to the customer's profile. The kiosks allow customers to build shopping lists and can print the store maps. If an item is not in stock in the current store but is available online or at other store locations, the kiosk will suggest alternative ordering/purchasing options, including home delivery, shipping to the current store, or pickup at nearby retail locations where the item is in stock. All customer searching, browsing, and purchasing activity on the store kiosks is combined with similar activities online and added to the customer's profile (see #11 below).

Figure 3. Customer User Interface for "Bookland" Service System

3. **Customer Service Help Desk.** Customers approaching the help desk with questions are asked to identify themselves with their loyalty cards or online customer IDs. Frontline employees use the bookstore management system's dashboard to display the customer's name, profile information including purchase and browsing history (both online and offline), and a list of tailored promotions for the customer. The dashboards also provide real-time inventory and location information for any item in the store.

4. **Checkout.** **Point-of-scale scanning** instantly updates the inventory system and the customer's purchase history in his profile.

5. **Bookstore Manager's Office.** The bookstore office contains the manager's workstation with various operational and management applications in addition to all of the services available in the kiosks and employee dashboards.

6. **Stock Room.** Merchandise in the stock room, like that in the bookstore, is managed using the RFID-driven inventory system that keeps track of locations. Low stock alerts for popular items automatically trigger orders to replace them. Employees can use terminals in the office or stock room or any of the kiosks to display dashboards for various operational and management services. The item alert service driven by transactional and location information is depicted in the top two panels of Figure 4; this is the same store map service that appears in the lower right panel of Figure 3, but in Figure 4 the map is "mashed up" with the locations of misplaced books so that the employee can restock them.

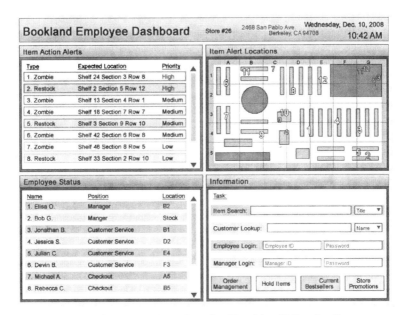

Figure 4. Employee User Interface for "Bookland" Service System

7. **Kiosks.** See 2.

8. **Online Store.** Visitors to the online store are encouraged to log in to receive personalized recommendations and promotions. Browsing and purchasing activity is added to the customer profile.

9. **Marketing and Promotions System.** Marketing and promotion services dynamically develop customized recommendations, coupons, promotions, and bundles for each customer. These will be displayed online when the user logs in or accesses kiosks in physical stores.
10. **Inventory System.** The real-time inventory system tracks the number and locations of all items in each store and warehouse. It generates fetch and restock alerts to employee dashboards and re-orders items according to business rules.
11. **Customer Profile.** All customer browsing and purchasing information (both online and offline) is fed to a customer's profile.

The In-store Service System from the Customer's Perspective

Figure 5 presents a service blueprint for the customer's in-store experience. It imposes a point of view on the service system information flow represented in Figure 2.

Physical Evidence	Kiosk	Welcome Screen / Members Card	Member Profile Screen	Member Profile / Search Interface	Book Directions / Map, Coupon	Books	Books / Receipt
User Actions	Customer approaches bookstore kiosk	Customer swipes members card, logs in to kiosk	Customer considers suggestions	Customer searches for book	Customer prints book location map and coupon discounts	Customer walks to book locations and retrieves books	Customer discards one book and purchases the rest
Front Stage		Welcome Screen	Members Profile Screen, Suggestions, Promotions	Kiosk search interface	Book location and tailored promotions		Checkout and registers
Back Stage		Kiosk software queries	Kiosk returns user profile, suggestions, promotions	Kiosk software queries	Kiosk returns book location, bundled promotional discounts		Systems logs customer purchases
Support		Customer Database	Marketing Database	Inventory DB / Location DB			Customer DB / Inventory DB

Figure 5. Customer-Centric Service Blueprint for "Bookland" Service System

The In-store Service System for the Employee's Restocking Tasks

Figure 6 presents a service blueprint for the bookstore employee, imposing a point of view that strongly contrasts to that of the customer in Figure 5. For example, some service system components that were invisible to the customer are now in the front stage, while others that were front stage to the customer are not visible to the employee. The bookstore blueprint shows the process of performing two kinds of restocking tasks. The first is to returning so-called "zombie" books that and have been left in the coffee shop, restroom, or any other location to their normal shelf locations.   The second is restocking books that have been sold and taken out of the store.

		Physical Evidence	Employee Dashboard	Employee Dashboard	Map / Book	Employee Dashboard	Employee Dashboard	Map / Books
User Actions	Employee checks computer screen	Employee sees zombie book action alert	Employee clicks on alert	Employee retrieves book and replaces it	Employee sees restocking action alert	Employee clicks on alert	Employee retrieves copies from stock and replenishes shelf
Front Stage		Employee dashboard alert section	Alert details link	Map with current book location	Employee dashboard alert section	Alert details link	Map with stock room and shelf book locations
Back Stage		Enterprise Service Bus (ESB) integrates RFID data, identifies zombie book	Employee system queries	Kiosk returns zombie book's current location	ESB integrates RFID data, identifies book that needs restocking	Employee system queries	Kiosk returns book's location in stock room and target shelf location
Support		Event Stream Processing (ESP), RFID Tracking tool, Inventory DB	Location DB		ESP, RFID Tracking tool, Inventory DB	Location DB	

Figure 6. Employee-Centric Service Blueprint for "Bookland" Service System

The differences between Figures 5 and 6 clearly demonstrate why it is useful to consider multiple points of view when designing a service system.   Neither of them alone captures the complexity of the information flow between the different design contexts shown in Figure 2.

Conclusions and Future Work

Many of the most complex service systems being built and imagined today combine person-to-person encounters, technology-enhanced encounters, self-service, computational services, multi-channel, multi-device, and location-based and context-aware services. The research reported in this paper has examined the characteristic concerns and methods for these seven different design contexts to propose a unifying view that spans them, especially when the service-system is "information-intensive." A focus on the information required to perform the service, how the responsibility to provide this information is divided between the service provider and service consumer, and the patterns that govern information exchange yields a more abstract description of service encounters and outcomes. This makes it easier to see the systematic relationships among the contexts that can be exploited as design parameters or patterns, such as the substitutability of stored or contextual information for person-to-person interactions.

This more abstract perspective on service design turns the different design contexts into building blocks that enable the incremental design of service systems. One typical trajectory for service system evolution starts with a person-to-person service and adds technology contexts to it. An alternative design trajectory adds customer-facing service contexts to exploit latent value from invisible back stage services.

More thorough analysis of existing and potential services will identify design patterns that encourage service innovation at the service system level while preserving the best practices embodied in each of the service design contexts. In addition, it should be possible to extend the unifying ideas about service interfaces and information exchange to better understand service encounters and outcomes that arise in the intersection of service systems. As examples: a business traveler interacts with transportation, hotel, restaurant, and various professional service providers during a business trip; a patient interacts with his physician, hospitals and medical laboratories, insurance companies, and the benefits office at his workplace. It is surely impossible to anticipate all of these ad hoc or dynamic service system compositions, but it is surely necessary to recognize their inevitability. Techniques for designing service interfaces that facilitate composition and substitution of contexts are under development and will become increasingly important.

References

Allmendinger, G., and Lombreglia, R. (2005). Four Strategies for the Age of Smart Services, *Harvard Business Review*, 83(10): 131-145.

Apple (2009). Apple iPhone3G App Store. http://www.apple.com/iphone/appstore/ (accessed 23 April 2009).

Apte, U. and Goh, C. (2004). Applying Lean Manufacturing Principles to Information Intensive Services. *International Journal of Services Technology and Management*, 5(5-6): 488-
506.

Apte, U. and Karmarkar, U. (2007). BPO and the Globalization of Information Intensive Services. In: U.M. Apte and U.S. Karmarkar, (Eds.), *Managing in the Information Economy:
Current Research Issues*, Springer, Norwell, MA.

Apte, U. and Mason, R. (1995). Global Disaggregation of Information-Intensive Services. *Management Science*, 41(7): 1250-1262.

Armstrong, A., and Hagel, J. III (2000). The Real Value of Online Communities. In: Lesser, E.,
Fontaine, M., and Slusher, J. (Eds.), *Knowledge and Communities*. Butterworth-Heinemann.

Baars, H., Kemper, H-G, Lasi, H., and Siegel, M. (2008). Combining RFID Technology and
Business Intelligence for Supply Chain Optimization – Scenarios for Retail Logistics, *Proceedings of the 41st Hawaii International Conference on System Sciences – 2008*.

Bendoly, E., Blocher, J., Bretthauer, K., Krishnan, S., Venkataramanan, M. (2005). Online/In-
Store Integration and Customer Retention, *Journal of Service Research*, 7(4): 313-327.

Benford, S., Giannachi, G., Koleva, and Rodden, T. (2009). From Interaction to Trajectories:
Designing Coherent Journeys Through User Experiences, *CHI'09*, 709-718.

Beyer, H. and Holtzblatt, K. (1998). *Contextual Design*. Morgan-Kauffman.

Bitner, M.J., Brown, S., and Meuter, M. (2000). Technology Infusion in Service Encounters.
Journal of the Academy of Marketing Science, 28(1): 139-149.

Bitner, M.J., Ostrom, A., and Morgan, F. (2008). Service Blueprinting: A Practical Technique
for Service Innovation. *California Management Review*, 50(3): 66-94.

Blinder, A. (2006). Offshoring: The Next Industrial Revolution? *Foreign Affairs*, 85(2): 113-
128.

Blong. D., Breitbart, J., Couhoult, J., and Santana, J. (2008). Smart Bookstore. *Team Project for
Information Systems and Service Design Course*, University of California Berkeley, Fall
2008.

Brohman, M., Watson, R., Piccoli, G., and Parasuraman, A. (2003). Data Completeness: A Key
to Effective Net-based Customer Service Systems, Communications of the ACM, 46(6): 47-
51.

Cockburn A. (2000) *Writing Effective Use Cases*. Addison-Wesley, Reading

Davis, S.M. and Dunn, M. (2002) *Building the Brand-Driven Business. Operationalize Your
Brand to Drive Profitable Growth*. San Francisco, CA: Jossey-Bass.

Dey, A., Abowd, G., and Salber, D. (2001). A Conceptual Framework and a Toolkit for Supporting the Rapid Prototyping of Context-Aware Applications. *Human-Computer Interaction*,
16(2): 97–166.

Dubberly, H. and Evenson, S. (2008). The Experience Cycle, *Interactions*, 15(3): 11-15.

Edmunds, A., White, R., Morris, D., and Drucker. S. (2007). Instrumenting the Dynamic Web.
Journal of Web Engineering, 6(3): 244-260.

Erl, T. (2004). *Service-Oriented Architecture*. Prentice Hall.

Falk, T., Schepers, J., Hammerschmidt, M., and Bauer. H. (2007). Identifying Cross-Channel
Dissynergies for Multichannel Service Providers. *Journal of Service Research*, 10(2): 143-
160.

Fitzsimmons, J. A., and Fitzsimmons, M. J. (2006). *Service Management*. McGraw Hill.

Florins, M. and Vanderdonckt, J. (2004). Graceful Degradation of User Interfaces as a Design
Method for Multiplatform Systems. *2004 International Conference on Intelligent User Interfaces*.

Frei, F. (2006). Breaking the Trade-Off between Efficiency and Service. *Harvard Business Review*, 84(11):93-101.

Glushko, R., (2009). Designing "Service Systems." Presentation for *"Seeing Tomorrow's Services: A Panel on Service Design,"* 19 March 2009.
http://people.ischool.berkeley.edu/~glushko/glushko_files/Glushko-20090319.pdf (accessed
23 April 2009)

Glushko, R. and McGrath, T. (2005). *Document Engineering: Analyzing and Designing Documents for Business Informatics and Web Services.* The MIT Press, Cambridge, MA.

Glushko, R. and Tabas, L. (2009). Designing Service Systems by Bridging the "Front Stage" and "Back Stage." *Information Systems and E-Business Management,* 7(4): 407-427.

Gronlund, A. (2002). *Electronic Government: Design, Applications and Management.* IGI.

Grudin, J. (1989). The Case Against User Interface Consistency. *Communications of the ACM,* 32(10): 1164-1173.

Gulati, R. and Garino, J. (2000) Get the Right Mix of Bricks & Clicks, *Harvard Business Review,* 78(3): 107-114.

Heskett, J., Jones T., Loveman, G., Sasser Jr., W., and Schlesinger, L. (1994). Putting the Service-Profit Chain to Work. *Harvard Business Review,* 72(2): 164-174.

Hill, D., Webster, B., Jezierski, E., Vasireddy, S., Al-Sabt, M., Wastell, B., Rasmussen, J., Gale, P., and Slater, P. (2004). Occasionally Connected Smart Clients. http://msdn.microsoft.com/en-us/library/ms998482.aspx (Accessed 24 April 2009).

Howe, J. (2008). *Crowdsourcing: Why the Power of the Crowd Is Driving the Future of Business.* Crown Business.

Iqbal, Z., Verma, R., and Baran, R. (2003). Understanding Consumer Choices and Preferences in Transaction-Based e-Services, *Journal of Service Research,* 6(1): 51-65.

Kelley, S. (1993). Discretion and the Service Employee. *Journal of Retailing,* 69(1): 104-126.

Kolesar, P. Van Ryzin, G. and Cutler, W. (1998). Creating Customer Value Through Industrialized Intimacy: New Strategies for Delivering Personalized Service. *Strategy and Business,* 12: 33-43.

Lashley, C. (1995). Towards an Understanding of Employee Empowerment in Hospitality Services. *International Journal of Contemporary Hospitality Management,* 7(1): 27-32.

Levitt, T. (1972). Production-Line Approach to Services. *Harvard Business Review,* 50(September-October): 41-52.

Lumsden, J. (Ed). (2008). *Handbook of Research on User Interface Design and Evaluation for Mobile Technology.* IGI Global.

MacKenzie, C., Laskey, K., McCabe, F., Brown, P., and Metz, R. (2006). Reference Model for Service Oriented Architecture 1.0, http://docs.oasis-open.org/soa-rm/v1.0/ (accessed 22 April 2009).

Maglio, P., Srinivasan, S., Kreulen, J., and Spohrer, J. (2006). Service Systems, Service Scientists, SSME, and Innovation. *Communications of the ACM,* 49(7): 81-85.

Massey, A., Khatri, V., and Montoya-Weiss, M. (2008). Online Services, Customer Characteristics and Usability Requirements, Proceedings of the 41st Hawaii International Conference on System Sciences.

Metters, R., and Walton, S. (2007). Strategic Supply Chain Choices for Multi-Channel Internet Retailers, *Service Business,* 1(4): 317-331.

Meyer, C. and Schwager, A. (2007). Understanding Customer Experience. *Harvard Business Review.* 85(2):116-126.

Mills, P. and Moberg, D. (1982). Perspectives on the Technology of Service Operations, *The Academy of Management Review,* 7(3): 467-478.

Neslin, S., Grewal, D., Leghorn, R., Shankar, V., Teerling, M., Thomas, J., and Verhoef, P. (2006). Challenges and Opportunities in Multichannel Customer Management. *Journal of Service Research* 2006; 9(2): 95-112.

Nielsen, J. (1994). *Usability Engineering.* Morgan Kauffman.

OnStar (2009). OnStar Services. http://www.onstar.com/us_english/jsp/explore/onstar_basics/services.jsp (Accessed 25 April 2009).

Osborne, D., and Gaebler, T. (1993). *Reinventing Government: How the Entrepreneurial Spirit is Transforming the Public Sector.* Plume.

Palmisano, S. (2006). The Globally Integrated Enterprise. *Foreign Affairs,* 85(3): 127-136.

Patricio, L., Fisk, R., and Cunha, J. (2008). Designing Multi-Interface Service Experiences: The Service Experience Blueprint. Journal of Service Research, 10(4): 318-334.

Pilone. D., and Pitman, N. (2005). *UML 2.0 in a Nutshell.* O'Reilly.

Programmable Web (2009). Top Mashup Tags. http://www.programmableweb.com/mashups (Accessed 24 April 2009).

Rao, B. and Minakakis, L. (2003). Evolution of Mobile Location-Based Services. *Communications of the ACM*, 46(12): 61-65.

Raper, J., Gartner, G., Karimi, H., and Rizos, C. (2007). Applications of Location–based Services: A Selected Review. *Journal of Location Based Services*, 1(2): 89-111.

Richter, K., Nichols, J., Gajos, K., and Seffah, A. (2006). The Many Faces of Consistency in Cross-platform Design. *Conference on Human Factors in Computing Systems*, 1639-1642.

Rohs, M., and Gfeller, B. (2004). Using Camera-equipped Mobile Phones for Interacting with Real-world Objects. *Proceedings of Advances in Pervasive Computing*, 265-271, Apr. 2004.

Segaran, T. (2007). *Programming Collective Intelligence.* O'Reilly.

Shafer, J., Konstan, J. A., and Riedl, J. (2001). E-Commerce Recommendation Applications. *Data Mining and Knowledge Discovery*, 5 (1/2): 115-153.

Shanableh, T. and Ghanbari, M. 2000. Heterogeneous Video Transcoding to Lower Spatiotemporal Resolutions and Different Encoding Formats. *IEEE Trans. Multimed.* 2(2): 101–110.

Shazam (2009). http://www.shazam.com/ (accessed 23 April 2009).

Sohraby, K., Minoli, D., and Znati, T. (2007). *Wireless Sensor Networks: Technology, Protocols, and Applications.* Wiley Interscience.

Sousa, R. and Voss, C. (2006). Service Quality in Multichannel Services Employing Virtual Channels. *Journal of Service Research*, 8(4): 356-371.

Spohrer, J., Maglio, P., Bailey, J. and Gruhl, D (2007). Steps Toward a Science of Service Systems. *IEEE Computer*, 40(1): 71-77.

Teboul, J. (2006). *Service is Front-Stage.* Palgrave Macmillan.

Tedeschi, B. (2007) Retailer's Shortcut From Desktop to Store, *New York Times.* 24 September 2007.

Tedeschi, B. (2009). Sprinting After the iPhone, and Starting to Close the Gap. *New York Times*, 8 April 2009.

Trimi, S., and Sheng, H. (2008). Emerging Trends in M-Government. *Communications of the ACM*, 51(5): 53-58.

Want, R. (2006). An Introduction to RFID Technology. *Pervasive Computing*, 5(1): 25-33.

Wiggins, A. (2007). Data-Driven Design: Using Web Analytics to Validate Heuristics, Bulletin of the American Society for Information Science and Technology, 33(5): 20-24.

Wine Snob (2009), http://www.iwinesnob.com/ (accessed 16 April 2009).

Zeithaml, V., Berry, L., and Parasuraman, A. (1998). Communication and Control Processes in Delivery of Service Quality. *Journal of Marketing*, 52: 35-48.

Zhang, D. (2007). Web Content Adaptation for Mobile Handheld Devices. *Communications of the ACM*, 50(2): 75-79.

Business Architectures for the Design of Enterprise Service Systems

Susanne Glissmann

    IBM Research - Almaden

Jorge Sanz

    IBM Research - Almaden

Business Architecture provides foundational and actionable concepts for enterprise service systems and their transformation. In practical terms, Business Architecture is an approach to formalizing the way an organization operates based on the convergence among strategy management, business process management and information technology. Partial perspectives on this convergence have received a great deal of attention from different disciplines in the last two decades. Companies and industries in regimes of fast technological change and innovation have made Business Architecture gain new emphasis, and thus, the discipline has been recently revisited intensively by companies, government, analysts, standards organizations, and researchers.

Business Architecture comprises three core components or dimensions, namely, conceptual model, methodology and tooling. Thereby, the variety of Business Architecture perspectives is wide and applications depend on purpose of adoption, scope of usage, and overall maturity of specific concepts. As Business Architecture involves different concepts and it has a strong multidisciplinary nature, it is common to find "different Business Architectures" in the literature. However, it is the different contexts for its application what makes Business Architecture appear as distinct.

With the goal of providing some practical assessment, this chapter reviews ten approaches to Business Architecture from the literature and evaluates them according to proposed measures of strength and weakness. Emphasizing the service system nature of an enterprise, the evaluation makes emphasis on the service concept as a main constituent of Business Architecture.

P.P. Maglio et al. (eds.), *Handbook of Service Science*, Service Science: Research and Innovations in the Service Economy, DOI 10.1007/978-1-4419-1628-0_12,
© Springer Science+Business Media, LLC 2010

Motivation

Growing global competition with constantly changing marketplaces and increasing customer demands has altered the way enterprises sell service offerings to their customers and collaborate with their partners (Friedman, 2007, 9). Consequently, in order to compete, enterprises must have a comprehensive knowledge about their business, must be able to quickly evaluate the business effect of external factors, and must be in a position to recognize new business innovations. Based on this knowledge, decisions can be made to adjust the enterprise accordingly, including the required modifications to the company's information systems. In this context Business Architecture (BA) has regained interest, providing an approach to analyze business concerns, align solutions to business priorities and communicate resulting actions and portfolios (Burton & Robertson, 2008)[1].

According to a recent study by Forrester, 50% of the analyzed companies claimed to have an active BA initiative, whereas 20% were planning to engage in BA work in the near future (Scott, 2008). However, despite the high interest in BA, there is not yet a common understanding of the main concepts (Burton, 2008). Furthermore, no holistic business architecture is available, and instead, various BAs have emerged, differing significantly in purpose, scope, level of detail, and maturity (BAWG, 2009a). For instance, some BAs are business-centric, focusing on business transformation and business capabilities necessary to realize change. Other cases of BA are IT centric, guiding the enterprise in IT strategy and IT investment decisions. Consequently, the strengths and weaknesses of current business architectures are often not clear, thus making it difficult for enterprises to determine the most suitable BA approach for their needs. With increasing relevance of a service-focus in enterprises (Spohrer et al., 2008), the need to understand how service components are represented in current business architectures is growing.

Thus, aiming at providing improved insights for the selection of business architectures, this chapter is structured as followed. The next section provides background information for our research, describing the notion of an enterprise service system and business architecture. We then introduce ten business architecture approaches that represent important trends in the literature. A comparative analysis identifies status quo, as well as BA's strengths and weaknesses regarding conceptual models, methodologies and tools. The last section draws some conclusions and proposes future research opportunities.

---

[1] Enterprise Architecture was likely the first context in which a Business Architecture was required (Minoli, 2007, 9). However, the architectural breadth of EA is broader than BA as the former also includes technology and application architectures (The Open Group 2009b). Much in the same way non-profits and government organizations may have found EA useful, the application of BA will also bring a number of unique advantages to these industries. While the word "business" suggests that the scope of BA be for-profit enterprises, such is not the case as the BA conceptual model definitions clearly prove. Whether an entire EA or Business Architecture is to be used depends on the problem and context at hand. This subject is complex and goes outside the scope of this paper.

Background

This section describes the notions of enterprise service systems and business architecture. The goal is to introduce some concepts and common language.

Enterprise Service System

Due to the increasing interest in service science amongst academic and practitioners, the term service system has gained momentum in recent years. A service system is defined as a dynamic collection of people, technologies and other resources, that interact with other service systems through shared information (Cambridge & IBM, 2007). Its goal is to create and deliver value together with the partnering service systems (i.e., customers, providers and other stakeholders). Examples of service systems include people, foundations, non-profits, non-governmental organizations, cities, nations, and enterprises (Spohrer et al., 2008). The focal point of the service system is the service, i.e., the value-cocreation phenomena that generates mutual benefits for two interacting service systems.

Service systems are decomposed into 'front stage' and 'back stage', (Glushko & Tabas, 2007; Spohrer et al., 2008; Teboul, 2006). The 'front stage' represents the provider-customer interactions that aim at ensuring customer satisfaction in multiple customer touch points and channels of contact. The 'back stage' addresses the operational efficiency. It is concerned with the optimization of the enterprise's productivity, which can be achieved through skilled employees, efficient processes and strong relationships with other players in the service network, i.e., partners and suppliers. Service performance depends similarly on front-stage and back-stage components. Thereby, the service system must identify the best design of these components in order to increase the overall service performance.

The service system considered in this chapter is the ***Enterprise***. As service system, the enterprise faces the ongoing challenge to remain competitive, providing cost-efficient and more valuable services to its customers. In order to create a sustainable front- and back-stage, the enterprise must determine necessary actions, analyzing its different business domains. Based on Tikkanen et al. (2005) the following four business domains can be defined for the enterprise.

1. ***Strategy & Structure*** defines the meaning and direction of an enterprise, governing its actions and structure. The domain is decomposed into three subdomains. First, Business Strategy which refer to the development of the enterprise's business models. Second, Organizational Structure, which describes the decomposition of the enterprise into organizational units. Third, Governance, which specifies internal and external commitments of the enterprise.
2. The ***Business Network*** describes the enterprise's interaction with its partners, as well as the partners' impact on the enterprise. It comprises four subdomains, in which the enterprise has varying roles. In the Customer Relation-

ship Portfolio the enterprise is the service provider, offering services to the final customers; in the Supplier Relationship Portfolio the enterprise itself is the customer, receiving services and resources from its suppliers; In the Product Development Portfolio the enterprise collaborates with other partners, designing and testing new products and services; finally in the Extra-Business Relationships the enterprise is impacted by its relationships to competitors, debtors, and equity holders.

3. *Operations* refer to the ongoing recurring activities, which consume resources and capabilities in order to produce the output of the enterprise. It is decomposed into three sub-domains. First, the enterprise's Offerings (i.e., products, services, or the combination of both), which create a value to the customer. Second, Process Architecture, which represents back stage and front stage processes, aiming at generating the best overall service performance. Third, Resources and Capabilities, which are used as input for the processes in order to create the enterprise's offerings.

4. The ***Performance and Revenue Model*** is concerned with the financial and performance aspects of enterprises. It covers aspects, such as the financial position of an enterprise, financial resources, value configuration, financial strengths, limitations, and goals, as well as financial metrics.

Business Architecture

"Architecture" is used in various disciplines, such as construction and information technology. Architecture helps manage the complexity of the work done in these disciplines by supporting design, change, communication, and realization of the objects of concern. According to ANSI/IEEE Std 1471-2000, architecture is "the fundamental organization of a system, embodied in its components, their relationships to each other and the environment, and the principles governing its design and evolution" (IEEE Standards Association, 2000).

Building on this generic architecture definition, various business-specific definitions have been proposed in recent years. Table 1 shows a summary of some of the definitions available from the literature. Business Architecture (abbreviated BA) is used to guide businesses-IT integration concerns, by pivoting on Business Strategy, IT Strategy, Business Process Management (BPM), and Service Oriented Architecture (SOA).

By using the context of house construction, Lankhorst presented an analogy of Architecture, which is also valid for the more specific notion of Business Architecture. "Suppose you contract an architect to design your house. You discuss how rooms, staircases, windows, bathrooms, balconies, doors, a roof, etc., will be put together. You agree on a master plan, on the basis of which the architect will produce detailed specifications, to be used by the engineers and builders. How is it that you can communicate so efficiently about that master plan? We think it is because you share a common frame of reference: you both know what a 'room' is, a 'balcony', a 'staircase', etc. You know their function and their relation. A 'room',

Table 1. Definitions of BA Approaches

Business Architecture Definitions
"A **Business Architecture** is a formal blueprint of governance structures, business semantics and value streams across the extended enterprise. It articulates the structure of an enterprise in terms of its capabilities, governance structure, business processes, and business information. The business capability is "what" the organization does, the business processes, are "how" the organization executes its capabilities. In articulating the governance and information." ... "In defining the structure of the enterprise, business architecture considers customers, finances, and the ever-changing market to align strategic goals and objectives with decisions regarding products and services; partners and suppliers; organization; capabilities; and key initiatives." (BAWG, 2009a)
Enterprise Business Architecture (EBA) represents the requirements, principles and models for the enterprise's people, financials, processes and organizational structure. As such, the EBA process should result in the creation of EBA artifacts, including requirements, principles and models, that business and IT people can use to evolve their business in the context of existing interrelationships. EBA is distinct from information and technology viewpoints but is deeply integrated with them in a holistic solution architecture. (Burton, 2008)
Business Architecture ..."describes the fundamental relationships between a business entity's business environment and its intent, value, capabilities, processes, and resources (human, IT, knowledge, capital, facility, and material)." (Strosnider et al., 2002)
"The concepts in the *Business Architecture* description provide a semantic framework for speaking about common business concerns. ... For our purposes, this semantic structure provides a common set of concept patterns to be able to understand the types of content that need to be supported in technology-based information systems. ...a set of generic concepts and their interrelationships organize business information content in terms of requirements on the business, the boundary of the business, and the business as a system for delivery of value." (McDavid, 1999)
"*BA* is the business strategy, governance, organization, and key business processes information, as well as the interaction between these concepts. ... A Target Business Architecture describes the product and/or service strategy, and the organizational, functional, process, information, and geographic aspects of the business environment, based on the business principles, business goals, and strategic drivers." (The Open Group, 2009b)
"We use the concept of *Business Architecture* to structure the responsibility over business activities prior to any further effort to structure individual aspects (processes, data, functions, organization, etc.). ... Business Architecture "..." is an architecture that is specifically meant to structure responsibility over economic activities by multiple organizations (supply chain level), by one organization (enterprise level) or by part of an organization (business unit level)." (Gerrit , Versteeg & Bouwman, 2006)

for example, serves as a shelter and is connected to another 'room' via a 'door'. You both use, mentally, an architectural model of a house" (Lankhorst, 2005, 1). Similar to the housing case, a Business Architecture specifies the core functions of an enterprise, how they are operated and how they collaborate. BA offers an abstract design, which ignores many details, such as the colors and detailed dimensions of the house. These details will be filled in later design stages of the business. In the context of this chapter, Business Architecture is defined as depicted in Figure 1. It is based on current BA definitions and foundational enterprise architecture work, such as the Generalized Enterprise Reference Architecture and Methodology (GERAM) developed by (IFIP-IFAC Task Force, 1999).

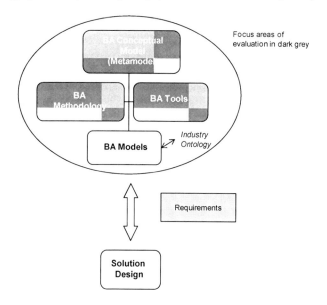

Figure 1. Focus of BA Evaluation

Business Architecture is divided into four core components, which together define a **Business Architecture Framework**. Three BA components were evaluated in depth in the following sections:

1. The *BA Conceptual Model*, also referred to as metamodel or modeling language, offers modeling constructs that cover, fully or partially, the four business domains of an enterprise (see section Enterprise Service System). Thereby, the core of the conceptual model can be represented in a business capability map and high-level business process models, using business goals and strategy as input and IT strategy and application portfolio contents as output (Scott, 2008). The constructs are applied in BA models (i.e., instances of the conceptual model) in the context of a real-world company or organization. The BA conceptual model should not be confused with "Business Model" as used in the business literature. Following (Osterwalder, 2004), a

Business Model is a conceptual tool that contains a set of elements and their relationships and allows expressing a company's logic of earning money.

2. The *BA Methodology* describes the development process of BA models, illustrating a company's transition from an initial state to a target state. In a process model or a structured procedure, the methodology explains the responsibilities to be defined, the activities to be executed and the principles to be considered. In the context of this chapter, design principles, best practices, reference models, or use case scenarios are part of the methodology.

3. The *BA Tools* support the engineering of the BA models of a particular enterprise. They should provide the functionality to develop, to visualize, analyze, and simulate the BA.

Using Business Architecture concepts, a particular enterprise creates BA models of the company's current and future states. These models illustrate the company-specific business concerns. The gap between the business and target states reveals the areas that need further improvement, and thus will guide the design of the final solution under considerations of the company's requirements designed for execution (Ross et al., 2006).

Introduction to Current BA Approaches

In recent years, various techniques that cover different Business Architecture Frameworks have been developed. To establish a better understanding of the current status quo of these BAs, an extensive literature review on enterprise and in particular Business Architecture was conducted. A wide range of publications on BA (i.e., specifications of current standards, contributions in scientific journals and conferences, as well as websites or whitepaper publications from practitioners) were identified, analyzed, and compared with each other. BA propositions differ significantly in terms of the degree of detail or their completeness. A sub-set of ten BAs was selected to be included in this chapter as they stood out due to their awareness levels, contributions to the BA community, application, maturity of the conceptual models, methodologies or supporting tools, as well as promising planned enhancements. The results of this evaluation were discussed with scholars and practitioners. The feedback was incorporated into the final evaluation results.

The overview of each BA is structured as followed:

- *General Information.* This criterion contains BA information about the publisher, the purpose, its application and degree of standardization.
- *Conceptual model.* This criterion is used to provide a short description of the elements defined by the conceptual model. Furthermore, it determines the maturity of the conceptual model considering syntax, semantics, and pragmatics.

- *Methodology.* This criterion describes the information available to guide the architect in BA initiatives (e.g., guidelines, responsibilities, activities, or structured procedures). Based on this information the maturity of the methodology can be identified.
- *Tools.* This criterion lists which tools support the usage of the particular BA.
- *Service Focus.* The service focus describes in how far the service concept is incorporated in the conceptual model, the methodology, or the supporting tools. (Sanz et al., 2007)

ArchiMate

Originally maintained by the ArchiMate Foundation, in February 2009 Archi-Mate(R) Version 1.0 was formally approved as technical standard by the Board of The Open Group. Today, consulting firms and tool vendors are engaged in its support, as well as the development of version 2.0. ArchiMate is an EA language that can be applied to formally describe business and IT concerns of enterprise operations (i.e., resources, process architecture, and offerings). It is used to identify requirements and to reason about the current and future structure and behavior of business and IT systems. ArchiMate is not however particularly designed to model the strategic, business network, financial, or performance aspects of an enterprise. The application of ArchiMate is published in various sources (e.g., ArchiMate Forum, 2009a; ArchiMate Forum, 2009b; Lankhorst, 2004; Lankhorst, 2005; The Open Group, 2009a).

Conceptual Model. The ArchiMate modeling language is decomposed into three tightly connected EA layers, i.e., the business layer, the application layer, and the technology layer. Thereby, the elements of each EA layer are bundled into three groups, i.e., elements representing an active structure, passive structure or the behavior. As illustrated in Figure 2, the Active Structure of the business layer consists of the business actor, which is assigned to a business role, working in internal or external collaboration with other business actors. The Behavior part includes the business service realized by business behavior elements. Finally, the Passive Structure connects the elements product, value, contract, and business object. The business object is an abstract element, which provides information about real objects of concern for the enterprise, such as a customer, an invoice, or a product. The business object is further described regarding its meaning and representation. Its linkage to the data element of the application layer is one example of how tightly the business layer is integrated with the other two EA layers. The modeling language can be described as mature. The elements and their relationships are clearly defined and extensively explained. Furthermore, to simplify the readability, ArchiMate provides a unique symbol for each EA element, as well various views, filtering the BA information for different stakeholders.

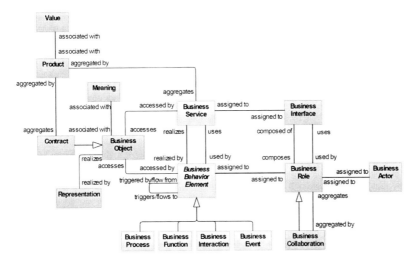

Figure 2. Business Layer of ArchiMate (The Open Group 2009a, 13)

Methodology. To guide the architect in creating EA models for a particular enterprise, ArchiMate describes a comprehensive sample case of an insurance company. It explains for each element which information needs to be defined. However, no management information is offered that describe how the EA models are used in a business transformation process.

Tools. The visualization of the ArchiMate-specific symbols is supported by various modeling tools, including BiZZdesign Architect by BiZZdesign, ARIS ArchiMate Modeler by IDS Scheer, Metis by Troux, Corporate Modeler by Casewise, and System Architect by IBM. Additionally, ArchiMate stencils to be used in MS Visio are available.

Service Focus. ArchiMate incorporates thoroughly the concepts of service orientation. On each layer a service element exists, namely the business service, the application service, and the technology service. The notation and the relationships of these service elements to other EA elements are formally explained. For instance, in the business layer, the business service is created by business behavior. The business service is externally visible to the environment and can be bundled to service groups that form together with a contract the product. Products and services create a value to a defined party, which accesses this outcome through a business interface. Finally, the business service uses the application service from the application layer as input.

Business Architecture Working Group

In 2007, the Business Architecture Working Group (BAWG) was founded as part of the Object Management Group (OMG). The BAWG aims at establishing industry standards, supporting the creation, and alignment of business blueprints. In this context, it is planned to develop a Business Architecture, connecting OMG's existing and proposed business standards (see Figure 3). The current status of the work is published in whitepapers and on the group's wiki (see e.g., BAWG, 2009b; BAWG, 2009a; or TSG, Inc., 2008). BAWG's BA ecosystem is planned to cover all business domains on an abstract and detailed level (i.e., strategy & structure, business networks, operations, and revenue & performance model). As the BAWG's BA is still in its infancy, it has not yet become a standard in BA.

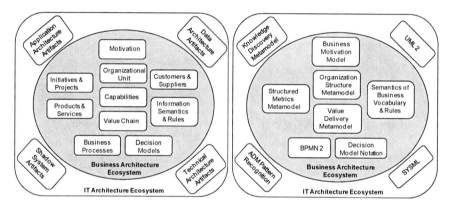

Figure 3. BA and IT Architecture Ecosystem: components and OMG standards (BAWG, 2009b)

Conceptual Model. Currently, the BAWG provides partially varying concepts about the key components of a BA ecosystem. The current status of the proposal of an integrated IT and BA ecosystem, published in BAWG's BA requirements for a standard, is illustrated in the following (BAWG, 2009b). In the proposal, the BA ecosystem covers aspects regarding the motivation, the organizational unit, capabilities, value chain, initiatives & projects, products & services, customer & suppliers, information semantics & rules, business processes, and decision models. As depicted in the figure above, these areas are addressed by existing and planned BA standards. As the standards represent silos, which are not connected, the planned BA work shall integrate these standards. As the work by the BAWG is still in an initial state, the maturity of the conceptual model can be described as low.

Methodology. In addition to the integration of standards in the BA and IT ecosystem, the Business Architecture Working Group has published business scenarios to illustrate the application areas and value of BA. Furthermore, a roadmap for the integrated BA ecosystem was defined and an overview of existing business models is given.

Tools. The current unfinished state of the BA cannot be supported by any tool.

Service Focus. The service is one conceptual area of the BA ecosystem. However, no further information is provided in the currently available documentation.

Business Motivation Model

In 2005, the Business Motivation Model (BMM) became a standard of the OMG (Object Management Group). The BMM is used for establishing, communicating, and managing business plans. As such, it defines the factors that motivate a business plan, the elements and the relationships of a business plan. The BMM is designed to model the strategy, governance and the business network of a company. The business operations are not addressed by this model, (Anderson Healy & Ross, 2007; OMG, 2006).

Conceptual Model. The elements of the BMM are divided into two groups. First, the Ends & Means define what an organization tries to achieve. Thereby, the ends (i.e., vision, goal, objectives) describe the planned accomplishments of an organization, whereas the means define the actions to achieve these goals. This includes the mission of a company, the course of action (i.e., strategy, tactic), and the directives (i.e., business policy, business rule). Second, in order to understand the context of the ends and means, the internal and external Influencers are an essential part of the BMM. Examples of internal influencers are infrastructure, assumption, issue, corporate value, resource, habit, and management prerogative. Examples of external influencers are environment, technology, regulation, supplier, customer, competitor, and partner. Influencers are neutral until their impact (i.e., the strength, weakness, opportunity for or threat against a company. The BMM model is described formally regarding the core elements and their relationships. Furthermore, BMM covers thoroughly the business domains to be modeled. Each element is explained with an extensive example, simplifying the understanding of the model. However, the BMM, does not provide recommendations on how to filter the modeled information in order to focus on specific stakeholder concerns.

Methodology. BMM's conceptual model provides for each element detailed examples, which serve as guidelines on how to develop the BA model for a specific company. It does not provide any methodology on how to develop company-specific BMM models.

Tools. Being a well-defined conceptual model, BMM can be modeled with any entity relationship modeling software. IBM Rational RequisitePro in combination with IBM Rational® Software Modeler also provide a BMM template which assigns to every definition a unique symbol.

Service Focus. The concept of a service is not represented as core element of the BMM model. However, it is used in combination with an action, as well as market and customer information to form the mission statement. For instance, "Provide (action) + car rental service (service) + across Europe for business and personal customers (market & customer)".

Business Process Modeling Notation

In 2004, OMG released the Business Modeling Notation BPMN 1.0 Specification. BPMN is based on prior efforts by the BPMI Notation Working Group. BPMN aims at linking business process model design and process implementation. As such, it shall be understandable from business analysts, to the technical developers, as well as the people involved in the management and control of the processes. BPMN can be used to describe business operations on a detail, as well as on a high-level. Thereby, it addresses in particular aspects of the process architecture, and only marginally resource and capability aspects. BPMN is a well accepted standard for process modeling. While in January 2009 the specification 1.2 was released, the BPMN specification 2.0 is in progress as of July 2009. The BPMN introduction given in this chapter is based on Lankhorst (2005) White (2004) and OMG (2008, 2009).

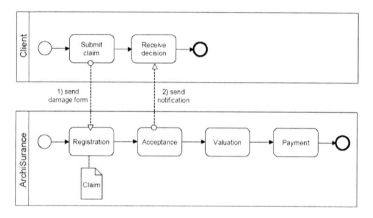

Figure 4. Example model in BPMN (Lankhorst 2005, 34)

Conceptual Model. The BPMN is based on four core element types. Flow Objects, the main element group, consists of events, activities, gateways and connections. These elements are linked to each other with different types of Connecting Objects, namely sequence flows, message flows, and associations. In order to provide the ability to cluster elements, two levels of groupings are available: Pool and Lane. Finally, Artifacts (i.e., data objects, group, and annotation) can be used to provide further information about the process. The BPMN elements are specified in further detail regarding their attributes, types, or sub elements. The BPMN is based on a clear syntax. Furthermore, it meets the defined purpose of building the bridge between business analysts and technical developers. As such, BPMN will furthermore be provided with an internal model that enables the generation of executable BPEL4WS. Due the simple set consisting of the four core elements, BPMN is easy to understand. However, it becomes more complex to manage if the numerous specifications of the elements are applied.

Methodology. The BPMN specification explains the notion of the elements in detail. Reference models, best practices, and guidelines on how to create the BPMN models however are provided in various books on BPMN, which are published independently from the OMG.

Tools. BPMN is supported by various SW vendor, as well as open source tools. Examples are System Architect from IBM, Lombardi Teamworks from Lombardi Software, or the BPMN modeler for Eclipse. The usage of these tools assures that the company-specific models are compliant with the BPMN syntax.

Service Focus. The concept of a service is addressed in the BPMN element 'task', a sub element of the element activity. Representing a single unit of work, the task can be of the type 'service task'. Service tasks are used to model automated services or web services.

Business Concepts

In 1996, McDavid introduced the business concepts as a business language that provides a technique to model common business concerns relevant for the development of information system (McDavid 1996, 1999). The business concepts are based on practical experiences gathered within IBM's initiative Enterprise Solution Structure (ESS), (Plachy & Hausler, 1999). They describe a generic Business Architecture, addressing on a high-level aspects of enterprise modeling, such as strategy, structure, business network, and operations. Against this, no particular focus is laid on the revenue and performance models of an enterprise. The BA concepts by McDavid represent a seminal introductory work in BA. As such, it has been laid the foundation for various BA concepts and practices. However, McDavid's business concepts needs to be further specified if they are used in practice.

Conceptual Model. McDavid defines a small set of nine business elements which are grouped into three interrelated parts. The Drivers of a Business describe the first part of the model, representing which requirements must be fulfilled by the enterprise as a system. Elements include the business situation, the business purpose, and the business outcome. The second part is the Business Boundaries. This part of the enterprise defines the business commitment, connecting the different role players in an ecosystem. The third part is the Business Delivery System. The business delivery system creates the value that was defined in the business commitments. It contains the elements business function, business resource, and business location. Between the before described elements various connection exists. Furthermore, the elements can be decomposed into sub-elements which can be connected on different levels of detail. The elements and their relationships of the conceptual model are well-defined elements. With the small set of nine elements describing different business domains, it serves the purpose of a high-level BA. Furthermore, it explains the general abstract relationships between business and IT systems. The business concepts do not provide further insights on how the different elements can be visualized in a final BA model.

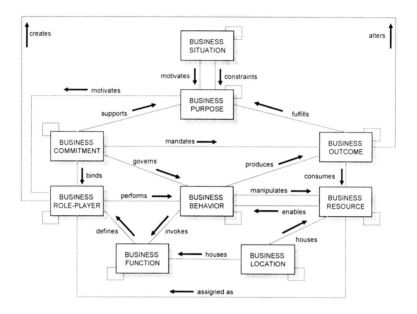

Figure 5. Business Concepts by McDavid (1999)

Methodology. McDavid does not provide a comprehensive methodology on how to develop Business Architectures. However, he describes in which documents, i.e., so-called work products, the business model can be captured: Classified business terms define the industry-and company-specific business terminology captured in interviews and available documents; context diagrams are used to model the relationships between the different role players; business process models explain the behavior of a company; business rule catalogs define the business commitments, and finally business object models capture the business concerns described in a more IT-related approach.

Tools. In order to support McDavid's business concepts with an entity relationship modeling tool the syntax of the model needs further specification.

Service Focus. McDavid defines outcome as one key element in a Business Architecture. The service is mentioned as a specific type of outcome. It is not explained in which way the service is connected to the outcome in general, or the other outcome types, i.e., interim outcomes, products and byproducts. Similarly, the relationship of the service to the other eight key elements is not specified, but can be derived from the element outcome. Thus, according to McDavid, a service fulfills a purpose, it is mandated by a commitment, produced by behavior, and it consumes resources.

Component Business Model

The component-based Business Architecture (CBM) has been developed by IBM and is actively applied in the consulting activities of IBM's Global Business Services (GBS). CBM is used for business transformation, by prioritization of strategic targets and their linkage to solutions through traditional packaged applications and SOA solutions (Cherbakov et al., 2005). CBM covers aspects of the operations and organizations such as a company's strategy, governance, operations, as well as revenue and performance models. Business network aspects are currently less prominent in CBM (Nayak et al., 2007).

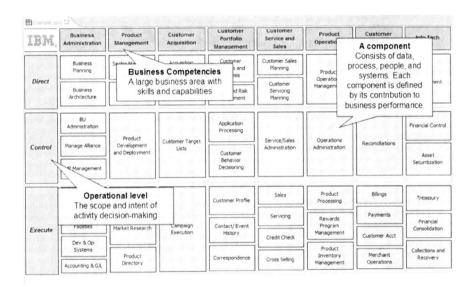

Figure 6. CBM map

Conceptual Model. The focal element of CBM is the business component. The business concepts serves as structuring element and has five dimensions: business purpose, activities, resources, governance model and business services (IBM, 2005). Business component dependences establish the loosely-coupled model of operations for the enterprise, thus enhancing the manageability of the conceptual model and the decision-making. (Sanz et al., 2006). Components are assigned to business competencies, which represent a large business area with skills and capabilities, as well as accountabilities levels, which are a simple framework for separating strategic decisions, control mechanisms, and business actions. All CBM elements and the relationships amongst them are well defined. Each element has a rich notation.

Methodology. In addition to the conceptual model IBM uses methods that guide GBS consultants in the use of BA for different type of client engagements. A CBM-related method is used for business transformation, a strategy and change method for strategy engagements, and an EA method for Enterprise Architecture initiatives.

Tools. Core tools support the above conceptual model, including IBM's publicly available WebSphere Business Modeler, as well as a CBM-specific tool.

Service Focus. CBM uses a business service concept. Business services are described in a business specification and assigned to operational goals. Composed of service functions, the business service is provided by the business component, i.e., it is part of an offering associated to the business value model.

Enterprise Business Architecture

Developed by Gartner, the Enterprise Business Architecture (EBA) is an integral part of an enterprise architecture. As such, its objective is to optimize business components along with information and technology in order to support the business strategy. EBA is a descriptive BA, which can be used as introduction to the BA topic. It covers in particular the structure and the operations of a company. Aspects, such as the business network and the performance models are less emphasized in the EBA. Publications on the EBA are available from 2008 (e.g., (Burton & Robertson, 2008, 2008b; Burton, 2009).

Conceptual Model. The EBA consists of five key dimensions. The Business Capabilities (also referred to as business functions or high-level business services) form the architecture foundation. Capabilities are realized by four key business elements: People who directly impact the scope of the EBA; Financials, which describe the financial situation of a company; Organization, which refer to the formal reporting structure, as well as the informal structure, including cultural hierarchy, virtual teams, and social networks; and finally Processes, which are composed of business activities. According to Gartner, these dimensions are impacted by several internal and external Influencing Factors. Although, Gartner intents to provide a BA that can be used to align business and IT concerns, the EBA lacks a formal descriptions of the linkages to other parts of the enterprise architecture (e.g., information or technology architecture). Regarding the maturity of the architecture, the syntax of EBA is rather ambiguous the relationships between the elements are not well-defined.

Methodology. In addition to the before described conceptual model, Gartner provides best practices, as well as requirements for an enterprise business architect. Moreover, Gartner defines a seven phase iterative procedure model for the development of enterprise Business Architectures (see Figure 7). In the first phase, i.e., Define & Scope, the scope of the EBA must be defined, and a common agreement and understanding of what EBA is must be reached. In the second phase, i.e., Organize, the EBA team must be determined. Afterwards, in phase 3, i.e., Future State, the vision of the future EBA is described, by creating the requirements, principles and models of the Business Architecture. Phase 4, Current State, aims at establishing a good understanding of the current state of the business, which is in the defined scope of the EBA. Based on the results of phase 3 and 4, in phase 5, a Gap Analysis is conducted. In phase 6, i.e., migration plan, initiatives, which aim at closing the gaps, are identified and selected according to priorities. Finally, phase 7, i.e., Iterate & Refine, describes the ongoing process of supporting and evolving the EBA.

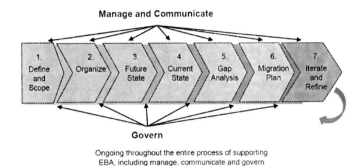

Figure 7. EA development process (Burton & Robertson, 2008)

Tools. In order to support Gartner's EBA model with an entity relationship modeling tool the syntax of the model needs further specification.

Service Focus. In the EBA, service components are not specifically addressed.

Event Driven Process Chain

As part of ARIS (Architecture of Information Systems), the Event Driven Process Chain (EPC) was originally developed within a research initiative lead by Prof. A. W. Scheer. EPC is a mature conceptual model, which is widely used for the documentation, and analysis of enterprise operations. The outcomes of these activities serve as foundation for the design of information systems. In particular, in the configuration and customization projects of the enterprise solution SAP, ARIS provides the standard modeling environment. The EPC was first introduced in 1992 in an article by Scheer (Scheer & Hars, 1992). Since then various scientific and practitioner contributions followed (e.g., Davis & Brabänder, 2007, Davis 2008; Scheer, 2000a, 2000b).

Conceptual Model. The EPC provides the subsequent four core elements for the modeling business processes. The first core element is the Event. This element, being of either internal or external nature, represents the changing state of an enterprise system. The second element is the Function. Triggered by events, functions are activities or tasks, which are carried out as part of a business process, create value for to the company. The third core element is the Rule. Rules connect events and functions, governing the process flow. Finally, Resources, also referred to as non-structurally relevant objects, form the fourth group of elements. Resources comprise sub-elements, such as organization, systems, data, knowledge, information carriers, products and services, objectives and measures, or general resources. In EPC, all elements are further defined by a set of attributes (e.g., the attributes costs and time for the element function). To model these resource elements about 150 symbols are provided by the EPC. The elements can be connected amongst each other, using five different relationship types. The EPC is of a high maturity, as its syntax is clearly defined, and the semantics of the elements are well explained. Furthermore, increasing the understandability of the EPC, to each element a unique symbol is assigned. Represented in the ARIS house, the following five views of the conceptual model are provided, focusing on different enterprise aspects, including the organization view, data view, control view, function view, and product service view.

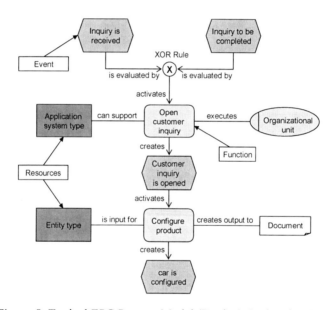

Figure 8. Typical EPC Process Model (Davis & Brabänder, 2007)

Methodology. Providing guidance for the development of company-specific ARIS models, the ARIS concept is supported by the ARIS build time phases that are incorporated into the ARIS house. Thereby, each view of the ARIS house is decomposed into a requirements definition phase, a design specification phase, and an implementation phase. Above all views lies the strategic phase. ARIS defines thereby for each phase and view a set of ARIS models to be developed (in total 150 models are available in ARIS). Due to its industry-wide application and its tight connection to SAP, in ARIS for numerous industry sectors reference models and best practices are available.

Tools. ARIS is supported by the ARIS Software platform, which is composed of the numerous tools of the strategy platform, design platform, implementation platform, and control platform. Thereby, the tools of the ARIS design platform provide the capabilities to model and manage the EPC business models. All tools of the ARIS platform are based on one data model repository, thus allowing the re-use of information from any tool. For instance, key performance indicators created in the balanced scorecard tool can be accessed in the ARIS Tool and connected to business process models.

Service Focus. The service concept is represented in the resource element product/service, which can be connected to a function as an output. Furthermore, ARIS proposes a product/service tree model, which aims at representing product hierarchies. In this model, the 'has' relationship describes the sub-components of a product/service, the 'substitution' relationship illustrates by which other products/services it can be replaced.

Enterprise Business Motivation Model

The Enterprise Business Motivation was developed by Microsoft's enterprise architect Nick Malik. It was first published in his blog, later also in Microsoft's The Architect Journal (Malik, 2009a, 2009b). The BA model aims at illustrating how the actions of a company are aligned with its objectives. It covers numerous aspects of enterprise modeling. A particular focus is thereby laid on the modeling of business models. As the EBMM was first published in 2009, little is known about the EBMM's actual application in companies, nor can it be today defined as a standard for BA.

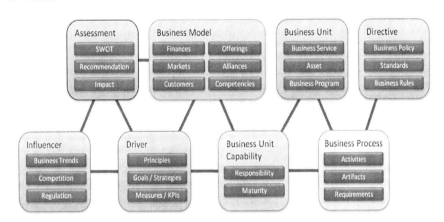

Figure 9. Enterprise Business Motivation Model (Malik, 2009b)

Conceptual Model. The EBMM is composed of the eight interrelated business areas illustrated in Figure 9. Thereby, the business area Assessment evaluates the Business Model and describes the impact of a company's Influencers. The assessment is furthermore defined as the impetus for the business Drivers. The drivers respond to the influencers, and motivate changes towards the business model. The business model defines the requirements for the Capabilities of the Business Units. Finally, implemented through the business unit capability the Business Process is performed by the business units and governed by the Directives. Each business area is decomposed into more detailed elements which are tightly connected to each other within one individual business area, or amongst different business areas. The conceptual model is comprehensive and well-defined. On a high-level it meets its purpose to explain comprehensively how the actions of a company are aligned to its goals. Against this, the notions of the business elements are explained in less detail. Thus, if more detailed information about the company has to be captured, the model needs further extensions. Regarding the understandability of the model, the detailed UML models provided by the author are essential.

Methodology. The EBMM explains the notations and relationships of the elements, it provides however little guidance on how the conceptual model is created.

Tools. The EBMM can be supported by any tool that provides ER modeling features.

Service Focus. The concept of a service is incorporated in the EBMM as a core element of the business model. It is a bundling of business capabilities that are offered to a customer or partner through a distribution channel. As such it is targeted in the value configuration. The business service is provided, as well as consumed by business units.

TOGAF Business Architecture

TOGAF (The Open Group Architecture Framework) is developed and maintained by the members of The Open Group working in the Architecture Forum (The Open Group, 2009b). TOGAF Version 1 was originally published in 1995 with a strong focus on IT architecture. In recent years, Business Architecture has become an essential part of TOGAF. In particular version 9.0, published in February 2009, shows various enhancements regarding conceptual model and guidelines for the creation of Business Architectures. Thereby, the Business Architecture in TOGAF addresses on a high level the organizational aspects strategy, structure, and operations. The business network, performance and revenue models are less covered in TOGAF. However, the maturity between the Business Architecture and other enterprise architectures still differs significantly. Nevertheless, TOGAF is a worldwide accepted standard for EA frameworks, which has been implemented for various industries.

Conceptual Model. TOGAF provides a so-called content metamodel which defines clearly the elements and relationships of the three enterprise architectures, i.e., Business Architecture, information system architectures, and technology architectures. The elements of the Business Architectures are decomposed into motivational, organizational, and functional groups (see Figure 10). Furthermore, TOGAF defines which diagrams can be used to model particular business aspects of the company. The metamodel does not define specific symbols for the elements of the metamodel. In order to support business IT alignment TOGAF defines the connection between the Business Architecture and the information and technology architecture. For instance, the business service is realized through an application component, and implemented on a technology platform.

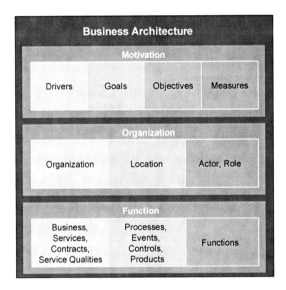

Figure 10. TOGAF Content Metamodel (The Open Group, 2009b, 375)

Methodology. Supporting a company in transitioning from a current to a target state, TOGAF provides the Architecture Development Method (ADM), which consists of eight iterative phases. Thereby, the Business Architecture is the second phase, which follows the phase architecture vision. The BA phase sets the foundation for the subsequent phases information systems architecture and technology architecture. It is composed into four sections, i.e., objective, approach, inputs, and steps. The steps section thereby describes the activities necessary to develop a Business Architecture. It first proposes the selection of reference models, viewpoints, and tools. Afterwards, the baseline and target BA description is developed, which are then analyzed in the gap analysis. Based on the results on the previous steps, the roadmap components are defined. In the subsequent phase, the target Business Architecture is evaluated regarding its impacts on the remaining architecture landscape. In the following two phases, stakeholders review the target BA to be then finalized by the architecture team. The BA phase concludes with the creation of an architecture definition document.

Tools. The ADM is supported by various tools, such as IBM System Architect, MDG Technology by Sparx Systems, or Metastorm Provision. Thereby, most tools support the modeling of conceptual EA models referenced by TOGAF. Furthermore, they provide a structure to organize the created company-specific models, according to the phases of TOGAF's ADM method.

Service Focus. Besides before described business-IT relationships, TOGAF defines the following relationships between business elements. The business service is realized by a process, it provides and consumes data entities, and it is owned and governed by the organization unit, and accessed by an actor.

Findings

As illustrated in the previous section, various kinds of Business Architectures can be applied for the design, change, communication and realization of enterprise service systems. The main goal of BAs is thereby to support enterprises in creating business solutions that combine their front stage and back stage in such a way that the system's overall service performance increases. The requirements which Business Architectures must fulfill to meet this goal depend significantly on the specific characteristics of an enterprise, as well as the particular objectives set for the transformation initiative. Thus, prior to every initiative, which requires the development of BA models, a careful comparison of the initiative's BA needs and the existing BA approaches is necessary in order to make a sound BA selection. To support enterprises in this selection process, the following BA comparison emphasizes the differences between the before introduced Business Architectures. It provides general guidelines to choose the most suitable BA for a specific problem area of an enterprise service system, considering general information, conceptual model, methodology, and tool support of the BA (status as of July 2009). Following enterprises' increasing change towards a service-orientation, a particular focus is laid on how well the service concept is integrated in the BA approach. Table 2 provides an overview this comparison.

General Information

Business Architectures are used to guide enterprise service systems in business IT integration concerns. Depending on the specific problem area enterprises focus differently on Business Strategy, IT Strategy, Business Process Management, and Service Oriented Architecture. For instance, for one enterprise information on the business strategy may be relevant for long-term IT investments decisions, determining which business areas need to be optimized. Other enterprises model in detail selected business processes in order to visualize cost reduction and value creation potentials of their business services. Additionally, often one transformation initiative must fulfill more than one modeling purpose, thus requiring the combination of different BAs.

Table 2. Overview of Current Business Architectures

Selected Business Architecture (July 2009)	ArchiMate	BAWG	BMM	BPMN	Business Concepts	CBM	EBA	EPC	EBMM	TOGAF BA
1. General Information										
• publisher	ArchiMate Foundation / The Open Group	OMG	OMG	OMG	McDavid	IBM	Gartner	IDS Scheer	Microsoft	The Open Group
• purpose	EA	Integration of OMG standards	Business Strategy	BPM	IT-Business Alignment	IT Strategy, IT-Business Alignment, SOA	EA	BPM, IT-Business Alignment, SOA	Business model, IT-Business Alignment, EA	EA
• available information										
• standardization / application										
2. Metamodel										
• scope										
– strategy & structure										
– business network										
– operations										
– revenue model & performance										
• integration with other architectures										
• maturity										
3. Methodology										
• scope										
– development of BA model										
– management: BA initiatives										
• structured procedure model										
• use case scenarios										
• best practices / reference models										
• maturity										
4. Tool Support										
• available tools	e.g. BiZZdesign Architect by BiZZdesign, ARIS ArchiMate Modeler by IDS Scheer, Metis by Troux, Corporate Modeler by Casewise, IBM System Architect, Visio by Microsoft	none, metamodel not yet defined	IBM System Architect	any entity relationship tool	none, metamodel extension would be necessary	WBM, CBM & SOMA	none, metamodel extension would be necessary	ARIS toolset	any entity relationship tool	any entity relationship tool that support the creation of the BA models referenced by TOGAF & methodology supporting tools such as IBM System Architect Technology by Sparx Systems or Metastorm Provision
5. Service Focus										
• service										

Current Business Architectures are developed and maintained by various parties, including vendor independent initiatives, companies, as well as individuals. Each party addresses one or several purposes in its BA. However, while the combined view of all models reveals a broad coverage of BA purposes, this view is not coherent. For instance, ArchiMate, EBA, EBMM, and TOGAF, are integral parts of an enterprise architecture, which guide in a top-down approach the design of the remaining architectures. Other BAs may have a more generic intent to align business and IT (e.g., business concepts by McDavid). Another purpose may be the support of business process management initiatives, which is for instance one goal of BPMN and ARIS. Another group of BAs is designed to illustrate the strategy and the motivations of a company, such as the business motivation model from OMG, or the enterprise motivation model from Microsoft. Additionally, ARIS and CBM amongst other purposes provide a modeling environment for SOA. Finally, the BA by BAWG aims at connecting different BA standards.

Furthermore, the amount and quality of available information explaining the particular Business Architecture varies. Whereas, more mature or standard BAs (i.e., ArchiMate, BMM, BPMN, CBM, EPC, TOGAF) have been explained extensively in various contributions, other not yet well-established BAs only provide introductory information (e.g., EBA, BAWG, business concepts). As a consequence, the models differ in how well they guide enterprises in describing their service system.

BA Conceptual Models

The purpose of a BA is tightly connected with the business domains and subdomains addressed in the BA conceptual models. For instance, to model the business strategy, it is necessary to specify aspects of the strategy, business network, as well as the performance and revenue model. Furthermore, the directions and value of the product and service offerings must be determined. Against this, SOA projects have a strong focus on the back stage and front stage operations of an enterprise, including the process architecture, resources, and service offerings. When selecting a BA conceptual model for an enterprise service system, the scope and level of the business domains must therefore be clear and aligned with the purpose of the BA model to be created.

Evaluating BA conceptual models regarding their applicability for a defined purpose, it must be taken into account that BA conceptual models have different scopes and levels of detail. As in the case of the ten introduced BAs, some conceptual models (e.g., BPMN, BMM) focus explicitly on one or two business concerns, whereas others (e.g., BAWG, TOGAF, or McDavid's business concepts) cover on a more abstract level a broader spectrum of business areas. In the following, it is described in how far the four business domains of an enterprise service system are addressed by the conceptual models.

1. *Strategy & Structure.* The sub-domains *Strategy* and *Governance* are addressed in very detail by the BMM from OMG. Thus, these models can be used to determine the value and focus of the enterprise's services, as well as to plan future service directions. Similarly, the EBMM from Microsoft has also a strong focus on the strategy and motivation of a company, but does not differentiate as extensively between directives, mission, vision, strategy, course of actions, policies and rules as the BMM does. The remaining BAs (e.g., ArchiMate, ARIS, business concepts) mostly cover the organizational aspects, and less the strategy aspects of a company.

2. *Business Network.* This business domain is only described on an abstract level by most of the evaluated BAs. BA elements used to specify the specifics of certain networks or the enterprise's differing roles as a service system (e.g., service supplier, customer, or partner) are not provided by these BAs. For instance, ArchiMate has the generic elements role and process that can be instantiated to define the supply chain process between the company and the supplier. The symbol of the role supplier and company however is the same as ArchiMate currently only offers one symbol for the superior element role. Against this, in the BMM by OMG and EBMM by Microsoft the customers, partners and suppliers are specifically mentioned as BA elements and can be used to describe their impact on an enterprise (e.g., the impact on their services). However, these BA elements are not used to define their involvement in the business processes to generate services or products.

3. *Operations.* Business *Operations* are addressed by all Business Architectures. Thereby, the level of detail of the elements for the process architecture, resources, and outcome differs however significantly between the conceptual models. For instance, the BMM, EBA and the business concepts define processes as a high-level element without information on how they are composed. Against this TOGAF, CBM, ARIS and ArchiMate define core components of a business process, such as events, functions, and connectors. Additionally, ARIS offers an extensive set of elements and element attributes to further specify the resources to be consumed and provided by a function. In contrast to the before described BAs, which also address other business domains, BPMN is exclusively designed to describe business processes. It provides a conceptual model which allows describing a business process in such level of detail that it can be transferred into executable business process language. The scope of the BPMN is limited as it does not extensively describe the resources and capacities, or the outcome of a business process. Consequently, to select a Business Architecture for the modeling of the service co-creation process, it must be considered in which level of detail the business processes must be described for the specific transformation initiative.

4. *Revenue* and *Performance Model.* This business domain is not a particular focus of the analyzed Business Architectures. Some conceptual models, such as CBM or EBMM define financial metrics for the modeling of Business Architectures. However, financial position, value configuration, or financial resources are less addressed by most conceptual models of the ten evaluated BAs. In order to increase the transparency of the impact, which a service has on the financial performance of an enterprise, most BA models must be extended.

Today's enterprise service systems depend heavily on information technology (IT) as many business services are created using IT services. In order to identify potentials for a better business-IT-alignment, it is therefore crucial to integrate Business Architectures with other enterprise architectures, such as technology, application, or data architectures. Although, most BAs claim to address these business and IT alignment issues, their integration abilities differ significantly between them. For instance, the Business Architectures BMM, EBMM, and EBA are not well connected to other architectures. Contrarily, the BAs BAWG, ArchiMate, BPMN, and EPC specify more extensively the connections to IT. BPMN connects, for example, web services to tasks, whereas EPC links applications to functions. The differences in the BA's integration to other EAs must be considered when choosing a conceptual model.

The maturity of BA conceptual models varies also in syntax, semantics, and pragmatics. Some conceptual models, being still in their infancy (e.g., BAWG) or serving as simple introduction to BA (e.g., EBA) describe the core elements of a BA but lack in describing the formal relationships between the elements. Against this, more mature BA conceptual models formulate clearly the elements, as well as their relationships. Thereby, the explanations about the elements differ. BPMN for instance describes each element on the level of attributes. Against this, the element description from McDavid is more abstract, providing small examples for each element. Improving the readability of the final BA models, conceptual models, such as ArchiMate, ARIS, and BPMN, assign to each element a unique symbol.

BA Methodologies

The modeling of enterprise service systems can be complex and error prone. Thus, in order to guide the business architects in the development of company-specific BA models it is essential to provide BA methodologies. BA methodologies explain ideally in process models or structured procedures the responsibilities to be defined, the activities to be executed, and the principles to be considered. Furthermore, methodologies may contain design principles, best practices, reference models, or use case scenarios.

The evaluation of the ten BA approaches reveals large variations in their methodologies. None of the analyzed BA methodologies guide business architects in similar ways through general BA project activities and concrete activities on how to develop BA models. The methodologies have either a focus on the first or the latter aspect. Furthermore, instead of well-defined procedures, most methodologies provide some kind of unstructured guidance. The information is mostly generic to be used in any context of BA development (e.g., business strategy, IT strategy, BPMN, EA, and SOA). As consequence, enterprises may be uncertain about which BA elements they should focus on and in which level of detail they should develop the BA models for a particular purpose. For instance, to analyze the value of business services in a business strategy project, it is essential to provide an abstract view of the final business services, the external customers consuming these services, as well as their importance for the enterprise. Against this, in a BPM initiative, it is helpful to decompose the final business service into a hierarchy consisting of detailed services that can be connected to business process tasks. The importance of the customer might be in this context less relevant.

Frameworks that stand out in their guidance regarding BA usage are the EBA from Gartner, the BA phase published in TOGAF, and the CBM method from IBM. TOGAF, for instance, defines several activities in its BA phase, ranging from activities to select reference models, viewpoints and tools, to develop the target and baseline architecture, to analyze the gaps, and to request the stakeholder agreement and finalize the BA. Similar activities are defined by Gartner's BA method. Gartner's and TOGAF's BA methods are strongly integrated into an EA development method. Thus, the BA phase requires input from previous phases (e.g., in TOGAF from the Vision phase) and produces output for the remaining architecture (e.g., information systems and technology architecture phases), as well as design phases (e.g., opportunities and solution, and migration planning phases).

Additionally, a few BA approaches also provide best practices, fictitious examples or reference models. For instance, the BMM illustrates with various sample mission statements of a car rental company, how the element 'mission' is described in BMM. ArchiMate also visualizes the relationships between its elements using a fictitious example of an insurance company. EPC is covered in various books providing reference models for different industries. Finally, the OMG BAWG provides business scenarios to guide companies in the evaluation of BA values.

BA Tools

BA Tools support enterprises in their development of BA models. Ideally, the tools provide functionality to develop, to visualize, analyze, and simulate the BA models. As such, they have a significant impact on the quality of the BA models.

Similar to the conceptual model and the methodology, the tool support varies among the BAs. Business Architectures, such as the EBA from Gartner, the current version of the BAWG from OMG and the business concepts from McDavid, do not provide the required syntax to be completely supported by a modeling tool. For other BA conceptual models, however, a broad variety of common entity-relationship (ER) modeling tools is applicable.

Additionally, some Business Architectures benefit from modeling tools that were enhanced, providing unique symbols for the BA elements. Examples are the ARIS software platform for EPC, or IBM's tool in support of CBM. In particular, the visualization of ArchiMate model is currently supported by several tools, such as BiZZdesign Architect by BiZZdesign, ARIS ArchiMate Modeler by IDS Scheer, Metis by Troux, Corporate Modeler by Casewise, Rational System Architect by IBM, and Visio by Microsoft.

While the conceptual model is already broadly supported by tools, only a few tools support the execution of BA methods. Rational System Architect is for instance a positive example that supports different Enterprise Architecture Frameworks, such as TOGAF, DoDAF, and MODAF. MDG Technology by Sparx Systems or Provision by Metastorm are further tool examples that support TOGAF. However, a closer look at these tools reveals that the support of BA methodologies still leaves room for improvement. For instance, most tools do not provide a workflow capability that guides the architect automatically through the development of a business or enterprise architecture.

Service Focus

The focal point of the enterprise service system is the service, i.e., the value co-creation phenomena that generates mutual benefits for the two interacting service systems. Thus, this section analyzes the incorporation of the service concept in the BAs, whereby a particular focus is laid on the conceptual models. Methodologies or tools are less discussed in this chapter as in the BAs no particular service orientation was recognizable.

To illustrate in which way the service element was represented in the conceptual models an integrated service model was developed, consisting of a business and an IT view. Figure 11 shows most service aspects of the business view, which were defined in the BAs. However, some relationships between service and other business elements were not integrated in the model as they were contradictory to parts of the conceptual model.

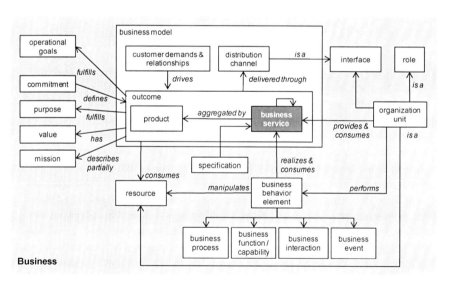

Figure 11. Integrated Service Model – Business View

Following Business Architectures contribute to the business view of the integrated service model. ArchiMate provides the detailed relationship between the business service, the product, and their value. Most BAs emphasized services and product offerings being an outcome of a business behavior. These behaviors are further specified by ArchiMate, ARIS, and BPMN. According to MS EBMM, the service is provided and consumed by the organization unit. McDavid defines more generically that the service consumes resources, e.g., capabilities of the organization unit. According to ArchiMate, the business unit is an interface and a role. Additionally, EBMM furthermore specifies that the organization unit, inheriting the characteristics from the interface, may be a distribution channel. EBMM also states that products and services are part of the business model and that they are driven by customer demands and relationships. Finally, according to BMM the business service is part of a mission statement. Inheriting from ARIS the business service can be decomposed into a service tree, whereby the 'has' relationships describes the sub-components of a service, the 'substitution' relationship defines by which other services the service can be replaced.

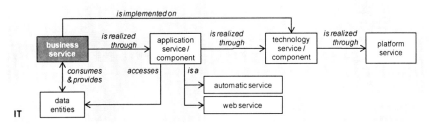

Figure 12. Integrated Service Model – IT View

As illustrated in Figure 12, the business service is often seen as a connection point to IT architectures. Both, ArchiMate and TOGAF, describe the relationship between a business service, an application service and a technology service. According to TOGAF, the business service consumes and provides data entities, which are accessed by the application service. Furthermore, the business service is directly implemented on a technology service, which again is realized through a platform service. Finally, BPMN further specifies the application service, also called service task in BPMN, as automatic or web service.

The proposed integrated service model provides a holistic view of all four business domains, as well as the integration points to the IT. Thus, it can serve as an integration model to the before introduced BA conceptual models. For instance, in a comprehensive transformation program an enterprise may choose the BMM by OMG to model the mission (which includes services) and other motivational aspects of the company. Using ARIS, the relevant business services can then be decomposed into more granular services, which then can be used with ArchiMate in order to specify the connection to the IT architecture. Similarly, other BA conceptual models can be integrated to better meet the BA purposes of a company.

Model integrations, such as the proposed integrated service model, should be used with cautious, as the simple connection of elements with the same name can lead to conflicts. For instance, unlike other Business Architectures, TOGAF differentiates specifically between a 'business function' and a 'business capability'. Thus, for the new service model the notation of this particular element needs to be newly defined. Furthermore, the combination of abstract and more concrete elements requires further specification. For instance, in the model the 'interface' is an abstract element, which can be instantiated by the more concrete element 'organization unit'. For these reasons, it is planned to evaluate the integrated service model in more depth, gaining further understanding on how it can be used for the development of real-life BA models, and how company benefit from it when applied for different BA purposes.

Conclusions

Current Business Architecture Frameworks differ in scope and maturity of their conceptual models. As determined before, the more mature BA approaches address only selected sub-areas of the four business domains 'Strategy & Structure', 'Business Network', 'Operations' and 'Performance and Revenue Model'. In general, these BAs represent silos which provide only limited guidance for the integration with other BAs. On the other hand, BA approaches addressing a broader spectrum of business concerns currently lack the syntax required for BA modeling in a practical context. For these reasons, when starting a business transformation initiative, which requires enterprise-wide BA models, it is essential to analyze carefully the different conceptual models with regard to how well they describe the involved business concerns. Additional development effort will be needed in both BA types. The BAs with a broader spectrum most likely need to be defined in further detail. As the example of the integrated service model shows that the connection of several conceptual models also involves a risk of linking business elements with similar names but different notations.

Whereas, conceptual models represent the dictionary for business concerns, the methodology aims at explaining how the business sentences, i.e., the BA models, are created. Today, most BAs provide only generic guidelines and only a few explain in more detail how a BA model should be created. Consequently, more sophisticated guidelines must be established in order to improve the support provided to business architects and to reduce the ambiguity of business modeling. In particular, well-defined procedures which respect the varying requirements for BA developments in different contexts (e.g., Business Strategy and IT Strategy, BPM, or SOA) would contribute considerably to the development of BA models.

Current modeling tools support in particular the development of BA models and less the execution of BA methodologies. Thus, current tools still reveal room for improvement in the support of both BA conceptual models and methodologies. For instance, guiding the business architects through a BA workflow supported by a BA modeling tool would allow to assign clearly tasks with defined goals, thus reducing potential mistakes in BA modeling and decreasing BA development times.

As identified in the previous section, the analyzed BAs incorporate the service concept to different extent. For the documentation and analysis of service components in an enterprise, BAs with a mature service orientation and best fit to the business context should be chosen.

References

AndersonHealy, K. & Ross, R.G., 2007. The Business Motivation Model - Business Governance in a Volatile World - Release 1.3.

ArchiMate Forum, 2009a. The Open Group ArchiMate Forum. Available at: http://www.opengroup.org/archimate/ [Accessed June 25, 2009].

ArchiMate Forum, 2009b. The Power of Enterprise Architecture. Available at: http://www.archimate.org/ [Accessed June 25, 2009].

BAWG, 2009a. Business Architecture Working Group. Available at: http://www.omgwiki.org/bawg/doku.php [Accessed July 5, 2009].

BAWG, 2009b. Defining Requirements for a Business Architecture Standard. Available at: http://bawg.omg.org/Bus_Arch_Ecosystem_White_Paper_Draft.pdf [Accessed July 5, 2009].

Burton, B. & Robertson, B., 2008. How to Develop Enterprise Business Architecture, Gartner.

Burton, B., 2009. Six Best Practices for Enterpries Business Architecture, Gartner.

Burton, B., 2008. Understand Enterprise Business Architecture to Realize Your Future State, Gartner.

Cambridge & IBM, 2007. Succeeding through service innovation -A service perspective for education, research, business and government. Available at: http://www.ifm.eng.cam.ac.uk/ssme/documents/ssme_discussion_final.pdf [Accessed June 23, 2009].

Cherbakov, L. et al., 2005. Impact of service orientation at the business level. IBM SYSTEMS JOURNAL, 44(4), 653-668.

Davis, R., 2008. ARIS Design Platform: Advanced Process Modelling and Administration: Rob Davis: Books 1st ed., London: Springer.

Davis, R. & Brabänder, E., 2007. ARIS Design Platform : Getting Started with BPM 1st ed., London: Springer.

Friedman, T.L., 2007. The World Is Flat 3.0: A Brief History of the Twenty-first Century, Picador.

Gerrit Versteeg & Bouwman, H., 2006. Business architecture: A new paradigm to relate business strategy to ICT. In Inf Syst Front. Springer Science+Business Media, pp. 91–102.

Glushko, R.J. & Tabas, L., 2007. Bridging the Front Stage and Back Stage in Service System Design. In Proceedings of the 41st Hawaii International Conference on System Sciences. Big Island, USA.

IBM, 2005. Component Business Models - Making Specialization Real, IBM Institute for Business Value.

IEEE Standards Association, 2000. IEEE Std. 1471-2000 Recommended Practice for Architectural Description of Software Intensive Systems.

IFIP-IFAC Task Force, 1999. GERAM: The Generalised Enterprise Reference Architecture and Methodology - Version 1.6.3. Available at: http://www.cit.gu.edu.au/~bernus/taskforce/geram/versions/geram1-6-3/v1.6.3.html#_Toc447291745 [Accessed June 27, 2009].

Lankhorst, M., 2005. *Enterprise Architecture at Work: Modelling, Communication and Analysis: Marc Lankhorst: Books* 1st ed., Springer.

Lankhorst, M., 2004. ArchiMate Language Primer - Introduction to the ArchiMate Modelling Language for Enterprise Architecture.

Malik, N., 2009a. Enterprise Business Motivation Model. Available at: http://motivationmodel.com/wp/index.php/home/ [Accessed July 6, 2009].

Malik, N., 2009b. Toward an Enterprise Business Motivation Model. *The Architecture Journal*, (19). Available at: http://msdn.microsoft.com/en-us/architecture/aa699429.aspx [Accessed June 27, 2009].

McDavid, D.W., 1999. A standard for business architecture description. *IBM Systems Journal*, 38(1), 12-20.

McDavid, D., 1996. Business Language Analysis for Object-Oriented Information Systems. *IBM Systems Journal*, 35(2), 23.

Minoli, D, 2007. Enterprise Architecture A to Z, Auerbach Publications

Nayak, N. et al., 2007. Core business architecture for a service-oriented enterprise . *IBM SYSTEMS JOURNAL*, 46(4), 723-742.

OMG, 2008. BPMN 1-1 Specification.pdf. Available at: http://www.omg.org/spec/BPMN/1.1/PDF [Accessed July 6, 2009].

OMG, 2006. Business Motivation Model (BMM) Specification - Draft Adopted Specification dtc/2006-07-02.

OMG, 2009. Business Process Modeling Notation (BPMN) - Version 1.2. Available at: http://www.omg.org/docs/formal/09-01-03.pdf [Accessed July 6, 2009].

Osterwalder, A., 2004. *The Business Model Ontology - a proposition in a design science approach* . HEC Lausanne. Available at: http://www.hec.unil.ch/aosterwa/PhD/ [Accessed June 25, 2009].

Plachy, E.C. & Hausler, P.A., 1999. Enterprise Solutions Structure. *IBM Systems Journal*, 38(1), 4-8.

Ross, J.W., Weill, P. & Robertson, D., 2006. *Enterprise Architecture As Strategy: Creating a Foundation for Business Execution*, Harvard Business School Press.

Sanz, J. L. C., Nayak, N., & Becker, V., 2006. Business Services as a Modeling Approach for Smart Business Networks, Conference Proceedings on Smart Business Networks, Putten Holland. Springer Verlag.

Sanz, J.L.C., Becker, V., Cappi, J., Chandra, A., Kramer, J. Lyman, K. Nayak, N., Pesce, P., Terrizzano, I., & Vergo, J., 2007. *Business Services and Business Componentization: New Gaps between Business and IT*, IEEE IEEE International Conference on Service-Oriented Computing and Appli-Applications, New Port Beach, California.

Scheer, A., 2000a. *ARIS - Business Process Frameworks* 3rd ed., Springer.

  Scheer, A., 2000b. *ARIS - Business Process Modeling: August-Wilhelm Scheer: Books* 3rd ed., Springer.

Scheer, A. & Hars, A., 1992. Extending Data Modeling to Cover the Whole. *Communications of the ACM*, 35(9), 166-171.

Scott, J., 2008. *Business Architecture's Time Has Come*, Forrester.

Spohrer, J. et al., 2008. The Service System is the Basic Abstraction of Service Science. In *Proceedings of the 41st Hawaii International Conference on System Sciences*. Big Island, USA.

Strosnider, J. et al., 2002. *IGS BizADS Handbook - IGS Business Architecture Description Standard (BizADS)* 1st ed., IBM.

Teboul, J., 2006. *Service Is Front Stage: Positioning Services for Value Advantage*, Palgrave Macmillan.

The Open Group, 2009a. Technical Standard ArchiMate® 1.0 Specification.

The Open Group, 2009b. TOGAF Version 9 - The Open Group Architecture Framework.

Tikkanen, H. et al., 2005. Managerial cognition, action and the business model of the firm. *Management Decision*, 43(5/6), 789-810.

TSG, Inc., 2008. Business Architecture: Scenarios & Use Cases. Available at: http://www.omg.org/cgi-bin/doc?bmi/08-04-01 [Accessed July 5, 2009].

White, S.A., 2004. Introduction to BPMN.

A Service Practice Approach

People, Activities and Information in Highly Collaborative Knowledge-based Service Systems

Cheryl A. Kieliszewski

IBM Research - Almaden

John H. Bailey

CA

Jeanette Blomberg

IBM Research - Almaden

In the practice of designing and engineering business systems, work is often defined and represented by a series of activities comprised of discrete tasks performed in a prescribed sequence, within a particular timeframe and set in the context of a particular technology. These elements are often reduced to a set of controlled system inputs and outputs, ignoring the complex interactions that need to be supported in highly collaborative work systems endemic of service systems. It is our position that designing and engineering service-based systems requires a new approach to understanding the interactions between the people, information technology and activities needed to enable services. We have approached service system design from the perspective of investigating and understanding work practices as the basis for system innovation. As such, our focus is on understanding what people actually do in practice, including their use of information, tools, methods and the relationships amongst these elements. This paper describes a practice-based approach for investigating work in service organizations. We argue for a need to understand work from the practice perspective, describe our practice-based approach, present a new way to represent work using practice diagrams, provide a case study as an example of our approach and make recommendations for future research.

P.P. Maglio et al. (eds.), *Handbook of Service Science*, Service Science: Research and Innovations in the Service Economy, DOI 10.1007/978-1-4419-1628-0_13,
© Springer Science+Business Media, LLC 2010

Introduction

Strategies to achieve greater workplace efficiencies and improved productivity often involve the decomposition of work into a series of granular tasks that can be automated and/or reconfigured. Well known strategies include time-and-motion studies and supply chain optimization practices. These strategies have attained success for work that can be characterized as linear, following step-by-step processes that take place in conjunction with other similarly structured work activities and where only limited iterative interaction between work processes occurs. However, it is our view that for highly collaborative, knowledge-intensive work, that is often characteristic of the service sector (Blomberg, 2009), an analysis and design approach based in the study of everyday work practices is needed. This paper describes such a practice-based approach for investigating work in service organizations and argues for its application in the design of informational, organizational and technological innovations for achieving service system transformation.

The paper is organized as three sections. The first describes our practice-based approach for studying work activities within highly collaborative, knowledge-based service systems. The second introduces the practice diagram, a representational form that helps convey the complex, interactive and iterative quality of service work. The third presents a case study where our practice-based approach was applied. The case is a description of the interactions and interdependencies that exist among work practitioners involved in designing and costing service delivery solutions for information technology (IT) outsourcing engagements. Our analysis points to the limits of representing work as a series of sequential steps where one component of the work concludes before the next begins (c. f. Bowers, Button & Sharrock, 1995; Dourish, 2001 for a related perspective on work). Through both our use of the practice diagram schema and our case study we show how work unfolds iteratively, cycling back-and-forth between components of the work until an eventual "end state" is achieved. We conclude by arguing for the benefits of a practice-based approach to understanding service systems and designing ways to achieve higher levels of service performance.

Practice-based Approach

Over the years, many approaches for infusing end-user perspectives into technology design have been developed, examples include user-centered design (Vredenburg, 2002), contextual inquiry (e.g., Beyer & Holtzblatt, 1997) and persona-based design (Cooper, 1998; Pruitt and Grudin, 2003). Another approach, the ethnographic study of work to inform technology and organizational innovations (Blomberg and Burrell, 2007; Hughes et al., 1995), focuses on what people do in practice including their interactions with one another and with artifacts. This practice-based, ethnographic approach is primarily concerned with understanding everyday practices and organizational relationships that enable work system performance and is less focused on requirements gathering, user likes/dislikes or task analysis. The practice-based approach involves observing work as it unfolds, underscoring relationships between people, between people and artifacts (including technologies and processes) and between artifacts.

As mentioned our practice-based approach to service system innovation has its roots in ethnography. Interest in ethnographic analytical frameworks and techniques as resources for technology design can be traced back to the early 1980s when computer technologies were moving out of the research labs and engineering environments and into mainstream office settings, call centers, manufacturing floors and educational institutions (Blomberg and Burrell, 2007). Designers were no longer able to rely exclusively on their own experiences to guide innovations, but instead looked for ways to immerse themselves in the everyday realities of people working within diverse contexts (Blomberg, Giacomi, Mosher & Swenton-Wall, 1991). Designers and developers sought ways of acquiring a firsthand view of - the here and now - of everyday work settings. Drawing on the key insight from the ethnographic tradition, that 'what people say they do' and 'what they actually do' are not the same (Rathje & Murphy, 1991; Whiting & Whiting, 1970; Corral-Verduga, 1997; and Rich, Lamolu, Amory & Schneider, 2000), the practice-based approach argues that it is not enough to simply ask people about their behaviors and activities through interviews, focus groups or questionnaires. To obtain valid understandings that reflect the experiences of those studied, opportunities to interact with people and observe their activities in everyday settings are critical.

Propelling the adoption of practice-based approaches to design has been the emergence of networked applications and devices, along with the widespread use of the Internet. These technologies and the services they enable oblige designers to look beyond supporting single, isolated users interacting with information technologies and towards systems that facilitate communication and exchange of information among people and organizations. Information technologies increasingly have become collaboration technologies that demand examination of the social interactions that take place across time and space (c.f. emerging field of CSCW Grief, 1988; Schmidt & Bannon, 1992. e.g., Bentley et al., 1992; Hughes, Randall & Shapiro, 1993; Hughes, King, Rodden & Anderson, 1994; Hughes, Rodden & Anderson, 1995). Today approaches rooted in ethnography, like our practice-based approach, have been widely adopted in industry (c.f. Cefkin, 2009 and proceedings of the Ethnographic Praxis in Industry conferences, 2005-2009).

Finally, with the recent emergence of service science which "…aims to explain and improve interactions in which multiple entities work together to achieve win-win outcomes or mutual benefits" (Spohrer and Maglio, 2009), the potential significance of practice-based approaches is even more compelling. Within the ethnographic tradition the foundational concept of "holism" or the view that activities must be understood within the larger context in which they occur, resonates strongly with the service science focus on service systems where interactions and interdependencies among entities are stressed. Historically the notion of holism maintained that societies were more than the sum of their parts, in other words, particular aspects of society (e.g., law or kinship) could only be understood in relation to the other aspects. Today, holism more generally argues that studying an activity in isolation, without reference to connections to other activities in time and space, provides a somewhat narrow and partial understanding of the activity. For example, investigating online search strategies without understanding how these strategies are integrated and connected with a broader set of activities (e.g., in the context of online trading, shopping or report writing) restricts the insights that can come from the study.

Our practice-based approach to the study of work, which attends to interactions and interdependencies within the broader organizational context, offers an approach to guide the design and transformation of service systems. Spohrer and Maglio (2009) have proposed that service systems, the primary unit of action in service value co-creation, are "...dynamic configurations of resources, which include.... people, organizations, shared information and technology (Spohrer et al., 2007)." Clearly the actions and interactions of people in relation to artifacts (technology and other objects) are the means by which resources are "dynamically configured". Examining work as practice-based is well suited for the analysis of service systems since value-creating activities are characterized by intra- and inter-organizational relations sustained through ongoing interactions (Stucky et al., 2009).

Work in service firms often involves interactions across both firm boundaries and internal organizational boundaries (e.g., service system entities). In the simplest case the service provider and the client must interact to co-create value (e.g., Vargo and Lusch, 2004). In more complex cases multiple entities interact in a constellation (Normann and Ramirez, 1993; Normann, 2001) and these value constellations construct "a new, coordinated set of activities resulting in a new kind of output" (Normann, 2001, p. 107). These value constellations organize relationship between entities enabling the integration of resources. The position of entities in the larger system facilitates and shapes value creation. A practice-based approach to understanding work within the context of service is well suited for understanding value constellations.

Data collection and analysis

As noted above, practice-based approaches seek to develop holistic views that require combining and juxtaposing different data sources (Agar, 1996). For example, onsite observations are usefully coupled with in-context interviewing and interviews can extend and deepen understandings originating from observations. Similarly, interviews inform observations, providing direction for the most appropriate activities or people to observe. Our practice-based approach is, in part, a corrective to the typical role people have played in work system analysis and design. Conventionally people are implicit objects in descriptions of work systems, but their actions and interactions have not been explicitly articulated. Our approach makes people first class actors in work systems, in particular representing people's role as active transformers of information in the system. In order to make the role of people explicit in service systems, our approach relies on onsite observations and interactions as part of the data collection strategy thus enabling access to the emergent and dynamic aspects of work.

Artifact analysis

Along with in-context interviews and observations, our practice-based approach includes the analysis of artifacts that are used in the accomplishment of work. These artifacts include such things as organizational charts, performance metrics, process diagrams, solution architecture diagrams and client-originated requests for proposals. These artifacts not only provide us with another perspective on the work, but they figure prominently in the coordination of work across departments and activity areas (see discussion of boundary objects below). Our analysis of these materials involves both reviewing the content and structure of the artifacts and conducting quantitative text analytics where appropriate.

Data analysis

Our practice-based approach results in large quantities of qualitative data, including audio recordings of interviews, video recording of observations, notes from both interviews and observations and documents used by work practitioners to describe their work and its execution. These data are systematically analyzed by identifying themes with supporting evidence and articulating the connections among activities, people and artifacts. At times these analyses are supported through the use of qualitative data analysis tools such as NVIVO7 (2006) and quantitative tools such as eClassifier (a classification and visualization tool for the analysis of unstructured text data sets). Central to the data analysis is the ability to trace the connections and maintain the linkages between the findings and the observational and interview data.

Representing practice

The practice-based approach described above begins with the view that it is difficult to specify the elements and entities of a service system without examining how work is enacted within the system. It then follows that a way of documenting and representing the work is needed to enable changes in those work activities based on the transformation of current practices, enabling technologies and processes. This section discusses the creation of a practice diagramming approach used to create a service practice schema to enable understanding of entities and interactions while keeping people as the central focus.

Our research on the response cycle to a Request for Proposal (RFP) in the engagement phase of an information technology (IT) outsourcing deal of business-to-business services led to the development of this new representational schema, practice diagramming (discussion of the engagement phase is provided in the Case Study section). The schema provides a means to represent the service practitioner in the system as an element separate from a task, technology or procedure. By representing practice as practice diagrams we are better able to characterize and communicate the dimensions of work carried-out by service practitioners and the interactions between the people and the technological and procedural elements within a service system.

The representation and communication of practice within a service system presents particular challenges due to the complexity of both the work and the diversity of the stakeholders involved in service system transformation. These stakeholders range from organizational business and process owners, program and project managers, technology designers and developers and the practitioners themselves. Without an accepted and widely used approach (e.g., object-oriented methodologies within computer science) to represent and communicate opportunities and recommendations for service system transformation the efficacy of practice-based inquiries is limited.

In a quest to improve how the work is coordinated, performed and delivered to realize greater efficiencies and decrease operational risk, earlier schemas have been created to represent people in work systems (whether they be manufacturing- or service-oriented systems) and more generally to understand the human element (e.g., Hendrick & Kleiner, 2001; Shostack, 1984; Wall & Mosher, 1994; Wemmerlöv, 1989). For example, the study of macroergonomics takes people into consideration within the context of a sociotechnical systems model where the focus is on understanding the organizational–technological relationship employed in the system and on optimizing the human–system relationship (Hendrick & Kleiner, 2001). Service blueprinting (introduced by Lynn Shostack (1984)) is another example of a schema, in this case for analyzing and representing service interactions within market entities. Blueprinting attempts to address and take account of the multiplicity of atomic service elements and interactions that define the behavior of a service system. However, service blueprinting does not provide specific representation of the human element and is based on the relationship (or bond) between the essential entities of the service element, product element and essential evidence. Although these schemas begin to address the issue of representing people as active entities of a system, our experience suggests that they are inadequate for analyzing and representing service practices to inform the creation of new technologies and the accompanying organizational and process changes.

In the development of our practice diagramming approach it was useful to revisit ideas developed in the context of sociotechnical systems theory. Sociotechnical systems are defined as having a technical subsystem and a personnel subsystem as the two primary components in system modeling (Hendrick, 1991). These two components are also assumed to comprise a service system, in addition to organizational processes (a third component). Cummings (1978), in his strategy for sociotechnical intervention, introduces a set of principles for sociotechnical analysis and design of an organization (i.e., hospital, school, factory, services). The principles he introduces aid the analyst in bounding the system to have (a) a clear delineation between the social and technological components of the organization, and (b) a clear definition of input and output states for particular activities that define a work unit's functionality. Without these system boundaries identified, the effectiveness and efficiency of the system cannot be determined. In our practice-based studies we focus on defining the people, technology and process components that comprise the service system, along with inputs, outputs and interactions that influence practitioner success.

In addition to sociotechnical systems theory, we draw upon the notion of boundary objects that was first introduced by Star and Griesemer (1989) and later applied in the business domain by Carlile (2002). According to Star and Griesemer, boundary objects "...are objects which are both plastic enough to adapt to local needs and the constraints of the several parties employing them, yet robust enough to maintain a common identity across sites. ... And that, the creation and management of boundary objects is a key process in developing and maintaining coherence across intersecting social worlds" (p. 393). In their research, boundary objects were represented by centralized records that were accounted for as nodes in a larger networked transactional structure.

Carlile (2002) extended this notion of boundary object and formalized it in his research on "knowledge in practice." For Carlile boundary objects are a pragmatic "...means of representing, learning about, and transforming knowledge to resolve the consequences [whether positive or negative] that exist at a given boundary" (p. 442). This use of boundary object provides a framework for the transfer of not just information in the form of a record that aids in the definition of a network, but the transfer of knowledge as a part of practice across organizational functions. The access and transfer of knowledge for multiple work purposes at a syntactic (or computational) level and at a semantic level between individuals and within the organization was a significant challenge for the success of our practice-based approach. The challenge resided in teasing apart practices for the identification and disclosure of individual and organizational routines and work-arounds that circumvented the prescribed tools and processes—mainly because some formal processes got in the way of accomplishing the work in a timely manner.

The notion of boundary objects provided us with a working definition for objects used for input and produced as output for particular activities in the service system. For our research, boundary objects were both important in the conduct of the inter- and intra-organizational work of responding to an RFP in the engagement phase of an IT outsourcing deal and in enabling us to communicate the results of our research to the multiple stakeholders who would have a say in service system transformation. The identification of boundary objects and relationships in our practice-diagram approach were augmented with a specific orientation to purpose, expectations, time, technology and access to individuals and information.

Communicating Practice

The audience and stakeholders for our research were technology-centric project managers, software architects and developers, and business owner executives. This made communicating the results of our people-centric research, focused on the everyday working practices of those developing IT outsourcing proposals in response to an RFP particularly challenging. The goal was to inform the development of organizational interventions (new technologies and processes) and to help anticipate their impact on the service system as a whole. To communicate what we were learning about these practices, the practice diagramming approach emerged to represent the what, who, and how of work performance within an organizational context. Practice diagrams grew out of a need to communicate how work is enacted through interaction and iteration with this diverse audience. This was not possible by focusing only on how individual tasks are performed (Kieliszewski, Bailey & Blomberg, 2007). That is, we needed an approach that would provide a systemic, integrative perspective on work.

Initial practice diagrams were generated from interviews with technical and business subject matter experts (SMEs). The diagrams were validated during a review with the SMEs. These early representations provided a general overview of the work, similar to a view of the work that would be provided through a business process diagram but with the central focus on the interactions and relationships between individual roles, occupational groups, information and technologies. Like business process diagrams, this perspective was helpful in showing general informational flow and illustrating pragmatic boundaries and transition points. A pragmatic boundary is exemplified by team members referencing past RFPs for response content and approaches they used in prior deals. Transition points are illustrated by passing the proposed technical solution back-and-forth between the Lead Technical Solution Manager, the Technical Solution Architects and the Quality Assurance Representative to ensure each domain perspective and expertise is properly represented. Where, each individual has a particular purpose for use of the RFP and interpretation of the contents, yet all must come to a consensus in the end to form a response.

Through further interviews and observations with work practitioners and additional analysis, we found that it was useful to view the work as chunked into clusters (Figure 1). The clusters were delineated by major semantic transition points which often were demarcated and enabled by boundary objects (Carlile, 2002). That is, the characteristic of the boundary object(s) was not computational (e.g., easily accessed and computed via automated means), but required explanatory communications between clusters to continue with the overall work effort of responding to the RFP.

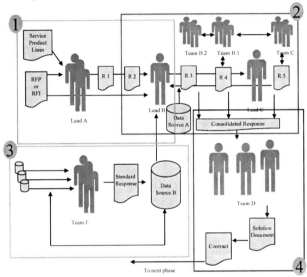

Figure 1. Practice diagram work clusters

Once we were able to represent the overall connections between clusters, we added annotations to the representations to capture more of the detail of everyday practices. The annotations represented four key attributes: (a) work and organization context description, (b) team members/actors, (c) informational resources and (d) events. These four attributes were data-driven and defined based upon information collected through the interviews and observations.

Attribute: Work and Organization Context Description

A general description of the work and organization was created to provide context for each of the diagram clusters. The general description is meant to be a very concise statement of desired outcome for a given cluster, basically the purpose and objectives of the work. For example, in the case study described below, there is a cluster to the strategic outsourcing engagement phase that was identified as "create a solution". Where, the objectives of the work were to (a) examine a proposal, (b) determine the costing aspects and (c) create the cost model. In addition to the purpose and objectives, generalized interactions between people, technologies and information were captured as one- and two-way flows between nodes in the diagram. The interactions could have been between people, between people and informational repositories (e.g., database or virtual team/activity space) or between informational repositories.

Attribute: Team Members/Actors

Another annotated attribute was team members or actors in the cluster. Recall that a primary reason for creating the practice-diagrams was to ensure that the roles of people were included in the understanding and design of service systems. The annotation for the team members was a concise description of roles, responsibilities and what or how information (as an object) was used and/or produced as part of the system. For example, in the case study that follows, the role of the Lead TSM (Technical Solution Manager) includes five primary responsibilities (define technical solution, coordinate technical solution activity, deliver consolidated case, proposal development, interact with customer as solution technical expert). In addition, two essential pieces of information that this role uses are called a 'win strategy' and a 'base case'. Information that is produced by the Lead TSM is a 'solution strategy' and a 'consolidated case'. Each of these elements (i.e., role, responsibilities and informational objects) is identified and provided a label for inclusion in the diagrams and subsequent analysis and recommendations.

Attribute: Informational Resource

Informational resources were elements of the system that afforded individuals and teams data and materials required to accomplish their work and align with the work of others. Examples of these resources include documents, files, databases and virtual team/activity spaces. Any individual informational resource was often used by multiple actors to communicate and disambiguate between client service needs as described in the RFP and provider capabilities. In essence, these resources acted as boundary objects as described by Star and Griesemer (1989). Five main annotations were captured for each informational resource.

1. The purpose or reason for the resource object, for example one purpose of the 'RFP' object was to assist with determining solution elements for detailing.
2. Inputs into and dependencies upon each of the resource objects by different team members to successfully contribute to the RFP response. An example of inputs and dependencies is the need by the Costing Representative, who creates the 'solution cost case' object

for input from the 'technical architecture' object created by the Technical Architect.

3. When and how inputs, dependencies or communications were typically received. We found early on that one of the primary complaints by the team members was the problem of coordinating intra-team dependencies. The Information Resource attribute would need to show when and how information was typically received versus ideally shared and accessed. A typical example is when a change to one technical architect specification (e.g., servers) has an impact on another technical architecture specification (e.g., networks) created by a different team member. Hence, if the Server Architect neglected to communicate changes to his/her specification (often times due to workload and time pressures to complete the specification) then the Network Architect would either be placed behind schedule due to a delayed communication or provide an incorrect specification due to a lack of communication.

4. Expectations held for each of the resource objects by the team. This was especially important for input and feedback coming from the client. Annotations included whether or not a resource object tended to be supplied at all, expectations for when it was supplied in the process, whether it tended to be complete when received and a description of what information was desired as a part of the resource.

5. Description of what information a resource object tended to provide for input into another resource object or for general reuse.

Attribute: Events

The last attribute for which annotations were created was special events. These included disruptions to getting work done, those unscheduled or unforeseen distractions that detract from accomplishing an activity such as a last minute request to attend a meeting that was inconsequential to the work or current issue being resolved. Everyday interruptions to getting work done were also identified. Some were scheduled or foreseen such as meetings and others were unscheduled such as phone calls or instant messages. Many of these interruptions were welcome with little consequence on the completion of the work. Another event was change in team composition when a member left or new member was added. The addition of a team member typically meant reviewing progress to bring the new member up-to-date. A team member leaving often resulted in aspects of project memory being lost, especially if the team member moved prior to project completion. Like the others, the identification of this attribute (along with the annotation types) was data-driven.

Transforming Practice

The details of how work is accomplished is not easy to represent and communicate (Suchman, 1995) to diverse stakeholders. The practice diagrams provided evidence for the sociotechnical pathway of work, recognizing that practice shapes and is shaped by processes and relationships within the organization. The diagrams aided in illustrating and communicating work dependencies: impacts of one set of work activities on another, informational expectations and short comings and short-cuts and work-arounds to standard procedures and processes. They also established evidence of the creative, collaborative, and individual aspects of the work and highlighted both formal and informal people-to-people relationships and informational resource pathways.

The ability to communicate work practices, relationships and organizational context through practice diagrams enabled us to better inform the design of business-to-business services. The iterative actions between actors, information and technology—often at odds with the formal business processes used to track and monitor progress—were acknowledged. Although the diagrams focused on the enactment of the work by practitioners, they also made reference to elements of formal business process and the use of technologies. In this way, the practice diagrams could be compared with prescriptive process diagrams and IT support and tooling diagrams to understand potential conflicts with formal processes and procedures and to identify new areas for innovation. To exemplify the value of using practice diagrams to represent work practices, a case example of our practice-based approach is provided in the next section. The case is focused on a description of the interactions and interdependencies that exist among work practitioners involved in designing and costing service delivery solutions for IT outsourcing engagements in response to client requests for proposals.

Case Study: Work in Organizational Context of IT Outsourcing

We designed and conducted a practice-based study to examine how work is enacted by a service provider in response to a request for proposal (RFP) from a potential client. This work was undertaken to gain a more detailed understanding of the work and organizational practices in information technology (IT) outsourcing towards the ends of improved technology designs and process innovations. The study took place over a period of about six months beginning in early 2007.

The business of IT outsourcing involves an IT provider who assumes responsibility for managing and maintaining an agreed upon set of IT functions for their client. The economic premise of an outsourcing deal is that the IT outsourcing provider has greater experience and superior know-how in IT. Thus, the provider can deliver value to their client primarily via cost reduction, and additionally through improved scalability, adaptability, availability, service quality and industry competitiveness.

As a brief overview to better understand the context of our study, IT outsourcing can be described in four phases:

- **Pre-sales** involves identifying and qualifying potential clients.
- **Engagement** is the sales phase, and involves the provider working with the client to develop a business and technical proposal, which will be embodied in a signed contract.
- **Delivery,** sometimes referred to as transition, involves transitioning the technical, business and human elements from the client to the provider organization.
- **Production,** sometimes referred to as steady state, involves the on-going IT operation and management by the service provider.

Our study was focused on the engagement phase of IT outsourcing (Figure 2). It is worth noting that outsourcing is not synonymous with off-shoring, which is the practice of moving work to a country with lower labor cost or available skills. Although an outsourcing deal may result in the service provider moving all or part of the work off-shore, it is not a requirement, and many deals do not include off-shoring.

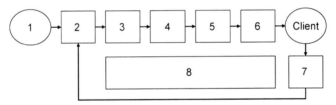

1. Initialize engagement
2. Requirements review
3. Design solution
4. Develop and document solution
5. Develop cost case
6. Final reviews
7. Due diligence
8. Develop client deliverables

Figure 2. Engagement phase process diagram

Method

We collected data by means of interviews, direct observation and gathering of artifacts. The two following sections describe the participant population and methodology for gathering information.[1]

Interviews

We interviewed people directly involved in the engagement phase of IT outsourcing. In general, their work involved developing a proposal in response to a request that corresponded to the outsourcing requirements of a potential client. Specifically, we interviewed technology experts who designed parts of the outsourcing solution (e.g. network, security, data center) and the technology leaders who managed the overall solution design efforts. The interviewees were located in North America, Europe and Asia Pacific (Table 1).

Table 1. Distribution of data collection efforts

Data Collection Effort	Community Studied	Americas Group	EMEA*	Asia Pacific
A	Subject Matter Experts	2	3	2
B	Technical Solution Managers	3	5	0
	Technical Solution Architects	3	3	0
C	Technical Solution Managers	3	1	1

*EMEA: Europe, Middle East and Africa

The interviews were semi-structured and composed of questions that would yield a general understanding of the interviewee's role, goals, activities, collaborators and perspective on aspects of their job and activities that could be improved. The interviews were scheduled to be one hour in length, although some went longer, and were conducted over the telephone by two researchers. One researcher led the interviews while the other took notes and helped keep the

[1] Acknowledgment: Brian Tsao, a summer intern and University of California Berkeley graduate student, helped us collect and analyze the data. We thank Brian for his methodological diligence and thoughtful analysis.

interview on track.   The resultant 25 hours of recorded conversation was transcribed by a vendor, and the transcripts were loaded into NVIVO7 (2006). We used NVIVO7 to find and mark topics of interest, yielding topical patterns and clusters across the interviews.   Topics of interest were not defined a priori, rather they were allowed to emerge in regards to advancing our understanding of the work and specific challenges, particularly challenges that might have been amenable to interventions.

Observations

We observed an engagement team while they developed an outsourcing proposal for a total of almost 40 hours.   Because of the confidential nature of the work and sensitivities of the people we observed, we did not capture video or audio recordings.   Instead, we relied on hand written notes.   The engagement team also gave us access to their knowledge repositories, which held hundreds of documents that we reviewed and referenced.   We were also able to get similar sample documents from previously completed engagements.

The engagement we observed took place over a period of about three months and included dozens of people with a diverse range of expertise such as sales, finance, technology, contract law and project management to name a few.   The team was geographically distributed, but co-located at a common physical location on several occasions in order to collaborate more effectively, especially when important milestones were due.   We observed two of these co-located meetings. In the second of the two meetings, which lasted over two days, we had two observers on-site and this allowed us to cross-reference our notes for accuracy and completeness.   It also allowed extended coverage to observe at least two engagement team groups during break-out working sessions.

When geographically distributed, the engagement team met regularly by teleconference.   As part of our observations, we listened to many of the regularly scheduled teleconferences, taking notes on topics of interest. These teleconference observations continued as the engagement team submitted the proposal, responded to follow-on requests and learned of the final response from the client.

Although our observations were limited to people and events on the provider side of the engagement, the client also had people with a wide range of skills (matching counterparts to the provider team) involved in the process. Additionally, the client had contracted a third party provider to manage the proposal bidding, response and selection process.   We did not directly collect observational or interview data on either the client or the third party provider, and thus they are not included in our analysis.   We mention them here for the sake of completeness, and because some findings may reflect inferred understanding from the provider perspective.

Analysis

We iteratively analyzed the data as it was collected, first working with the data from the interviews and then with notes from the observations. As previously described, the interviews yielded topical patterns and clusters. These were then combined with the descriptive data from the observations along with analysis of artifacts to yield insights about the work of RFP solution development within the engagement phase of IT outsourcing. The primary purpose of our analysis was to identify both the obvious (already known to the organization) and non-obvious (new discoveries) practices that impact IT outsourcing engagement to inform the design of new technologies and processes for a more efficient and effective engagement phase cycle. We placed an emphasis on identifying practices and activities that challenged expected and accepted understanding. The lens through which we viewed the data also focused on critical, but overlooked, interactions among people, process and technology.

The complete analysis across all of the data resulted in a large set of findings that we expressed in short phrases as snippets of interview conversation, observation notes or text from artifacts. There were considerable overlap and interconnectedness among the findings and an affinity clustering exercise was conducted to structure and organize the findings (Figure 3). This exercise helped us reduce the number of unique findings to twenty (which fell into one of three groups) where we could focus our recommendations for proposed practice, technology and/or process interventions.

Figure 3. Example of affinity cluster analysis

Additionally, as we went through our analysis we developed and iterated on the practice diagrams, which allowed us to portray people as active participants in creating, processing and transforming information and to communicate our early descriptive findings to stakeholders. The practice diagrams represented one- and two-way information flows and boundaries within the service system. Collectively, these representations allowed us to visualize the elements in the IT outsourcing work system during the engagement phase, yielding insights that fed into the final findings.

Findings

Contrary to commonly held views of IT outsourcing engagement phase work as aligned and conducted as a sequential process (Figure 2), we found that the activities were iterative, parallel and highly collaborative (Figures 4 and 5). Not surprisingly, the tooling and formal process descriptions were not well adapted to the enactment of the work, resulting in sometimes inefficient, yet creative and resilient adaptations by the people doing the work.

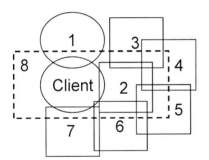

1. Initialize engagement
2. Requirements review
3. Design solution
4. Develop and document solution
5. Develop cost case
6. Final reviews
7. Due diligence
8. Develop client deliverables

Figure 4. Engagement phase diagram showing parallel and interdependent relationship among activities

Process View	Practice View
• Serialized, staged	• Parallel, Iterative
• Process stages are central	• Client deliverables are central
• Work and information compartmentalized	• Information flows back and forth freely, work is collaborative

Figure 5. Comparison of process and practice views of engagement phase work

Collaborative Disambiguation

A majority of the important work of disambiguating the RFP happened outside of the standard tooling with little or no technology to support the activity. Disambiguation was done iteratively and often in parallel by practitioners reviewing the RFP documents independently or in small groups. The activity was conducted in this manner to discover specific statements that might be interpreted differently by people with diverse domain expertise or to identify statements that had unspecified implications across multiple domains. This work was performed by reading the printed RFP documents while highlighting questionable statements or, if working in a small group, projecting the documents onto a screen where they could be read collectively. This slow and tedious work required the careful attention of experienced professionals to ensure that nothing was missed. Even the smallest of details were inspected.

For example, a small group representing technical, legal and financial experts found a statement about a requirement that the provider would remove certain types of assets for the client. This statement raised a number of questions that dealt with the technical implications of removal, the subsequent disposal or redeployment of the removed assets and the financial responsibilities associated with disposal. The outputs from these types of disambiguation activities would later be captured in the tools being used to support the team as a change to the outsourcing solution. This practice of doing the real work outside of the tooling and then capturing the results in the tools at a later time was less efficient than it could have been, introducing opportunities for errors and mis-communications, and was not aligned with the formal engagement phase process.

Tracking Dependencies

Outsourcing proposals are often very complex, as was the one we observed being crafted. They involve multiple, interrelated technical and non-technical components with numerous dependencies amongst the components. The management of these relationships and dependencies often occurred outside the official technical systems. The chore of tracking dependencies and keeping related parts of the solution synchronized was done manually by email or telephone. If someone failed to notify their counterparts of a change, or the recipient of a notification failed to react, then the components of the solution were temporarily out of alignment, potentially leading to costly redesign and time lost later in the process.

Tracking Assumptions

Another finding, related to the previously mentioned work of disambiguation, was the manual tracking of assumptions. Assumptions were made frequently during iterations on the solution designs and proposal development. The assumptions were necessary because of the incomplete, misleading and ambiguous nature of the RFP. However, once again, there was no central technology for tracking and maintaining assumptions. Instead, the common practice was for assumptions to be recorded manually and communicated during meetings and via emails. Missed, lost and conflicting assumptions were corrected by having several technical leads sit down together to go through all the various lists of assumptions, creating a consolidated, accurate list. This revised list would then be distributed to the team so that they could check their designs to ensure the assumptions were accurately reflected in their piece of the solution design.

Summary

The work of developing a response to a complex outsourcing RFP involved the manual recording, coordinating and processing of design elements. The success of producing the response relied on the skills and experience of the provider response team. Because outsourcing solutions are often very large—comprised of many technical, process, financial and human functions—the work of developing the response proposal was conducted in parallel with dozens of specialists working simultaneously on their individual pieces. While everyone on the team used general purpose tooling (e.g., word processing, spreadsheets, email, instant messaging, presentation tools, telephone), the specialized tooling was primarily used for solution specifications along with associated costs and price of the deal. These tools represented savings in effort (as compared to a similar manual process) and provided some consistency across engagements. However, they did not support the iterative, parallel and collaborative work practices that we found to be fundamental in performing critical activities of disambiguation and tracking of dependencies and assumptions.   Our research showed there were many opportunities for improvements in how these collaborative activities were supported which could dramatically improve work efficiency and quality of the outsourcing proposal.

Discussion and Future Directions

This paper describes a practice-based design approach for the study of everyday work practices that provides a systematic and robust way of investigating and understanding work in service organizations. A challenge that service organizations pose to system transformation and optimization is that work is performed in an iterative, non-linear manner with complex interactions within and across provider and client organizations. Viewing work this way challenges the canonical supply chain and operations research techniques of process optimization. Our practice-based approach represents work in a holistic manner and takes into consideration the relationships, boundaries and layers of dependencies that compose work in a service organization. This provides a vehicle for identifying relationships that impact the service system. The emphasis of this paper is how the investigation and understanding of work practices can effectively be communicated to relevant stakeholders to shape service system transformation. The results of our work were recommendations to transform the engagement phase of the service system through improvements to work practices, organizational process and technology-based support tools. However, in the spirit of full disclosure, we did encounter barriers by the business to the uptake of our research findings and implementation of our recommendations. As we continue to develop our practice-based approach and techniques of practice diagramming we will need to explore ways to more closely couple our activities with those of the people responsible for designing the next generation of enterprise tools and processes. Below we outline some of the contributions our approach gives to service system transformation.

Contributions of Practice-based Approach

Our approach demonstrates that the practices of highly collaborative, knowledge-intensive works cannot be reduced to a set of controlled system inputs and outputs. Ways of representing the creative, collaborative and iterative aspects of the work are essential. Representing work as overly sequential and linear has consequences for the design and specification of information requirements, skills definition and technologies intended to support the work. Our practice-based approach builds on the ethnographic tradition and adopts concepts from sociotechnical systems theory, research on boundary objects and service blueprinting representational practices. These foundational constructs informed the practice diagramming approach. This allowed for the identification and communication of key attributes describing work and organizational practices. The practice diagrams also allowed for the identification of informational and technological resources that are employed and potential areas for improvement.

Our practice diagramming approach supports Cummings (1978) view of the importance of clearly defining the social and technological components. However in our case, part of the research was to identify and define potential interventions for system transformation. To aid in defining work practices, we found identifying boundary objects (Star and Griesemer, 1989; Carlisle, 2002) and how they are used as both syntactic entities within the context of a technology or semantic entities within the context of knowledge transfer are important. Understanding the handling of boundary objects was key in identifying inefficiencies in work practices that impacted the effectiveness of the service system. We also found the need to include attributes of context, practitioners, information and events to understand the critical and extended interactions needed to accomplish goals that go beyond the traditional representational practices.

Expressing Opportunity Costs to the Organization

Some of our findings and recommendations to the business were not surprising (e.g., alleviating redundant communications: implement collaborative tools and practices, such as wikis and RSS feeds that allow for a pattern of information acquisition that is one-to-many as opposed to one-to-one); while others were directly informed by the attention we paid to how work was actually performed (e.g., improving the speed and quality of disambiguation of client RFP via an automated processing of client documents using a text analytics technology). One of the barriers we encountered in implementing our recommendations that had the potential of transforming the service system (especially ideas that would require considerable change to either a technology or process) was the identification and communication of opportunity costs to the organization that were associated with both foregoing or supporting transformational changes.

A danger in the approach we took (as with related qualitative approaches) is that without having a quantitative rationale for the changes, usually related to cost savings or revenue growth, it is difficult to convince the business to take the risk of transformation. We did not measure elements of the work system such as labor-hours or time-on-task or quality of outputs that would benefit from supporting collaboration and interaction as they related to specific activities. The addition of some sort of measurable metric would have been helpful in arguing for our recommendations to the business, particularly as the business was considering trade-offs with other business initiatives.

Broadening the Scope of Service System Analysis

Our practice-based approach allowed us to examine and communicate a significant and important aspect of the IT outsourcing service system while focusing on people as the central element in the system. As we look to the future we realize the value of broadening the scope of our analysis to include the larger service system that encompasses interactions with clients and third party contract negotiators. This broader scope would have deepened our understanding of service system constellations as they relate to the engagement phase of IT outsourcing. We look forward to applying our practice-based approach to understanding value-creating interactions that occur among and across service system entities broadly defined.

References

Agar, M. (1996). *The Professional Stranger (2nd ed.).* San Diego, CA; Academic Press.

Bailey, J., Kieliszewski, C., & Blomberg, J. (2008). Work in organizational context and implications for technology interventions. *Proceeding of Human Factors in Organizational Design and Management* (ODAM 2008). Sao Paulo, Brazil. March 2008.

Beyer, H. & Holtzblatt, K. (1997). *Contextual design: Defining customer centered systems.* San Francisco: Morgan Kaufmann.

Blomberg, J. (2009). Work in the service economy, In W. Karwowski and G. Salvendy (eds.) *Introduction to Service Engineering.* John Wiley.

Blomberg, J., Giacomi, J., Mosher, A., & Swenton-Wall, P. (1993). Ethnographic field methods and their relation to design. In *Participatory Design: Perspectives on Systems Design, D. Schuler and A. Namioka (eds.).* Hillsdale, NJ: Lawrence Erlbaum Associates, pp. 123-154.

Blomberg, J., Burrell, M., & Guest, G. (2003). An ethnographic approach to design. In J. Jacko & A. Sears (Eds.), *Human-computer interaction handbook: Fundamental, evolving technologies and emerging applications.* Lawrence Erlbaum Associates, Inc., New Jersey, pp. 965-984.

Bowers, J., Button, G., & Sharrock, W. (1995). Workflow from within and without: Technology and cooperative work on the print industry shopfloor. *Proceedings of CSCW '95* (pp.51-66), New York: Kluwer.

Carlile, P.R. (2002). A pragmatic view of knowledge and boundaries: Boundary objects in new product development. *Organization Science, 13*(4), 442-455.

Cefkin, M. (2009). *Ethnographers at work: New social science research in and of industry,* Berghahn Books.

Chi, L., & Holsapple, C.W. (2005). Understanding computer-mediated interorganizational collaboration: A model and framework. *Journal of Knowledge Management, 9*(1), 53-75.

Cooper, A. (1999). *The inmates are running the asylum: Why high tech products drive us crazy and how to resotre the sanity.* Indianapolis, IN: Sams-Pearson.

Corral-Verduga, V. (1997). Dual 'realities' of conservation behavior: self reports vs. observations of re-use and recycling behavior. *Journal of Environmental Psychology, 17,* 135-145.

Cummings, T.G. (1976). Sociotechnical systems: An intervention strategy. In W. Warner Burke, *Current Issues and Strategies Organization Development,* pp. 187-213.

Dourish, P. (2001). Process descriptions as organisational accounting devices: The dual use of workflow technologies. In C. Ellis & I. Zigurs (Eds.) *Proceedings of the International ACM SIGGROUP Conference on Supporting Group Work.* (pp. 52-60), Boulder, CO.

eClassifier (2009). Information available at : http://www.almaden.ibm.com/asr/projects/biw/publications/eClassifier-Brochure.pdf

Hendrick, H.W. (1991). Ergonomics in organizational design and management. *Ergonomics, 34*(6), 743-756.

Hendrick, H.W., & Kleiner, B.M. (2001). *Macroergonomics: An Introduction to Work System Design.* Santa Monica, CA: Human Factors and Ergonomics Society.

Hughes, J. A., Rodden, T., & Anderson, H. (1995). The role of ethnography in interactive system design. *ACM Interactions, 2*(2), 56-65.

Kieliszewski, C., Bailey, J., & Blomberg, J. (2007). Early reflections on practice diagrams to facilitate service design. *Emergence 2007* (September 7–9), Pittsburgh, USA.

NVIVO7 [Computer Software]. (2006). Australia: QSR International Pty Ltd.

Pasmore, W.A. & Sherwood, J.J. (1978). *Sociotechnical Systems: A Sourcebook.*

Pruitt, J. & Grudin, J. (2003). Personas: practice and theory. In *Proceedings of the 2003 conference on Designing for User Experiences.* New York, NY: ACM

Rathje, W.L. & Cullen Murphy, C. (1991). *Rubbish! the archaeology of garbage.* New York: HarperCollins.

Rich, M., Lamola, S., Amory, C., & Schneider, L. (2000). Asthma in life context: video intervention/prevention assessment (VIA). *Pediatrics, 105*(3), 469-477.

Shostack, G.L. (1984). How to Design a Service. *European Journal of Marketing, 16*(1), 49-63.

Spohrer, J. & Maglio, P. (forthcoming). Service Science: Toward a smarter planet. In W. Karwowski & G. Salvendy (eds.) *Introduction to Service Engineering.* John Wiley.

Star, S. L., & Griesemer, J. (1989). Institutional ecology, "translations" and boundary objects: Amateurs and professionals in Berkeley's Museum of Vertebrate Zoology 1907-39. *Social Studies of Science 19*(3), 387-420.

Stucky, S., Cefkin, M., Rankin, Y., Shaw, B., & Thomas, J. (2009). Business Value in Service Engagements: Realization is Governed by Interactions, *Hawai'i International Conference on System Sciences (HICSS 09) Conference Proceedings.*

Suchman, L. (1995). *Making work visible.* Communications of the ACM. *38*(9), 56-64.

Vargo, S. L., & Lusch, R. F. (2004). Evolving to a new dominant logic for marketing. *Journal of Marketing,* 68, 1-17.

Vredenburg, K. S., Isensee, et al. (2002). *User-centered design: An integrated approach.* Upper Saddle River, NY: Prentice Hall.

Wall, P., & Mosher, A. (1994). Representations of work: Bringing designers and users together. *In PDC '94: Proceedings of the Participatory Design Conference (Palo Alto, Calif), R. Trigg, S. I. Anderson, and E. Dykstra-Erickson, Eds.* (pp. 87-98). Computer Professionals for Social Responsibility.

Wemmerlöv, U. (1989). A taxonomy for service processes and its implications for system design. *International Journal of Service Industry Management, 1*(3), 20-40.

Whiting, B. & Whiting, J. (1970). Methods for observing and recording behavior. In R. Naroll & R. Cohen (Eds.), *Handbook of method in cultural anthropology* (pp. 282-315). New York, NY: Columbia University Press.

Part 4
Research and Practice: Operations

The Neglect of Service Science in the Operations Management Field

Richard Metters

Goizueta Business School

Emory University

Services have dominated Western economies for over half a century. Worldwide, services are now the largest economic sector, recently replacing agriculture. Services are now a larger portion of the economy than manufacturing for every nation on Earth. Yet, much of the scholarly work in Operations Management (OM) still addresses manufacturing issues. While Western economies are 70%-85% services, less than 10% of OM research done by Western academics is dedicated to services. Here, we examine some causes for this state of affairs: The attitude that "service = servile", the rise of supply chain as an organizing paradigm, and the research methods needed for services.

Introduction

Most introductory sections in Operations Management (OM) academic papers that call for more research into services start with the laundry list of facts regarding the size and scope of services. However, the audience of this work already is aware of the dominance and importance of services in the world economy. The intellectual scandal of OM scholarship is that, unlike other business disciplines, OM research continues to focus on manufacturing despite this fact. This, too, is well known to the readers of this article, but permit me a short paragraph from Metters and Marucheck (2007, 200) to make the point:

> Amoako-Gyampah and Meredith (1989) noted service operations was the subject of only 6% of manuscripts in 10 journals from 1982 to 1987. Pamnirselvam, Ferguson, Ash, and Siferd (1999) stated that service operations was the topic in only 3% of publications in seven OM journals from 1992 to 1997. Of the 23 OM sessions at the Decision Sciences Institute National Meeting in 1984, only one session featured services (Decision Sciences Institute, 1984). Machuca, Gonzalez-Zamora, and Aguilar-Escobar [2007] surveyed 10

P.P. Maglio et al. (eds.), *Handbook of Service Science*, Service Science: Research and Innovations in the Service Economy, DOI 10.1007/978-1-4419-1628-0_14,
© Springer Science+Business Media, LLC 2010

OM journals from 1997 to 2002 and found service operations composed 7.5% of all articles. Prasad and Babbar (2000) reviewed 548 "international operations management" articles in 28 journals published from 1986 to 1997. They note that "few articles on international services appeared in the set of journals reviewed" (p. 229). The main topic of "service" was listed for only 14 of the 548 articles.

This article picks up where Metters and Marucheck left off, assessing why this has occurred and what can be done about it.

The attitude of the OM research community towards manufacturing is like that of post-civil war U.S. Southerners who claimed that "the South will rise again." Despite the clear rise of services worldwide, the OM research community continues to pour vast resources into researching the ever dwindling role of manufacturing. This has consequences. In the words of the venerable Harvard professor, Robert Hayes (2008, 567), "I am concerned that the field of production and operations management is losing direction and cohesion, as well as the battle for the best new faculty, student enrollments, and research funding." (As a side note, Dr. Hayes' most famous book is titled "Restoring our competitive edge: Competing through manufacturing," published in 1984 when manufacturing was about 20% of the U.S. economy and sinking.)

We are certainly losing the battle for students. On the websites of Harvard and Wharton it is reported that less than one percent of their graduates find employment in OM. A course in OM remains in the core, required curriculum of top business schools, but we now find ourselves relegated to second class citizen status in many schools. The OM class is frequently the target of a "flexible" core where students take, say, "3 of 4" of a select group of "core" courses. Oddly, finance and marketing never seem to be part of the flexible core, and the number of finance and marketing elective courses usually dwarf the number of OM electives.

We are losing the "new faculty" battle as well. As reported in Metters and Marucheck, the percentage of OM faculty in business schools peaked between 1993-1998 and has been in decline since then.

Toward a more modern allusion, imagine the hordes of bitter OM scholars, left behind in the strategic visions of their employers, with few students taking their classes, clinging to their job shop scheduling and MRP research as though they were religion and guns.

Business schools are designed to have a dual mission. Like the liberal arts, we are supposed to teach students how to think. Critical thinking skills in business education can be honed around inventory issues just as they can be honed around in a philosophy class. In this realm, the thought processes involved in solving a three-machine scheduling problem can be educational, even though the problem is not actually found in practice. However, we have a second mission: Enhancing society through businesses that run better. Given that mission, we must teach actionable skills that can be used by our students. Overwhelmingly, our students will get jobs in service firms. For those students who work for manufacturers, the vast majority will work in the service functions of those firms. Far more of our students will be running shop floors of accounts receivable departments rather than shop floors full of 100 ton presses.

We explore how it came about that the "home" of OM research remained in manufacturing, and how change can be accomplished.

Reasons For OM Research Neglect Of Services

Many reasons were given for the neglect of services in Metters and Marucheck (2007) that will not be repeated here, such as the managerial view that services do not contain processes (which was never true), the historical lack of scale of service firms (that no longer exists), and the effect of standardization on service performance.

Here, new thoughts are offered on two topics contained in Metters and Marucheck: the problem of defining "services" and the societal view of services as not contributing to economic growth.   Further, the rise of "supply chain management" is also traced, as it provided a research alternative to services for OM faculty.

The Definition of Services – Give it up already!

There is no consensus on a general definition of services.   The government usually defines services by what it is not: Services is not manufacturing or extraction (mining, fishing, agriculture).   The definition of services as "non-manufacturing" is emotionally unsatisfying or even offensive to those who spend their life researching the topic.

For some, this is a never-ending problem that needs to be addressed. At the 2008 INFORMS meeting a 90 minute session was dedicated to the navel-gazing process of defining what "services" mean. Scott Sampson (2008) presented a history of the published work trying to define services, claiming the first definition published in an academic journal was a two page article in the Journal of Marketing by Judd (1964) dedicated to defining services. Sampson noted that many definitions have followed. The various definitions distinguish services from manufacturing   based   on   intangibility,   customization,   simultaneity   of production/consumption, perishability, ownership versus rental, and customer contact involved, just to name a few. Academic articles providing definitions of services continue to this day.

None of the definitions are satisfactory. As a broad stroke, the definitions tend to include clear manufacturing tasks with services (e.g., customization, customer contact), or exclude many clear services from the definition (e.g., intangibility).

Service researchers have wandered through the definition desert for 44 years now. It took less time for Moses to find the promised land. It is time to take a stand: Give up. Move on. We don't need a definitive definition. The time for navel-gazing is over, and the time for action is at hand. To misquote the famous jurist on certain illicit services, I propose that the operating definition of services is: "I know it when I see it." By simply aiming our research can(n)ons at the actual problems facing businesses, we will be practicing service science 90% of the time.

Attitude: Manufacturing is important. Services is just being servile

I am the lead author of a service operations textbook (Metters, King-Metters, Pullman and Walton, 2006). The first chapter presents the historical view that the backbone of economic progress depends on manufacturing (e.g., Cohen and Zysman, 1987). Reading this causes my students - taking a course titled "service operations" — to think that there must be some primordial basis for commerce, something behind it all. They often come to the erroneous conclusion that the "something" is manufacturing.

It seems to be inbred in humans that labor creating a thing is work but labor creating a service is, well, something else. Historically, attitudes towards services have followed this path. According to Spohrer (2006), Adam Smith defined service work as "unproductive labor" and manufacturing work as "productive labor" in his 1776 book, An Inquiry into the Nature and Causes of the Wealth of Nations.

In more modern times, services have also been viewed differently than manufacturing. The U.S.S.R. ruler Stalin was fixated on manufacturing, overemphasizing it compared to services because he believed that manufacturing brought more "prestige" to his nation (Sabillon, 2000, 213). Similarly, Mao Zedong's "Great Leap Forward" policy in China in the late 1950s focused on increasing manufacturing (Yang, 1996) and led to the Great Leap famine that killed between 16 and 40 million Chinese. While the Great Leap Forward ended in 1961, the fixation on manufacturing continued through the 1970's, greatly holding back China's economy. As an example, the country of China had only 137 hotels in 1978 – all government owned (Zhang, Pine and Lam, 2005, 97).

Western Europe was not immune to this disease, with Kaldor (1966, 1967) advising post-World War II European governments that manufacturing was the key to economic growth.

The U.S. has also displayed this attitude. In the early 1900s F.W. Woolworth, creator of the Woolworth's retail chain, was one of the wealthiest people in America. However, because he was a mere "shopkeeper" he was not included on the "A" list social scene (Plunkett-Powell, 2001, 80). Even the U.S. Supreme Court has opined that services are not "commerce." In the 1922 decision that allowed baseball to be exempt from anti-trust law, Oliver Wendell Holmes wrote for the majority that "personal effort not related to production is not a subject of commerce" (Supreme Court, 1922). The opinion continues by giving examples of other services, such as lecturers or legal services, that even though the service providers cross state lines, it is not interstate commerce.

Unfortunately, this attitude pervades even today among OM researchers. An editor of the journal M&SOM claimed at a conference presentation that services were defined as "doing something for someone that they could do for themselves." This definition implies "services = servile" rather than involving expertise.

A key to moving forward is changing the collective mindset. We must not be shy in recognizing the role of services. Certainly, economic events in 2008 should bring to our attention the primacy of services. The U.S. government sets aside $800,000,000,000 to rescue commercial banks and insurance companies because they are central to the economy, while providing far less funds for ailing automobile manufacturers. The minds of our students have changed – the jobs most coveted are not with Fortune 500 manufacturers, but with service firms in consulting and investment/commercial banking. McKinsey & Co. has an "operational consulting" practice staffed by a few hundred consultants. Despite the popularity of these careers, I could find only one elective at one school offered on these topics: Mike Pinedo's "operations of financial services firms" at NYU.

Renaming Old Paradigms – The Rise of Supply Chain Management

From my perspective, the OM field looked poised to make a surge into services in the mid-1990's. The "Services Mini-conference" of the Decision Sciences Institute was attracting triple digits of attendees. The "service operations" research tracks at conferences were expanding.

Then, "supply chain" struck.

To my knowledge, the first textbook with the term "supply chain" in the title was a 180 page book by Handfield and Nichols (1999). Now, there are over a dozen such textbooks available, and an elective class with the words "supply chain" in the title is the most common OM elective among the top 20 schools (my investigation counted 26 such classes). The supply chain track at the Production and Operations Management Society conferences is now the largest by volume of presentations. A supply chain track did not exist a little over a decade ago. Searching the ABI/INFORM database for the journals Management Science, Operations Research, Journal of Operations Management, Production and Operations Management, and IIE Transactions, the first article with the words "supply chain" in the title appeared in 1993. Two more appeared in 1997 – both "bullwhip effect" papers. The Department of Supply Chain Management was inaugurated in

Management Science in 1997. There were only three such articles in 1998. Between 2003-2008 there were 167.

Supply chain has been an organizing principle for the field. The academic journal International Journal of Purchasing and Materials Management renamed itself the Journal of Supply Chain Management in 1999. The professional society National Association for Purchasing Management, around since 1915, changed its name to the Institute of Supply Management in 2001.

The promise of studying supply "chains" rather than individual firms is the study of how organizations act at the boundaries. The relationships between firms, rather than within a firm, is the focus of study. The concept of supply chain management has reinvigorated the OM field, spawning hundreds of research articles on the bullwhip effect, revenue sharing and other supply chain contracting methods, and strategic sourcing.

However, the rise of supply chain as a concept has had a dark side. It has allowed those who do not wish to move forward to stay where they are, and it has pushed service operations to the side. Research on a small tweak to inventory theory is now titled "How a Small Tweak to Inventory Theory Changes Supply Chain Management." Likewise, course offerings that were titled "production planning and control" or "inventory management" were simply renamed "supply chain management." The "supply chain" textbooks have many of the same inventory, logistics, and scheduling work that the old production planning texts had – plus a chapter on the bullwhip effect.

Expectations of Service Research

Journal editors can act as the gatekeepers of academic publications, either by immediately rejecting academic manuscripts before they are sent on to peer review, or by setting a tone at the journal they edit. Consequently, their personal opinions can be important. At a conference session dedicated to the publication of services articles, an editor of M&SOM declared that services were "too familiar" to reviewers, since we all tend to be more intimate customers and observers of services than manufacturers. As a consequence, according to this journal editor, unrealistic assumptions made on articles involving services are questioned more thoroughly than unrealistic assumptions made on articles involving manufacturing issues.

While it is always best to have realistic assumptions, often some abstraction from reality is excused in research articles if insight is provided despite the lack of reality. For example, over a thousand inventory research articles have been published assuming a linear cost in lost sales or backorders. In layman's terms, the "linear" assumption means that if your grocery store does not have your favorite item one time, you simply buy it at another store. If that item is missing 10 times, you buy it at another store 10 times – a linear relationship. The "linear" assumption means that you never think of switching stores, that a store that is always out of stock on your favorite item loses more than just the profit margin of that item after awhile. Although we all know this assumption is not correct, and there has been research that has empirically measured the nonlinearity of lost sales cost, it is permitted to continue as an assumption in the inventory literature. Further, it is allowable to assume 100% backorders or 100% lost sales. However, we know that partial lost sales/backordering actually occurs in practice. These are allowable abstractions because they make the analysis tractable and we realize that, although the specific policy mentioned in the research might not be what is truly optimal in practice, something very similar probably is. The list of "allowable abstractions" in manufacturing research is quite long, including deterministic or unvarying demand over time; single machine job shops (I've never visited a job shop with only one machine); flexible manufacturing systems that never break down, produce a defect, or need maintenance; labor that never takes a break, is absent or on vacation, etc.

This courtesy is often absent in services research. Regardless of how services are defined, many services require customer contact, which causes human behavior to be an input. Assumptions regarding human behavior that are made in a manuscript for the sake of making analysis tractable often lead to manuscript rejection. Survey work that asks a question in a way we find objectionable, or has difficulty explaining non-response bias is simply rejected. Due to the nature of survey work, it is impossible to change something and simply run it again, like many academic analytic or simulation models on manufacturing issues. Rather than stating the imperfections of the work and allowing publication, the work is merely rejected. Since academics need a certain volume of publications to retain their jobs (i.e., get tenure) and get pay raises or bonuses (e.g., "summer support" based on research productivity), the clear implication is to steer away from this risky work on services and, instead, grind out another tweak on the non-existent single-machine job shop problem.

What To Do

For the OM field to thrive, we must teach and research topics that have meaning to society and our students. We must be on the left side of the decimal point. Topics such as health care, revenue management, and professional services do not see the coverage in our classrooms that is remotely close to their impact on society. Since our students are going to be employed in the service sector, methods for managing service firms should be taught.

The research-teaching connection is an important one. Our field can be schizophrenic in regard to the research-teaching interface – with some of us never bringing our research into the classroom. It is difficult to research manufacturing then step into the classroom and teach services. If we begin to research service topics, it will lead to more service courses, more student enrollments, and a reinvigorated field.

The problem is, getting there may be difficult.

Accord Services the Respect Deserved

There was some scoffing when the journal Manufacturing & Service Operations Management was named. Certainly, the name is a bit unwieldy. However, the point was made explicit that "services" was part of the journal. The word "services" used to be in the name of a department of Management Science. It no longer is. Now, a services manuscript is sent to the department of "Operations and Supply Chain Management."

There is still a latent assumption on the part of our deans, colleagues in other departments, and students that operations = manufacturing. We must be explicit on the contribution that operations scholars can make to managing services.

Tool-up

My own doctoral training in research methodologies consisted of linear programming, Markov chains, dynamic programming, and simulation. This training is perfectly adequate for research into many manufacturing issues, and I have made a career in service operations with that background, but it falls short for truly addressing the pressing issues in services. Many of the most interesting services problems must be addressed by surveys, case studies, interviews, and attendant methods such as principal components analysis, structural equation modeling, and content analysis, among others. Our field must change its tool set.

Get Out of the Office

A standard formula for producing research in manufacturing is to reduce the problem to mathematical symbols, then manipulate the symbols to get a result. Often this could be done in one's office with no knowledge of the actual business situation. Representative of this is the empirical work on Flexible Manufacturing Systems by (Vineyard, Amoako-Gyampah and Meredith, 1999). They were the first authors to empirically determine the actual downtime of such systems. The dozens of papers on such systems prior to that merely assumed some functional form of downtime without empirical justification.

While manufacturing issues such as those are aided by empirical data, much of service research is completely dependent on getting real data. Since human interaction is at the core of what happens in services, it has to be observed and measured.

Give Services Manuscripts an Even Playing Field

As referees of academic papers the temptation is to search for reasons to reject. Journals brag about their low acceptance rates, so it encouraged from editors. Further, a revised article keeps coming back to us, increasing our workload, while rejected articles just go away.

As noted previously, services manuscripts are often held to a higher standard than manufacturing work. This has the indirect effect of driving scholars away from the field. Rather than looking for the one "fatal flaw" by which a manuscript can be discarded, I encourage service researchers to find the insight in a manuscript that is not perfect. Since many service manuscripts contain empirical data that cannot be reworked, the "fatal flaw" concept makes the labor involved in researching services too risky for the reward. Authors must still be held accountable for flaws, but the flaws can be acknowledged, rather than rejecting work because of them.

Embrace Service Science

The Operations field has a window of opportunity. Rather than hunker-down in the trenches of our own self-defined narrow set of topics, we can break out. The concept of "Service Science" allows us to invigorate and enlarge our domain by working on new problems with new colleagues. Services Science has been announced to practitioners (Chesbrough, 2005), and to the varied academic communities of information systems (Chesbrough and Spohrer, 2006; Maglio, Kreulen, Srinivasna and Spohrer, 2006), operations (Spohrer, 2006), marketing (Bitner and Brown, 2006), and engineering (Tien and Berg, 2003). "Interdisciplinary research" has been likened by many to the mythical Yeti, as they are both often talked about but rarely seen. By design, Service Science can force us from our foxholes to interact with those of other disciplines to attack real problems.

References

Amoako-Gyampah, K., & Meredith, J. R. (1989). The operations management research agenda: An update. *Journal of Operations Management, 8*(3), 250–262.

Bailey, M., Farrell, D., & Remes, J. (2006). The hidden key to growth. *International Economy, 20*(1), 48–55.

Bitner, M. & Brown S. (2006). The evolution and discovery of services science. *Communications of the ACM, 49*(7), 73-78.

Chesbrough, H. (2005). Toward a science of services. *Harvard Business Review, 83*, 16-17.

Chesbrough, H., & Spohrer, J. (2006). A research manifesto for services science. *Communications of the ACM, 49*(7), 35–40.

Cohen, S., & Zysman, J. (1987). *Manufacturing matters: The myth of the postindustrial economy.* New York: Basic Books.

Dasgupta, A., & Singh, D. (2006). *Manufacturing, services, and premature deindustrialization in developing countries: A Kaldorian analysis.* United Nations University, WIDER, research paper 2006/49.

Decision Sciences Institute. (1984). *Decision Sciences Institute National Meeting Proceedings.* Atlanta, GA: Decision Sciences Institute.

Handfield, R., & Nichols, Jr, E. (1999). *Introduction to Supply Chain Management.* Upper Saddle River, NJ: Prentice Hall.

Hayes, R. (2008). Operations Management's Next Source of Galvanizing Energy? *Production and Operations Management, 17*(6), 567-572.

Judd, R. (1964). The Case for Redefining Services. *Journal of Marketing, 28*(1), 58-59.

Kaldor, N. (1966). *Causes of the slow rate of economic growth of the United Kingdom.* Cambridge, UK: Cambridge University Press.

Kaldor, N. (1967). *Strategic factors in economic development.* Ithaca, NY: Cornell University.

Machuca, J. A. D., Gonzalez-Zamora, M., & Aguilar-Escobar, V. G. (2007). Service operations management research. *Journal of Operations Management, 25*(3), 585-603.

Maglio, P. P., Kreulen, J., Srinivasan, S., & Spohrer, J. (2006). Service systems, service scientists, SSME, and innovation. *Communications of the ACM.* 49(7), 81–85.

Metters, R., King-Metters, K., Pullman, M., & Walton, S. (2006). *Successful Service Operations Management,* 2nd ed. Cincinnati, OH: Cengage Publishing.

Metters, R., & Marucheck, A. (2007). Service Management - Academic Issues and Scholarly Reflections from Operations Management Researchers, *Decision Sciences*, 38(2), 195-214.

Pamnirselvam, G. P., Ferguson, L. A., Ash, R. C., & Siferd, S. P. (1999). Operations management research: An update for the 1990s. *Journal of Operations Management,* 18(1), 95–112.

Plunkett-Powell, K. (2001). *Remembering Woolworth's: A Nostalgic History of the World's Most Famous Five-And-Dime.* NY: Macmillan.

Prasad, S., & Babbar, S. (2000). International operations management research. *Journal of Operations Management,* 18(3), 208–247.

Sabillon, C. (2000) *Manufacturing, Technology, and Economic Growth.* London: M.E. Sharpe.

Sampson, S. (2008) The Core Principle of Services: 1964-2008. Presentation at INFORMS National Meeting.

Smith, A. (1776). *An Inquiry into the Nature and Causes of the Wealth of Nations.* London: W. Strahan and T. Cadell.

Spohrer, J. (2006). Services science. *Presentation at the 2006 meeting, Production and Operations Management Society Services College.*

Spohrer, J, Maglio, P.P., Bailey, J., & Gruhl, D. (2007). Toward a Science of Service Systems. *Computer,* 40(1), 71-77.

Supreme Court. (1922). supreme.justia.com/us/259/200/case.html accessed November 11, 2008.

Vineyard, M., Amoako-Gyampah, K., & Meredith, J. (1999).   Failure rate distributions for flexible manufacturing systems: An empirical study. *European Journal of Operational Research*, 116(1), 139-155.

Yang, D. (1996). *Calamity and Reform in China: State, Rural Society and Institutional Change Since the Great Leap Famine*. Stanford, CA: Stanford U. Press.

Zhang, H., Pine, R., & Lam, T. (2005) *Tourism And Hotel Development In China: From Political To Economic Success*. Binghampton, NY: Hayworth Press.

Death Spirals and Virtuous Cycles

Human Resource Dynamics in Knowledge-Based Services

Rogelio Oliva

Mays Business School
Texas A&M University

John D. Sterman

Sloan School of Management
Massachusetts Institute of Technology

While the productivity and quality of manufactured products steadily improve, service sector productivity lags and quality has fallen. Many service organizations fall into "death spirals" in which pressure to boost throughput and control costs leads to worker burnout and corner cutting, lowering service quality, raising costs while revenue falls, forcing still greater cuts in capacity and even lower quality. We present a formal model to explore the dynamics of service delivery and quality, focusing on the service quality death spiral and how it can be overcome. We use the system dynamics modeling method as it is well suited to dynamic environments in which human behavior interacts with the physics of an operation, and in which there are multiple feedbacks connecting servers, managers, customers, and other actors. Through simulations we demonstrate that major recurring problems in the service industry—erosion of service quality, high turnover, and low profitability—can be explained by the organization's internal responses to work pressure. Although the reinforcing feedbacks can operate as virtuous as well as vicious cycles, the system is biased toward quality erosion by basic asymmetries and nonlinearities. We show how, with the right mix of policies, these same feedbacks can become virtuous cycles that lead to higher employee, customer satisfaction and additional resources to invest in still greater service quality improvement.

P.P. Maglio et al. (eds.), *Handbook of Service Science*, Service Science: Research and Innovations in the Service Economy, DOI 10.1007/978-1-4419-1628-0_15,
© Springer Science+Business Media, LLC 2010

Introduction

Increasing class size and teacher burnout, shorter hospital stays and longer waits for emergency care, long waits on hold and unsatisfying conversations with customer service agents—these are all symptoms of poor quality in knowledge-based services. Despite the growing importance of services and service quality as sources of competitive advantage, the quality of service delivery in the United States is not improving and in many cases is falling. Complaints about poor service are staples in the popular press and online (see, for example, Aho, 2008; McGregor et al., 2009). While the quality of most manufactured products has improved over the past few decades, the American Customer Service Index fell to 72.5 in 2008, down 4% from its 1995 level (see http://www.theacsi.org). What explains the divergence? Why has quality improved so much for products but fallen on average for services? Here we develop an integrated dynamic model to explore the sources of persistent low service quality.

Services differ from manufacturing because they cannot be inventoried, so balancing capacity and demand is more difficult than in manufacturing. More important, services differ from manufacturing because they are produced in the context of a personal interaction between the customer and the server. Services are often produced in front of customers and often in direct collaboration with them, thus bringing employees and customers physically and psychologically close. The quality of a service interaction is necessarily a subjective judgment made by the individual customer. Feelings and emotions matter. Because customers have different backgrounds, knowledge, needs, and expectations, services are harder to standardize than manufacturing. Perceptions of procedural fairness and respect are important. Customers do not evaluate service quality solely in terms of the outcome of the interaction (e.g., did the doctor correctly diagnose my illness?) but also consider the process of service delivery (e.g., did the doctor take the time to hear me out, listen with empathy and treat me with respect—or rush through the appointment as quickly as possible to get to the next patient?).

Customers' perceptions of the service experience are not only affected by the conditions under which the service is delivered, but also by employee attitudes towards the customer. Similarly, employees' attitudes towards and perceptions of their job are influenced by customers' attitudes and behavior. The co-evolution of perceptions and expectations is further confounded by the fact that services are intangible, thus making it difficult to assess customer requirements and to fix an objective service standard.

The study of services therefore requires an interdisciplinary approach that integrates the physical and technological characteristics of service delivery with the organizational and behavioral features of the social systems in which service delivery is embedded. Such interdisciplinary studies are coming to be known as "services sciences" (Chesbrough, 2005; Chesbrough and Spohrer, 2006; Horn, 2005; Maglio et al., 2006). Here we use the system dynamics modeling method (Sterman 2000) because it is well suited to dynamic environments in which human behavior interacts with the physics of an operation, and in which there are multiple feedbacks connecting servers, managers, customers, and other actors.

We seek to understand the persistence of capacity problems in services and the persistent failure of service quality to improve over the past few decades. The tools of process improvement and the quality movement have been applied to service delivery just as they have to manufacturing, yet the quality gap continues to widen. Why? Since services are produced and consumed simultaneously, with no finished goods inventory, service providers are particularly vulnerable to imbalances between supply and demand. The problem of balancing supply and demand in services, however, is not simply a matter of absorbing short-term variations in customer orders. Rather, chronic undercapacity persists for two reasons. First, organizations facing growing service demands struggle to acquire capacity fast enough. Over the last fifty years, the service sector has consistently been the fastest growing in the economy. Second, service-sector productivity improves slowly compared to manufacturing (Baumol et al., 1991). Technological progress has dramatically increased output per person in manufacturing, but one taxi driver is still needed per taxi. Low productivity growth drives service organizations to seek efficiency gains and impose cost containment initiatives. The continuous pressure to "do more with less" pushes service organizations to operate with little margin to accommodate demand variability. We show that such policies not only lead to poor quality when demand temporarily rises, but can trigger a set of self-reinforcing processes that lead to the persistent, continual erosion of service quality, service capacity, and the customer base. These positive feedbacks operate as vicious cycles that can drag an organization into a death spiral of declining quality, customer loss, budget cuts, higher work pressure, poor morale, higher employee attrition, and still lower quality. Poor service can destroy a firm's brand and erode sales. In contrast, high quality service boosts customer loyalty, repeat business and favorable word of mouth that can increase growth and market share.

Here we present a formal model to explore the dynamics of service delivery and quality, focusing on the service quality death spiral and how it can be overcome. The work builds on foundations presented elsewhere (e.g., Oliva, 2001; Oliva and Bean, 2008; Oliva and Sterman, 2001; Sterman, 2000, Chapters 12 and 14), but adds additional structure we have identified over the last ten years working with organizations that provide knowledge-based services. We present the model iteratively, beginning with the dynamics of human capital. We then add additional structures, including the interactions of employees and customers, the workweek, standards for customer service, hiring and training, customer responses to service quality, and budgeting. We explore how the dynamics change as the model boundary expands. A documented version of the model is available for experimentation under different assumptions.[1]

The paper is structured as follows. We first present a structure that captures the dynamics of the experience learning curve. We then introduce notion of work pressure, the gap between required and available service capacity, and explore the service providers respond to imbalances. We next expand the model to include the

---

[1] http://iops.tamu.edu/faculty/roliva/research/service/handbook/.

feedback effects of performance on the market and we then add budgeting and financial constraints on hiring. We close with policy recommendations.

Service capacity

We begin with the service organization's human capital, including hiring, training, and learning-by-doing. Learning-by-doing is well documented in diverse settings, including services (Argote and Epple, 1990; Darr et al., 1995). The importance of customization suggests potential for significant learning in high-contact service settings. When services involve personal and customized interaction between individual servers and customers, much of the learning gained through experience is embodied in the skills and behaviors of the individual workers.

Experience chains and learning curve

We model the individual learning curve of new employees as an "experience chain" (Jarmain, 1963). The workforce is divided into two populations: experienced and recently hired "rookie" employees (Figure 1). New hires are less productive than experienced employees, but gradually gain skills through experience, on-the-job coaching and mentoring. The effective workforce, measured in fully trained equivalent employees, is given by

Effective Workforce = Experienced Employees + Rookie Productivity Fraction *
Rookie Employees.   (1)

The stocks of rookie and experienced employees accumulate their respective flows of hiring, assimilation, and quits.[2] The model is initialized in equilibrium to facilitate testing.

Rookie Employees =
INTEGRAL(Rookie Hire Rate – Rookie Quit Rate – Assimilation Rate,
Initial Workforce * Rookie Fraction$_{ss}$)   (2)

---

[2] We present the model with a minimum of mathematical notation, using "friendly algebra" in which the variables are named for the concepts they represent and correspond exactly to the simulation model. The INTEGRAL function denotes an accumulation, specifically:

Stock = INTEGRAL(Inflow –Outflow, Initial Stock)

is equivalent to

$$Stock_T = \int_{t_0}^{T} (Inflow - Outflow)dt + Stock_{t_0}$$

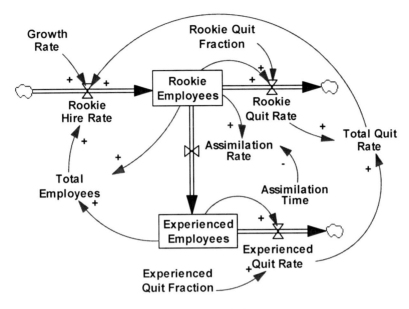

Figure 1. Experience chain structure

Experienced Employees = INTEGRAL(Assimilation Rate – Experienced Quit Rate,
        Initial Workforce * (1 – Rookie Fraction$_{ss}$))   (3)

where Rookie Fraction$_{ss}$ is the equilibrium fraction of rookies (eq. 13). Formulating the flows as first-order processes yields

Rookie Quit Rate = Rookie Employees * Rookie Quit Fraction   (4)

Experienced Quit Rate = Experienced Employees * Experienced Quit Fraction   (5)

Assimilation Rate = Rookie Employees / Assimilation Time.   (6)

Average worker productivity is:

Average Productivity = Effective Workforce / Total Employees.   (7)

Two parameters determine the speed and strength of the learning curve: the rookie productivity fraction—the productivity of rookies relative to fully trained employees—and the assimilation time—how long it takes rookies to become fully experienced. Figure 2 shows two simulations of the learning process. The solid line represents a setting where the service tasks are not difficult to master (e.g., a fast food restaurant). New hires have an initial productivity equal to 80% of a fully trained employee and an assimilation time of three months. The hashed line represents a more complex setting (e.g., financial services) where rookie productivity is only 20% of experienced employees and it takes an average of one year to become fully productive.

Finally, the total quit rate is the sum of quits from each employee cohort, total employees sums the stock of employees in each experience-level cohort, and the rookie fraction is the ratio of rookies to total employees:

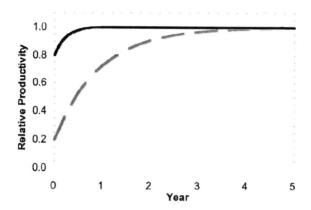

Figure 2. Examples of learning curves

Total Quit Rate = Rookie Quit Rate + Experienced Quit Rate   (8)

Total Employees = Rookie Employees + Experienced Employees   (9)

Rookie Fraction = Rookie Employees / Total Employees.   (10)

For purposes of testing, assume for now that the workforce grows at a constant exponential rate. That is, the firm replaces all those who quit and adds a fraction of the current total workforce:

Rookie Hire Rate = Total Quit Rate + Growth Rate * Total Employees.   (11)

Below we replace this simple hiring formulation with an endogenous hiring rule that accounts for the adequacy of service capacity.

Despite its simplicity, the structure above illustrates fundamental dynamics of human resources. Figure 3 shows the effect of higher employee turnover on productivity. We assume a rookie productivity fraction of 30% and an assimilation time of 1 year. The simulation begins in equilibrium with headcount growth of 20%/year.

Figure 3a assumes an annual turnover rate of 20% while 3b assumes 80% annual turnover. In both cases the firm grows to 270 employees after five years. However, the employee mix in the two scenarios is quite different — the rookie fraction increases from 29% in the base case to 50% with high turnover. Growth causes significant experience dilution. Oliva et al. (2002) show how this structure caused service quality problems for a rapidly growing airline.

To understand the effects of the parameters on productivity, consider the rookie fraction when the system reaches steady state, i.e., when, the ratio of rookies to

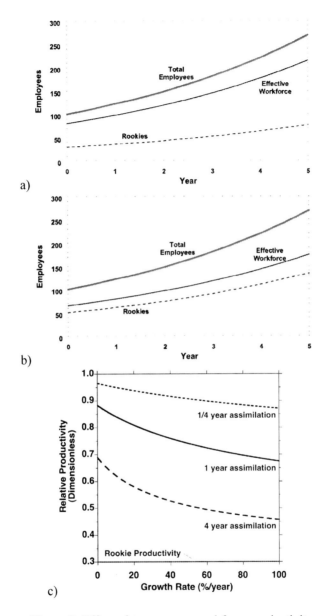

Figure 3. Effect of turnover on workforce productivity

experienced workers becomes constant (total labor might still be growing). Average productivity can be expressed as:

Average Productivity =
    (1 – Rookie Fraction) + Rookie Productivity Fraction * Rookie Fraction.   (12)

The steady state rookie fraction is easily shown to be:

Rookie Fraction$_{ss}$ = Assimilation time*(Experienced Quit Fraction + Growth Rate)/
    (1 + Assimilation Time * (Experienced Quit Fraction + Growth Rate)).   (13)

Figure 3c shows steady-state average productivity as a function of headcount growth for three different assimilation times, assuming rookie productivity is 30% and turnover is 20%/year. Slower assimilation or faster growth increases the steady-state rookie fraction, reducing average productivity. Without growth, average productivity is 97%, 88% and 69% of the fully experienced level with assimilation times of one-quarter, one, and four years, respectively, but drops to 91%, 62%, and 51% when headcount grows at 50%/year.

Mentoring

Rookies typically learn with the help and mentoring of experienced employees. On-the-job training, however, is not free. Mentoring reduces the time experienced personnel can allocate to their own work as they supervise rookies, demonstrate proper procedure and answer their questions. The effective workforce is thus determined by the effective number of experienced employees, which is the number of experienced workers net of the time they devote to mentoring:

Effective Workforce = Effective Experienced Employees +
    Rookie Productivity Fraction * Rookie Employees   (14)

Effective Experienced Employees = MAX (0, Experienced Employees –
    Rookies * Fraction of Experienced Time Required for Training).   (15)

Effective experienced employees are constrained to be nonnegative to control for the extreme case where the on-the-job training impact of rookies exceeds the available time of experienced personnel.[3]

Mentoring does not affect the steady state rookie fraction (eq. 13), as the flow of people through the experience chain remains the same. Mentoring, however, does lower average productivity:

Average Productivity = ((1 – Rookie Fraction) + (Rookie Productivity Fraction –
    Fraction of Experienced Time Required for Training) * Rookie Fraction).   (16)

The effect of mentoring on average productivity is proportional to the number of rookies that need to be trained. Thus, it can have a dramatic impact in situations where the rookie fraction is high, when the organization is growing rapidly. Figure 4 shows a simulation with the same parameters used in Figure 3b, but now assum-

---

3 A more robust formulation would gradually reduce the mentoring rookies receive as the workload of experienced employees grows, lengthening the assimilation time for rookies.

ing each rookie requires mentoring by the equivalent of 0.4 experienced people. Average steady state productivity drops from 0.65 to 0.45 FTEs per employee.[4]

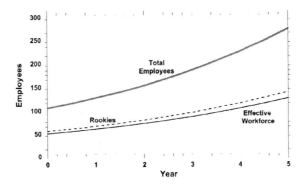

Figure 4. Effect of mentoring on workforce productivity

Task processing and work pressure

In this section we present the structure for the arrival, accumulation and processing of customer orders and link it to the service capacity sector.

Tasks accumulate in a backlog until they are processed and delivered to the customer (Figure 5). The service backlog could be pending loan applications, tasks in a consulting project, the inbox of any administrative process, a physical queue of customers awaiting service at a bank or doctor's office, or the number of customers on hold at a call center. For now we assume an exogenous arrival rate.

Service Backlog =
INTEGRAL(Task Arrival Rate – Task Completion Rate, Service Backlog$_{t0}$).(17)

Following Little's law, the average delivery delay (service time) is the ratio of the backlog to the completion rate:

Delivery Delay = Service Backlog / Task Completion Rate.   (18)

The completion rate is the lesser of (i) the potential completion rate based on the effective workforce (eq. 14) or (ii) the maximum completion rate, based on the number of tasks in the backlog and the minimum time needed to process each task.

Task Completion Rate =
MIN(Maximum Completion Rate, Potential Completion Rate)   (19)

Maximum Completion Rate = Service Backlog / Minimum Delivery Delay   (20)

---

[4] An interactive version of this structure is available for experimentation at
http://forio.com/resources/learning-curve-for-service-organizations/.

Potential Completion Rate =
        Service Capacity * Standard Workweek / Standard Time per Task   (21)

Service Capacity = Effective Workforce.   (22)

The desired completion rate depends on the backlog and the organization's delivery time goal:

Desired Completion Rate = Service Backlog / Target Delivery Delay.   (23)

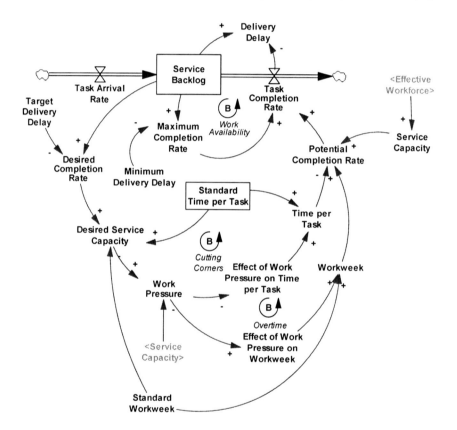

Figure 5. Feedbacks from Employee's responses to work pressure

The organization must adjust service capacity (measured in person-hours of work effort available per week) to complete tasks at the desired rate. We define work pressure as the ratio of desired to actual service capacity. Desired capacity depends on the desired completion rate, the standard workweek and the standard time required to complete each task:

Work Pressure = Desired Service Capacity / Service Capacity   (24)

$$\text{Desired Service Capacity = Desired Completion Rate * Standard Time per Task /}$$
$$\text{Standard Workweek.} \tag{25}$$

Work pressure greater than one indicates the service center is under stress as there are more tasks in the backlog than the center can process within the target delivery delay, given the number and productivity of employees, the standard workweek and the current standard for the time that should be allocated to each task. Work pressure less than one indicates excess capacity.

High work pressure should signal management to increase service capacity. However, service capacity responds with long lags: management must recognize the increase in work pressure, decide it is large and persistent enough to justify capacity expansion, authorize the new positions, then recruit, select, hire and train the new employees—and acquire the complementary capital stocks they need to become effective (office space, IT infrastructure, etc.). Until this occurs, employees are forced to handle high work pressure by either working harder (longer hours, fewer breaks) or by cutting corners (spending less time with each customer than needed to provide high quality service).

Employee responses to work pressure: working overtime and cutting corners

While management responds slowly to changes in work pressure, employees usually respond quickly: a bank teller sees the line of customers; a call-center representative knows when people are on hold; engineers know when their designs are late—and all know they must quickly boost throughput.

The first option for service providers facing high work pressure is to increase work intensity, that is, to work harder through overtime and by cutting the number and length of breaks. Thus, workweek is an increasing function of work pressure:

$$\text{Workweek = Standard Workweek * Effect of Work Pressure on Workweek} \tag{26}$$

$$\text{Effect of Work Pressure on Workweek} = f(\text{Work Pressure}). \tag{27}$$

Service providers can also respond to high work pressure by reducing the time per task. Speeding up might be as simple as reducing the time spent in pleasantries with the customer, but often involves "cutting corners", for example, failing to provide informative responses to customer queries, offer ancillary services, collect relevant information from the customer, check for errors, document the work or complete required reports. Time per task falls as work pressure increases:

$$\text{Time per Task =}$$
$$\text{Standard Time per Task * Effect of Work Pressure on Time per Task} \tag{28}$$

$$\text{Effect of Work Pressure on Time per Task} = f(\text{Work Pressure}). \tag{29}$$

The potential completion rate, eq. 21, now depends on service capacity modified by work intensity and actual time per task:

$$\text{Potential Completion Rate = Service Capacity * Workweek / Time per Task.} \tag{21'}$$

These responses create balancing feedbacks through which servers attempt to keep work pressure within certain limits. High work pressure boosts task completion through greater work intensity, reducing the backlog and work pressure (the Overtime loop in Figure 5). Similarly, high work pressure leads servers to cut corners, reducing time per task and speeding task completion, thus reducing the service backlog and work pressure (the Cutting Corners loop in Figure 5).

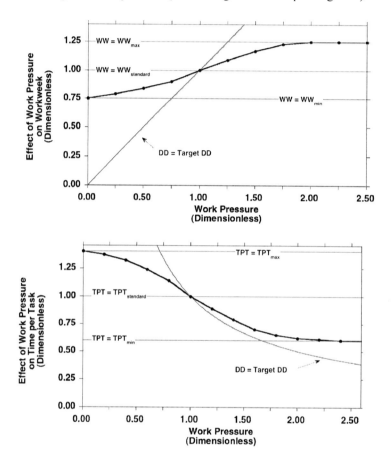

Figure 6. Employee's responses to work pressure

Figure 6 shows the effect of work pressure on workweek and time per task estimated from a detailed field study of a retail lending operation in a UK bank (see Dogan, 2007; Oliva, 2001; Sterman, 2000, §14.3, for details on the estimation process). In that bank, management required all tasks to be processed within one day. Employees used both overtime and corner cutting to meet this goal. Interestingly, the data show employees were twice as willing to cut corners as to work overtime. Note that both workweek and time per task saturate at extreme levels of work pressure: work hours cannot be increased beyond some level, and time per task cannot be cut below some minimum level, even when work pressure is very high; similarly, the workweek does not fall to zero and time per task reaches some maximum even when work pressure is very low.

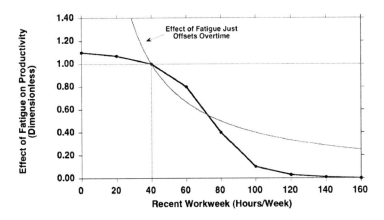

Figure 7. Effect of fatigue on productivity

Side effects of overtime: fatigue and burnout

While higher work intensity boosts output in the short run, extended overtime causes fatigue that eventually undermines the benefit of longer hours (Homer, 1985; Thomas, 1993):

$$\text{Service Capacity} = \text{Effective Workforce} * \text{Effect of Fatigue on Productivity.} \quad (22')$$

The effect of fatigue on productivity is a decreasing function that reduces service capacity when the recent workweek is greater than 40 hours/week, but increases only marginally above its normal operating point when the workweek falls below normal (Figure 7). Fatigue builds up and dissipates over time; we model fatigue as an exponentially weighted moving average of past work intensity. The longer the fatigue onset time the longer it takes for burnout to set in and for employees to recover when work intensity falls.

$$\text{Effect of Fatigue on Productivity} = f(\text{Recent Workweek}) \quad (30)$$

$$\text{Recent Workweek} = \text{SMOOTH}(\text{Workweek, Fatigue Onset Time}) \quad (31)$$

where Output = SMOOTH(Input, Averaging Time) denotes first-order exponential smoothing of the input with a mean delay of the Averaging Time (see Sterman 2000, ch. 11 for details).

Extended periods of high work intensity also increase employee turnover. The effect of fatigue on turnover is an increasing function of burnout, and affects both types of employees:

Rookie Quit Rate = Rookie Employees * Rookie Quit Fraction *
    Effect of Fatigue on Turnover   (4')

Experienced Quit Rate = Experienced Employees * Experienced Quit Fraction *
    Effect of Fatigue on Turnover   (5')

Effect of Fatigue on Turnover = f(Long Term Workweek).   (32)

Like the effect of fatigue on productivity, extended overtime increases attrition with a delay, but with a longer time constant: long workweeks quickly reduce productivity, but people will tolerate high overtime much longer before quitting.

Long Term Workweek = SMOOTH(Workweek, Burnout Onset Time).   (33)

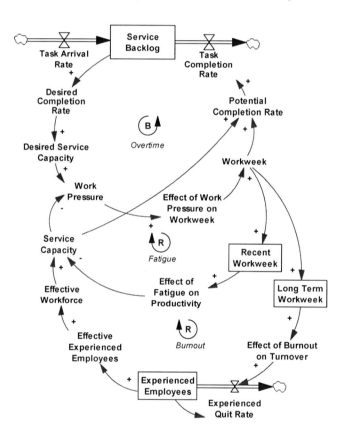

Figure 8. Consequences of sustained work intensity

These two 'side effects' of high work intensity create a pair of reinforcing feedbacks that can trap the organization in substandard performance. Fatigue and burnout reduce service capacity (directly and indirectly, as attrition both lowers headcount and increases the rookie fraction), which—*ceteris paribus*—lowers task completion, pushing the service backlog up, further increasing work pressure and forcing service providers to work even harder (the Fatigue and Burnout loops in Figure 8).

To illustrate, Figure 9 shows the impact of a 15% increase in task arrivals for one quarter, starting from equilibrium and assuming workweek is the only adjustment process (holding time per task constant). Hiring is set to replace total quits, so the workforce remains constant throughout. When arrivals increase, the backlog and work pressure grow, and employees immediately increase their workweek. Task completion rises, though not enough to match the arrival rate. Backlog continues to accumulate, and work pressure grows further. By week 15 the effects of fatigue overcome the benefits of longer hours and the completion rate begins to drop. By week 20 employees reach the maximum possible workweek (see Figure 6). In week 23 the arrival rate drops back to its original level. Work completion

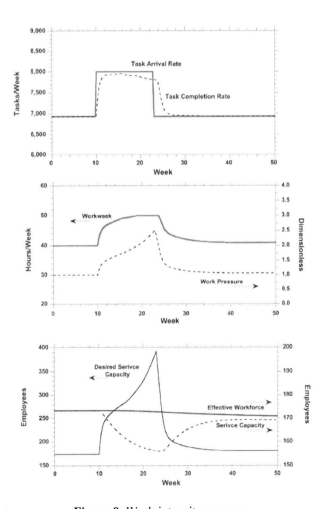

Figure 9. Work intensity response

gradually falls as the backlog drops, reaching its desired level in approximately 5 weeks. Note, however, that the system settles into a new equilibrium. Burnout from extended overtime increased turnover, shifting the employee mix to include more rookies. With the base case parameters the steady-state rookie fraction rises from 16.6% to 18.2%, causing a 1.4% drop in average productivity. As a result, work pressure does not return to normal: the same number of less productive employees are forced to maintain a slightly longer workweek. A *temporary* surge in work volume caused a *permanent* drop in productivity.

Side effects of cutting corners: lower quality and standard erosion

While cutting corners immediately increases output, it does so at the cost of the quality of the customer's experience and a higher likelihood of errors. We begin with the impact of corner cutting on service operations; below we consider how corner-cutting feeds back to affect the firm's competitiveness and customer base.

Effects of lower quality

A common way to cut the time spent on each task is to skip steps and cut quality assurance. The obvious unintended impact is a higher error rate, leading to customer dissatisfaction and costly rework. Errors are typically not detected immediately: A waiter in a hurry may take the customer's lunch order without reading it back for confirmation, but the error is not discovered until the customer receives the tuna surprise instead of the tofu burger. Credit card billing errors are typically discovered only after customers examine their monthly statements. Errors therefore accumulate in a stock of undiscovered rework until they are discovered (Lyneis and Ford, 2007; Sterman, 2000, ch. 2).

$$\text{Undiscovered Errors} = \text{INTEGRAL}(\text{Error Generation Rate} - \text{Error Discovery Rate}, \text{Undiscovered Errors}_{t_0}). \tag{34}$$

The error discovery rate is assumed to be a first-order process with a constant average error discovery time:

$$\text{Error Discovery Rate} = \text{Undiscovered Errors} / \text{Time to Discover Errors}. \tag{35}$$

Error generation depends on the total completion rate and the probability that each task contains an error:

$$\text{Error Generation Rate} = \text{Task Completion Rate} * \text{Probability of Error Generation}. \tag{36}$$

We assume that the probability of errors depends on three factors: corner cutting (time per task), fatigue, and average employee experience. Cutting the time spent on each task increases the probability of error as employees hurry, skip steps, and fail to check their work. Fatigue increases the chance of error and cuts the chance of detecting and correcting it at the time. Inexperienced personnel make more errors. For simplicity we assume these sources of error are independent. The probability a task is done incorrectly is then the complement of the probability that no error was introduced by any of these factors:

Probability of Error Generation $= 1 - \prod_{i \in \{F\}}$ Probability of Error Free$_i$ (37)

Probability Error Free$_i = f(F_i)$ (38)

where $F \in$ {Time per Task, Recent Workweek, Average Productivity}.

When errors are discovered they are added to the service backlog to await reprocessing. Thus, equation 17 is modified to

Service Backlog =
        INTEGRAL(Task Arrival Rate + Error Discovery Rate – Task Completion Rate,
        Service Backlog$_{t_0}$). (17')

Corner cutting also influences employee attrition. Employees will endure more pressure and develop greater loyalty to the organization if they perceive that they deliver a high-quality service (Schneider, 1991; Schneider et al., 1980). Alternatively, if employees perceive low levels of service quality they are more likely to leave the organization. The effect of quality on turnover modifies the fractional attrition rate for all employees:

Rookie Quit Rate = Rookie Employees * Rookie Quit Fraction *
        Effect of Fatigue on Turnover * Effect of Quality on Turnover (4")

Experienced Quit Rate = Experienced Employees * Experienced Quit Fraction *
        Effect of Fatigue on Turnover * Effect of Quality on Turnover. (5")

The effect of quality on turnover is modeled as an increasing function of the quality perceived by employees. Employees are assumed to adjust their perception of service quality after a short delay. We model this perception process as a first order exponential average of the actual quality delivered:

Effect of Quality on Turnover $= f$(Perceived Quality$_E$) (39)

Perceived Quality$_E$ = SMOOTH(Delivered Quality, Time to Perceive Quality$_E$). (40)

Service quality is, by definition, determined by the customer's subjective experience with the service organization. We model quality as a function of the performance gap—the difference between the time allocated per task and the customer's expectation of what that time should be. Delivered quality is one when the performance gap is zero, that is, when time per task matches customers' expectations (Figure 10). The existence of a "tolerance zone" for service quality (Strandvik, 1994; Zeithaml et al., 1993) suggests that the function is relatively flat when the performance gap is small, but grows progressively steeper with the gap.

Delivered Quality = f(Time per Task – Customer Expected Time per Task) /
Customer Expected Time per Task).   (41)

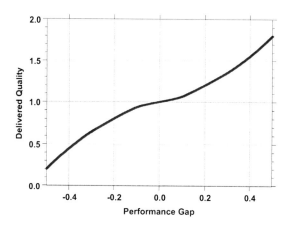

Figure 10. Effect of preformance gap on delivered quality

The introduction of rework creates another performance trap. Corner cutting eases high work pressure, but also causes quality to drop while increasing errors. When the errors are discovered they must be reworked, further increasing work pressure and pushing employees to cut corners still more (the Rework loop in Figure 11). Low quality also boosts attrition, reducing average productivity, creating another positive feedback (the Disappointment loop in Figure 11).

The unintended consequences of corner cutting are similar to those of increased work intensity: the effect of quality on turnover is structurally identical to the effect of burnout on turnover and the effect of errors similar to the productivity losses from fatigue. The strength and time constants for these effects differ from the workweek impacts analyzed in Figure 9, but the resulting behavior is qualitatively similar. After a temporary increase in task arrivals, the system reaches equilibrium with more inexperienced employees, causing sustained work pressure. The higher rookie fraction is the result of the increased turnover caused by lower quality. With fewer experienced people, work pressure remains above normal, leading to more errors and lower service quality.

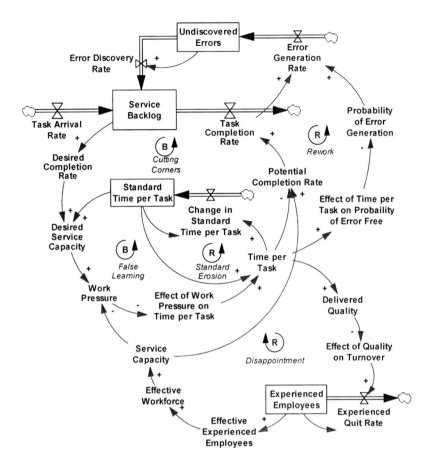

Figure 11. Consequences of sustained corner cutting

Erosion of service standards

Services are intangible and quality is difficult to measure. In the absence of compelling external feedback on service quality, an organization's internal standards for service quality tend to drift with past performance. The expectation formation literature suggests that performance standards are adjusted based on an anchoring and adjustment heuristic (Lant, 1992; Lewin et al., 1944). We model the adjustment process for the standard time per task, the time employees would allocate to each task in the absence of work pressure, as an asymmetric process. Asymmetric adjustments have been used in the organizational and psychological literature to represent biased formation of expectations and goals, and are normally formulated with different time constants governing the adjustment process depending on whether the aspiration level is above or below actual performance:

Standard Time per Task = INTEGRAL((Time per Task − Standard Time per Task) /
Time to Adjust Standard, Standard Time per Task$_{t0}$)   (42)

Time to Adjust Standard = IF(Time per Task < Standard Time per Task,
Time to Adjust Down, Time to Adjust Up).   (43)

Oliva and Sterman's (2001) financial services field study showed that the organization's standard time per task adjusted downward much faster than it adjusted upward. Management interpreted any reduction in time per task as cost-saving productivity improvement rather than as a sign of poor quality. Upward adjustments of standard time per task, in contrast, were resisted as they imply a reduction in productivity. Indeed, Oliva and Sterman found that the best estimate of the downward adjustment time for quality standards was 19 weeks, while the upward adjustment time was essentially infinite—temporary corner cutting was quickly embedded in organizational norms for standard time per task, while increases in time per task did not result in upward revision of quality norms.

Incorporating dynamic quality norms creates a new reinforcing loop that can trap the firm in substandard performance. As high work pressure causes temporary corner cutting, standard time per task begins to fall (eq. 42). If work pressure remains high, however, employees seeking to clear the backlog faster will cut time per task below the new, lower standard, causing still more erosion of the quality norm (the Standard Erosion loop in Figure 11).

Furthermore, since management uses the standard time per task to estimate required service capacity (eq. 25), reductions in the standard, *ceteris paribus,* reduce required capacity, thus easing work pressure. That is, management interprets erosion in the time needed per task as permanent productivity improvement due to learning (the False Learning loop in Figure 11). Goal erosion provides another negative feedback through which high work pressure can be eliminated.

Figure 12 shows the impact of corner cutting and standard erosion, holding the workweek constant (thus eliminating the impact of overtime on task completion, errors, productivity, and turnover). The system begins in equilibrium with enough capacity to deliver high quality work with no errors. In week 10 task arrivals rise by 15% for one quarter, then fall back to the original value.

The surge in arrivals causes the backlog to grow, increasing work pressure. Employees respond by reducing time per task, but the completion rate remains below arrivals, so the backlog continues to grow. The unanticipated side effects of corner cutting soon appear: less time per task increases errors; after a delay, these are discovered, increasing the backlog still further. Low quality increases employee turnover, reducing effective capacity as rookies replace experienced staff. Lower effective capacity forces work pressure up still more. Finally, the standard for time per task gradually falls as workers and management become habituated to spending less time with each customer, cut quality checks, reduce effort to understand the customers' needs and cross-sell additional services, and fail to document their work. Eroding quality standards eases work pressure even though the service backlog continues to grow (the False Learning loop in Figure 11).

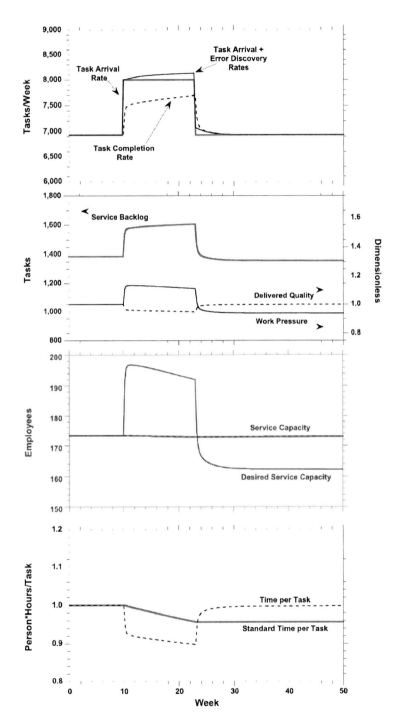

Figure 12. Consequences of sustained corner cutting

When task arrivals fall back to the original value, the backlog and work pressure quickly fall, and time per task increases. In the new equilibrium work pressure is less than one, indicating excess capacity. Standard time per task fell during the period of high work pressure, but does not rise when work pressure is low. Since headcount remains constant throughout the simulation, lower standards (higher perceived employee productivity) mean service capacity eventually exceeds demand. With low work pressure, employees can restore service quality close to its original level. However, in reality, management would not long tolerate such excess capacity.

Management response to work pressure: adjusting service capacity

In reality, management is likely to respond to imbalances between desired and actual service capacity by altering the workforce. If the workforce could adjust quickly and fully in response to changes in required capacity, overtime and corner cutting, with their unintended harmful consequences, would be minimized. However, expanding the workforce is expensive and time consuming, and it is costly and disruptive to reduce headcount. Managers of service operations often face severe budget constraints and pressure to meet financial targets. Capacity expansion is, therefore, often the response of last resort.

To capture capacity adjustment endogenously we now replace the constant-headcount hiring policy (eq. 11) with a more realistic decision rule that adjusts the workforce in response to the gap between desired and actual service capacity. First, hiring takes time—time to create and advertise vacancies, review applicants, interview candidates, and fill positions. The difference between the rates at which new positions are authorized and filled accumulate in a stock of unfilled vacancies. We assume the average time to hire is constant (in reality it varies with labor market conditions, rising when labor markets are tight and falling when unemployment is high):

Rookie Hiring Rate = Employee Vacancies / Time to Hire   (11')

Employee Vacancies = INTEGRAL(Labor Order Rate – Rookie Hiring Rate,
   Desired Vacancies).   (44)

Orders for labor – the rate at which vacancies are created – are normally determined by the desired hiring rate corrected for any discrepancies between the desired and actual number of vacancies. If, however, there were an extreme surplus of workers labor orders could become negative, forcing existing job openings to be canceled. In such a situation, vacancy cancellation is constrained to be no faster the rate determined by the average time required to cancel open vacancies:

Labor Order Rate =
   MAX(Desired Hiring Rate + (Desired Vacancies – Vacancies) / Time to Adjust
   Workforce, – Employee Vacancies / Time to Cancel Vacancies).   (45)

The number of vacancies needed to hire at the desired rate is, by Little's Law, proportional to the desired hiring rate and average delay in filling vacancies:

Desired Vacancies = Desired Hiring Rate * Time to Hire.   (46)

The organization seeks to replace those employees who have quit and correct any discrepancy between desired and existing labor. The responsiveness of the policy is given by the time to adjust the workforce:

Desired Hiring Rate = Total Quit Rate + Workforce Adjustment Rate   (47)

Workforce Adjustment Rate =
(Desired Workforce – Total Employees) / Time to Adjust Workforce.   (48)

The desired workforce is determined by desired service capacity and management's belief about average productivity. However, because labor is costly and slow to change, management does not act instantaneously on labor requirements. Instead, the desired workforce adjusts with a lag to the level indicated by desired service capacity and perceived employee productivity. The lag, modeled here by first-order exponential smoothing, ensures that capacity and hiring do not overreact to temporary variations in service demand:

Desired Workforce =
SMOOTH(Desired Service Capacity / Perceived Employee Effectiveness,
Time to Adjust Desired Workforce).   (49)

Furthermore, employee effectiveness is not perceived instantaneously, since it takes time to measure, report and assess changes in productivity. We model that process with exponential smoothing of actual employee effectiveness:

Perceived Employee Effectiveness = SMOOTH(Service Capacity / Total Employees,
Time to Perceive Productivity).   (50)

Note that perceived employee effectiveness is an aggregate measure based on the data management actually has available: productivity is the ratio of service capacity (which is the task completion rate converted to labor requirements using the standard work week and standard time per task) to total staff. Consequently, managers' beliefs about employee productivity adjust gradually to variations in productivity caused by changes in the rookie fraction, fatigue, and erosion of the standard time per task.

Management's decision rule for hiring acts to eliminate discrepancies between desired and actual service capacity, creating another negative feedback loop through which the organization can regulate work pressure.

Figure 13 shows the impact of all three ways workers and managers respond to work pressure: overtime, corner-cutting, and hiring. From an initial equilibrium there is a sudden, unanticipated, permanent 10% increase in task arrivals. Figure 13 shows the contribution to task completions from each response, along with the change in throughput resulting from service standard erosion. The combined responses are capable of immediately boosting task completions to match the arrival rate. However, the timing and strength of the responses differs substantially.

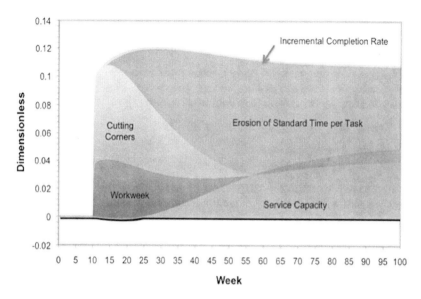

Figure 13. Response to a 10% increase in demand

First, as estimated by Oliva and Sterman (2001) and shown in Figure 6, employees are twice as willing to cut corners as to work overtime. The reduction in time per task, along with fatigue and experience reduction, cause errors to grow; as these are discovered the task arrival rate rises beyond the 10% exogenous shock (eventually peaking 11.4% above the initial rate). At the same time, internal quality standards (standard time per task) begin to erode. Longer hours and lower quality cause higher turnover, lowering effective service capacity. Lower standards for time per task ease work pressure somewhat, but it remains well above normal.

The service standard continues to erode as employees respond to continued work pressure by still more corner cutting. Meanwhile, management responds to the high workload by increasing the desired workforce, but the lags in recognizing and responding to the need, and in filling vacancies, mean service capacity begins to increase only after week 25. Service capacity reaches the desired level by week 58, then overshoots. Service capacity overshoots because of the delays in perceiving the adequacy of service capacity and in filling vacancies. Further, even as hiring slows, the many rookies hired in response to the demand surge continue to gain experience, raising effective capacity. Excessive capacity causes work pressure to fall below one. Employees then spend more time with each customer than the (now lower) service standard indicates, and reduce their workweek (taking longer breaks, using more work time for personal business, etc.). The inertia of the hiring process causes service capacity to peak two years after task arrivals increase, and the delays in the learning curve and in changing perceptions of productivity mean it takes almost five years for the system to return to equilibrium.[5]

Most important, the new equilibrium reached by the system is very different from the original equilibrium. While task arrivals rise by 10%, capacity does not expand by 10%. Rather, most of the growth in throughput results from a permanent reduction in the organization's internal quality standard. With the base case parameters, capacity expands in equilibrium by only 2.1%, with permanent standard erosion providing the rest of the "capacity" needed to meet the increase in demand. Note also that the drop in the equilibrium time per task causes a rise in errors and rework contributing an additional 1.3 percentage point increase in task completion compared to the original level, and that the lower quality increases employee turnover, causing the rookie fraction to increase by one percentage point, to 17.7%, lowering productivity and increasing costs.

To assess system response under more natural conditions than a single increase in demand, we subject the model to random variations in the task arrival rate. We assume arrivals are determined by a pink noise process with a standard deviation of 5% and first-order autocorrelation time constant of four weeks (Figure 14). Most people intuitively believe that, since orders are stationary, the firm's initial resources should, on average, be sufficient to maintain the service standard and desired delivery delay. Instead, the system exhibits persistent erosion in the service standard (in this case, an average of 2.1%/year). The asymmetric adjustment of the standard time per task is responsible. When task arrivals exceed the mean, work pressure rises, time per task falls, and the standard drops a bit. However, when task arrivals are lower than the mean and work pressure falls below one, time per task rises, but the standard does not adjust upward. Management responds to the small, but cumulative, decrease in person-hours per task by gradually raising their estimate of workforce productivity, leading them to reduce desired service capacity accordingly. As service capacity falls, work pressure rises, which in turn leads to further corner cutting and standard erosion, thus locking the system into a vicious cycle.

Market feedback

Until now we have assumed task arrivals are exogenous, corresponding to a captive customer base. Such scenarios are approximated in many settings, for example, health care, financial services, and hardware help desks, where customers must seek medical care from the doctors in their existing health plan, file claims with their existing insurance policy, and seek service from the help desk of the firm from which they bought their new laptop. However, even in such captive

---

[5] The adjustment to equilibrium is also slowed by the assumed low attrition rate of 20%/year and assumption that the firm does not lay off excess staff. Many service operations, particularly low-wage settings such as retail, entry-level financial services, fast food, and call centers experience far higher turnover. The model can also be easily expanded to allow for layoffs (Sterman 2000, ch. 19).

situations, customers usually have the option of switching to other providers over the long term. We now expand the boundary of the model to incorporate the main market feedbacks that drive the customer base and task arrivals.

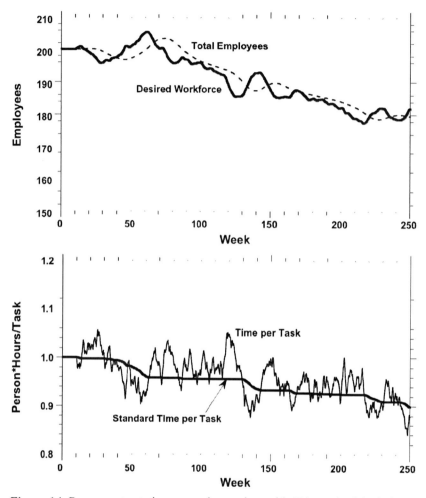

Figure 14. Response to stationary random orders with 5% standard deviation

We assume tasks arrive at a rate proportional to the customer base:

Task Arrival Rate = Customer Base * Task Requests per Customer.   (51)

For simplicity we assume task requests per customer are exogenous. The customer base is formulated to increase at a rate that depends on perceived service attractiveness. When service attractiveness is greater (less) than one, the customer base will gradually rise (fall) as the firm wins or loses customers to competitors:

Customer Base = INTEGRAL(Base Customer Growth Rate +
(Customer Base * Service Attractiveness – Customer Base) /
Time to Adjust Customer Base, Customer Base$_{t_0}$)   (52)

where the Base Customer Growth Rate is an exogenous fractional increase in customers, to allow for growth in the underlying market. Service attractiveness responds with a delay to the product of four attributes of the service encounter: errors, balking, the service delivery time, and delivered service quality. The delay represents the time required for customer beliefs about service quality to change, and for a new level of service attractiveness to persist long enough to induce customers to switch providers:

Service Attractiveness = SMOOTH($\prod\limits_{j \in \{A\}}$ Effect of Attribute$_j$ on Attractiveness,

Time to React to Service Attractiveness)   (53)

Effect of Attribute$_j$ on Attractiveness =
(Actual Performance Attribute$_i$ / Standard Attribute$_i$)$^{\text{Sensitivity of Attractiveness from Attribute}_j}$

(54)

where Attribute A$_i$ ∈ {Error Discovery Rate, Balking Rate, Delivery Delay, Delivered Quality}.

Finally, the balking rate—the rate at which customers abandon the service backlog because of excessive waiting time   depends on an increasing function of the delivery delay relative to the customers' standard for wait time:

Balking Rate = Service Backlog * Normal Balking Rate *
Effect of Delivery Delay on Balking   (55)

Effect of Delivery Delay on Balking =
f(Delivery Delay / Customer Standard for Delivery Delay).   (56)

The service backlog is now:

Service Backlog =
INTEGRAL(Task Arrival Rate + Error Discovery Rate –
Task Completion Rate – Balking Rate, Service Backlog$_{t_0}$).   (17")

For simplicity, we assume that customers who balk do not return to the queue at a later time. However, the higher the rate of balking, the lower are customer perceptions of service quality (eq. 53), which feed back to the customer base (eq. 52).

Figure 15 shows the service center's response to a 10% increase in tasks requested per customer. As before, the surge in workload leads to overtime and corner cutting. These responses, along with eventual hiring, together allow the service center to process the higher load in the normal delivery time, so the impact of wait time on balking and customer perceptions of service attractiveness is minimal.

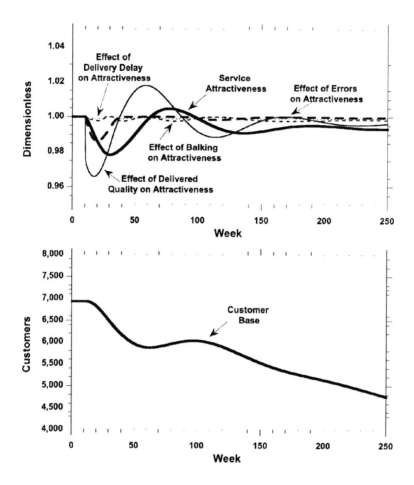

Figure 15. Response to a 10% increase in demand with market feedback

However, overtime and corner cutting increase errors and lower the quality of service the customers experience. It takes time for customers to perceive the drop in service attractiveness, but as they do, the customer base begins to erode.

The drop in customer base and slight increase in service capacity eventually bring capacity in line with service demand, and attractiveness returns to normal (week 35). With a delay, customers react to the improvement in quality, and the customer base stabilizes, which then starts to rise as excess service capacity temporarily improves quality. However, the reduction in time per task during the period of high work pressure caused throughput per worker to rise. Observing this increase in task completions per person, management raises their estimate of worker productivity (as in Figures 12 and 14), leading desired service capacity to fall more than the drop in work volume arising from the erosion of the customer base. The resulting drop in capacity then raises work pressure, leading to additional corner cutting and lower quality, further eroding the customer base. The organization is captured in a vicious cycle: high work pressure erodes service standards and lowers capacity, ensuring that work pressure remains high and standards continue to erode.

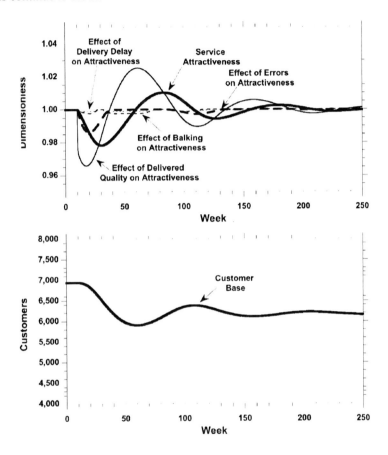

Figure 16. Response to a 10% increase in demand with market feedback and the possibility to improve Standard Time per Order

As discussed above, these results could be in part explained by the asymmetric adjustment of the service standard documented in Oliva and Sterman (2001): standards can fall, but not rise. To test the sensitivity of the results to this assumption we ran the same test as before, but allowing standard time per task to increase when time per task rises above the standard. We set the time constant for upward adjustment equal to 150% of the value for downward adjustment—an optimistic estimate of managements' ability to recognize the benefits of the increased level of service and to build them into organizational practices. As in the previous scenario, the surge in demand triggers overtime, corner cutting and standard erosion, leading to a drop in the customer base (Figure 16). Unlike the previous case, however, during the period of excess service capacity, the service standard rebounds. The system reaches an equilibrium in which service capacity matches demand and employees deliver the standard time per task working the standard week. Note that while the standard time per task returns to its original value, it does so only after the firm permanently loses nearly 10% of its customer base. Upward adjustment of the quality standard allows the firm to halt the death spiral, but, rebuilding the customer base would require the firm to increase service quality and standards above the original levels; the interactions of the routines for assessing worker productivity and hiring do not create such conditions.

Financial pressure

Up to now the organization has been free to hire as many people as it deems necessary to meet demand. We now expand the model boundary to include financial constraints on hiring. To do so, we revise the workforce adjustment to respond to the authorized workforce, defined to be the lesser of the workforce needed to meet demand or what the organization can afford given its budget:

Workforce Adjustment Rate =
(Authorized Workforce – Total Employees) / Time to Adjust Workforce   (48')

Authorized Workforce = MIN(Desired Workforce, Affordable Workforce) *
Margin for Reserve Capacity.   (57)

The margin for reserve capacity represents a nominal fractional level of excess capacity built into budgets and staffing. A margin of $1+m$ indicates that the staff target for the service organization is m% higher than the level just sufficient to meet demand, and that the budget to cover this reserve capacity is also made available. The desired workforce continues to be driven by throughput requirements described above. The affordable workforce is determined by the operating budget and fully-loaded cost per employee. Again, because labor is costly and slow to change, management does not react instantaneously to budget changes. Like the desired workforce, the affordable workforce adjusts to the level indicated by the budget and cost per employee with a lag:

Affordable Workforce = SMOOTH(Budget / Salary per Employee,
Time to Adjust Affordable Workforce).   (58)

The operating budget is assumed to have a fixed component and a component dependent on generated revenues:

Budget =
MAX(0, Base Budget + Revenue * Fraction of Revenue for Operations).   (59)

The budget formulation allows a wide range of service organizations to be modeled. A single customer support call center in a firm may generate no revenue; such centers are typically managed as cost centers and must live within a given base budget each year. At the other extreme, when the model represents an entire firm, the budget must then come (nearly) entirely from revenue.

For simplicity we model revenue as proportional to the customer base and the average revenue generated per customer per month, independent of the number of service requests each customer generates, an approximation of many settings in which customers pay a certain monthly fee, such as insurance premium payments or account maintenance fees in financial services:

$$\text{Revenue} = \text{Customer Base} * \text{Revenue per Customer}. \tag{60}$$

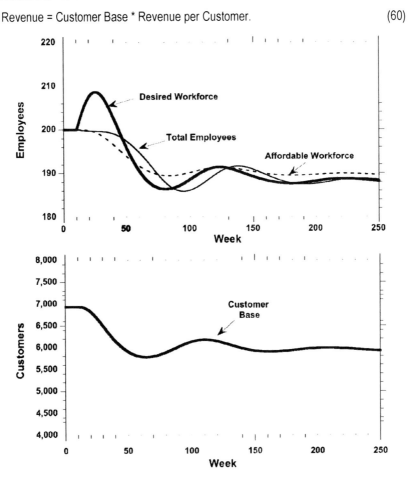

Figure 17. Response to a 10% increase in demand with market feedback, the possibility to improve Standard Time per Order, and financial constraints on hiring

For the base case, we start the system in equilibrium with the budget set to cover the cost of the work force exactly, i.e., no margin for reserve capacity. Figure 17 shows the evolution of the desired, affordable and actual workforce for the same scenario as Figure 16, but with the budgeting process active. The financial constraint means the workforce does not rise after the surge in demand. As before, the increase in work pressure causes overtime and corner cutting that reduce service attractiveness, causing a gradual drop in the customer base. Now, however, the drop in revenue caused by the loss of customers forces the workforce down as the budget falls. Capacity remains inadequate, forcing employees to cut corners further. The customer base drops still more. Like the simulation in figure 16, the system reaches equilibrium with attractiveness returning to normal. However, because the budget constrained hiring during the transient, the customer base drops 14.6% instead of 8.9%. The death spiral in this simulation halts only because the base budget of the service center creates a floor for the affordable workforce. Results are worse if the organization must rely on revenue for its budget to a greater degree.

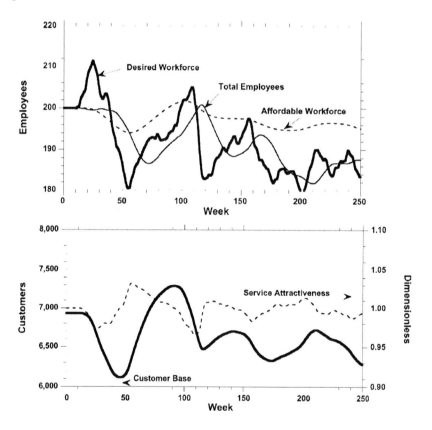

Figure 18. Response to stationary random orders with 10% standard deviation – Full model (base case)

To assess the full system response under more realistic conditions, we subject it to random variations in the task arrival rate. We assume arrivals are determined by a pink noise process with a standard deviation of 10% and first-order autocorrelation time constant of four weeks. The system begins in equilibrium with a time constant to adjust the standard time per task upward equal to 150% of the downward adjustment time. While the system is capable of maintaining service attractiveness very close to its normal operating point, it does so mainly by driving customers away until demand falls enough to reduce work pressure and stop the erosion of service quality (Figure 18). During temporary periods of high demand, the resulting drop in quality drives some customers away and causes some erosion of the service standard, forcing the workforce below initial levels. Temporary periods of low demand increase quality, and can win back some customers, but due to the asymmetry in standard adjustment, lags in adjusting the workforce, and other nonlinearities (e.g. in the customers' response to quality), service attractiveness spends more time below normal than above, resulting in persistent erosion of the customer base and a subsequent reduction of the workforce.

Policy recommendations

The simulation results show that service organizations are vulnerable to a wide range of self-reinforcing processes that can act as death spirals. In each case, the short-term benefits of an action, whether overtime, corner-cutting, service standard erosion or hiring, can trigger harmful long-term effects that either lead to insufficient capacity, drive away customers, or reduce the organization's budget, forcing further service capacity erosion. Although in principle these positive feedbacks can act as virtuous cycles, progressively improving service capability, leading to higher standards, more customers and revenue, and still greater service capacity, in practice, and as verified by empirical studies, the system is biased towards quality erosion. Workers are typically more willing to cut corners than increase their work effort, norms for the time that should be devoted to each customer fall more readily than they rise, management is more willing to raise its estimates of labor productivity than to cut them and to downsize rather than hire. Policies to reduce the strength and likelihood of quality erosion death spirals must overcome each of these processes.

Expediting capacity acquisition: Because the erosion of the internal service standard occurs when work pressure is high, one obvious policy is to ensure that service capacity is acquired before the standard can erode. Capacity expansion can be expedited by having a more responsive hiring process or reducing the delays governing capacity acquisition. Other strategies to increase the responsiveness of service capacity include hiring employees with greater initial effectiveness, accelerate the learning process by task routinization, maintaining a contingent workforce that can be deployed quickly when demand surges, and coordinating capacity management with other actions that affect demand such as marketing campaigns and product promotions. Unfortunately, these options are rarely available in high-contact services that require job-specific knowledge.

Reducing the effect of work pressure on time per task: Reducing employees' willingness to cut corners should slow the decline of service standards. Of course, if the time spent with customers were completely unaffected by work pressure, there could be no quality erosion. Such a rigid policy is unrealistic, however, because customer needs differ, individual servers have considerable autonomy in selecting how they respond to each customer, and the overtime required to hit throughput targets with no flexibility in service would be prohibitive. A more realistic policy is to distribute employee responses to work pressure more evenly between corner cutting and overtime, while still responding fully to changes in work pressure. This can be done by reducing the flexibility of the service encounter (through process standardization and documentation, such as checklists in medical care) or by increasing the relative attractiveness of overtime (by creating high empathy with customers or increasing overtime compensation).

Creating quality pressure: Because service quality is intrinsically subjective and difficult to measure, there is little pressure from quality norms to counteract cuts in service induced by high work pressure. Surveys of customer experience are infrequent, less salient, and appear to be less consequential than the throughput, cost, and productivity feedback workers and service center managers receive every day. Though service providers often report some discomfort with their performance, we found no evidence in our fieldwork that low quality had any impact on the time employees devoted to each customer. Creating quality pressure requires management to become aware of the implications of poor service—lost sales, rework, and customer defections—and then, through training, incentives, measurement, and example, persuade employees that avoiding these costs is a priority and that they will not be punished for slowing their work to correct any quality problems they detect.

Maintaining a reserve margin of capacity: Even if the policies above are instituted, they will have little impact if the budget for service is continually tightened. Many of the executives responsible for customer service in organizations we have worked with continually face pressure to cut their expenses, even as the load on the service organization increases. It is common for managers at all levels, from supervisors to the CIO, to be told "technology is improving, and our shareholders expect double digit net income growth. You have to do more with less." The long delays in adjusting service capacity coupled with unpredictable variations in service demand mean an organization must maintain a strategic margin of reserve capacity to avoid the corner cutting, standard erosion, and other behaviors that trigger the death spirals. However, to many senior managers, reserve capacity looks like waste, leading to continual pressure to reduce budgets and headcount. Worse, financial stringency often prevents organizations from undertaking the process improvement initiatives that could lead to genuine improvements in productivity (Repenning and Sterman, 2001, 2002).

Figure 19 implements the policies suggested above. The hiring delay is cut from 20 to 10 weeks. Because corner cutting is not likely to be fully eliminated, we assume employees, through changes in training and incentives, are now twice as willing to work overtime as to cut corners. Quality norms are more resistant to erosion (the time for the standard to erode is lengthened from 20 to 25 weeks, still shorter than the 30 weeks for upward adjustment). Finally, a 5% margin of reserve capacity is built into the budget and staffing levels. Figure 19 shows the results of 1,000 monte-carlo simulations with different realizations of the random process for task arrivals.

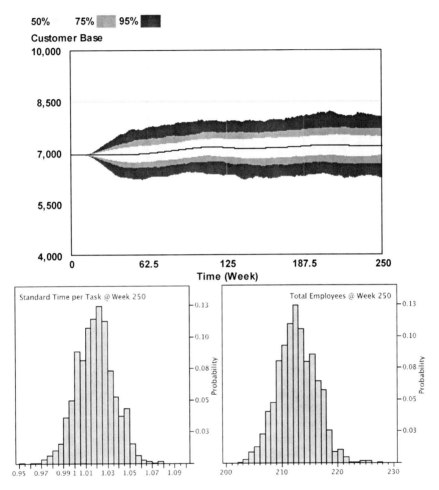

Figure 19. Response to stationary random orders with 10% standard deviation – Full model (policy recommendations)

On average the policies result in a rise in service standards and an increase in the customer base. The margin of reserve capacity lowers work pressure enough to enable servers to spend enough additional time with customers to push service quality up. Management is assumed to pay more attention to quality feedback, so the service standard also gradually increases. Higher average service quality gradually builds the customer base, and with it, the budget. The margin of reserve capacity also means that the growth of the customer base and therefore the task arrival rate does not immediately lead to high work pressure despite the lags in building service capacity. When random variations in task arrivals push work pressure above normal, service quality does not fall as much as before because servers are less willing to cut corners. These policies reverse the vicious cycles that previously create the potential for a self-reinforcing death spiral; now the same positive feedbacks operate as virtuous cycles, leading the organization to progressively higher quality, longer employee tenure, higher productivity and lower error rates, building the customer base and revenue.

Concluding remarks

Despite the growing importance of services and service quality as sources of competitive advantage, the quality of service delivery in the United States is not improving and in many sectors is falling. Poor service quality contrasts sharply with the generally rising quality of manufactured products. Service delivery is intrinsically dynamic, involves multiple feedbacks among servers, customers, managers, and other actors. In this paper we develop a dynamic, behavioral model with a broad boundary to capture the structural characteristics of the service delivery process, management's and employees' decision-making processes, and the formation of expectations for customers and employees. Like any model, it is imperfect and can be extended; we provide full documentation and the model itself online so that others can replicate, extend, and improve it. Additional scenarios can be tested easily and tend to strengthen the results shown here. In particular, the propensity for capacity to become inadequate, triggering the positive feedbacks identified here, is greater in the presence of absenteeism and, especially, rapid growth in demand (e.g., Oliva et al., 2003).

To develop intuition for the dynamics of the service delivery process, we built the model up in stages to highlight the dynamics of each major sector – human resources, work flow, standards for quality, hiring, customer reactions to quality, budgeting, etc. By gradually expanding the boundary of the model we identify the many self-reinforcing feedbacks that can lead to persistent undercapacity and quality erosion. These feedbacks operate at the level of individual servers' responses to work pressure, in the interactions between hiring and experience, in the routines management uses to assess productivity and set staffing levels, and in the interactions between service quality and customer retention. High work pressure leads to overtime that causes fatigue and burnout, increasing errors and rework, lowering productivity, and increasing absenteeism and attrition, all of which feed back to worsen work pressure. High work pressure leads to corner cutting by employees, but the improvement in processing rates is interpreted by management as productivity growth, leading to staff cutbacks that raise work pressure further. Low quality causes customers to defect, cutting revenues and forcing further staff reductions. And so on.

Through simulations of the model we demonstrate that major recurring problems observed in the service industry—erosion of service quality, high turnover, and low profitability—can be explained by the organization's internal responses to work pressure. The manner in which a service firm responds to work pressure determines whether the system will disappoint customers, employees, and shareholders. Although in principle the positive feedbacks can operate as virtuous as well as vicious cycles, the system is biased toward quality erosion by basic asymmetries and nonlinearities. Workers are typically more willing and able to cut corners (reduce the time spent with customers, cut back on preparation, documentation and other procedures to ensure fairness and quality) than to work overtime to maintain quality. Norms and standards for quality erode more easily than they rise. Because quality is subjective and difficult to measure compared to the relentless pressure to hit cost and throughput targets, management tends to interpret improvements in the customers processed per server as signs of productivity improvement even when they arise from corner cutting that harms the customer experience and erodes revenue. Hiring and building a skilled workforce is slower and more difficult than laying people off and losing skilled and motivated workers through burnout and voluntary attrition. Budgets are cut more readily than raised. And so on. These asymmetries mean service organizations are more likely to tip into death spirals in which the many positive feedbacks in the system operate as vicious cycles than to experience self-reinforcing improvement.

However, we also present policies that can reverse the death spiral and convert the vicious cycles into virtuous cycles of continuous improvement. Although quality, costs, and employee satisfaction are normally perceived as tradeoffs, we find successful policies that simultaneously delight customers, employees, and shareholders.

References

Aho, K. (2008). The customer service hall of shame. Retrieved 3/24/08, from http://articles.moneycentral.msn.com/SmartSpending/ConsumerActionGuide/TheCustomerServiceHallOfShame.aspx

Argote, L., & Epple, D. (1990). Learning curves in manufacturing. *Science, 247,* 920-924.

Baumol, W., Blackman, S. B., & Wolf, E. (1991). *Productivity and American Leadership*. Cambridge, MA: MIT Press.

Chesbrough, H. (2005). Toward a science of service. *Harvard Business Review, 83,* 16-17.

Chesbrough, H., & Spohrer, J. (2006). A research manifesto for services science. *Communications of the ACM, 49*(7), 35-40.

Darr, E., Argote, L., & Epple, D. (1995). The acquisition, transfer and depreciation of knowledge in service organizations: Productivity in franchises. *Management Science, 41*(11), 1750-1762.

Dogan, G. (2007). Bootstrapping for confidence interval estimation and hypothesis testing for parameters of system dynamics models. *System Dynamics Review, 23*(4).

Homer, J. B. (1985). Worker Burnout: A Dynamic Model with Implications for Prevention and Control. *System Dynamics Review, 1*(1), 42-62.

Horn, P. (2005, January 21). The new discipline of services science. *Businessweek*.

Jarmain, W. E. (Ed.). (1963). *Problems in Industrial Dynamics*. Cambridge, MA: MIT Press.

Lant, T. K. (1992). Aspiration Level Adaptation: An Empirical Exploration. *Management Science, 38*(5), 623-644.

Lewin, K., Dembo, T., Festinger, L., & Sears, P. S. (1944). Level of Aspiration. In J. M. Hunt (Ed.), *Personality and the Behavior Disorders* (pp. 333-378). New York: The Ronald Press Company.

Lyneis, J. M., & Ford, D. N. (2007). System dynamics applied to project management: a survey, assessment, and directions for future research. *System Dynamics Review, 23*.

Maglio, P. P., Kreulen, J., Srinivasan, S., & Spohrer, J. (2006). Service systems, service scientists, SSME, and innovation. *Communications of the ACM, 49*(7), 81-85.

McGregor, J., McConnon, A., & Kiley, D. (2009, March 2, 2009). Customer service in a shrinking economy. *BusinessWeek*.

Oliva, R. (2001). Tradeoffs in responses to work pressure in the service industry. *California Management Review, 43*(4), 26-43.

Oliva, R. (2002). *Southwest Airlines in Baltimore (TN)* (Teaching Note No. 603-055). Boston, MA: Harvard Business School.

Oliva, R., & Bean, M. (2008). Developing operational understanding of service quality through a simulation environment. *International Journal of Service Industry Management, 19*(2), 160-175.

Oliva, R., & Sterman, J. D. (2001). Cutting corners and working overtime: Quality erosion in the service industry. *Management Science, 47*(7), 894-914.

Oliva, R., Sterman, J. D., & Giese, M. (2003). Limits to growth in the new economy: Exploring the 'get-big-fast' strategy in e-commerce. *System Dynamics Review, 19*(2), 83-117.

Repenning, N. P., & Sterman, J. D. (2001). Nobody ever gets credit for fixing problems that never happened. *California Management Review, 43*(4), 64-88.

Repenning, N. P., & Sterman, J. D. (2002). Capability traps and self-confirming attribution errors in the dynamics of process improvement. *Administrative Science Quarterly*, 265-295.

Schneider, B. (1991). Service Quality and Profits: Can you have your cake and eat it, too? *Human Resource Planning, 14*(2), 151-157.

Schneider, B., Parkington, J. J., & Buxton, V. M. (1980). Employee and Customer Perceptions of Service in Banks. *Administrative Science Quarterly, 25*(2), 252-267.

Sterman, J. D. (2000). *Business dynamics: Systems thinking and modeling for a complex world.* Boston: Irwin McGraw-Hill.

Strandvik, T. (1994). *Tolerance zones in perceived service quality.* Helsinki: Svenska handelshögskolan.

Thomas, H. R. (1993). *Effects of Scheduled Overtime on Labor Productivity: A Literature Review and Analysis* (Source Document No. 60). University Park, PA: Pennsylvania State University.

Zeithaml, V. A., Berry, L. L., & Parasuraman, A. (1993). The nature and determinants of customer expectations of service. *Journal of the Academy of Marketing Science, 21*(1), 1-12.

Service Science —

A Reflection from Telecommunications Service Perspective

Eng K. Chew

Faculty of Engineering and Information Technology

University of Technology, Sydney

An initial set of requirements for a proposed next-generation telecom service innovation model is derived by viewing telecommunications service in the context of the emergent service science principles. An in-depth review of the industry-standardized telecom business operations, eTOM, the next-generation network (NGN) architecture and advances made by global leading service providers yields the basic constructs for the proposed model which is centered on collaborative innovation, particularly customer collaboration. The proposed model is broadly described, and an initial review of challenges and recent advances in customer cocreation of service offering is provided.

Introduction

Telecommunications (telecom) is a complex technology-based service industry. Contemporary telecom service industry, while highly customer-oriented, tends to be viewed from a product-centered perspective[1] (TMF, 2004). This paper reflects on the telecom service industry and its future trends from a *service-centered perspective*. It uses the emerging *service science concepts and principles* (IfM and IBM, 2007) to highlight the *multidisciplinary* nature of service at the heart of telecom industry. From these service-centered insights the paper aims to synthesize from the literature an emerging *open collaborative* approach to telecom service innovation.

---

[1] For example, TMF (2004, 24) states "a key input to the service strategy arises from the enterprise's market and product portfolio strategy and forecasts" suggesting a somewhat "subordinate" role of service to product.

P.P. Maglio et al. (eds.), *Handbook of Service Science*, Service Science: Research and Innovations in the Service Economy, DOI 10.1007/978-1-4419-1628-0_16,
© Springer Science+Business Media, LLC 2010

This paper will show that telecom service industry indeed resonates well with the emerging service science concepts which have evolved, over two decades, from a series of seminal work from disparate disciplines (Levitt, 1976; Chase, 1978; Shostack, 1984; Schmenner, 1986; Normann and Ramirez, 1993; Schneider and Bowen, 1995; Boisot, 1998; Prahalad and Ramaswamy, 2000; Gadrey and Gallouj, 2002; Gallouj, 2002; Bryson et al., 2004; Karmarkar, 2004; Vargo and Lusch, 2004; Womack and Jones, 2005; Anderson et al., 2006; Chesbrough and Spohrer, 2006; Maglio et al., 2006; Fitzsimmons and Fitzsimmons, 2007; IfM and IBM, 2007; Spohrer et al., 2007; Maglio and Spohrer, 2008; Lusch et al., 2008; Vargo and Lusch, 2008; Vargo et al., 2008; Bitner et al., 2008; Maglio et al., 2009). The service-centered view is reinforced in the modeling of the emergent next-generation network (NGN) architecture (Knightson et al., 2005). Telecom service providers around the globe are migrating towards the NGN with the view to offering enormously flexible *service capabilities* to meet their current and future customer needs.

This paper first briefly reviews service science concepts and principles from the perspective of a generic telecom service model. From this review an initial set of requirements for a proposed telecom service innovation model is derived. Next, through the lens of service science principles, it reviews the industry-standardized telecom service process known as eTOM (enhanced Telecom Operations Map; TMF, 2004), and the emergent service-oriented next-generation network architecture. From these developments and a review of recent advances made by global leading service providers and service science research, the paper synthesizes a proposed emergent telecom service innovation approach – one that emphasizes open innovation (Chesbrough, 2003; Huston and Sakkab, 2006), particularly customer collaboration. The paper concludes by briefly describing a generic service innovation process and reviewing the challenges and recent advance made in customer co-creation of service offerings.

Service Science Concepts and Principles

Service science is an emerging field of research (Chesbrough and Spohrer, 2006), which aims to understand and systematize service innovation (IfM and IBM, 2007; Maglio and Spohrer, 2008; Vargo et al., 2008). As indicated above, it has evolved from over two decades of study by disparate service-related disciplines (IfM and IBM, 2007, 18). This has resulted in services being viewed from the perspective of the *service-dominant (S-D) logic* (Vargo and Lusch, 2004; Lusch et al., 2008; Vargo and Lusch, 2008; Vargo et al., 2008) and of service systems (Maglio et al., 2006; Spohrer et al., 2007; Maglio and Spohrer, 2008; Maglio et al., 2009). A service-centered view is inherently customer-oriented and relational (Gallouj, 2002; Gadrey and Gallouj, 2002; Fitzsimmons and Fitzsimmons, 2007). Service is a process of applying the provider's competence (knowledge and skills) for the benefit of, and in conjunction with, the customer (Schneider and Bowen, 1995; Gallouj, 2002; Fitzsimmons and Fitzsimmons, 2007; Vargo and

Lusch, 2004, 2008). Service systems are the basic unit of analysis of service (Maglio and Spohrer, 2008). Broadly, a service system (Spohrer et al., 2007) or service world (Bryson et al., 2004) is a complex adaptive system of people, and technologies working together to create value for its constituents.

Telecom industry is a complex market-facing technology-based service system. A telecom service might be as simple as establishing a reliable end-to-end communication link (telephone or data) on behalf of the client to another party on demand, anytime, anywhere in the globe. It might also be as complex as establishing a network solution for a large multinational enterprise client. In both cases, the 'proposed or expected' value of the service can be realized only upon action *initiated by the client* to use the service (enabled by the provider). Thus the client always plays a central role in value co-creation (Schneider and Bowen, 1995; Gallouj, 2002; Gadrey and Gallouj, 2002; Fitzsimmons and Fitzsimmons, 2007; Vargo and Lusch, 2004, 2008).

Service science is concerned with the study of service systems with the view to creating a basis for systematic service innovation (IfM and IBM, 2007). This study would require a *multidisciplinary integrative* understanding of the ways organization, human, business and technology resources and *shared information* may be combined to create different types of service systems. And how the service systems may interact and evolve to co-create value (Maglio and Spohrer, 2008). A service system is defined by Spohrer et al (2007) as "a value co-creation configuration of people, technology, other internal and external service systems, and shared information (such as language, processes, metrics, prices, policies, and laws". Service systems are connected by value propositions (Maglio and Spohrer, 2008). A service system has a service provider and a service client or beneficiary (Maglio et al., 2006). The provider and the client can be further modeled as two separate service system entities.

Service is a *process*, by which value is co-created by the client with the service provider (Normann and Ramirez, 1993; Fitzsimmons and Fitzsimmons, 2007). A service offering is produced using the firm's resources including both tangible (such as goods) and intangible (such as knowledge, competence and relationship) assets (Arnould, 2008). The value characteristics of the service provisioned, however, are co-created through the interactions of the client's competences with that of the service provider (Gallouj, 2002, 57). Thus the client is active in a service interaction; it co-creates value (for itself) with the provider (Gallouj, 2002; Gadrey and Gallouj, 2002; Fitzsimmons and Fitzsimmons, 2007).

A resource is called an *operand* resource "on which an operation or act is performed to produce an effect", or an *operant* resource "which acts on other operand or operant resource to produce an effect" (Vargo and Lusch, 2004). Operant resources are *dynamic*, which include *competences* or *capabilities* that can be nurtured and grown in some unique ways to provide competitive advantage to firms (Madhavaran and Hunt, 2008). Prahalad and Hamel (1990) have used the terms competence and capability interchangeably, which is defined as a bundle of skills that are "often routines, actions, or operations that are tacit, causally ambiguous, and idiosyncratic" (Vargo and Lusch, 2004).

Prahalad and Hamel (1990) define *core* competence as a bundle of (strategic) skills and technology that enable a firm to provide significant benefits to customers in a competitively unique (and inimitable) way. Core competence provides the firm with potential access to a wide variety of markets. Core competences are the firm's emergent (cross-functional) integration and configuration skills that enable organization-specific integration of technologies to yield benefits to customers (Boisot, 1998, 183-4). Firms gain competitive advantage by transforming their key business processes, which link and transcend disparate business units and functions, into *strategic capabilities* that consistently provide superior value to the customer (Stalk et al., 1992). Competitive advantage is determined by the performance of one firm's application of its operant resources to meet the needs of the customer relative to another firm's (Lusch et al., 2007).

Highly innovative firms possess *"masterfully developed"* operant resources accumulated over a long period from institutionalized learning practices (Madhavaran and Hunt, 2008). They allow the firm to effectively manage *co-evolution* of knowledge, capabilities, and products or services to sustain its competitive advantage. Ulrich and Smallwood (2004) identify eleven types of organizational capabilities (such as customer connectivity, collaboration, innovation) that firms need to master to sustain their competitive advantage. Lusch et al (2007) similarly identify *collaborative competence* as a pivotal operant resource for sustained service innovation – one that assists in the development of two additional meta-competences: *absorptive competence,* and *adaptive competence* to enable the firm to, respectively, absorb new knowledge and information from partners, and adapt to the complex and turbulent environments using external partners. These operant resources are key components of a service system which is a resource integrator (Spohrer et al., 2007). It is the people's unique knowledge and skills and organizational competences that make service systems *adaptive* to and *sustainable* with the changing market environments (Spohrer et al., 2007; Vargo et al., 2008).

From a service perspective, customer is at the *heart* of value creation and service is about relationship with the customer (Edvardsson et al., 2005). Service innovation consists of four dimensions: a new service concept, a new customer interface, a new service delivery system and the technology options (den Hertog, 2002, 226). The customer interacts with the service provider via the interface through which information, knowledge, emotions and civilities are exchanged to co-create value (Gallouj, 2002). Value is wholly determined by the customer and in the *context* of, service usage (and customer experience), in which the competence (operant resource) of the provider is *integrated* with the competence (operant resource) of the customer to (perform 'a job' to) create (business) value with the customer. The service provider cannot deliver value, but only offer value propositions (Vargo, 2008). To win the service game, the value proposition must consistently meet the customer expectations and behavioral needs (Schneider and Bowen, 1995). This can be assured by co-opting the customer competence in co-creating the service offering with the provider (Prahalad and Ramaswamy, 2000). However, the customer may only *choose* to collaborate with the provider in co-creation of core service offerings if there are benefits. Six key factors influence the extent of customer participation in co-creation of service offering: expertise, control, physical capital, risk taking, psychic benefits, and economic benefits (Lusch et al., 2007).

The above principles are evidently reflected in telecom service where service is seen as an offering provided by the service providers. Products are an abstract term (names) used to denote the service offerings. Telecom service is subscribed by the end-user (client) under a service contract. Each service offering (contract) has a predefined set of capabilities representing its value proposition (with a specific level of quality of service obligation) for a given rate plan (and price-point). For example, a simple telecom service offering might have a value proposition of "ubiquitous connectivity" for the customer. But the provider cannot 'deliver' the value without the instigation of the customer to initiate and use the connection. Value is *only* realized by the end-user as and when they use the subscribed service (e.g., making a mobile call) – "value-in-use". The *'true'* value of telecom service however is determined by the end-users based on their *"perceived" capabilities* of the subscribed service experienced during usage balanced against the *end-user efforts* (or 'burdens') required to use it; *plus* their *end-to-end service relationship experience* with the provider at each contact-point from pre-sales assistance on choosing the 'fit-for-purpose' offering (e.g. mobile rate plan) to post-sales service-provision (activation), and on-going customer care (e.g. service problem resolution, billing inquiries, or prepaid refill) over the life of the service.

Thus, in telecommunications, as in any service business, value is always uniquely and experientially determined by the customer (Edvardsson et al., 2005; Vargo and Lusch, 2008). This observation suggests that service innovation must be concerned with effectiveness of value co-creation between the provider and beneficiary. It recognizes the principle that a proposed value by the provider, in the context of the client, is actually a composite of benefits and burdens (or costs), which can be evaluated using a *customer value equation* (Fitzsimmons and Fitzsimmons, 2007, 69). Burdens relate to the service's usability (or its relative ease-of-integration with the client's resources or activities to *"perform the job the service is hired to do"*) – the more user-friendly it is the less the burden and the greater the user experience. This is akin to the design principle of a software system for the benefits of the end-users. It follows, thus, the most compelling service with the best "value for money" to the client is one that has the largest "benefit-to-costs" ratio. This would suggest that user involvement in co-creating the service offerings (or co-designing the value propositions) with the provider would more likely create 'fit-for-purpose' service for the client and thereby maximizing the benefit. Thus, S-D logic focuses on the service's *effectiveness* in responding to the customer's requirements rather than the *efficiency* of producing the service as espoused by the traditional goods dominant logic.

Service firms must therefore "consider not only the employees' productivity but also the 'productivity' and experience of the customer" (Schneider and Bowen, 1995; Womack and Jones, 2005; Fitzsimmons and Fitzsimmons, 2007; Lusch et al., 2008). From a service system viewpoint, value, created as a result of integrating the provider's resources with the client's, increases the client system's adaptability and survivability to fit with its changing environment (Vargo et al., 2008). According to Normann and Ramirez (1993), a service firm is defined by its *value-*

creating system in which a *constellation of economic actors* (customers, suppliers, business partners and the like) *collaborate* to co-create value. And, the firm's competitive advantage is sustained by its ability to "reconfigure the roles and relationships among this constellation of actors...... to create an ever-improving fit between (enterprise) competencies and customers". This will require the firm to realign its strategy, redesign its business processes and restructure its organization to connect to the customers so as to deliver consistently high-quality service (Karmarkar, 2004).

The above observation in the context of emerging service science principles suggests telecom service innovation needs to address the following requirements:

- Proactive collaboration with the customer to gain insights on the customer's business/lifestyle contexts/objectives, continuous learning of customer experience and the effectiveness of value-in-use, and to co-create new offerings to improve "fit between competences and customer" to deepen relationship and grow market share.
- Collaboration with suppliers, third-party service providers, and partners to identify disruptive technologies, business models to co-create new radical offerings to meet current customers' unserved needs and/or to those of un-addressed market segments.
- Collaboration with the regulatory body and competitors to accelerate the economies of scale for mutual benefits.
- Nurture a continuous learning culture through a seamless feedback loop system to grow the provider's customer knowledge and related core competences and the customer's knowledge of the provider's service offerings.
- A simple service innovation process to accelerate the speed to market of innovative service ideas.

The next three sections will review the current telecom service development process, the telecom service process standard, and the future, next generation networks (NGN), architecture – all in the context of the above service innovation requirements using service science and related concepts.

Telecom Service Development

Telecom services are commonly developed using the *collaborative competence* (Lusch et al., 2007) and *product innovation competence* (Madhavaram and Hunt, 2008) of experts from the marketing, network, IT and customer-care organizations working as a team for the benefit of the customers.

The network provides the technological operant resources with diverse ubiquitous communications capabilities which can be configured *in conjunction* with IT operant resources (business processes and information systems to support service utilization) into innovative service offerings which can be *'provisioned'* (for a price) for the end-user customers to meet their business or lifestyle needs. Telecom network capabilities are co-created[2] (co-configured) often in collaboration with the network technology suppliers, though largely bounded by the software capabilities of the supplier's network equipment. Software enabled application development platform (Reeve et al., 2007) supported by the switching networks allow telecom service providers to collaborate with third-party application developers to offer their digital services over the network services to the provider's customer base using mutually beneficial business models (more detail later).

Marketing uses market and customer insights (competences) to define the desirable telecom service offerings by packaging suitable sets of telecom network capabilities each with a clear value proposition that customers are willing to purchase and use. Customer insights are mainly gained through data mining of vast arrays of voluminous customer data collected in various databases associated with customer contact-points (e.g., customer care centers, network switches, billing systems, etc.).

IT defines and implements the service management business processes with the attendant operations support and business support systems (OSS and BSS respectively) – operant resources – which must be *integrated* (using *technological and collaborative competences*) with the network capabilities to *co-create* the value propositions. OSS and BSS support and enable business to engage the customer over the complete service lifecycle of presales, service fulfillment and activation (upon sales completion), billing and post-sales (quality of service) support. Thus IT implements information systems (OSS and BSS) to provide superior customer service (contribute to *knowledge management competence and customer response capability*); they account for all customer touch-points (hence experience) across the whole service lifecycle, with the exception of in-service usage whose quality is solely determined by network performance (TMF, 2004). The operant resources are all components of the service provider service system, as illustrated in Figure 1.

---

[2] From a service system perspective, this is a value co-creation between the client (telecom service provider or telecom carrier) service system entity and the provider (the equipment supplier) service system entity. Telecom network design and construction activities are often collaboratively performed between the telecom service provider's engineers and the network equipment supplier's engineers. It is their *collaborative competence* that co-creates the new network capabilities (value to the service provider). From a service system standpoint, broadly speaking, this is represented by the integration of the provider's (supplier) 'soft' Intellectual Property (engineers) and 'hard' IP (equipment) operant resources with the client's (telecom carrier) 'soft' IP (engineers) and 'hard' IP (the network to which the new equipment will be integrated). The client's (carrier) *service experience* will be determined by both the actual capabilities (functionality and flexibility etc) of the network equipment *and* the knowledge, technical and social skills of the supplier's engineers – across the whole end-to-end spectrum of network development lifecycle.

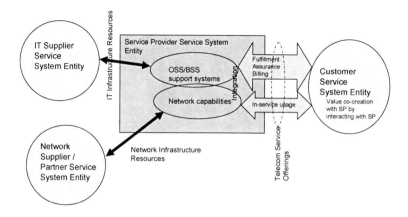

Figure 1. Simplified Telecom Service Systems Model

Customer-care is concerned principally with post-sales support of service fulfillment and activation, billing and other general enquiries and service support. Its key role (e.g. *customer response capability* and *learning platform capability*) is to help the customers resolve usage issues or problems and to use the telecom service effectively so as to fully realize its benefits with pleasant experience. Significant technology investments by service providers are prevalent to ensure speedy and effective customer response, capture customer knowledge and reduce total cost-to-serve through automation and self-service technologies. Despite these investments, customer-care success in terms of customer experience however is still centered on the customer-care agents' interpersonal and technical skills, mindsets and overall service culture (Schneider and Bowen, 1995). The principle of value co-creation (efficient and effective problem resolution with grace and courtesy often under stressful circumstances) with the customer underpins the service culture and end-to-end service process design competence[3], which in turn will contribute to the firm's performance and competitive advantage (Madhavaram and Hunt, 2008).

A telecom service provider's competitive advantage is attained by *its collaborative competence* and *organizational learning capability* to define the *unique way* it can combine its marketing, network, IT and customer care (operant) resources,

---

[3] Plus the above two capabilities plus organizational learning capability and market orientation-innovativeness capability (Madhavaram and Hunt 2008).

the operant resources of their suppliers (network, IT, advertising agency etc.) and those of the government regulatory and competitors to create a diverse range of innovative telecom services for the benefit of its clients and itself.

Telecom Service Process

Telecom Business Process Reference Framework (eTOM)

Service is by nature process-centric (Shostack, 1984; Fitzsimmons and Fitzsimmons, 2007; Lusch et al., 2008). Service firms thus need superior process management competences. The industrialization of service (Levitt, 1976) has advanced to a stage where some business processes are now becoming commoditized and standardized (Davenport, 2005). Outsourcing and offshoring of these non-core business processes to lower-cost service providers have become a common phenomenon. Service firm thus needs an appropriate sourcing strategy to sustain its competitive advantage (Karmarkar, 2004).   Business strategic goals are achieved by meeting the customer needs through a differentiated customer value proposition (Kaplan and Norton, 2004). The customer value proposition defines the *'strategic fit'* criteria for all the enterprise's business processes, systems and intangible assets (Porter, 1985). And, it is the enterprise's internal business processes (business operations) which implement the strategy to "deliver[4]" on the value proposition (Kaplan and Norton, 2004).   Telecom service process is similarly configured to align with the provider's business strategy in order to deliver the provider's distinctive value proposition.

Telecom service creation critically depends on the service designer's understanding of the provider's service process to ensure effective value co-creation accompanied by excellent customer experience. This requires an end-to-end modeling of the provider's operations across all organizational functions. The end-to-end model will ensure seamless linking of inter- and intra-organizational processes which constitute the service process for *effective* value co-creation with the customers – in accordance with their distinctive customer value proposition (Kaplan and Norton, 2004; Anderson et al., 2006). To that end, the telecom industry (TMF, 2004) has specified a standard framework of telecom service provider business processes, known as eTOM (enhanced Telecommunications Operations Map). The eTOM is a generic telecommunications reference framework for categorizing all the business activities that a service provider will use. The reference framework is used by providers to specify firm-specific service processes, and to source commercial-off-the-shelf standards-based OSS/BSS software systems to support and,

---

[4] This term, which is a G-D logic view of customer value proposition, is used by Norton and Kaplan (2004).

where appropriate, automate the specified service processes (business operations). As shown in Figure 2, eTOM has three core process areas:

1. strategy, infrastructure and *product[5]* – it addresses infrastructure and product planning and lifecycle management (associated with development and delivery);
2. operations – it addresses the core of customer (and network) operational management, which is the heart of service provider operational business;
3. enterprise management – it addresses corporate or business support management.

The *former two* core process areas are of primary interest to service design. They are comprised of four functional process blocks representing four *organizational functions*:

- market, product and customer processes – including sales and channel management, marketing management, product and offer management, and customer-facing operational processes (such as service order, problem handling, SLA management and billing);
- service processes – including service development, delivery of service capability, service configuration, and operational processes such as service problem management, quality analysis and rating;
- resource processes – including development and delivery of resource (network and IT) infrastructure, and associated operational management processes such as provisioning, trouble management and performance management;
- supplier/partner processes – including processes for dealing with enterprise's interactions (for service capability co-creation purposes) with suppliers and partners such as supply chain management[6] of product and infrastructure; and operational interfaces with suppliers and partners.

---

[5] Product has been modeled by eTOM as a superordinate to service; that is service arises from, and as a part of, product – a G-D logic worldview (Vargo and Lusch, 2004).

[6] Supply chain is also viewed from a G-D dominant logic perspective.

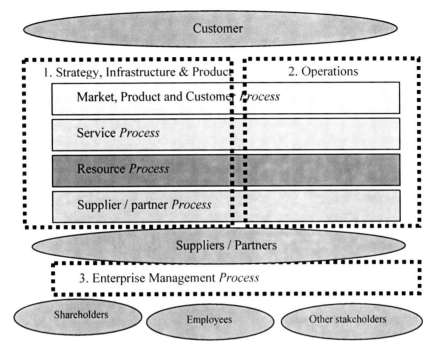

Figure 2. eTOM Framework (source: TMF, 2004)

From a service system modeling perspective (Maglio et al., 2006; Vargo et al., 2008), the service development and delivery processes (within the service process layer) perform the *resource integrator role* (applying the collaborative competence) for the telecom service provider which integrates its own resources (resource process layer) with those sourced (either network, IT resources or third-party products/services) from the suppliers/partners (supplier/partner layer) to co-create service capabilities (i.e. *value* to service provider as the client) that can be made available to the provider's customers. From the provider's *customer perspective*, this is co-creation of service offerings between the provider and its suppliers. This is the service design, development and implementation phase of service/product development lifecycle (left-hand side core process of Figure 2), which is (mostly) invisible[7] to the provider's customers. Once the service is fully tested and launched into production, it is 'managed' by the Operations core process (right-hand side of Figure 2) and its performance becomes highly *visible* to the customers. The service is now available for the customers to access and integrate with their own resources to perform "the jobs" and thus co-create value (with the provider) for themselves.

[7] It becomes visible when the customer is co-opted to collaborate with the provider to co-create the service offering.

End-to-end Customer-centered Telecom Service Processes

Customer experience is a combined result of *what* is offered (i.e. function and outcome of the product or service) and *how* it is offered (i.e. process of usage, context of use, and emotional components of interaction; Patricio et al., 2008). It is represented by the provider's distinctive value proposition to the client (Selden and MacMillan, 2006). Service providers should therefore focus on "designing service settings and orchestrating service clues that enable customers to co-create unique experiences" (Patricio et al., 2008, 320).

To put customer experience in the center of service design, it is important to model the *customer's 'outside-in' view* of the *vertical* end-to-end process, which links the four horizontal core process blocks *contiguously* to support service creation (for provider) and value co-creation (with customer). Four vertical end-to-end processes are particularly relevant to service design: one (as noted above) from the *"strategy, infrastructure and product"* core process – product (service) lifecycle management process; and three from the *"operations"* core process – service fulfillment process, service assurance process, and service billing process (Figure 3). These are core competences or strategic capabilities that the service provider must possess to stay in competition.

The product lifecycle management vertical end-to-end processes are responsible for the definition, planning, design and implementation of all *products* or *services* in the service provider's portfolio. They deliver new products/services or product/service enhancements, and manage products/services to required customer satisfaction and quality commitments (TMF, 2004). As mentioned above, the service provider collaborates with the suppliers and partners to integrate their operant resources (network infrastructure or products/services) to co-create new products/services for the SP's own customers.

Fulfillment vertical end-to-end processes are responsible for value co-creation with the customers by activating the customer-requested services within industry best practice response time. For complex business customer requirements, it provisions the 'fit-for-purpose' solutions using the provider's product/service portfolio. The solutions are co-created with the client as part of the sales contract agreement, using an appropriate client co-creation management process (Bettencourt et al., 2002). The contract will stipulate the service level agreements for service fulfillment, assurance and billing processes. Thus the fulfillment process must keep the customers informed of the status of their service order, and activate the solutions within the contracted timeframe (TMF, 2004). All these activities will be orchestrated by the provider to make easy the efforts required by the customers to integrate the service offerings with their own resources to "do the job" so as to achieve good customer experience.

Assurance vertical end-to-end processes are responsible for ensuring that service performance, such as availability and reliability, satisfies the contracted Service Level Agreement (SLA) or Quality of Service (QoS) performance levels. This is achieved by performing proactive and reactive maintenance activities. They monitor performance and resource status to proactively detect possible failure or identify potential problems and resolve them without impact to the customer (TMF, 2004).

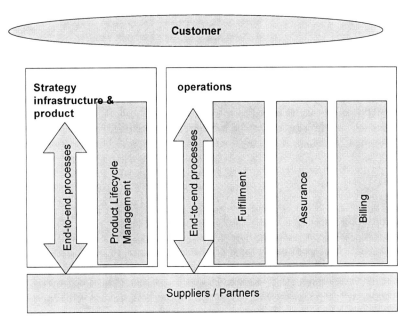

Figure 3. End-to-end Customer-oriented Service Processes (adapted from TMF, 2004)

Billing vertical end-to-end processes are responsible for the collection of appropriate usage records, production of timely and accurate bills, provision of pre-bill use information and billing to customers. They process customer payments and perform payment collections. They handle customer billing inquiries, provide billing inquiry status and resolve billing problems to SLA to ensure high level of customer satisfaction (TMF, 2004).

Telecom Open Service Innovation

While eTOM recognizes the need for managing customer experience, it does not specify how this could be done. Telemanagement Forum (TMF, 2008) has recently initiated a program to manage the end-to-end quality of customer experience for new services, such as Mobile TV, IPTV or Telephone over IP. This program seeks to deliver high quality customer experience over complex value networks. This, in turn, requires cooperating service partners to jointly develop standardized solutions for: (a) measuring customer satisfaction; (b) pinpointing problems across the value network / ecosystem; (c) apportioning payments and maintaining security; and (d) policing service level agreements (TMF, 2008).

Telecom service providers commonly use eTOM as a reference framework to map out their own enterprise-specific end-to-end business processes as part of developing their enterprise architectures which embody and articulate the enterprises' business strategies and business models. The enterprise architecture also takes into account the SP's network strategy towards NGN such that an integrated coherent blueprint for the enterprise's business process and technology directions is articulated to guide capital investment for future growth (Strang, 2005). Target OSS/BSS systems architectures to represent the future state of the SP's business operations are defined, as part of the enterprise architecture, to support and where appropriate automate the end-to-end business processes by functional areas (e.g. fulfillment, assurance, billing, customer relationship management, and so on). The technologies for OSS/BSS are trending toward convergent OSS or BSS system platforms which will support business processes of the same functional area (e.g. billing) for multiple disparate (e.g. fixed and mobile) core networks. OSS/BSS systems functions will be componentized to enable reuse by multiple disparate services, accessible via a service-oriented architecture (SOA) to which the NGN service delivery platform is also connected. Integrating OSS/BSS systems with NGN service delivery platform will increase speed of service development and reduce costs (Strang, 2005; Crane, 2005). These new transformational OSS/BSS systems will be invested and developed in line with the SP's strategic objectives for growth. SPs often collaborate with external resources (IT systems integrators) to undertake the development of these large scale transformational programs (i.e. IT outsourcing). This in turn creates another network of collaborative service systems (Maglio et al., 2006).

In the case of closed, in-house innovation, an innovative telecom service idea is internally conceived, validated, designed and implemented (applying *product innovation competence and technological competence*; Madhavaram and Hunt, 2008) by integrating the requisite set of network capabilities with the OSS/BSS systems that support the end-to-end business processes of fulfillment, assurance and billing (Figure 1). The set of network capabilities is typically configured from the service provider's own resources, having had co-created a priori the network infrastructure with the network suppliers. In this case, innovation can be regarded as internal creative idea + commercialization (Sato, 2008). This IT/network integration allows:

- the network capabilities (what is offered) to be acquired (ordered then activated to put in service) by the customers (end-users);
- in-service quality to be efficiently and effectively assured (proactive monitoring of service quality to ensure continuous availability of service at the required quality of service by rapid resolution of any service problems encountered during service usage); and
- service usage to be accurately and timely billed.

In the case of open innovation through collaboration with third parties, the set could be a result of integration of the service provider's network resources with those of other service providers, suppliers and partners (Figure 4). In this case, the fulfillment, assurance and billing processes and associated OSS/BSS systems must incorporate the third parties' business requirements (based on pre-negotiated contractual business model and service level and quality agreements). Open innovation can be regarded as external disruptive idea + integration (of the idea with SP's resources) + timing (of market launch) + commercialization (Sato, 2008).

In both cases, the customer care agents must be fully trained with both 'what is offered' and 'how should it be offered and supported' to ensure delightful customer experience. This implies that the service/product manager who conceives and is responsible for the commercialization of the service idea together with the service design engineers must have an in-depth understanding of the customer (experience) requirements to make the service (provider's operant resource) easy to integrate with the customer's operant resources to 'to do the job' effectively. That is the service designer must not only be concerned with the service co-creation (with the suppliers/partners) but also the value co-creation with the customers (across all service processes).

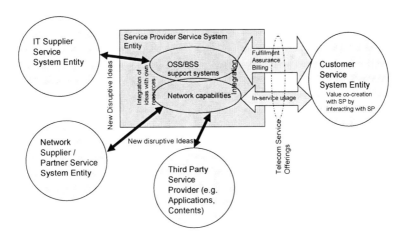

Figure 4. Telecom Service Creation through Open Innovation with Third-party Partners or Service Providers

Bitner et al (2008) observe that "services are fluid, dynamic, and frequently co-created in real time by customers, employees and technology, often with few static physical properties". Haskett et al (2008) have shown that highly satisfied customers drive growth and profitability of service firms. This is achieved by effectively managing the firm's *service-profit chain*: all the links in the firm's operation that affect customer satisfaction. They show that customer satisfaction is directly related to employee satisfaction in value co-creation with the customers. The human factors (from both customer's and employee's perspectives) of customer experience are therefore a critical success factor of service system design. Telecom service system design is likewise concerned with co-creation of memorable customer experience with the customers. The challenge, however, is to model not only the technology or organizational interactions but also the people and their roles as knowledge workers in the service system (Maglio et al., 2006).

Customer experience management requires an end-to-end analysis of service processes that support customer interactions with the service provider. It focuses on managing the customer touch-points with the firm which makes value co-creation with the customers a simple, effective, distinctive and memorable experience – i.e. maximum benefits with minimum efforts from the customer. It requires cross-functional views of value co-creation across the provider organization, with all functional areas focused on co-contributing resources to achieving the same customer experience goal. The end-to-end service delivery process is commonly modeled by *service blueprint* to ensure superior customer experience (Shostack, 1984; Fitzsimmons and Fitzsimmons, 2007, 71; Bitner et al., 2008).

Next-Generation Network

Telecom full-service providers presently offer multiple diverse services to the public using vertically integrated, service-specific *silos* of disparate telecom networks – e.g. public switched telephone network for fixed line service and GSM network for mobile service. The network silos are in turn supported by their own service-specific OSS/BSS support systems. Telecom industry is thus burdened by high operating cost, inflexible service and poor customer experience (Reeve et al., 2007). This shortcoming will be remedied by the Next-Generation Network (NGN) architecture which leads to network convergence (Knightson et al., 2005; Reeve et al., 2007). NGN is designed specifi cally to functionally separate the service layer from transport layer to enable changes in one layer without impacting the other (Figure 5). The transport layer consists of two sub-layers: *core access network* capable of supporting a common access by a multiplicity of diverse set of *end-user devices* (e.g., fixed, wireless or mobile handset, PC, digital TV set-top boxes) at the network edge; and *a single IP core network* layer to provide the ubiquitous end-to-end *transport* connectivity between these devices and between an application or content services (e.g. providing directory or infotainment contents services) and the end-user devices. The NGN service layer also consists of two sub-layers:

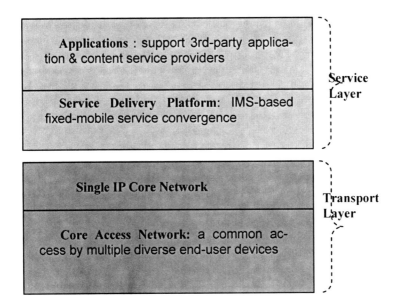

Figure 5. Next Generation Network Architecture

- *Service delivery platform* sub-layer, enabled by Internet Multimedia Sub-system IMS, supports fixed-mobile convergence of services allowing multiple types of services to be available across all networks (Knightson et al., 2005; Crane, 2007). It provides *generic service support capabilities* such as authentication, presence, location to the service provider transparently of the complexity of the underlying networks (Carugi et al., 2005). IMS maintains the registered user profiles, so is user-centric and allows access to multiple disparate services that can be tailored to user preferences (Yahia et al., 2006; Crane, 2007). IMS could be conceptualized as a service system entity with a set of service support capabilities (operant resources) as its components, which themselves could be modeled as service system entities (perhaps at an atomic, service object level).
- *Applications sub-layer* offers the service provider a flexible, efficient and *open* environment to rapidly develop, test and deploy new innovative services by reusing the *'published'* generic service support capabilities of the service delivery platform through open application program interfaces (APIs).

Rapid NGN service provisioning also benefits from the convergence of the IMS-based service execution and eTOM-based OSS/BSS service management *componentized* service frameworks towards *service-oriented architecture* with a common middleware and a common information model across all domains (Crane, 2007; Strang, 2005). Thus the NGN architecture comprises sets of *standardized building blocks* known as *capabilities*. The transport layer is comprised of a set of *basic capabilities* which include network management, routing, network authentication and authorization, accounting, traffic class and priority management (Carugi et al., 2005). The service layer is comprised of *service support capabilities*, which include presence, location, group management, message handling, broadcast/multicast, push, session handling and device management (Carugi et al., 2005). These service capabilities could be conceptualized as components of a service system, each with a well defined service (with an addressable interface as in the object based service model). A new service can be rapidly produced by configuring[8] the selected requisite set of basic and service support capabilities and accompanying componentized OSS/BSS customer-service systems capabilities including the customer interface (Crane, 2005; Strang, 2005).

The *open* application environment of the service layer allows third party service providers *equal* access, subject to authorization and attendant security control, to the same service support capabilities. This creates opportunities for *new business models* and revenue streams for the provider. The provider can now also offer the *"application environment as a service"* to entrepreneurial third-party service providers to create and offer their innovative services to the market using the provider's generic service support capabilities and the underlying network capabilities, under a variety of *negotiated* business models and associated service agreements (Darling and Sauvage, 2005). The third-party service provider becomes both a *customer* (to *co-create* customer value with) and a *partner* (to *co-create* innovative *service offerings* to the market at large) of the service provider. The appropriate OSS/BSS service management components must be selected to make good the value propositions stipulated in the negotiated contractual service agreements. The open application environment also offers the possibility of future extension into a user-friendly simple online (resource configuration) tool to allow telecom end-users to co-produce or personalize their own services (Crane, 2007).

NGN provides a diverse ecosystem of flexible new services from multiple providers with attendant user-defined selective end-to-end quality of service (QoS) across disparate underlying networks to give end-users superior service experience (Reeve et al., 2005). It allows easy access to any service offering by any customer anywhere using any device (either fixed or mobile) subject to authentication and authorization by the service provider (Lee and Knight, 2005).

---

[8] Dynamically configuring 'componentized' capabilities into groups of higher level service capabilities is analogous to Madhavaram and Hunt's (2008) organization of the intangible and dynamic operant resources into composite or interconnected operant resources.

Telecom Service Innovation

Service Innovation Model

From the above review we can synthesize a potential NGN-based next-generation telecom service innovation model as shown in Figure 6. The next-generation telecom service innovation model has three important characteristics:

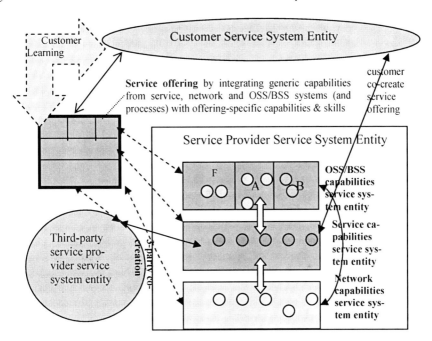

Figure 6. A Proposed Model for Telecom Service Innovation

1. The service provider's enterprise technical architecture define a technology-based componentization of service, network and system (OSS/BSS) capabilities that maximize reuse and enable rapid new service creation through configuration of capabilities. These capabilities (software objects) are easily identified by a standard naming convention, and interconnected via service-oriented architecture (SOA). The network, service, system domains of the provider service system can be conceptualized as individual internal service system entities each containing a *repository* of generic service capabilities (common to all offers) and its attendant technical experts to

maintain the service system entity's sustainability and adaptability with changing business conditions. Each service system entity 'publishes' its clearly defined service offers to the other system entities and interface points through which the service will be offered. These internal service system entities may interact by either 'client-server' or 'peer-to-peer' protocols via SOA middleware at a capability-integration (implementation and production) level or technical document transfer between experts at higher technical design level. The service and network capabilities are as described in the previous section. OSS/BSS capabilities are centred on componentizing the service fulfilment (F), assurance (A) and billing (B) systems, being the three with end-to-end processes that handle customer encounters and thus directly impact customer experience. Service offering is produced by configuring the requisite generic capabilities from the service, network and systems repositories and integrating them with any new capabilities to be developed in either the service layer or OSS/BSS layer for the service offer. The same service creation process will be followed in the case of service offering co-creation with a third-party service provider or with the customer. Thus the service offering shown in Figure 6 could be the output of an in-house innovation, or a collaborative innovation with a third party provider or with the customer.

2. The new service innovation process (common to all offers) requires a high degree of *collaborative competence* (Lusch et al., 2007) to undertake collaborative innovation with third party service providers, suppliers, partners, as well as customers. Service offering co-creation with third party service providers and customers is supported through the service layer. Subject to stringent security control, the repository of generic service capabilities would be made available to these collaborators upon contract agreement. Self-selection of NGN standard-based service and network capabilities by the external party from these repositories would be relatively straight forward compared to those of OSS/BSS, as the latter requires more in-depth knowledge of the provider's service processes. Expert advice by the provider may be necessary.

3. A comprehensive *customer learning* (and research) system and associated competences are institutionalized to increase the provider's understanding of the effectiveness of the co-created value in the context of the customer's resource integration process, and the customer's knowledge of the service offering and associated provider competences so as to maximize the value created for the customer and deepen relationship with superior customer experience.

To successfully exploit this innovation model the telecom service provider requires *market orientation-innovativeness capability* and *product/service innovation competence* (Madhavaram and Hunt, 2008) to configure their operant resources including human intellectual (knowledge and skills), service, network, OSS/BSS systems, distribution channels and other resources in some unique ways that will differentiate their service offerings from the competition. In particular, the service provider creates a *unique service value proposition*, representing the customer experience (Selden and MacMillan, 2006; Patricio et al., 2008), which take into account not only the *"contents"* (the service capabilities[9]) of the offerings but also the "unique way" they *interact*[10] with the service providers in acquiring, using and paying for this service. Thus telecom service providers compete on the basis of the customer experience of the end-to-end service from presales to service usage to post-sales customer care.

Service Innovation Process

Service innovation *competence* is a crucial operant resource for the firm's competitive advantage. Service innovation practice depends critically on a streamlined and flexible process for *internal* and *external* resource coordination and integration to achieve *effective* and *efficient* customer value co-creation. Service innovation process generally (Thomke, 2003; Engel et al., 2006) consists of five phases:

- Create ideas – this phase defines the idea, its scope and business benefits
- Evaluate and select ideas – this phase prioritizes the portfolio of ideas and develops the selected idea into a (low cost low risk) experiment to test its feasibility; go/no go decision is made quickly to speed up the chance of identifying a feasible idea (or conversely the rate of failures of infeasible ideas)
- Plan, design, develop and implement ideas – this phase takes the feasible idea through a rigorous service development lifecycle
- Commercialize the ideas – this phase launches the service
- Review the impacts – this phase reviews the results of the innovation to improve current performance and as a feedback for future process improvement

There are two basic types of service innovation: (a) enhancement for incremental growth; and (b) new growth idea (Anthony et al., 2008), or new service idea that could become a new growth platform (Laurie et al., 2006). The process above is designed for new innovation where success is less certain. Whereas service enhancement has a somewhat more predictable outcome – incremental growth leading to economies of scale – and is managed with an abbreviated process. New service idea once launched will lead to further (continuous) improvement through

---

[9] For instance, a multimedia conference capability that can be established on any device, anywhere and anytime.

[10] For instance, the knowledge and skills and responsive behaviors of the customer care agents and the simplicity and ease of use of the telecom service.

learning with the customers and feedback (review phase) from the value co-creation process. Strategic fit of the new service idea with the core business is also assessed to either scale up or, if mismatch with core as is often the case with a new growth platform whose business model is radically different from the core business (Laurie et al., 2006), to create a separate business (Anthony et al., 2008).

Innovation depends on customer insights and the ingenuity of the service provider to flexibly configure the layered network resources together with the intellectual resources (human and organizational capabilities) to co-create innovative services that meet the customer needs. Innovative ideas could be internally or externally sourced. Internally sourced ideas arise from the service provider's market- and customer-insights. Increasingly, telecom service providers are beginning to adopt open innovation (Reeve et al., 2007; Sato, 2008; Nesse, 2008) by sourcing ideas from suppliers, partners or customers. This remainder of this paper will review the prevailing customer collaboration practices.

Customer Collaboration

As service is always determined by the customer, new creative ideas must be developed from the customer's *outside-in* view (Edvardsson et al., 2007; Payne et al., 2008). Successful firms are co-opting customer involvement in service and value co-creation (Prahalad and Ramaswamy, 2000). Customer involvement in a mobile service design has been found to improve the provider's customer understanding and create more innovative ideas (Magnusson et al., 2003). Customer value creation process is a dynamic, interactive, non-linear and often unconscious process (Payne et al., 2008). Value is in the context of the performance outcome of the customer's *resource integration* practice. For example, the value-in-context of a 3G mobile data service may be different when used as part of the enterprise customer's mobile sales-force resource coordination, from one used as a part of the customer's wireless real-time heart monitoring device linked to the customer's online health-care application managed by the physician. To maximize customer value, the service offer must fit with and improve the customer's resource integration practice. Customer value is determined by the relationship experience arising from the customer's *cognition, emotion* and *behavior* with the service encounters *over a duration* (Payne et al., 2008). These encounters are serviced by the provider's cross-organizational functions (e.g. marketing, sales, activation, assurance, billing and customer care), which must be managed *integratively* to ensure a consistent relationship experience, as exemplified in Figure 1 previously and Figure 6 above. The requisite value proposition, to match the experience requirements, can be co-designed *collaboratively* by the provider with the customer, e.g. using a prototype of the encounter processes calibrated by appropriate performance metrics (ibid). Continuous learning is required by both the customer and the provider from the respective processes of value co-creation. Learning enhances the customer's competence in seamlessly integrating the value proposition with their lives, objectives and aspiration (ibid). Organizational learning about customer's value creation processes deepens customer insights. Organizational learning is a crucial process for nurturing the provider's *collaborative competence* to improve the provider's innovation capability and competitive advantage (Edmondson, 2008).

Service offer co-creation is directly linked to customization (Etgar, 2008). Customization of telecom service solutions to enterprise and wholesale customers' business problems is a common practice. The service process is similar to that IT outsourcing example described in Maglio et al (2009). With the availability of broadband fixed and wireless digital networks and particularly the emergent NGN, direct participation by 'consumer' customers in service offering co-creation is becoming more cost-effective and commercially attractive for both the provider and the customer. Etgar (2008) defines a five stage dynamic model of customer co-creation process towards successful personalization of service: 1) establishment of antecedent conditions for customer to participate; 2) development of motivations or customer benefits; 3) cost-benefit evaluation; 4) activation of co-creation process by choosing the stages of the "production-consumption" activity chain[11]; and 5) evaluation of the effectiveness of the co-creation strategies against the cost-benefit analysis. It is prudent for the provider to institute a continuous learning process with the customer from the co-creation experience to improve their service-usage competence.

The emergence of a digital ecosystem enabled by the NGN capabilities allows telecom service providers to empower online service end-users to co-create service offer and value by offering them easy-to-use tools to interact with the provider and amongst themselves. Blazevic and Lievens (2008) find that in the online world, customers can play three different roles, viz. *passive, active* and *bi-directional creators*, as exchange partners in joint knowledge creation (Vargo and Lusch, 2004). And that each role produces distinctive declarative and procedural knowledge characteristics and a distinctive impact on the three innovation phases of new service ideas *detection, development* and *deployment*. Moreover, knowledge co-creation not only gives the provider the cost advantage but also incorporates solutions for future performance improvements. Finally, Blazevic and Lievens (2008) find that bi-directional dialogs between firm-customer and customer-customer provide contextual knowledge that allows detection of latent customer needs that in turn will contribute to both incremental and radical innovations.

Increasingly, innovative service providers are investing in customer R&D (Selden and MacMillan, 2006) to understand what customers want and create innovation that benefits them. Customer R&D requires the service provider to build a deep relationship with core customers by developing mutually beneficial value propositions that exceed the customers' expectations (ibid). To retain these core customers and acquire new customer segments against the competition, however, the customer value proposition must *'resonate'* with the customer's most critical value requirements (Anderson et al., 2006). This means the provider's key points of differentiation will create the greatest value (compared to the competition) to

---

[11] Adaptation of the G-D logic based model to S-D logic based to fully align with the S-D logic is for future research.

the customer in the foreseeable future (ibid; Lusch et al., 2007). Deep relationship with core customers is sustained by close and constant interaction with customers through customer feedback, proactive service usage monitoring and problem resolution, and overall general customer care. All will contribute to the provider's deep customer insights – a strategic capability. Customer R&D leverages these insights to, on one hand, extend and create new capabilities to serve the unmet needs of the customer; and extend and create new segments to meet the needs of the unserved market (Selden and MacMillan, 2006). Customer R&D enables the service provider to sense and detect shifts in customer needs and potential disruptive capability threats (ibid), for which a timely strategic response can be instituted to retain its competitive market position.

Conclusion

Telecommunications industry is a complex service system. The multidisciplinary nature of telecom service has been shown to resonate well with the emerging service science concepts.

An initial set of requirements for a proposed next-generation telecom service innovation model is derived by viewing telecom service in the context of the emergent service science principles.

In response to these initial requirements, an in-depth review of the industry-standardized telecom business operations, eTOM, the next-generation network (NGN) architecture and advances made by global leading service providers is described using the service science concepts and principle.

The review yields the basic constructs of the proposed next-generation telecom service innovation model, which is *customer-centered,* and comprises three characteristics: (a) service creation by integrating componentized capabilities (operant resources) from three internal service system entities: service, network and OSS/BSS; (b) a simple service innovation process that incorporates collaborative innovation with the suppliers, partners, third-party service providers and customers; (c) an institutionalized customer learning system. The proposed model advocates for *collaborative innovation with customers*, which is not yet well developed in telecommunications industry.

As an initial small step, the paper provides a preliminary review of the challenges and recent advances in customer co-creation of service offerings. More in-depth service science-based research is required to fully develop the proposed telecom service innovation model towards a potential future industry application.

References

Anderson, J. C., Narus, J. A., and van Rossum, W. (2006), Customer Value Propositions in Business Markets, *Harvard Business Review, March, 91 – 99.*

Anthony, S. D., Johnson, M. W., and Sinfield, J. V. (2008), Institutionalizing Innovation, *MIT Sloan Management Review, Vol. 49, No. 2, Winter, 45 – 53.*

Arnould, E. J. (2008), Service-dominant logic and Resource Theory, *Journal of the Academy of Marketing Science, Vol. 36, 21 – 24.*

Bettencourt, L. A., Ostrom, A. L., Broan, S. W., and Roundtree, R. I. (2002), Client Co-Production in Knowledge-Intensive Business Services, *California Management Review, Vol. 44, No. 4, Summer, 100 – 128.*

Bitner, M. J., Ostrom, A. L., and Morgan, F. W. (2008), Service Blueprinting: A Practical technique for Service Innovation, *California Management Review, Vol. 50, No. 3, Spring, 66–94.*

Blazevic, V., and Lievens, A. (2008), Managing Innovation Through Customer Co-produced Knowledge in Electronic Services: An Exploratory Study, *Journal of the Academy of Marketing Science, 36, 138 – 151.*

Boisot, Max H. (1998), *Knowledge Assets: Securing Competitive Advantage in the Information Economy.* Oxford University Press, Oxford, UK.

Bryson, J. R., Daniels, P. W., and Warf, B. (2004), *Service Worlds: People, Organizations, Technologies.* Routledge, London.

Bughin, J., Chui, M., and Johnson, B. (2008), The Next Step in Open Innovation, *The McKinsey Quarterly, July, 1 – 8.*

Carugi, M., Hirschman, B., and Narita, A. (2005), Introduction to the ITU-T NGN Focus Group release 1: target Environment, Services and Capabilities, *IEEE Communications Magazine, October, 42 –48.*

Chase, R. B. (1978), Where Does the Customer Fit in a Service Operation?? *Harvard Business Review, 56 (6), 137 – 142.*

Chesbrough, H. (2003), A Better Way to Innovate, *Harvard Business Review, July, 12 – 13.*

Chesbrough, H. and Spohrer, J. (2006), A Research Manifesto for Services Science, *Communications of the ACM, July, Vol. 49, No. 7, 35 – 40.*

Crane, P. (2007), A New Service Infrastructure Architecture, *BT Technology Journal, Vol. 25, Nos 3 & 4, July/October, 185 – 197.*

Darling, J., and Sauvage, A. (2005), The Application Environment, *BT Technology Journal, Vol. 23, No. 1, 82 – 89.*

Davenport, T. (2005), The coming commoditization of processes. *Harvard Business Review, June, 100–108.*

Den Hertog, P. (2002), Co-producers of innovation: on the role of knowledge-intensive business services in innovation. In Gadrey, J., & Gallouj, F. (Eds). *Productivity, innovation and knowledge in services: New economic & socio-economic approaches.* Edward Elgar Publishing, Cheltenham, UK.

Edmondson, A. C. (2008), The Competitive Imperative of Learning, *Harvard Business Review, July-August, 60 – 67.*

Edvardsson, B., Gustafsson, A., and Enquist, B. (2007), Success Factors in New Service Development and Value Creation through Services. In Spath, D. and Fahnrich, K-P. (Eds), *Advances in Services Innovations. 166 – 183.*

Edvardsson, B., Gustafsson, A., and Roos, I. (2005), Service Portraits in Service Research: A Critical Review, *International Journal of Service Industry Management 16*(1), 107-121.

Engel, J F., Thompson, A M., Nunes, P F., and Linder, J C (2006), Innovation Unbound. *Accenture Publication, Outlook* 2006, No. 1, pp 28-37.

Etgar, M. (2008), A Descriptive Model of the Consumer Co-production Process, *Journal of Academic Marketing Science, 36, 97 – 108.*

Fitzsimmons, J. A. and Fitzsimmons, M. J. (2007), *Service management: Operations, Strategy, Information Technology.* Sixth edition, McGraw-Hill Irwin, New York, NY.

Gadrey, J., and Gallouj, F. (2002), *Productivity, innovation and knowledge in services: New economic & socio-economic approaches.* Edward Elgar Publishing, Cheltenham, UK.

Gallouj, F. (2002), *Innovation in the service economy: The new wealth of nations.* Edward Elgar, Cheltenham, UK.

Haskett, J. L., Jones, T. O., Loveman, G. O., Sasser, W. E., and Schlesinger, L. A. (2008), Putting the Service-Profit Chain to Work, *Harvard Business Review, July-August, 118 – 129.*

Huston, L., and Sakkab, N. (2006), Connect and Develop – Inside Procter and Gamble's New Model for Innovation, *Harvard Business Review, March, 58 – 66.*

IfM and IBM. (2007), *Succeeding through Service Innovation: A Discussion Paper.* Cambridge, United Kingdom: University of Cambridge Institute for Manufacturing. ISBN: 978-1-902546-59-8.

Kaplan, R.S., and Norton, D.P. (2004), *Strategy Maps.* Harvard Business School Press, Boston, MA.

Karmarkar, U. (2004), Will you survive the services revolution? *Harvard Business Review, June, 101 - 107.*

Knightson, K., Morita, N, and Towle, T. (2005), NGN Architecture: Generic Principles, Functional Architecture, and Implementation, *IEEE Communications Magazine, October, 49-56.*

Laurie, D. L., Doz, Y. L., and Sheer, C. P. (2006), Creating new Growth Platforms, *Harvard Business Review, May 2006, 80 – 90.*

Lee, C. S. and Knight, D. (2005), Realization of the Next-generation network, *IEEE Communications Magazine, October, 34 –41.*

Levitt, T. (1976), The Industrialization of Service. *Harvard Business Review.* September-October, 74.

Lusch, R. F., Vargo, S. L., and O'Brien (2007), M. Competing Through Service: Insights from Service Dominant Logic, *Journal of Retailing, January, 83, 5 – 18.*

Lusch, R. F., Vargo, S. L., and Wessels, G. (2008), Towards a Conceptual Foundation of Service Science: Contributions from Service-Dominant Logic, *IBM Systems Journal, Vol 47, No. 1, 5 – 14.*

Madhavaram, S. and Hunt, S. D. (2008), The Service-Dominant Logic and a Hierarchy of Operant Resources: Developing Masterful Operant Resources and Implications for marketing Strategy, *Journal of the Academy of Marketing Science, 36, 67 – 82..*

Maglio, P. P. and Spohrer, J. (2008), Fundamental of Service Science, *Journal of the Academy of Marketing Science, 36, 18 – 20.*

Maglio, P. P., Srinivasan, S., Kreulen, J. T. and Spohrer, J. (2006), Service Systems, Service Scientists, SSME and Innovation, *Communications of the ACM, July, Vol. 49, No. 7, 81-85.*

Maglio, P. P., Vargo, S. L., Caswell, N., Spohrer, J. (2009), The Service System is the Basic Abstraction of Service Science, *Information Systems E-Business Management, Springer Online Publication.*

Magnusson, P. R., Natthing, J., and Kristensson, P. (2003), Managing Use Involvement in Service Innovation, *Journal of Service Research, November, 6, 2; 111 – 124.*

Nesse, P. J. (2008), Open Service Innovation in Telecom Industry – Case Study of Partnership Models enabling 3rd party Development of Novel Mobile Services, *online publication.*

Normann, R. and Ramirez, R. (1993), From value chain to value constellation: Designing interactive strategy. *Harvard Business Review, July – August, 71,* 65 – 77.

Payne, A. F., Storbacka, K., and Frow, P. (2008), Managing the Co-creation of Value, *Journal of the Academy of Marketing Science, 36, 83 – 96.*

Patricio, L., Fisk, R. P., and Cunha, J. F. (2008), Designing Multi-Interface Service Experiences: The Service Experience Blueprint, *Journal of Service Research, 10, May, 318 – 334.*

Porter, M.E. (1985), *Competitive Strategy,* The Free Press, New York, NY.

Prahalad, C.K. and Hamel, G. (1990), The Core Competence of the Corporation, *Harvard Business review, January – February, 68, 79 – 91.*

Prahalad, C. K., and Ramaswamy, V. (2000), Co-opting Customer Competence, *Harvard Business Review, 78 (1), 79 – 87.*

Reeve, M. H., Bilton, C., Holmes, P. E., and Bross, M. (2007), Networks and Systems for BT in the 21st Century, *BT Technology Journal, Vol. 25, Nos 3 & 4, July/October, 181 – 184.*

Sato C. E. Y. (2008), Organizing Innovation in Services: The Case of Telecommunications Next generation Networks (NGN), *Innovation in NGN – Future Network and Services, ITU-T Kaleidoscope Academic Conference, May 12-13.*

Schmenner, R. W. (1986), How Can Service Businesses Survive and Prosper? *Sloan Management Review.* 27(3).

Schneider, B. and David E. B. (1995), *Winning the Service Game.* Harvard Business School Press, Boston, MA.

Selden, L., and MacMillan, I. C. (2006), Manage Customer-Centric Innovation – Systematically, *Harvard Business Review, April, 108 – 116.*

Shostack, L. (1984), Designing Services that Deliver, *Harvard Business Review, Jan-Feb, 133-9).*

Spohrer, J., Maglio, P. P., Bailey, J., and Gruhl, D. (2007), Steps Towards a Science of Service Systems", *IEEE Computer 40, No. 1, 71–77.*

Stalk, G., Evans, P., and Shulman, L. E. (1992), Competing on Capabilities: The new Rules of Corporate Strategy, *Harvard Business review, March-April, 57 – 69.*

Strang, C. J. (2005), *BT Technology Journal, Vol. 23, No. 1, January, 55 – 68.*

Thomke, S. (2003), R&D Comes to Services – Bank of America's Pathbreaking Experiments, *Harvard Business Review, April, 71 – 79.*

TMF (2004), Enhanced Telecom Operations Map (eTOM): The Business Process Framework, *GB921, TeleManagement Forum Approved Version 4.0, March.*

TMF (2008), Customer Experience: e2e Service Quality Management Program – Managing Quality of Customer Experience – Charter, *TeleManagement Forum Version 0.8, September.*

Ulrich, D. and Smallwood, N. (2004), Capitalizing on Capabilities, *Harvard Business review, June, 119 – 127.*

Vargo, S. L. and Lusch, R. F. (2004), Evolving to a New Dominant Logic for Marketing, *Journal of Marketing, Vol. 64, January, 1-17.*

Vargo, S. L. and Lusch, R. F. (2008a), Service-dominant logic: continuing the evolution, *Journal of the Academy of Marketing Science, 36 (Spring), 1-10.*

Vargo, S. L. and Lusch, R. F. (2008b), From Goods to Service(s): Divergences and Convergences of Logics, *Journal of Industrial Marketing Management, 37, 254 – 259.*

Vargo, S. L. and Lusch, R. F. (2008c), Why "Service"?, *Journal of the Academy of Marketing Science, 36 (Spring), 25 – 38.*

Vargo, S. L., Maglio, P. P., and Akaka, M. A. (2008), On Value and Value Co-creation: A Service Systems and Service Logic Perspective, *European Management Journal, 26, 145 – 152.*

Womack, J. P. and Jones, D. T. (2005), Lean Consumption, *Harvard Business Review, March, 58 – 68.*

Yahia, I. G. B., Bertin, E. and Crespi, N. (2006), Next/New Generation Networks Services and Management, *IEEE Xplore.*

Service Engineering

Multiperspective and Interdisciplinary Framework for New Solution Design

Gerhard Gudergan

FIR RWTH

Aachen University

In order to compete in a global economy organizations are forced to regard their worldwide activities as an integrated collaborative activity. In-sourcing supporting capabilities through collaboration with external service suppliers is now crucial to deliver high quality solutions to customers at any time and any place in the world. The aim of this article is to provide a framework which enhances the existing scope of the discipline of service engineering. Existing research shows that industrial services and service based relationships are characterized by complex and unique aspects that require a broader and more comprehensive view on designing service based solutions and establishing the organizational prerequisites for successful innovation with service based solutions. Therefore an integrated framework and understanding of service organization's new service design process and its interactions and interdependencies with the organizational structures is crucial for today's service based solution providers to succeed. An appropriate, framework is illustrated and relevant aspects to enhance the concept of service engineering are proposed.

This research has been made possible with funding provided by the German Bundesministerium fuer Bildung und Forschung (BMBF), grant number 01FD0674.

P.P. Maglio et al. (eds.), *Handbook of Service Science*, Service Science: Research and Innovations in the Service Economy, DOI 10.1007/978-1-4419-1628-0_17,
© Springer Science+Business Media, LLC 2010

Introduction - Industrial transformation towards the economy of solutions

Solutions as unit of exchange in business markets

The importance of the services sector can simply be justified by its sheer weight in the economy. Services account for around 70% of the GDP in developed regions and countries. In Europe, business-related services constitute the largest sector of the economy employing around 55 million persons in 2003 - or nearly 55 % of total employment in the EU market economy. Since business-related services are the dominant part of the European market economy, the sector is important in its own right for the economy.

However, the most important feature of business-related services is that they are present in - and integrated into - every stage of the value adding supply chain. There is a fundamental necessity for the existence of all enterprises, whether in manufacturing or logistics, micro or large enterprise. They are inextricably linked to manufacturing industry.

All goods contain elements of services and their contribution to the value added of any manufactured product often determines its attractiveness to the market. Providing business related services more and more means to solve a customer problem and deliver an individualized solution that is able to substitute a customer process or function rather than just to deliver a single service in a single transaction. For example, the automotive industry uses pre-production services such as design services and research and development, production-related services (such as engineering and IT services), after-production services (transport and distribution services) and financial services and finally other business services such as accounting or legal services. These services are often bundled into an integrated offering which is configured by different tangibles such as capital goods, spare parts and services such as repair services, remote services, joint project management and others. It often ends in lasting relationships which are characterized by collaborative engineering efforts and emotional elements which closely link providers and customers.

The analysis of the service sector shows that the services sector consumes more than half of the output going to intermediate demand from business-related services, compared to a share of less than one-third consumed by manufacturing as shown in the figure below.

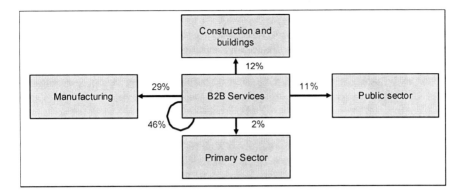

Figure 1. business related services for different economic sectors (Source: European Commission, 2003)

The figure illustrates that besides the service sector by its own, manufacturing industry is an important user of business-related services, as nearly 30 % of the inter mediate output from the sector is consumed by manufacturing companies. Nevertheless, crucial for understanding the growth of business-related services in the last decades is the demand for business-related services created by the sector itself as a consequence of the penetration of these services into the value chain of all enterprises.

Growth of business-related services is usually explained by the migration of employment from manufacturing industry to services due to the outsourcing of the services functions previously produced in-house. The process of externalisation of services functions has been an important driver of the growth in the services sector.

Reasons for the growth are multiple and not just restricted to the ongoing outsourcing practices of business processes: outsourcing decisions are not solely driven by labour costs aspects, but frequently by the need to gain access to specialised skills (quality aspects) in order to increase the demanding companies' effectiveness. Changes in production systems, more flexibility, stronger competition on international markets, the increasing role of ICT and knowledge as well as the emergence of new types of services are other important factors which finally lead to solution based offerings as illustrated in Figure 2.

Providing business related services consequently more and more means to solve a customer problem and deliver an individualized solution that is able to substitute a customer internal process or function rather then just to deliver a single service in a single transaction. For example, the automotive industry requires pre-production services (such as design services and research and development), production-related services (such as maintenance and IT services), after-production services (transport and distribution services) and financial services and finally other business services such as accounting or legal services.

In business to business settings of producing companies, these services are usually integrated into an well coordinated offering which is configured by different tangibles such as capital goods, spare parts and intangibles such as repair services, remote services, joint project management and others (Womack and Jones, 2005; Schuh and Gudergan, 2008). This concept is characterized by its inherent integration within the components and the integration with the customer's processes and systems as well.

It has been well realized that this integration of high quality services, business related services in particular, is crucial for successful differentiation and the competitiveness. Thus, producing companies increasingly link products, parts, after sales services and valued added services such as training, business consulting and engineering services into a integrated solution system as illustrate to successfully differentiate from worldwide competition (Schuh, 2004; Belz, 1997). Founded on the underlying strategy in industrial markets is to substitute the subsequent and single offerings by integrated value adding solutions which lead to lasting relationships to closely link providers and customers.

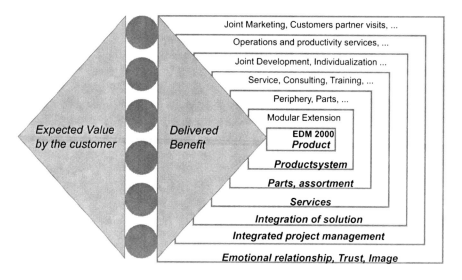

Figure 2. Solution system to deliver value to the customer
(own illustration, based on Belz, 1997)

These often are characterized by collaborative engineering efforts and even link providers and customers on an emotional level. Belz has first introduced the term solution system to describe the integrative character of the solution delivered (Belz, 1997). Companies in the future have to develop and establish solution systems to generate superior value to the customer (Anderson, Narus and Rossu, 2006; Schuh, Firedli and Gebauer, 2004). The corresponding concept is illustrated in the following picture. It should be pointed out, that a solution system is not considered to take place in single transactions but contains and integrates all offerings, processes and interactions which are exchanged between provider and customer within the relationship. This leads to a unique value to the customer of the relationship. A solutions is not understood as a bundle of services due to its integrative character and the real value resulting for a customer organisation is based on this integration and the closely linked relationship between the parties.

Corporate interdisciplinary integration needs

The transformation towards a solution provider however has tremendous impact on the whole company. It is not only important to formulate the appropriate strategy including for successful differentiation, it is the integration of all relevant company activities which has to be achieved: strategy, product definition, marketing concept and the solution design process itself have to aligned and inherently linked. In addition, all organisational structures and the company culture and employee behaviour have to be changed towards a more customer and solution orientated characteristics. E.g. there is a need for decentralised structures which concentrate the relevant competencies where they are needed near the customer.

Figure 3 illustrates the interdisciplinary integration needs and direction as mentioned for four important company activities: differentiation strategy, solution concept and configuration, solution marketing and communication and finally the solution design activity. The integration as illustrated means that all of these activities have to be changed simultaneously towards a solution, customer needs supporting and value driven orientation. This simultaneous shift is the prerequisite to successfully implement a solution orientation within a producing company. An unbalanced change in organisational transformation processes will cause tension and finally the fail of the initiative (Bleicher, 2004).

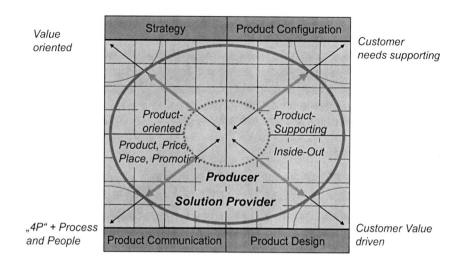

Figure 3. Required integration and orientation of company activities
for successful transformation

We here concentrate on the methodological foundation of the solution design process. Designing solution systems as illustrated in Figure 2 is a challenging task. There are challenges to facilitate the rich interactions and cohesion between the different services or solutions and the customers. There are challenges to ensure flexibility and reconfigurability of services and solutions in processes and structures (Gudergan, 2008). Unfortunately, managers of service organizations are facing tremendous difficulties in meeting these challenges. The high degree of integration and synchronization needed in services and solutions causes complexity which is not understood and generates need for new approaches and perspectives in service research (Chesbrough and Spohrer, 2006). Neither within the structure service based solutions nor in implementing new service processes (Gudergan and Luczak, 2003).

There is first a need for a comprehensive understanding of the nature of solution systems and second a need for systematic design processes. Otherwise, it will not be possible to properly handle the complexity in today's and future service based solutions and relationships.

Customer Value perspective on integrative solutions

Value is an important concept in the management literature for years and is becoming more and more attractive to explain exchange relationships. The term value is used in several very different contexts. From the perspective of managing an organization and is considered to be an important means in order to increase the value of an organization (Woodruff, 1997; Rust, Lemon and Zeithaml, 2004).

From a different point of view, the term customer value takes the perspective of an organization's customers. This perspective considers what customers want and what they believe that they get from buying and using an organizations product or service offering. This perspective is central to the resource based view of strategic management, which considers value to the customer to be the dominate prerequisite to produce a sustainable competitive advantage based on the companies resources and competencies. Only if resources and competencies are used to deliver a solution which is valuable to the customer, these resources and competences can be considered to be of significant relevance for a companies competitive position.

The customer value perspective is coherent with the perspective applied in this paper and existing definitions of integrative offerings of products and services such as the IPS² concept (IPS² Industrial Product Service Systems). In this context, an IPS² are understood as integrated product and service offering that delivers values in different a use and application contexts (see also Baines, 2007).

Value is the underlying concept of solution systems as illustrated in Figure 2. There exists a brought variety of divers definitions of the term customer value. "Customer value is a customer's perceived preference for and evaluation of those product attributes, attribute performances, and consequences arising from use that facilitate (or block) achieving the customer's goals and purposes in use situation" (Woodruff, 1997).

This definition emphasizes the customer perspective of value. It incorporates both desired and perceived value and emphasizes that value originates from customers' perceptions, preferences, and evaluation. It also links together products or services with use situations and related consequences.

Customer value can be classified in several ways (Woodruff, 1997). One possible classification suggests to specify types of value regarding to their contexts within a customer's evaluation process and distinguishes product value, value in use, possession value, and overall value (Woodruff, 1997). Value in use, for example, reflects the use of a product or service in order to achieve a certain goal or set of goals. Hassle free supplier relationships or a proactive services are examples for value in use. Possession value reflects the inherent meaning of the product or service to the customer. For example, value to an industrial customer may be resulting from the rate of return or cost reduction earned on the purchase of a new piece of equipment or on the use of an industrial service. If the cost reduction or revenue enhancements generated by the product or service purchase justify the price, value has been created. This purchase process can be objectively valued. In the case of value in use, this process is subjective, but benefits and costs are still compared so that in industrial settings value for the customer often means the difference between the benefits customers realize from using a product and the costs they incur in finding, acquiring and using it. If the benefits exceed the costs, then a customer will at least consider purchasing a product or service. To increase the understanding of the term customer value the model of three hierarchical levels of value as illustrated in Figure 4 serves as a useful explanation (see also Woodruff, 1997).

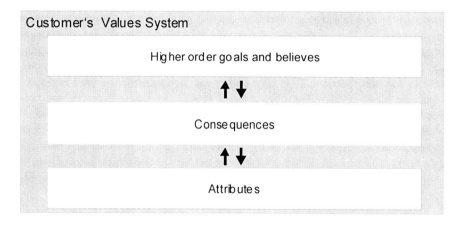

Figure 4. Customer values hierarchy (based on Woodruff, 1997)

The customer value hierarchy as depicted suggests that customers experience value at different levels when they expect a desired value and when they perceive value as well. This hierarchical structuring is important to systematically designing solution systems as illustrated in Figure 2: The structuring i.e., allows to specify requirements for the different elements (tangible or intangible elements) of the solution system in a hierarchical manner and thus allows the application of systematic design approaches as illustrated in this paper.

Service Engineering: Framework for systematic approaches to solution design

Service Engineering framework

Handling complexity in solution design requires frameworks and methods which help to systematize and structure complex tasks into pieces which can be overseen and handled properly. In the following, service engineering is considered to be the scientific discipline and a foundation to solution design. Architecture for services design is introduced as an initial starting point to design service based solutions. This architecture as illustrated comprises steps for successful design and development of services and has been introduced by Gill in 2002 (Gill, 2002).

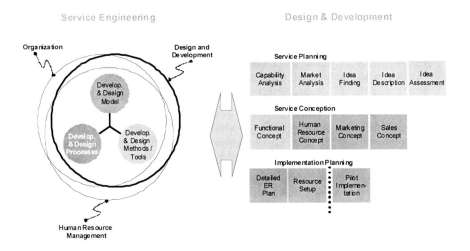

Figure 5. Perspectives of service engineering and phases of the design and development of services

The term Service Engineering becomes more and more prominent in the scientific literature as the discipline covering the development and design of new services (Gustafsson and Johnson, 2003; Bullinger, 2005). Service Engineering can be defined as the engineering discipline which covers the systematic design of services. Service Engineering covers the following perspectives (Luczak and Keith, 2002; Gill, 2002):

- Service engineering as systematic design and development task
- Service engineering as a organizational function
- Service engineering in the context of human resource management.

These perspectives are illustrated in Figure 5. The term "Service Engineering" implicates its basis on engineering knowledge and stems from the assumption that services can be designed and redeveloped in a similar manner as physical products (Cooper and Scott, 1999; Bitran and Pedrosa, 1998; Meyer and DeTore, 1999; Luczak et al., 2000).

Accordingly, engineering procedures, methods and tools build the core of this approach (VDI, 1980; VDI, 1993). Service engineering comprehends what Ramaswamy (1976) established as 'Service Design', but has a wider focus with regard to the breadth of the innovation process and the 3 aspects addressed above. From this point of view, Service Engineering differs to some extent from the related research field of New Service Development (NSD) which also deals with the issues of how to develop new service products (Easingwood, 1986; Bowess, 1989; Scheuing and Johnson, 1989; Edvardsson and Olsson, 1996; Sundbo, 1997; Edvardsson et al., 2000). NSD has its roots in service quality research. Quality is said to strongly contribute to the understanding of the service logic and the drivers of customer satisfaction (Parasuraman et al., 1988). In contrast to Service Engineering, NSD in many cases has addressed consumer services rather than business-to-business (B2B) services and approaches the issues of service innovation from a marketing perspective (Johne and Storey, 1998).

Within Service Engineering the process of service design and development consists of three major phases, namely the service planning, service conception and service implementation planning as shown in Figure 5 (Luczak et al., 2003). The first phase, service planning, is centered on idea generation, forming and evaluation. During the subsequent phase, service conception, these ideas become more precise regarding content, so that in the end of this phase the service is ready to launch.

The design and development perspective

The design and development perspective of service engineering as illustrated in Figure 5 covers the phase model of the service engineering process and the architecture of service engineering as first introduced by Gill (Gill, 2004). The process model of service engineering supports in structuring the different design and development tasks in a timely manner. The overall process is organized into three sub processes: service planning, service conception and implementation planning. In the following the planning phase will be described in detail. The architecture structures the overall service engineering task while linking tasks with the methods and tools required performing the tasks.

The phase of service planning starts with a systematic idea generation. The use of the contradictory expressions "Systematic generation" and "idea" might cause confusion. Certainly, the search for ideas can only be supported by systematic approaches; however it can not be systematized in the sense of an automatic generation. Generating ideas will always remain a creative process.

Depending on the size and the strategic goals of a company, the idea generation might have different focuses. One can distinguish the resource-oriented and the market-oriented idea generation (Luczak et al., 2000). The starting point of a resource-oriented idea generation is a firms set of capabilities and new possibilities to utilize them. During the planning process this input focus moves to the needs of the market.

In the B2B sector these needs are mainly determined by the customer problems in the sense of services being a problem solution as illustrated in the introduction of this paper. The market-oriented approach starts with the analysis of market opportunities and customer problems as source for ideas and subsequently takes necessary capabilities and resources into account (Luczak et al., 2000; Luczak et al., 2003). An adequate method, which brings both mentioned aspects together, is the policy deployment (Alyao, 1991). In any case, both the company's core capabilities and customer problems serve as seed crystal for an idea generation. The main criterion for identifying and selecting core capabilities is their potential to redound to the company's sustainable competitive advantage. According to Barney (1991) this is the case if the resources are rare, valuable and can neither be imitated nor substituted. A Value Chain Analysis helps to gather these input data (Sontow, 2000). Result of the analysis with respect to the Barney criteria is a catalogue of sustainable and superior core capabilities and underlying resources.

For gathering customer problems internal as well as external information sources can serve as input. Departments with a high degree of interaction with the customer, i.e., sales or after-sales service, usually have huge amounts of information about customer problems and customer needs. Even if this knowledge is rarely documented it can be processed by means of workshops and other kinds of interpersonal interaction and linkages.

Especially for professional services business relations and interactions with customers are close and intimate. Thus, customer visits and interviews provide with another valuable source to problem analyses. Goal of this analysis of customer problems is to gain a deeper understanding of what the problems are, what effects they have and how new service based solutions can solve customer problems.

By bringing sustainable competitive capabilities and problems (what?) together with the help of Interdependence Analysis method, the creation of ideas (how?) takes place systematically. Thus, combinations of sustainable competitive capabilities that highly contribute to the solution of a severe customer problem build an attractive basis for a service idea. The actual creation of an idea, again, is a matter of creativity suitably assisted by creativity techniques like Brainstorming, Mind-Mapping or the 6-3-5 Method. The description of the addressed customer problems, the necessary capabilities and resources and a rough description of the solution process together build the service idea and conclude the phase of service planning.

An architecture for service concept development

Service engineering architecture components

The architecture of service engineering as illustrated in the following figure structures the overall service engineering task while linking tasks with the methods and tools required performing the tasks (Gill, 2004). The architecture as shown in Figure 6 consists of five essential components for designing and developing business related services:

The Service Development Process Model (SDPM) comprises development steps that are necessary to determine requirements and to form the functions and processes that fulfill these requirements. This model also contains steps to identify the skills and resources that are essential to perform these processes profession-ally. The steps included in the SDPM will be described in detail in the following sections.

The architecture component Service Development Methods (SDMe) comprises methods that enable a systematic approach to the development targets. Which methods are suited to support the design and development will also be shown in depth in the subsequent sections.

The architecture component Service Development Tools (SDTo) contains only tools that directly support distinct methods. In the understanding of this architec-ture, the tools of the SDTo operationalize the methods of the SDMe.

The Service Development Result Description Model (SDRDM) documents the specific outcome of design and development steps as well as of the service work itself. Thereby, this model builds a common understanding among the design and development team members at the same time. The SDRDM combines functional and graphical aspects of the representation of development results.

The Service Development Management Model (SDMM) integrates the four other components. The SDMM connects the development steps of the SDPM with the methods and tools of the SDMe and SDTo respectively in order to achieve the development result represented in the SDRDM.

To keep the complexity of a development project as low as possible, it is not useful to construct the service in detail from the start. Instead, the development can be stated in such a way, that the requirements for the service system are im-plemented first in a general concept. Afterwards, the general concept can be di-vided into components. The determined characteristics of the general concept re-sult in requirements for those components.

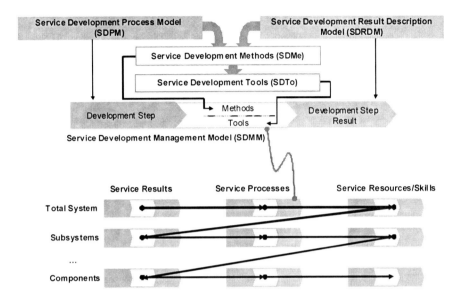

Figure 6. Architecture for service engineering: essential components
(Source: Gill, 2004; Luczak and Gill, 2003)

Each component can then be considered independently. This procedure of specifying concepts into partial concepts and their subsequent configuration can be continued at all levels of detail in the same way. An appropriate method to detail a service system is the Function Tree Analysis under consideration of Suh's axiomatic design. Suh states that one can only detail a function tree with the embodying concept in mind (Akiyama, 1991; Suh, 1990).

Based on the essential characteristics of professional services the architecture itself is divided into three partial models with regard to the characteristic elements of services: results, processes and resources. The partial models are intimately connected in the sense of means-end relationships. Since results are generated by a set of processes, which still has to be specified, a determined service result implies requirements for the service processes. Hence, service processes are means which generate predetermined results. The processes in turn necessitate resources for their implementation. For this reason processes and resources represent a means end relationship. Therefore, a complete service concept always contains a result concept, a process concept and a resources concept.

The service result branch of the architecture

This partial model of the architecture comprises activities to incorporate the external requirements of customers as well as the internal requirements; to check their plausibility, to prioritize and to detail them. The result branch and the corresponding methods are illustrated in the following three figures.

The first step on this level is the investigation into the customer and company requirements. It is recommended to employ the Advanced Sequential Incident Method (Parasuraman et al., 1988; Kamiske, 1997). In this method individual process steps are identified along the chronological course of the service creation on a level, at which customers and suppliers have direct contact. In the following development step "plausibility analysis of the service requirements" requirements from the perspective of customers and the company are brought together and analyzed with respect to their plausibility.

The Qualitative Interdependence Analysis is employed to show the mutual dependence between requirements which are regarded as coequal by analyzing the reactions of the elements to changes in one element (Clausing, 1994; Schütze, 2001). For this purpose the requirements for the service from the perspective of the customer are confronted and compared with those from the perspective of the company in a matrix.

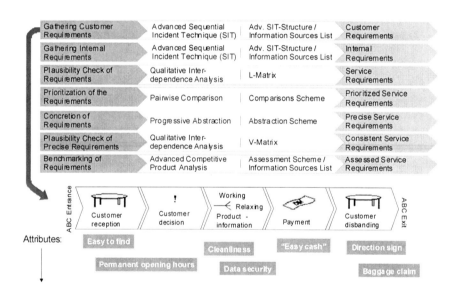

Figure 7. The result branch of the service engineering architecture part 1

Criteria for the Qualitative Interdependence Analysis are "target-neutrality", "target-harmony" and "target-conflict". The results of this development step are consistent service requirements from the perspective of customers and the company.

As a next step, the service requirements are prioritized from the customer perspective with respect to their impact on the success of the service. The Pair wise

Comparison has been identified as a suitable method for this prioritization (Eversheim et al., 2002). For this purpose the service requirements are confronted with each other and two at a time are compared. Finally, a ranking order of the service requirements based on the sum of the lines in the matrix can be constituted.

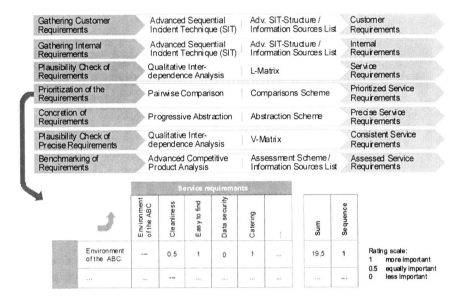

Figure 8. The result branch of the service engineering architecture part 2

In the development step "concretion of the service requirements" the method of Progressive Abstraction is used in the architecture. With the Progressive Abstraction the requirements in terms of their benefit of use are edited and the levels of measures are revealed which contribute to a large extent to the achieved objectives of the development (Botschen and Mühlbacher, 1998). The results are requirement-solution combinations, which are more exact and more precise than the originally formulated requirements.

Since service requirements could have changed while implementing the Progressive Abstraction, a new Plausibility Analysis has to be conducted. In the last step within the result section of the service development architecture the processed requirements are compared with the characteristics of services already available on the market. For this evaluation, the Advanced Competitive Product Analyses has been identified as a suitable method (Hildebrandt and Klapper, 2000). For this purpose it is first necessary to identify competitive services. Integrating aspects of customer expectation into the evaluation enlarges the perspective towards a rival service. The criteria used for this are the characteristics "must-be requirements", "revealed requirements" and "exiting requirements", introduced by Kano (1984).

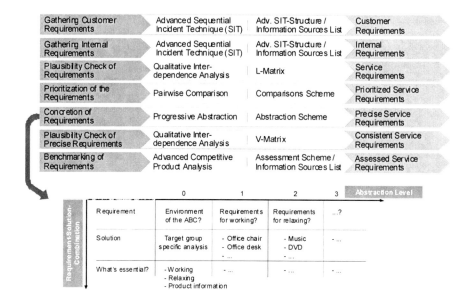

Gathering Customer Requirements	Advanced Sequential Incident Technique (SIT)	Adv. SIT-Structure / Information Sources List	Customer Requirements
Gathering Internal Requirements	Advanced Sequential Incident Technique (SIT)	Adv. SIT-Structure / Information Sources List	Internal Requirements
Plausibility Check of Requirements	Qualitative Inter- dependence Analysis	L-Matrix	Service Requirements
Prioritization of the Requirements	Pairwise Comparison	Comparisons Scheme	Prioritized Service Requirements
Concretion of Requirements	Progressive Abstraction	Abstraction Scheme	Precise Service Requirements
Plausibility Check of Precise Requirements	Qualitative Inter- dependence Analysis	V-Matrix	Consistent Service Requirements
Benchmarking of Requirements	Advanced Competitive Product Analysis	Assessment Scheme / Information Sources List	Assessed Service Requirements

Abstraction Level

		0	1	2	3
Requirement		Environment of the ABC?	Requirements for working?	Requirements for relaxing?	...?
Solution		Target group specific analysis	- Office chair - Office desk - ...	- Music - DVD - ...	- ...
What's essential?		- Working - Relaxing - Product information	- ...	- ...	- ...

Figure 9. The result branch of the service engineering architecture part 3

As an evaluation criterion for the degree of performance by the rival product the ordinal rating scale "better performance" and "worse performance" is used respectively. The objective is the design of marketable services. Therefore, specifications of the requirements have to be undertaken as long as the sum of the revealed and exiting requirements, which are already fulfilled by the competitive service, is smaller than the one of the service to be developed. No further design should be considered in case this measure could not be achieved. Otherwise this section of the architecture "determination of the service result" is completed.

The service process branch of the architecture

Starting from the service requirements, the respective tasks are identified and defined. The leading question for this task can be formulated as follows: "How can the individual service requirements be implemented?" After having found implementation methods for each requirement, the requirements are summarized hierarchically with the help of Transfer Graphs as a tool of the Affinity Method (Schaude, 1992). The results of using this method are hierarchically structured service tasks, which are deduced from the requirements. The process branch of the architecture is illustrated in the following Figure 10, Figure 11, and Figure 15.

In the next step the service tasks have to be analyzed with respect to their type. By allocating the service tasks to the types "overall task, "primary task" and "secondary task" distinctions can be made. The overall task shall be defined as to meet a maximum amount of service requirements the customer is willing to pay for. The primary task fulfils at least one service requirement and can also be priced.

Although a secondary task must also fulfill at least one requirement functionally the customer is often not willing to pay for that. In order to benefit from synergies, an alignment of service tasks, which are already implemented, and the service to be developed need to be conducted. For this purpose the Interdependence Analysis is again a suitable method. Therefore, all primary service tasks should be evaluated by an ordinal rating scale, which distinguishes target is covered by existing task" and "target is not covered by existing task" respectively.

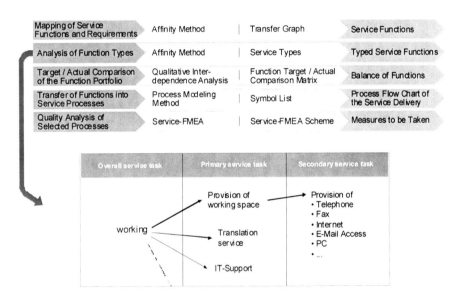

Figure 10. The process branch of the service engineering architecture part 1

In the following development step "transfer of service tasks into service delivery processes" those primary service tasks, which are necessary to fulfill the customer requirements, are further detailed by a Process Modeling Method. As a supporting tool for this the Service Blueprinting of Shostack (1984) has been identified. The Service Blueprinting is a flow chart particularly for the service delivery process, which distinguishes several ways of customer interaction and visually separates them by so called lines-of-visibility. The customer section contains only processes the customer is directly involved in. The onstage processes are visible to the customers but they do not take an active part in it. The third section of the process flow chart comprises the backstage activities that are entirely performed by the employees without any contact to the customer. With this differentiation the service delivery processes can be adjusted with respect to performance reproducibility (Fitzsimmons, J. A. and M. J. Fitzsimmons, (2007).

For a detailed analysis of potential risks associated with service delivery processes, the application of the Service-FMEA (Failure Mode and Effects Analysis) is implemented into the architecture. Using the Service-FMEA in a first step, potential failures linked to the process steps are determined and rated on a 1 - 10 scale with respect to their severity (S) and their detectability (d) (DIN, 1990; Eversheim, 2000).

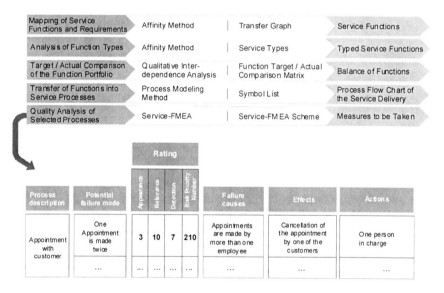

Figure 11. The process branch of the service engineering architecture part 3

For processes with direct customer interaction as ascertained in the Service Blueprinting the detectability is irrelevant since there is no chance to prevent the customer from experiencing the failure. Afterwards, the causes of each potential failure need to be discovered and evaluated with regard to their probability of occurrence on a 1 - 10 scale as well. Subsequently these three values of severity, occurrence and detectability, if applicable, are multiplied.

The result is the so called Risk Priority Number (RPN), which identifies the greatest areas of concern and indicates what kind of corrective actions should be taken. Particularly, preventive measures can be taken, which helps to avoid cost intensive failures before they might occur. Once the development steps for all identified primary service tasks have been undertaken the development of the service delivery concept is complete.

The service skills and resources branch of the architecture

This partial model of the architecture helps to develop a concept for the essential service resources. The skills, which are necessary to perform the identified service tasks and service processes, are identified first with the help of the Affinity Method and hierarchically structured by means of a Transfer Graph. The result of this development step is a target skills profile, which should be understood as the sum of skills necessary to deliver the service. The skills and resource branch of the architecture is illustrated in the following Figure 12, Figure 13 and Figure 16.

Afterwards, the individual skills are analyzed regarding to their type: professional competence, social competence, personality competence and method competence can be distinguished. Besides the allocation of the identified skills to these types, a qualitative evaluation with regard to the marks "no competence necessary", "basic understanding necessary", "first practical experience and advanced understanding necessary" as well as "management, practical experience and distinct understanding necessary" is conducted.

In order to benefit from synergies a target/actual comparison should be conducted with the skills, which are already available throughout the company and the determined skill profile. A suitable method for this is again the Interdependence Analysis.

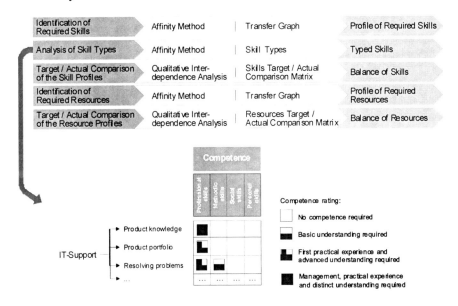

Figure 12. The service skills and resources branch of the architecture part 1

Subsequently, the key resources related to the skills for the Service delivery have to be identified with the help of the Affinity Method. It is important to find as many resources as possible, which embody the required skills. A Transfer Graph is again an adequate tool for the structuring.

Afterwards, a target/actual comparison is conducted between those resources that are necessary for the Service delivery and those that are already available throughout the company. Again, an adequate method is the Interdependency Analysis with an ordinal rating scale of "target is covered by existing resources" and "target is not covered by existing resources" respectively. In case of resource coverage or a resource excess, the service which should be developed can be generated with the already available resources of the company. In case of a resource deficit the corresponding resources have to be obtained.

When the development steps for the identified competencies and resources are finished, the development of a potential conforming service provision concept is completed.

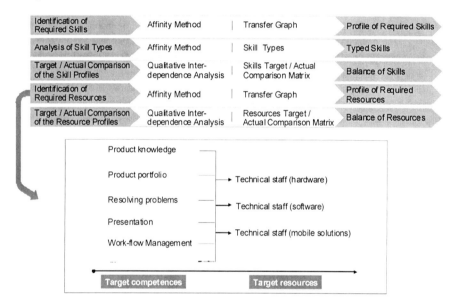

Figure 13. The service skills and resources branch of the architecture part 3

Service engineering framework and architecture application potential for solution engineering

Integrative industrial solutions such as delivering a comprehensive assembling line are more complex in their nature than single services and thus require an even more structured and systematic approach for their development or engineering. In the following we illustrate how the framework and architecture as presented can be used to systematically develop solution systems. We here take an example from the capital goods industries, which is a company delivering assembling system, as turnkey solutions and offering the operation as well. The solution delivered by the company can be best described with the term "assembling capability". The company designs and produces complex assembling systems, i.e., for the automotive industry. The unique capability of the company is to design the assembling systems based on a physical model or digital model of the part to assemble. The company then fully integrates the assembling systems into the customer's production processes. The company offers leasing arrangements for their solutions and different service contracts including the operation of the assembling system at the customer's site. Challenges the company has to overcome are illustrated in the following figure.

Design of solution portfolio and system	Design of engineering process for hybrid solutions
Design of organizational structure for solution delivery	Design of change management towards solution orientated behavior

Figure 14. The potential to apply service engineering framework and architecture: producing company transformation

One major challenge when designing a solution as described is to exactly specify the behavioural skills needed to successfully implement the solution concept into practice. Employees need very specific skills, in particular when the solution as described here is i.e., operated at the customer's site. Employees then need specific communication or language skills. As illustrated in the following figure, the architecture supports to systematically identify the adequate method to identify a skill profile for the service technician.

Another challenge when designing solutions such as the described assembling system is to design the required flows of activities and communication. Solutions as illustrated often require remote service concepts which require complex interaction and communication flows between the customer's site and provider's site. At the provider's site, processes have to be handled with customer interaction or by the back-office employees.

Designing the process and communication structure requires methods and tools which allow structuring and systematic drawing. The figure illustrates how the architecture supports to identify the right methods and tools to design process and communication flows. Both examples for application of the service engineering framework and architecture demonstrate that both, the framework and architecture, can support the engineering of complex solution systems.

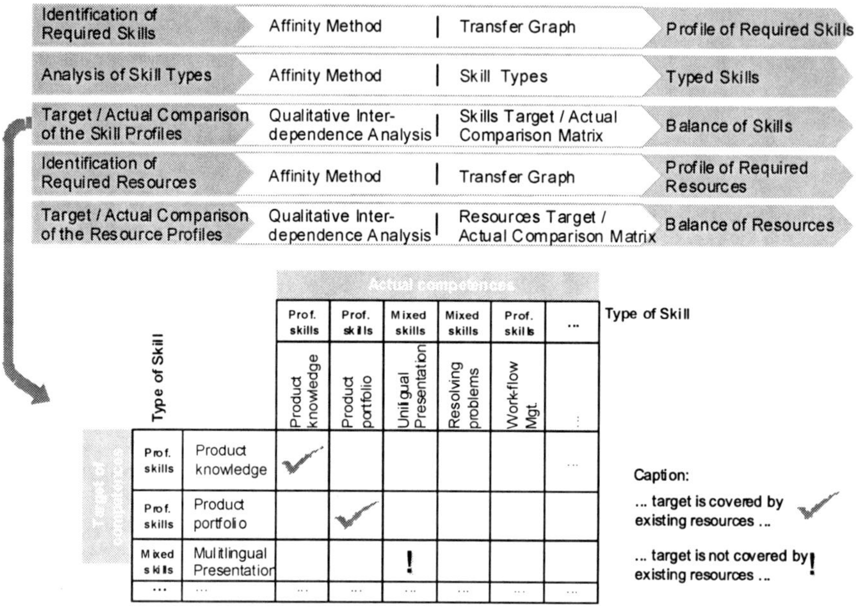

Figure 15. Architecture of service engineering to develop a skill profile in the conception phase (skills and resources branch of the architecture part 2)

The main contribution is to reduce the complexity in engineering complex solutions as the architecture supports structuring the associated planning and design steps for the single components which are put together into the overall solution after their design. In addition, the architecture contributes with the suitable methods and tools to design the single services of the overall solution system.

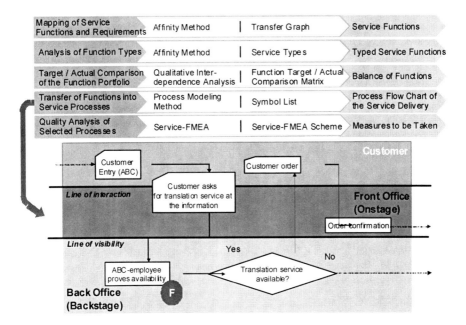

Mapping of Service Functions and Requirements	Affinity Method	Transfer Graph	Service Functions
Analysis of Function Types	Affinity Method	Service Types	Typed Service Functions
Target / Actual Comparison of the Function Portfolio	Qualitative Inter-dependence Analysis	Function Target / Actual Comparison Matrix	Balance of Functions
Transfer of Functions into Service Processes	Process Modeling Method	Symbol List	Process Flow Chart of the Service Delivery
Quality Analysis of Selected Processes	Service-FMEA	Service-FMEA Scheme	Measures to be Taken

Figure 16. Application of service engineering architecture to identify methods and tools to designing process and communication flows (process branch of the architecture part 2)

Organizational perspective: The transition of producing companies

Impact of the organizational structure on innovation

From the methodological perspective the complexity of designing services per se and the overall solution system can be handled with the methodological framework as illustrated. The question arises how companies can make use of the planning procedures and methods as illustrated and introduced here in the development architecture to successfully implement a service or solution engineering into organizational practice.

Having the methods and tools at hand in a structured way cannot be considered the only success factor to implement the engineering of services or solutions. Organizational integration of the planning steps is the second factor needed to successfully integrate service and solution engineering into the company. The organizational design literature proposes strong linkages between organizational design variables and innovation capability.

The question is how the illustrated methodological framework of service and solution engineering can be implemented into organizational structures that allow to make use of service engineering as a planning concept and to include the creative potential of the organization to come up with new, innovative solutions which consist of a configuration of different services and service components which deliver value to existing or new customers.

In the following a concept is illustrated which aims to answer the question how service planning as suggested by service engineering and facilitated by the architecture as described can be successfully linked with structural elements of a service organization to come up with innovative solutions as introduced in the beginning of this paper.

As introduced the term service engineering accounts to the systematic development of new services including corporate integration and resource development. Based on this view it seems to be helpful to align to innovation research to more in depth link service engineering with organizational structures and finally analyze how structural components are linked to planning procedures as introduced here.

The term of innovation has a broad use, but nevertheless, the constitutive character of innovation is the novelty which means that a product or service is considered to be new for a customer (Macharzina, 1995). Schumpeter differentiates between invention (the creative mental conception of an idea) and innovation (the successful implementation of an idea) (Schumpeter, 1912; Fischer, 1982). In this context innovations can refer to new products and services and to internal aspects of the organization (Tuominen and Myvönen, 2005).

The organizational structure is considered as one of the most important factors for the innovation ability of enterprises (Osterloh, 1993). Since the studies of Burns and Stalker, who in 1961 differentiated the organization into mechanistic and organic forms, the economical literature sees the innovation ability of an organization in dependence of its organizational design.

New studies derive that team based lateral coordination and the application of planning instruments and systems have — beside culture — the biggest and most significant impact on the ability to develop new solutions in industrial service organizations (Gudergan, 2008). Thus, an increased attention must given to this variables when successfully developing and implementation new service based solutions systems. Appropriate planning systems for service based solutions have to be designed and advantages of these have to be combined with the advantages of the lateral coordination achieved by team and project structures. The first aspect has been illustrated in the service engineering section of this paper. The second aspect — the connection of planning procedures in services with an integrated organizational structure — is illustrated in the following.

Organizational architecture for new solutions

The architecture of service engineering as described provides a rich and comprehensive set of methods and tools to develop new services. The architecture is based on findings and research in the area of business related services which are provided to solve an often complex and comprehensive customer problem with an adequate service based solution. Planning and conception of new services is supported by the architecture in a structured and systematic fashion.

Taking into account the empirical results on organizational success factors for new solution development, the integration of both aspects — systematic development and integration of planning procedures with teams — within an interdisciplinary framework — seems to be a promising approach to make companies more successful when developing new, service based solutions. The resulting organizational concept is introduced in the following.

The following outlines the underlying logic of the SERDUCT concept which are based on the findings of Gudergan 2008; Luczak and Gudergan, 2009). Empirical results as described imply to combine the positive effects of team based structures with planning instruments and systems. The underlying logic is that both variables are synergetic in their effects on a company's ability to develop new solutions. This implies to connect structures which are based on democratic decision making with adoptable and planning procedures and systems in a way that decisions can be made in flexible structures but based on profound information provided. This requires distributing information stored in planning systems and transformed in planning procedures into team based structures. Second, team based structures are required which are dedicated to take part in different planning steps and thereby are involved into the overall planning procedure.

This form of connecting planning procedures with team based structures combines hierarchical elements of organizations with democratic, flexible elements and would allow to take advantage of both. Taking the Service Engineering procedure as illustrated in the first figure as a systematic task the SERDUCT concept of organizational integration in new solution development is illustrated in the following figure (Figure 17).

The proposed structure highlights two aspects: The one is on the informed design of team based structures in solution design and the other is to more formalized team based work itself. According to the SERDUCT logic, team based structures need for a certain degree of formalism in order to interlink with planning procedures which are installed to support cross functional work and decisions. SERDUCT thus contributes to the need for a better integration of democratic, team based structures with bureaucratic structures (Schreyögg, 2006, 197). It has be pointed out that the SERDUCT concept as introduced here has to be differentiated from the concept introduced by Likert who is focusing on multiple, overlapping groups over hierarchical levels. SERDUCT is explicitly focusing on the integration of team based structures with planning procedures and systems to support service based solution development.

The concept as introduced is embedded in a company culture which is characterized by shared values and believes shared mindsets and a sense of positive critics. Thus, the SERDUCT concept basically is near to the concept of heterarchical organizational forms. However, the SERDUCT concept as introduced here differentiated in the way that is more formalized and that this is a strong integration with planning procedures and systems. The concept integrates cross hierarchical and cross functional team members into a team based structure which is interactively linked with different stages of systematic planning procedures.

The concept systematically integrates Service Engineering planning and conception procedures with team structures. The service engineering process provides the guiding structure for task execution. Team members get access to methods and instruments provided for service engineering and structured in the service engineering architecture as described in this paper.

The SERDUCT concept allows team members to get access to methods and tools as they are required for the engineering tasks. As the empirical analyses shows assembling the teams from different functional departments finally leads to an organizational capability to designing customer orientated and integrative solutions rather than just single services.

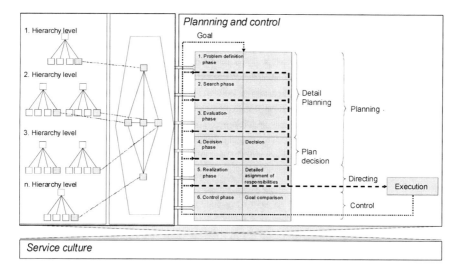

Figure 17. The SERDUCT concept for integrated service-product solution development

Summary

The aim of this article is to provide a new multiperspective and interdisciplinary framework which enhances the existing scope of the discipline of service engineering. Existing research shows that industrial services and service based relationships are characterized by complex and unique aspects that require a broader and more comprehensive view on designing service based solutions and establishing the organizational prerequisites for successful innovation with service based solutions. Therefore an integrated framework and understanding of service organization's new service design process and its interactions and interdependencies with the organizational structures is crucial for today's service based solution providers. An appropriate framework is illustrated and relevant aspects to enhance the concept of service engineering are proposed.

The discipline of service engineering is enhanced accordingly by first specifically addressing two relevant perspectives on service engineering – the methodological design and development perspective and the organizational perspective and second integrating these into one integrative framework. The SERDUCT concept is introduced which allows integrating the three perspectives. Two aspects provide the foundation of the concept introduced here: Service Engineering is considered to originate from engineering and design theory and the discipline of Service Engineering provides processes and architecture for the systematic planning of solutions in a business to business context. Organizational design theory provides evidence that an informed integration of planning procedures with cross functional team based structures is a prerequisite for the successful development of new solutions. Both aspects integrated lead to the concept introduced here: The SERDUCT concept for solution design.

References

Anderson, J. C., Narus, J. A., and van Rossu,W. (2006) Customer Value Propositions in Business Markets. *Harvard Business Review*. Spring, 90-99.

Baines et al. (2007) State-of-the-art in product-service systems. *JEM. Proc. IMechE* Vol. 221 Part B: J. Engineering Manufacture

Barney, J. (1991) Firm Resources and Sustained Competitive Advantage *Journal of Management*, 17(1), 99-120.

Bitran, G., and Pedrosa, L. (1998) A Structured product development perspective for service operations, *European Management Journal*, 16(2), 169- 189.

Botschen, G., and Mühlbacher, H. (1998) Zielgruppenprogramm – Zielgruppen-orientierung durch Nutzensegmentierung (Target groups program - Targeting groups by benefit segmentation) In A. Meyer (Eds,) Handbuch Dienstleistungs-Marketing, I . Stuttgart: Schäffer-Poeschel, 681-692.

Bowers, M. (1989) Developing new services: Improving the process makes it better, *Journal of Services industries*, 15-20.

414 G. Gudergan

Chesbrough, H., and Spohrer, J. (2006) A research manifesto for services science. *Communications of the ACM*. 49(7), 35-40.

Clausing, D. (1994) *Total Quality Development A Step - By - Step Guide to World - class Concurrent Engineering*, New York: ASME.

Cooper, R. G. and Edgett, S. J. (1999) *Product Development for the Service Sector: Lessons from Market Leaders*. Cambridge, MA: Basic Books.

DIN (1990) Ausfalleffektanalyse (Fehler-Möglichkeits und Einfluss-Analyse), (Failure Mode and Effects Analysis) Berlin: Beuth.

DIN (1981) DIN-Fachbericht 75 - Service Engineering, Entwicklungsbegleitende Normung (EN), Berlin, Wien, Zürich: Beuth.

Easingwood, C. J. (1986) New Product Developrnent for Services Cornpanies *Journal of Product Innovation Management*, 3 (4), 264-275.

Edvardsson, B., Gustafsson, A., Johnson, M. D., and Sanden, B. (Eds) (2000) *New Service Development and Innovation in the new Economy*, Lund: Studentliteratur.

Edvardsson, B., and Olsson, L. (1996) Key concepts for new service development. *Service Industries Journal* 16(2), 140-164.

Eversheim, W. (2000) Qualitätsmanagement für Dienstleister - Grundlagen, Selbstanalyse, Umsetzungshilfen (Quality management for service providers) , Berlin: Springer.

Eversheim, W. , Kuster, J. and Liestmann, V. (2003) Anwendungspotenziale ingenieuwissenschaflicher Methoden für das Service Engineering (Application potential of engineering specific methods for Service Engineering), in: H-J Bullinger and A. W. Scheer (Eds), Service Engineering - Entwicklung und Gestaltung innovativer Dienstleistungen, Berlin, Heidelberg, New York: Springer, 417-442.

Fitzsimmons, J. A. and Fitzsimmons, M. J. (2007) *Service management: Operations, Strategy, Information Technology*, Sixth edition, New York, NY: McGraw-Hill Irwin.

Gudergan, G. (2008) Erfolg und Wirkungsmodell von Koordinationsinstrumenten für industrielle Dienstleistungen (Model of performance and causal effects of coordination in industrial services). Schriftenreihe Rationalisierung und Humanisierung. Shaker Verlag, Aachen 2008, 239.

Gudergan, G., and Luczak, H. (2003) Coordination mechanisms in industrial service organizations, in: Human Factors in Organizational Design and Management – VII, H. Luczak and K. J. Zink (Eds).

Gustafsson, A., and Johnson, M. D. (2003) *Competing in a Service Economy: How to Create Competitive Advantage Through Service Development and Innovation*. San Francisco, CA: Wiley/Jossey-Bass.

Hildebrandt, L., and Klapper, D. (2002) Wettbewerbsanalyse (Comeptition Analysis) In. S. Albers and A Hermann (Eds), Handbuch Produktmanagement, Wiesbaden: Gabler, p. 461-485.

Johne, A., and Storey, C. (1998) New Service Development - A Review of Literature and Annotated Bibliography, *European Journal of Marketing*, 32 (3), 184-251.

Kamiske, G. (1997) Qualitätstechniken für die Dienstleistung (Quality techniques for services), München, Wien: Hanser.

Kommission der Europäischen Gemeinschaften (2003) Bericht der Kommission an den Rat und das Europäische Parlament. Der Stand des Binnenmarktes für Dienstleistungen - Bericht im Rahmen der ersten Stufe der Binnenmarktstrategie für den Dienstleistungssektor Luxemburg Amt für amtliche Veröffentlichungen der Europäischen Gemeinschaften.

Kano, N., Serahu, N., Takahash, F., and Tsuji, S. (1984) Quality and Must-Be Quality, Hinshitsu, 39-48.

Liestmann, V., and Kuster, J. (2002) Applying a Platform Approach to Redesign Industrial Services, paper presented at the Quis8 - Quality in Service Crossing Borders, Victoria, Canada.

Liestmann, V., and Meiren, T. (2002) Service Engineering in der Praxis. Kurzstudie zur Dienstleistungsentwicklung in deutschen Unternehmen, Stuttgart, Fraunhofer.

Liestmann, V., Keith, H., Kuster, J., Scherrer, U., Schmitt, I. and Thimrn, S. (2002) Dienstleistungsentwicklung durch Service Engineering - Von der Idee zum Produkt (Development of

Services by Service Engineering – From the idea to the product), in: H. Luczak, FIR+ IAW Praxis Edition Vol 2, Aachen: FIR.

Luczak, H., Liestmann, V., and Gill, C. (2003) Service Engineering Industrieller Dienstleistungen (Service Engineering of industrial Services), In: H -J. Bullinger and A. Scheer (Eds.), Service Engineering: Entwicklung und Gestaltung innovativer Dienstleistungen (Service Engineering: Development and confirmation of innovative services), Berlin, Heidelberg, New York: Springer, 443-466.

Luczak, H., and Gill, C. (2003) Service Engineering Industrieller Dienstleistungen (Service Engineering of industrial Services), In: Proceedings of the 7th Southeast Asian Ergonomics and 4th Malaysian Ergonomics Conference (SEAMEC), 19-22 May 2003, Eds.: Khalid, H.M.; Yong, L.T.; Kion, L.N., University Malaysia Sarawak, Kuching, Sarawak, Malaysia 2003, 346-353.

Luczak, H., and Gudergan, G. (2009) *The evolution of service engineering - towards the implementation of designing integrative solutions, Introduction to Service Engineering,* Whiley 2009.

Luczak, H., Kuster, J., Reddemann, A., Scherrer, U., and Sontow, K. (2000) Service Engineering – Der systematische Weg von der Idee zum Leistungsangebot (Service Engineering – from the idea to the service offer), München: TCW.

Meyer, M. H., and DeTore, A. (1999) Product Development for Services, *Academy of Management Executive,* 13 (3), 64-76.

Ramaswamy, R. (1996) *Design and Management of Service Processes - Keeping Customers for Life.* Reading: Addison-Wesley.

Rust, R.T., Lemon, K.N., and Zeithaml, V.A. (2004, January) Return on marketing: Using customer equity to focus marketing strategy. *J. of Marketing* 68, 109–127.

Schaude, G. (1992) Kreativitäts-, Problemlösungs- und Präsentationstechniken Eschborn: RKW.

Scheuing, E. E., and Johnson, E. M. (1989) A Proposed Model for New Service Development, *Journal of Service Marketing* 3 (2), 25-34.

Schutze, A., (2001) Ansatz zur prozessorientierten Planung Industrieller Dienstleistungen (Approach to process-oriented planning of industrial services), Dissertation, Dortmund.

Shostack, L. (1984) Designing services that deliver, *Harvard Business Review,* 62 (1), 133-139.

Schuh, G., Friedli, T., and Gebauer, H. (2004) Fit for Service: Industrie als Dienstleister, Carl Hanser Verlag, München, Wien.

Schuh, G., and Gudergan, G. (Eds.) (2007) Fakten und Trends im Service 2007 (Facts and trends in services 2007), Klinkenberg, Aachen.

Schuh, G., and Gudergan, G. (Eds.) (2008) Fakten und Trends im Service 2008 (Facts and trends in services 2008). Verlag Klinkenberg, Aachen.

Sontow, K. (2000) Frühe Phasen des Service Engineering - Dienstleistungsplanung in Unternehmen des Maschinen- und Anlagenbaus, Dissertation Aachen: Shaker.

Suh, N. P. (1990) *The Principles of Design,* New York: Oxford University Press.

Sundbo, J. (1997) Management of Innovation in Services *Service Industries Journal* 17 (3), 432-455.

VDI (1980) VDI-Richtlinie 2220 - Produktplanung - Ablauf; Begriffe und Organisation (Planning the product - development, terms and organization), Düsseldorf: VDI.

VDI (1993) VDI-Richtlinie 2221- Methodik zum Entwickeln und Konstruieren technischer Systeme und Produkte (Methodology for the development and construction of technical systems and products), Dusseldorf: VDI.

Womack, J. P. and Jones, D. T. (2005) *Lean Solutions: How Companies and Customers Can Create Value and Wealth Together.* New York, NY: Free Press.

Woodruff, R.B. (1997) Customer Value, The Next Source for Competitive Advantage, in: *Journal of the Academy of Marketing Science,* 25(2), 139-153.

Zeithaml, V. A., Parasurarnan, A., and Berry, L. L. (1985) Problems and Strategies in Service Marketing. *Journal of Marketing,* 49 (2), 33-46.

Part 5
Research and Practice: Delivery

The Industrialization of Information Services

Uday S. Karmarkar

Anderson School of Management

University of California, Los Angeles

Almost all major economies in the world are already dominated by services. A more recent trend is their evolution towards becoming information economies. The confluence of these trends is leading towards the growth of information intensive services which is already the major part of many developed economies. This change is being accompanied by a technology driven process of "industrialization" in information services that has some similarities to the industrialization of manufacturing, but also some important differences. Outcomes of industrialization include increases in productivity, standardization and mass markets. The consequences for industry structure, sector size and growth, employment and management practice are significant and again have both similarities to and differences from what occurred in manufacturing. One difference for industry structure is the tendency towards vertical de-integration and lateral dominance, as the role of transport media diminishes, and transaction costs reduce.

Introduction

The United States has become a service economy. This is not a new trend; it has been in progress for many decades. Today, about 85% of economic value as measured by the GNP and over 85% of the jobs in the United States are in the service sector (Apte, et al., 2008). This is also largely true of other developed economies around the world, though they may not be quite that far along. However, the trend is inexorable. Even the less developed nations are moving rapidly towards becoming service economies in terms of GNP and economic value if not in employment. For a review of services in world economies see Daniels (2003).

A second major trend that is just as important though perhaps less obvious, is the evolution to an information economy. Early studies of this trend were by Machlup (1962) and Porat and Rubin (1977). The United States is already an information economy with about 65% of GNP attributable to information products and services, and about 45% of employees engaged in information work while capturing about 55% of all wages paid (Apte, et al., 2007; Wolff, 2006). Similar

P.P. Maglio et al. (eds.), *Handbook of Service Science*, Service Science: Research and Innovations in the Service Economy, DOI 10.1007/978-1-4419-1628-0_18,
© Springer Science+Business Media, LLC 2010

trends are visible in other developed economies as well. The developing economies are not yet quite there in relative terms, but in absolute terms it is already the case that China has the world's biggest telecom sector and the largest number of internet users. India in 2007 and 2008 was adding cell phone subscribers at a rate of over 6-7 million a month.

"Information Services" is where these two trends come together. This aggregate sector includes financial services, telecommunications, entertainment and media services, business services, professional services, education, parts of health care and retailing, and information intensive components from other sectors (Apte and Nath, 2007). It now comprises over 55% of the US economy, with over 40% of the employment and about 45% of the wage bill. What is more, this appears to be an ongoing trend, with respect to GDP share as well as the shares of jobs and wages. More and more value will continue to accrue to services, to the information sector and to their intersection: information services.

Apart from these observations about changes in the aggregate economy, there are very significant consequences at the level of economic sectors. The information technologies that are pervasive in information services are beginning to have an impact on the basic structure and conduct of businesses and industries in this sector. The nature of the change can be thought of as "industrialization."

Industrialization in Manufacturing

The term "industrialization" can mean very different things to different people. Often it is taken to mean the change from an agrarian to an organized manufacturing economy. We will be using the term to address the structure of how goods and services are produced, and then to draw analogies between the industrial revolution of the late 18th and 19th centuries, and the recent and ongoing changes in information services. The purpose is to identify the drivers of the changes, the effect on industry structure and the consequences for competition, for jobs and wages, and for the strategies that companies need to employ to succeed in the changing environment.

So by industrialization, we mean changes in the underlying processes of production driven by the appearance and implementation of new technologies. In the small, this refers to changes in the way tasks and processes are carried out in a firm. In the large, there can be substantial changes in the way sectors and industries are organized.

In the manufacturing sector, industrialization was driven by a set of complementary factors

- The application of sources of power such as water, steam and electricity
- The mechanization and automation of processes to leverage human ability
- Improved precision and reliability in process operations

- Reliable sources of inputs and materials of uniform quality
- Increases in the efficiency of transportation and logistics using rail, roads and shipping
- A process of standardization starting with products, going to processes, and leading to mass production
- Precision of specification and measurement, to support standardization

The outcomes of industrialization included increases in productivity, mass cost-effective production, improved product quality, mass markets, increased consumer welfare and wealth and a growing "industrial" sector due to market growth.

Standardization of products started long before the industrial revolution. The earliest manifestation was probably with weapons, armor and other military equipment. For consumer markets product standardization was necessary to enable both mass production and the mass markets that would absorb the output of that production. The next step was standardization of parts that pushed manufacturing from a craft to a managed process. An early event in that process was Eli Whitney's famous 1801 demonstration of musket assembly from interchangeable parts, and his subsequent development of the high volume production of firearms. Whitney was actually following the example of Honoré Blanc (Alder, 1997) who had made a similar demonstration 18 years earlier. This system, which permitted the decoupling of parts production from final assembly, was the pre-requisite for a number of important process innovations, including specialization and the division of labor, the assembly line and the geographical distribution of production, eventually leading to today's global supply chains.

A natural consequence of parts standardization and the resulting specialization of tasks and workers was the standardization of processes, initially associated with pioneers such as Frederick Taylor and Frank Gilbreth. Today, this has evolved into the standardization of capabilities at the level of entire manufacturing systems as exemplified by quality and delivery standards.

Industrialization of Information Processes

All the driving factors for industrialization in manufacturing have now appeared in information production processes as well. Clearly there have been vast increases in basic processing capability as exemplified by Moore's Law. Correspondingly, the ability to automate and leverage human capabilities in data and information processing has increased, starting with mechanical devices such as card sorters and calculators, and going to computers.

The increases in transportation efficiency for information have taken an interesting path. The telegraph, radio, TV and telephone were big leaps in capacity that occurred decades ago. But they all had their limitations, and none could integrate with computers very well. Major advances came very recently with packet switched data networks, the internet and the world-wide web. These innovations, enabled by protocols and standards even more than hardware, created the explosion of information logistics in the 1990's. What is new about modern data communications systems is that they integrate seamlessly and digitally with the processing and storage resources, allowing for end to end integration of information chains.

The process of standardization is also occurring in information production for goods and services, but the path is different. By and large, the starting point has been the standardization of the representation of information. The next step has been the standardization of processes. For example, with languages, the first step was the standardization of symbols for the representation of information on physical media like clay, papyrus or paper. The next step was the creation of a standardized process of production: printing with blocks or movable type. The two together allowed the mass production of books. Process capability initially exceeded the availability of and the demand for products. The earliest surviving printed book (from 870 AD) is a Chinese block printed translation of the Diamond Sutra, a Sanskrit Buddhist text. It is pretty easy to guess at the first substantial printed product in Europe: the Gutenberg bible around 1455 AD. The Diamond Sutra and the Bible had both existed for centuries already, with a known audience. But what would be the next products? They included an account of a pilgrimage to Jerusalem, and a world history. It took time to develop a steady stream of what we would now call "content" to fill the new channel. Some of the new attempts eventually included "novels" and "essays."

For the mechanical processing of information too, the symbolic representation of numbers in early number systems was the first step. This was closely followed by early calculating aids like the Babylonian, Egyptian and Chinese abacuses, and much later by the mechanical calculators of Schickard and Pascal in the 17th century. Modern computational tools of course depended upon binary arithmetic and Boolean algebra. Binary representation made electronic computing feasible and robust, since only two system states sufficed for representation rather than say, ten. Just as an alphabet makes typesetting much more efficient than a character (Chinese) or pictographs and hieroglyphics, so too the binary representation is very powerful for both representation and processing. Production, storage and processing tools evolved from the mechanical, to the electro-mechanical and to the electronic. Symbolic representation too, went from that suited for humans as in the decimal system, to that suited for machines.

So the standardization process for information products and services can be thought of in stylized form as

- standardization of information representation in symbolic form
- standardization of processes of production (e.g. printing), storage (books) and processing (calculators, cash registers and computers)

- standardization of processing and processes at the machine level (punched cards, programmable machines, software)
- standardization of products and services (books and newspapers, packaged software including operating systems, data bases and applications, websites and server based applications)

The standardization of information products has happened rather quickly. But that for services is still evolving.

Just as with physical production, an eventual consequence of standardization has been modularization. Again, this has first occurred in processes as exemplified early on by printing, and more recently with object oriented software, client-server and multi-tier architectures, and distributed computing. Today we are in the middle of a new wave with service oriented architectures, syndication, mash-ups and web services.

The standardization of information processes at the machine or "shop floor" level, is now visibly migrating upwards into transaction handling and business processes. The most systematic example on the transaction side has perhaps been in telecommunications. At a basic level, standardization of business transactions has been widespread in banking and other financial services, and in inter-firm transactions facilitated with standards like Electronic Data Interchange (EDI). With higher level business processes, the degree of agreement is far lower, but companies like SAP, IBM, Microsoft are competing to define business standards. It looks as though Apple and Google may also play a significant role in this area in the future.

Drivers of Service Industrialization and Industrialization Strategies

Industrialization could as well be thought of in large part, as the creation and application of new technologies. Whether it is in the enhancement of processing power (computers), or in more effective logistics (telecommunications), new technologies are involved. The process of creating, commercializing and adopting technologies is a part and parcel of industrialization, and inseparable from it. Issues like standardization (for example, communications protocols) enable the commercialization and adoption of technologies, just as they support industrialization. We might say that technology development and adoption processes are a major part of industrialization, though not all of it.

One driver of industrialization is the process of technological development from scientific discoveries, to invention, product development and commercialization. This is the "push" aspect of technological development and of industrialization. The impact of new technologies on service industrialization can be examined in terms of three ongoing processes:

- the application of new technologies to improve performance in existing processes. An example is the invention of digital cameras and their use in image capture. Another is the development of software that leverages human effort (word processing) or substitutes for it (online services).
- the creation of infrastructure and systems that improve existing processes or enable new ways of executing certain processes. An example would be the development of telecommunications and the application to business transactions.
- the reconstruction of information and service chains, enabled or even forced due to the use of new technologies

The decisions and actions underlying these processes occur in the firms that develop, commercialize and sell new technologies in the form of new products and processes, as well as in the firms that use these new technologies to create new businesses, ranging from infrastructure (telecommunications networks) to business services (hosting and email) to technology products and services (hardware, software and IT services).

The "pull" aspect of industrialization, as with technological development, comes from the actions of firms both established and new, to compete more effectively and to create markets and profits. In practice, service firms industrialize to compete more effectively, and to increase or maintain profitability. The strategies that we observe (Karmarkar, 2004), include

- Automation (often directly related to new technologies)
- Outsourcing
- Geographic re-distribution of tasks (off-shoring)
- Process reengineering including modularization
- Service redesign; standardization of designs
- Operations and task shifting in the information processing chain
- Self-service (a specific version of task shifting)

Most of these are very analogous to the approaches that were visible in manufacturing starting with the industrial revolution and continuing till today. However, operations shifting and self service are much more viable in information production and information services. These are also very complementary to automation.

The Consequences of Industrialization

From an economic perspective, the process of industrialization has certain consequences. It is generally associated with an increase in productivity. There is now a body of research demonstrating productivity increases in services in the last dec-

ade in the service sector as a whole, and more specifically, in information intensive services down to the firm level (Stiroh, 2001; Jorgenson and Stiroh, 2000;
Brynjolfsson and Hitt, 1996). Productivity increases are generally seen as beneficial from a macro-economic perspective since they increase total wealth in an
economy. However, they can have consequences for employment patterns and
sectors which can be painful for some. Higher productivity naturally means lower
levels of resource usage (e.g. labor) at a given level of output. At the firm level, as
noted above, productivity increases might be achieved by means such as automation - the substitution of capital for labor, or by re-organization of industry sectors
through means such as outsourcing. So if productivity increases in a certain sector
are not accompanied by a corresponding growth in demand, there is likely to be a
reduction in employment in that sector. Furthermore, it is also possible that the
sector can shrink relative to the rest of the economy, in terms of the value produced (Karmarkar and Rhim, 2008). It can also be the case that income inequality
increases.

It is worth noting that the term "productivity" can be used in different ways
with different meanings and implications. For discussions of service productivity
see Baumol (1985) and Gadrey (2002). Due to the technical difficulties in measuring multi-factor productivity, it is not uncommon to think of productivity in a
monetized sense as the ratio of revenue to cost. Of course, this is a fundamentally
different measure. As an example, off-shoring software production may actually
mean lower labor productivity in the basic sense. However, it can cut costs so that
the monetary version shows an increase. Or it may allow for more effort to be allocated towards customization. Global production and delivery can also allow for
24 hour working cycles and improved customer response. So in addition to productivity changes or cost improvement, other performance measures may improve. And sometimes, workforces in different countries can have superior skills
at certain tasks, so that productivity and quality can indeed also improve.

There are several other consequences of the industrialization process for information services that are readily observed. One is the de-integration of information
"chains" in sectors like financial services. For example, the mortgage banking industry has seen a steady process of de-integration and specialization (Jacobides,
2005; Chaudhary, et al., 2007). Even within a firm there is a tendency to modular-
ize processes, for ease of automation. Legacy processes sometimes combine tasks
into jobs in ways that are not efficient in the context of new technologies. In many
cases, modularization helps not only redefinition of jobs to be more consistent, but
also the consideration of automation, process engineering, outsourcing and possibly relocation to advantageous sites. Again, mortgage banking is an example. We
discuss the effects on industry and sector restructuring further in a later section.

As service processes become standardized, so do services themselves. There is
a convergence in service design, and certain dominant designs begin to emerge.
Web sites that do similar things start to look similar, partly because of copying
and reverse engineering, partly because the underlying technology favors certain
formats, partly because certain designs are more effective, and partly because of

the use of common components. The systematization of the underlying processes and their heightened visibility on the web makes reverse engineering easy. So for example, banking or retail sites eventually tend to look similar and to have similar functionality.

An extreme consequence of convergence in design is a slide into commoditization, so that differentiation across services is reduced and many suppliers are able to provide essentially the same service; for example, see Davenport (2005). On the one hand, this helps in the development of mass markets, following from a common understanding of what certain services deliver. On the other hand, the lack of differentiation can lead to an intensification of competition with an emphasis on competing with low costs.

Physical products could always be transported and distributed over long distances and large geographies. However, many information intensive services were and often still are localized. A well known consequence of modern communication technologies (especially the web and Internet) is the loss of localization, and of local monopolies, again leading to an intensification of competition (Cairncross, 1997). This is really not a new phenomenon, since many older technologies ranging from printing to the telephone, radio and recording media have helped us down this road. But the new technologies are intensifying these effects, and bringing them into sectors like financial services.

Industrialization and Employment

As noted earlier, increased productivity is a major consequence of industrialization. Another is the development of mass production enabled by standardization. The last has perhaps been more obvious in manufacturing than in services, but is clearly both possible and evident in information services. A third factor is the appearance of new services and indeed entire industry sectors. These factors all directly affect jobs and employment in terms of the distribution of jobs, the distribution of wages and the nature of the jobs themselves.

Mass production and sector growth enabled by standardization are of course key outcomes, since without them industrialization would not be economically significant. Mass production is only feasible with mass markets, which in turn require low prices, common usefulness, reasonable quality and good distribution. With physical products, military equipment, household goods and building materials such as bricks were early pre-industrial examples. For physical service sectors, transportation and distribution, driven by industrial development are prominent. In information sectors, printing and publishing are leading early examples. Telecommunications and broadcasting are later examples. Web based consumer services such as online retailing and search are very recent.

Growth in well defined industry sectors also created well defined jobs. The standardization of production processes made jobs and tasks standard as well. This in turn simplified hiring and training, and created the clusters of well paid worker communities which were joined by their work rather than by other allegiances. While automobiles and mass transportation caused some dispersion of these communities, the effects remain with us to a great extent. In information services, the picture is not quite the same. The labor input for industrial products, though reduced by the processes of industrialization, remained quite large. The scale of production was also large. With information, the proportion of labor inputs dropped very drastically. Information intensive processes were in many cases more capital and equipment intensive in terms of the proportion of equipment cost to labor costs. Printing is a good example, as are broadcasting (radio, TV) and telecommunications. Furthermore the proportion of costs attributed to distribution (rather than production) is also much larger for information sectors. So we do indeed see a substantial growth in employment in sectors such as printing and broadcasting though it does not result in the same kinds of communities and clusters.

Information intensive industries have become a major source of employment and jobs in developed economies. In the US economy, this trend started some decades ago, and continues to the present day (Apte, et al., 2008). In our most recent studies, we see that for the United States in 2007, information related work is increasingly the source of both jobs and wages (Apte, et al., 2009). For the entire economy, about 48% of jobs (equivalent) and 57% of wages are attributable to information intensive work. Looking at services alone, information intensive work comprises slightly over 50% of jobs and almost 59% of the wage bill.

While growth can be expected as an early consequence of industrialization, the increases in productivity can cause somewhat perverse effects. While the manufacturing sector grew during and after the industrial revolution, it began to shrink in the United States after the 1960's. The size of the manufacturing sector in comparison to services, in terms of relative GNP contribution, as well as the share of jobs and wages has been dropping steadily since then. The reasons for this shift were clearly identified by Baumol (1967) as high productivity growth in manufacturing relative to services resulting in the growth of costs in services. Even earlier, Clark (1940) had conjectured that employment in services would rise relative to manufacturing due to lower productivity in the former relative to the latter.

As noted earlier, service productivity has begun to show increases. However, manufacturing productivity also continues to grow. As of 2006, the net effect appears to be a continuing growth of the service sector, and a shrinking manufacturing sector. There is one small sign of a changing pattern in services: after 2004, the rate of increase of jobs in the service sector has dropped. It remains to be seen whether this is a lasting change, and the recent recession has confounded the picture.

Within the service sector, industrialization and productivity growth due to information and communication technologies can be expected to favor information intensive services rather than physical services. The impact of this relative increase could eventually mean that the size of the information services sector, and employment in that sector could show declines relative to other (non-information or physical services). Indeed this is the case for employment in certain sectors. For example, the financial services sector showed a decrease in employment growth rates around the late 1980's. This could be due to the extensive use of computers in the "backroom." One might expect some decrease in financial services in the future due to technology effects in "front office" functions as well. However, this has not yet (as of 2007) shown up in the aggregate data. Another sector which showed a dramatic decrease in employment after 2000 was the information technology sector. But this may have been more of an unwinding of excessive employment in the run up to the 2000 recession with the following dot.com crash.

Finally, one effect of technology driven industrialization is in the creation of new jobs. Just as the industrial revolution created many new jobs like machine tool operators, the industrialization of information services has created many new jobs related to new technologies. In addition there are new jobs related to new services. The jobs range from chip designers and programmers to medical sonographers to web designers. Not all of these show up in the official labor statistics as yet, but this is an ongoing process that is likely to continue. The number of new job categories for which statistics are collected by the Bureau of Labor Statistics in the United States has gone from about 400 in the late 1980's to well over 800 after 2000, a very rapid increase.

Restructuring of Industry Sectors

As an example of the industrialization of information product and service sectors, consider what has happened with consumer imaging (Apte and Karmarkar, 2007). By this I mean the capture and distribution of images for personal and family use or perhaps a family portrait for the living room. At one time this would have required the services of an artist; an expensive option that was only affordable to the wealthy. Photography changed all that, and put the capability into the hands of anyone with a camera. We have now been through another change as film based photography is supplanted by electronic and digital means. Table 1 shows how the steps in the imaging process have changed recently in terms of the technologies that are employed at various stages of the process.

Table 1. Technology and Process Change in Consumer Imaging

Process Step	Photochemical Process	Digital Process
Capture	Camera	Digital Camera
Store and Transport	Film	Disk, card (digital media)
Process	Photofinisher	Computer, software
Archive	Album	Digital storage, media
Transport	Mail	On-line, Media transport
Display	Photo (print)	Screen, print

This sector presents a nice example of some of the consequences of industrialization. First, the photochemical process (silver halide chemistry based capture and printing of images) was itself an excellent example of industrialization and of conversion of a service into a new product based industry. The skills required in capturing an image by drawing or painting were replaced by an automated process that required very little skill, and could be done by anyone with a camera. Developing film and printing were done as third-party services. The result was a huge explosion of picture taking, and the growth of a multi-billion dollar industry that included products (film, cameras, photofinishing equipment) and services (developing and printing). The industry was dominated by a small number of companies (Kodak, Fuji, Agfa Gevaert), and it was the medium of film that was the key, not the camera hardware. Looking at the digital version of the process, it is apparent that even more of the process has passed to the hands of the user. There is no single firm that dominates the new version of the chain, since the technologies used in the chain cut across industry sectors. So there are indeed some dominant firms in certain sectors, but that dominance is lateral (or horizontal) rather than vertical. This is because of one form of convergence that has occurred in information logistics including storage, transport and processing. The degree of localization in the process had already been greatly reduced; it was essentially present primarily in the photofinishing step in going from film, to "negatives," to prints. This step is now to some extent unnecessary (though many people still prefer printed photos), to some extent in the hands of the user (using photo management software and desktop printing) and to some extent a service not limited to any locality, since it can be accessed remotely from anywhere through a website.

As another example consider diagnostic imaging in medicine (Apte and Karmarkar, 2007), including radiology, MRI scans, ultrasound, and other such technologies. Now this process was already high in technological sophistication and automation. The capture of images has always been more a matter of equipment than of individual skill. However the traditional X-ray film process, was usually co-located with other process steps including imaging, reading, and transcription in one place, typically a hospital or a large clinic. Today, with digitization of the information (image), co-location is not necessary. We begin to see geographical distribution and de-integration of this process. First the capture point can move closer to the customer, especially with conventional radiology, where equipment has become quite portable. The image can be transported anywhere for analysis and diagnosis. Diagnosis can be outsourced, and there is a potential for some automation. Transcription of the diagnosis from a recording to typed form can be partially automated, and can be done anywhere; it is indeed being outsourced and off-shored from countries like the United States. Finally there is the possibility of part of the diagnosis by-passing the specialist altogether, since it is simple to send a copy of the image to the referring physician. In this example, we see many industrialization strategies appearing, with very significant consequences for the organizations and individuals in the process.

Similar changes have either occurred already, are occurring now or will start to be visible, in every information intensive sector. We have already seen the impact for the B2C layer in retailing (Amazon) and services (news, banking and brokerage). Other sectors like publishing, education and professional services are beginning to show these trends in both front offices and back rooms.

Convergence, Vertical De-integration and Lateral Integration in Information Chains

"Convergence" or "digital convergence" is by now a common phrase used to describe the digitization of information of all types. It is sometimes used more generally to describe the blurring of boundaries between what used to be distinct activities and sectors. Looking a bit more closely at this phenomenon, we can identify a sequence of different kinds of convergence. The first is of course "digital," or convergence in form and representation. This in turn leads to the convergence in logistics and processing methods mentioned earlier. This convergence includes software and hardware assets, since the same methods and tools can be used in different sectors. The commonality and convergence in equipment and appliances extends to the user and the consumption of information, not just its production and delivery. As a result there is a form of convergence on the supply side of information sectors, where the same companies now play the same role across sectors. An obvious example is the use of telecommunications for transportation of digital material. As a result of convergence in the appliances used in consumption, there is a kind of convergence in behavior, where formerly distinct use patterns start to overlap.

As an example, visualize all the streams of information going into a home. They include books, telephones, newspapers, magazines, TV broadcasts, DVD's and many others. Each of these information flows ends in a different way, with a different consumption pattern, different content, a different consumption location and often a specialized appliance. With convergence in form and logistics, these streams are gradually being replaced by a common digital pipe. One can safely say that the end appliances and consumption locations will also begin to converge to some extent. Going further it is not unreasonable to conjecture that consumer behavior could also converge, or at least overlap in terms of the place, time and pattern of consumption of information. Indeed for many, this is already the case.

On the supply side, industry sectors were separated and often dominated by the media used for storage and distribution. This effectively separated the music business more or less completely from the publishing business. Even the frequency of distribution of different types of media led to different industry sectors, so that newspapers were very distinct from say weekly newsmagazines, or from books. The economics of storage, distribution and transportation were highly scale dependent. As a result, many information intensive sectors were dominated by a few companies. Like the imaging example of the previous section, this was the case with newspapers, television and the phone service. Where there were common third parties available for distribution (like the postal service), there was more fragmentation, as with magazines.

The historical pattern, driven by the scale economies of logistics and distribution with traditional information sectors, was often of a few dominant companies, with a significant degree of vertical integration. Newspapers, voice phone service and TV broadcasting are prime examples. However, as we have already seen with the imaging, and mortgage banking examples of previous section, this structure cannot survive "convergence." The general consequence is a shift from vertical dominance and integration driven by distribution economics, to lateral dominance and integration based on technologies and assets (Karmarkar, 2009).

The structure of the converged chain for the delivery of information in the form of products and services can be described in a stylized way as having the following stages (many seen earlier in our discussion of the imaging example):

- Creation and capture
- Processing
- Assembly (including aggregation)
- Storage
- Distribution
- Server based B2B services
- Server based B2C services
- Local distribution and access
- Consumption enablers (appliances and software)

At each stage there may be one or more companies or entities involved. The degree of economic power is closely related to the number of companies, and the degree to which their role in the stage is differentiated from others at that stage. So for example, the capture or create stage is highly differentiated with a very large number of entities. And as far as one can foretell, this is likely to remain the case due to low entry costs and high heterogeneity. On the other hand, at the distribution stage, the fixed costs of systems are very large and the service is a near commodity. There are very few large players, and the profit margins are relatively low.

While vertical de-integration is a general trend, there are some exceptions that are worth noting where certain new forms of vertical integration have appeared. NTT DoCoMo's iMode and related consumer services are an example of a telecom company that not only provides voice communication and content transportation and distribution, but also brands the consumer appliance and provides server based consumer services (Natsuno, 2003). Another example is that of Apple's iPod and iTunes store, where Apple was able to integrate backwards from the appliance to server based service. Now with the iPhone and iTouch, Apple is extending this business model to other server based applications, to become an "applications retailer."

While lateral strength and integration are a general trend, there is considerable variation in the strategies that we see. Firms like Google, Yahoo, Amazon, Microsoft, and NTT DoCoMo have exploited their positions to expand laterally, though again to varying degrees and with differing models and strategies. On the other hand, many telecommunications companies seem not to have recognized the opportunities that were and still are open to them.

It remains to be seen as to what mix of lateral and vertical structures will eventually survive, and which firms will be the dominant players. However, the strongest contenders appear to be the server-based consumer companies that have built strong brands, like Google, Amazon and eBay (Karmarkar, 2008).

Scale, Scope and Structure in Information Services

The evolution of the US economy towards information is very apparent not only in the aggregate statistics, but in many visible ways. The lists of the wealthy are increasingly filled by founders and leaders of technology-centric companies. The lists of the largest companies also include many information intensive firms. However here too, there are some differences in the economic consequences of industrialization.

With manufactured products, industrialization and mass production were typically associated with large economies of scale. The reason for this was the employment of new sources of power and the use of machines and equipment using those power sources to substitute for or leverage human effort. This required high initial fixed costs to acquire and install equipment. The ongoing development of machinery to use more power and to operate at higher volumes led to a further shift in the direction of larger scale. The economy of scale also tended to act as a barrier to entry, with the result that sector structure over time tended towards fewer larger firms, with higher profitability.

In information intensive industries, there were similar scale effects in the distribution and transportation oriented sectors. The most obvious case is that of telecommunications, which was widely regarded as a natural monopoly because of the large investment required and the relatively high capacity that could be reached by one supplier. In addition, though perhaps not well recognized initially, there were also substantial positive network externalities that favored the early mover.

Scale economies are also present in TV broadcasting, cable and satellite distribution system, radio broadcasting. In many other information sectors too, scale economies played a role in distribution and media. We have already noted the cases of newspapers, imaging and printing.

However, digitization and the resulting convergence are changing the economics of many information intensive sectors. Most importantly, the economics of information processing (as distinct from transportation and logistics) are not particularly scale dependent. The effect of Moore's law for information processing, and the analogues for other functions such as storage and display, have resulted in drastically reduced fixed costs for information processing.

So first of all, the cost of information capacity is closer to linear than concave. It also, in the modern parlance, scales well. That is to say, it is easy to add capacity when needed, without large jumps in cost. Low cost logistics through networking and communications systems, combined with modern software techniques, has made it feasible to distribute processing locally across clusters of computers, and globally across networks of machines. At the same time, convergence as described earlier provides significant economies of scope in the sense that the same equipment can perform a very wide range of tasks.

The combination of these factors — low scale economies, high scope economies, high network externalities in logistics — makes for a very different industrialization path and a different industry structure from that for physical products.

First we have already noted the tendency toward vertical de-integration and lateral integration or dominance. This can be regarded as direct consequence of low logistics costs, low interface costs, lower scale economies in logistics combined with high scope economies (convergence) in both logistics and processing. Next the locus of innovation can be in very small firms due to the low costs of processing power. Entry is also much simpler. However, particularly in consumer applications, branding and network externalities can combine to create significant first mover and scale advantages.

The economics of information production, distribution and delivery are complex and still in the process of change. There are more complete discussions elsewhere (Whinston, et al., 1997; Shapiro and Varian, 1998). Here we have briefly touched upon some of the issues related to the industrialization perspective. Broadly speaking, the picture for industrialized information services could be quite different from that of industrial manufacturing. While the latter has developed towards large centralized processing plants, and distinct vertical sectors, the information sector is likely to consist of smaller, widely distributed plants, relatively low vertical integration, and rapid innovation and entry perhaps with rapid exit as well. At the same time, scale economies do apply to very basic services like storage, search and cloud computing. As noted above, with a high degree of commoditization in these, brand recognition will play a role.

Summary

The US economy along with other developed economies is in the middle of a long term steady evolution towards an information economy. In the US, this trend is now more pronounced than the trend to services and at the confluence of these trends, information services have shown substantial and sustained growth in the past two decades. One of the major emerging features of this evolutionary picture is a process of industrialization of the information intensive service sectors which already constitute the major portion of the US economy. This process of industrialization shares some features with the industrial revolution and industrialization of manufacturing. But there are some significant and fundamental differences in the process of industrialization, as well as the end result of the process. The underlying mechanism of standardization in services has naturally started at the process level, and appears to be migrating "upwards" to business processes and business structure. In the evolving and eventual structure of information industry sectors, we see the dominance of scope economies rather than scale. This tends to favor vertical de-integration and lateral dominance or integration. In combination with low cost logistics, we observe geographically distributed information chains, just as we have already seen with manufactured goods. Finally there are significant consequences for employment and wages. For now the trend there is towards growth. However, it is possible that eventually, increasing productivity will lead to lower employment levels in some sectors. This is already visible in sectors such as information technology and financial services. An important factor in ameliorating some of these outcomes will lie in service innovations and in the creation of new services and new service jobs that may not even exist today.

References

Alder, K. (1997). Innovation and amnesia: engineering rationality and the fate of interchangeable parts manufacturing in France. *Technology and Culture*, 38(2), 273–311.

Apte, U., Karmarkar, U., Nath, H.K. (2008). Information services in the US economy: value, jobs and management implications. *California Management Review*, 50(3), 12–30.

Apte, U., Karmarkar, U., Nath, H.K. (2009). Jobs and wages in the US economy: the dominance of information intensive work. UCLA Anderson School, BIT Working Paper.

Apte, U., Karmarkar, U. (2007). Operations management in the information economy: products, processes and chains. *Journal of Operations Management*, 25(2), 438–453.

Baumol, W.J. (1967). Macroeconomics of unbalanced growth: the anatomy of urban crisis. *American Economic Review*, 57(3), 415–426.

Baumol, W.J. (1985). Productivity policy and the service sector, in R. P. Inman (Ed.), *Managing the service economy: prospects and problems*, Cambridge, UK: Cambridge University Press.

Brynjolfsson, E., Hitt, L. (1996). Paradox lost? Firm-level evidence on the returns to information systems spending. *Management Science*, 42(4), 541–558.

Cairncross, F. (1997). *The death of distance*. Boston: Harvard Business School Press.

Chaudhary, S., Green, M., Mahmoudi, R., Ting, V. (2007). The impact of new information technology on the US mortgage industry. In U. Karmarkar & V. Mangal (Eds.), *The Business and Information Technologies (BIT) project: a global study of business practice* (pp. 251–288). World Scientific Press.

Clark, C. (1940). *The conditions of economic progress*. London: McMillan.

Daniels, P.W. (1993). *Service Industries in the World Economy*. Blackwell Publishers, Cambridge, MA

Davenport, T. (2005). The coming commoditization of processes. *Harvard Business Review*, 83(6), 100–108.

Gadrey, J. (2002). The misuse of productivity concepts in services: Lessons from a comparison between France and the United States. In J. Gadrey & F. Gallouj (Eds). *Productivity, Innovation, and Knowledge in Services: New Economic and Socio-economic Approaches*. Cheltenham UK: Edward Elgar, pp. 26–53.

Jacobides, M.G. (2005). Industry change through vertical disintegration: how and why markets emerged in mortgage banking. *Academy of Management Journal*, 48(3), 465–498.

Jorgenson, D. W., Stiroh, K. J. (2000). Raising the speed limit: U.S. economic growth in the information age. *Brookings Papers on Economic Activity*, 1, 125–211.

Karmarkar, U.S. (2009). Convergence and the restructuring of information intensive industries. UCLA Anderson School, BIT Working Paper.

Karmarkar, U.S., Rhim, H. (2008). Industrialization, productivity and the effects on employment, wealth, equality and sector size. UCLA Anderson School, BIT Working Paper.

Karmarkar, U. (2004). Will you survive the services revolution? *Harvard Business Review*, June 2004.

Machlup, F. (1962). The production and distribution of knowledge in the United States. Princeton, NJ: Princeton University Press.

Natsuno, T. (2003). *i-mode Strategy*. Wiley.

Porat, M.U., Rubin, M.R. (1977). *The information economy (9 volumes)*, Office of Telecommunications Special Publication 77-12. Washington, DC: U.S. Department of Commerce.

Shapiro, C., Varian, H. (1998). *Information rules: a strategic guide to the information economy*. Boston: Harvard Business School Press.

Stiroh, K.J. (2001). Investing in information technology: productivity payoffs for U.S. industries. *Current Issues in Economics and Finance*, 7(6).

Whinston, A. B., Stahl, D. O., & Choi, S. (1997). *The economics of electronic commerce*. MacMillan Publishing Company.

Wolff, E. N. (2006). "The Growth of Information Workers in the US Economy, 1950-2000: The Role of Technological Change, Computerization, and Structural Change." *Economic Systems Research*, 18(3), 221–255.

Workforce Analytics for the Services Economy

Aleksandra Mojsilović

Business Analytics and Mathematical Sciences

IBM Research

Daniel Connors

Business Analytics and Mathematical Sciences

IBM Research

Central to the notion of services operation are concepts of labor and people – the deployment of knowledge, skills, and competences that one person or organization has for the benefit of another. In the new economics of services, the ability to manage skills and resources more effectively and efficiently is becoming the critical driver of success for any organization. As a result, forward-thinking businesses are beginning to invest in workforce optimization methodologies as a major competitive differentiator, and are looking for novel solutions to help optimize their workforce to yield greater business value. For the client serving businesses, the requirements for the next generation workforce management systems are expanding – they are not only expected to make the most effective use of the global workforce through improved planning, scheduling, deployment and resource management, but to also drive the best career environment in the industry while optimizing responsiveness to client needs. This article describes some of the workforce management challenges in services operations and discusses opportunities that could be addressed through the use of operations research, computer science, mathematics and management science methods.

P.P. Maglio et al. (eds.), *Handbook of Service Science*, Service Science: Research and Innovations in the Service Economy, DOI 10.1007/978-1-4419-1628-0_19,
© Springer Science+Business Media, LLC 2010

Introduction

The services sector has grown over the last 50 years to dominate economic activity in most advanced industrial economies (Chesbrough and Spohrer, 2006). The existing literature offers a number of formal definitions of *services* (Lovelock and Wirtz, 2007), (Fitzsimmons and Fitzsimmons, 2003), (Lusch and Vargo, 2006). Yet, in all cases, central to the notion of services operation are concepts of *labor* and *people* – the deployment of knowledge, skills, and competences that one person or organization has for the benefit of another. Therefore, the ability to manage skills and resources more effectively and efficiently was always the critical driver of success for any service organization. This is becoming even more important in the recent years with the "industrialization" of services, characterized by enormous demographic and technological changes, growing labor costs, automation, customer self-service and global competition presenting both a threat and significant opportunity for all services companies (Karmarkar, 2004). Top-level executives of outstanding organizations understand that in the new economics of service, in addition to customers, frontline workers need to be the center of management concern (Heskett, et al., 1994). Successful service managers realize that investment in people and technology that supports them is the key factor behind growth, profitability and client satisfaction in this new paradigm. As a result, forward-thinking services businesses are beginning to invest in workforce optimization methodologies as a major competitive differentiator, and are looking for novel solutions to help optimize their workforce to yield greater business value.

Over the past several decades mathematical models of traditional manufacturing and logistics systems have been developed and used for business optimization, resulting in significant gains in efficiency (Dietrich and Harrison, 2006). *Manufacturing Resource Planning* (MRP), which automated the calculations of material requirements within manufacturing, evolved into *Enterprise Resource Planning* (ERP), which monitors all manufacturing enterprise processes, and formed the information base for advanced planning and e-commerce. However, such technologies and analytical models behind them cannot be directly applied for workforce management in services industries, given that human resources are far more complex to model than machines and parts, and new models are required to understand and represent these complexities. Furthermore, the term workforce management applies to a broad range of problems (including skill demand forecasting, resource capacity planning, demand/supply matching, scheduling, long-term strategic planning, talent optimization) and even broader range of scientific disciplines. Changing the landscape of workforce management in services sector calls for collaboration and scientific contributions across disciplinary boundaries. This article describes some of the challenges in services operations and discusses opportunities for workforce management that could be addressed through the use of operations research, computer sciences, mathematics, management science and service science methods.

The case for workforce management – a deeper view

In the new services economy organizations are recognizing that they are once again competing not only for product superiority but also for talent to help them bring products and services to the market. Creation of new products and markets is requiring new skills, both in make up and quantity, and recent analyst research indicates that many organizations have difficulties filling positions or are facing talent shortages (IDC, 2007). As employee costs continue to rise, companies are beginning to look into unique ways to control cost and maximize business value (IDC, 2006). With economic growth in regions such as India, China and a number of other emerging markets, companies are being drawn outside their "traditional" boundaries for customers, suppliers and employees. Embracing the challenges brought by the new economic models and global integration will require a fundamentally different approach to production, distribution and workforce deployment. Planning and operating a globally integrated enterprise will involve understanding the cost/value of differentiation in product, delivery, and service, geographic dependencies to sourcing, production, and consumption, standardization of processes and labor, and modeling global skill demand/supply such that effective training, deployment and monitoring of resources is possible (Palmisano, 2006).

Today, the *human capital management* (HCM) market is at a turning point. Following tactical investments in core HR and ERP systems, companies are now in a position to use this enterprise data coupled with advanced analytics to pursue more strategic, personnel driven improvements (AMR, 2006a). The *workforce analytics* (WFA) market has been steadily growing for more than ten years. However, it is still a relatively small market primarily due to the fact that the implementation of advanced WFM solutions and the deployment of workforce application require significant maturity levels in terms of data, process and business understanding. This paper will discuss the issue of organizational workforce maturity and review the requirements for the successful implementation of WFA solutions in the enterprise.

In the current market, the risks of not using analytics to drive workforce management can directly affect key business goals. In contact centers, it may mean dropped calls, higher attrition and decreased customer satisfaction. In service delivery, it could mean inadequately staffed projects, or the inability to meet project demand, both impacting the bottom line and the ability to serve the client. In retail organizations, it can result in long checkout lines, sending customers to shop elsewhere. For manufacturers, it means idle production lines and suboptimal production output (AMR, 2006b). Therefore, workforce management is gradually transitioning from simple time, attendance and absence management, to include tracking workers, forecasting, scheduling and optimization capabilities to meet the business objectives in the "best" possible way. By reviewing methodologies and algorithms behind such solutions, this paper provides an insight into the state of the art workforce analytics and a vision for integrated workforce planning across the services lifecycle.

While the state-of-art analytics provides a solid foundation for advanced work-force management, it has largely been based on the supply chain ideas, and has yet to tap into the "human" aspects and complex relationships within the workforce. People are typified by phenomena like learning response curves, burnout, accel-erations/slowdowns, sensitivity towards fairness in workload, absenteeism, etc. As more and more organizations recognize that their talent is a true competitive dif-ferentiator in the new service economy, there is an increased interest in tools and methodologies that will support the transition to this new model, where the chal-lenge is not just cutting the cost and providing the lowest cost services to beat the competition, but fostering collaboration, cross-training, providing the best career environment, and optimizing responsiveness to client needs. We present the vision for the next generation workforce analytics. These new solutions will require and drive significant advances in diverse technical areas — some examples are hig-lighted in the concluding section, together with the next steps and closing remarks.

Foundations for Workforce Analytics: An IBM Case Study

The ability to implement an advanced workforce management solution in a ser-vices organization calls for tremendous focus on developing proper labor man-agement foundation, an effort that includes process development and re-engineering, new business practices, as well as significant investment in support-ing information technology (IT) infrastructure and data collection. This section re-views the key foundational initiatives through a case study of IBM Workforce Management Initiative (WMI), a recent workforce transformation at IBM Corpo-ration ("The 2008 Workforce", 2008 October).

In the early 2000s, as services became a larger and larger part of IBM's reve-nue, it was recognized that the company must better manage its workforce in order to more effectively and efficiently deploy the appropriate resources to meet cus-tomers' needs. WMI was established, bringing together expertise from IBM's Human Resources (HR), Global Services (GS) business units, Integrated Supply Chain (ISC) and Research organizations to establish a set of processes and tools that would manage IBM's workforce to ensure that "the right person with the right skills and the right cost is assigned to the right assignment".

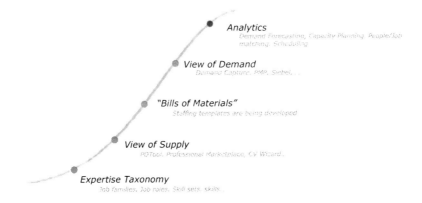

Figure 1. The organizational workforce maturity curve, representing the
key steps in the workforce management transformation,
which will enable the use of advanced analytics

The initiative drew upon IBM's own supply chain management expertise,
drawing many parallels between managing a supply chain and managing an enterprise workforce. Questions such as "how many resources are needed to meet the
demand", "are there shortages or excesses of resources", "from where should resources be sourced" all had analogies in the supply chain realm. IBM had previously transformed its supply chain with a set of common processes, enterprise
tools and data standards, and IBM's WMI relied on a similar approach. This transformation process is shown in Figure 1, representing the IBM *workforce maturity
curve*, and a blueprint for the application of advanced WFM analytics in any organization.

The first step was to establish the *Expertise Taxonomy* (ExT), a common taxonomy
for describing the job roles performed by the workforce and the associated skills.
Prior to having a standardized taxonomy, IBM had "application developers",
"software engineers" and "programmers". They were further categorized by different salary bands, raising questions like "is an advisory software engineer in India equivalent to a band 7 application developer in Canada?" In the early days of
product development, IBM ISC understood the advantages of using a common
part naming convention, thus transforming IBM's supply chain from several incompatible requirements planning systems to a common enterprise planning platform. The similar approach was taken in the development of Expertise Taxonomy
to achieve the standardization of jobs and skills required to deliver IBM products
and services.

The next step was to develop a *supply inventory system* to monitor and track
the availability of practitioners. IBM built the *Professional Marketplace* (PMP)
tool, which contains a central repository of IBM's talented resources, described in
common way via the ExT. Project managers who need to staff an engagement can

search PMP for resources, or create an *open-seat* describing the needs of the position in both structured and unstructured terms.

The third step was to describe the services work in standardized way. Much like the way "bill-of-materials" are used in IBM's supply chain to define, in terms of parts, how products are built, IBM developed staffing models to describe the "bill-of-resources", also known as *staffing templates*, for the products and service offerings delivered by their services businesses. (Details of how staffing templates are developed are given in subsequent sections).

As the final step, WMI created a repository for capturing the demand for products and services. By integrating the views of ongoing engagements, signings and market opportunities, on-going work, signed work and forecasted work now make up the demand that is stored in this repository, thereby creating inputs for advanced planning processes.

This workforce transformation laid the foundation for advanced analytics from IBM's Research Division. Research scientists worked closely with HR, ISC and GS to develop novel workforce management tools. These solutions and the underlying algorithms will be described in detail. Today WMI continues to work as a management and measurement system that monitors process implementation and the usage of the tools. However, this is not the end of the journey. With constantly evolving service products, new business processes and delivery models, the workforce management transformation continues, driving significant advances in diverse technical areas in order to support continually evolving services business.

Integrated Workforce Analytics for the Services Lifecycle

The services sector is undergoing a major transformation, where the primary change driver behind this new "services revolution" is technology (Karmarkar, 2004). One way to realize competitive advantage is through innovative and integrated workforce management technologies that will extend beyond just tracking employees' time/attendance or project participation, to span the entire talent cycle of the organization, starting from forecasting the labor demand, planning coverage of business operations and tasks, scheduling individuals and teams to efficiently fulfill them, and linking the talent-related decisions to real business outcomes. This section provides an overview of each step in this integrated workforce management approach and describes novel analytical models behind them.

Automated generation of staffing templates for resource demand forecasting

A good view into future resource needs is essential for driving profitability in a service-oriented business. Services engagements typically require multiple resources, each having different skills. Not having resources with the appropriate skills to carry out a project when needed, as well as having too many under-utilized resources, both result in the loss of profits to the business. However, services offerings/opportunities are commonly specified in terms of revenue and solution, without a linkage to resource needs. A more accurate view of resource and skill requirements can be obtained via standardized staffing templates, which allow for planning of staffing decisions at earlier stages of the engagement process, more reliable forecasting of resource needs and better workforce planning. This template-based approach calls for the creation of a project categorization scheme, which would link a set of project attributes, captured in the early stages of negotiations with a client, to typical resource requirements over the project lifecycle. Such an approach requires the development of a systematic method for creating a *solution taxonomy*, and estimating *staffing templates* (i.e., the specification of staffing needs in terms of required hours of each skill each week for the planned project) automatically, on the basis of key engagement characteristics.

Hu, et al. (2007) describe a methodology based on statistical clustering techniques for generating groups of similarly staffed projects, using information on reported labor hours from a large number of historical projects from the enterprise labor-claim management system. The approach utilizes a variant of the hierarchical-k-means algorithm proposed by Chen, et al. (2005), to identify homogeneous groups of projects with respect to the resource utilization vectors. Once the statistical cluster analysis is complete, the next step is to create the representative solution taxonomy, by: (1) examining the distribution of values of project attributes in each cluster, (2) creating appropriate name and description for each cluster, and (3) validating cluster assignment and refining taxonomy labels and class descriptions through discussions with subject matter experts. In many practical situations resource requirements are not static, and can vary over the life of a project as it enters different phases. Datta, et al. (2007) extend the above approach to identify time-varying staffing templates by applying a novel sequence clustering algorithm, where each sequence represents a project, and each observation in the sequence represents the weekly distribution of project labor hours across job role categories.

Matching

Service providers operate in a very dynamic environment. Every day new engagements are starting requiring resources, existing engagements are continuing to use resources, and some engagements are concluding freeing up resources. The time horizon of engagements can vary from weeks to several months to many years in duration. Matching highly skilled people to available positions is a high-stakes task that requires careful consideration by experienced resource managers. A wrong decision may result in significant loss of value due to understaffing, under-qualification or over-qualification of assigned personnel, and high turnover of poorly matched workers. While the importance of quality matching is clear, dealing with pools of hundreds of jobs and resources in a dynamic market generates a significant amount of pressure to make decisions rapidly. Naveh, et al. (2007) present *Optimatch*, a novel solution designed to bridge the gap between the need for high-quality matches and the need for timeliness.

Optimatch can match requests for resources that contain both structured and unstructured information. The organizational expertise taxonomy provides the basis for much of the structured information. A request specifies the job-role and skill-set, coming from the expertise taxonomy, salary band, start and end dates, language requirements, location requirements, and other needs which can be expressed in structured terms. The request also permits descriptive text such as project and position descriptions, and required and "nice to have" skills. These descriptive fields are often used to provide additional information about the position that are not adequately addressed by the structured data. Optimatch could also consider "people" skills, as described in Butler and Waldroop (2004), if the resources can be categorized and the open-seat requests can specify the people skills.

The Optimatch tool is implemented at IBM to assist the staffing of services engagement. The IBM implementation relies on the *Professional Marketplace* PMP tool, which serves as a repository of the skills, resumes, availability information and other key data of its professional service resources. This typical use of the PMP tool to identify qualified candidates for the position is labor intensive. When generating a list of candidates for a position, managers may not have access to other positions that could be better suited for the candidates. They may not be aware that a candidate they are considering has unique skills that are needed for another position. Furthermore, at any given time there are often dozens to hundreds of open-seats and resources, making the identification and matching problem of resources to open-seats very difficult to impossible for the project and resource managers. Optimatch is specifically developed to address this large-scale, enterprise matching problem. It takes as input a pool of resources and open-seats, and a set of matching rules, and produces as output an assignment or a prioritized list of candidate resources for each open-seat. The matching rules specify the attributes of the resources and open-seats which must match (mandatory rules) and the attributes which are prioritized. For example, "the salary band of the resource must be band 8", is a mandatory rule, while a prioritized rule is "a preference for a Java programmer over a C programmer", or "a preference for resources who are located closer to the engagement site". Optimatch relies on constraint programming methodology, whose expressive language is rich, natural and modular, contains many types of constraints, and therefore allows the rapid development and maintenance of models (Naveh, et al., 2007). Additionally, the strong algorithmic foundation of constraint programming allows for fast execution and good optimality.

Scheduling

An increasingly large number of enterprises are outsourcing their infrastructure support and business process requirements to service providers. In many cases, the support is provided by people working in large service centers that serve customers located around the globe. Due to the varied geographic locations of the customers, and the time zone differences, such support must be provided in shifts, 24 hours a day, seven days a week. Service center environments are characterized by the fluctuations in demand depending on the day of the week and time of the day, making the creation of shift schedules that minimize the costs of service provision, while maintaining the required service quality a significant challenge.

Due to issues such as demand and load forecasting, complex business rules (e.g. "the night shifts should be distributed evenly among all the agents in Group 3"), intra-day scheduling, on-line crisis management (no-show or sudden rise in the demand), the shift scheduling problem is complex, versatile and rich in mathematical, algorithmic and performance challenges. Typical services scheduling applications involve pools of homogeneous resources and periodic needs for specific skills. For example, when scheduling an call center that is providing 24/7 support, workload analyses may indicate there is a need for a specific number of call center advisors who have certain skills in order to meet the required Service Level Agreement (SLA). The schedule must be feasible against applicable government work rules, negotiated union contracts, seniority rules, vacation schedules and many other factors. Gilat, et al. (2006) describe *Shift Work Optimized Planning and Scheduling* (SWOPS), a scheduling tool designed to address complex scheduling issues. SWOPS consists of three main components: 1) Forecasting the workload, 2) Computing the resource requirements, and 3) Building the schedule. Forecasting the load applies statistical and machine learning techniques to predict for each type of load item how many load items will arrive, when they will arrive, and what will be the amount of work required by each item. Statistical techniques are used to generate the forecast. In the IT call center the forecast includes how many problem tickets will arrive in a given hour, the amount of work required for a specific ticket, as well as the handling process followed by this ticket. Given the predicted load, computing the resource requirements entails calculating how many support representatives, and with what skills, will be required at each point in time, in order to meet the required service level. Analytical or simulation based queuing network models are used for this purpose. Building the schedule consists of creating the actual operational schedule, which takes as input the staffing requirements, and scheduling rules (for example, maximum consecutive work hours, maximum number of shifts per week) in order to create the operational schedule. Heuristic algorithms and mathematical programming techniques are used to create the schedule. More details on these operations can be found in Gilat, et al. (2006) and Wasserkrug, et al. (2007).

One particularly interesting scheduling problem in services organizations, especially support and call centers is scheduling of the third-level support. A typical support service includes three main types of support: *first-level*, *second-level* and *third-level* support. First-level support services (e.g. resetting a user's password) require very little skill, second-level support calls for higher skill level and additional knowledge, while third-level support requires deep specialization in specific product platforms. Shift scheduling for first-level call center support is a topic that has been extensively researched from a wide variety of aspects (Brusco and Jacobs, 2000), (Gans, et al., 2003), (Mason, et al., 1998), and several commercial products that support the scheduling of such work are available. However, very little research has been carried out into the scheduling of the third-level support, which is characterized by relatively low number of load items per interval and a large amount of work required to resolve each such item. These characteristics violate many of the assumptions used in "traditional" scheduling models. Wasserkrug, et al. (2007) review the issues associated with forecasting and scheduling third-level shift work. They also present an end–to-end methodology for forecasting and scheduling this type of work, and discuss it in the context of a specific case study. The unique characteristics involved in providing third-level support work, as well as the increasing need to schedule shifts for such work, will continue to require new and specific forecasting, staffing and scheduling methodologies.

Capacity Planning

Efficiently managing and planning a large workforce is a challenge faced by all service companies, as their revenue is largely accounted by the billable time charged from the employees' commitment on business engagements. A typical service engagement consists of different tasks, simultaneously executed by resources (workforce) with different attributes (skills). Any shortage of the required resources can result in the failure of the entire engagement. This section focuses on analytics and models that can be used to perform workforce capacity planning in services operations.

Deterministic planning and gap/glut analysis

Supply chain optimization techniques have long been used to model the behavior of manufacturing supply chains (Voss and Woodruff, 2003). Although there is a strong analogy between MRP and resource capacity planning, a typical off-the-shelf MRP engine cannot be directly applied to later problem -- people are not parts and fundamental models and assumptions used in MRP/ERP engines are not suited for modeling human resources. People resources often have multiple skills, they can change and acquire new skills, and become more productive through experience. Furthermore, people are capacity resources, meaning that if a resource is not used during a period of need that capacity is lost. Although MRP systems have some capability to model capacity parts, underlying models are not rich enough to adequately describe people resources.

Gresh, et al. (2007) extend the MRP paradigm and apply it for human resource management. They describe the *Resource Capacity Planning* (RCP) engine, developed for the planning of the services workforce. Given the demands for service offerings and products, "bill-of-resources" (or staffing templates), and resource availability, the RCP engine determines the shortages (gaps) and excesses (gluts) of resources over the planning horizon. The RCP engine relies on Watson Implosion Technology (WIT), a set of general resource capacity planning models, algorithms for solving capacity planning problems, and an API for creating resource capacity planning problems (Wittrock, 2006). The RCP model differs from the standard supply chain models in that the business planners involved in talent decisions typically want to include a rather complex set of substitution possibilities in the model. In many cases it is not necessary to "exactly" match a human resource to a job -- depending on the particular engagement, some amount of flexibility may be allowable. In addition, "what-if" scenarios may be explored, in which the impact of ignoring the effect of particular resource attributes on gaps and gluts can be investigated interactively. The decision-maker may discover, for example, that a strict requirement to match people to jobs within line-of-business boundaries has a large impact on overall efficiency. The wide variety of substitution possibilities made this problem different from the case of industrial production, in which typically only one part (or perhaps one from a small set of parts) is suitable for substitution.

The RCP engine supports deterministic planning, and assumes that the demands and supplies are known. The engine offers two approaches for solving the capacity planning problem. The first approach is priority-based: Given business rules on the use of resources such as preferences and priorities, a heuristic algorithm implements the desired allocation rules. The second solution approach is based on linear programming, which is a method for optimizing a mathematically expressed objective given mathematically expressed equations and inequalities such as those ensuring that consumed capacity is less than available capacity. Given costs for using resources, costs of resource actions (such as hiring, retraining, transferring or letting go) and rewards for meeting the demands, a mathematical programming model is formed and solved. Optimization-based approaches require more complete economic data on all of the relevant costs, such as salaries, severance or hiring costs, and engagement revenues. Heuristic models, while not "optimal" in a mathematical sense, are easier to understand, and more closely follow the human method of assigning preferences to different actions.

Risk-based capacity planning

Uncertainty in the engagement demand, process delivery and resource supply, is one of the fundamental characteristics of services business. Demands are streams of engagements. Each engagement requires the service of several different classes of resources for certain amount of time. After the completion of the engagement, a reward is collected, and the resources are free to be assigned to other engagements. For example, to fulfill an IT service contract, a team of a project manager and several IT specialists are needed for three months of time. If there are not enough resources to fulfill the demand of an engagement, the engagement will be lost and financial penalty will be incurred for the loss. It is a typical model for the business processes in consulting service, hospitals and government. Therefore, in addition to computing the desired capacity levels (i.e. gaps and gluts) the users might be interested in modeling the overall workforce capacity planning process, and providing performance analysis and decision support to make it more effective.

One approach to performing the capacity planning process is to formulate it as a stochastic planning problem with multi-type demand and multi-attribute supply. Such model assumes that projects arrive according to some random process in time, and require resources of different types for a random, not known a priori, amount of time. Different customers are characterized by their resource requirements, their willingness to pay, statistical properties of their arrival processes and processing times. An arriving customer must be either accepted or rejected at the moment of arrival. If accepted, the required amount of resources is committed for a random processing time; otherwise, the customer is lost. There is an enormous variety of modeling, analytic and optimization problems one can address in the framework described above. One of the most relevant to the service provider is maximizing the expected profit in two scenarios: (1) by controlling skill capacities subject to service levels, i.e., bounds on customer loss probabilities; and (2) given fixed skill capacities, suggest an "optimal" customer selection policy.

Although stochastic loss networks are an extensively studied model for telecommunication networks, (Kelly, 1986), (Kelly, 1987), (Kelly, 1988), (Kelly, 1990), (Kelly, 1991), there are significant differences between the "traditional" loss networks and the stochastic workforce model. First, compared to circuit-switched boards, human resources display a much higher degree of flexibility. For example, an engagement can require only 20% of a certain resource and the same resource can be used to handle multiple engagements. The second difference is time scale. In telecommunications networks the duration of the calls are more homogeneous and small compared to the planning horizon, while services engagement duration can vary in a large range, from several hours to one or two years, and the planning horizon is usually a month or a quarter. The third difference is the action lead time. The actions in the planning problem include *increase* (hire), *decrease* (lay-off) and *reallocate* (retrain) the capacity, with significant lead times and uncertainties associated to these actions. Such differences are considered in the stochastic network models for workforce management described in Lu, et al. (2006), Lu et al. (2007) and Bhadra, et al. (2007). This work represents the capacity planning process as a stochastic loss network and calculates the minimum capacity required for high percentage of engagements to be fulfilled. The authors formulate an overall performance optimization problem, which along with satisfying the serviceability constraints and finance objectives, produces desired capacity levels. They also formulate a stochastic dynamic programming model to incorporate resource actions (hiring, lay-off, retraining, etc.) over time, and lead to optimal long term performance (e.g., profit maximization).

Next Generation Workforce Analytics

As companies continue to implement WFM solutions, besides supporting skills demand forecasting, matching, scheduling and capacity planning, there will be a need for even more advanced workforce analytics, analytics that will go beyond the "bill-of-resources" model and tap into the "human" aspects of the workforce to leverage information on workforce dynamics, incentives, patterns of interaction, knowledge sharing, productivity and innovation. As mentioned previously, specificities of human resources make workforce models vastly different from the ones applied in inventory control, supply chain and revenue management. Human resources share characteristics such as flexibility (resources could have multiple skills, or work on multiple projects at the same time); projects can be outsourced and resources can be borrowed; reusability (once released from a project, human resources can be assigned to another), etc. Concepts such as hiring, training and acquisition of new skills fundamentally influence the characteristics of the relevant optimization problems, making them more difficult to model and solve, but more realistic, and therefore of critical importance to practical implementations. Humans as resources are typified by phenomena like learning response curves, burnout, accelerations and slowdowns, sensitivity towards fairness in workload, teaming, collaboration, etc. All of these may affect performance and workforce availability and therefore must be incorporated into a realistic workforce management solution.

As ERP systems continue to grow, more and more workforce-related data is captured and available for modeling, and will drive better and more human-oriented analytics. The future workforce models will therefore focus not only on "standard" demand/ supply relationships, but will also include evolving information about employee project activities, career progression, incentives, productivity, etc. Examples of such data include: (1) employee information (skills, organizational hierarchy, etc.), (2) information regarding job transitions (e.g. past job history and project involvement), (3) CVs and career background, (4) project experience (project assignments, tasks accomplished, related client satisfaction and billing information, etc.), (5) project-related blogs, jams, wikis, etc. and (6) professional activities (joint authorships, conference sessions, with whom they worked externally, certifications, society memberships, patents, etc.). In the remaining sections, we describe several emerging research areas and novel solutions for talent planning and management that are driven by this explosion of the workforce-related data.

Strategic Workforce Planning: Workforce Evolution

In a service-oriented business model, trends in the labor market critically affect organizational ability to deliver on business objectives and remain competitive. Furthermore, as organizations encounter the era of rapidly changing demographics, shifting business models and volatility in economic environments, managing human capital relative to strategic business objectives will be of paramount importance. Therefore the area of strategic workforce management based on proactive use of data and analytics will be one of the key levers of organizational success.

The two key requirements for the strategic HCM analytics are: (1) provide visibility into future workforce trends and (2) create linkages between the talent profile and policies and organizational goals and success. Additional benefits include the ability to identify, assess and mitigate workforce risks, proactively respond to changing workforce demographics and trends, plan for change, mergers, acquisitions or restructuring, and synchronize financial and operational workforce strategies. Sharma, et al. (2008) describe a novel approach for the analysis of workforce trends under conditions of high uncertainty. They develop the *Workforce Evolution & Optimization* (WEO) methodology, which allows users to predict and understand future workforce trends (evolutions), analyze workforce evolutions under different actions, policies and conditions, and determine the optimal workforce evolution with respect to user-specified business objectives (e.g. maximize revenue or minimize cost).

In the WEO approach, employees are grouped by geography, band, job role, skill set, etc. into *workforce states*, and the overall workforce is represented as a *network topology* of dynamic transitions among states. The model assumes that there are costs, rewards and penalties, associated with each workforce state and transition between the states. The costs (e.g. salary, office, pension, hiring, attrition, learning, promotion), rewards (incremental revenue, productivity, etc.) and penalties (lost rewards and additional costs due to not having enough people) are functions of the number of people in each state and making each transition. The historical HR information on hiring, attrition, and employee movements (e.g. changes in band, skill, or organizational transfers) is used to estimate the transition probabilities, which then serve as the base model parameters for estimating future workforce profiles. Stochastic models are then applied to determine evolution, target state and path (actions of hiring, attrition, retraining, promotion, etc. with lead times) for the workforce network, and compute the "optimal" path that maximizes financial/business objectives.

WEO users can view workforce trends extrapolated from historical data and study alternatives through what-if scenario capabilities. The tool allows for a specific profitability target to be established and shows the amount of revenue needed to support the amount of resources on board. One can organize the analysis of workforce evolution under current and alternative composition, policies, actions, and scenarios to understand impact of demographics, globalization, aging workforce, other forms of turnover, etc. over time, or study longer-term effects of operational policies, skill development policies, and various forms of business dynamics.

Expertise Location and Recommendation

As services organizations become increasingly global in their operations and market presence, they are beginning to face new challenges and consequences of having global workforce and clients. A major issue for large and dispersed organization is expertise location – the ability to find the right people for the job, right experts for a particular question, or connect people sharing the same goal or business objective. By tapping into a global view of how people interact in the organization, tools based on social network analysis can significantly enhance information-flow and knowledge sharing within the enterprise, beyond what can be offered by traditional information sources. Social network analysis and expert finding systems offer a variety of toolkits to satisfy a compelling need for expertise location and knowledge sharing in large organizations (Luce, 1950), (Seidman and Foster, 1978), (Alba, 1973), (Ackerman, et al., 2002), (Kautz, et al., 1997), (Dom, et al., 2003), (Zhang, et al., 2007).

Chenthamarakshan, et al. (in press) leverage instantiations of corporate social networks to address two key aspects of workforce management: (a) *project staffing*, which is the problem of appropriately assigning professionals, or *subject matter experts* (SMEs), to ongoing projects where their expertise is needed, and (b) *expert recommendation*, which is the problem of appropriately connecting SMEs to other employees who can benefit from their expertise or answer a specific technical question.

Enabling better staffing decisions through social network analysis

In order to assist with project staffing decisions, Chenthamarakshan, et al. (in press) leverage SNAzzy (Dasgupta, et al., 2008), a set of algorithms for identifying communities in large social networks, to discover social communities between *resource deployment managers* (RDMs). They develop Connect2Staff, a tool that allows RDMs to locate one another while making assignment decisions. Connect2Staff uses data on past RDM interactions to derive a social network graph, where RDMs represent nodes (vertices) and their intercommunications represent edges. They focus on three types of "communities". (1) *Clique*, a community where each RDM from the community interacts with every other RDM. A clique implies a close tie between the RDMs, bringing out a possibility that most RDMs are already working together as a group, or have worked as a group earlier, and are likely to be aware of demand and supply of different job profiles within the clique. (2) The *densest subgraph* structure, indicating the most globally active RDM community – these RDMs collectively have the best visibility into the overall demand/supply status. (3) *Star,* a structure where one central RDM, *hub*, connects many RDMs, *spokes*, who have not communicated with each other. Thus the hub RDM can establish contact between two spoke RDMs if there is a demand and supply match. The hub RDM is likely to be a repository of formal and informal institutional knowledge and a potential point of focus if one wants to reach out to many RDMs who are socially not well connected. Such social constructs are used to provide profiling information about the RDMs, aid their decision making process, profile communities of which they are a member, the stars that they relate to, their role within the organization, and individuals/communities most likely to help them move beyond established boundaries. The network also provides a social proximity score and allows for matching the job profiles in demand/supply of an individual RDM, with the RDM performing the job search.

The architecture of Connect2Staff tool therefore comprises of two components: *RDM Direct Interaction Analyzer*, and *RDM Recommendation Engine.* In the RDM Direct Interaction Analyzer the history of social interactions is used to build the RDM interaction graph in the form of an adjacency list, and to identify communities. The RDM Recommendation Engine accepts RDM queries, either from a search request or from a browsing activity. The sample queries include *"recommend me for all communities that have an opening for SAP Manager"* or *"Find all communities that are at distance 3 or less from me".*

Finding and recommending experts in the enterprise

In many services organizations, intranet applications, project wikis, message boards and discussion forum are becoming standard tools of doing business and addressing specific work issues. In these online communities, participants frequently act as information seekers (by posting a question) or information providers (by providing an answer or opinion). Such knowledge sharing mechanism creates content on a variety of topics that can be indexed by search engines to support further information retrieval and expertise location needs, which are otherwise hard to satisfy.

A novel approach to connect knowledge seekers and knowledge providers is described in Singley, et al. (2008). The work introduces *BlueReach*, a synchronous chat tool with automatically created, topic-dependent buddy lists, that enables a question-asker to link with a predetermined set of question-answerers who have agreed to be available. When a topic is selected, the application displays a list of people who are currently available and have enrolled themselves as experts on this topic. The user then composes a question and selects a name which launches a chat session. The question is immediately presented to the expert. If the question is not a good match for his/her expertise, both parties can quickly establish this fact. At the end of the chat, both parties can optionally rate their satisfaction with the interaction on a scale of 1 to 5.

Chenthamarakshan, et al. (in press) describe an extension of the work, which focuses on enhancing the overall effectiveness of the synchronous chat tool, via a recommendation system that ranks experts according to their suitability to answer a given question on a specific topic. The first step in the expert recommendation methodology is to construct a BlueReach social interaction graph, whose nodes are community members, while directed edges go from an expert to a user representing all sessions between them. Given a new or existing user with a new question on a topic, the goal is to rank experts enrolled in that topic in decreasing order of potential match, taking into account the following: (a) past interactions and ratings if available and (b) internal information about members such as job profiles, description of project engagements etc. A good ranker is one which encourages user-expert interactions that lead to highly rated sessions, thus driving-up the net quality of the network. The recommendation engine requires two steps to be configured for the real-time use. The first step is designed to overcome the problem of sparse expert and user ratings, by using sessions labeled with rating information to train a binary classification model capable of producing probabilistic outputs. This classification model is then applied to score each unrated session with the probability of being a positive interaction. In the second step, standard information retrieval tools are applied to index the collection of member profiles and historical session transcripts, and also store the probabilistic scores produced by the binary classification model for the sessions (Chenthamarakshan, et al. (in press)).

Although the approaches based on automated skill matching can be applied to solve the expertise recommendation problems, the solutions based on the network models demonstrate that social relationships play an important role in many workforce problems, and hence superior recommendations can be obtained by combining traditional skill matching with rich social interaction data.

Methodologies for improving the quality of workforce-related data

The availability and quality of the workforce-related data is the single-most critical factor for the adoption of advanced WFM analytics. Oftentimes, due to constantly evolving nature of business processes and supporting IT, enterprise data is not fully aligned or supportive of newly developed solutions. As a result, no matter how sophisticated the analytics engine might be, without accurate inputs, the results and recommendations generated are of little value. Therefore, in addition to rigorous data collection and updating mechanisms, during the development of workforce management analytics there should be a great focus on methodologies for automated data refinement, re-labeling or error-discovery. In this section we provide examples of several data-quality issues that are frequently encountered in ERP systems, and algorithms used to address these issues and improve the inputs into the WFM solutions.

Information "boosting"

As already mentioned, one of the key requirements for the implementation of advanced WFA solutions is the existence of an ERP/HCM solution across the organization. For most of the companies the development of an ERP system represents a significant financial and time investment, involves substantial changes to the infrastructure, and calls for introduction of new business models and processes. Therefore, such investments are typically made over long periods of time (e.g. several years), and are influenced by different architects/decision-makers. This frequently results in redundancies or disconnects among different components of the system, and oftentimes presents challenges for the implementation of advanced analytics. It is especially prominent when there is a lack of compatibility and linkages among various workforce data, such as employee, skill and project/product information, which is used as input in all operations of the workforce management lifecycle. Such data is used to produce demand and workload forecasts, perform assignments for ongoing projects, determine resource requirements for future projects, and compute business metrics to assess project success.

From the workforce management perspective the three most important data components of an ERP system are: 1) *Employee information*, describing the supply of resources and their skills; 2) *Project claims*, describing which projects have been conducted in the past and how they were staffed; 3) *Project templates*, describing different types of projects and their average bill of resource requirements. In practice, none of the three data sources is "perfect". Employee information is prone to many types of errors, including missing employees, and missing/incorrect skill information. Although new projects should be staffed according to the project template specification, the actual staffing can often differ depending upon the availability of resources. Moreover, project claims often indicate only the number of hours each employee spent on a project, without specifying which skills were deployed, causing an ambiguity when employees have multiple skills. As a result, project claims typically exhibit significant deviation from the project templates. Project templates also need additional improvement, as they are usually provided once by subject matter experts without taking into account the inconsistencies in actual staffing or changes/updates in employee skill information. As a result, the implementation of any analytics solution often calls for a data-cleaning and pre-processing step to address missing information, perform error-discovery and correction, increase the reliability of different data inputs, and improve the quality of bills of resources estimation and other information used for workforce forecasting and planning. One such pre-processing approach is described in the work by Hu, et al. (2008 June). They propose an information-boosting methodology that exploits various relationships in workforce data to infer missing information and identify incorrect entries. The algorithm consists of three steps. It first estimates the most likely usage of resource skills on past projects, given the employee skill vectors and the recommended staffing from project template data. Using the obtained information, it then identifies and corrects errors in the employee skill data. In the final step the newly computed information is used to adjust and update the project templates. The algorithms also allow for iteration among the three schemes, through which the information is subsequently refined until certain convergence criteria are met.

Semi-supervised engagement clustering

A crucial component of the resource forecasting and planning process is the analysis of current and (anticipated) future workload to estimate expected demand for various types of projects and associated skills. In order to accomplish this accurately, each project must be labeled to reflect the pre-defined solution category it belongs to, since different solution categories have different staffing requirements and different cost profiles, etc. However, because of dynamic business environments in services business and changing customer needs, solution portfolios are constantly evolving and are frequently redefined, limiting the ability of project managers to categorize projects accurately. Hence, often there is a need for an automated methodology to either map projects into a set of predefined, but highly dynamic, solution categories, or to re-label the old data every time the solution taxonomy changes.

Hu, et al. (2008 August) describe a new approach to solving this problem by formulating it in a semi-supervised clustering framework. They propose a solution wherein text-based matching between solution category and unstructured project descriptions is used to generate "soft" seeds, which are subsequently used to guide clustering in the basic feature space. As the basic feature for each project they use the *skill allocation vector*, computed from the actual hours billed for resources of various skills on that project. The clustering is then performed via a new variation of the *k*-means algorithm, called *Soft Seeded k-means*, which makes effective use of the side information provided by seeds with a wide range of confidence levels, even when they do not provide complete coverage of the pre-defined categories.

Discussion and next steps

Talent/skill management is becoming one of the most important factors in a company's ability to deliver projects, grow revenue, be more profitable and embrace challenges of global integration. This is especially true for service oriented businesses, and as a result, forward-thinking organizations are beginning to invest in advanced workforce analytics as a major competitive differentiator. For the client serving businesses, the requirements for the next generation workforce management systems are expanding – the WFM tools are not only expected to make the most effective use of the global workforce, but also to drive the best career environment in the industry while optimizing responsiveness to client needs. With today's market focus on innovation and individual productivity, the key asset to leverage for sustained business growth is human capital and the new applications will emerge in support of these requirements. We envision analytics and applications that will take an advantage of a wealth of workforce related data to derive the representation of the workforce beyond just the numbers or skill distributions, to understand the patterns of interaction, knowledge sharing and innovation, and to identify optimal workforce decisions and strategies that will benefit both the company and the employees. The future solutions will enable the "best performing teams" and support creation of successful projects while taking into consideration human interaction and synergy, as well as long term objectives such as on-the-job training and relationship building. Emerging models and analysis of work complexity and workgroup composition (Man and Lam, 2003) will support better team building. Workforce productivity and quality (Oliva and Sternan, 2001) will also be incorporated into future comprehensive workforce planning systems. The future solutions will be able to support collaborative environments and help employees manage their careers: suggest personalized career paths, identify "ideal" mentors/mentees, connect people with question to people who can answer them. We envision applications that will determine optimal policies to achieve desired workforce composition, using information on teaming, work relationships, career background and experiences.

These new capabilities will require and drive significant advances in diverse technical areas. Due to the heterogeneous and sparsely labeled nature of the data inputs, and due to the complex and dynamic characteristics of the multiple relationships, to learn models from such complex data, and to use these models to perform workforce optimization will require novel contributions to data mining, statistical modeling, machine learning, social network analysis, and stochastic optimization. Some of the most critical areas of exploration will include:

Semi-Supervised Learning, an emerging research area that focuses on methodologies that can effectively learn from vast amount of unlabeled data coupled with limited, imperfect knowledge, using techniques such as low-density methods of classification, graph regularization, constrained k-means clustering and metric learning (Zhu, 2008 July). The semi-supervised methodologies are particularly relevant to the applications involving the modeling of teams and communities, as there exists a wealth of historical data such as past projects and jamming sessions, while only a small portion are categorized with interesting properties such as types of engagement, customer satisfaction, project success level, individual performance, team/community productivity, "innovativeness" of ideas, etc.

Statistical Relational Learning, which addresses the challenge of applying statistical inference to problems involving rich collections of objects linked together in complex relational networks (Perlich and Provost, 2006). In the workforce management setting, such relationships could be people-to-people (worked on same project before), people-projects (manager of a specific project), project-offering (instance of a specific service product), and translating these complex relationships into a form suitable for predictive modeling is a challenging research subject.

Temporal Graph Modeling, which refers to an emerging collection of techniques that allow for modeling of causal relationships among variables given time series data, and where new advances are needed to identify accurate and scalable ways to derive both static and time varying relationships (Arnold, et al., 2007 August).

Optimal Stochastic Control, referring to research into techniques that enable analysis and optimization of complex stochastic networks over time (Bertsekas, 2001). The networks encountered in workforce applications tend to involve extremely high dimensions with complex dependencies among the dimensions, posing challenging optimization problems that are notoriously difficult to solve. Furthermore, the solutions need to be mapped to policies/actions that will "incentivize" desired workforce/human behaviors.

Multi-Objective Optimization, which aims to develop a unified optimization framework to address competing objectives in an integrated manner (Bertsekas, 2001). While most workforce modeling and optimization to date takes a top-down approach to maximize company benefits, for the next generation systems, there will also be a need to incorporate a bottom-up approach to maximize individual/group benefits.

Competing in today's environment requires companies to focus on building a more responsive, flexible and resilient workforce. To do so, organizations will have to be more effective in sourcing talent, allocating resources across competing initiatives, measuring performance and building key capabilities and skills. But developing a broad workforce management agenda requires an enterprise-wide commitment and investment on a number of fronts (data, IT, process). As pointed out by the The Global Human Capital Study 2005, individually, organizationally, and nationally, human capital management is at a crossroads -- deficiencies in skills, talent and leadership have to be addressed by a refocusing and, in many cases, by fresh thinking on "the capability within" ("The capability within", 2005). By helping companies attract, maintain and make most productive use of high value skills, and by impacting the business metrics such as cost, revenue growth, product/service delivery excellence and workforce satisfaction, workforce analytics has a potential to be among the key drivers of corporate success.

References

Ackerman, M., Wulf, V., Pipek, V. (Eds.). (2002). *Sharing expertise: beyond knowledge management*. Cambridge, MA: MIT Press.

Alba, R. (1973). A graph-theoretic definition of a sociometric clique. *Journal of Mathematical Sociology*, 3, 113–126.

AMR. (2006a). *The human capital management applications report, 2005–2010*. (AMR Research report). Boston, MA.

AMR. (2006b). *Workforce management landscape: the right people in the right place at the right time*. (AMR Research report). Boston, MA

Arnold, A., Liu, Y., Abe, N. (2007 August). *Temporal causal modeling with graphical granger methods*, Proceeding of the Thirtheenth ACM DIGKDD International Conference on Knowledge Discovery and Data Mining, KDD'07, San Jose, CA.

Bertsekas, D. (2001). *Dynamic programming and optimal control, Volume II*. Belmont, MA: Athena Scientific, 2001.

Bhadra, S., Lu, Y., Squillante, M. (2007). *Optimal capacity planning in stochastic loss networks with time-varying workloads*. Proceedings of the 2007 ACM SIGMETRICS international conference on measurement and modeling of computer systems, San Diego, CA.

Brusco, M., Jacobs, L. (2000). Optimal Models for meal-break and start-time flexibility in continuous tour scheduling. *Management Science*, 46(12), 1630–1641.

Butler, T., Waldroop, J. (2004). Understanding 'people' people. Harvard Business Review, June 2004, 78-86.

Chen, B., Tai, R., Harrison, R., Pan, Y. (2005). *Novel hybrid hierarchical-K-means clustering method (H-K-Means) for microarray analysis*. Proceedings of the 2005 IEEE Computational Systems Bioinformatics Conference Workshops, BCSBW'05, Stanford, CA.

Chenthamarakshan, V., Dey, K., Hu, J., Mojsilovic, A., Riddle, W., Sindhwani, V. (in press). Leveraging social networks for corporate staffing and expert recommendation. *IBM Systems Journal*.

Chesbrough, H., Spohrer, J. (2006). A research manifesto for services science. *Communications of the ACM*. 49(7), 35-40.

Dasgupta, K., Singh, R., Viswanathan, B., Chakraborty, D., Mukherjea, S., Nanavati, A., Joshi, A. (2008) *Social ties and their relevance to churn in mobile telecom networks*. Proceedings of the 11th international conference on extending database technology: advances in database technology, EDBT 2008, 668–677.

Datta, R., Hu, J., Ray, B. (2007). *Sequence mining for business analytics: building project taxonomies for resource demand forecasting*. Proceedings of the Workshop on Data Mining for Business, PAKDD, Nanjing, China.

Dietrich, B., Harrison, T. (2006 April). Serving the services. *ORMS Today*, 33(3).

Fitzsimmons, J., Fitzsimmons, M. (2003). *Service management*. New York, NY: McGraw-Hill.

Gilat, D., Landau, A., Ribak, A., Shiloach, Y., Wasserkrug, S. (2006 August). *SWOPS (shift work optimized planning and scheduling)*. Proceedings of the 6th International Conference on the Practice and Theory of Automated Timetabling, PATAT 2006, Brno, Czech Republic.

Gresh, D., Connors, D., Fasano, J., Wittrock, R. (2007). Applying supply chain optimization techniques to workforce planning problems. *IBM Journal of Research and Development*, 51(3/4), 251-261.

Dom, B., Eiron, I., Cozzi, A., Zhang, Y. (2003).*Graph-based ranking algorithms for email expertise analysis*. Proceedings of the 8th ACM SIGMOD workshop on Research issues in data mining and knowledge discovery, San Diego, CA.

Gans, N., Koole, G., Mandelbaum, A. (2003). Telephone call centers: tutorial, review and research prospects. *Manufacturing and Service Operations Management (M&SOM)*, 5(2), 79-141.

Heskett, J., Jones, T., Loveman, G., Sasser, W., Schlesinger, L. (1994). Putting the service profit chain to work. *Harvard Business Review*, 72, 164-174.

Hu, J., Ray, B., Singh, M. (2007). Statistical methods for automated generation of services engagement staffing plans. *IBM Journal of Research and Development*, 51(3/4), 281-294.

Hu, J. Lu, Y., Mojsilovic, A., Radovanovic, A., Squillante, M. (2008 June). *"Information boosting" methodologies for multiple data sources in workforce management*. Paper presented at Manufacturing & Service Operations Management, MSOM 2008, Adelphi, MD.

Hu, J., Singh, M., Mojsilovic, A. (2008 August). *Using data mining for accurate resource and skill demand forecasting in services engagements*. Paper presented at the KDD Workshop on Data Mining for Business Applications, Las Vegas, NV.

IDC. (2006). *Worldwide workforce analytics software 2006-2010 forecast*. (IDC Report #201577). Framingham, MA.

IDC (2007) *Worldwide Workforce Performance Management 2007-2011 Forecast*. (IDC Report #206281). Framingham, MA.

Karmarkar, U. (2004 June). Will you survive the services revolution? *Harvard Business Review*, 82, 100-107.

Kautz, H., Selman, B., Shah, M. (1997). Referral web: combining social networks and collaborative filtering. *Communications of the. ACM*, 40(3), 63-65.

Kelly, F. (1986). Blocking probabilities in large circuit-switched networks. *Advances in Applied Probability*, 18, 473-505.

Kelly, F. (1987). One-dimensional circuit-switched networks. *Annals of Probability*, 15(3), 1166-1179.

Kelly, F. (1988). Routing in circuit-switched networks: optimization, shadow prices and decentralization. *Advances in Applied Probability*, 20, 112-144.

Kelly, F. (1990). Routing and capacity allocation in networks with trunk reservation. *Mathematics of Operations Research*, 15(4), 771-793.

Kelly, F. (1991). Loss networks. *Annals of Applied Probability*, 1(3), 319-178.

Lovelock, C., Wirtz, J. (2007). *Services marketing: people, technology, strategy*. Upper Saddle River, NJ: Prentice Hall.

Lu, Y., Radovanovic, A., Squillante, M. (2006 June). *Workforce management in service via stochastic network models*. Presented at the 2006 IEEE International Conference on Service Operations and Logistics, and Informatics, SOLI, Shanghai, China.

Lu, Y., Radovanovic, A., Squillante, M. (2007). Optimal capacity planning in stochastic loss networks. *ACM SIGMETRICS Performance Evaluation Review*, 35(2), 39-41.

Luce, R. (1950). Connectivity and generalized cliques in sociometric group structure. *Psychometrika*, 15(2), 169-190.

Lusch, R., Vargo, S. (2006). *The service-dominant logic of marketing*. Armonk, NY: ME Sharpe.

Man, D., Lam, S. (2003). The effects of job complexity and autonomy on cohesiveness in collectivistic and individualistic work groups: a cross-cultural analysis. *Journal of Organizational Behavior*, 24(8), 1979-1001.

Mason, A., Ryan, D., Panton, D. (1998). Integrated simulation, heuristic and optimization approaches to staff scheduling. *Operations Research*, 46(2), 161-175.

Naveh, Y., Richter, Y., Altshuler, Y., Gresh, D., Connors, D. (2007). Workforce optimization: Identification and assignment of professional workers using constraint programming. *IBM Journal of Research and Development*, 51(3/4), 263-279.

Oliva, R., Sternan, J. (2001). Cutting corners and working overtime: quality erosion in the service industry. *Management Science*, 47(7), 894-914.

Palmisano, S. (2006). The globally integrated enterprise. *Foreign Affairs*, 85(3), 127-136.

Perlich, C., Provost, F. (2006). *Distribution-based aggregation for relational learning with identifier attributes*. Machine Learning, 62(1-2), 65-105.

Seidman, S., Foster, B. (1978). A graph-theoretic generalization of the clique concept. *Journal of Mathematical Sociology*, 6, 139-154.

Sharma, M., Lu, Y., Squillante, M. (2008 October). *Stochastic analysis and optimization of workforce evolution*. Paper presented at the INFORMS Annual Meeting, Washington, DC.

Singley, K., Lai, J., Kuang, L., Tang, J. (2008). *Bluereach: harnessing synchronous chat to support expertise sharing in a large organization*. Paper presented at the Conference on Human Factors in Computing Systems, CHI 2008, Florence, Italy.

The capability within: the global human capital study 2005. (2005). IBM Global Services Study.

The 2008 Workforce Management Optimas Awards (2008 October). *Workforce Magazine*.

Wasserkrug, S., Taub, S., Zeltyn, S., Gilat, D., Lipets, V., Feldman, Z., Mandelbaum, A. (2007 August). *Shift scheduling for third level IT support: challenges, models and case study*. Proceedings of the 2007 IEEE/INFORMS International Conference on Service Operations and Logistics, and Informatics, Philadelphia, PA.

Voss, S., Woodruff, D. (2003). *Introduction to computational optimization models for production planning in a supply chain*, Berlin, Springer.

Wittrock, R. (2006). *An introduction to WIT: watson implosion technology*. (IBM Research Report RC-24013). Yorktown Heights, NY.

Zhang, J., Ackerman, M., Adamic, L. (2007 May). *Expertise networks in online communities: Structure and algorithms*. Proceedings of WWW 2007, Banff, Alberta, Canada.

Zhu, X. (2008 July). *Semi-supervised learning literature survey*. Retrieved April 22 2009 from http://pages.cs.wisc.edu/~jerryzhu/research/ssl/semireview.html.

Understanding Complex Product and Service Delivery Systems

William B. Rouse

Tennenbaum Institute

Georgia Institute of Technology

Rahul C. Basole

Tennenbaum Institute

Georgia Institute of Technology

This chapter considers alternative views of complex systems that deliver products and services to consumers and other constituencies. Holistic views of complex systems are discussed in the context of several public-private systems and a notional model is introduced that relates complexity to the number of enterprises in a domain and the levels of integration required for these enterprises to function successfully. Reductionist views of complexity are discussed, including the basic premises underlying axiomatic models of complexity. An information theoretic model is introduced for calculating the complexity of value delivery networks and applied to assessing the complexity of several enterprise domains. The use and value of models of complex systems are discussed.

Introduction

This chapter considers complex product and service delivery systems. Some of these systems are focused on product delivery. A good example is systems that design, develop, manufacture, and sustain aircrafts and automobiles. These systems are laced with services, but the focus is on creating and sustaining the product. In contrast, there are systems that focus on service delivery. Examples include networks that provide healthcare, education, defense, finance, and food (Basole & Rouse, 2008). While there are many products that enable the services

P.P. Maglio et al. (eds.), *Handbook of Service Science*, Service Science: Research and Innovations in the Service Economy, DOI 10.1007/978-1-4419-1628-0_20,
© Springer Science+Business Media, LLC 2010

in these networks, the focus is on the services provided. Note that none of the examples just discussed are purely product or service delivery systems, although they are often seen and managed that way.

We seek to understand the complexity of these types of systems in order to better design, operate, and maintain them (Rouse, 2003, 2007a). This chapter considers definitions and models of complexity, as well as the application of these models to particular systems. Models based on both holistic and reductionist views of these systems are considered. We argue that the reductionist approach provides important insights but is not sufficient due to emergent properties of complex systems. Hence, a balance between reductionist and holistic approaches is necessary to understand and gain insights into design, operation, and maintenance of these systems.

This chapter proceeds as follows. The next section considers holistic views of complex systems in the context of several public-private systems. A notional model of complexity is introduced that relates complexity to the number of enterprises in a domain and the levels of integration required for these enterprises to function successfully. The following section discusses reductionist views of complexity. The basic premises underlying axiomatic models of complexity are discussed including typical definitions of the structure and state of a system. An information theoretic model is introduced for calculating complexity in terms of the number of bits of information that must be processed to estimate the state of a complex system. This model is applied to assessing the complexity of several enterprise domains. The chapter concludes with a discussion of the use and value of models of complex systems.

Holistic Views

The reductionist approach, discussed later in this chapter, attempts to decompose a system into its structural elements to understand how these elements function together to yield the behavior of the system. In contrast, the holistic approach considers the characteristics and functioning of the overall system with little if any decomposition.

When one compares holistic views of aircraft manufacturing and healthcare delivery, for example, it quickly becomes evident that these are quite different types of systems. Aircraft manufacturing is an example of a complex product delivery system where many things have to come together into one smoothly functioning entity, such as an airplane or automobile. In the case of an airplane, for example, companies collaborate and interact during the design process and form global supply relationships to provide and deliver major components, such as the wing, the fuselage or engine. In this type of domain, the physical products or "goods" are the center of this kind of complex system.

Healthcare delivery, in contrast, is an example of a complex service delivery system where the complexity is due to the many organizational seams that hinder alignment of objectives and incentives, as well as information flow. There are many products that enable the services provided in such systems but, unlike complex product delivery systems, these products are not a primary source of the complexity of such systems. The socio-technical nature of the system is the primary source of complexity (Rouse & Baba, 2006). In other words, people and organizations, rather than technology, are dominant (Rouse, 2007b).

Large-scale public-private systems provide interesting opportunities to elaborate holistic views of complex systems. Such systems involve numerous private enterprises operating in a marketplace that is heavily influenced by government policy and, in some cases, by government funding. Examples include:

- *Defense*: Many interdependent private enterprises with integrated delivery of products and systems for public use, one source of payment, and substantial and integrated public oversight
- *Education*: A large number of independent, mostly public, enterprises with distributed delivery of products and services, many from private enterprises, as well as distributed payment and distributed public oversight
- *Finance*: Many interdependent private enterprises with integrated delivery of shared services, but distributed delivery of products and services to consumers, and distributed payment with integrated public oversight
- *Food*: A large number of independent private enterprises with integrated delivery systems, but distributed products and payment, with integrated public oversight of products, but less so services
- *Healthcare*: A very large number of independent private and public enterprises with distributed delivery of products and services but, for older and poor consumers, one source of payment, and integrated public oversight of products, but less so services

Note that *Defense* is a complex private sector product delivery system, embedded in a complex public sector service delivery system. *Education* and *Healthcare*, in contrast, are primarily complex service delivery systems, with both private and public sector service providers. *Finance* and *Food* predominantly involve private sector product and service delivery, with public sector oversight, albeit quite intense of late for *Finance*.

Table 1 summarizes the holistic characteristics of public-private enterprises discussed above. *Defense* is the most integrated while *Education* is the least integrated of these enterprises. Note that while oversight is integrated for *Finance*, *Food*, and *Healthcare*, the level does not approach that of *Defense*.

Table 1. Characteristics of Public-Private Enterprises

	No. of Enterprises	Delivery	Products/ Services	Payment	Oversight
Defense	1,000	Integrated	Integrated	Integrated	Integrated
Education	100,000	Distributed	Distributed	Distributed	Distributed
Finance	10,000	Integrated	Distributed	Distributed	Integrated
Food	100,000	Integrated	Distributed	Distributed	Integrated
Healthcare	1,000,000	Distributed	Distributed	Integrated	Integrated

In order to assess and contrast the complexity of these five domains, consider the following notional model of complexity C.

$$C = f(NE, DI, PSI, PI, OI) \qquad (1)$$

where NE is the number of enterprises, DI is the level of delivery integration, PSI is the level of product/service integration, PI is the level of payment integration, and OI is the level of oversight integration.

Delivery integration refers to the extent that the flow of resources across the value network is managed as a single or integrated entity. Product/service integration refers to the extent to which the consumer receives a single product/service. Payment integration refers to the extent that a single user pays for the products/services received. Oversight integration refers to the level of influence, management, and control of product and service delivery by a third-party constituent.

Note that integrated information systems are key to the other types of integration, particularly DI and PI. This is also the case for PSI when the product or service involves access to and use of information, such as in online financial services. The level of information integration differs substantially across types of enterprise. *Finance* has the highest level of information integration; *Healthcare* the lowest. The consequence is the well-known enormous paperwork burden experienced by *Healthcare*.

We would expect C to increase with NE and levels of integration – DI, PSI, PI, and OI – either required for success or imposed by oversight. *Education* is the least integrated enterprise and, hence, the least complex despite the large number of independent enterprises. It seems reasonable to argue that *Finance* is less complex than *Food* as it is a much less diverse industry and, until recently, oversight was less complicated; a case in point is the contrast of the Federal Reserve with the Food and Drug Administration.

Considering *Healthcare*, the fragmentation of provider enterprises and the third-party payment system, via either employers or government, contributes substantially to the complexity of this enterprise (Rouse, 2008). The lack of standard processes and practices can be contrasted with *Food* or, in general, *Retail* (Basole & Rouse, 2008). Hence, the complexity of *Healthcare* exceeds that of *Food*.

It could be argued that *Defense* has the greatest complexity due to the levels of integration imposed across all aspects of the enterprise. However, relatively few enterprises are involved and standard processes and practices are dictated by the single customer. Consequently, it can be argued that *Health* exceeds *Defense* in complexity.

Relationship (2) summarizes this notional analysis of the complexity of these public-private enterprises.

$$C_{Healthcare} > C_{Defense} > C_{Food} > C_{Finance} > C_{Education} \qquad (2)$$

Later in this chapter, we discuss a model that enables going beyond the ordinal relationship in (2) and quantifying complexity.

To probe a level deeper into holistic views of complexity, consider the differences between enterprises that produce airplanes and automobiles, and enterprises that deliver healthcare. Also, consider how the complexity of these enterprises differs depending on their relationship with the government. Table 2 summarizes these contrasts.

Table 2. Contrasts of Complexity

	Government	Non-Government
Airplanes & Automobiles	2nd in complexity due to processes imposed by government	3rd in complexity due to number of things that must function together
Healthcare Delivery	4th in complexity due to single organization provider and payer	1st in complexity due to many organizational seams

Healthcare delivery in the private sector is the most complex due to the many organizational seams that hinder alignment of objectives and incentives, as well as information flow. In contrast, healthcare delivery in the government via the Military Health System and Veterans Administration is the least complex because a single organization provides and pays for the care. Clearly, the nature of the enterprise, such as characterized in Table 1, has an enormous impact on these two enterprises providing the same products and services.

Enterprises that provide custom-designed airplanes, automobiles, and other systems to the government are the second most complex because of the processes and practices imposed by the government (Pennock, Rouse, & Kollar, 2007). Enterprises that provide the same types of systems to non-government customers are less complex because their processes and practices are designed to minimize overhead rather than maximize scrutiny. In this case, the product or system is evaluated or rated, but not the process that created it.

In summary, holistic views of complex systems can enable qualitative analyses that provide insights into sources of complexity. Such analyses are particularly useful when they enable benchmarking one type of systems versus another. We can see from the foregoing why the complexity of various public-private systems differs.

Reductionist Views

Reductionist approaches to modeling involve decomposing a system into its elements, determining the relationships among these elements, and composing these relationships into an overall model of the system. In this section, we apply this approach to developing an axiomatic model of the complexity of a system using network models and information theory.

Basic Premises

It is important to begin by discussing a few basic premises. First, and perhaps foremost, complexity is not a property of a system independent of its context. More specifically, complexity is related to the intentions (or objectives) and expertise of the observer relative to the system of interest (Rouse, 2007a). Thus, for example, a large aircraft that is used as a paperweight is not complex; it is simply a large mass. If, on the other hand, one's intention or objective was to operate and maintain this aircraft, it could be quite complex.

Elsewhere we have argued that complexity is the amount of information that must be processed to achieve the objectives of interest, expressed in bits or bits/second (Basole & Rouse, 2008). Observers' objectives and requisite expertise can differ for the same system, for example:

- Design and develop an airplane or automobile
- Manufacture and assemble an airplane or automobile
- Drive or fly an airplane or automobile
- Maintain an airplane or automobile
- Ride in an airplane or automobile

Thus, riding in an airplane or automobile is not very complex, but designing and developing these vehicles is likely to be quite complex, especially if one has little expertise in performing these design and development tasks.

A generalized objective with respect to a complex system is to determine its state, perhaps in order to influence or control the system. While achieving this objective is premised on the system being observable and controllable, consideration of these constructs is beyond the scope of this chapter (Sage & Rouse, 2009). Consequently, we define complexity as the amount of information that must be processed to determine the state of a complex system, expressed in bits (or binary units) (Basole & Rouse, 2008).

Models of Complex Systems

In order to operationalize this definition, a model of the system of interest is needed. An enterprise system can be modeled as a highly interconnected and layered network of physical, economic, informational, and social relationships. It is rooted in the idea that many natural, social and economic phenomena are in fact complex networked systems (Arthur, 1999). In the sciences, for example, biologists have examined networks of interactions between genes and proteins to study the behavior of organisms, to model diseases, or to explore the dynamics of food webs (Cohen, Briand, & Newman, 1990; Kauffman, 1969; Newman, 2003). Engineers and computer scientists have studied information and technological networks, such as the electric power grid, telecommunications networks, and the Internet (Broder, et al., 2000; Newman, 2003; Strogatz, 2001). Networks have also been studied in the social sciences. Sociologists, for example, have examined the connections among people to understand the functioning of human society (Wasserman & Faust, 1994). Economists have investigated how innovations diffuse through a network of individuals and organizations.

Along the same lines, the conceptualization of product and service delivery systems as complex networks is not new. It is based on the fundamental thinking that individuals and organizations do not merely operate in dyadic relationships, but are deeply embedded in complex economic and social systems consisting of numerous inter- and intra-organizational relationships. This perspective replaces the traditional view of value chains proposed by Porter which suggested a linear value flow from raw material suppliers to manufacturers to consumers (Normann & Ramirez, 1993; Porter, 1985).

Today, however, value is provided by a myriad of multidirectional relationships across and between businesses and consumers. As a result, products and services are designed, created, delivered, and provided to customers via complex processes, exchanges, and relationships (Chesbrough & Spohrer, 2006; Fitzsimmons & Fitzsimmons, 2001; Vargo & Lusch, 2004) This has led traditional value chains to evolve to value networks (Allee, 2000; Bovet & Martha, 2000; Kothandaraman & Wilson, 2001; Parolini, 1999), which are characterized by a complex set of direct and indirect ties between various participants, or actors, all delivering value either to their immediate customer or the end consumer. The value network construct thus assumes the organization to be part of a larger complex networked system of organizations, or extended enterprises, that together create (i.e., co-create) value. (Allee, 2000; Basole & Rouse, 2008; Brandenburger & Nalebuff, 1997; Dyer, 2000; Stabell & Fjeldstad, 1998).

Complex systems in a broad range of domains tend to exhibit some common characteristics. Generally speaking, complex systems consist of a large number of interacting entities, e.g., components or agents (Arthur, 1999). Each entity's behavior is commonly governed by a set of rules, which may range from physical principles to economic or social rules. The relationships among these entities and their consequent interactions can often lead to complex "emergent" structures and dynamic behaviors.

Modeling a complex system, such as a product or service delivery system, requires specification of the entities and relationships that embody a system's structure and enable the dynamics of system behavior. When the model is represented as a network diagram, the basic building blocks of models of complex systems are nodes (entities) and links (relationships). Note that if we were to adopt another representation (e.g., differential equations or if-then rules), the building blocks used to depict the system would be quite different.

Nodes represent agents or actors (e.g., people or firms), while links represent relationships, or ties, between actors in a complex networked system (Moody, McFarland, & Bender-deMoll, 2005). An axiomatic model must also take into account the existence of conflicting objectives among nodes (e.g. capture largest market share, minimize supply cost, etc.). Similarly, nodes in complex systems have the ability to learn and self-organize (i.e., add, remove, and change the nature of links). A robust axiomatic model would, ideally, capture this. Relationships among nodes can also be of varying nature.

Traditionally, network studies have captured flows of both tangibles and intangibles, such as raw materials, components, goods, services, information, money, and people. However, there are also numerous non-flow relationships among nodes. These often include contracts, competition, technology, geography, and industry. In the context of product and service delivery systems, there also may be a stochastic nature of supply and demand as well as changes in the system structure due to adaptation to internal and environmental factors that must be considered.

Beyond the simple indication of a relationship between nodes, there are also context-specific attributes of interest for the network models we have adopted to represent product and service delivery systems. For instance, while traditional node-link diagrams assume a single relation between two nodes, previous product and service delivery research has shown that for a pair of organizations, multiple types of relationships, or compound relationships, often may exist (Ross & Robertson, 2007). A firm may therefore be a customer, supplier, partner, and competitor of another firm all at the same time. Thus, the number of relationships can be an attribute of interest in complex systems research.

Table 3 provides a non-exhaustive summary of potentially relevant network elements and their attributes that should be considered when visualizing complex product and service delivery networks.

Table 3. Salient Node-Link Characteristics of Enterprise Networks (adapted from Basole, 2009)

Element	Description
Node	Actor (Organization), Player, Entity in the Product and Service Delivery System
- Label	Actor Name (e.g. Company A, Company B)
- Type	Type or Class of an Organization (e.g. Supplier, Partner, Complementor, Competitor)
- Attribute (Class)	Industry Segment (e.g. Insurance Provider, Pharmaceuticals, Medical Equipment Supplier, Health Providers, R&D Laboratories, Automobile Manufacturer, Engine Supplier), Organization Size, Organization Revenue, Geospatial Position (e.g. Country, Location)
Link	Relation (Alliance, Partnership, JV, Buyer / Supplier / Customer); Contract; Technology Dependence
- Attribute (Class)	Strength of Relation, Type of Relation, Length of Relation, Type of Value Exchanged (e.g. Information, Raw Material, Components, Goods, Services, Knowledge, Money, Material, People)
- Direction	Directed (e.g. flow from source to destination node), Undirected

Visualizing Complex Systems

Product and service delivery systems, or value networks, contain five types of actors: consumers, service providers, tier 1 and 2 enablers, and auxiliary enablers (Basole & Rouse, 2008). Value in such systems is created and delivered through a complex set of business-to-business (B2B), business-to consumer (B2C), and consumer-to-consumer (C2C) relationships, and influenced by the social, technological, economic and political context in which it is embedded. Figure 1 depicts the nature of such networks.

The following examples illustrate the characteristics of the retail domain and healthcare delivery domain. Specifically, we have focused on the Fortune 1000 to identify salient industry segments and companies in each segment of these domains. It should be noted that this approach inevitably eliminates many innovative small companies from the analysis. It is however our belief that this limitation is acceptable given the comparative nature of the examples and analyses we present in this chapter.

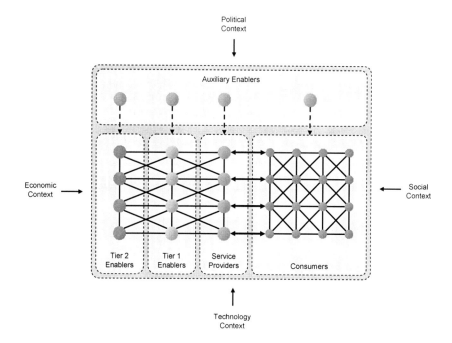

Figure 1. A Conceptual Model of Service Value Networks

Retail Example

The retail market is immense. The five markets depicted in our earlier paper (Basole & Rouse, 2008) involve roughly one-half of the Fortune 1000; retailers and their suppliers involve one-half of these companies. Service delivery systems such as *Retail*, as well as *Healthcare*, differ from product delivery systems in terms of the nature of transactions. When one buys or uses an airplane or an automobile, one can reasonably expect that after the purchase one will receive all the parts of the vehicle. In contrast, it would be very unlikely to buy one of everything in a retail store, or avail oneself of every treatment is a hospital. Consequently, the product and service delivery system (Figure 2) has a more varied set of relationships between suppliers and retailers.

As the complexity assessments in the next section indicate, *Retail* is very complex. However, as will be seen, the consumer does not have to address this complexity. A very efficient user interface has been created: stores, both brick-and-mortar and online. Increasing B2B complexity has resulted in decreasing B2C complexity. Increased convenience and decreased prices have driven consumer value (i.e., B2C value), enabled by B2B value.

Healthcare Example

The *Healthcare* value network is one of the most complex of the five domains discussed in (Basole & Rouse, 2008). This network can be described as a loose federation of independent enterprises, all trying to optimize the market from their perspective and for their benefit (Figure 3). No single enterprise or type of enterprise dominates. Further, enterprises from private and public sectors, as well as academia and nonprofit organizations, are laced throughout the value network (Rouse, 2008).

This can result in very confused customers, often receiving conflicting guidance from different players. However, this situation will inevitably change, and the Internet has enabled highly informed customers to make well-informed choices. As more information on provider performance — and availability — becomes accessible, consumers will have greatly increased leverage. It can be expected that the extreme fragmentation of the industry will not persist, if only because the projected economics of the industry as it is are not tenable.

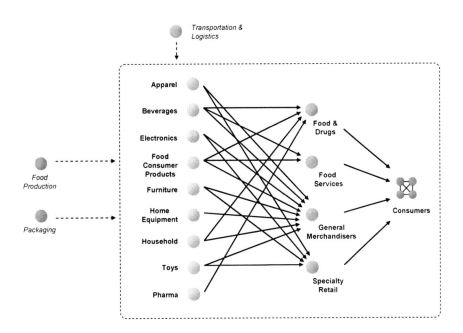

Figure 2. Retail Enterprise

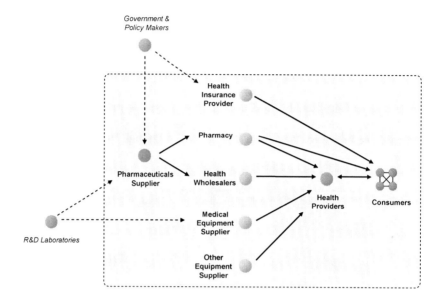

Figure 3. Healthcare Enterprise

In addition, there are a large number of providers of services with many dimensions. Consequently, service is uneven, costs are high, and consumers are often confused and frustrated. The providers and enablers that can fix the B2C value proposition, while also reducing B2C complexity, are likely to reap enormous benefits. At the same time, the push for ''consumer directed'' healthcare may result in increased complexity for consumers, which has not proved successful in the other four markets. Innovations that increase B2B complexity in order to reduce B2C complexity are more likely to be successful.

Complexity Assessment

In order to assess the complexity of networks such as depicted in Figures 2 and 3, this representation can be generalized as shown in Figure 4. As discussed earlier, the objective for which complexity is to be assessed has to be specified. The objective of interest is the state of the network. In this section, we present an axiomatic model of the complexity associated with determining network state, based on the axioms of network, probability, and information theories.

The state can be defined as the identity of all nodes involved in any randomly chosen transaction, t_m, where $m = 1, 2, 3, ,T$. Each type of transaction can be selected with probability pt_m. The complexity of the network can be defined as the amount of information that has to be collected to determine the state of the network, i.e., the identity of the nodes involved in the transaction of interest. To determine this, one needs to know the conditional probabilities that particular nodes are involved given the type of transaction of interest. From Figure 4, one can see that the conditional probabilities cascade from right to left depending on which paths exist from left to right. In general, not all enablers are suppliers of all providers. Therefore, these conditional probabilities are not uniform.

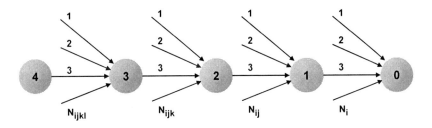

N_i = No. of 1st tier suppliers to i^{th} product/service outlets

N_{ij} = No. of 2nd tier suppliers to ij^{th} product/service outlets

N_{ijk} = No. of 3rd tier suppliers to ijk^{th} product/service outlets

N_{ijkl} = No. of 4th tier suppliers to $ijkl^{th}$ product/service outlets

Figure 4. General Network Model

Given knowledge of the conditional probabilities of interest, equation (3) shows how complexity C can be calculated using Shannon's calculation of entropy in information theory (Shannon, 1948). This measure has since been applied in domains ranging from failure diagnosis (Golay, Seong, & Manno, 1989) to manufacturing (Deshmukh, Talvage, & Barash, 1998; Kaimann, 1974) to sociology (Butts, 2000) as a measure of the observational and/or computational effort involved to assess the state of a system. Indeed, all measures of complexity are based on the characteristics of a representation of a system (Rouse, 2007b), with network representations the most common (Casti, 1995).

$$C = \sum_{m=1}^{T} pt_m \left\{ \begin{array}{l} \displaystyle\sum_{i=1}^{N_i} - p(n_i \mid t) \log[p(n_i \mid t_m)] \\[2ex] \displaystyle+ \sum_{i=1}^{N_{ji}} - p(n_j \mid n_i t) \log[p(n_j \mid n_i t_m)] \\[2ex] \displaystyle+ \sum_{i=1}^{N_{jik}} - p(n_k \mid n_i n_j t) \log[p(n_k \mid n_i n_j t_m)] \\[2ex] \displaystyle+ \sum_{l=1}^{N_{jikl}} - p(n_l \mid n_i n_j n_k t) \log[p(n_l \mid n_i n_j n_k t_m)] \end{array} \right\} \tag{3}$$

where N_i, N_{ij}, N_{ijk} and N_{ijkl} are the number of nodes at each "tier" of the network and $p(n \mid n\ n\ n\ t)$ is the conditional probability that a particular node is involved given the transaction is type t_m, and the logarithm is to the base 2.

The measure of complexity resulting from the above equation is binary digits, or bits. Intuitively, it represents the number of binary questions one would have to ask and have answered to determine the state of a value network. This measure is not without subtlety. For example, if one claims, as we do below, that the complexity of the entire *Retail* market is over 30 bits, there will undoubtedly be many skeptical responses. However, once one explains that this means that more than one billion binary questions would be needed to determine the state of the system, people begin to understand the implications of this measure of complexity.

Note that equation (3) has repeated terms of the form $- p\ log\ p$. If the network of interest included only one upstream node, with probability p of being involved in the transaction and *(1-p)* of not being involved, then the complexity calculation would be of the form $- [p\ log\ p + (1-p)\ log\ (1-p)]$. This value is maximum for *p* = *1/2*. In general, if there are N upstream nodes and the probability of each being involved in a transaction equals *1/N*, then uncertainty and, hence, complexity is maximized.

This observation implies that complexity, as we have defined it, can be decreased by greatly simplifying supply chains, i.e., having only one supplier for each element of the system. Unfortunately, this tends to reduce variety and can lead to increased risk of losing the sole supplier for an element of the system. A better strategy may be to allow increased complexity as long as it can be managed by, for instance, enhanced back office information systems. Indeed, this has been the strategy in *Retail*.

Using publicly available data from the Fortune 1000, we were able to identify the number of companies in each node of Figures 2 and 3, as well as for three other domains – aerospace, automotive, and telecom (Basole & Rouse, 2008). The probabilities associated with each company being involved in any given transaction were calculated in one of two ways. The predominant way was simply to estimate the probability as one divided by the number of supplier or manufacturers. In a few cases, we adjusted the probabilities to reflect the fact that a Fortune 1000 supplier must be supplying at least one Fortune 1000 manufacturer. The results are shown in Figure 5.

Several observations are important. First, highly fragmented markets are much more complex than highly consolidated markets. There are relatively few aerospace and automotive providers compared to retailers and consumer products companies. While manufacturers of airplanes and automobiles are likely to claim that their products are complex, consumers do not have to address this complexity and these industries benefit from this. Many more people fly on airlines and drive automobiles than design and develop such systems.

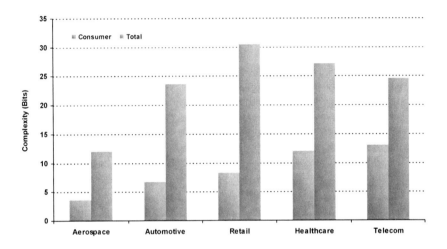

Figure 5. Complexity Assessments

Second, consumer complexity can be reduced by either market consolidation, so there are fewer choices, or by increased B2B efficiency that reduces B2C complexity. The aerospace and automotive industries are examples of the former and the retail industry is an example of the latter. Note that the telecom industry is clearly employing both mechanisms, while healthcare, via consumer-directed healthcare, is moving away from both mechanisms. This suggests that new intermediaries will emerge in healthcare to manage complexity for consumers.

Of particular interest is the comparison of *Retail* and *Healthcare*. *Retail* is the most complex domain because, as indicated earlier a very large number of companies are in the retail industry. However, the consumer does not experience this complexity because of a high degree of back office automation. *Healthcare* includes fewer enterprises, but the lack of integration results in consumers having to deal with much more of the network. If *Retail* operated the same way as *Healthcare*, buying a toaster or can opener at a retailer would result in the consumer receiving ten or more bills from suppliers of components, probably many months later, with little explanation of why this supplier was involved in creating the appliance. This would not make for happy consumers.

Note that this conclusion regarding the complexity of *Healthcare* is consistent with our earlier conclusions based on more holistic analyses. The fragmentation of this domain contributes greatly to its complexity, especially for consumers. Thus, we see that the qualitative and quantitative analyses can be quite complementary.

Use and Value of Models

There are many benefits of developing models of complex systems. In general, a model tends to serve as an abstraction, or approximate representation, of phenomena of interest. Models enable researchers, designers, and managers to explicitly identify, describe, and analyze the key underlying elements, principles, and properties that define and shape complex systems.

The resulting models thus allow us to illuminate core dynamics, predict future states, suggest dynamical analogies, identify uncertainties, discover new questions, and challenge existing theories (Epstein, 2008). They also enable us to formulate and address tradeoffs and suggest efficiencies.

Beyond the value in the final resulting model, there is tremendous, and often ignored, value in the modeling process itself; it provides critical insight into the salient underpinnings of product and service delivery systems and exposes the importance of the enabling assumptions. In other words, modeling of complex systems enables us to open dialog and communicate our cognitive map of the product or service delivery system of interest.

By laying out complex system elements and their relationships in detail, we are able to study why, how, and potentially when observed and anticipated phenomena may occur. In the context of product and service networks, for example, it allows us to study policies, interventions, and strategies at various points and stages of delivery life cycles. It enables researchers and managers to make informed tradeoffs across design and development, manufacturing and assembly, operations, maintenance and consumption, as well as suggest efficiencies and strategies to mitigate risks. It also enables uncovering the complexities that either accelerate or impede the product and service delivery network. Consequently, complex system models of product and service delivery networks enable us to better design and manage these networks.

Furthermore complex system models enable us to benchmark processes, enterprises, and markets and make competitive comparisons. Such comparisons were central to the results presented in this chapter. Models can also provide insights into the dynamics of innovation and the factors that lead to competitive advantage in product and service delivery networks.

Last but not least, developing models of complex systems also provides the basis for visualization of ecosystems and their dynamics. Using visualization, decision and policy makers can analyze and understand the structure of complex enterprise systems, identify roles (e.g. hub, broker, bridge, niche) that actors play, and the potential evolution of the industry (Basole, 2009).

Mapping actor relationships enables us to understand and identify patterns and structures of firms engaged in innovation and value creation. The use of visualization models also provides one a platform to differentiate complex networked systems by purpose, in terms of the ways firms compete and collaborate (Kambil, 2008).

Visualization also enables one to explicitly map actors into a decision space. We can see how actors relate to each other. Identifying coordinates within a visual framework will provide insight into the nature of firms' placements, what these positions mean, and consequently provide a more systematic way to understand the structure and evolutions of inter-firm networks over time.

In summary, complex system models have tremendous value for both researchers and practitioners. They enable exploration, identification, discovery, and communication of complexities that previously were often ignored. The knowledge gained can both extend the state of the art and provide competitive advantage.

Conclusions

This chapter has discussed the complexity of product and service delivery systems. This involved considering holistic views of complex systems in the context of several public-private systems. A notional model of complexity was introduced that relates complexity to the number of enterprises in a domain and the levels of integration required for these enterprises to function successfully. Reductionist views of complexity were also considered. The basic premises underlying axiomatic models of complexity were discussed including typical definitions of the structure and state of a system. An information theoretic model was introduced for calculating complexity in terms of the number of bits of information that must be processed to assess the state of a complex system. This model was applied to assessing the complexity of several enterprise domains. The chapter concluded with a discussion of the use and value of models of complex systems.

The overarching conclusion of this chapter is that understanding of complex systems can be advanced by both holistic and reductionist approaches. Indeed, these approaches are complementary as illustrated by our conclusions regarding the complexity of *Healthcare*. We can learn a lot by considering both the forest and the trees. The holistic view enables seeing emergent phenomena and connections, while the reductionist view enables seeing how the pieces of a network come together to achieve the objectives for which they were designed.

The reductionist results presented in this chapter are predominantly quantitative, while the holistic results are rather qualitative. The reductionist complexity model, built upon axioms of network, probability and information theories, enabled deduction of the complexity metric of bits of information needed to determine network state. In contrast, the holistic complexity model relied upon knowledge of the broad characteristics of particular complex systems. Had we sought data on these characteristics, this model could have been parameterized, quantitative results measured, and statistical inferences made. The result would have been an empirical holistic model.

It would also be possible to frame an axiomatic holistic model. This might take the form of a macroeconomic model perhaps represented in terms of differential equations, from which characteristics such as stability and response times could be deduced. Thus, the distinction of deduction vs. inference, while very important, is not synonymous with holism vs. reductionism, nor qualitative vs. quantitative approaches. Perhaps the crucial distinction is between deriving conclusions from basic principles versus inferring conclusions from observations of phenomena. Our basic argument in this chapter is that both approaches are needed and complementary.

It is also important to revisit a basic premise of the model of complexity presented here, namely, that complexity can only be modeled relative to the intent of the modeler – in our case, determining the state of the network. The complexity metric employed does not capture the effectiveness, strength, or basis of relationships between entities in the system; it merely captures the conditional probability that two nodes are linked. For example, two nodes may be connected with each other based on a supply relationship, but the extent to which this link is effective is not reflected in our model. Hence, we can have a network that is very complex but ineffective (e.g., *Healthcare*) or very complex and extremely effective (e.g., *Retail*). Of course, we might also have networks low in complexity, but very ineffective in some cases and very effective in others.

This issue was not as limiting for the holistic model because we could incorporate a broader set of knowledge into the line of reasoning. We know that *Healthcare* is ineffective and the reasons underlying this assessment (Reid, Compton, Grossman, & Fanjiang, 2005; Rouse, 2008). Similarly, we know the overhead burden imposed by government oversight of *Defense*. Thus, to a great extent, the holistic model was based on simply organizing a wealth of knowledge of the characteristics of these domains, finding common attributes among these characteristics, and then positing how these attributes would affect complexity. In other words, we organized observations rather than deriving results.

These contrasts raise questions of how best to represent and visualize complex product and service delivery systems. How can one represent and visualize the nature of relationships among entities in order to derive – or just observe – the effectiveness of a network? How might one assess current effectiveness or project future effectiveness? How might one infer or deduce likely areas of future innovation from the nature of the entities and relationships portrayed?

Our sense is that no single type of representation or visualization will be sufficient. The analyst or the decision maker will need multiple views of the value network. At a minimum, these views will need to include at least one holistic view and at least one reductionist view. Put another way, at least one top-down view and one bottom-up view will be needed. Beyond this minimum, we expect that the necessary views will include financial, material, behavioral, social, and geographical portrayals. With such a portfolio of views, people will be able to truly understand complex value delivery networks.

References

Allee, V. (2000). Reconfiguring the Value Network. *Journal of Business Strategy, 21*(4), 36-41.

Arthur, W. B. (1999). Complexity and the economy. *Science, 284*(5411), 107-109.

Basole, R. C. (2009). Visualization of Interfirm Relations in a Converging Mobile Ecosystem. *Journal of Information Technology. 24*(2), 144-159.

Basole, R. C., & Rouse, W. B. (2008). Complexity of Service Value Networks: Conceptualization and Empirical Investigation. *IBM Systems Journal, 47*(1), 53-70.

Bovet, D., & Martha, J. (2000). *Value Nets: Breaking the Supply Chain to Unlock Hidden Profits.* New York: John Wiley and Sons.

Brandenburger, A. M., & Nalebuff, B. J. (1997). *Co-opetition.* New York: Double Day.

Broder, A. Z., Kumar, R., Maghoul, F., Raghavan, P., Rajagopalan, S., Stata, R., et al. (2000). Graph Structure in the Web. *Computer Networks, 33*(1), 309-320.

Butts, C. T. (2000). An Axiomatic Approach to Network Complexity. *Journal of Mathematical Sociology, 24*(4), 273-301.

Casti, J. L. (1995). The Theory of Networks. In D. Batten, J. Casti & R. Thord (Eds.), *Networks in Action: Communications, Economics, and Human Knowledge* (pp. 3-24). Berlin: Springer-Verlag.

Chesbrough, H., & Spohrer, J. (2006). A Research Manifesto for Services Science. *Communications of the ACM, 49*(7), 35-40.

Cohen, J. E., Briand, F., & Newman, C. M. (1990). *Community Food Webs: Data and Theory.* Berlin: Springer-Verlag.

Deshmukh, A. V., Talvage, J. J., & Barash, M. M. (1998). Complexity in Manufacturing Systems, Part 1: Analysis of Static Complexity. *IIE Transactions, 30*(7), 645-655.

Dyer, J. H. (2000). *Collaborative Advantage: Winning through Extended Enterprise Supplier Networks.* New York, NY: Oxford University Press.

Epstein, J. M. (2008). Why Model? *Journal of Artificial Societies and Social Simulation, 4*(11), 1-5.

Fitzsimmons, J. A., & Fitzsimmons, M. J. (2001). *Service Management: Operations, Strategy, Information Technology* (Third Edition ed.). New York: Mc-Graw Hill.

Golay, M. W., Seong, P. H., & Manno, V. P. (1989). A Measure of the Difficulty of System Diagnosis and its Relationship to Complexity. *International Journal of General Systems, 16*(1), 1-23.

Kaimann, R. A. (1974). Coefficient of Network Complexity. *Management Science, 21*(2), 172-177.

Kambil, A. (2008). Purposeful Abstraction: Thoughts on Creating Business Network Models. *Journal of Business Strategy, 29*(1), 52-54.

Kauffman, S. A. (1969). Metabolic Stability and Epigenesis in Randomly Constructed Genetic Nets. *Journal of Theoretical Biology, 22*(3), 437-467.

Kothandaraman, P., & Wilson, D. T. (2001). The Future of Competition: Value-Creating Networks. *Industrial Marketing Management, 30*(4), 379-389.

Moody, J., McFarland, D., & Bender-deMoll, S. (2005). Dynamic Network Visualization. *American Journal of Sociology, 110*(4), 1206-1241.

Newman, M. E. J. (2003). The Structure and Function of Complex Networks. *SIAM Review, 45*(2), 167-256.

Normann, R., & Ramirez, R. (1993). From Value Chain to Value Constellation: Designing Interactive Strategy. *Harvard Business Review, 71*(4), 65-77.

Parolini, C. (1999). *The Value Net: A Tool for Competitive Strategy*. Chichester: John Wiley.

Pennock, M. J., Rouse, W. B., & Kollar, D. L. (2007). Transforming the acquistion enterprise: A framework for analysis and a case study of ship acquisition. *Systems Engineering, 10*(2), 99-117.

Porter, M. E. (1985). *Competitive Advantage: Creating and Sustaining Superior Performance*. New York: The Free Press.

Reid, P. P., Compton, W. D., Grossman, J. H., & Fanjiang, G. (2005). *Building a Better Delivery System: A New Engineering/Health Care Partnership*: National Academies.

Ross, W. T., & Robertson, D. C. (2007). Compound Relationships Between Firms. *Journal of Marketing, 71*(July), 108-123.

Rouse, W. B. (2003). Engineering complex systems: Implications for research in systems engineering. *IEEE Transactions on Systems, Man, and Cybernetics – Part C, 33*(2), 154-156.

Rouse, W. B. (2007a). Complex Engineered, Organizational, and Natural Systems. *Systems Engineering, 10*(3), 260-271.

Rouse, W. B. (2007b). *People and Organizations: Explorations of Human Centered Design*. New York: John Wiley and Sons.

Rouse, W. B. (2008). Healthcare as a complex adaptive system. *The Bridge, 38*(1), 17-25.

Rouse, W. B., & Baba, M. L. (2006). Enterprise Transformation. *Communications of the ACM, 49*(7), 67-72.

Sage, A. P., & Rouse, W. B. (Eds.). (2009). *Handbook of systems engineering and management* (2nd Edition ed.). New York: Wiley.

Shannon, C. (1948). A Mathematical Theory of Communication. *Bel Systems Technical Journal, 27*, 379-423.

Stabell, C. B., & Fjeldstad, O. D. (1998). Configuring Value for Competitive Advantage: On Chains, Shops, and Networks. *Strategic Management Journal, 19*(5), 413-437.

Strogatz, S. H. (2001). Exploring Complex Networks. *Nature, 410*, 268-276.

Vargo, S. L., & Lusch, R. F. (2004). Evolving to a new dominant logic for marketing. *Journal of Marketing, 68*(1), 1-17.

Wasserman, S., & Faust, K. (1994). *Social Network Analysis: Methods and Applications*. New York: Cambridge University Press.

A Formal Model of Service Delivery

Guruduth Banavar

IBM Research - India

Alan Hartman

IBM Research - India

Lakshmish Ramaswamy

Computer Science

University of Georgia

Anatoly Zherebtsov

XJ Technologies

St. Petersburg, Russia

We define a *service delivery system* as a set of interacting entities that are involved in the delivery of one or more business services. A service operating system manages the processes and resources within a service delivery system. This paper develops a formal model for these concepts, with the goal of clearly and precisely describing the delivery behavior of service systems. The model lays the groundwork for reasoning about the scenarios that occur in service delivery. We evaluate the model by capturing the structure and behavior of some realistic service delivery systems — a credit card service, a hospital, an IT problem service and a hotel reception desk — and reason about key performance indicators.

P.P. Maglio et al. (eds.), *Handbook of Service Science*, Service Science: Research and Innovations in the Service Economy, DOI 10.1007/978-1-4419-1628-0_21,
© Springer Science+Business Media, LLC 2010

Introduction

Services are frequently described as *performances by a provider that create and capture economic value for both the provider and client* (Chesbrough & Spohrer, 2006). Everyday services range from healthcare and restaurants to call centers and a host of other examples. The full range of services makes up a significant portion of modern economies all over the globe (Chesbrough & Spohrer, 2006; Lovelock, Witz & Chatterjee, 2006). Thus, precisely understanding the nature of systems that support services enables us to understand the main drivers of modern economies.

Services are described in terms of four major characteristics, conveniently remembered through the acronym CHIP (Lovelock, Witz & Chatterjee, 2006): *coproduction* (both provider and client participate in the act), *heterogeneity* (clients generally tend to have heterogeneous requirements), *intangibility* (many services are nothing more than experiences), and *perishability* (most services cannot be inventoried). One classification of services was given by Lovelock et al. (2006), and is reproduced in Table 1.

Theatre performances are often used as a metaphor for services, in the sense that clients interact with the front-stage (e.g., the dining room of a restaurant), and the back-stage is where the materials required for the service are produced (e.g., the kitchen of a restaurant). The front-stage could be thought of as taking a client as input and producing the same client as output, but transformed by the experience of working with the providers and possibly other clients. The back-stage is where raw materials (including information) go in as input, and finished products come out as the output. This characterization has led some to state that 'every business is a service... more or less' (Teboul, 2006).

A *service system* (Chesbrough & Spohrer, 2006; Spohrer, Vargo, Caswell & Maglio, 2008) has been defined as a network of providers and clients co-producing value through service performances. For a given (set of) service provider(s), we define a *service delivery system* as a set of interacting entities, such as people, processes, and products, that are involved in the *delivery* of one or more services. Examples of service delivery systems are hospitals, universities, banks, and call centers. The delivery of a service utilizes resources and produces outcomes that are valuable to the client. Outcomes are domain dependent, and eventually translate into value for the client, some of which is transferred into value for the provider.

Our experience from other fields of science suggests that a conceptual tool that supports formal representation and analysis of service delivery systems could be immensely useful to service providers in their quest for optimizing the value of their services. While several models have been developed for business, economic and social interactions in services settings (Alter, 2008; Lusch & Vargo, 2006;

Spohrer, Vargo, Caswell & Maglio, 2008; Tian, Ray, Lee, Cao & Ding, 2008; Vargo & Lusch, 2004), there are no formal models for service delivery systems to the best of our knowledge.

Table 1. Services classification Lovelock et al. (2006)

	People processing	*Possessions processing*
Tangible actions	Services aimed at people's physical body, e.g., healthcare and transportation	Services aimed at material items, e.g., shipping and cleaning
Intangible actions	Services aimed at people's minds, e.g., education and entertainment	Services aimed at information, e.g., banking and legal

We believe that a good model of service delivery must help us answer questions such as: (1) *How to utilize the available resources in the most cost-efficient way?;* (2) *How to schedule and execute the services such that contract-deadlines are met?;* (3) *What metrics and mechanisms are necessary for monitoring the health and performance of a service delivery system?;* (4) *How can the performance of various services be predicted with reasonable accuracy?;* (5) *How to analyze the resiliency of the system, and how do we minimize failures?*; and (6) *How do we plan the capacity of a service delivery system assuming that we know the anticipated services workload it has to support?*

Each of the problems listed above is a research challenge in its own right, and these questions will be explored as the research in this area matures. However, we contend that one of the most fundamental requirements for research in this emerging discipline is to develop a formal model for effectively representing the delivery of services.

Towards addressing the above challenge, this paper makes three unique contributions. First, we propose a formal model for a *service delivery system* that lays the foundation for answering the above questions. Our conception of a service delivery system is inspired by formal models of computing systems such as State Machines and Turing Machines (Knuth, 1997; Turing, 1936). Our model will, at a minimum, provide a clear and precise way to describe the delivery behavior of service systems. Second, we propose the concept of a *service operating system* as a component that manages the resources of the service delivery system and enables service processes to execute on the system. *Service processes* are the step-by-step procedures followed by entities in the service delivery system in response to service requests. Third, by applying our model to real-world services, we demonstrate the utility of the model in analyzing and optimizing service delivery systems, as well as designing new service architectures.

Comparing Service Delivery Systems and Computing Systems

Computing is a well understood paradigm. Theoretical models such as the Turing model (Turing, 1936) have provided a foundation upon which results like undecidability, NP completeness, and complexity theory have been developed for understanding the limits of computing as well as analyzing the time and costs associated with various tasks (Knuth, 1997). Further, experimental computer science (Tucker, 1996) has studied various practical questions such as: (1) How to execute multiple computing tasks on the platform simultaneously? (2) How to manage various resources available in the system? (3) How to schedule the computing jobs on the platform? and (4) How to manage large-scale inter-related data?

Our quest for a formal model of service delivery begins by asking similar questions in the services arena. Thus, we start by comparing service delivery systems with computing systems, and identify the analogies, similarities and differences between the two.

The main similarity between the computing and service platforms is that both involve a set of tasks that needs to be executed in a framework consisting of various resources. However, the resources in a service platform are much broader, and include IT resources (including computing, communications, and information), people resources, facilities (such as workspaces and equipment), and "products" (such as consumables).

An algorithm (or program) provides the step-by-step procedure for achieving a computation. Analogously, a service process (or workflow) is an abstraction that provides a stepwise procedure for executing a service request, thereby transforming the service client. However, there are three key differences between these two analogous elements. First, algorithms operate upon data whereas service processes operate on various entities such as data, other processes, organization structures, and system design. Second, a program must be completely specified before its execution. In contrast, a process may be partially specified at the beginning of the execution of the service request, and it may evolve on the basis of its initial execution. Third, algorithms are predominantly deterministic (except for randomized algorithms), whereas service processes may be inherently non-deterministic due to the involvement of human resources.

These differences have important implications on the design and performance of a service delivery system. For example, there is a significant "warm-up" time associated with the human resources involved in the service platform. This means that these resources will not be operating at their full capacity when they enter the system. The human factor also complicates the modalities of failure. For example, failures can be permanent (such as attrition), temporary (e.g., illness), due to misunderstanding/mismanagement, or even malicious. In addition, the service platform faces an inherent scalability challenge, as human expertise cannot be obtained on short notice. Thus, there is not only a greater need for capacity planning, but the transient overloads might be difficult to handle as well. Furthermore, it may be impossible to provide hard guarantees on the outcome or the performance of a service. Rather, the guarantees would be statistical.

The Proposed Model

Figure 1 shows a high-level architectural diagram of a service delivery system (represented as SDS). The service delivery system consists of a set of resources and a set of processes that are executed on the available resources. Recall that the processes transform the service client thus enhancing its value, part of which is transferred to the service provider. Corresponding to these fundamental concepts our service delivery model consists of three major parts, namely, a resource model, a process model, and a value model. The client can browse the service catalog in order to discover which services are provided. The module in the service delivery system that is responsible for managing the resources and processes to arrive at the desired value outcome is called the *service operating system*. A service request arrives at the operating system which performs the functions of instantiating service processes, allocating and managing the resources, and scheduling the tasks of the instantiated processes.

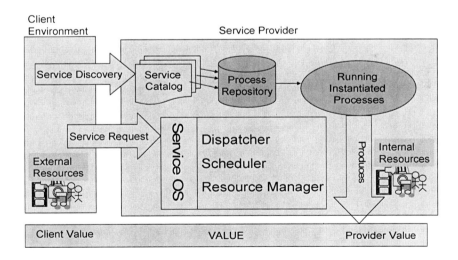

Figure 1. Service System Architecture

Process Model

A service delivery system consists of a set of *service process instances* P = {p_1, p_2, ..., p_n} needed to deliver a set of *service requests SR*. Each service request instantiates a process instance from one of a collection of process *types* {PT_1, PT_2, ...,PT_m} which reside in the process repository. A process type is a collection of tasks T_i and interconnections among them, organized as a directed graph.

Figure 2 shows a process with tasks T_1 through T_6. Each arc can be labeled by probability or by a Boolean expression. (An unlabelled arc is assumed to have probability 1 or Boolean value TRUE.) A process instance is always in a current 'state'. A task takes a process from one state to another. Transitions are taken either deterministically – when there is a single Boolean expression evaluating to TRUE on the arcs leaving a state; or non-deterministically – when there is a probability on the arc, or when more than one arc carries an expression that is TRUE.

Service requests or events in other processes trigger processes to be instantiated. Process instantiation occurs in the following manner. Service requests are trapped by a *dispatcher* (note that the dispatcher can be a human). The dispatcher parses and recognizes the request. It then chooses the best process for handling the service request and instantiates it. When a process is instantiated, the dispatcher provides it with the resources needed for handling the request.

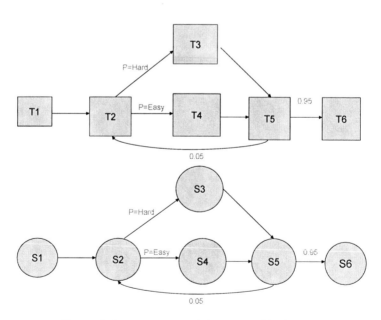

Figure 2. Process type and the states of its instance

State-Space Representation

An instantiated process is always in exactly one of a set of states. The possible set of states of a process is represented as PS = $\{S_0, S_1, ..., S_N\}$. A subset of these states are specialized initial states IS = $\{S_0, S_1, .., S_L\}$. A just-instantiated process can be in one of these states (S_1 in Figure 2 is an initial state). Analogously, a process terminates in one of the final states FS = $\{S_i, .., S_N\}$ (S_6 in Figure 2). The set of all arcs leaving a state S_i must satisfy either one, but not both of the following conditions:

1) The arcs are all labeled by a real number, p, in the interval $[0,1]$, and the sum of all the labels is 1.

2) The arcs are all labeled by Boolean expressions, at least one of which is TRUE for any input to the process.

The state machine transitions from one state to another with a certain probability. The probability of transitioning from S_i to S_j is the value of the label on the arc from S_i to S_j, in case 1. In the second case, if n of the arcs have labels evaluating to TRUE, then one of these arcs is taken with probability $p = 1/n$.

The state machine in Figure 2 shows the arcs with a non-zero transition probability. The numbers near the arcs emanating from S_5 indicate the probability of transitioning along that edge. The arcs emanating from S_2 are labeled by Boolean expressions in the parameter P that is passed to the executing process. If a state has only one outgoing edge, the associated transition probability is assumed to be 1.

Each state in the state machine has three distinct sets of actions associated with it, namely *entry actions*, *core actions*, and *exit actions*. Core actions correspond to the tasks that must be accomplished in the state as specified by the process. Entry actions are the actions taken in preparation for core actions. Entry actions include obtaining the capabilities needed for the performing the core actions by contacting the resource manager. If entry actions cannot be executed (because, for example, the requested capabilities are not available), then the process cannot proceed to the core actions, and it remains blocked (dormant state). Exit actions are the housekeeping operations that are needed to maintain the SDS in a consistent state, including releasing capabilities that would not be needed in the next state.

A process in a particular state requires a certain set of capabilities in order to complete the core tasks of the state. The capabilities are classified into various *types*, represented as CT = $\{C_0, C_1, ..., C_M\}$. Each type has one or more levels of quality (competency) associated with it. For example, an employee might have working knowledge of DB2 or he may be an expert. For simplicity, we assume that the quality levels are discrete, finite, and predefined. $x = C_p$ represents a unit of resource of the category "p" at the quality level "x".

When a process is in a certain state, say S, it requires at least some quantities of various capability types at particular competency levels in order to complete the tasks associated with that state and transition to the next state. This is modeled through a *minimum capability vector (MCV)*. MCV(S) is a vector indicating the minimum quantities of types and qualities of capabilities needed for transitioning out of the state S. $MCV(S) = (\lambda_0, \lambda_1, ..., \lambda_p, ..., \lambda_M)$ indicates that the minimum amount of capability C_p needed to transition out of the state S is λ_p. As an example, the development of certain customized software may require a Linux expert, a DB2 expert and 4 Java programmers.

Each state of a service instance is also associated with an ideal capability vector (ICV). $ICV(S) = (\mu_0, \mu_1, ...\mu_p, .., \mu_M)$ indicates the quantities of types and competencies of capabilities that the process would ideally want to possess in that state so that it can complete the tasks and transition out of the state in the minimal amount of time. While performing the entry actions of a state S, the service instance requests capabilities by sending MCV(S) and ICV(S) to the resource manager. The resource manager provides capabilities based on the available resources and its allocation policy. If the resource manager cannot allocate enough capabilities to satisfy MCV(S), the process is blocked and becomes dormant.

Resource Model

Resources embody one or more capabilities, and delivering a service utilizes a set of resources, both within the service delivery system and in the client's environment. Thus, resources constitute the fundamental entities of the service delivery system.

Resources as Capability Containers

Resources are characterized by the capabilities they manifest. Hence, in our model, an individual resource is described by a vector, called the *Resource Capability Vector (RCV)*, which identifies the capabilities of the resource. The resource capability vector of a resource R is represented as $RCV(R) = \{C_0, C_1, ..., C_q \}$, where $y = C_j$ represents the capability C_j, at the competency level "y". Each resource contains at least one capability. Furthermore, for any particular capability, RCV(R) only contains the highest level of competency that R contains. In other words, if R contains $y = C_j$, it is implicitly assumed that R supports $z = C_j$ for any $z \leq y$.

In the simplest case, a resource has a single capability. An employee who just has the skills of a waiter and nothing more is an example of a resource with a single capability, whereas a DB2 expert who also has the basic Java skills is a resource with two capabilities.

The resources employed by a service delivery system can be contained within the system or they may be external to the system. The resources contained in the service delivery system are called *internal resources.* The resources outside the service delivery system are referred to as *external resources.* External resources can be either in the client's environment or with a third party. We explain the mechanisms for accessing external resources later in the section.

Resource Utilization Model

The resource manager allocates resources to service processes that need them for their execution. When a process enters a state, it requests the capabilities needed by sending the ICV and MCV to the resource manager. The resource manager implements a resource allocation policy which dictates which resources are allocated to the process. In the best case (from the requesting process's perspective), the resource manager allocates a set of resources such that the union of all their capabilities satisfies the corresponding ICV. If that is not possible, the resource manager attempts to allocate resources such that the union of their RCV at least satisfies the MCV. In the case where even that is not possible, the process enters a dormant state, and is woken up when enough resources are available.

When a resource is allocated to a process all its capabilities are available to the process. In other words, in our model, it is not feasible to split a resource into various capabilities and allocate individual capabilities to different concurrently executing processes at the same time instant. Analogously, when a process intends to exit a state, it frees entire resources and not individual capabilities of the resources. When a resource is unavailable (due to failure), all its capabilities become unavailable.

The above is the static resource model for a particular invocation of a service. In general a service is invoked many times, and in order to deal with the service value over time and its reliability, we can also introduce a dynamic resource model with a time parameter. This enables us to model the increase in capabilities over time as service providers gain experience and expertise. The *set of all resources available to the SDS at time t* will be denote by $\Re(t)$.

External resources: Since services are *co-produced*, service delivery processes need to access resources that are external to the service provider's environment.

These external resources may be present in the client's environment, or they may be a third party resource. For example, in a credit card service scenario, a new-credit-card request to an outsourced call center (service delivery system) requires access to the bank's database (an external resource at the service client) as well as the credit history of the applicant (a third party resource).

Our model supports two modalities for accessing external resources. First, the actual external resources may be physically provided to the service provider at the time of the service invocation – we call this *explicit resource passing*. This is suitable for tangible services aimed at people's physical bodies or physical possessions (refer to Table 1), such as in a hospital or an automobile service station.

Second, for many intangible services, it is not possible or appropriate to explicitly pass the physical resources at service invocation time. For example, services that require access to very large databases or to information embedded within physical objects such as servers in a customer data center. For such resources, we introduce the *implicit resource passing* method, in which service processes access the resource via *access-credentials*. An access-credential is a tuple of four values: AC(ER) = (&ER, CS(ER), OP(ER), CFT(ER)). &ER is a reference to the resource, which can be used to locate it. CS(ER) is a set of states of the service process in which it can access the resource (see Section 3.1 for a discussion on processes and states). The third parameter indicates the operation that the process is allowed to invoke on the resource ER. CFT(ER) is a certificate proving the rights of process to access the resource. At the time of their instantiation, the processes are provided with the capabilities they need.

Evaluating Time and Cost

With the above resource and process models, we can now evaluate the time and cost of service delivery.

The time required for transitioning through a state S depends upon the quantities and levels of capabilities allocated to it. However, the required time is not a deterministic function, due to involvement of human resources and client variability. Suppose $\xi = (\xi_0, \xi_1 ..., \xi_p,..., \xi_M)$, denotes the capability vector of the resources available to the state S. The function $\omega_T(S, \xi, t)$ represents the probability distribution function (PDF) and $\tau_T(S, \xi, t)$ denotes the cumulative distribution function (CDF) of the time t required to transition through S with resource vector ξ. In other words, the PDF indicates the probability that the transition through S would take exactly t time units and the CDF indicates the probability that the transition through S would be completed within t units of time. The CDF satisfies the condition that $\tau_T(S, \xi, t) < 0$ for all $t < \infty$ if for at least one capability the available quantity is less than the corresponding value in the MRV. This means that if the availability of one of the resources is less than its minimum required amount, the time to transition through S will take infinitely long. In fact the process goes into a waiting mode, until such time as resources become available, and the dispatcher allocates the resources to the process.

There is a finite, positive cost associated with each resource. C(R) denotes the cost of employing R for one unit of time. C(R) depends upon the capabilities and skill levels R possesses. Intuitively, C(R) is higher if R has multiple capabilities and at higher competency levels. Thus, the total cost of resources per unit of time incurred by the services delivery system is Σ_R C(R). Note that some resources may incur a cost only when they are actively in use by a service process, but others may contribute to the cost of the SDS even when idle.

We can also analyze the costs associated with the transition through each state. Suppose that the transition takes place in t time units and that $\Re$ is the set of resources allocated to state S. The cost associated with this transition is $C = t \, {}^*\Sigma_{R \in \Re}$ C(R). Thus, the function $\tau_C(S, \xi, C)$ indicates the CDF of the costs of transitioning through S with resource vector ξ.

Value Model

A central aspect of a service delivery system – *value co-creation* – is the manner in which the value associated with the service provider and client changes during the process of service delivery.

Our model captures two values: (1) A value associated with the service client, which we call *Client Value* (CV); and (2) A value associated with the service provider, which we call the *Provider Value* (PV). These two values are at a certain level when a service process is initiated – *Initial Client Value (ICV)* and *Initial Provider Value (IPV)*. IPV and ICV are among the input parameters provided to the instantiated process. After the transition through a state S of a service process the current values of CV and PV are updated. The values that these two parameters acquire at the end of the process are called the *Final Client Value (FCV)* and the *Final Provider Value (FCV)*. The difference between FCV and ICV is termed as *Client Value Appreciation (CVA),* and the difference between FPV and IPV is the *Provider Value Appreciation (PVA).*

Different invocations of the same service may result in different values for either CVA or PVA. Even different invocations of the same service by the same client with the same request may result in different values of CVA and PVA, depending on the load on the delivery system, the availability of external resources, or other factors.

The individual client is interested in maximizing his expected CVA.

A possible goal of a service provider service is to maximize the accumulated PVA for the delivery process over time, subject to the expected CVA > 0. This represents an opportunistic and greedy approach to service provision. It may well be the case that if the expected CVA is too low, this will have the effect of reducing the frequency of service requests, and thus the PVA over time will also decrease. However in the case of a monopoly service, this may well be the optimal business strategy.

A more realistic goal for the service provider may be to maximize the accumulated PVA over time, subject to CVA being bounded below by some constant which depends on the market conditions, taking into account competitors' offerings and client volatility.

If we assume a certain probability distribution for the arrival times of service requests, the expected CVA is defined as the average CVA over all outcomes of the service invocations. The accumulated PVA over time is measured by the sum of all CVA outcomes in a fixed time period (long relative to the service time, and mean arrival time).

We illustrate the use of this value model in conjunction with the earlier time/cost model, through an example. Consider two scenarios – a person P1 who repairs a car himself, and a person P2 who 'outsources' the repair to a service center. P1 puts herself through a training process and eventually repairs the car at a cost C1 (say $300) which includes the cost of the training, and thus increases her own value by V (she now has a working car, which she can potentially sell for $500). In this case, P1 is both the service provider and client. P1's overall value gain (CVA) is G1 = V – C1 ($200 in this case). P2, on the other hand, spends C2 (C2 < C1, say $200) on a repair service S2, which in turn spends CS2 (CS2 << C1, and CS2 < C2, say $100). P2 also increases his value by V ($500), and has a gain (CVA) of G2 = V – C2 ($300, in this example), which is greater than G1. Moreover, the service provider S2's gain (PVA) is GS2 = C2 – CS2 ($100). Overall, the gain in the system as a whole (CVA+PVA), G2 + GS2 ($400), is larger than G1 ($200).

Qualitative Applications of the Model

We now evaluate our model by applying it to two example services. In order to better represent the wide variety of services, we choose one service from each of the first and the fourth quadrants of the tangibility/recipient matrix shown in Table 1. The services here are analyzed in a qualitative way, based on the formal model described in the previous section.

Credit Card Service

A credit card service is a good example of "intangible actions on possessions" (see Table 1). The services that fall into this category are usually related to information processing, e.g., banking, accounting, research, and customized software development.

Many credit card companies outsource the end-user request handling (call center) part of their business. This part of the business involves receiving client calls and performing the required actions. Typical actions include applying for a new credit card, canceling an existing card, changing the details of a card, and reporting a lost/stolen card.

The procedures for handling specific types of client requests, e.g., new credit card application, credit card cancellation, card detail changes, etc., are modeled as processes in the service delivery system. The service provider is paid a certain amount for handling a specific type of request. This amount is the PVA associated with that service. The type of value gain for the client depends upon the type of request. For example, the successful completion of a new credit card application increases the profit potential of the company. In contrast, the successful completion of a lost/stolen card reporting request mitigates the risks associated with abuse of the stolen card. While changing credit card details or canceling an existing card does not result in explicit value creation, they nevertheless increase the future profit potential if a high client satisfaction is maintained.

The resources in the service delivery system (internal resources) include service professionals, IT resources, and other physical infrastructure. Required external resources in the client environment are primarily databases storing credit card related information, whereas the credit history of card holders and applicants is a third-party external resource. An example of external resource access capabilities provided to the process is the consent given by the card applicant to check his/her credit history.

The state space of the new credit card application process is shown in Figure 3. S_0 is an initial state and, S_5, S_8, and S_{10} are final states. The states belonging to the front stage and the back stage of the service are also identified. The client value is measured in terms of the total number of credit card users as well as the perception of the users about the quality of service. The provider value appreciation is the amount paid by the client for handling the new application request. As discussed in Section 3.4, both CVA and PVA may depend upon the final state reached and the path taken to get there.

The transitions from S_1, S_3, S_6, and S_9 are deterministic, whereas the transitions from S_2, S_4, and S_7 are non-deterministic. When the transition is non-deterministic, we indicate the transition probability of various outgoing edges. In this example, the probability of the process terminating in S_{10} is 0.42 (0.6 * 0.7).

Let us construct the MCV of state S_4. Besides IT and physical infrastructure, one service professional and access to the credit history of the applicant are needed to complete the tasks of S_4, thus constituting MCV(S_4). The time taken to transition depends upon the available resources and the quality of resources. For example, the time to transition through S_4 depends upon the time needed to access the credit history. However, the transition time is not deterministic. For example, the time required to obtain credit history varies depending upon the load at the credit reporting agency.

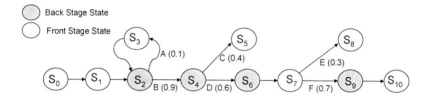

S_0 – call received	S_1 – data collection	S_2 – data validation	S_3 – data verification
S_4 – credit history check	S_5 – decline application	S_6 – determine credit level	S_7 – offer card terms
S_8 – terminate call	S_9 – order and dispatch card	S_{10} – terminate call	A – invalid data
B – valid data	C – unacceptable history	D – acceptable history	E – reject terms
F – accept terms			

Figure 3. State-Space of New Credit Card Application Process

Hospital Service

A hospital is a good example of a "tangible action on humans" (see Table 1). Other services in this category include hotels, restaurants, passenger transportation, and beauty salons.

Some of the resources in the hospital service delivery system are doctors, nurses, equipment, medications, and physical infrastructure. The external resource is the patient's body. The various treatment procedures followed in the hospital form the processes. The reception unit at the hospital which receives the patients and their phone calls is the dispatcher. Treatment procedures for a specific condition (such as surgery) are processes, which would be instantiated by other processes (such as diagnostics). The client value appreciation is in terms of improved health and/or reduced health risks. The hospital charges correspond to the service provider's value appreciation.

Figure 4 illustrates the state space of the treatment process for a non-emergency patient. Upon arrival, a patient records file is created for each new patient. For existing patients, their respective files are retrieved. Following these states, the vital statistics (temperature, blood pressure, etc.) of the patient is collected. Next, information about the patient's illness is collected, which is followed by diagnosis. If the illness is perceived as non-routine, the patient is referred to a specialist. In addition, the patient might be provided with in-hospital medication and/or prescriptions take at home. For routine illnesses, the patient may be provided with in-hospital medication and/or some prescription. Finally, the patient is billed (state S_9).

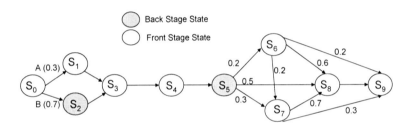

S_0 – patient registration	S_1 – patient file creation	S_2 – patient file retrieval	S_3 – vital statistics collection
S_4 – information collection from patient	S_5 – problem diagnosis	S_6 – specialist referral	S_7 – in hospital medication
S_8 – issue prescriptions	S_9 – record update and billing	A – new patient	B – existing patient

Figure 4. Non-emergency Treatment Process

MCV varies widely among states. For example, S_0, S_1, and S_2 require the capabilities of a receptionist/clerk. S_3 and S_4 require a nurse's capabilities, S_5, S_6, S_7, and S_8 need a doctor's skills, whereas S_9 requires accountancy skills. Similarly, the equipment needs also differ from state to state. The time required for transition depends upon several parameters including the resource availabilities and the patient's health and type of illness. Observe that the probabilistic function for transition time, provided by our model, is well suited for the hospital service.

Analysis of Service Architectures

We now illustrate how the proposed model can be used to analyze possible architectures (or resource availability functions) for a given service with respect to different criteria, which would help in choosing an architecture that best suits the design requirements. We consider a simplified state representation of a healthcare clinic containing four states $\{S_0, S_1, S_2, S_3, S_4\}$. The state S_0 corresponds to patient registration and record retrieval, state S_1 corresponds to vital statistics and information collection from the patient and preliminary tests, S_2 represents problem diagnosis and prescribing medication, S_3 represents insurance billing and record update, and S_4 corresponds to patient exit. In the interest of simplicity, let us assume that each state in the state space is connected only to the next state in the numerical logical order (S_0 is connected to S_1, and so forth).

Besides equipment and infrastructural resource capabilities, states S_0, S_1, S_2 and S_3 require single units of human capabilities - C_0, C_1, C_2 and C_3 respectively. C_0 would be the skill of a receptionist, C_1 a nurse's skill, C_2 a doctor's skill and C_3 would be administrative assistant skill. Let us assume that the clinic can hire only four personnel including the doctors. Now, we analyze two possible resource availability architectures for this service. In the first architecture, there are four doctors who are also knowledgeable in receptionist, nurse and administrative duties. The doctors handle all patients throughout the process. The second architecture comprises a dedicated (expert) receptionist, nurse, doctor, and administrative assistant. In the second architecture, the tasks associated with states S_0, S_1, and S_3 are performed by an expert (represented as R_i^1 for state S_i), whereas in the first architecture, they are performed by a person who has working knowledge in the respective processes (represented as R_i^0 for S_i).

Let us assume that the transition time through state S_0 is exponentially distributed, and let the mean transition time be 12 minutes, if an R_0^0 (person with working knowledge of receptionist duties such as a doctor who is also acting as a receptionist) is employed. However, if we were to employ R_0^1 (expert receptionist), the mean transition time would be 10 minutes. Similarly, let us assume that the mean transition times through S_1 and S_3 are 16 and 20 minutes respectively if R_1^0 and R_3^0 are employed at the respective states. However, let the transition times be 11 and 12 minutes for states S_1 and S_3 if respective experts (R_1^1 and R_3^1) are employed. The average transition time for the state S_2 is 12 minutes for both architectures, as tasks of this state can only be performed by a doctor.

We now analyze the two architectures, first with respect to their throughputs and later with respect to their failure resilience characteristics. In the first architecture, the mean total time needed to complete the service is 1 hour (sum of individual transition times since they are exponentially distributed). If we assume that the clinic operates 10 hours per day, the throughput from one doctor is 10 patients per day, and the average throughput from the entire system is 40 patients per day.

In the second architecture, as each person is handling the services that are in a particular state, the throughput of the system is determined by the most costly (in terms of time) state, which in our case is S_2 or S_3. The throughput of the system is 50 patients per day. Therefore, the second architecture is clearly better than the first one in terms of the system throughput. Further, hiring a doctor is more expensive than other employees. Thus, the second architecture is also better in terms of cost effectiveness.

However, in the second architecture, if the sole doctor does not report to work, the clinic stops functioning. If one of the doctors fails to turn up for work in the first architecture, the system will continue to provide the service, but with lower throughput (30 patients per day). In fact, the system will continue to function, albeit in a degraded state, even if 3 of the four doctors fail. Thus, the first architecture is significantly better than the second with respect to failure resilience.

This example illustrates the utility of the proposed model in analyzing competing architectures and quantifying their relative pros and cons with respect to various different performance parameters. Further, the model also helps us evolve better architectures. Our analysis suggests that a hybrid architecture, wherein there is an experienced doctor, an intern (who performs the routinely performs the activities associated with state S_1, but can also substitute for the doctor in his absence), together with a receptionist and a billing expert who also have working knowledge of each other's duties is likely to combine the strengths of both architectures while overcoming their weaknesses.

Simulation Experiments with Services

In this section we describe a method for converting the structures described above into simulation models, thus enabling more detailed quantitative analysis, and the evaluation of complex what-if scenarios.

Input data required for simulation

In order to build a simulation model for a service delivery system, we need a minimal set of quantitative inputs. These include:

1) A list of all service requests (SR) together with the distribution function for their arrival times.
2) A set of capability types (CT) and a set of resources $\Re$ each of which is associated with a capabilities vector.

3) A set of service processes (P) for handling each service request – each process comprises a set of states, transitions and the transition probabilities.
4) Each state (task) is qualified by a minimum capabilities vector (MCV), an ideal capabilities vector (ICV), and a function for estimating the CVA increment, PVA increment, task time (ω_T), and any other statistics from a given resource vector.
5) A time dependent resource availability function.
6) A *dispatcher algorithm* (DA) for deciding how to handle the requests for service and how to allocate resources.

Simulation Procedure

On arrival of a request it is added to the dispatcher queue. The dispatcher looks at all requests in the queue and the current free resource vector and decides which resources to allocate to which items on the queue and updates the free resource vector. Items on the dispatcher queue include requests for processes to initiate, and processes waiting to enter a new state.

Processes, on receiving resources to enter a new state, increment their time counter, PVA and CVA. After the task time has elapsed, they notify the dispatcher that the resources not required in the subsequent state are free, and enter a new request for any additional capabilities needed for the state they are about to enter. The dispatcher receives resources from processes, updates the free resource vector, and returns to scanning the queue.

The simulation software can compute global statistics like resource utilization, queue lengths at each state (to determine bottlenecks), mean and standard deviation of service times, CVA, and PVA, system throughput, etc.

The simulation software used for our experiments is the AnyLogic tool from XJ Technologies. This tool is readily customized to deal with all of the features we have described in the formal model in a natural way, enabling experimentation with different service processes, resource allocations, request scheduling algorithms, and more.

IT Infrastructure Maintenance Service

The service described here is a simplification of a real service offered by IBM. The analyses have a significant business value, since they provide accurate predictions of the service performance, cost, and profitability.

1) The service requests (SR) in this example are IT problem tickets in three classes, trivial, easy, and complex. Tickets arrive according to a Poisson process. Percentages of trivial, easy and complex tickets are configurable parameters of the simulation.

2) The capability types (CT) are expert capability C_0, and ordinary capability C_1. The resources $\Re$ each have one of two capability vectors (1,2) for experts and (0,1) for standard personnel.

3) The service process (P) for handling each service request is simple with each ticket being serviced by a single resource.

4) Trivial tickets can be solved by either an expert or standard resource, easy tickets can be solved by either type of resource, but a standard person would take longer than an expert for solving an easy ticket. The complex tickets can only be solved by an expert resource. Each ticket is also associated with a severity, which determines the deadline within which the ticket has to be solved in order to avoid SLA violations. The severity can range from 1 to 3. Severity-1 tickets have a time-window of 2-3 hours. Severity-2 tickets have time window of 4-6 hours and Severity-3 tickets have a time window of 24 hours. The PVA for a particular ticket is computed as follows. The income for resolving a ticket depends on its complexity. Simple tickets provide a lower income than more complex tickets; however no income is recorded for tickets which miss their deadlines. The total income for the provider in a particular time period is the sum of income from all tickets that were resolved (with no SLA violations) in that period. The costs for the service provider include the salaries of the personnel, infrastructure costs (building rent, electricity costs, etc). PVA for the time period is the difference between the income and the costs incurred by the service provider.

5) The numbers of expert and standard resources are configurable parameters for the simulation but remain constant over the duration of a simulation run.

6) The dispatcher algorithm (DA) for deciding how to handle the requests for service is dependent on the currently available resources. The dispatcher assigns each arriving ticket into trivial, easy, or complex queues. If an expert resource is available, the dispatcher assigns him to the ticket on the complex queue with the earliest deadline. If there are no complex tickets waiting, and there are no standard resources available, the expert resource will be assigned to the earliest deadline ticket on the easy queue – and if there are no easy tickets waiting, then he will be assigned to the earliest deadline ticket on the trivial queue. If a standard resource is available he will be assigned to the earliest deadline ticket on either the easy or trivial queues.

The service delivery system was simulated with a variety of input parameters to compute the expected PVA over a period of one year with different staffing configurations. The arrival rate of tickets was fixed at 40 tickets per hour, with 5% of these being complex tickets, 30% easy, and the remainder trivial. The income from trivial, easy and complex tickets was fixed at 30, 50, and 300 units, and the costs of staffing were set to 3000 and 2000 units per month for experts and standard resources respectively, with 10000 units per month as infrastructure expenses.

Table 2. Infrastructure maintenance simulation results

Number of experts	Number of standard staff	%age of missed deadlines				Average PVA per ticket
		trivial	easy	complex	total	
10	10	0	0	13.4	0.1	40.1
2	6	0	0	99.6	4.9	34.5
3	5	44.2	0	99.4	33.7	25.9
4	4	85.3	0	99.2	60.4	17.9
5	3	97.6	0	99.0	68.3	15.6

The easy tickets never seem to miss their deadline, since they are handled by both experts and non experts. The service of complex tickets degrades first, followed by a degradation of service to the trivial tickets as staffing levels go down. The surprising result is that when the total number of staff is kept constant, but the number of experts is increased the service level for complex tickets improves only marginally, and the PVA goes down drastically.

Hotel Reception Desk Service

The service described here focuses on two processes performed at a hotel reception desk: check-in and check-out. A typical hotel reception desk would also have other processes, for example, answering telephone queries from clients, and taking orders for taxis.

The input to the simulations was as follows:

1)   The service requests (SR) consist of clients with various properties arriving at the hotel. A client arrives at the hotel and initiates the check-in process, and schedules a check-out process for a particular date. The client attributes include whether or not the client is a loyalty club member, has a previous booking, pays by cash or credit, etc. The distribution of clients with differing properties is an input to the simulation. Arrival times follow a biased distribution, with a tendency to more arrivals in the evening hours, and check-outs skewed towards the morning hours.

2) The capability types (CT) consist of human administrative capacity C_0, human low skilled capability C_1, internal IT capability C_2, hotel infrastructure (rooms) C_3 and external IT capability C_4. The internal resources are reception clerks of differing profiles with capability vector (1,0,0,0,0) or (2,0,0,0,0) – the hotel manager or shift supervisor has capability (2,0,0,0,0) also. Bellboys have capability vector (0,1,0,0,0). The internal IT systems resource (accounting, client database, key issue) has capability vector (0,0,1,0,0). Each hotel room has capability vector (0,0,0,1,0), and an external credit card system has capability vector (0,0,0,0,1).

3) The service processes (P) for handling each service request are given in the Appendix. Note that these processes are entirely deterministic dependent on the client attributes.

4) For each task, the minimum capability vector (MCV), which equals the ideal capability vector (ICV) is given in the Appendix, which also contains the task time distribution (ω_T).

5) The resource availability function for reception clerks, supervisors, and bellboys is time dependent, depending on time of day. All other resources are continuously available, with service times dependent on the system load. The parameters of these functions are an input to the simulation.

6) The dispatcher algorithm (DA) removes resources from the pool in the order listed in the MRV in the Appendix for each task, and each task is processed when all its resources have been acquired.

The simulation was run without taking into account shift work, and with fixed probabilities of prior booking (80%), previous stay (50%), credit card payment (90%), and credit card valid (90%). The arrival rate of clients at check-in was 24 clients per day, with the majority arriving between noon and 6pm. The hotel was populated by 50 people occupying rooms at the start of the simulation. The duration of stay of each client was set randomly to between 1 and 5 nights. The number of managers on duty is set to 1, the simulation was run with varying numbers of reception clerks, there were one internal IT system, 2 external credit card checking systems, and 300 hotel rooms available in total.

Table 3. Hotel simulation results

Number of reception clerks	50% of check in processes complete within (time units)	90% of check in processes complete within (time units)	50% of check out processes complete within (time units)	90% of check out processes complete within (time units)
3	60	90	240	480
6	25	35	240	480
9	20	30	150	420
12	15	20	150	300

Discussion and Related Work

This section briefly discusses the strengths and limitations of the proposed model. Our model has several inherent advantages. First, by providing a formal representation, the proposed state space model lets service designers clearly identify the various aspects of a service process, and the resources needed at each stage. Second, a major goal in service delivery is to maximize the determinism (of outcome, time, and costs) of a given service. With our model this abstract goal can be more concretized - at each state the transition probability should be heavily biased towards a small number of other states, which ensures that the service process progresses in a predictable way. Third, minimizing the costs associated with a service is one of the most important goals of a service provider. A major factor in minimizing costs is to allocate optimal amount of resources. The proposed framework enables us to model this problem as a stochastic optimization problem, for which there are well-known techniques.

One problem with the application of the model is the availability of reliable data or good statistical models of the arrival times of service requests, the distribution functions of time and cost, and other inputs needed to do a formal analysis of a service delivery system. In most cases such data is only available after the service has been running for some time, or can be obtained only from similar but not identical services offered by the service provider. Moreover, these inputs to an analysis of a service are seldom static, and can change with the business climate, or other imponderable factors. However the fact that such assumptions must be specified explicitly will improve the risk analysis and mitigation before the implementation of a service.

Another difficulty with the model comes from our simplistic model for value. We assume that there are only two parties in the service system for which value is computed, the provider and client. Complex service systems usually involve a network of entities in the supply chain each of whom wishes to derive value from participating in the service network. We also assume that value is generated by each task in a service process, and that these values are additive, ignoring side effects like customer satisfaction and its impact on future value generation. Caswell et al. (2008) give a more detailed value model which computes the value increment for each participant in a service network as a combination of the profits derived in a time interval, plus the expected value of transactions in the next time interval. Such computations are feasible within our model and require appropriate modifications of the functions used for value computation.

One final limitation of our model is its emphasis on service delivery processes which are predefined. This is appropriate for a large variety of services, but is not applicable to knowledge intensive services like business consultancy or research services. The process for such services is more complex, amorphous, dynamic, and usually impossible to define before the performance of each service instance

Related Work

Service science, despite being a relatively new discipline, has attracted considerable attention from various fields (Chesbrough & Spohrer, 2006; Lovelock, Wirth & Chatterjee, 2006). We limit our discussion to prior literature that is closely related to the work reported in this paper. As with any emerging discipline, the early literature mainly focused on laying the foundation for the field through definitions and conceptualizations (Carlzon, 1989; Cherbakov, Galambos, Harishankar, Kalyana & Rackham, 2005; Hill, 1977; Teboul, 2006).

Formal modeling of services has been a topic of several recent research efforts. Most of these models are concerned with economic, business, and social aspects of services (Alter, 2008; Lusch & Vargo, 2006; Spohrer, Vargo, Caswell & Maglio, 2008; Tian, Ray, Lee, Cao & Ding, 2008; Vargo & Lusch, 2004). The service-dominant logic (Lusch & Vargo, 2006; Spohrer, Vargo, Caswell & Maglio, 2008; Vargo & Lusch, 2004) has been the predominant conceptual tool in modeling service economics. Tian et al (2008) use a role-based paradigm for modeling the ecosystem of interconnected businesses. Alter (2008) argues for a service system model that is comprised of three independent but interacting frameworks, namely work system framework, service value chain framework, and work system life cycle model. The ISPAR model proposed by Spohrer et al. (2008) provides a representation of interaction between the service provider and the client. They also provide important characterizations and classifications of services and resources, which can be used in conjunction with different formal models. Researchers have also used game theory and multi-agent systems to model the behavior of competing and cooperating business entities in a service system (Constantine & Lockwood, 1999; Gilder, 1989; Gronroos, 2007). There is also a considerable body of knowledge on queuing models and simulation of services (Gans, Koole & Mandelbaum, 2003). What distinguishes our approach from these works is our systematic approach to defining a method of creating queuing and simulation models from models of services and their delivery systems.

However, none, to our best knowledge, has proposed a model for representing and reasoning about service delivery, which forms a very important and integral component of service systems. Thus, our work is not only unique, but also a significant step towards evolving a comprehensive model for service systems.

Conclusions

Formal models play an important role in designing and analyzing services. This paper proposes a new model for service delivery, which includes formal models for resources, processes, and the values associated with a service delivery system.

The effectiveness of the proposed model is evaluated by representing real-world service delivery systems, and analyzing competing service architectures with respect to key performance parameters.

References

Alter, S., (2008). Service system fundamentals: work system, value chain and life cycle. *IBM Systems Journal*, 47(1), 71-86.

Carlzon, J., (1989). *Moments of truth*, Harper Collins, New York.

Caswell, N. S., Nikolaou, C., Sairamesh, J., Bitsaki, M., Koutras, G. D., & Iacovidis, G., (2008). Estimating value in service systems: a case study of a repair service system. *IBM Systems Journal*, 47(1), 87-100.

Cherbakov, L., Galambos, G., Harishankar, R., Kalyana, S., & Rackham, G., (2005). Impact of service orientation at the business level. *IBM Systems Journal*, 44(4), 653-668.

Chesborough, H., & Spohrer, J., (2006). A research manifesto for services science. *Communications of the ACM*, 49(7), 35-40.

Constantine, L. L., & Lockwood, L. A. D., (1999). *Software for use: a practical guide to the models and methods of usage-centered design.* Addison Wesley, Boston, Massachussets.

Gans, N., Koole, G., & Mandelbaum, A., (2003). Telephone call centers: tutorial, review, and research prospects. *Manufacturing & Service Operations Management*, 5, 79–141.

Gilder, G., (1989). *Microcosm.* Touchstone Books, New York.

Gronroos, C., (2007). *In search of new logic for marketing: foundations of contemporary theory.* John Wiley and Co., Chichester, England.

Hill, T. P., (1977). On goods and services. *The Review of Income and Wealth*, 23(4), 315-338.

Knuth, D. E., (1997). *The Art of Computer Programming – Volume 1, 3rd ed.* Addison-Wesley, Reading, Massachussets.

Lovelock, C., Writz, J., & Chatterjee, J., (2006). *Services Marketing: People, Technology, Strategy,* Pearson Education Ltd., New Jersey.

Lusch, R. F., & Vargo, S. L., (2006). Service-dominant logic: reactions, reflections and refinements. *Marketing Theory*, 6(3), 281-288.

Spohrer, J., Vargo, S. L., Caswell, N., & Maglio, P. P., (2008). The service system is the basic abstraction of service science. *Proceedings of the Hawaiian international conference on systems science. HICSS-2008.*

Teboul, J., (2006). *Services is front stage: positioning services for value advantage.* Palgrave Macmillan, New York.

Tian, C. H., Ray, B. K., Lee, J., Cao, R., & Ding, W., (2008). BEAM: A framework for business ecosystem analysis and modeling, *IBM Systems Journal* 47(1), 101-114.

Tucker, A. B. Jr., [Ed.] (1996). *The computer science and engineering handbook.* CRC Press Inc., Boca Raton, Florida.

Turing, A. M., (1936). On computable numbers, with an application to the entscheidungs problem. *Proceedings of the London mathematical society*, 2(42), 230-265.

Vargo, S. L. & Lusch, R. F. (2004). Evolving to a new dominant logic for marketing. *Journal of marketing*, 68(1), 1-17.

Appendix 1 Summary of Notation

A *service delivery system* SDS comprises the following elements:

Set of service requests SR

Service process instances $P = \{p_1, p_2, ..., p_n\}$

Set of process states $SS = \{S_0, S_1, ..., S_N\}$.

Initial states IS⊂SS , *final states* FS⊂SS

Capability types $CT = \{C_0, C_1, ..., C_M\}$

Minimum capability vector to process state S MCV(S)

Ideal capability vector to process state S ICV(S)

Set of all resources in SDS at time t $\Re(t)$

Resource capability vector of a resource R RCV(R)

Access-credentials of an external resource ER AC(ER) = (&ER, CS(ER), OP(ER), CFT(ER)).

Reference to external resource ER &ER

Set of states which can access ER CS(ER)

Operations invokable on ER OP(ER)

Certificate providing access to ER CFT(ER)

Probability distribution function of the time to transition state S with capability vector ξ $\omega_T(S, \xi, t)$

Cumulative distribution function of the time to transition state S with capability vector ξ $\tau_T(S, \xi, t)$

Cost of using resource R for one time unit C(R)

Cumulative distribution function of the cost to transition state S with capability vector ξ $\tau_C(S, \xi, t)$

Client value CV, *Provider value* PV

Initial client value ICV, *initial provider value* IPV

Client value appreciation CVA, *provider value appreciation* PVA

Dispatcher algorithm DA

Appendix 2 Details of Hotel Example

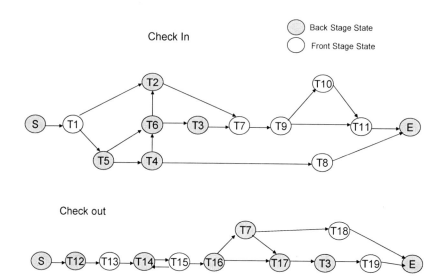

Task	Task Description	MCV	ω_T (in time units)
T1	Initiate Check in	(10000)	Uniform[1,3]
T2	Retrieve Client Record	(10100)	Uniform[0,1]
T3	Create/Update Client Record	(10100)	Uniform[1,3]
T4	Check Room Availability	(10100)	Uniform[0,1]
T5	Check Prior Booking	(10100)	Uniform[0,1]
T6	Check Previous Stay	(10100)	Uniform[0,1]
T7	Check Credit Card	(10001)	Uniform[0,3]
T8	Reject Booking	(10000)	Uniform[1,3]
T9	Issue Key	(10110)	Uniform[0,1]
T10	Issue gift	(10010)	Uniform[1,3]
T11	Baggage	(01010)	Uniform[1,5]
T12	Draft Invoice	(01110)	Uniform[1,3]
T13	Initiate Check out	(10000)	Uniform[1,3]
T14	Update Invoice	(10100)	Uniform[1,3]
T15	Validate Invoice	(10000)	Uniform[1,3]
T16	Issue Invoice	(10100)	Uniform[0,1]
T17	Issue Receipt	(10100)	Uniform[1,3]
T18	Defaulting Client	(20101)	Uniform[1,5]
T19	Complete Check out	(11000)	Uniform[1,3]

Transition	Condition on transition
T1→T2, T9→T10	Client is a loyalty club member
T1→T5, T9→T11	Client is not a loyalty club member
T5→T6	Client has a prior booking
T5→T4	Client has no prior booking
T6→T2	Client has previously stayed at the hotel
T6→T3	Client has not previously stayed at the hotel
T15→T16	Invoice is valid
T15→T14	Invoice needs correction
T16→T7	Credit card payment
T16→T17	Cash payment
T7→T9, T7→T17	Credit card transaction OK
T7→T8, T7→T18	Credit card transaction not allowed

Part 6
Research and Practice: Innovation

Service Innovation

Ian Miles

Manchester Institute of Innovation Research

Manchester Business School

The University of Manchester

Innovation is widely recognized to be a critical contributor to economic growth, quality of life, and industrial competitiveness. Accordingly, a whole discipline of "innovation studies" emerged during the last quarter of the twentieth century, with major impacts on economic policymaking, management thinking, and approaches to science and technology studies. But innovation research was overwhelmingly focused on technological innovation in manufacturing sectors – and in particular, on high-tech sectors such as pharmaceuticals, electronics, and aerospace. It was not until the last decade of the twentieth century that serious and sustained attention to service industries and firms, and their innovation processes and outcomes, was more than the province of a few pioneers. We now have almost two decades of such analysis, and this chapter reviews highlights of the literature. Since the area covered by "services" and "service innovation" is so vast, and because the literature is fragmented across many disciplines, the aim is to give a broad overview rather than to synthesize the literature into a new grand theory. It is apparent that there are many ways in which service innovation parallels the processes described for manufacturing activities, and that some of the "new" features that are brought to light are ones that also exists in manufacturing firms but that have typically been neglected. The study of service innovation leads us to reconsider how we think about innovation more generally.

P.P. Maglio et al. (eds.), *Handbook of Service Science*, Service Science: Research and Innovations in the Service Economy, DOI 10.1007/978-1-4419-1628-0_22,
© Springer Science+Business Media, LLC 2010

Introduction: The Double Ambiguity

"According to a study by the National Academy of Engineering, services in 2003 represented 80 per cent of the US's gross domestic product. And according to the OECD, they account for a similar percentage of economic activity across all advanced industrial economies. Despite this, most analyses of innovation tend to focus on products, not services. It is now time to update our curriculum for teaching and researching innovation to address the dominant sector of economic activity. The National Academy of Engineering study surveyed the contribution of academic research to industrial performance in seven industries. In the five product-based sectors - network systems, communications, medical devices, equipment and aerospace - academic research was found to have had a very significant effect. However, in the two service industries - transportation and financial services - it had only a limited impact. Further, the study concluded that "the academic research enterprise has not focused on or been organised to meet the needs of service businesses." At this early stage, academic research about innovation in services is not well defined. (There is even an active debate over the proper definition of the term "services".) Any useful understanding of the opportunities and risks that are unique to services innovation will invariably involve business process modelling, business models, systems integration and design. More deeply, questions of complexity in systems design, cognitive processing of information, and the role of codified and tacit knowledge will also be involved. The design of choice sets and experience points in facilitating interaction with customers will also be a rich vein of inquiry." (Chesbrough, 2004)

As with practically all discussions containing the words "service" or "services", "service innovation" is a topic where ambiguity runs rife. Are we talking about service activities or processes? About services as products, things supplied by or through products, or as relationships? About service as customer service, as work (from service occupations or professions?), as the domain of service firms and industries? "Service" can be any or all of these things, but too often we assume that our understandings about what we are discussing at any one moment are convergent – when they are anything but.

Thus Service Innovation (SI) can refer to innovation in **service products** – this includes the topic of new service development, as well as covering more incremental innovations in service products (closely related to the topic of service design) and the context in which they are supplied (sometimes, especially in the context of experiential services, described as the servicescape). Relevant research will tend to focus on the innovation processes (creation of new ideas, management of the development or change process, implementation, diffusion and roll-out of innovations, ex ante and ex post evaluation of innovations, etc.) and innovation dynamics (trajectories of change, success factors, market development, user inputs and feedback, etc.).

SI can refer to innovation in **service processes**, in the production of services in new or improved ways – though often service production and service product are hard to readily differentiate. Innovation studies frequently analyze processes and dynamics of process innovation alongside similar analyses of product innovation. While service products tend to be distinctive as compared to the products of, say, mining, manufacturing, construction – they are often intangible, or at least the share of value created by tangible elements of the service (e.g. the physical CD-ROM, the paper on which a report or design is printed, or the dental filling implanted in a patient) is usually a small proportion of the total cost involved.

In practice, SI research conducted from an innovation studies perspective has tended to focus on *innovation in service firms and sectors*, with much research contrasting service organizations' innovation processes with those of manufacturing or other organizations. Such research may be conducted by survey analysis, where there is often a focus on the frequency with which innovations in service products and processes is reported, or by case study research, where there is more often attention to the variety of innovations and innovation processes within specific organizations. A distinctive body of work, which can be undertaken using either methodology, attends more to rather broad classes of (usually technologically-enhanced) service activity, by exploring the diffusion and development of specific innovations (for example, Knowledge Management Systems, electronic Customer Relationship Management Systems, or even Information Systems more generally).

But there is an important feature of many services that makes the service innovation literature incomplete. Many services are extremely variable in nature, with no two service relationships being identical. In some cases, practically every service product will be in many respects unique, in many respects there will be novelty in the supplier-customer relationship and/or in the service that is ultimately provided. From one perspective, just about any service interaction involving new elements could be regarded as innovative. Thus a great deal of research into non-routine services will inevitably be dealing with innovations, and could be examined or re-examined as such. But a common reaction from innovation researchers to such a suggestion is that novelty as such is not necessarily innovation – the argument is that we only see innovation where the new elements are reproduced, where there has been learning and creation of replicable practices. The debate here tells us that the concept of "innovation" is itself as ambiguous as is that of "service". "Innovation" can refer to a process of creating something new, or the actual result of this process. Some scholars and practitioners adhere to a strict demarcation between invention, innovation, and diffusion – indeed, some would restrict attention only to "successful innovation" (though the definition of success opens up new areas for debate). Some would see all of these stages – together with other elements such as search for new ideas, implementation and configuration of acquired new products, reinvention, and so on – as all parts of the innovation process.

Exploring Service Innovation, then, means grappling with the combination of two ambiguous and multifaceted concepts. The relevant bodies of research and practice are fragmented and often poorly interconnected. While there are many limitations in existing research, there have been substantial achievements - despite the double ambiguity. This review will attempt to indicate major lines of work and to suggest some fruitful ways of gaining an overview of the SI field.[1] It can be situated within the wider literature on the evolution and nature of services, and efforts to create a new "service science" or SSME (Service Science, Management, and Engineering) discipline.[2]

Innovation in Service Activities, Industries and Firms

Many service activities share common features, such as the **intangibility** of their core offering or product, and the **interactivity** between the service supplier and client. These are liable to shape innovation processes in various ways – there may be less to attach a brand to, to patent, there may be more need to take account of customer location and other characteristics. Much discussion of service marketing, trade and quality focuses on these features, and several authors have examined them in an innovation context – e.g. Berry et al (2006) who differentiate between four classes of major service innovation, varying in terms of how they address the benefit offered by the service (an important new core benefit versus new delivery that revolutionizes customers' access to the core benefit) and the degree of service "separability" (whether the emphasis is on service delivery at the supplier's time and place, or there is more of a "separable" solution that can be consumed at any time or place). [3] As the issue of separability indicates, service activities span a huge range. Some basic differentiation among sets of service activities can help give insight into different innovation dynamics.

A very simple classification of service activities differentiates between them on the basis of what it is that they are transforming. (1) The first set of services mainly transforms physical artifacts. They may be moved, stored, maintained,

---

[1] Two early collections of studies of SI are Guile and Quinn (1988a, b). There have been many reviews of the field more recently, including several chapters in BERR/DIUS (2008), Bryson and Daniels (2007), DTI (2007), Gallouj (2002), Kuusisto and Meyer (2003) Miles (1994, 2004), NESTA (2008), OECD (2001), and many more. The field has seen explosive, if belated, growth recently.

[2] Classic reviews and compilations on the topic of services include Bryson et al. (2004), Bryson and Daniels, (2007), and Daniels and Bryson (1993) – see their chapter in the current volume. On service science and SSME, see, for example, Chesbrough (2005) , Chesbrough and Spohrer (2006) Springer Publisher's series on "Service Science: Research and Innovations in the Service Economy" (e.g. Hefley and Murphy, 2008), the journal Service Science, and many resources available from SSME sites such as http://www-304.ibm.com/jct01005c/university/scholars/skills/ssme/ university.htm and http://www.ssmenetuk.org (both accessed 29 June 2009). IfM/IBM (2007), and Maglio et al (2006) discuss service innovation in relation to SSME.

[3] Miles (1993) discussed how various defining characteristics of services were associated with innovation trajectories that often led to the services more closely resembling manufacturing industries. One of the inspirations for this approach was the pioneering work of Theodore Levitt (1976) on industrialization of services – it is instructive to compare` this to current discussions of the "servicisation" of industry. See also Karmarkar's chapter in this volume.

manipulated (the *making* of artifacts is more a matter for manufacturing, construction, etc.). (2) The second set of services mainly transforms people. Services intervene to affect their health, social welfare, and personal appearance (along with their physical location, where passenger transport and freight transport share some similarities). (3) The third set of services mainly transforms symbols and data. These may be created or captured, communicated, processed, displayed, etc. Miles (1987) used such a framework to describe major innovation trajectories across different service sectors, since different industrial sectors tend to centre more on one or other set of transformations as their main activity.[4]

(1) Physical services have long been adopters of innovations based on motor power and readily applicable energy – new transport systems, new industrial equipment (washing machines, ovens, etc.) A wave of innovations based on such technologies swept these services for much of the twentieth century. Some sectors, such as air transport, were subject to intense innovation involving specific types of vehicle and infrastructure, and the network nature of many transport industries means that these were ready users of new communication systems and Information Technologies.[5] By the last quarter of the century, and in some cases earlier, many consumer services were challenged by what Gershuny (1978) had termed self-service. By this he meant consumers acquiring equipment that produced services for them (e.g. providing entertainment) they could use to produce their own services (e.g. transport) at low cost and or high convenience/high quality. This was seen as leading to a relative decline in some service industries as consumers switched to "self-service". Often there was an intermediate form of self-service, as epitomized by the launderette, where customers produced their own services, or at least controlled the machinery that was producing these services, while the equipment and often the premises belonged to a private firm. The launderette supplanted the private laundry, and was in turn supplanted by the consumer washing machine – though all modes of service production and delivery still persist. (This also draws our attention to the fact that much service employment till the middle of the twentieth century consisted of domestic service workers: this went into sever decline in most industrial countries as (a) new job opportunities for service workers opened up elsewhere in the economy and (b) new consumer equipment and consumables meant that tasks of cleaning and cooking required substantially less effort.

---

[4] Miles (2008) explores input-output data as a source of indicators for classifying services into these broad groups: another approach might be to utilize data on the tasks performed by specific occupations, such as those provided by O*NET (see http://online.onetcenter.org/skills/ accessed June 29 2009), and relate the incidence of occupations, and thus of tasks, to specific sectors.

[5] There is an important line of work on innovation in large technical systems that was largely kicked off by the historical studies of Thomas Hughes (cf Hughes, 1983, 1984, Mayntz and Hughes (1988). A rather different body of literature examines "Complex Product Systems", which include service operations such as airports, together with many other systems that combine services, technologies, and built infrastructure – see for example Davies and Hobday (2005), Gann and Salter (2000), and Hansen and Rush. (1998).

(2) Human services were being shaped in various ways by a combination of sector-specific innovations, such as pharmaceuticals and surgical instruments for health services, and the application of more powerful information processing for better capture and use of data on the complexities of specific individuals and circumstances.   Major developments may be expected in these services through the application of knowledge currently emerging from genomics and neurosciences, but there is much scope for more use of portable computers and mobile networking.   One of the key features of services in general, but especially human services, is their **interactivity** – the relation between service firms and their clients. Interactivity involves information flows (even in services performing biological transformations like surgery and hairdressing, and those providing personal care and often physical transformations like hotels and restaurants, but also in those effecting sociopsychological transformations like counseling and education), and this creates opportunities for use of new Information Technology (IT).   Francophone researchers, in particular, produced many studies with the service relationship as the focal point of analysis,[6] some using the term "servuction" to describe the processes underpinning service relationships.   The activities and procedures involved in producing and sustaining supplier-client relations were seen as much more important to service firms than to those in other sectors.   One early study of innovation in services (Belleflame et al, 1986) suggested that innovations could involve servuction and/or production, classifying innovations from service companies in these terms.[7]   There is also a large literature focusing on service quality, with important Scandinavian and American contributions, and often focusing on Human Services.[8]   Attention to quality means identifying problem areas, and this may stimulate innovation; while and examining component parts of the service process for quality control can foster an engineering approach to service activities.

(3) Information-focused services, which had been major users of traditional office technologies, were being transformed through the use of new information technologies (IT), allowing for a range or product and process innovations.   A rapid expansion of IT use was following the development of microprocessor-based systems in the last quarter of the twentieth century.   One of the most influential accounts of SI, from Barras (1986) actually focused on these services.[9]   Barras argued that they were "industrializing" through the use of new information technologies, but that whereas we are used to the "product cycle" as describing the trajectory of innovations, in service industries we see a "reverse product cycle".   This account, which has been taken up by many subsequent researchers, suggested that

---

[6] A fairly recent study is Gadrey & de Bandt (1994).

[7] Gallouj & Weinstein (1997) provide a useful review, comparing "servuction" to a number of other formulations. See the chapter by Edvardsson et al in this volume for a discussion of customer co-development of services.

[8] For reviews of the Service Quality literature see Asubonteng et al (1996), Gummesson (1998), Seth et al (2005).

[9] Several US researchers also focused on these, for example, Faulhaber, Noam and Tasley (1986).

service industries first introduce new IT to improve the efficiency of their operations (mainly back-office operations); then use them to improve service quality; and finally learn that new services can be created and delivered using the new systems. Miles noted that office work is common to all sectors, so their symbol/data service activities may be subject to similar innovation trajectories related to the adoption of new IT. Licht and Mocht (1997) confirmed the importance of such innovation: in a survey of innovation in German service firms, finding that all firms that reported innovative activities included new IT-based innovation among these.

Howells and Tether (2004) elaborated the classification above into four groups of service industries. In addition to those engaged in: (1) physical transformation, particularly of goods (e.g. road transport, handling and storage), (2) the transformation of people providing physical and/or mental/emotional changes (e.g. care for the elderly), (3) the transformation of information (e.g. data processing services), they added a fourth category – (4) knowledge creating services, supplying knowledge-based services (e.g. design and related services). They undertook a survey of firms in the four groups (focusing on the examples given in parentheses above), studying around 1300 firms from 15 EU (European Union) countries, the United States and Canada. Though the set of services covered is rather small, the study explored various types of innovation, and produced results that should be extended, and provocative analyses from these.

Eight types of innovation were explored, covering changes in the last 3 years to: (a) the products or services provided; (b) the means of producing services; (c) the means of delivering services; (d) the technologies used to produce or deliver services, (e) the skills of the workforce used to produce or deliver services; (f) the organizational structure of the business; (f) customer inter-relations; and (g) other business inter-relations. In an analysis focusing on the European data, Tether and Howells (2007) reported both similarities and differences across the four sectors. Almost half the firms reported significant or complete changes found in the *technologies* used to produce or deliver services (only 17% claimed their technologies had remained unchanged); over a third of the businesses claimed their *products or services* had changed completely or significantly (a quarter that they remained unchanged), and a very similar pattern emerged for changes to the means of *producing* services. The extent of change reported to the *skills* used to produce and deliver services was also remarkably similar to the extent of change to the firms' services and their means of producing and delivering services, with a third of the businesses claiming the skills they used had changed completely or significantly in the last three years. Slightly fewer firms reported extensive change to their means of *delivering* services, and a fifth reported complete or significant changes to *organizational structures*, and to *inter-relations with other businesses* (including customers). Some differences across sectors were statistically noteworthy: the extent of change to technologies was much greater amongst information processing companies than amongst those providing elderly care, for example, while the extent of change to services was similar across the two sectors. This implies that technology plays very different roles in (changing) service provision across these sectors, as we would expect contrasting a human-transformation and a symbol-transformation service.

This study was able to examine interrelationships between the different dimensions of innovation, and Tether and Howells (2007) reported that design firms with technological change (services, processes, technologies) were likely to also report significant or complete changes in all the other types of innovation (including the organizational ones); but organizational change, in contrast, did not render firms more likely to be undertaking technological change. Among the elderly care firms, in contrast, there were fewer complementarities, and the main locus of change was seen to be around skills, organizational arrangements and services to clients. In the design, road transport and information processing services, the main locus of innovation appears to be around technologies, processes, services and skills in combination. Principal components analysis differentiated for the latter three sectors between two sets of innovations – those involving changes to the processes of service provision and delivery (including the technologies used in these processes), and those associated with organizational changes (in the structure of the business and how it inter-relates with its clients and other businesses.) Changes to the services provided and to the skills of the workforce are more closely associated with changes to processes than organization in these three sectors. For the Elderly Care firms, the picture was less clear, hence the results for that sector are not reported here.

There have been numerous survey studies contrasting firms in different service sectors, but few of these have included human-transformation services. Thus we cannot make any strong assertions about how far the sorts of results reported here would apply to other such services (for example, to hospital services). However, some of the available survey studies do cover a wide variety of service firms. In the EU over the past decade and more there has been a series of Community Innovation Surveys (CIS), which have been progressively extended to cover more facets of innovation and more service sectors. The CIS depends upon respondents (managers) being able to judge whether they have introduced new products or processes in the last three years, which inevitably involves a subjective element. At the time of writing, there have been five rounds of the CIS; all but the first covering some marketed service sectors (such as transport, business services, communications, and trade services). Social and community services, personal services, hotels and restaurants, many creative and entertainment activities, and public services in general have been excluded. This makes it difficult to examine the more human-oriented services with the CIS instrument. But contrasts between more physical and more informational services, and subcategories within these, are readily available.

Three other limitations to the CIS surveys are service-relevant. First, only enterprises with more than ten employees are sampled – services firms are typically smaller than manufacturers, and contain many microbusinesses. (Typically, survey analysis finds larger firms reporting more innovative activity and resources – interestingly, one exception is the computer services sector (Tether et al, 2002) – though the ratio of innovative effort to employees is higher for smaller firms

(Baron, 1993.) Second, only one respondent is addressed at the companies studied, and it is unlikely that even a designated innovation manager (which often is not a job title) will know about the range of new activities being introduced across the organization. This may mean that we have some bias towards information on classic technology innovations, and away from "softer" forms of change.   The third point is related to this: the CIS uses a simple question at the outset about whether product (including service) or process innovations have been introduced in the last three years. Later questions in the survey (introduced only in the fourth round of CIS, CIS4, in 2005) ask about new organizational and marketing strategies. But this is after a series of questions about innovation activity – various types of expenditures associated with innovation, of sources of innovative information, of collaborative activity, of barriers to innovation, and so on – but these will presumably be answered mainly in terms of more technological product and process innovations. Despite these reservations, and the continuing improvements in CIS-5 and later there is a great deal that can be derived from CIS-type surveys, and here we can only touch upon a few highlights of the results.

Several researchers have used multivariate analysis to classify service sectors, or firms, into various clusters or statistical groups, based on such survey results. One particularly interesting German study by Hipp and Grupp (2005) differentiated between knowledge-intensive, network-intensive, scale-intensive and external innovation-intensive patterns in services. (These categories follow rather closely the classification of services by Soete and Miozzo, 2000, which was designed as a riposte to the traditional view of services as supplier-dominated, in other words as innovating only on the basis of absorbing inputs from manufacturing.) The knowledge-intensive pattern, for instance, was particularly marked in technical and R&D services and computer services, the network-based model in banking, the supplier-dominated model in other financial services.   But they also found, as they stressed, that every type of innovator can be found in every service sector.

The general picture from such surveys is that the information- and knowledge-transforming service sectors have much higher rates of innovation than more physical services, and indeed than manufacturing (where they resemble high-tech sectors). Detailed analysis of CIS2 data explicating this point was provided by Tether et al (2002), and a recent summary of CIS4 results (Eurostat (2008) notes that the share of firms reporting innovation in transport, storage and communication is noticeably lower than the average for the sample. (These are mainly engaged in physical transformations, though telecommunications may be included here.) In contrast, information- and knowledge-transforming services report innovation more frequently than other sectors (including manufacturing). There are high shares of innovative enterprises in financial intermediation services (banks, insurance, etc.) and for "economic activities classified in NACE section K core coverage" (computer and related activities - NACE 72,[10] architectural and engineering activities - NACE 74.2, and technical testing and analysis - NACE 74.3; these are

---

[10] NACE is the Standard Industrial Classification now in use in the EU, substantially similar to North America's NAICS.

often referred to as the TKIBS, technology-based knowledge-intensive business services. 53% of the enterprises in the K core coverage are innovative by this account, with the highest shares of innovative enterprises among computer and related activities.

Tether et al (2002) reported high levels of innovation in other business services which are part of section K (this includes the PKIBS, professional KIBS such as legal and accountancy, advertising and market research firms, but also less knowledge-intensive business services such as secretarial, security and cleaning services). One interpretation of such results is that the physical transformation activities of many services have already been subject to innovation associated with motor technologies – though this is not to rule out the scope for substantial future innovation here, for example associated with energy efficiency and pollution control, with new materials, etc. In contrast, the information and knowledge processing service activities are still undergoing rapid change associated with new IT. Indeed, we would speculate that even if there were to be no more fundamental innovation in IT hardware and operating system software, there could be decades of rapid innovation as services continued to exploit, and learn how to better use, the technological capabilities that are available.

What of nontechnological innovations?[11] Howells and Tether (2004) used data from the INNOBAROMETER survey of innovating EU firms (in 2002), which allowed them to contrast manufacturing and services sectors in terms of product, process and organizational innovation. This led them to conclude that some services (unfortunately they were not able to examine more detailed sectors) seem unusually focused on organizational innovation as compared to manufacturers. More than a third of top managers of services firms considered their main innovative activities to have been solely organizational, compared to less than a tenth of manufacturing firms). CIS4 contains some questions on organizational change, which researchers have begun to examine - typically reporting rather less dramatic results than the Howells/Tether ones. Kanerva et al. (2006) reported that services firms (especially financial and wholesale sectors) are more prone to initiate organizational change. Schmidt and Rammer (2006) examined plotting technological (product and/or process) innovation against organizational change (including marketing change) for German CIS4 data, and Miles (2008) for UK data: both studies found that while more technologically innovative sectors tend to be more organizationally innovative, manufacturing tends to emphasize technology-based product and process innovation, while most services emphasize organizational innovation. Exceptions are services sectors focused on IT, which are particularly innovative and tend to focus more on technological innovation. ("Physical services" are the converse, and the few services more focused on transforming people are also more oriented to organizational change.)

Other studies qualify these results: Arundel et al (2007) divide services into KIBS and "other services" – roughly information and knowledge service sectors

---

[11] For a conference focusing on such innovations, with several service-focused contributions, see 6 Countries Programme (2008).

versus physical service sectors. On all four dimensions of innovation (product, process, organizational and marketing) KIBS are outstandingly more often innovators than other services with manufacturers, achieving an intermediate position. The overall conclusion is that nontechnological innovation is less predominant in more physical services as in manufacturing firms, though the overall patterns look quite similar across manufacturing and services in general. If we look just at those firms that do report innovation, however, a rather different picture emerges. The "other services" innovators are more prone to report organizational and marketing innovations than the innovative manufacturers (and indeed, report more marketing innovation – and more process and less product innovation – than the KIBS). There do seem to be clear differences in emphasis of innovation across sectors, then, but these need further exploration .

The survey studies discussed above focus on service firms and sectors. As is well-known, services of various sorts are produced by firms in all sectors of the economy – and in addition to those that are produced for internal consumption by the firms themselves, there are many services supplied to clients, of which after-sales is only one example.   There is some evidence to support the arguments of management studies[12] that an emphasis on "service" is growing across the economy (e.g. Lay, 2002, finds this among German manufacturers).

Hollanders (2008) explored what this might mean in terms of innovation using another European survey (of innovative firms with over 20 employees), the 2007 Innobarometer, which asked whether, in the last two years, the firm had introduce new or significantly improved goods and whether it had introduced new or significantly improved services. The results are striking. 42% of all firms introduced both new goods and services; 24% new services only, 34% new goods only. Among manufacturers, only about 50% innovated only in goods; over a third introduced new services as well as goods, and around 10% had introduced new services only! (Also, a majority of the services firms reported also, or only, introducing goods – we can speculate that these might involve such tangible accompaniments to services as phones and terminals, loyalty and cash cards, and the like). While it is possible to trace out broad differences between manufacturing and services sectors, then, and while these may tell us something about striking features of service innovation, we need to be attentive to the fact that there are many overlaps between the broad sectors, and that their products are frequently composed of a mixture of goods and services, supplied through "product-service systems".

Another way of exploring service innovation via large-scale surveys involves examining the experience of the workforce. Over the years there have been many surveys exploring the use of new IT at the workplace, with some quite detailed examination of the use of computer systems for specific functions. Recently, another set of European surveys, this time based on interviews with employees (and self-employed people) concerning their working conditions gives some insights

---

[12] E.g. Mathe and Shapiro (1993), Quinn et al (1990), Zemke (1990). For complementary perspectives, see Kuusisto (2000), Kuusisto and Metyer (2002).

into not only technology use, but also into the extent to which they are being creative in their work. The European Working Conditions Survey can be used to examine working conditions across sectors and occupational groups (Parent-Thirion et al 2007). As we would expect, the data indicate that service sectors involve more contact with people such as customers. Information-transforming services (finance, real estate and business services, and public services like education feature relatively large shares of jobs where the employees report complex tasks, problem-solving, learning new things on the job, computer and internet use, and so on, and relatively low shares of people reporting monotonous work. The reverse tends to be the case for transport and trade services, and hotels, restaurants and catering services. These trends more or less follow the pattern of educational credentials that are displayed across sectors, in terms of the shares of the workforce with higher or lower levels of qualification. In terms of occupations, it is the three higher levels of ISCO (the International Standard Classification of Occupations) that emerge as more complex, involving learning new things, and involving problem-solving (which presumably means more innovative). These categories are what we can describe as knowledge-intensive service workers - senior managers, professionals, and associate professionals.[13] While many service jobs – catering, sales, etc. – are very mundane, these higher-level service jobs – which include R&D workers, designers, and many more – are particularly important sources of creativity and innovation.

Management of Service Innovation

From the survey and case study literature – mainly in Europe, and mainly on innovation in service firms and sectors – some fairly clear results have emerged about the management structures associated with various types of service. Such studies as Arundel et al (2007), Dialogic et al (2006), FhG-ISI (2003), IOIR (2003), Kanerva et al (2006) Miles (2007) PREST et al (2006), and Tether et al (2002) suggest that typically the innovation budgets of service firms tend to be lower than those of comparable manufacturers (controlling, for instance, for size). This is especially the case for R&D expenditure. But T-KIBS firms, like high-tech manufacturing firms, tend to have large budgets. Several recent studies examine R&D and R&D-like activities in services.[14] The term R&D is often not recognized, or seen as referring to market research, by many service firms. In much of the service sector, it is rare to find firms that have R&D departments, or that employing specialized R&D workers and managers: more often what R&D is accomplished is done through special project-based teams. Again T-KIBS, such as computer services, are exceptions. Very large service firms in other sectors (such as finance and trade services) do, however, quite often feature R&D depart-

---

[13] For the analysis of these data, see Miles and Jones (2009).
[14] den Hertog et al, 2006; Miles, 2007; NIST, 2004; PREST et al, 2006

ments (which may also be found in some public services and government agencies).

What are the origins of innovative ideas? CIS-type studies enquire as to the sources of information used in innovation (not quite the same thing!). Compared to manufacturing, most services (surprisingly) report less use of suppliers and customers as sources of information for innovation.[15] Business Services do report more use of clients; and Trade Services of suppliers. Services recruit many employees from Universities, but (with the marked exception of Business Services, especially T-KIBS) make relatively little use of them as sources of information for innovation, and as potential collaborators. They make slightly more use of consultancies and competitors as information sources. Sundbo and Gallouj (2000) usefully differentiate between several types of service innovation framework, characterizing different firms ands sectors. Reworking their account somewhat, we can see seven broad patterns. (1) Some do follow a classic R&D pattern, with specialized departments conducting research of a strategic nature – this is often the case in large technology-based service organizations. (2) A "Services Professional Pattern" often applies in knowledge-intensive organizations whose professionals generate solutions for clients that are often ad hoc and highly customized; here, the innovation process is rarely formalized, relying on employees' professional skills. Much innovation intelligence may flow through professional networks and associations, or other communities of practice. Many consultancy firms, and parts of the "creative industries" such as advertising and design follow such a model. One major challenge for these firms is "capturing" and replicating innovations that are made in practice by professionals, and much attention in knowledge management is directed to this. (3) A Neo-Industrial Pattern lies between patterns (2) and (3): alongside a specialized R&D or innovation department, there is much more distributed innovation in the course of professional practice. This often characterizes, for example, health services and some large consultancies. (4) A pattern often encountered in large service firms, such as airlines, hotel chains, and retailers, is the "Organized Strategic Innovation Pattern", where innovation is organized in the form of projects that are directed by more or less transitory cross-functional teams, working through distinct steps of project management, and often with strong leadership from marketing groups. (5) An "Entrepreneurial Pattern" commonly involves start-up firms that offer services based on more or less radical innovations: these may be technological or rely more on new business models: many so-called gazelles, online services, and others follow this pattern, across many sectors: typically it is short-lived and they move into one of the other innovation modes. (6) An "Artisanal Pattern" is found in many smaller scale and low-tech physical ("operational") services, such as clearing and catering. These are classic supplier-driven sectors, where major innovations are imported from other sectors (e.g. manufacturing), though innovation may also be driven by regulations and demand. Employees and managers may be sources of (typically incremental) innovation. Finally, (7) a "Network Pattern" involves on a network of firms acting together,

---

[15] Arundel et al (2007), IOIR (2003).

with franchising being a common organizational structure in services such as fast food (but network structures are also found in some professional sectors). There may be a dominant company that follows, for example, patterns (1) or (3), and rolls out innovation to members of the network (sometimes in the form of new standards).

This account describes some recognizable patterns at the firm level, but it is still quite possible for particular service innovations to be organized in different ways within the same firm. Thus, examining (Finnish) KIBS firms Toivonen and Tuominen (2006), describes five innovation patterns, which varied in terms of their formality and collaborative nature. These were (1) Internal processes without a specific project – here, innovations emerge in an unintentional, unplanned, and incremental way; existing services are gradually adapted to new problems; (2) Internal innovation projects carried out deliberately within the firm - usually focused on improvement of the service production system, but sometimes including innovations in service content; (3) Innovation projects where a pilot customer supplies resources, sponsorship, critical evaluation and information relevant to a new service idea; (4) Innovation projects tailored for a client who has presented a specific problem, the innovation possibly being one-off or further developed possible with client support; and (5) Externally funded innovation projects, which are usually formal and research-oriented (possible funded through national or international programmes in   part), which usually involve several collaborators, and which are intended to generate new service concepts or platforms that benefit the whole sector or cluster.

One final set of results from the SI literature based on surveys or multiple case studies concerns Intellectual Property. The overall picture is that the *patent* mechanism is rarely used (except by some T- KIBS, such as engineering services). Patents are still most oriented to tangible innovations in most countries, Business Process Patenting in the USA may be leading to changes here, but this is not employed in the EU. *Trademarks* are very important for some services, and while a new trademark does not necessarily signify a product innovation (it can just be rebranding), trademarking and innovation have been shown to be associated in many sectors. *Design rights* are important in a few sectors, for instance, to protect innovative engineering and architectural designs.[16]

It is notable that alongside the SI literature, are two related bodies of work that are inherently associated with SI, but whose theory and practice are often poorly related to it. First is the field of Service Design, which for a long time seemed to be largely dominated by informatics practitioners, but which of late has begun to attract much wider attention – especially from those in design industries who are facing the challenges of deindustrialization and the rise of a service-dominant logic in the markets they serve. A Service Design Network and journal have recently come into being,[17] studies are available on design of services as varied as

---

[16] See Arundel et al (2007), FhG-ISI (2003), Miles et al (2003).

[17] The network website is: http://www.service-design-network.org/ from which useful publications can be accessed, and there is linkage to the journal Touchpoint. (The journal name embod-

technology-based services (Candi, 2007)[18] and theatre (Stuart and Tax, 2004); and (very different) reviews of the field have been prepared by Moritz (2005) and Saco and Goncalves (2008 - in an issue of in an issue of Design Management Review,(vol. 19 no 1, devoted to design for service industries).[19]

Second, there is a substantial body of research and practice on "New Service Development" (NSD). This has taken up various themes – differences between services and new product development more generally, involvement of customers in the NSD process, factors leading to success and failure in NSD projects, and more. It still seems an underdeveloped body of work as compared to work on product development of goods (this is argued in the review by Page and. Schirr, 2008, who found only 4% of the articles reviewed to focus on NSD), but there is still substantial material here which could be the subject of a review in its own. Indeed, already in 1998 Johne and Storey were able to produce a pioneering review of the NSD field, in which they argued that a particular feature of NSD was the need to manage three groups for an NSD project to be effective. As well as the NSD staff themselves, those employees involved in the customer interface were vital points of reference, whose insights and cooperation were important. Additionally, the customers' themselves were critical. In all innovation, understanding of user needs is a vital element: in the case of NSD, cooperation may be required from customers in that the quality of the service outcome is very dependent on their inputs into the process. Earlier still, Edvardsson and Olsson (1996) had prepared an overview very much linking NSD to quality issues, and differentiating between strategies for development of the service concept, the service system, and the development of the service process.

Martin and Horne (1993, 1995) published a pair of papers examining successful and unsuccessful NSD, in one case across firms and in one case within firms. They found that there were rarely specialized innovation functions in service firms (indeed, there may have been problems to do with the loss of service champions (as compared to the product champions described for manufacturing); successful service innovations were not typically the result of a few specialists, working in isolation (though this may reflect the types of firm they studied. What did emerge as conducive to successful NSD was (not surprisingly) greater direct customer participation in the process, and strategic use of customer information at specific stages in the process; together with increased managerial and other employee involvement in the NSD. An overview of recent studies by concluded that NSD management needs to look beyond a technology-centric view of innovation and explore innovation in service concepts, client interfaces, and delivery systems.

---

ies a term from one tradition of service design work.) A pioneer in this area was Lynne Shostack, e.g. Shostack (1984).

[18] See also the research reports from the project Designing for Services in Science and Technology-Based Enterprises, available at: http://www.sbs.ox.ac.uk/D4S

[19] See Glushko's chapter in the present volume. For a discussion of how service design relates to SSME, see Holmlid and Evenson (2008); see also Holmlid (2007) on interaction design.

Rather than being a random flash of genius, various organizational characteristics, related to people and structure, influence the pace and success of NSD. The innovative climate should be nurtured by, for example, workers sharing information and using frequent external contacts, and structures being established that provide strategic focus, staff training and education, opportunities to learn through task rotation, and relevant information systems. For effective implementation of new services, key people must be mobilized and involved (frontline employees, potential service champions, senior management supporters), and firm structures should be established that permit multi-functional project teams to be developed, using appropriate project management tools and deploying sufficient resources, with serious attention being given to prototyping, to testing and issues of marketing and roll-out.

The growing role of "service" across all sectors means that issues of NSD, and of enhancing the service elements of operations, are being confronted very widely, and not only in service firms. (Of course, some firms have shifted from being manufacturing firms to being predominantly service firms, too.) This underpins the argument that a service-dominant logic is most appropriate for marketing (e.g. Hunt 2004, Vargo and Lusch 2004b) – whatever you are selling, it is the service that the customer receives that is vital. Similar philosophies are apparent in manufacturing and engineering research, for example in Jay Lee's "dominant innovation" approach, which frequently advises goods producers to focus on innovation concerning the services supplied by and through their goods (e.g. Lee 1998, 2003). Howells (2001) discusses "servicisation", the trend for manufacturing and extractive firms to provide services related to the goods they produce. Rather than offering simply goods to business customers or consumers, a wider product, involving a service component, is supplied. Two main forms of this are (1) to complement the good with services such as finance, insurance, maintenance; and (2) to sell not the good itself, but the functionality that the good would ultimately fulfill (e.g. aircraft miles travelled to time, rather than engines). These strategies leads to firms thinking more about the consumption of the material good - and the way they conduct innovation, design and NSD. The pattern of use and disposal, the life span of the good, come to the fore. This can change the logic of innovation in the good itself – for instance leading to new emphasis on embedded systems for error reporting and diagnosis, or for supporting service functions associated with maintenance and disposal. Again, it is product-service systems that rise to the fore, even as we stress a service-dominant logic. And the close link between service innovation (and design and development) to service engineering[20] is also apparent.

---

[20] For instance, Bullinger et al (2003), Ganz (2006). See Gudergan's chapter in the current volume.

Conclusions and Implications

We have reviewed a large body of literature, and this is just an aerial view of the tips of several widely scattered icebergs. There is a major challenge involved in pulling this literature together, and in integrating it. As argued elsewhere, we need to examine SI not as something that is radically demarcated from innovation in general, but as representing a challenge to innovation studies to develop a more synthesized viewpoint, capable of handling NSD and SI as well as innovation in manufacturing products and processes.[21]   This is liable to mean rethinking the metrics of innovation research (from innovation surveys to R&D measurement), exploring novel sites of innovation (which can involve essentially any business process and product feature), and examining various "hidden" forms of innovation management.

The growing attention to SI has not treated all sectors equally. Some sectors and services have been looked at in detail and/or from many perspectives – for example financial services (e.g. Consoli, 2005a, b, Uchupalanan, 2000). Some are relatively neglected. It is remarkable how little scholarly work has concerned *Public Services* – though this has exercised policymakers, with much practitioner discussion of the topic. (Examples of more academic research include Halvorsen et al, 2005, Windrum and Koch, 2008.) What are known as *"Creative Sectors"* have also received little attention from the innovation studies community until relatively recently, perhaps because of concerns about getting involved in aesthetic judgments – but with the economic prominence of "experience industries" this is beginning to change, too.[22] It is likely that these services will involve patterns of innovation and practices of design rather similar to those in professional and large service systems, but there are also likely to be surprises as we investigate largely uncharted territory.

The growth of service sectors, and the rise of "service", in modern economies and management practice means taking SI, in all its forms, seriously. We cannot assume that it follows the patterns and is organized through the mechanisms familiar in manufacturing activities. Our approaches to innovation will have to extend beyond emphasis on artifacts and technological innovation, and pay more attention to changes in business processes and market relationships that involve service and organizational as well as technological dimensions. Understanding SI means a substantial widening of approaches to explaining, measuring and managing innovation. Academics and management training courses have been slow to wake up to this fact, as Chesbrough (2004) noted in the remarks quoted at the outset of this chapter. But many practitioners have not – thus we see lively discussions on

---

[21] For instance, Camacho and Rodríguez (2005), Coombs and Miles (2000)), de Vries (2004), Drejer, (2004) Flikkema et al (2007), Miozzo and Miles (2003), and Salter and Tether (2006).

[22] Studies include Green and Miles, 2008, Sundbo and Darmer (2008), and the very interesting survey study by Muller et al (2009). Work on the creative industries is clearly linked to that on the "experience economy" – cf. Pine II and Gilmore (1999).

SI in such locations as the Consortium for Service Innovation, and discussions about service design are beginning to engage wide audiences. There is also growing interest in the policy issues surrounding service innovation, for example whether R&D and innovation policies need to be reoriented to better fit the challenges of the service economy.[23] The pace of development of the research literature, is quite possibly not as rapid as the pace of activity and accumulation of experience in NSD, in service design, and in SI itself. But the literature is growing so rapidly that we can expect substantial contributions to knowledge in the coming years. The biggest challenge is likely to be that of integrating these burgeoning bodies of knowledge.

References

6 Countries Programme (2008). *Non-Technical Innovation - Definition, Measurement and Policy Implications*. Workshop held 16-17 October 2008, Karlsruhe, Germany presentations available at http://www.6cp.net/workshops/karlsruhe08.html Accessed 10 June, 2009.

Arundel, A. , Kanerva, M., van Cruysen, A. and Hollanders. H. (2007). *Innovation Statistics for the European Service Sector* UNU-MERIT, INNO-Metrics Thematic Papers at: http://www.proinno-europe.eu/index.cfm?fuseaction=page.display&topicID=282&parentID=51 Accessed 10 June, 2009.

Asubonteng, P., McCleary, K.J. and Swan, J.E. (1996). "SERVQUAL revisited: a critical review of service quality", *The Journal of Services Marketing*, Vol. 10 No. 6, pp. 62-81.

Baron, J. (1993). "The Small Business Technology Transfer (STRR) program: Converting Research Into Economic Strength". *Economic Development Review,* 11(4), 63-70.

Barras R. (1986). "Interactive Innovation In Financial And Business Services: the vanguard of the service revolution", Research Policy, vol. 19, pp215-237

Barras, R., (1986). "Towards a Theory of Innovation in Services" *Research Policy* vol 15 (4) 161-173.

Belleflamme, C., Houard, J. & Michaux, B. (1986). *Innovation and Research and Development Process Analysis in Service Activities* Brussels, EC, FAST. Occasional papers no 116.

BERR/DIUS (2008). *Supporting Innovation in Services* London: Departments for Business Enterprise and Regulatory Reform, and of Universities, Innovation and Science, at: http://www.berr.gov.uk/files/file47439.pdf Accessed 16 June, 2009

Berry, L.L., Shankar, V., Turner Parish, J., Cadwallader, S. and Dotzel, D. (2006). Creating New Markets through Service Innovation *MIT Sloan Management Review* 47(2), 56–63.

Bryson, J.R., Daniels, P.W., & Warf, B. (2004). *Service worlds: People, organisations, technologies*. Routledge: London

Bryson, J.R. .and Daniels, P W. (2007). (eds) *The Handbook of Service Industries* Aldershot, Edward Elgar

Bullinger, H.-J., Fähnrich, K.-P. and Meiren, T. (2003). "Service Engineering – Methodical Development of New Service Products" *International Journal of Production Economics* vol.85 no.3, pp275-287.

Camacho, J. A. and Rodríguez, M. (2005). "How innovative are services? an empirical analysis for Spain" *Service Industries Journal*, 25(2), pp.253-271

---

[23] For example, den Hertog and Segers (2003), Rubalcaba (2006); for a view from OECD, see OECD (2005).

Candi, M. (2007). "The role of design in the development of technology-based services" *Design Studies* vol 28 pp559-583

Chesbrough, H. (2004). "A failing grade for the innovation academy" *Financial Times* September 24 2004 at http://www.ft.com/cms/s/2/9b743b2a-0e0b-11d9-97d3-00000e2511c8,dwp_uuid=6f0b3526-07e3-11d9-9673-00000e2511c8.html Accessed 10 June, 2009.

Chesbrough, H. (2005). " Toward a science of services" *Harvard Business Review*, 83, 16-17.

Chesbrough, H. and J. Spohrer (2006). "A research manifesto for services science" *Communications of the ACM*. Vol 49 no 7. July. pp35-40.

Consoli, D. (2005a). "Technological cooperation and product substitution in UK retail banking: the case of customer services" *Information Economics and Policy* 17(2), 199-216.

Consoli, D. (2005b). "The dynamics of technological change in UK retail banking services: an evolutionary perspective" *Research Policy* 34 (4), 461-480.

Coombs, R., & Miles, I. (2000). "Innovation, Measurement and Services: the new problematique" pp83-102 in J S Metcalfe & I Miles (eds) *Innovation Systems in the Service Economy* Dordrecht: Kluwer

Coppetiers, P., Delaunay, J-C., Dyckman, J., Gadrey, J., Moulaert, F., & Tordoir, P. (1986). *The Functions of Services and the Theoretical Approach to National and International Classifications* Lille, John Hopkins University Centre (mimeo)

Daniels, P.W. and Bryson, J.W. (1993). (eds) *Service Industries in the Global Economy*. (2 vols) Cheltenham UK: Edward Elgar

Davies, A. and Hobday, M. (2005). *The Business of Projects: Managing Innovation in Complex Products and Systems*. Cambridge University Press: Cambridge

de Jong, J.P.J. and Vermeulen, P.A.M. (2002). *Organizing Successful New Service Development: A Literature Review* SCALES -paper N200307 electronic working paper series of EIM Business and Policy Research.at http://www.entrepreneurship-sme.eu/pdf-ez/N200307.pdf Accessed 16 June, 2009

de Vries, E.J. (2004). *Innovation in services: towards a synthesis approach*, PrimaVera Working Paper 2004-20, Universiteit van Amsterdam, Department of Business Studies available at: http://imwww.fee.uva.nl/~pv/PDF 9docs/2004-20.pdf Accessed 16 June, 2009

den Hertog, P. and Segers J. (2003). *Service Innovation Policies: A Comparative policy Study*, Paper within the framework of the SIID Project, DIALOGIC, Utrecht, http://www.eco.rug.nl/GGDC/ dseries/SIIDfrontpage.shtml

Dialogic, IAS ,PREST, SERVILAB (2006). *Research and Development Needs of Business Related Service Firms (RENESER Project)* Delft: Dialogic innovatie & interactie, report to DG Internal Market

Drejer, I. (2004). "Identifying innovation in surveys of services: a Schumpeterian perspective" *Research Policy* vol. 33, no.3 pp551-562

Edvardsson, B.and Olsson, J. (1996). "Key concepts for New Service Development" *The Service Industries Journal*, vol 16 pp. 140 - 164

Eurostat (2008). *Science, Technology and Innovation in Europe* Luxembourg: Office for Official Publications of the European Communities

Faulhaber G., Noam, E. & Tasley, R. (1986). (eds.) *Services in Transition: the impact of information technology on the service sector* Ballinger, Cambridge Mass.

FhG-ISI (2003). Patents In The Service Industries, Karlsruhe, FhG-ISI, March 2003, EC Contract No ERBHPV2-CT-1999-06, available at: ftp://ftp.cordis.lu/pub/indicators/docs/ind_report_fraunhofer1.pdf Accessed 12 June, 2009

Flikkema, Meindert, Jansen, Paul and Van Der Sluis, Lidewey, (2007). 'Identifying Neo-Schumpeterian Innovation in Service Firms: A Conceptual Essay with a Novel Classification', *Economics of Innovation and New Technology*, 16:7, 541 – 558

Gadrey J., de Bandt J. (1994). *Relations de service, Marchés de service*, Paris, CNRS éditions

Gallouj C., and Gallouj, F. (2000). "Neo-Schumpeterian Perspectives on Innovation in Services", in Boden, M. & I. Miles (eds.) *Services, Innovation and the Knowledge Economy,* London, Continuum.

Gallouj, F. and Weinstein, O. (1997). 'Innovation in services', *Research Policy*, **26**, 537-556.

Gallouj, F. (2002). *Innovation in the Service Economy – The New Wealth of Nations,* Edgar Elgar, Cheltenham, UK

Gann D. M. and Salter A. J. (2000). Innovation in project-based, service enhanced firms: the construction of complex products and systems, *Research Policy* 29, 955–72.

Ganz, W. (2006). "Germany: service engineering". *Communications of the ACM* vol. 49 no.7 pp78-79.

Gershuny, J.I. (1978). *After Industrial Society?* London : Macmillan

Guile B. R., Quinn, J. B. (eds.), (1988a). *Managing Innovation: cases from the services industries,* Washington DC, National Academy Press.

Guile, B. R. and Quinn, J. B. (eds.), (1988b). *Technology in Services* Washington DC, National Academy Press.

Gummesson, E. (1998). "Productivity, quality and relationship marketing in service operations", *International Journal of Contemporary Hospitality Management*, Vol. 10 No. 1, pp. 4-15.

Halvorsen, T., Hauknes, J. Miles I., and Røste, R. (2005). *On the Differences between Public and Private Sector Innovation* Oslo: NIFU STEP, Publin Report D9 (http://www.step.no/publin Accessed 12 June, 2009)

Hansen, K.L., and Rush, H. (1998). "Hotspots in complex product systems: Emerging issues in innovation management." *Technovation, 18*, no. 8/9, 555–61

Hefley, B. and Murphy, W. (eds) (2008). *Service Science, Management and Engineering Education for the 21st Century,* Norwell, MA : Springer Academic

Hipp, C. and Grupp, H. (2005). "Innovation in the service sector: The demand for service-specific innovation measurement concepts and typologies", *Research Policy*, 34, 4, 517-535.

Hollanders, H. (2008). "Measuring Services Innovation: Service Sector Innovation Index" presented at 6 Countries Programme (2008) *Non-Technical Innovation - Definition, Measurement and Policy Implications* available at: http://innovatiecentrum.gorilla.ys.be/page_attachments/0000/0814/Hollanders.pdf Accessed 16 June, 2009

Holmlid, S. (2007). "Interaction Design and Service Design: Expanding a Comparison of Design Disciplines" *Design Inquiries* Linköping, Sweden: Human-Centered Systems, Linköpings Universitet, at: http://www.nordes.org/data/uploads/papers/143.pdf

Holmlid, S. and Evenson, S (2008). "Bringing Service Design to Service Sciences, Management and Engineering" pp 341-345 in Hefley, B. and Murphy, W. (eds) *Service Science, Management and Engineering Education for the 21st Century,* Norwell, MA : Springer Academic

Howells, J. and Tether, B. (2004). *Innovation in Services: Issues at Stake and Trends* Inno Studies Programme (ENTR-C/2001), Brussels:.Commission of the European Communities http://www.cst.gov.uk/cst/reports/files/knowledge-intensive-services/services-study.pdf Accessed 16 June, 2009

Hughes, T.P. (1983). *Networks of Power: Electrification of Western Society 1880–1930.* Johns Hopkins Univ. Press, Baltimore, MD.

Hughes, T.P. (1984). The evolution of large technological systems. in: Bijker, W., Hughes, T., Pinch, T. (Eds.), *The Social Construction of Technological Systems.* MIT Press, Cambridge.

Hunt, S. D. (2004). "On the Service-Centered Dominant Logic of Marketing" *Journal of Marketing*, 68, pp18-27.

IfM and IBM (2007). *Succeeding through Service Innovation: A Discussion Paper.* Cambridge, United Kingdom: University of Cambridge Institute for Manufacturing. ISBN: 978-1-902546-59-8 available at http://www.ifm.eng.cam.ac.uk/ssme/documents/ssme_discussion_final.pdf Accessed June 29 2009

IOIR (Institute of Innovation Research) (2003). *Knowing How, Knowing Whom: A Study of the Links between the Knowledge Intensive Services Sector and The Science Base* IOIR, University of Manchester; Report to the Council for Science and Technology available at:

http://www.cst.gov.uk/cst/reports/files/knowledge-intensive-services/services-study.pdf   Accessed 20 June 2009

Johne, A. and Storey, C. (1998). "New service development: a review of the literature and annotated bibliography" *European Journal of Marketing*, Vol. 32 No. 3/4, 1998, pp. 184-251

Kanerva, M., Hollanders, H. & Arundel, A. (2006). *Can We Measure and Compare Innovation in Services?* Luxembourg: European TrendChart on Innovation, 2006 TrendChart report

Kuusisto, J. and Meyer, M. (2002). *Insights into services and innovation in the knowledge-intensive economy* Helsinki: Finnish Institute for Enterprise Management, National Technology Agency, Technology Review 134/2003

Kuusisto, J. and Meyer, M. (2003). 'Insights into services and innovation in the knowledge intensive economy', *Technology Review* 134/2003, Tekes, Helsinki

Kuusisto, J. (2002). *The Determinants of Service Capability in Small Manufacturing Firms*, PhD thesis, Kingston University Small Business Research Centre, Kingston, United Kingdom.

Lay, G. (2002). *Serviceprovider Industry: Industrial Migration From Manufacturing To Selling Products And Services - Trends And Impacts* Karlsruhe: Fraunhofer Institute for Systems and Innovation Research (ISI-A-13-02) German language version available at: http://www.isi.fhg.de/publ/pi_en.htm

Lee, J. (1998). "Teleservice engineering in manufacturing: challenges and opportunities" *International Journal of Machine Tools and Manufacture* Volume 38, Issue 8, pp. 901-910

Lee, J. (2003). "Smart Products and Service Systems for e-Business Transformation," Special Issues on "Managing Innovative Manufacturing," *International Journal of Technology Management* Vol. 26, No. 1, pp. 45-52

Levitt, T. (1976). 'The Industrialisation of Service' *Harvard Business Review* vol. 54 no. 5 pp. 63-74.

Licht, G. and Moch, D. (1997). *Innovation and Information Technology in Services*, ZEW Discussion Paper No 97-20, ZEW, Mannheim

Maglio, P. P., Kreulen, J., Srinivasan, S., and Spohrer, J. (2006). "Service systems, service scientists, SSME, and innovation" *Communications of the ACM*. 49(7). July. 81–85.

Martin, C.R. and Horne, D. A. (1995). 'Level of success inputs for service innovations in the same firm', *International Journal of Service Industry Management*, Vol. 6 No. 4, pp. 40-56.

Martin, C.R. and Horne, D.A. (1993). "Services innovation: successful versus unsuccessful firms", *International Journal of Service Industry Management*, Vol. 4 No. 1, pp. 49-65

Mathe H. and Shapiro, R. D. (1993). *Integrating Service Strategy into the Manufacturing Company* London: Chapman & Hall

Mayntz, R., Hughes, T.P. (Eds.) (1988). *The Development of Large Technical Systems*. Campus Verlag, Frankfurt.

Miles I. (1993). "Services in the New Industrial Economy" *Futures* Vol. 25 No 6 pp. 653-672,

Miles, I. (2008). "Patterns of innovation in service industries" *IBM Systems Journal* Vol 47 No. 1 pp115-128 at http://www.research.ibm.com/journal/sj/471/miles.html

Miles, I. (1987). "Information Technology and the Service Economy" in P Zorkosky (ed) *Oxford Surveys in Information Technology 4* Oxford: Oxford University Press

Miles, I. (1994). "Innovation in Services" in Dodgson, M. amd Rothwell, R. (eds) *Handbook of Innovation* Aldershot, Edward Elgar

Miles, I. (2004). "Innovation in Services", in Fagerberg, J., Mowery, D., and Nelson, R. (eds) *The Oxford Handbook of Innovation* Oxford: Oxford University Press

Miles, I. and Green, L. (2008). *Hidden Innovation in the Creative Industries* London, NESTA Research report HICI/13   available at http://www.nesta.org.uk/hidden-innovation-in-the-creative-industries/

Miles, I. and Jones, B. (2009). *Innovation in the European Service Economy – scenarios and implications for skills and knowledge* Brussels: ETEPS European Techno-Economic Policy Support Network, to be published and put only by JRC-IPTS, Seville.

Miles, I. Andersen, B., Boden, M. and Howells, J. (2000). 'Services Processes and Property', *International Journal of Technology Management*, Vol 20.1/2 pp. 95-115.

Miles. I. (2007). "R&D beyond Manufacturing: the strange case of services' R&D" *R&D Management* vol 37, no 3 pp. 249-268

Miozzo, M., and Miles, I., (eds) (2003). *Internationalization, Technology and Services* Aldershot, Elgar

Moritz, S. (2005). *Service Design – Practical access to an evolving field* Cologne: Koln International School of Design, available at: http://stefan-moritz.com/Stefan%20Moritz/Service%20Design.html Accessed June 29 2009

Müller, K., Rammer, C. and Truby, J. (2009). *The Role of Creative Industries in Industrial Innovation*, Mannheim, Germany: Centre for European Economic Research (ZEW), ZEW Discussion Paper no. 08-109, available at: *ftp://ftp.zew.de/pub/zew-docs/dp/dp08109.pdf*

NESTA (2008). *Innovation in Services* London: National Endowment for Science, Technology and the Arts, at http://www.nesta.org.uk/innovation-in-services/

NIST (2004). Measuring Service-Sector Research and Development, Gaithersburg, Maryland: NIST (Planning Report 05-1, Prepared by Michael Gallaher, Albert Link, and Jeffrey Petrusa of RTI International for National Science Foundation and National Institute of Standards & Technology)

OECD (2001). *Innovation and productivity in services*, OECD: Paris

OECD (2005). *Promoting Innovation in Services*, OECD: Paris available at http://www.oecd.org/dataoecd/21/55/35509923.pdf Accessed June 29 2009

Page, A.L., and. Schirr, G.R. (2008). "Growth and Development of a Body of Knowledge: 16 Years of New Product Development Research, 1989–2004" *Journal of Product Innovation Managament* vol 25 pp. 233–248

Parent-Thirion, A., Fernández Macías, E., Hurley, J., and Vermeylen, G., (2007). *Fourth European Working Conditions Survey,* European Foundation for the Improvement of Living and Working Conditions, Dublin available at: http://www.eurofound.europa.eu/pubdocs/2006/98/en/2/ef0698en.pdf Accessed 16 June, 2009

Pine II, B. J., and Gilmore, J. H. (1999). T*he Experience Economy: Work is theatre and every business a stage.* Harvard Business School Press: Cambridge, MA

PREST, TNO, SERVILAB, ARCS (2006). *The future of R&D in services: implications for EU research and innovation policy* Brussels, European Commission DG Research (S&T Foresight Unit) Directorate K Unit K2 EUR 21959 ISBN 92 79 01209 6

Quinn, J B, Doorley T.L.& Paquette, P.C. (1990). "Beyond Products: services-based strategy" *Harvard Business Review* March 1990, pp 58-67

Rubalcaba, L. (2006). Which policy for innovation in services?; *Science and Public Policy* 33(10), 745-756.

Saco, R. M.and Goncalves, A. P. (2008). "Service Design: An Appraisal" *Design Management Review* vol.19 no.1 pp. 10-19

Salter, A. and Tether, B.S. (2006). *Innovation in Services: Through the Looking Glass of Innovation Studies*, Background paper for Advanced Institute of Management (AIM) Research's Grand Challenge on Service Science, April 7, 2006.

Schmidt, T. & C. Rammer (2006). *The determinants and effects of technological and nontechnological innovations – Evidence from the German CIS IV* mimeo Centre for European Economic Research (ZEW), Department of Industrial Economics and International Management, Mannheim, Germany

Seth, N. Deshmukh, S.G. and Vrat, P. (2005). "Service quality models: a review" *International Journal of Quality & Reliability* Management Vol. 22 No. 9

Shostack, L. (1984). "Designing Services that Deliver", *Harvard Business Review*, vol. 1 no.i Jan-Feb, pp.133-139

Soete, L. and Miozzo, M. (2001). "Internationalization of Services: A Technological Perspective" *Technological Forecasting and Social Change* 67, 159–185

Stuart, F. I. and Tax, S. (2004). "Toward an integrative approach to designing service experiences. Lessons learned from the theatre" *Journal of Operations Management* Vol 22 No 6 pp. 609 -627

Sundbo, J. and Gallouj, F. (2000). "Innovation as a Loosely Coupled System in Services," in S. Metcalfe and I. Miles (eds.), *Innovation Systems in the Service Economy*, Dordrecht:Kluwer.

Sundbo, J. and Darmer, P. (eds.) (2008). *Creating Experiences in the Experience Economy*, Cheltenham: Edward Elgar

Tether B. and Howells J. (2007). Changing understanding of innovation in services, Chapter 2 in DTI, *Innovation in Services* DTI Occasional Paper no. 9 London: Department of Trade and Industry (now BERR) available at: http://www.berr.gov.uk/files/file39965.pdf   Accessed 2 June, 2009

Tether, B., Miles. I., Blind, K., Hipp, c., de Liso, N., and Cainelli, G. (2002). *Innovation in the Service Sector: Analysis of Data collected under the CIS2* University of Manchester, CRIC Working paper no 11 ISBN 1 8402 006X – available as http://www.cric.ac.uk/cric/pdf Accessed 16 June, 2009s/wp11.pdf Accessed 16 June, 2009

Tordoir, P. P. (1996). *The Professional Knowledge Economy : The Management and Integration of Professional Services in Business Organizations* Dordrecht, Kluwer Academic

Uchupalanan, K. (2000), "Competition and IT-based Innovation in Banking Services" *International Journal of Innovation Management* vol. 4 no 4 (December 2000) pp. 455-490

Vargo, S. L. and Lusch, R. F. (2004a). "Evolving to a New Dominant Logic for Marketing" *Journal of Marketing* vol 68 (January), pp. 1-17

Vargo, S. L. and Lusch, R. F. (2004b). "The Four Services Marketing Myths: Remnants from a Manufacturing Model", *Journal of Service Research* (May), pp. 324-35

Windrum, P. and Koch, P. (eds.), (2008). *Innovation in Public Services: Management, Creativity, and Entrepreneurship*, Cheltenham: Edward Elgar

Zemke, R. with Schaaf, D. (1990). *The Service Edge: 101 Companies that Profit from Customer Care* New York, Plume (Penguin Books)

Innovation in Services and Entrepreneurship

Beyond Industrialist and Technologist Concepts of Sustainable Development

Faridah Djellal

University François Rabelais of Tours

Clersé-CNRS and Gercie, Tours, France

Faïz Gallouj

Université of Lille 1

Clersé-CNRS, Villeneuve d'Ascq, France

The questions of innovation in services, on the one hand, and sustainable development, on the other, are relatively recent concerns for economic theorists and public policymakers alike. They have become key issues, which pose considerable academic, economic and political challenges. However, these two questions, and the problems they raise, have evolved independently of each other. The present chapter seeks to link them by considering innovation in and by services and innovation-based entrepreneurship in services in terms of their relationship to sustainable development. Our hope in so doing is that we can play a part in moderating the industrialist, technologist, environmentalist and curative concept of sustainable development that is, paradoxically, still dominant in our service economies.

This chapter draws on a research carried out for the European Commission, ServPPIN project (FP 7).

P.P. Maglio et al. (eds.), *Handbook of Service Science*, Service Science: Research and Innovations in the Service Economy, DOI 10.1007/978-1-4419-1628-0_23,
© Springer Science+Business Media, LLC 2010

Introduction

Innovation in services, on the one hand, and sustainable development, on the other, are relatively recent concerns for economic theorists and public policymakers alike. However, they are no longer marginal issues but fundamental questions which, along with the academic, economic and political challenges they pose, are arousing increasing interest. Both questions deserve a special attention in the 'service science' agenda (IBM 2004, Maglio et al. 2006, Chesbrough 2005, Chesbrough and Spohrer 2006, Spohrer et al., 2007).

Thus the question of innovation in services has left the *non-recognition* phase, during which only innovation in manufacturing industry was taken into account (Djellal and Gallouj 1999). It could not be otherwise in economies dominated by services. Three different approaches can be identified in the current debate (Gallouj 1994, 1998, C. and F. Gallouj 1996 and more recently Gallouj and Savona 2009): *assimilation*, in which the differences between innovation in services and in manufacturing are minimised or eliminated, *differentiation* of one from the other and, thirdly, attempts to *integrate* the first two approaches[1]. The question of sustainable development, for its part, has gone beyond its earlier status as a militant, utopian demand to become a controversial but fundamental theoretical category, a socio-economic goal of vital importance globally and a society-wide movement, a defining purpose and ambition for society at large.

The aim of this chapter is to link these two questions and the problems they pose by investigating innovation *in* and *by* services and innovation-based entrepreneurship in services in the context of sustainable development. Although the links between services and innovation in services, on the one hand, and sustainable development, on the other, are now obvious and manifold (both positive and negative), these two problematics have, in essence, evolved independently, with the primary concern being to establish academic and institutional recognition for both of them.

The notion of sustainable development developed essentially as a reaction to the initially environmental and then socio-economic damage associated with economies based on manufacturing industry and intensive agriculture (exhaustion of non-renewable resources, proliferation of waste, pollution, desertification, deforestation, climate change, social exclusion in the rich countries and increased inequality between North and South). It still has a strong *industrial connotation*, even though certain services (tourism, transport, etc.) are major contributors to environmental damage and the rise to prominence of the social or socio-economic aspect of sustainable development has paved the way for greater recognition of services.

The notion of sustainable development is also frequently associated above all with technological innovation. This *technologist bias* is not unconnected with the

---

[1] The 3 approaches framework was later widely adopted in the service innovation literature: see, e.g., among others Coombs and Miles (2000), Miles (2002), Tether (2005), Howells (2007).

earlier sectoral bias. After all, technological innovation is often regarded as the main instrument for the intensive exploitation of natural resources in manufacturing industry and agriculture, and also as the main lever of economic growth. This emphasis on technological innovation has led to underestimation of the non-technological forms of innovation, which are particularly important in a service economy and can play an essential role in economic growth and sustainable development.

Even though the threefold environmental, economic and social dimension of sustainability is recognised, an *environmentalist bias* still prevails. Taking services into account (introducing a service dimension into the notion of sustainability) has been an important factor in shifting attention towards the socio-economic components of sustainability.

The notion of sustainable development is further characterised by a fourth bias, which is closely linked to the previous three. After all, the dominant concept of sustainability does seem to be a *curative or defensive* one. Sustainable development is considered primarily in terms of the reactive objective of reducing or repairing the essentially environmental pollution and damage caused by industrial or technological civilisation. Drawing on a database of technological innovations developed in order to foster sustainable development, Patris et al. (2001) note that the main purpose of these innovations is, firstly, the reduction of environmental pollution and, secondly, remediation. And indeed, so-called 'end of pipe' innovations and remediation account for almost 55% of their sample.

Nevertheless, services (and innovation in services) play a major role in guiding economies towards sustainable development. However, this role is still too frequently underestimated. And yet, in many respects, the expansion of the service sector in contemporary economies would seem to lead 'automatically' to increased sustainability. After all, the expansion of the service sector has led to an increase in activities whose very nature means that their 'environmental footprint'[2] is, at least for the moment, lower than that of manufacturing and agricultural activities. Thus in France, the service sector (excluding transport) consumes only 16% of total energy. The expansion of the service sector has also led to an increased emphasis on activities whose fundamental purposes are social and civic in nature: these are service activities (public, private or non-profit) aimed at reducing unemployment or promoting human development and social cohesion. More generally, however, since they are the main suppliers of jobs in contemporary developed economies, services are, automatically, the main factors in reducing inequalities. Thus it can be hypothesised that the expansion of the service sector in our economies is helping to reduce the *environmentalist bias* in approaches to sustainability by shifting the emphasis towards socio-economic concerns. It is true, as Gadrey (2010) notes, that this positive relationship between the expansion of the service sector and sustainability can be questioned, from a long-term perspective, and that in the future, the structure and extent of the service society are likely to be strictly

---

[2] A population's environmental footprint is a simple indicator based on the area of the planet on which that population depends in order to sustain its economic activities.

determined by its environmental footprint. Whether the relationship is considered in positive or negative terms, the lesson to be remembered is that such a relationship does indeed exist. The expansion of the service sector and sustainable development are not unconnected with each other, far from it.

The slackening of the industrialist bias and the increased emphasis on the role of services in approaches to sustainable development leads automatically to a reduction in the technologist bias. After all, one of the conclusions of the recent literature on innovation in services, as well as that on innovative entrepreneurship, is that non-technological innovation (i.e. organisational, methodological, social and strategic innovation) and the corresponding forms of entrepreneurship (particularly social entrepreneurship) play an essential role. They should, therefore, play an equally essential role in approaches to sustainable development in a service economy. We would also hypothesise that this shift in the focus of the preoccupations linked to sustainable development (tertiarisation of preoccupations) should eventually lead to the emergence of a less reactive and more 'natural' or proactive approach to this notion.

In sum, in economies dominated by services and in view of these activities' (passive or active) role in sustainability, the industrialist, technologist, environmentalist and curative connotations of sustainable development, which have historical origins, should gradually become blurred. This chapter seeks to contribute to this process.

The chapter is divided into four sections.

The first section consists of a brief review of the traditional definitions of services and of sustainable development. We attempt to identify, presumptively, some possible links between the characteristics of services and those of sustainability and to highlight a certain number of convergences and common preoccupations.

The second part is given over to the question of innovation *in* services as it relates to sustainable development. The 'assimilation, differentiation and integration' analytical framework (Gallouj 1994, 1998, Gallouj and Weinstein, 1997), which is used to tackle many problems in the economics, management and politics of services[3], provides a valuable heuristic for approaching this particular question as well.

Even though there are obvious links between them, the subject of innovation *in* services must be distinguished in analytical terms from that of innovation *by* services. After all, service activities are not confined to innovating on their own behalf: they can also exert a decisive influence on innovation in other firms and sectors of the economy (induced innovation). In the third section of this chapter, therefore, we examine the question of sustainable innovation (*induced*) by services.

---

[3] This framework was recently used to address European public policy for service innovation (Rubalcaba and Den Hertog, 2010) and productivity strategies within services firms (Djellal and Gallouj, 2008).

This question of innovation in and by services is closely linked to that of entrepreneurship. In the fourth section, therefore, we tackle the question of the new types of innovation-based entrepreneurship in services, several particularly dynamic forms of which are also closely linked to the issues surrounding sustainable development.

Services and sustainable development: analogies and conceptual convergences

Independently of the innovation issue, comparison of the definitions of the various notions of service and sustainable development reveals a number of interesting relationships between the nature of services and sustainability. First of all, a number of analogies are revealed between the definitions of services and those of sustainable development. It also becomes clear that some of the technical characteristics of services can be closely linked to certain aspects of sustainability. Finally, the two research agendas (i.e. those relating to services and sustainable development respectively) are shown to be overlapping and mutually enriching with regard to the question of performance (both its definition and measurement).

The definition of services and of sustainable development: some analogies

In contrast to a good, which is a material or tangible artefact, a service is generally defined as a change in the state of a medium, whether it be an object, codified information, an individual or an organisation (Hill 1977; Gadrey, 1996a). The process of transformation is generally intangible and interactive (Chase 1978, Berry 1980, Grönroos 1990, Gustafsson and Johnson 2003 among many others). It cannot, by its very nature, be easily stored. Thus the 'product' or output of a service is an act, a process, the definition and designation of which are determined by convention, on the basis of a multiplicity of complementary or competing evaluation systems. Furthermore, this output can be broken down temporally, with a distinction being made, to use Gadrey's terminology (Gadrey 1996a), between a short-term output (the immediate act of delivery) and a long-term output (the mediate output or outcome).

A number of analogies between the definitions of services and of sustainable development can be identified. The concept of sustainable development, which was popularised by the Brundtland Report, is by definition located within an even longer time horizon, since it is defined as 'development that meets the needs of the present without compromising the ability of future generations to meet their own needs'. Furthermore, sustainable development, as defined in the Bruntland Report, has three dimensions: it is not only environmental, but also economic and social, which brings into play, here too, a pluralist (complementary or competing) evaluation system. In a way, sustainable development is concerned with the transformation of a collective entity's (in this case humanity's) support medium, whether it be its material medium (i.e. its physical environment at both local and global level), its economic medium (i.e. the way it conceives of and creates wealth) or its social and symbolic medium (equity in the redistribution of wealth). In a way, it also includes, the coproduction and interaction dimension that lies at the heart of the definition of services. After all, citizens' participation (e.g. in selective waste sorting) plays an important part in any approach to sustainability.

Typology of services and sustainable development

To the best of our knowledge, there is no typology of services that takes account of the problems of sustainable development. The definition of services alluded to above suggests a relatively simple one. After all, the sustainability of service activities (and the component concerned) depends to some extent on the nature of the mediums that these activities are seeking to transform. Thus services can be divided into four broad categories: those concerned primarily with processing materials, information, knowledge or persons. Table 1 provides a number of illustrations of services belonging to these four categories.

Table 1. Typology of services and sustainable development

Medium or dominant function of the service	Examples	Dimension of sustainability affected	
		environmental	socio-economic
Material	Transport of goods, water, gas, electricity, large-scale retailing, restaurants, collection of household waste, cleaning, decontamination	++	+
Individual			
• spatial location	Passenger transport, tourism	++	
Individual			
• aesthetic state, health	Health services, elderly care services, hairdressing		++
• knowledge	Education		++
Codified information	Banking, insurance		++
Knowledge of organisations	Consultancy in all its forms		++

A number of hypotheses can be formulated regarding the nature of the relationships between these categories of service and the problems of sustainable development. However an analysis of this kind has certain limitations that should be noted at the outset. The first is that, in reality, all service activities affect a number of different mediums: they are combinations, that vary in both time and space, of functions, associated with different mediums (material, informational, cognitive and relational functions). The second is that sustainability is also a composite category that has economic, environmental and social dimensions. Sustainability is a trade-off between these three dimensions and it is difficult to envisage a one-to-one relationship between a type of service and overall sustainability. The third limitation is that the economic dimension of sustainable development is not a structuring factor in our analysis, since all types of services are affected by this dimension, whose role in sustainability is confined to the way in which it takes the other two into account. For simplicity's sake, our analysis will in most instances be confined to the distinction between environmental and socio-economic sustainability.

With due account being taken of the limitations outlined above, a number of hypotheses can be formulated about the relations (positive or negative) that exist presumptively between the various types of services and the problems of sustainable development.

• Material processing services (such as goods transport, and water, gas and electricity supply) are often associated with sustainability from the environmental perspective. After all, these activities cause significant environmental damage (pollution, congestion, etc.). Nevertheless, some of them also have a negative impact on social sustainability: this applies to large-scale retailing (productivist pressures on agriculture) and fast-food restaurants (junk food/unhealthy eating).

Note should be taken of the particular case of cleaning or decontamination, which are material processing services directly associated with environmental improvement. The same is true of a number of public environmental services, such as the maintenance of public parks, garden and woodlands.

It might also be asked whether, all other things being equal, some material processing services, including some of the most environmentally destructive, might also evolve structurally to include activities with a lower environmental footprint. After all, the material components of their output are declining in favour of other (informational and cognitive) components that are, on the face of it, less environmentally damaging. This could apply, all other things being equal, to road freight transport (Djellal 2001) or even to retailing (C. Gallouj 2007). In the case of road freight transport, this hypothesis would appear to fit with the abandonment in European sustainability policies of the modal shift principle and a reorientation towards co-modality (Zéroual 2008). This new approach no longer seeks to substitute the most sustainable modes of transport for the least sustainable but to find the most effective possible combination of the different modes. It favours a broader definition of road freight transport as a logistical system.

Services whose target medium for processing is individual human beings are not homogeneous as far as their relationship with sustainability is concerned. They do vary, after all, depending on the nature of the processing involved. It is hardly surprising that services that transform individuals' location in space (e.g. passenger transport and tourism) have a similar relationship to sustainability as some material processing services (freight transport). They also affect environmental sustainability. On the other hand, services that transform the aesthetic, physiological and cognitive aspects of individuals (e.g. local services, health and education services) tend rather to affect socio-economic sustainability.

Information-processing services (particularly financial services: banking and insurance) seem to be associated with the question of sustainable development largely from the socio-economic point of view. After all, the process whereby their outputs are produced is not generally associated with environmental damage that is perceived as significant. On the other hand, these services do have a considerable influence on direct and indirect social sustainability, which they may impact adversely (indebtedness, unfairness in granting of credit, etc.) but can also help to restore (mutual or cooperative banks, microcredit).

Services that process (organisational) knowledge seem not to have any direct consequences for environmental sustainability. On the other hand, they do influence social or socio-economic sustainability by contributing to the development of the knowledge economy, which is replacing the material (tangible) economy.

• Sustainability considered from the environmental perspective seems to be inversely proportional to materiality. The more intangible (cognitive, informational) a service is, the less it seems to pose problems for this aspect of sustainability. Conversely, the more closely a service is linked to tangible mediums, the more it appears to pose direct environmental problems (e.g. transport and tourism) and/or indirect problems, by exerting pressure on other sectors. Thus large-scale retailing, for example, exerts productivist pressures on its suppliers, but it also has a direct, and negative, effect on the urban and suburban environment. In these cases, however, sustainability can be pursued through its environmental dimension, as well through other, particularly social dimensions (e.g. fair trade).

Considered from the social perspective, sustainability seems to be positively linked to the intangible and relational aspect of services. The more intangible a service is (this is the case with informational and cognitive services) and/or the more relational it is (this applies to many services for individuals, e.g. support services for the elderly), the more the social aspect of sustainability seems to occupy an important position.

The problem of defining and measuring performance in a service economy: from growth to (sustainable) development

The question of measuring and evaluating the 'output' of services also provides fertile ground for the dialogue between the problems posed by services and those posed by sustainable development. Whatever name we give it, the post-industrial, information, knowledge, "permanent innovation" or "quality" economy, comes up against certain technical and conceptual problems when it comes to measurement, which bring into play the informational/cognitive and service-based component and the notion of sustainability in its various facets (environmental, social and economic).

Thus numerous arguments can be advanced in support of a multi-criteria, pluralist and flexible approach to wealth and performance and thus of the abandonment of the absolutism of GDP and productivity (Gadrey 1996b, 2002, Djellal and Gallouj 2008). The use of GDP and productivity for evaluation purposes is based on volumes or quantities of ouputs. However, the service economy is characterised by a considerable increase in the cognitive content of economic activities and by a proliferation of service-based social relations between providers and customers. In an economy of this kind, the quantities or volumes of outputs matter less than their long-term utility effects. In other words, the outcomes and mechanisms that create trust are often more important than any measurement of output or productivity. Furthermore, some volumes should not be included in any measure of wealth, namely those equating to expenditure on making good environmental damage. The drive for growth and productivity produces negative externalities, which have to be deducted. It can give rise to a number of costs, both social (stress and health problems) and environmental (in the form of environmental damage), that are not included in measurements of growth and productivity.

Overall, it would increasingly seem that the level of the production of goods and services is neither the only indicator of a society's well-being nor necessarily the best. Consequently, in an attempt to reflect more accurately the creation of wealth and well-being in contemporary post-industrial societies, a considerable number of alternative indicators of development that seek to measure the various dimensions of sustainability are currently being developed.

Innovation *in* services and sustainable development

There is an extensive literature dedicated to analysis of the link between technological innovations and sustainable development, considered essentially from an environmental perspective. This technologist bias in analyses of the relationship between innovation and sustainable development is reinforced by the ambivalent status of technologies, which are regarded both as a source of the problem (e.g. a cause of pollution) and as a solution (technologies used to make good damage or clean up pollution).

Innovation in services, as it relates to sustainable development, is not immune to this bias. In services as well, it is very often the technologies deployed that are the sources of environmental problems (polluting means of transport, for example), and hence it is in technological innovations adopted by services that the solution to these problems is sought. The aim of this section is to highlight other forms of innovation in services that are linked in some way to sustainable development. In this way, it will be shown that innovation in services is usually, given the intangible and relational nature of the output, sustainable innovation.

There are three approaches to tackling the question of innovation in the economics of services (Gallouj 1994, 1998, 2002): *assimilation*, in which innovation in services is reduced to the adoption of technical systems, *differentiation*, in which the aim is to identify the specificity of innovation in services, and *integration*, the aim of which is to develop common models for industrial and service-sector innovation. These three approaches also provide starting points for investigating services in terms of sustainable development.

Assimilation

The assimilative approach is based on a technologist concept of innovation, in which services are limited to adopting the technological innovations produced in manufacturing industries, for example, means of transport, cooking and refrigeration equipment, automatic dispensing machines, computers, etc. (Gallouj 1994, 1998). This approach also seems to be widespread, indeed dominant, in studies of innovation in services considered in terms of their relationship to sustainable development.

A number of remarks can be made with regard to this dominant assimilative approach.

1) It reflects a view that services play a subordinate role when it comes to innovation. They are supposed to be "supplier-dominated" (Pavitt, 1984). For example, a local authority that buys gas-powered or electric vehicles for its public transport system, on the grounds that they are clean, quiet and need little maintenance, is not, strictly speaking, the innovator but simply the adopter of an innovation. In this case, services' role in environmental damage and its repair is located not in the production of innovation but rather in its use.

2) From this assimilative perspective, environmental innovation targeted at environmental problems is the most obvious form of innovation. However, this should not blind us to the development of technologies aimed at the social dimensions of sustainable development. Thus technological innovations developed in response to the problems faced by the elderly (e.g. domestic robots, 'smart' homes, tele-surveillance, etc.) constitute a powerful innovation trajectory in ageing service societies (Djellal and Gallouj 2006). Within these tangible technologies that

lie at the heart of the assimilative approach, a distinction can be made between *environmental technologies* and *social technologies*.

3) The assimilative approaches to innovation in services have placed great emphasis on the pervasiveness of ICTs in services, and the main theories of innovation in services are based on the dynamic of ICTs (cf. Barras's model 1986, Quinn et al. 1987, Scheer and Spaths 2004). Since ICTs are regarded as low-MIPS[4] technologies, and in view of their pervasive diffusion in services, it can be said that they foster sustainability and that, more generally, the information society is consistent with sustainable development. Within services, innovation in ICTs (often in combination with other environmental or social technologies) is also playing (or is likely to play) an increasing role in sustainable development. The most frequently cited examples include the use of videoconferencing as a substitute for physical travel (business travel) and the introduction of new modes of work (e.g. teleworking). ICTs are also a powerful tool for measuring, checking and monitoring the problems of sustainable development. They also play a part in other aspects of sustainability (particularly the social dimension). For example, they can be used to question the public authorities and to mobilise citizens at short notice.

4) The assimilative approach can also be interpreted, from the strategic point of view, as an attempt to eliminate the specificities of services, so that they differ as little as possible from goods. To do so, it is necessary to make them less fuzzy or intangible, to reduce or eliminate the periods of interactivity (in other words, the service relationship) and to make them less immediate by establishing certain forms of stockability. The ultimate goal is to reduce the diversity of possibilities and to create a product or quasi-product that can be embodied in an explicit contract. This is sometimes referred to as the industrialisation of services (Levitt 1976, Shostack 1984). This process of industrialisation, whether it involves a gradual move towards the production of tangible goods, to the detriment of the provision of intangible services, or the implementation of a certain mode of production (Gadrey 1996b), has helped to ensure the success of the Fordist growth regime. It is often regarded as a factor that has had a negative influence on the notion of sustainable development. The best-known examples are fast food, low-cost airlines, discount stores, mass tourism and large-scale food retailing.

Differentiation

The assimilative approach is incapable of providing a full account of innovation in services. It is the cause of what might be called the '*innovation gap*' (NESTA, 2006). There are, after all, many forms of non-technological innovations that are not captured by the traditional indicators. They are often described as 'hidden' or 'invisible' innovations. This innovation gap has been the object of an

---

[4] The MIPS indicator (material intensity per service unit) measures the amount of non-renewable natural resources used to produce a good or service.

expanding literature for the past fifteen years (Gallouj 1994, 2002, Sundbo 1997, 1998, Miles 2002, various contributions in Gallouj and Djellal 2010).

This gap also affects service-sector innovations linked to sustainable development (Seyfang and Smith 2006). The assimilative approach focuses on technological innovations to the detriment of less spectacular innovations, which are, nevertheless, numerous and of considerable importance in the sphere of sustainable development. These innovations are non-technological and, in particular, social in nature and are generally ignored in the economic literature.

All in all, in order to capture invisible or hidden (sustainable) innovation, an approach based on differentiation has to be adopted, one that seeks to reveal the particular forms of service innovations linked to sustainability, whether it be economic, social or environmental in nature.

Table 2 provides examples of sustainable innovations in services, as revealed by adopting a differentiating approach, i.e. one that is not focused on the technological dimension.

As far as material processing services are concerned, examples include, among others, car sharing and waterless cleaning, where in both cases the objective is an environmental one, and fair trade, the growing number of producer outlets and community supported agriculture schemes or even the maintenance of water, gas and electricity supplies to groups living in hardship, all of which are pursuing socio-economic goals.

Some forms of sustainable tourism and many innovative initiatives in the care of the elderly or of young children are examples of non-technological innovations in services in which individuals constitute the medium to be processed or changed.

Table 2. Examples of innovations from a differentiating perspective

Type of service	Examples of innovations in the various dimensions of sustainable development	
	Environmental	Socio-economic
• Materials processing Goods transport, water, gas and electricity distribution	Car sharing, cleaning without water, materials recycling	No gas, water or electricity cut-offs, fair trade, producer outlets, community supported agriculture schemes
• Processing of individuals Transport, personal services, health, education	Work integration enterprises, sustainable tourism (agro-tourism, cycling, industrial tourism)	Work integration enterprises, sustainable tourism (linked to local social fabrics), care of the elderly, services for individuals living in hardship, cooperative nurseries
• Information processing Banking, insurance, family allowance offices, local authorities	Information on environmental and social situation, loans at preferential rates	Microcredit, PIMMs (points d'information et de médiation multi-services/information and multi-service mediation points, Points Services Publics/Public Service Points (PS), 'Maisons des services'/public service and advice centres
• Processing of organisa-	New area of expertise (environ-	New area of expertise (social law,

tional knowledge Consultancy services	mental law, sustainable development consultancy services), ad hoc innovation, methodological innovations (MIPS, PER model)	sustainable development consultancy services), ad hoc innovation, methodological innovations

As far as information processing services are concerned, examples might include financial innovations designed to promote sustainable development, such as microloans in response to the problem of exclusion from banking services and loans at preferential rates in order to encourage firms to install environmentally-friendly machinery. Mention could also be made of the development by local authorities (possibly in partnership with private companies, particularly in areas where services to individuals are inadequate) of facilities ('one-stop shops') providing services for people in hardship: PIMMs (multi-service information and mediation points), Points Services Publics (PS/public service points) and public service and advice centres.

The innovations produced by knowledge intensive business services would seem, by definition, to be 'environmentally friendly'. They involve the provision of cognitive solutions without any particular direct adverse impact[5] on sustainability, particularly on its environmental dimension. Thus Gallouj (1994, see also Gadrey and Gallouj 1998) identifies three types of innovation in consultancy activities: *ad hoc innovation* (the joint development, with the client, of an original solution to a problem), *new expertise field innovation* (i.e. the identification of an emerging field of knowledge and the provision of advice in that field) and *formalisation innovations* (the implementation of methods with a view to making a service less ill-defined). This typology of innovation can readily be applied to sustainable development. After all, there are lot of examples of ad hoc solutions provided by consultants to social and environmental problems. Sustainable development, in all its various facets, is a new field of expertise that has given birth to many specialist consultancies, in environmental and social law, for example, as well as in sustainable development itself. Finally, there have been large numbers of methodological innovations in the field of sustainable development. The MIPS indicator already mentioned above can be cited by way of example.

This differentiating approach also gives rise to a number of observations.

1) We referred above to the mistake of linking technological innovations too closely with environmental and ecological objectives, since such innovations can also purport to have economic and social aims (solving problems for the elderly and handicapped, for example). The same argument can be deployed here as in the case of non-technological innovations. Their end purpose is not exclusively social: it may also be economic and environmental. This applies, for example, to certain

---

[5] Some cognitive solutions provided by consultants can have a negative impact on social sustainability, particularly when they involve plant closures or redundancies.

forms of sustainable tourism, which seek not only to preserve the environment but also to promote economic development and to enhance and preserve local socio-economic fabrics.

2) From this differentiating point of view, innovation in services, as far as its relationship with sustainability is concerned, overlaps and merges with the vast and prolific field of social innovation (which, nevertheless, remains little explored in economic theory). Thus the assimilative perspective can be said to promote a 'top-down' approach to technological innovation as it relates to sustainable development. On the other hand, in view of the intangible and not necessarily spectacular nature of the innovations it reveals, the differentiating perspective promotes a 'bottom-up' approach to innovation. Seyfang and Smith (2006) use the expression 'grassroots innovation' (in contrast to 'green mainstream business innovations') to denote the devising, by individuals or organisations, of 'bottom-up' innovative and sustainable solutions that respond to local problems and are in keeping with the interests and values of the communities concerned.

3) While the assimilative approach is associated with the industrialisation of services, the differentiating approach is associated with another form of innovation-producing rationalisation, which Gadrey (1996b) terms professional or cognitive rationalisation, in contradistinction to industrial rationalisation. This cognitive rationalisation, which is at work in some consultancy companies, for example, can be embodied in three strategies: the standardisation of cases, the formalisation of problem-solving procedures (methods) and the use of individual or organisational routines. In contrast to industrial rationalisation, professional rationalisation does not seem to have any negative effect on the notion of sustainable development.

Integration

In the integrative approach to innovation, it is regarded as possible, indeed necessary, to use the same tools to analyse innovation in goods and services (Belleflamme et al. 1986, Barcet et al. 1987, Gallouj and Weinstein 1997, Gallouj 2002a, de Vries 2006, Windrum and Garcia-Goni 2008). This approach takes into consideration technological innovation as well as non-technological forms of innovation, particularly social innovation (Harrisson and Vézina 2006, Harrisson et al. 2010). The integration of goods and services (the transition from an economy based on the production and consumption of goods to one based on the production and consumption of hybrid solutions or packages) is a factor in sustainability. After all, by adding services to their product or by increasing the service content of their goods, firms are reducing the relative share of material processing activities, which are causes of environmental damage.

This integration is based on several observations that suggest that the boundary between goods and services is becoming blurred (Bressand and Nicolaïdis 1998, Furrer 1997, Bryson 2010 among others). The first of these is that goods and services are increasingly less likely to be sold and consumed separately, but more and more likely to be sold as solutions, systems or functions. Secondly, the service or the information provided is the main component of many goods (Vargo and Lusch, 2004). A number of studies have sought to identify and measure the informational or service value of goods, or even the increasing prominence of the service dimension in goods. Studies of this type have focused on manufacturing, particularly the automotive industry (Lenfle and Midler 2003) and on agriculture (Le Roy 1997) or construction (Carassus, 2002 ; Bröchner, 2008a, 2008b). Others (Broussolle 2001) have shown that NICTs (as technical systems shared by both manufacturing industry and services) are contributing to this 'blurring'.

However, a further argument in favour of integration is to be found in the notion of sustainable development itself. After all, the very definition of this concept encourages a synthetic or integrative approach to innovation. The notion of sustainable development has economic, environmental and social aspects; sustainable innovation should, in consequence, link these various dimensions and thus encourage an integrative concept of innovation.

The blurring of boundaries that can be observed naturally leads to a theoretical analysis, with the aim of developing integrative interpretative frameworks. Gallouj and Weinstein (1997) (cf. also Gallouj 2002a) make use of this theoretical perspective by adopting a Lancasterian approach to the product (adapted to services). They define the product (whether it is a good or a service) as the conjunction of vectors of characteristics and of competences: service characteristics [Y], internal technical characteristics [T] and external technical characteristics [T']^6 and internal competences [C] and external competences [C'] (cf. Figure 1).

The general representation in Figure 1 can be used very flexibly. It makes it possible to include in the analysis both tangible artefacts, such as cars or computers, and intangible products (insurance contracts, financial products or consultancy services). It can be used to include pure services ([C']—[C]—[Y]), as well as less pure services ([C]—[T]—[Y]) or even self-service arrangements ([C']—[T]—[Y]). And it is also capable of illustrating the provision of hybrid solutions (goods or services), for example a car and various associated services, both upstream and downstream (insurance, maintenance, finance, guarantees, etc.).

---

[6] The inclusion of clients' technical characteristics was suggested by De Vries (2006) in order to take account of the new channels of consumption and delivery (e.g. when consumers use their own technologies to access a service on the web).

Service provider's direct competences

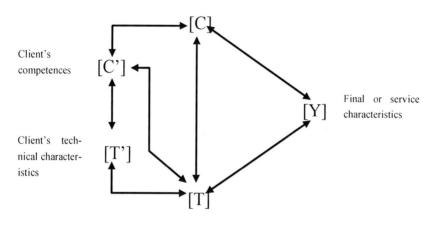

Figure 1. The product as the conjunction of characteristics and competences
(after Gallouj and Weinstein 1997).

This approach to the product also makes it possible to take account of certain
aspects of sustainability. Sustainable service characteristics on both the socio-
economic and environmental levels, can be incorporated (for example, socio-civic
service characteristics), as can the corresponding technical competences and characteristics. The following socio-civic characteristics in the case of postal services
can be cited by way of example: fair treatment for users (counters, delivery
rounds), fairness in accessibility, non-discrimination (e.g. young people or foreigners) in customer contact, assistance for marginalised populations, social prices
and social banking services (accounts for low-income earners, reasonable penalties, advice for individuals living in hardship). Negative externalities (pollution
and congestion in the case of motor vehicles, for example) can also be included in
the service characteristics vector.

Thus on the basis of this representation of the product, innovation emerges as a
change in the (technical, service or competence) characteristics brought about by
one of a number of mechanisms: addition, subtraction, association, dissociation or
formatting. This definition makes it possible to identify several models of innova-

tion, which can be applied without difficulty to sustainable service innovations. These models are radical, ameliorative, incremental, recombinative and formalisation innovation (cf. Gallouj and Weinstein 1997, Gallouj 2002a).

Radical innovation denotes the creation of a new set of characteristics and competences. The introduction of wind turbines would, at the time, have been an example.

Ameliorative innovation reflects an increase in the prominence (or quality) of certain characteristics, but without any change in the structure of the system of competences and characteristics. The aim here is to increase the prominence or significance of a sustainable technical characteristic or competence, in other words to improve a sustainable service characteristic. The components targeted may make the product in question more environmentally friendly (by improving energy efficiency, for example, or reducing pollution levels) or they may be socio-civic in nature (for example, an increase in assistance for disadvantaged groups).

Incremental innovation denotes the addition (and possibly also the elimination or replacement) of characteristics. So-called 'add-on' technologies fall within the scope of this form of innovation. Another common example is the addition of services to an existing product. This form of innovation 'automatically' increases the sustainability of those firms that make use of it, since it contributes to the 'dematerialisation' of their activities, which in turn enhances environmental sustainability. However, the 'add-ons' may also be social or civic characteristics and competences (cf. the examples listed above for postal services).

Recombinative innovation is a form of innovation that relies on the basic principles of dissociation and association (i.e. the splitting or combining) of final and technical characteristics.

Formalisation innovation, finally, is based on the formatting and standardisation of characteristics. One illustration would be the development of numerous methodologies aimed at increasing sustainability.

Innovation *by* services and sustainable development

In the previous section, we tackled the question of innovation within service firms and industries. This section, in contrast, focuses on the way in which service firms or organisations induce innovation in other firms or sectors (innovation by (as opposed to in) services). This mainly concerns two groups of activities, namely knowledge-intensive business services (KIBS) and public services. These two sectors share the particular characteristic of innovating for themselves while at the same time contributing in different ways to innovation in other sectors.

KIBS, induced innovation and sustainable development

The term KIBS denotes a number of service activities, the particular characteristic of which is that knowledge is their main input as well as their main output (Miles et al. 1994, Gallouj 2002b, Toivonen 2004). They include many consultancy, R & D and engineering services, as well as certain aspects of other activities, such as financial and insurance services, etc. These activities are among the most innovative in their own right, as the results of the Community Innovation Surveys (CIS) indicate. However, one of their main characteristics is that they also provide support for innovation in client organisations (Muller and Zenker 2001, Gallouj 2002b, Sundbo 2002, Toivonen 2004, Wood, 2005).

This support can take various forms. For example, consultants may be involved in the introduction of new environmental standards. Thus Nicolas (2004) analyses the way in which the introduction of eco-label standards (e.g. the organic farming standard) has given rise to an organisational learning process for firms, which is based on the use of external knowledge-intensive services (e.g. training services). Another example is those knowledge-intensive services that contribute to the development of sustainable innovation on behalf of clients, generally with the latter's participation (co-production). These innovations may be based on material sciences and technologies (in the case of R&D activities) or on the humanities and social sciences and organisational engineering. Thus they may be technological innovations, but also non-technological and, particularly, social innovations. One final example of the support knowledge-intensive services can provide for sustainable innovation is that of the banks, which can play a decisive role as catalysts of innovation by offering financial products that encourage sustainable development (e.g. loans at advantageous rates).

Public authorities, which are the subject of the next section, can also facilitate the use of knowledge-intensive services with a view to fostering sustainability. This applies, for example, to the regional authorities that have put in place 'incentive programmes' in order to encourage upgrading, compliance with standards and innovation in the sphere of sustainable development through mechanisms such as the regional consultancy support funds (Maubrey 2003).

Public services, induced innovation and sustainable development

The links between sustainable development and public services (whether national, regional or local) can be considered from various points of view. The first has already been mentioned above: it is that of public services as suppliers (in a variety of ways) of products (water, energy, transport) that are likely to pose problems of sustainability that can be tackled by innovations. The second point of view is that of local, national or supranational public authorities as producers of laws, regulations and norms with which organisations and users have to comply. In this case, public authorities, via the legislation they enact, act as drivers of change and innovation in the sphere of sustainability. The third and final perspective, and the one that concerns us here, is that of public policies intended to promote and support sustainable innovation.

These public policies aimed at inducing sustainable innovation can take a variety of forms. Just as with innovation in services, the 'assimilation, differentiation, integration' (ADI) framework provides a satisfactory basis for analysis[7].

Many public policies intended to promote and support innovation in services as it relates to sustainable development do, after all, fall within the scope of a type A (assimilative) approach. In services, as elsewhere, the aim here is to support sustainable technological innovations, on both the production and consumption sides. This support can take various forms: funding, taxation (e.g. by granting tax credits for clean or energy-saving technologies), public purchasing, the diffusion of information, etc.

D-type approaches (differentiation policies), for their part, emphasise the specificities of sustainable innovation in services. Generally speaking, they favour non-technological innovations, particularly social innovations. One example that can be cited is local authority support for business incubators nurturing firms specialising in environmental or social problems.

In the case of the UK, Seyfang and Smith (2006) identify two sustainable development strategies that clearly illustrate at a national level this distinction between type A and type D approaches: on the one hand, environmental modernisation and technological innovation and, on the other, local action and the social economy. According to these authors, these two types of sustainable development strategies have been investigated in separate bodies of literature, one on technological innovation aimed at fostering sustainable production and consumption (Fusslar and James 1996, Smith et al. 2005) and the other on local activities and civil society (Amin et al. 2002, Seyfang 2001).

Finally, some public policies fall within the scope of I-type approaches. These are integrative policies aimed at supporting categories that are regarded as cutting across sectoral boundaries. This would seem to apply, for example, to public strategies intended to encourage the development of certain forms of sustainable governance (corporate social responsibility). The promotion of an innovation culture can also be regarded as falling within the scope of an I-type approach, since it transcends sectoral boundaries. Patris et al. (2001) provide a number of illustrations of national and European programmes targeted at this same objective, for example the National Action Plan for Environmental Education for a Sustainable Future launched in the year 2000 by the Australian government.

---

[7] See Rubalcaba and Den Hertog (2010) for a general application of the framework to service innovation support public policy.

Innovation-based entrepreneurship in services and sustainable development

Concerns about sustainable development and the particular forms of innovation examined in the previous sections also raise the question of innovation-based entrepreneurship (in services) in so far as it relates to sustainable development. A not inconsiderable part of this Schumpeterian entrepreneurship falls within the scope of a sustainable development perspective. Four new types of sustainable entrepreneur/innovator in services can be identified: the 'cognitive' entrepreneur, the 'social' entrepreneur, the 'environmental' entrepreneur and what might be called the 'entrepreneurial' entrepreneur.

1. The 'cognitive' entrepreneur. 'Cognitive' entrepreneurs are experts who establish their companies on the basis of new fields of knowledge that they themselves have helped to develop (*researcher-entrepreneurs*) or of which they make good use without actually having contributed to it (*consultant-entrepreneurs*). The latter are closely linked to what we have termed new expertise field innovation (cf. above). This new knowledge may be derived from the natural sciences or engineering, or from the humanities and social sciences. The cognitive sphere of sustainable development is fertile ground for the development of this form of entrepreneurship. Examples might include expertise in environmental labelling, North-South cooperation, environmental law, consultancy in sustainable development, etc. Cognitive entrepreneurs play an active role in the diffusion of knowledge within firms and, more generally, in knowledge-based societies.

2. The 'social' entrepreneur. The 'social' entrepreneur's sphere of action is the social and solidaristic economy. Social entrepreneurship involves the establishment of new organisations in order to take responsibility, in innovative ways, for disadvantaged or vulnerable groups in the population: young children, the elderly or people suffering from handicaps of various kinds, whether socio-economic, physical or psychological. In other words, the aim of social entrepreneurship is to find innovative solutions to social problems.

3. The 'environmental' entrepreneur. The 'environmental' entrepreneur's sphere of action is the preservation of the environment and the quest for sustainable development. The tourism industry and the various component parts of this composite service (hotels, restaurants, leisure activities, etc.) provide many examples of entrepreneurs of this type, who have carved out market niches for themselves, by steering tourism in new directions linked to local social fabrics or by introducing new forms of exploration, such as agro-tourism, industrial tourism, cycle touring, etc. Another group is the one that is emerging around the exploitation of what are sometimes called 'green technologies', i.e. tangible or intangible (methods, protocols) technologies that contribute to preservation of the environment.

4. The 'entrepreneurial' entrepreneur. We use this term to denote business incubators. Incubators are programmes designed to encourage and support, in various ways, the gestation, birth and first steps of firms and thereby to improve their viability. They are organisations providing a complex service, whose aim is to create entrepreneurs. They are, as it were, 'entrepreneurs in entrepreneurship'. Many experiments in entrepreneurial entrepreneurship are based on the principles of sustainable development (regional development, local redevelopment and restructuring, etc.). Thus in the USA in particular, there are examples of incubators that specialise in female entrepreneurship, ethnic minorities, not-for-profit associations, etc.

Conclusion

The notion of sustainable development is characterised by four interdependent biases: it is industrialist, technologist, environmentalist and defensive. As an instrument of militant protest and then as a major theoretical category, it was born and grew to maturity in an environment dominated by an all-powerful manufacturing industry reliant on continuous technological innovation that impacted on the environment. Before it acquired its social or socio-economic dimensions, sustainable environment was (and continues to be to some extent) primarily ecological and environmental; its main concern was manufacturing industry's devastating effects on non-renewable resources and the environment. However (and this is a consequence of the four interdependent biases), this notion of sustainable development is also 'defensive', that is it is fundamentally concerned with the repair of damage (essentially to the environment).

These four biases persist in economies in which services are the main sources of wealth and jobs. However, services alter the terms of the sustainable development problematic. They play (and will increasingly be led to play) an important role in sustainable development, both statically and dynamically, that is through the innovations they produce or induce. The present chapter has argued in favour of a service-based approach to sustainable development, which involves a loosening of the various biases in question.

Thus it is in the dominant service sector that the future of the sustainable development question will be played out, whether positively or negatively. At the moment, a large proportion of service activities have a fairly small environmental footprint compared with manufacturing industries, while at the same time producing essential socio-economic effects: it is services that generate most jobs in contemporary economies. They are also the main users of information and communications technologies, which are regarded as having a relatively low MIPS. However, as Gadrey (2010) notes, none of these characteristics is irreversible over the long term and the future of the service society (the nature of its constituent sectors and their size) is closely correlated with the environmental variable.

Furthermore, non-technological (particularly social) innovation occupies an essential place in a sustainable service society. Many new services, which may possibly be delivered through new forms of entrepreneurship (and this has been recognised by public policy), are sources not only of jobs (economic solutions) but also of solidarity (services to individuals living in hardship).

Finally, whether the innovation is technological or non-technological, environmental or socio-economic, services play an active role in the production of innovations, not only those that cure or repair damage inflicted on the environment or on individuals' socio-economic well-being but also those that are preventive and proactive (education of populations, training related to environmental norms or labels, etc.).

References

Amin, A., Cameron, A., Hudson, R. (2002). *Placing the social economy*, London: Routledge.
Barcet, A., Bonamy, J., Mayère, A. (1987). Modernisation et innovation dans les services aux entreprises, Report for Commissariat général du Plan, Paris, October.
Barras, R. (1986). Towards a Theory of Innovation in Services. *Research Policy*, 15, 161-173.
Belleflamme, C., Houard, J., Michaux, B. (1995). Innovation and Research and Development Process Analysis in Service Activities, IRES, FAST report, August.
Berry, L. L. (1980). Services marketing is different. *Business,* (May-June), 24-29.
Bressand, A. and Nicolaïdis, K. (1998). Les services au cœur de l'économie relationnelle. *Revue d'Economie Industrielle,* 43, 141-163.
Bröchner, J. (2008a). Construction contractors integrating into facilities management. *Facilities,* 26(1-2), 6-15.
Bröchner, J. (2008b). Client-oriented contractor innovation. in P., Brandon and S.-L. Lu (eds). *Clients driving innovation* (pp. 15-136). Chichester: Wiley-Blackwell.
Broussolle, D. (2001). *Les NTIC et l'innovation dans la production de biens et services : des frontières qui se déplacent.* 11th RESER conference, Grenoble, October.
Bryson, J. (2010). Service innovation and manufacturing innovation: bundling and blending services and products in hybrid production systems to produce hybrid products. In F. Gallouj F. and F. Djellal (eds). *The handbook of innovation and services.* Cheltenham: Edward Elgar (forthcoming).
Carassus, J. (2002). *Construction: la mutation: de l'ouvrage au service.* Paris: Presses des Ponts et Chaussées.
Chase, R. B. (1978). Where Does the Customer Fit in a Service Operation? *Harvard Business Review,* November-December (1), 137-142.
Chesbrough, H. (2005). Toward a science of services. *Harvard Business Review,* 83, 16-17.
Chesbrough, H., Spohrer, J. (2006). A research manifesto for services science. *Communications of the ACM,* 49(7), July, 35-40.
Coombs, R. and I. Miles (2000). Innovation, Measurement and Services: The New Problematique. In J.S. Metcalfe and Miles, I. (eds). *Innovation Systems in the Service Economy: Measurement and Case Study Analysis* (pp. 85-103). Dordrecht: Kluwer Academic Publishers.
De Vries, E. (2006). Innovation in services in networks of organizations and in the distribution of services. *Research Policy*, 35(7), 1037-1051.
Djellal F., & Gallouj F. (2008). *Measuring and improving productivity in services: issues, strategies and challenges.* Cheltenham and Northampton: Edward Elgar.
Djellal, F. (2001). Les trajectoires d'innovation dans les entreprises de transport routier de marchandises. *Revue Française de Gestion,* 133, April-June, 84-92.

Djellal, F., Gallouj, F. (1999). Services and the search for relevant innovation indicators: a review of national and international surveys. *Science and Public Policy*, 26(4), 218-232.

Djellal, F.; Gallouj, F. (2006). Innovation in care services for the Elderly. *The Service Industries Journal*. 26(3), 303-327.

Furrer, O. (1997). Le rôle stratégique des "services autour des produits". *Revue française de gestion*, March-May, 98-107.

Fusslar, C., & James, P. (1996). *Driving eco-innovation: understanding wealth creation*. London: Pitman.

Gadrey, J. (1996a). *L'économie des services*. Paris: Repères, La découverte.

Gadrey, J. (1996b). *Services : la productivité en question*. Paris: Desclée de Brouwer.

Gadrey, J. (2002). The misuse of productivity concepts in services: Lessons from a comparison between France and the United States. In J. Gadrey & F. Gallouj (Eds). *Productivity, Innovation, and Knowledge in Services: New Economic and Socio-economic Approaches* (pp. 26 – 53). Cheltenham UK: Edward Elgar,

Gadrey, J. (2010). The environmental crisis and the economics of services: the need for revolution. In F. Gallouj, F. Djellal, F. (Eds) *The handbook of Innovation and Services*. Cheltenham and Northampton: Edward Elgar Publishers (forthcoming).

Gadrey, J., Gallouj, F. (1998). The provider-customer interface in business and professional services. *The Service Industries Journal*, 18(2), 1-15.

Gallouj, C. & Gallouj, F. (1996). *L'innovation dans les services*. Paris: Economica.

Gallouj, C. (2007). *Innover dans la grande distribution*. Bruxelles: De Boeck.

Gallouj, F. & Djellal, F. (2010). *The handbook of innovation and services*. Cheltenham: Edward Elgar (forthcoming).

Gallouj, F. (1994). *Economie de l'innovation dans les services*. Paris: L'Harmattan.

Gallouj, F. (1998). Innovating in reverse: services and the reverse product cycle. *European Journal of Innovation Management*, 1 (3), 123-138.

Gallouj, F. (2002a). *Innovation in the Service Economy: the New Wealth of Nations*, Cheltenham, UK, Northampton MA, USA: Edward Elgar Publishers.

Gallouj, F. (2002b). Knowledge intensive business services : processing knowledge and producing innovation. In J. Gadrey and F. Gallouj (Eds), *Productivity, Innovation and knowledge in services* (pp. 256-284). Cheltenham, UK, Northampton MA, USA: Edward Elgar Publishers.

Gallouj, F. and Savona, M. (2009). Innovation in Services. A Review of the Debate and a Research Agenda. *Journal of Evolutionary Economics*, 19, 149-172.

Gallouj, F., Weinstein, O. (1997). Innovation in services. *Research Policy*, 26(4-5), 537-556.

Grönroos, C. (1990). *Service management and marketing*. Lexington, MA: Lexington Books.

Gustafsson, A. & Johnson, M. D. (2003*). Competing through Services*. San Francisco, CA: Jossey-Bass.

Harrisson, D., Klein, J.-L., P. Leduc Browne (2010). Social innovation, social enterprise and services. In F. Gallouj and F. Djellal (eds). *The handbook of innovation and services* (forthcoming).

Harrisson, D., Vézina, M. (2006). L'innovation sociale: une introduction». *Annals of Public and Cooperative Economics*, 77(2), 129-138

Hill, P. (1977). On goods and services. *Review of Income and Wealth*, 23(4), 315-338.

Howells, J. (2007). Services and innovation: conceptual and theoretical perspectives. In J.R Bryson and P. W. Daniels (eds). *The Handbook of Service Industries* (pp. 34-44). Cheltenham: Edward Elgar.

IBM Research (2004). Services science: a new academic discipline?. A 120-page report of a two-day summit entitled Architecture of On-Demand Business, May 17-18.

Le Roy, A. (1997). *Les activités de service: une chance pour les économies rurales? vers de nouvelles logiques de développement rural*. Paris: L'Harmattan.

Lenfle, S., Midler, C. (2003). Innovation in automative telematic services: characteristics of the field and management principles. *International Journal of Automative Technology and Management*, 3(1/2), 144-159.

Levitt, T. (1976). The Industrialization of Service. *Harvard Business Review*, September-October, 41-52.

Maglio, P. P., Kreulen, J., Srinivasan, S., Spohrer, J. (2006). Service systems, service scientists, SSME, and innovation. *Communications of the ACM*. 49(7). July. 81-85.

Maubrey, R. (2003). Les problèmes et solutions pour accéder aux innovations environnementales au sein d'entreprises et de collectivités. *Innovations, Cahiers d'économie de l'innovation*, 18,113-138.

Miles, I. (2002). Services innovation: Towards a teriarization of services studies. In J. Gadrey & F. Gallouj (Eds). *Productivity, Innovation and Knowledge in Services, New Economic and Socio-Economic Approaches* (pp. 164-196). Cheltenham, UK: Edward Elgar.

Miles, I., Kastrinos, N., Flanagan, K., Bilderbek, R., den Hertog, P., Huntink, W., Bouman, M. (1994). *Knowledge-Intensive Business Services: Their Role as Users, Carriers and Sources of Innovation*, PREST, University of Manchester.

Muller, E., Zenker A. (2001). Business services as actors of knowledge transformation: The role of KIBS in regional and national innovation systems. *Research Policy*, 30 (9), 1501-1516.

NESTA (2006). *The innovation gap : why policy needs to reflect the reality of innovation in the UK*, National Endowment for Science, Technology and the Arts, Research Report.

Nicolas, E. (2004). Apprentissage organisationnel et développement durable. La norme AB. *Revue française de gestion*, 2(149),153-172.

Patris, C., Valenduc, G., Warrant, F. (2001). *L'innovation technologique au service du développement durable*, Report for Services fédéraux des affaires scientifiques techniques et culturelles (SSTC), Fondation Travail-Université, Namur, Belgium.

Pavitt, K. (1984). Sectoral patterns of Technical Change: Towards a Taxonomy and a Theory. *Research Policy*, 13, 343-374.

Quinn, J. B., Baruch, J. J., Paquette, P. C. (1987). Technology in Services. *Scientific American*. 257(6), December, 50-58.

Rubalcaba, L., Den Hertog, P. (2010). Policy frameworks for services innovation: a menu-approach. In F. Gallouj and F. Djellal (eds) (2010). *The handbook of innovation and services*. Cheltenham: Edward Elgar Publishers (forthcoming).

Scheer, A.-W., Spath, D. (2004). *Computer-Aided Service Engineering*. Berlin: Springer [In German].

Seyfang, G. (2001). Community currencies: small change for a green economy. *Environment and planning*, 33 (6), 581-593.

Seyfang, G., Smith, A. (2006). *Community action: a neglected site of innovation for sustainable development ?*, CSERGE Working Paper EDM 06-10.

Shostack, G. (1984). Service Design in the Operating Environment. In G. William, M. Claudia (Eds). *Developing new services (*pp. 27-43). American Marketing Association, Proceedings Series.

Smith, A., Stirling, A., Berkhout, F. (2005). The governance of sustainable socio-technical transitions. *Research Policy*, 34(10), 1491-1510.

Spohrer, J, Maglio, P. P., Bailey, J., Gruhl, D. (2007). Toward a Science of Service Systems. *Computer*, 40(1), 71-77.

Sundbo, J. (1998). *The organisation of innovation in services*. Copenhagen: Roskilde University Press.

Sundbo, J. (2002). Innovation as a strategic process. In Sundbo & J., Fuglsang, L. (Eds), *Innovation as strategic reflexivity* (pp. 57-80). London and New York : Routledge.

Sundbo, J., 1997. Management of innovation in services. *The Service Industries Journal*, 17(3), 432-455.

Tether, B. (2005). Do Services Innovate (Differently)?: Insights from the European Innobarometer Survey. *Industry and Innovation*, 12, 153-184.

Toivonen, M. (2004). *Expertise as business: Long-term development and future prospects of knowledge-intensive business services*, PhD, Helsinki University of Technology.

Vargo, S. L. & Lusch, R. F. (2004). Evolving to a new dominant logic for marketing. *Journal of Marketing*, 68, 1-17.

Windrum, P., Garcia-Goni, M. (2008). A neo-Schumpeterian model of health services innovation. *Research Policy,* 37(4), 649-672.

Wood, P. (2005). A service-informed approach to regional innovation - or adaptation? *The Service Industries Journal,* 25(4), 429-445.

Zéroual, T. (2008). *Vers une réévaluation des politiques de transport durable de marchandises,* Séminaire du programme SITE, Clersé, University of Lille 1, 28 February.

Service Innovation and Customer Co-development

Bo Edvardsson

CTF-Service Research Center
Karlstad University, Sweden

Anders Gustafsson

CTF-Service Research Center
Karlstad University, Sweden

Per Kristensson

CTF-Service Research Center
Karlstad University, Sweden

Lars Witell

CTF-Service Research Center
Karlstad University, Sweden

Customer co-development is a core concept to understand service innovation. Our point of departure is that there is an untapped business potential from customer co-development, i.e. integration of customers, throughout the service innovation process. From a service logic perspective, the customer has an important role both in service production and service innovation. Most of the focus thus far has been on the role of the customer in production. We argue that there should be a relationship between the role of the customer in service production and the potential role of the customer in service innovation. When there is a change in the process of service production it ought to be followed by a change in the service innovation process. Customers can be integrated as interpreters and translators during various phases of the service innovation process. Companies must be able to understand and manage various customer roles as they complement one another; close and in-depth integration of customers throughout the innovation process is important but at the same time also challenging.

P.P. Maglio et al. (eds.), *Handbook of Service Science*, Service Science: Research and Innovations in the Service Economy, DOI 10.1007/978-1-4419-1628-0_24,
© Springer Science+Business Media, LLC 2010

Introduction

An innovation is aimed at producing some kind of benefit for both the customer and the organization, e.g. profits, growth, increased customer loyalty or the creation of a new business. Service innovation can be based on a new role for the customers as co-creators, a new customer interface, technological options or new ways of resource integration as a basis for the service process. In a service-driven economy, companies try to increase their competitiveness through service innovations that create value for existing customers, attract new customers and at the same time produce shareholder value (e.g. Edvardsson, Gustafsson, Johnson & Sandén 2000; Gustafsson & Johnson 2003). Service as a science is an emerging discipline developing the knowledge needed to succeed in the service economy (Glushko, 2008). Chesbrough and Spohrer (2006) argue for a services science discipline to integrate across academic silos and advance service innovation more rapidly.

Companies compete by developing, offering and delivering superior customer value. Value designed-in during service production and exchanged with customers is now challenged by a view that value through service is co-created with the customer. The service is assessed on the basis of value in use or the resulting consumption experiences. Service is what products or services do for people or oganzations. Within service research and service science, customer co-creation of value is a central theme or a perspective on how to view a business. This view should also be taken into the innovation process.

Innovation viewed from the perspective of a service logic includes a strong focus on changes in value creation that occurs for a customer during the consumption process. In other words, innovation regards how a "situation" has changed for a customer, i.e. the extent to whether the customer is able to do things better, more smoothly, faster, cheaper, with higher satisfaction, together with others, learn new things and so forth. In contrast to a goods logic, it does not focus on new technology, attributes or features that are being produced within a company. If value is created in the use situation, the customer is the resource that holds the competence and knowledge about value. Such a resource should be central to the success of the development of service innovations. A question we address in this chapter is if, how and when to integrate customers as co-developers in the service innovation process.

By customer integration as co-developers, we mean being proactive and "getting close to customers" in order to learn from and with them beyond what traditional market research methods, such as focus groups, questionnaires and interviews can provide. Our point of departure is the significant business potential from integrating customers and learning with them as co-developers throughout the service innovation process. The customer as a co-developer of service innovation is a growing concept in service research, with relevance for not only service companies and public service providers but also for manufacturing companies in the transition from product to service orientation.

In this chapter, we will share some of our insights from various projects carried out at the CTF-Service Research Center, Karlstad University, Sweden. The empirical foundation is a survey of Swedish service firms as well as a number of case studies and experiments carried out in cooperation with multinational companies such as Telia, Ericsson and Whirlpool. We begin by looking at the service logic to better understand what service innovation is and the importance of customer co-development for service innovation. We then take the perspective of a service logic and discuss the customers' role in value creation through service and continue with different views on the possible roles of the customer in service innovation. We continue with examples from companies of customer co-development in service innovation and finally, we present some guidelines about how to change the locus of attention and how to manage customer co-development in service innovation.

The service logic and customer co-developed value

Definitions and Service perspectives

Grönroos (2008) argues that there are at least three different aspects of the concept of service as it is used in the literature: (1) service as an activity; (2) service as a perspective on the customer's value creation; and (3) service as a perspective on the provider's activities (business logic). "Service as an activity is what is traditionally meant by the term service in the literature. It is a process where someone does something to assist someone else and his or her everyday practices (activities or processes). A cleaner washes and irons a customer's business shirts and, thus, enables him to go to his office; a lunch restaurant provides a meal for him or her during the lunch break, so that he or she will be able to manage the afternoon's tasks successfully. In both cases, the firms' activities are providing something of value for a customer" (Grönroos 2008:300). Assisting everyday practices means that a service activity should support some activities or processes of a customer. The second and third aspects of service are according to Grönroos (2008) perspectives that can be applied as a foundation for customers' purchasing and consumption processes (customer service logic) and for organizations' business and marketing strategies (provider service logic), respectively. These perspectives or logics of service have been proven useful to better understand how value is created in many businesses today, ranging from traditional service companies, the public sector and manufacturing companies.

Grönroos (2008:311) argues that "the service logic, interaction rather than exchange is the fundamental construct in marketing – exchange is not geared towards customers' value creation, but towards transactions and value facilitation only. Interaction is focused on customers' value creation and value fulfillment, and moreover, it enables the firm's co-creation of value with its customers. Exchange conceals the importance of customers' value creation and the opportunities for the firm to perform as value co-creator"

According to Vargo and Lusch (2008) service is an interactive process of "doing something for someone" and this process is being valued. Service becomes the unifying purpose of any business relationship, seen from any perspective, through resource procurement, production, distribution, and consumption (Vargo & Lusch, 2006). Vargo and Lusch believe that the new perspectives are converging to form a new dominant logic for marketing, one in which service provision rather than goods are fundamental to economic exchange. Products are platforms which enable service when used by customers. Products form the basis for services such at the telephone, invented by Graham Bell and Elisha Gray, for communication services. Using modern technology and infrastructures in new ways formed the basis for Skype many years later. A new and more cost effective service was invented. Many service innovations are driven by technology development and new ways of using products and infrastructure.

The service dominant logic

Value for customers is created in somewhat different ways if the focus is on a service or a product e.g. the transportation solution versus the car. The focus on the car suggests a Goods Dominant Logic (GDL) to understand value creation while the transportation solution needs a Service Dominant Logic (SDL) to describe and understand the customer value being created. Further more, the goods dominant logic suggests that value is embedded in the physical products during manufacturing. Lusch, Vargo and Wessels (2008) suggest that service-dominant logic is a more robust framework for service science than the traditional goods-dominant logic.

A service business based on SDL is essentially customer-oriented and relational (Vargo & Lusch 2004; 2008). SDL is resource-centered: Operant resources can act on or in concert with other resources to provide benefit/create value; It is a shift from output towards mutually satisfying interactive processes; It also represents a shift from static resources as plant and equipment to employees, competences of enterprise, other value-creation partners and customers; Finally service points toward co-creation of value through resource integration (Vargo & Lusch 2008).

A key assumption in Vargo and Lusch's logic is that resources – operand and operant - do not "have" value per se, but value is rather co-created with customers when resources are used. Operand resources are static in nature whereas operant resources can be rejuvenated, replenished, and newly created, thus dynamic in nature. According to service dominant logic the culture and the employees of an organization must be treated as operant resources. This will result in more empowered employees in their role as value co-creators. The leader must be a servant-leader, who serves the employees, in order for the employees to develop new ways of providing service (Lusch et al. 2007). Exchanging an individuals application of knowledge and skills (operant resources) for knowledge and skills not specialized by the individual is a central notion of service dominant logic, and according to Vargo and Lusch (2006) it is fundamental to human well-being. The focus thus far in SDL has mostly been on production rather than innovation and development of services.

Customer integration, co-development and customer value

We argue that integrating customers in order to learn from and with them in the service innovation process is a key success factor. Co-development is about co-opting customers' competence and bringing the customer into the innovation process and design shop. According to Norton and Ariely (2007), people value the objects they create more than things others produce, even when the things produced by others are, objectively speaking, higher in exchange value. Co-developing service with customers and co-opting their competence is a core area within service science. The dual role of customer as a 'prosumer' (producer and consumer) is not new. Prosumer was coined by Alvin Toffler in 1980. What is new is when in the process we think it emerges. In our case we argue that presumption must be taken into the development process. By introducing the concept co-development, we bring the customer into the service innovation process as a key player.

We view value as being interactive and co-invented (Normann & Ramirez 1998) through a strong interrelationship with stakeholders and "balanced centricity" (Gummesson 2008). The key stakeholder in this chapter is the customer and value-in-use in the context of the customers'. There are many definitions of customer value propositions (Anderson et al. 2006) but most often a customer value proposition is defined from the customer perspective (promise the customer value in use) and it has a strategic role within the company in creating a competitive advantage or business success. Grönroos emphasize the time dimension of value and argues that: "value for customers is created throughout the relationship by the customer, partly in interactions between the customer and the supplier or service provider. The focus is not on products but on the customers' value-creating processes where value emerges for customers and is perceived by them" (Grönroos 2000:24-25). In a global, changing and competitive environment, the logic of value creation is changing.

The changing role of the customer

The changes in the logic of value creation means that the role of the customer is changing and that employees in many businesses no longer meet the customer on a daily basis. The traditional face-to-face service interactions have been replaced by technology-based service encounters. Many service innovations have the consequence of a changing role for the customer in service production. A paradox arises because the new technology creates a distance between the company and their customers, i.e., customers do not interact with employees - they meet technology. Technology not only increases the distance between customers and employees making it more difficult for employees to understand the customer, but also influences customers' ability to articulate what they need and want – they do not understand the possibilities and limitations that a complex technology may convey.

The changing role of the customer in service production also has consequences for the role of the customer in the development process of products and services. Technology makes it possible to touch and learn from customers' actual behaviours over time and on an individual level. To understand the customer, it is no longer sufficient simply to conduct interviews or surveys; the customer must become an active participant and co-developer in the service innovation process. As a result, employees can better understand the customer and therefore the customers' potential as a source of new ideas can be better utilized.

Consequently, customer co-development has been suggested as one such new and important way of listening to the customer and translating customer information into value-creating offerings (Alam 2002; Edvardsson et al. 2006). In the literature, co-development generally denotes everything from a company using questionnaires, i.e., gathering of customer information, to an innovation developed by customers, i.e., lead user approach. There is limited knowledge about better means for understanding the customer. There is a need for future research, especially in the relationship between the implementation of such means and the financial performance of an organization.

Our goal is to be as close as possible to the customers' real life, not only when a new service is tested but also during the early phases of the service innovation process. A company needs to have access to the sticky information, i.e., information from the customers' everyday life that is difficult to transfer to a company because their actions may not be triggered by deliberate thought. The information may only emerge as a customer is using a service but they may not think of it afterwards.

The customers role in value creation through the service dominant logic

SDL is inherently customer-oriented and relational. Operant resources used for the benefit of the customer place the customer in the centre of value creation, implying relationship dynamics and a new way of organizing value co-creation that includes the customer as an active participant and resource in the value-creation system. Organizations exist to combine specialized competences into complex services that provide desired solutions and attract customer value-in-use. SDL suggests that service innovation is about developing value propositions and prerequisites for customers so they can co-create value for themselves by providing resources with their knowledge and skills resulting in attractive customer value and favourable customer experiences.

In summary, SDL emphasizes the key and active role of the customers in co-creating service and it should also be valid in co-development. The customers' individual knowledge, skills experiences and values are important for understanding service and how the service is assessed on the basis of value-in-use in the customer's own context. Adopting SDL instead of GDL has major implications for the management of service innovations. Customer integration in the innovation process becomes natural in the design of value propositions, service concepts and service processes. Service developers must pay attention to the role of the customer to realize customer value - as defined and experienced by the customer - while in GDL, service innovation pertains to the designed-in quality of value propositions, service concepts and service processes as defined by the provider.

Looking at the customers' role in value creation through the perspective of a service dominant logic has a number of consequences regarding the more active role that a customer can take as a resource in the service innovation process.

- Customers for purposes of innovation
- Customers as value creators
- Customers as idea creators

First, with co-development in the innovation process, the result is intended to be innovate, and not solely customized. Traditionally, the customers' role in a development project has been bound to the end of the development cycle, implying that customers are allowed to make suggestions for incremental changes to an almost completed prototype. In this role, the customer is usually cast in a reactive mode of responding to questions posed by the manufacturer. In contrast, customer co-creation implies that the customer takes part as a co-developer from the beginning of the innovation process. As stated by Vargo and Lusch (2004), customers are naturally more familiar with their own context and are therefore better at evaluating the value in use of a product. The difference between 'co-creation' and 'traditional customization' lies in the degree of involvement of the customer; in general, the customer plays a less active role in customization than is the case in co-development. Thus, the concept of co-development incorporates a more market oriented perspective to the question of innovation than is the case with mere customization.

Second, the main benefit claimed with co-development regards the possibility to develop a service innovation with unique benefits and better value in use (Alam 2002). Thus, customer co-development implies that ideas generated – at the front end of a service innovation project – will be more unique and valuable than ideas would be if they would be created in other ways. If ideas early in an innovation project do not come from customers they would presumably come from inhouse developers. Clearly, two immediate questions that arises regards if customers really outperform in-house developers in being creative and why customers are better in identifying value. There are several studies that empirically examine the question of whether customers are more creative than in-house developers (e.g. Kristensson, Gustafsson & Archer 2004; Kristensson, Matthing & Johansson 2008, Kristensson, Magnusson & Matthing 2002). In a field experiment 74 customers were equipped with mobile phones and a short lecture about future mobile phone services. During thirteen days they were assigned to be attentive to difficulties and problems that occurred to them and to reflect on if and how a mobile phone service could solve their recently occurred problem. After the experiment all ideas were handed in and compared with ideas that in-house developers also had produced. The ideas from the customers came up as being more original and valuable but the in-house developer's ideas were more realizable (Kristensson et al. 2004). Thus, the concept of co-development incorporates customers as a novel source of innovative ideas to be utilized throughout the service innovation process.

Third, the ability of the customer to identify and translate manifest and more importantly latent needs is central for customer co-development. This aspect is important as there are numerous studies in the history of marketing that claim market fit, i.e., the correct identification, translation, and application of customer needs, as one of the key ingredients in successful product and service development (Rothwell 1994). As the customer is viewed as a resource, and latent needs are documented difficult to identify, the customer are provided with solution information (from the manufacturer) and are then asked to do the "need" search. Such need search is likely to be much more effective as the customer can carry out their search in their own setting of use, where a possible future product or service is supposed to have a valuable role. Thus, the concept of co-development incorporates an active customer as a resource throughout the service innovation process.

Organizational views of the customer

The organizational view of the customer reflects a company's attitude towards their customers. There are several possible roles of the customer both in service production (Lengnick-Hall 1996) and in service development (Alam 2002). At one end of the continuum, the customer is viewed as a mere product with little to contribute and the organization is seen to have all the expertise. For certain services or during certain phases of a service innovation process customers may actually have little to add in terms of knowledge. At the other end of the continuum, a customer is viewed as a resource that possesses knowledge critical for the development of future services. In this respect, there may be strongly held beliefs that customers are competent and an important ingredient in the production or development of service. In summary, due to the distance between these two views it seems important to note that the view of the customer may vary across different time-periods, development projects, types of services, or parts of an organization.

The customer in service production

Gershuny and Rosengren (1973) provided one of the first models covering the different roles of the customer in service production. They argued that the customer could have four different roles: resource, worker (co-producer), buyer, or beneficiary (user). Building on this work, Lengnick-Hall (1996) concludes that the customer can be viewed as a resource, a co-producer, a buyer, a user or a product. The customer as a resource and the customer as a co-producer are input-based roles because they directly or indirectly influence the operations and outcomes of an enterprise. The other three roles are on the output side of the system.

As a resource, the role of the customer has mainly been to supply information and/or wealth. Customers are often the raw material of the production process and the more impersonal the service process, the more discretionary the number, intensity and continuity of the customer-resource contacts. If customers provide information that is incomplete or inaccurate, or if they make commitments of funds or time that they do not meet, their input reduces service performance.

The customer as a co-producer means that the customer is a co-creator of value when utilizing a service. The more customers who are co-producers, the more influence they have on the quality of the work processes. In these cases the production is largely dependent on the knowledge, motivation and experience of the customer. If customers know what they are intended to do and how they are supposed to do it, they are more likely to perform well.

Lengnick-Hall (1996) has three views of the customer as output: (1) the customer as a buyer, (2) the customer as a user and the (3) customer as a product. These three views all focus on constructs related to service delivery such as expectations, customer satisfaction and intention to buy.

Customer participation has been defined as "the degree to which the customer is involved in producing and delivering the service" (Dabholkar 1990). In relation to this definition, Meuter, Ostrom and Bitner (2000) distinguish among three types of customer participation: company production, co-production and customer production (wordings changed from Meuter, Ostrom & Bitner, 2000). Company production implies a product made entirely by the firm and its employees, with no participation by the customer. Co-production implies both the customer and the firm's contact employees interacting and participating in the production. Customer production is a product made entirely by the customer, with no participation by the firm or its employees.

Some of these customer roles are specific to service production, while some of them are more general and applicable in the context of service innovation. In addition, there are consequences for the choice of role for the customer in the production process as to what and how the customer can contribute to the service innovation process.

The customer in service innovation

Within development work, additional models have been developed viewing the customer as buyer, subject of interest, provider of information, expert and co-developer (e.g. Finch 1999; Nambisan 2002). Alam (2002) suggests a model based on the degree of communication between the organization and the customers throughout the development process. In his model, the intensity of the communication ranges from passive acquisition of input, information and feedback on specific issues and extensive consultation with customers, to representation of customers in the development team. It is explained that organizations that treat their customers only as users, will lose out to other firms that integrate their customers in a variety of roles that expand and deepen the relationship.

Voss (1985) suggests five categories of customer integration: (1) User developed, not transferred, (2) User developed, transferred, (3) User innovation, (4) User initiated supplier innovation and (5) Supplier innovation. It is noteworthy that the main source of idea generation in the first three categories is the user, while the supplier is the dominating party in the last two categories. As idea generation is likely to be the determining activity for the subsequent progress of the service innovation process, it seems likely that if the user takes on an active role in the early phases and generates ideas then this participation will be a defining occurrence in a service innovation project (e.g. Kristensson et al. 2004).

Voss (1985) takes the innovation as his point of origin, but we prefer to look at the organizational view of the customer. Based on the models previously mentioned, we suggest a classification system showing a gradually changing view of the customer ranging from the customer as buyer, the customer as a subject of interest, a customer as a provider of information, the customer as co-developer and finally the customer as developer.

When customers are seen as buyers, the company also sees them as passive recipients of a new service. The company may therefore have a technology push belief, or they may believe that service innovation is driven by their own ideas or capabilities, created in the absence of any specific need that customers may have. In technology push situations, innovations are created and then appropriate applications or user populations are sought that fit the innovation. Methods used are often forms of internal idea generation that rely on the know-how of the R&D department as the source for new services.

When customers are viewed as subjects of interest, an organization uses passive information such as customer complaints or sales force knowledge. In these cases the development is more driven by the things gone wrong than by future opportunities. The logic is that the company is not actively searching for information; instead, they passively wait for feedback. Often, a company is stuck in day-today activities and has difficulty finding time to create service innovations. Commonly used methods are customer comment cards, problem detection studies and critical incident studies.

When customers are seen as providers of information, traditional market research techniques are often used as a viable means for gaining knowledge about their needs. Common market research techniques include in-depth interviews, surveys or focus groups where a company questions a customer about present needs. Another common scenario involves the company testing almost finished prototypes in order to understand what final steps need to be taken ahead of launch. Some companies would argue that using market research implies a form of co-creation with customers. This is seldom the case, however, as often the company has come a long way in their development work and the customer only speaks when spoken to (i.e., the customer takes a reactive role in the innovation process).

When customers are viewed as co-developers, there is a change in their role in the service innovation process from being reactive to proactive. Often the customer is involved earlier in the service innovation process and the involvement can be carried out over several phases of the development process. Companies and lead customers have joint roles in education, shaping expectations and co-creating market acceptance for products and services. Customers are part of the enhanced network; they co-create and extract business value. They are collaborators, co-developers and competitors at the same time. Successful innovations come from matching technical knowledge about a certain platform with knowledge about usage (where value occurs). Since needs arise from within the operating conditions that surround a user, it seems reasonable that users are competent enough to co-produce the service innovations of tomorrow. After all, the user represents a substantial part of the knowledge that is crucial for innovation.

From a company perspective, customers as developers seem to take over the responsibility of service innovation. It can be a rewarding strategy since the costs of service innovation are low or nonexistent, but it is also a risky strategy. Taken too far, customers can become more knowledgeable than the company specialists and start to develop innovations without the company and start to market, distribute and sell the innovation themselves. Linux is a good example where the customers are developers. It started in 1991 with an email from Linus Torwald, a young student in Finland. He asked for reactions and feedback on an idea for a new computer operative system, based on open source. Linux had a market share of 6.8% in 1997, 24% in 2003 and it is still growing. Companies such as IBM, HP, Intel, Volvo and Motorola are now using Linux. A network of customers forms a group of innovators and innovation takes place on a continual basis. The system is developed based on the users' needs, solutions to their problems and particularly the customers' expertise.

Relationships between the customers role in service production and innovation

We argue that there should be a relationship between the role of the customer in service production and the potential role of the customer in service innovation. When there is a change in the process of service production, for instance, the customer takes over a larger responsibility of the workload through technology, which ought to be followed by a change in the service innovation process. There are several reasons to pursue such a change. First, by changing from company production to co-production or customer production, the knowledge of the developers is reduced and the distance between the company and the customer increases. Second, the number of service encounters is decreasing therefore limiting the number of face-to-face interactions. Less face-to-face interactions mean less opportunity to learn from the customer and possibly weaker customer relationships.

One example of a change in service production is IKEA and their creation of a kitchen planner. By using the kitchen planner, a customer can test-drive the kitchen before purchase and consumption. The customer can build different models of a kitchen suited to the measurements in their kitchen and test these models in a virtual environment. As such, a customer's interaction with a hyperreal service can create an experience which is more distinct and clearer than the reality we know, i.e., a hyperreality (Edvardsson et al. 2005). If this service is only used for the customers' benefit, then the change occurs only in the production process. If information is gathered in a systematic way, however, then letting customers test-drive service experiences can be used in service innovation (e.g., Edvardsson et al. 2005, see Figure 1).

In an example of microwave ovens, Whirlpool changed the customers' role in the innovation process while leaving the production process unchanged. To be able to get customers to generate new ideas about functions, services and features related to a microwave oven, customers were allowed access to a new microwave that was not available in stores. Customers received a bag with instructions about how to use the microwave, a camera, a diary, a bag of popcorn and a cake to bake in the microwave. Customers were told to use the new microwave oven for a week and during this time write a diary about how they used it. Each time a customer had an idea related to how to buy, use or dispose of a microwave oven, the customer was supposed to write this idea in a specific section of the diary. At the end of the week, the microwave ovens and the diaries were collected. During one week, 30 customers were enabled to use a new microwave oven. During this period, the customers generated 108 ideas related to microwave ovens (see Figure 1).

One illustration of a change in both dimensions is the introduction of the LEGO Digital Designer in 2004. It is an Internet service where the customer can build LEGO in a 3D CAD program online. The customer can create a customized model in the program, see the cost of it and order it online. As a result, the production process is changed from company production of LEGO models to customer production. Customers create new, virtual models by interacting with one another online. The innovations are available on LEGO's website, and other customers can add suggestions and input. The virtual models are further developed by other customers. Some models are considered innovative and well-designed and can be mass produced and marketed by LEGO. The customer then receives royalty. This service enables a change at LEGO from "100 designers to 100.000 innovators". The 100.000 innovators are new and existing customers. In this case, the change in service production was followed by a change in service innovation, where the role of the customer changed from subject of interest to co-developer (see Figure 1).

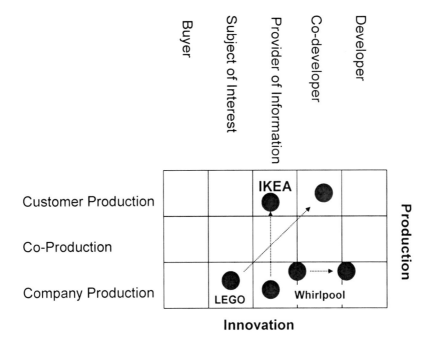

Figure 1. Changes of the role of the customer in service production and innovation

Most organizations use the customers as co-developers to a different extent in different kinds of projects. As an example, Whirlpool in many projects still view the customer as a subject of interest and a study by Sandén, Gustafsson and Witell (2006) shows that this is the dominant perspective on customers throughout the product and service innovation process. In the long run, a position where customers produce their own service (customer production) is not consistent with viewing the customer as a buyer in the service innovation process. There are several examples on e-services such as customer portals and customer clubs that have been developed this way and where the outcome has been a complete failure.

Discussion and Conclusions

A change of the locus of attention

In this chapter, we have described the rationale for the relation between service innovation and customer co-development throughout the service innovation process. The Service-Dominant Logic suggests a new way of approaching innovation as it starts out from how the customer co-creates value and not from the manufacturers' value propositions. What, then, are the implications of such a change on looking at how service innovations should be developed?

With a Service-Dominant Logic as the perspective on innovation new opportunities arise for managers and decision makers. Innovation is now not only related to various activities conducted within a product or service development department but may arise anywhere in the company and also (nota bene) outside the company as customers contribute and facilitate the co-creation of value among other customers (i.e. compare Facebook). To exemplify with a manufacturer for car tires new opportunities for innovations does not only regard chemical mixtures (at the product development department) in order to produce gum in a better way but also to teach customers how to supply them with better service (reduce wear), facilitate change to winter tires (avoid cueing) and facilitate storage (be spared having them in your house etc) and also with providing customers an opportunity to exchange views on driving by providing the platform for a user community (where users exchange wisdoms, ideas and emotional experiences).

In this chapter, we have shown how customers can be integrated in co-development throughout the service innovation process. There is a trend in most industries and especially among the leading and successful companies to come closer to their new and existing customers. Companies can do this by using proactive methods to learn more about how to increase realized value-in-use in the customer's context, the customer's behaviour, drivers of favourable customer experiences, value creators and value destroyers as defined by customers and important customer values. Integrating various customers into the service innovation process will provide useful and critical information to make sure that the resulting new services will be 'wanted', 'chosen', and 'preferred'. Customer involvement in 'the service design shop', however, is no guarantee for commercial success but rather one important success factor in a service-driven economy.

Guidelines for customer co-development for service innovation

We will now conclude with five guidelines for customer co-development in service innovation based on our research and the literature on service development and service innovation.

First, in the modern service-driven economy, customers trade time for money to buy services and experiences directly. The new services, often based on self-service technologies, must be renewed in a structured and planned way to result in value-in-use over time. Therefore, the emphasis on renewal will be even more important in the future, especially in the market for B2B services. In order for companies to manage the renewal processes efficiently, customers' need to be involved, e.g., by contributing with ideas on what is most important for further development. Companies and other organizations must plan how to renew the service and service experiences over time to arrive at favourable customer experiences and stay competitive.

Second, SDL emphasizes the key role of customers in the co-creation of service as well as service assessed on the basis of value-in-use in the customers' own context. The customers' knowledge, skills and experiences have a major impact on perceived customer value. Therefore, new service cannot require more of the customers than they are willing or able to do within their role as co-creators of the service. Since the customers often do not know how to use the full potential of a service, customer competence development or developing the customers' context should be seen as an important area in service innovation. This development will broaden the scope of how service innovation is framed and how new challenges and opportunities are introduced making it even more natural to involve customers. Developing the customers' competence, resources and capabilities to use services to improve realized customer value should be emphasized more often.

Third, there are differences in organizational views about the customer in the innovation process. We have described five different roles: a buyer, a subject of interest, a provider of information, a co-developer and a developer. We suggest that companies and other organizations should be able to understand and manage these roles and that they complement one another. We claim that customers as providers of information are often not enough in the service innovation process, especially when the goal is to create new kinds of experiences for customers. Customers should also be involved as co-developers of personalized experiences. Customers are part of the enhanced network; they co-create and extract business values. They are collaborators, co-developers and competitors. Understanding various customer roles is crucial for long-term success in service innovation. Companies and other organizations must understand and manage various customer roles as they complement one another; close and in-depth integration of customers throughout the innovation process is important but at the same time challenging.

Fourth, when the basic requirements are met, favourable service-driven customer experiences become a powerful competitive weapon in service competition.

Service innovation already focuses on new, individualized and attractive service experiences and will continue even more so in the near future. Test-drives or simulated service contexts allow customers to be involved in the creation of such services and to test-drive the service before purchase and consumption. In the case of IKEA, the stores are designed as a service landscape (servicescape) to host experience rooms, e.g., living rooms, kitchens or bedrooms. The furniture and other items are means to ends, resources and enablers for "solutions to real life problems at home". Customers are triggered and can experience the solutions in the store, in the catalogue and at the website. The customers can test-drive the solutions with the customer's own furniture, size of kitchen etc. using the simulation tool kitchen planner provided by IKEA. The customer can also get help and advice from an architect or other expert in the store. Make it possible for customers to create their own, individualized service and to test-drive the service before purchase and consumption.

Fifth, technology makes many new opportunities possible for customer integration in service innovations. In this chapter, we have mentioned the creation of hyperrealities, simulations, service test-drives and open source. Technology also makes it possible to track and store data about customer's actual behaviours over time on websites, in various chat rooms and on blogs. These somewhat new sources are becoming more and more important in service innovation and customers can play an important role in interpreting and translating the information into action in service innovation. It is possible to capitalize on new sources of in-depth and fruitful customer information by integrating customers as interpreters and translators during various phases of the service innovation process.

References

Alam, I. (2002). An exploratory investigation of user involvement in new service development. *Journal of the Academy of Marketing Science*, 30 (3), 250-261.

Anderson, J. C., Narus, J. A, & Rossu van, W. (2006). Customer Value Propositions in Business Markets. *Harvard Business Review*, 84 (3), 90-99,

Chesbrough, H. & Spohrer, J. (2006). A Research Manifesto for Services Science, *Communications of the ACM*, 49 (7), 35-40.

Dabholkar, P. (1990). How to Improve Perceived Service Quality by Improving Customer Participation, Developments in Marketing Science, B.J. Dunlap, (Ed.), Cullowhee, NC: *Academy of Marketing Science*, 483-87.

Edvardsson, B., Gustafsson, A., Johnson, M. D. & Sandén, B. (2000). *New Service Development and Innovation in the New Economy*. Studentlitteratur, Lund.

Edvardsson, B, Enquist, B. & Johnston, B. (2005). Co-creating customer value through hyperreality in the pre-purchase service experience. *Journal of Service Research*, 8 (2) 149-161.

Edvardsson, B., Gustafsson, A., Kristensson, P., Magnusson, P. & Matthing, J. (Eds.) (2006). *Involving Customers in New Service Development*. Imperial College Press, London.

Finch, B. J. (1999). Internet discussions as a source for consumer product customer involvement and quality information: an exploratory study. *Journal of Operations Management*, 17 (5), 535-556.

Gersuny, C., & Rosengren, W.R. (1973). *The Service Society*. Schenkman, Cambridge, MA.

Glushko, R. J. (2008). Designing a Service Science Discipline with Discipline, *IBM Systems Journal*, 47 (1), 15-38.

Grönroos, C. (2000). *Service Management and Marketing*. New York, John Wiley and Sons.

Grönroos, C. (2008). Service logic revisited: who creates value? And who co-creates? *European Business Review*, 20 (4), 298-314.

Gustafsson, A. & Johnson, M. D. (2003). *Competing through Services*, San Francisco. CA: Jossey-Bass.

Gummesson, E. (2008). Extending the New Dominant Logic: From Customer Centricity to Balanced Centricity. Commentary for Special Issue of *The Journal of the Academy of Market-ing Science (JAMS)* on the New Dominant Logic, 36 (1), 15-17.

Kristensson, P., Gustafsson, A. & Archer, T. (2004), Harnessing the creative potential among users, *Journal of Product Innovation Management*, 21 (1), 4-14.

Kristensson, P. Matthing, J. & Johansson, N. (2008). Key strategies for successful involvement of customers in the co-creation of new technology-based services. *International Journal of Service Industry Management*, 19 (4), 474-491.

Kristensson, P. Matthing, J. & Magnusson, P. (2002). Users as a hidden resource for creativity: findings from an experimental study on user involvement. *Creativity and Innovation Management*, 11 (1), 55-61.

Lengnick-Hall, L. (1996), Customer Contributions to Quality: A Different View of the Customer-Oriented Firm, *Academy of Management Review*, 21 (3), 791-824.

Lusch, R. F., Vargo, S. L. & O´Brien, M. O. (2007), Competing through service: Insights from service-dominant logic, *Journal of Retailing*, 83 (1) 5-18.

Lusch, R. F., Vargo, S. L. and Wessels, G. (2008), Toward a conceptual foundation for service science: contributions from service-dominant logic. *IBM Systems Journal*, 47 (1): 5-13.

Meuter, A. L., Ostrom, R. I. & Bitner, M. J. (2000). Self-Service Technologies: Understanding Customer Satisfaction with Technology-Based Service Encounters. *Journal of Marketing*, 64 (3): 50-64.

Nambisan, S. (2002). Designing virtual customer environments for new product development: toward a theory. *Academy of Management Review*, 27 (3) 392-413.

Normann, R. & Ramirez, R. (1993). From value chain to value constellation: Designing interactive strategy. *Harvard Business Review*, 93 (4), 65-77.

Norton, M. I. & Ariely, D. (2007). Less Is More: The Lure of Ambiguity, or Why Familiarity Breeds Contempt. *Journal of Personality & Social Psychology*, 92 (1) 97-105.

Rothwell, R. (1994). Towards the Fifth-generation Innovation Process. *International Marketing Review*, 11 (1), 7-25.

Sanden, B., Gustafsson, A. & Witell, L. (2006). The Role of the Customer in the Development Process. In Edvardsson, B., Gustafsson, A., Kristenson, P., Magnusson, P. & Matthing, J. (Eds.). *Involving Customers in New Service Development*. Imperial College Press, London.

Toffler, A. (1980). *The Third Wave*, New York: Bantham.

Vargo, S. L. & Lusch, R. F. (2004). Evolving to a new dominant logic for marketing. *Journal of Marketing*, 68 (1) 1-17.

Vargo, S. L. and Lusch, R. F. (2006), Service-Dominant Logic: What It Is, What It Is Not, What It Might Be. *The Service-Dominant Logic of Marketing: Dialog, Debate, and Directions*, Lusch, R. F. & Vargo, S. L. (Eds.), Armonk, New York: M. E. Sharpe, 43-56.

Vargo, S. L. & Lusch, R. F. (2008). Service-dominant logic: continuing the evolution. *Journal of the Academy of Marketing Science* (on line version).

Voss, C. A. (1985). The role of users in the development of applications software. *Journal of Product Innovation Management*, 2 (2), 113-121.

Advancing Services Innovation

Five Key Concepts

Henry Chesbrough

Haas School of Business

UC Berkeley

Andrew Davies

Innovation and Entrepreneurship Group

Imperial College Business School

Imperial College London

As the many chapters in this volume agree, there is growing awareness of the importance of services innovation to the prosperity of advanced economies in the 21st century. In this chapter, we explore the challenges that services innovation poses, as well as the potential value it may create. The conceptual differences between products and services are also outlined. We pay particular attention to five key concepts in systems integration: the role of complexity; the role of dynamics; the role of systems integration; the role of openness; and the structure of organizations.

Introduction

As is evidenced by the many chapters in this book, it is well known that most leading economies in the world are increasingly dominated by services businesses. Yet we know surprisingly little about how such businesses advance and improve over time. Most of what we know about innovation comes from decades of research into the creation of new products and technologies. But services are not the same thing as products and technologies. They are not physically tangible, they are usually consumed when delivered, they cannot be inventoried, and they often require close interaction between the provider of the service and the consumer. If

P.P. Maglio et al. (eds.), *Handbook of Service Science*, Service Science: Research and Innovations in the Service Economy, DOI 10.1007/978-1-4419-1628-0_25,
© Springer Science+Business Media, LLC 2010

we are to continue to advance innovation in the 21st century, we must learn how to advance innovation in services businesses.

This is not an easy task. Understanding services innovation requires us to re-think business in fundamental ways. Product-based businesses utilize artifacts to convey to suppliers what requirements are needed, and those same artifacts help customers determine whether or not the product meets their needs. In services businesses without those artifacts, the relationship with customers and suppliers shifts. The company cannot fully specify its needs in advance to the supplier. And the company cannot describe fully its capabilities to meet the needs of its customers.

And a services perspective makes for some strange bedfellows. Customers become partners, as do suppliers. Competitors become collaborators. Strangers become important, even vital. As we shall discuss below, the role of integration, of bringing together a variety of possible items on behalf of one's customers, becomes a source of value in such a world.

Such drastic changes are costly, risky, and time consuming for companies. Yet they are clearly worth it. Companies who have embraced a services logic to organize their business have found new sources of growth and profit. Consider IBM in enterprise computing. Or Rolls-Royce and GE in aircraft engines. Or Xerox in copiers and printers. Or Philips in electronics and (now) health care. Each of these companies used to treat services as peripheral to their core business. Now services are at the core of their new, larger, faster growing business.

Services can also strengthen a company's competitive position, making it harder to attack. Consider the iPhone and iPod. Companies like Dell, Microsoft, and Google have tried valiantly to unseat Apple in the cell phone and personal music player markets. To date, though, their efforts have been unavailing, and services are the reason why. For the Apple iPod and iPhone are no longer merely products. Instead, they are platforms for the distribution and delivery of a range of services that make Apple's devices far more valuable for their customers. So a competitor cannot succeed in an attack against Apple on the basis of a better product alone. Instead, that competitor must orchestrate an alternative array of services on the competitor's device (a capability we explore below as "systems integration") that collectively deliver a superior experience for users.

Services innovation clearly matters. But realizing this is only the first step on a long journey to actually creating sustainable innovations in services. How to innovate in services is a challenging question, in part because research has only recently begun to address this question. Even the companies at the forefront of services admit that they lack a deep understanding of how to keep advancing their services offerings over time.

That is the focus of this chapter. We will explore five important conceptual points in services innovation:

- the role of complexity
- the role of dynamics
- the role of modularity and systems integration

- the role of openness
- the structure of organizations

Prior Literature

Before investigating our five conceptual points, we wish to ground our discussion in the considerable academic work that has preceded us. Our chapter must be seen in the wider context of a collective effort to articulate the nature, scope and antecedent literature of an emerging discipline of service science (Chesbrough, 2005; Horn, 2005; Chesbrough and Spohrer, 2006; IfM and IBM, 2007). There are at least four specific strands of literature which have contributed to the underlying argument developed in this chapter concerning the emerging role of integrators in the co-production of products and services.

First, there are the early studies of the role of services in the general management literature (Levitt, 1976; Drucker, 1991; Quinn et al., 1987, Quinn, 1992, Schmenner, 1986) which attempted to understand and transcend the key distinction between manufacturing and services. Levitt (1976) emphasized the industrialization of services through automation, standardization of processes and adoption of new technologies. Drucker (1991) argued that the greatest management challenge facing developed economies in the 21st century is to raise the productivity of knowledge and service workers. Quinn (1992) made a strong case to move beyond the traditional product-service dichotomy, arguing that any activity including R&D and manufacturing becomes a service when it is outsourced and sold to external customers. Working with an inversion of product and process life cycle model originally developed by Hayes and Wheelwright (1984) for manufacturing, Schmenner (1986) develops a 'service process matrix' to identify the logic of industrialization of services.

Second, there is a strand of literature concerned with how value is added in a series of activities – from raw materials through to the final consumer – to provide products and/or services as solutions to customers needs. The original services literature helped to draw attention to the specific characteristics of service-based value chains (Heskett et al., 1994) or value networks (Basole et al., 2008). It is now understood that the entire value-creating system must be reconfigured as a 'value constellation' that mobilize suppliers and customers in the co-production of solutions (Norman and Ramirez, 1993; Norman, 2001). Wise and Baumgartner (1999) identified four downstream business models for manufacturers that are integrating forwards in the value chain to provide services. Waste and inefficiencies can be minimized when supply chains are organized to provide 'lean solutions' that are designed around the final customers' needs (Womack and Jones, 2005).

Third, closely related to this reconfiguration of value chain around the customer, suppliers are moving from product-centric to customer-centric service-based solutions (Slywotzky, 1996; Slywotzky and Morrison, 1998). Under the traditional product-centric approach – the dominant logic of manufacturing during the 20th century – the supplier concentrated on enhancing the performance the activities involved in making, selling and delivering products that were 'handed over the wall' to the customer. By contrast, customer-centric approach works back from the needs and priorities of the customer. The supplier must acquire a detailed understanding how value is created 'through the eyes of the customer'. Engaging in a close dialogue and 'bonding relationship' with the customer, suppliers must first identify the customer's needs and experiences (Hax and Wilde, 1999; Prahalad and Ramaswamy, 2000). They must then develop the capabilities and resources to offer a specific combination of products and services that link uniquely well with the customer's requirements. New types of organizational forms are required to support customer-centric solutions (Galbraith, 2002).

Fourth, building on the early contribution of Levitt (1976 & 1983) and others, the marketing literature has long been at the forefront in articulating the role of services in the economy. Recent marketing literature has emphasized a shift in 'dominant logic' from goods to services (Vargo and Lusch, 2004; Lusch et al., 2008). The dominant logic of the 20th century centred on the exchange of goods focused on tangible resources, value embedded in physical products and transactions. This is giving way to a new dominant logic centred on the provision of services based on competencies to market offerings, perform processes and provide outcomes. In this view, products must be seen as artifacts around which customers have experiences (Pine and Gilmore, 1999). Service-dominant logic also emphasizes the importance of collaborating with and learning from customers, while being adaptive to their specific needs.

Having identified important prior academic contributions to the domain of service innovation, let us now proceed to develop our five conceptual points.

I. The role of complexity

One significant challenge of services innovation is the intangible nature of the services activity. Both agricultural and manufacturing economies produce tangible outputs in the form of products that are the primary focus of exchange in the economy. Crucially, key information comes embedded in the products being traded.

Services exchange is qualitatively different from both earlier eras. It involves a negotiated exchange between a provider and an adopter (supplier and customer) for the provision of (predominately) intangible assets. While there may be tangible artefacts transferred as well, they are no longer the central focus of the exchange.

This lack of a central product raises an important and interesting corollary: each party in the exchange needs the other's knowledge in negotiating the exchange. On the one hand, the provider lacks the contextual knowledge of the customer's business and how the customer is going to leverage the offering to compete more effectively in the market. At the same time, the customer does not know the full capabilities of the provider's technologies or its experience from other transactions in assessing what will work best. (Alert customers will also worry that the contexts in which the supplier's experiences with previous clients occurred may not correspond to their own specific context. Similarly, alert suppliers will be concerned with whether or not their previous experiences apply to the present exchange.)

This contextual difficulty should not be carried too far. The prevalence of services in advanced industrial economies shows that suppliers and customers usually are able to exchange enough information to accomplish the exchange. When the service provided is modest in complexity and repeatedly provided over time (think of a haircut in a salon, for example), the provider and customer need to exchange only limited amounts of information, and can do so over many repeated attempts, so that errors at one exchange can be corrected in the next.

When the complexity of the exchange becomes very large, and when the exchange is repeated only seldom or not at all (think of installing and operating an enterprise resource planning system for your company), the technical complexity and the lack of repeated experiences between the parties makes the full exchange of information vitally important to achieve, yet daunting to accomplish.

As technical complexity rises, the services customer becomes a co-producer of a service innovation, intimately involved in defining, shaping and integrating the service into his organization. The supplier of the service can extend an offer of what is to be provided, but as we shall see below, it cannot entirely specify the requirements of the service. Instead, the supplier designs its processes to elicit this information from its customers, and modifies the offering in response to customers' needs before sale. In turn, customers select their service provider on the basis of the capabilities they offer, and the extent to which the customer is able to shape those capabilities to serve their particular needs.

This leads to a consideration of the nature of the knowledge involved in a services exchange. Both codified and tacit knowledge must be considered before an exchange. Codified knowledge represents information that is well-understood by providers and adapters. For example, owing to common language, customs, media and culture, a great deal of information is known by both supplier and customer. Codified knowledge is also developed within more technical areas, when technical standards represent the codification of knowledge across multiple entities, such as the html and http protocols in the Internet, or the Digital Video Disk format for movies. These standards enable information to transfer between physical devices such as computers or TVs and DVD players in ways that are predictable in advance. When knowledge is standardized in this way, parties can exchange services with each other even though they may be otherwise not known to each other.

Tacit knowledge is quite different. Tacit knowledge is experiential knowledge that has not been reduced to a codified form. A classic example of tacit knowledge is learning to ride a bicycle. This form of knowledge is difficult to transfer, particularly when parties do not know each other already. This difficulty of transmission greatly complicates the services exchange. It limits the ability of each party to fully comprehend the needs and abilities of the other. Even in technical domains, tacit knowledge is vital. Professional associations, school ties, convention gatherings and the like provide face-to-face experiences that help to transfer tacit knowledge.

II. The role of dynamics – from products to services

Innovation matters to service businesses. If they don't alter their offerings or change the way they create and deliver those services, often provided in combination with products, their survival and growth will be threatened. Competitive pressures to innovate in services may be stronger than in manufacturing because new ideas in services are easier to imitate and harder to protect. For example, despite being much smaller than its rivals, Southwest Airlines' strong position in the US as a low-cost airline was achieved by innovation in operational processes, such as rapid aircraft turnaround times and a simple "no thrills" service. The stable world of airline travel was radically transformed by the influx of many new firms such as EasyJet and Ryan Air that emulated this low-cost business model.

If a business is unable or unwilling to build on an initial innovation, it risks being left behind as other firms change their offerings, modify their processes and underlying models which drive their business. This is why dynamics are so important to understand. Models of innovation have largely been derived from studies of manufacturing rather than services. But, as we have seen, the provision a service is distinct from making a physical product. It is important to consider, therefore, whether managing and organizing the innovation process in services represents a different or similar model to manufacturing. Recent progress in our understanding of service innovation has been achieved by identifying influential dynamic models of innovation that, with appropriate modifications, can be applied to services.

The product life cycle (PLC) developed by William Abernathy and James Utterback is perhaps the most influential model for understanding how firms manage the innovation process (Abernathy and Utterback, 1978; Utterback, 1994). The PLC model depicts innovation as a dynamic process, focusing on the rate of innovation in physical products and production processes. It describes the main phases in the life cycle of a product from birth to maturity.[1]

This pattern helps understand why organizations often find it difficult to cope with disruptive innovation. They have built their capabilities to deal with a particular trajectory of innovation and can find it hard to move to a new one, especially during the mature stages of the product life cycle.

---

[1] There are three main phases in the PLC: (1) a fluid phase, when product innovation prevails, and many small firms offer competing product designs; (2) a transitional phase, when process innovation dominates, which is initiated by the emergence of a 'dominant design' and the shakeout as the industry becomes dominated by a few large firms that concentrate on cost-advantages obtained by high-volume production of standardized products; and (3) a specific phase when the rate of product and process innovations declines.

Although originally devised for manufactured products, the model also works well for some services. For example, the early days of Internet banking were comparable to a fluid phase with many different services offerings. The emergence of a dominant design characterized by a standard bundle of services with levels of security and privacy support ushered in a transitional phase.

There are also differences, evidenced by the attempts to adapt the PLC model in order to explain the dynamics of innovation in services. Richard Barras (1986) developed a "reverse product life cycle" by emphasizing the interactive nature of innovation in services in response to technological opportunities and changes in market demand. More recently, Cusumano and Suarez (2007) have extended the PLC model to incorporate the role of services in combination with physical products at different stages in the evolution of an industry. They cite the example of IBM, which since the early 1990s has attempted a shift from improving "processes" to offering services to enhance its products, through systems integration, technical support and maintenance. In this "product, process and service" (PPS) life cycle, services are increasingly important in the mature stage of the life cycle. Services associated with maintaining an installed base of existing and shrinking line of products begin to decline in importance, while services associated with a new line of products become increasingly important.

The PLC model helps to show how products are progressively industrialized as an industry evolves by developing standardized and repetitive processes and standardized products. However, many firms have experienced enormous difficulties in achieving improvements in services that compare with productivity gains in manufacturing processes. IBM, for example, is attempting to improve service productivity and innovation by emulating the systematic and replicable product development and production processes found in manufacturing. Yet little is known about how firms are turning the different services they provide from ad hoc, one-off offerings into repeatable and scalable processes; what specific managerial processes are developed to package, simplify and reuse service offerings; and whether techniques developed for manufacturing can be easily transferred to the service sector.

It is well known, however, that firms strive to improve the performance of service provision by substituting technology for service workers (automation), or standardizing service processes. As Levitt (1976) recognized, a service can be industrialized using hard, soft and hybrid technologies:

- hard technologies and physical processes replace people (e.g. ATM replacing a bank clerk);
- soft technologies involve carefully planned industrial systems and procedures that can replace individual service operatives (e.g. self-service restaurants replacing waiters in cafés and diners); and
- hybrid technologies combine hard and soft technologies often into a new style of production system to improve the efficiency of service provision (e.g. ICT logistics and distribution networks for just-in-time delivery).

The dynamics of innovation also help to resolve the tension in services between full customization on the one hand, and vertical specialization on the other hand. In the initial stages of a new technology, much of the underlying knowledge is poorly understood, and not well codified. This is the natural domain of systems sellers (whom we discuss in the next section of this chapter). Over time, however, the degree of understanding about the technology advances and diffuses outwardly to many others. This enables outside participants to contribute to a service in ways that do not disrupt the integrity of that service. In this latter stage of understanding the system seller must give way to a new entity, the system integrator. The systems integrator can use its well codified knowledge to simultaneously deliver a satisfactory solution, while drawing from a variety of internal and external sources.

The product-process matrix (PPM) developed by Hayes and Wheelwright (1984) helps us to understand how products are industrialized by moving to progressively higher and more efficient stages of production. It is useful to consider whether this framework is relevant for the industrialization of services, which also vary considerably across industries depending on the volume and variety of output. As shown in Figure 1, the PPM examines the co-evolution of production processes and products. There are four main stages of production process:

- job shop – unit or project-based production
- batch – small and large batch production
- assembly line techniques – mass production
- continuous process – flow production

These stages are linked to changes in the evolution of the PLC described in Abernathy and Utterback's research. The PPM is useful because it identifies the key challenges and capabilities required at different stages in the life cycle. It also shows how firms can alter their position in the PPM by making product and process choices. As firms move towards the supply of a few, more standardized products and higher volume processes, the focus of competitive advantage shifts from capabilities based on production flexibility and customization to standardization and cost reduction. Some firms may prefer to remain in one stage of the PPM, rather than evolve from product variety to process standardization as suggested in the PLC model.[2]

Although developed to understand manufacturing, Hayes and Wheelwright pointed out that the PPM also applies to services, referring to the example of restaurant industry. Fine dining restaurants, such as Michelin starred establishments,

---

[2] See also Schmenner (1986), who developed a similar model showing how service businesses move diagonally within a service-process matrix. In his inversion of the PPM, improvements in productivity are gained by moving from a bottom right (high customization and high labor intensity) to a top left quadrant (low customization and low labor intensity).

located in the top-left corner of the PMM, offer high-quality bespoke meals at high-prices. The traditional short-order café uses a batch process to make low volumes of a variety of standardized food items. Fast-food restaurants are positioned in the bottom right corner. For example, McDonalds and Burger King have successfully adopted technologies from mass production to provide a standardized menu in high volume at low cost.[3]

Product Structure Process Lifecycle Stages	I Low Volume/low standardisation one-of-a-kind	II Low Volume, Multiple products	III Higher Volume Few major products	IV High Volume, High Standardisation, commodity products
I Jumbled Flow (Job Shop)	Classic French Restaurant	Traditional Restaurant		
II Disconnected Line Flow (Batch)		Short Order Cafe		
III Connected Line Flow (Assembly Line)			Steak House Pizza Hut	
IV Continuous Flow				Burger King / McDonalds

Figure 1. Incorporating services in the Product-Process Matrix.

This example shows that mass production technologies cannot be applied to provide a customized service to meet the varying needs of individual customers. Fast food chains operate in an almost continuous flow model, while fine dining restaurants must operate on a job shop or craft basis to cope with the highly specific needs of each customer.

The PPM can be used to map different types of service businesses by separating their activities according to volume and variety. Retail banking and low-cost airlines deal in high volume markets and are often standardized and cost driven, whereas knowledge-intensive professional services provided by firms like PWC or McKinsey have a client orientation where service quality and customized solutions are more significant drivers. The revised PPM shows how service industri-

---

[3] But these two fast food chains have traditionally followed slightly different strategies. McDonalds 'produce to inventory' by offering standardized products using automated assembly processes. Burger King 'produce to order' offering a little more flexibility and customization by cooking hamburgers in response to individual orders, allowing customers to select their own pickles, onions and condiments. The customer's perception is the main difference between these two service offerings. Burger King tried to change the customers' perceptions by offering product or service options that had little impact on the process.

alization is made possible by adopting technologies to move towards higher volume service processes and standardized offerings.

The PPM can also be used to examine products and services offered in combination as a bundled package or integrated solution (Wise and Baumgarnter, 1999; Davies, 2004; Davies et al., 2006). These are services that wrap around and add value to the physical product in order to solve an individual customer's specific problem or operational needs. These product-service combinations range from one-off to fully standardized offerings. For example, Rolls-Royce competes in low volume markets by providing individual airlines with highly customized "power-by-the-hour" solutions. This involves selling or leasing jet engines, operating a global IT network to monitor each engine's in-flight performance, and providing services to maintain, repair, and upgrade them.

In high-volume markets, products are combined with standardized after-sales services, such as consumer credit, maintenance contracts and short-term warranties purchased along with a new car, fridge or household boiler. Depending on their needs, each consumer selects one or more services from a standardized menu of options. For example, the survival of SKF, the Swedish manufacturer of industrial bearings (devices to reduce friction in mechanical movement), has been threatened by commodization as manufacturers in low-cost economies can produce bearings at much lower cost (Marsh, 2007). SKF has responded to this threat by improving the company's ability to solve problems for its customers and add value to its products. The company's sales engineers are responsible for discovering a customer's requirements and providing the right technical and service solution from five platforms – bearing products, lubricants, seals, electronics and service-related technologies – which can tailored to each customer's needs.   The internet has increased the scope for offering value added services in combination with standardized goods. For example, the iPod and iTunes is provided as an integrated product-service bundle for downloading music from the internet.

As we move from the lower right to the upper left quadrant in the diagram, the nature of knowledge moves from being highly standardized and codified (enabling replicable modes of service production, even the franchising of service businesses) to becoming more dependent on customized processes and tacit knowledge associated with the experience and insights and professional expertise of single individuals such as a Michelin-star chef. The appropriability of this codified knowledge is low, while the dependence on tacit knowledge creates cultural and practical challenges in terms of productizing offerings or industrializing their delivery. This is a major challenge for a service business that seeks to industrialize its offerings while continuing to differentiate its services competitively. Service businesses that compete on cost leadership and market focus can improve their offerings within a given quadrant in the matrix, rather than by changing their position.

III. Modularity and systems integration

By developing a standardized product design based on modular components that can easily be configured and reconfigured for a variety of customers needs, firms can combine the cost advantages of high-volume production (components) with high flexibility or customization of final product. Components of a product can be standardized and the interfaces linking components into a system made compatible so that multiple components can be specified, adjusted and integrated in various predetermined ways to the varying customer or market demand. Modularity provides a resolution to the tradeoff between price and customization: offering the cost advantages of economies of scale and scope in standardized component production, while providing a higher degree customization of the final product.

Product modularity and platform approaches (Baldwin and Clark, 2000; Gawer and Cusamano, 2002; Cusumano and Gawer, 2002) are now used to standardize components and/or final products in a range of high-volume industries. In standardized consumer goods, for example, cars, PCs and cellular phones are based on a modular design, composed of standardized components that can easily be integrated into the final product as long as they conform to the pre-determined design. However, there are limits to modularity in low-volume complex product industries, such as defence systems, chemical plants, cellular networks and aero-engines). The need to customize the final product for specific operational requirements requires a high degree of customization at the product, component and interface levels (Brusoni et al., 2001; Prencipe et al., 2003).

Although the literature on modularity and platforms is almost exclusively concerned with manufactured products, the early industrial marketing literature suggests that such approaches can be applied to combinations of product-service offerings (Mattson, 1973; Hannaford, 1976; Davies et al., 2007). Each combination forms a complete system of product and service components:

- hardware or "product components" are the physical pieces of technology that form a specific function in the overall system; and
- software or "service components" are the knowledge or intangible human efforts to solve customer's problems by performing activities to design, build, operate and maintain a product.

Like product components, services can be developed into standardized, simplified and routinized methods of operation. Rather than being offered on an ad hoc basis at the request of a each customer, services can be developed and "packaged" into routines and performed as repeatable processes. For example, companies like IBM and Ericsson have developed standardized portfolios of services to support the design, integration and ongoing management of physical products embedded in each customer's operations. However, as with products, there are limits to standardization in highly complex service situations, because services are often individually designed and tailored to a specific customer's needs - such as an airline, telecoms operator or railroad company – and uniquely provided to address phases in life of a specific product, such maintaining and support a fleet of trains.

The nature of systems provision depends on a customer's make or buy decision. As we illustrate in Figure 2, the industrial marketing literature distinguishes between "component selling" (products or services) and "systems selling". Components sellers focus on one or a few components and seek to gain economies of specialization by supplying a narrow range of components to many customers. Systems sellers are vertically integrated and provide all components in a system. An entire system can be purchased from an external vendor or a customer can buy in components from external suppliers, integrate them into a system, and develop the specialized skills and resources in-house required to operate and maintain the system. For example, in the 1980s and 1990s, IBM's customers – such as American Express – performed integration in-house by bringing together components from many different suppliers into workable solutions (Gerstner, 2002).

A systems seller's offering is an example of a "closed model of innovation" (Chesbrough, 2003), based a single-vendor – or "seller-designed" – system incorporating internally developed technology, products, services and proprietary interfaces. The systems seller takes over responsibility for systems previously operated in-house as part of a customer's operational activities, such as inventory control systems, IT, aircraft engine or flight simulator. When a system is outsourced in this way, the customer does not simply buy a system, but the "expectations of benefits" a system provides for a customer over time, such as operating an IT network (Levitt, 1983). A systems seller is responsible for identifying ways of creating value for customers by reducing purchasing costs, improving operational performance and facilitating system growth by incorporating new products and services.

Given the potential value in identifying, assembling, connecting, integrating and testing complex services, the evolution towards services is ushering in a new kind of value-added participant: the systems integrator. This is the lead organization in a supply chain. It is more than an assembler of product components because it is responsible for the overall system design, selection and coordination of product and service components supplied by a network of external suppliers, the integration of components into a functioning system, and the continuing development of knowledge to keep pace with future generations of technology and system upgrades (Brusoni et al., 2001; Prencipe et al., 2003). This external network expands the capabilities and range of components that can be combined to create value for customers (Galbraith, 2002b). For example, while Boeing continues to design and manufacture core airframe components, it is primarily a systems integrator for airframe assembly, contracting out up to 80% of component production to specialist manufacturers around the world.

In an industry characterized by outsourcing and "open innovation", a systems integrator is uniquely positioned to link or couple upstream developments in technology and products with downstream requirements of customers and rapidly changing markets (Chesbrough, 2003; Chesbrough 2006). The systems integrator model of industrial organization emphasizes the advantages of specialization at the systems and component levels, based on modular components supplied by many external companies, standardized interfaces, and an ability to integrate multi-vendor sources of technology, products and services (Prencipe et al., 2003; Davies et al., 2007). Systems integrators have moved beyond the traditional domain of systems selling – taking over a customer's design, build and operational activities – to providing higher value added integrated solutions, including offering strategic consultancy advice and financial support to help a customer develop its business in existing and new markets (Davies, 2004).

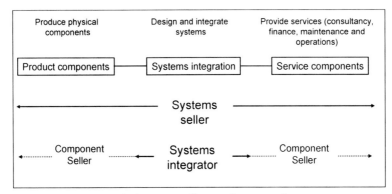

Figure 2. Systems sellers and systems integrators.

Over the past decade, a growing number of systems sellers have been transitioning from "being vertically integrated (doing everything in-house) to being an integrator of somebody else's activities" (Hobday et al., 2003; Hobday et al., 2005). IBM illustrates one company's transition from a systems seller to systems integrator. In the 1960s and 1970s, IBM was a vertically integrated systems seller. The IBM System/360 was based on a modular design, but the software components and interfaces were proprietary. Once a customer had purchased an IBM computer, the complex operating system made it difficult to switch to another vendor's system. The customer was locked in to IBM's hardware, software and service support. By the 1980s, a new organizational model challenged the traditional advantages of vertical integration. Many specialized suppliers of modular components began to challenge IBM's dominant position. Rather than mirror the structure of the industry by breaking up IBM to create a number of specialized suppliers, Louis Gerstner, IBM's CEO executed a strategy to move into services, while reducing its dependence on in-house technology by offering to design, integrate and support a competing vendor's products (e.g. HP, Microsoft and Sun) if this was required to provide integrated solution to customer needs.[4]

---

[4] Gerstner's (2002) account of this move highlighted his previous experience as a large customer of IBM's when he was at American Express. As a customer of IBM's who relied on information

A systems integrator must understand what component activities can be successfully outsourced, while maintaining the capabilities in-house to integrate core technology, products and services. At root, their job is to ensure that the value of the complete solution is greater than the sum of its component parts. Systems integration is attractive to service businesses as well as manufacturers. For example, companies such as BT, EDS, LogicaCMG and Atkins with no in-house manufacturing capability are focusing on being systems integrators of products and services sourced from many external suppliers.

To see this from another vantage point, think of Apple's iPod. None of its component parts are particularly new. But the speed and ease of use of the device, combined with the iTunes online service, has been enormously valuable, not least to Apple's shareholders. As a recent tear-down analysis of the iPod showed,[5] most of the value added in an iPod went to Apple, with little profit going to the component makers who supply parts to the system (with the partial exception of the hard disk drive, which came from Toshiba).

To architect new and useful systems in services, system integrators must learn how to deconstruct complex knowledge, and how to integrate, recombine and reuse it from one instance to another. As the number of potentially reusable bits of codified knowledge expands, the wider the scope of potential services that can be produced from those reusable bits. This is potentially a mixed blessing: the same increase in these knowledge elements exponentially increases the number of possible ways that these elements can be combined. This means that the gains in scope could be outweighed (in theory at least) by the even greater increase in complexity.

As we discuss below, a key challenge facing systems integrators is to understand how to strike a balance between customization and standardization of components and the final product or system. When should a module be reused, instead of employing a custom-engineered piece of knowledge, to serve a customer need? The former will cost less to develop, since it has already been created (and is therefore codified). It is also easily scaled to higher volumes of activity. The latter will be more tightly connected to the context of the customer's problem (and will therefore involve substantial tacit knowledge). This also limits its scalability, as important contextual elements will likely vary from one instance to another.

Understanding the customer's business process is necessary, but not sufficient to the challenge of innovating in services. As noted above, the customer must interact with the supplier at various points in the services process. So, a second necessity to business process mapping is the idea of experience points. These are

---

technology as a key part of Amex's operations, Gerstner well knew how complicated the IT world was. From his experiential (aka tacit) knowledge, he knew the potential value IBM could deliver to its customers by helping customers accomplish their mission critical tasks in this bewilderingly complex environment.

[5] For a detailed analysis of the bill of material for an Apple iPod, and the resulting allocation of profit, see, "Who Captures Value in a Global Innovation System? The case of Apple's iPod" by Greg Linden, Kenneth L. Kraemer, Jason Dedrick, a Personal Computing Industry Center (PCIC) working paper, UC Irvine, June 2007.

points of contact between customers and suppliers in the exchange of services, where each entity's respective processes must interact in order to accomplish the exchange. At these experience points, customers select paths from sets of choices constructed by suppliers, and the exchanges branch into different domains depending on the choice made by the customer. Even customers within the same industry will not necessarily share the same experience points.

Here is where integration becomes so important in services. Product-based businesses leave it to the customer to perform the final installation and integration of the item into the customer's process. Service businesses deliver the benefit to the customer by taking over the integration of the item. Thus, effective integration by the supplier can enable co-creation with the customer. One such example is the systems integrator, Alstom, which provides the cars for much of the London Underground. Working with the London Tube Authority, the company identified 250 product improvements that increased the uptime of the cars, and reduced their lifetime service costs. This enabled the Tube Authority to reduce the number of redundant cars kept on hand as spares, while improving uptime availability of the service.

The management of complexity over the PLC also presents important challenges to the design and implementation of business models for services. How is it that the supplier can take on the challenges of systems integration, while still giving a better deal to the customer? This can only occur if the customer is able to alter its own processes, as a result of having the supplier provide a complete solution. The customer may no longer require an in-house maintenance crew, or an internal IT staff, etc. This change in processes can lead to win-win outcomes in services innovation. This is a further dimension in co-creation between customer and supplier, the dimension of streamlining customer processes and taking out costs in the system.

IV. The Role of Openness

In an open model of innovation, firms use internal and external sources of knowledge to turn new ideas into commercial products and services that can have internal and external routes to market. Firms can initiate internal projects, while tapping into new sources of ideas from outside the firm. While Chesbrough (2003) is primarily concerned with manufacturing firms that use open innovation to develop and commercialize new products, this approach can be usefully applied to services. For example, traditional broadcasting companies like the BBC face the challenge of successfully responding to the proliferation of new digital media technologies and markets (Bessant and Davies, 2007). Acknowledging that it no longer has on the "R&D" capacity in-house to maintain its leading position, the BBC set up a kind of open source community to engage with numerous external individuals and firms through a process of open innovation experiments called "BBC Backstage". External developers are encouraged to use its website established in May 2005 – offering live news feeds, weather and TV listings – to create innovative applications.

As one moves from being a systems seller to a systems integrator, openness takes on a far more important role in the innovation process of a services firm. In the earlier phases of the PLC, there is insufficient knowledge for an integrator to accomplish the integration task, except through the integrator's own knowledge and resources. This effectively means that the integrator is functioning as a systems seller. Later, as the innovation becomes more widely understood, tacit knowledge is gradually transformed into more codified knowledge, enabling customers and suppliers to adequately communicate their needs and capabilities respectively.

The dynamics of innovation in product-service offerings is illustrated in a highly simplified way in Figure 3. Although each product-service combination has its own particular life cycle profile, the figure helps to show how the emphasis moves over time from the provision of closed, highly customized systems-seller solutions in the early phase of the life cycle to more open and standardized solutions, delivered by a range of specialized component suppliers and systems integrators in a later phase of development.

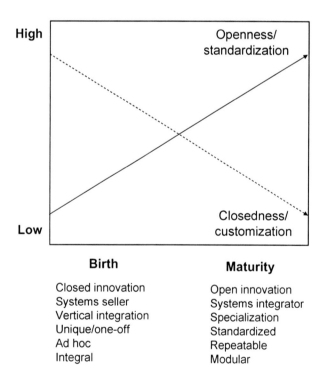

Figure 3. Product-Service Life Cycle Dynamics.

Here is where openness becomes quite valuable. An innovation is now able to be deconstructed into its constituent parts, and changes in one part have little or no impact on the rest of the system. Modularity reigns supreme here, as vertical specialization enables advances in price and performance. This is the natural domain of the systems integrator. Co-creation is quite feasible here, with the added proviso that much of what is customized is transferable to other customers with little additional cost.

A related benefit from modularity comes from the participation of many more firms in the market. With the diffusion of more knowledge to more participants in the industry, more companies can experiment in parallel with possible ways of utilizing and combining knowledge (Baldwin and Clark, 2000). No integrator can hope to compete with this external explosion of potential offerings with its own internal knowledge. While internal knowledge and resources may be deep, they are necessarily limited in scope. Combination and experimentation proceeds in series within the firm, rather than in parallel in the market. The only way forward is for systems sellers to become integrators of both internal and external knowledge.

Performing the integration function effectively requires a high degree of systems knowledge, of how the various elements of a system work, and how they might be combined together in useful ways. Firms that focus only on particular parts of the system without regard to the overarching system (and its further development), are at risk of falling into a "modularity trap" (Chesbrough and Kusunoki, 2000). In this trap, the design rules and interfaces that connect the specific part of the system to the overall system evolve over time in ways that disadvantage firms who have lost essential knowledge of the system's architectural evolution.

Systems integrators must develop the knowledge in-house to accomplish the complex interactive coupling process involved in matching upstream sources of technology and product supply with downstream market demands, needs and expectations. Although many service businesses have no formal R&D departments, they do undertake a similar activity in order to identify, create and deliver innovation to meet a customer's expectations and needs. Openness towards signals from customers may be more even important than technology in triggering and shaping how innovation occurs in services. An in-depth knowledge of a user's needs, an ability to identify and solve individual client problems, and a capacity to co-create solutions with customers are some of the capabilities that are essential to successful the successful development of customer or "market-facing innovations". As well as continuous streams of revenue and higher margins than physical products, the provision of high-value services build long-term relationships with customers and end-users of an installed base of products. This creates opportunities for customer lock-in by creating long-term loyalty and a source of innovation over an extended period of time.

Customer feedback is no longer confined to business-to-business relationships in the co-production of complex industrial goods. Customer experiences can be fed back via the internet to front-end designers to co-create customized mass products (Lampel and Mintzberg, 1996) or personal experiences for consumers (Voss, 2003). Such mass customized solutions provide services along with the product as standardized options that can be configured to address individual needs.

So openness for the integrator requires extensive systems knowledge. Armed with this knowledge, and also with the necessary connections to the many outside suppliers and customers who might contribute useful offerings, the integrator is able to provide "one stop shopping" to its clients. The customer is able to alter its own processes as a result, and there are net savings in cost or in new capabilities that the integrator facilitates. Thus, the integrator leverages economies of scope through openness in serving its market.

V. The Role of Structure

The elements of services that we have identified, including the mixture of codified and tacit knowledge, the role of complexity, the ability to systematize codified information through increasingly scalable architectures, and the co-creation with customers, all have powerful implications for organizing services innovation. One the one hand, organizations need to provide intimacy with the customer, to enable the customer to co-create solutions to their specific needs. The organization likely will want to offer a broad services integration capability to its customers, enabling access for the customer to a vast array of offerings through the organization. In this sense, the organization will need to generate substantial economies of scope in serving the many and diverse needs of its customers.

Such orchestration of various elements brought together at the behest of customers offers powerful vehicles for both value creation and also value capture. Value creation arises first and foremost out of the ability to craft "one stop shopping" solutions for customers. This saves substantial time and hassle for customers, and allows better support and service after the initial sale and installation as well. Customers are likely to be willing to pay a premium for such capabilities (or, to be more precise, many customer segments in the market will pay a premium for such capabilities), which allow the organization to charge on the basis of value, rather than cost.

New forms of organizational structure are emerging to provide customer-focused services and solutions based on a range of standardized and customized offerings. As previously mentioned, these new structures are designed to resolve the trade-off between standardization and customization. They are responsible for developing standardized "solutions-ready" components, that can be combined and recombined at much less cost than solutions comprised of entirely customized components (Galbraith, 2002a,b). Each solution can be tailored to a customer's unique requirements using standardized, reusable and easy-to-deploy modular products and components.

Some large companies that have developed growing services businesses – such as IBM, Sun Microsystems, ABB, Nokia and Ericsson – have reorganized to form "front-back" structures designed for efficient and repeatable solutions provision (Galbraith, 2002a,b; Davies et al., 2006). In a shift away from traditional structures with operational units organized along product, brand and geographic lines, these businesses have formed "front-end" customer-facing units to develop, package and deliver customized solutions for individual clients. Traditional product based divisions have been reorganized into "back-end" providers of standardized solutions-ready components, often developed as common technology and product platforms that can easily be configured for individual customers. In addition, some companies have set up service divisions – such as IBM Global Services and Ericsson Global Services – as back-end providers of services, capabilities, processes, guarantees for service reliability, pricing and resources. Services must be developed into simplified, consistent, and easy to understand portfolios that can be easily combined with products as customized solutions. Both types of back-end units provide solutions-ready components that can be mixed and matched in different combinations by the front-end units. A "strategic centre" manages the interfaces and flows of knowledge and resources between the two operational units. This "reconfigurable organization" can adapt and respond to continuous changes in technology, sources of component supply and customer needs. For example, since 1999 Ericsson (the world's largest supplier of cellular phone networks) has created back-end units – Ericsson Gobal Services and Ericsson Systems – and formed 28 market units and individual front-end units – such as Ericsson Vodafone – dedicated to the requirements of its large cellular network customers.

Within vertically-integrated systems sellers, these organizational units remain in-house. While many systems integrators are creating their own back-end divisions, they often enter into partnerships with external suppliers to provide long term and reliable sources of sources of back-end capabilities in technologies, products, applications and services. The front-end units can provide solutions using a platform of products and pre-developed services selected from a portfolio, rather than develop new configurations for each customer. Ericsson estimates that up to 75% of the service component of its solutions can be based on off-the-shelf reusable components. The remaining services must be customized by the front-end unit at the point of contact with the customer.

The proportion of standardized and customized components in a solution will vary according to the nature of the market (e.g. industrial products or consumer goods). In high-volume industries, the product is usually offered as only as standardized bundle including a pre-defined set of services. In the provision of complex industrial goods industries, the solution offered varies considerable depending on the needs, capabilities and sophistication of the large business, institutional or government customer organizations. Less experienced customers - such as Virgin Mobile and Virgin Trains – with limited internal systems-related capabilities often demand solutions comprised of entirely standardized offerings. More experienced or sophisticated customers, may be find that their needs are not met by a standardized solution.

The emphasis on customization and standardization changes over the PLC. In the early phases of PLC development, there is a powerful incentive to provide entirely customized solutions, since this offering distinguishes a firm from its competitors. Although the front-end units are driven by the need to meet each customer's expectations for unique and innovative solutions, too much emphasis on customization can hinder efforts to provide repeatable solutions. As the technology and product mature, standardization and replication become more important. The knowledge gained from initial customer experiences must be shared, codified and reused across a growing number of customer projects. The costs of developing initial solutions are recouped by replicating components until they become standardized or mature offerings, used repeatedly for many customers at lower cost. For example, Ericsson works closely with lead customers such as Vodafone and T-Mobile in the early stages of the product life cycle to develop highly customized solutions for commercializing new generations of technology. As the technology matures, customers are provided with a customized solution from an increasingly standardized set of modular products and services.

The keys to success in organizing the back end of the organization derive from economies of scale (in contrast to the economies of scope that are essential to the front end of the organization's structure). Processes that receive more and more transactions become very efficient in processing those transactions. Companies can invest in greater automation and process improvement to design and implement these processes. Higher volumes allow the fixed costs of designing and setting up the processes to be amortized over more transactions, making the cost per transaction less and less as volume increases. At the same time, companies will invest in process engineering to make the processes highly reliable and highly available, enabling these processes to scale to meet demand.

Organizing the back end includes being able and willing to utilize processes that handle the very highest volumes of transactions. For it is these which have the lowest costs, highest reliability and greatest availability. Only a small number of organizations receive enough activity to sustain these "best in class" processes at very large scale. Most others will need to partner with an organization that provides such capabilities. Alternatively, some organizations will need to offer its back end to other organizations in order to attract enough volume to reach this scale of transactions – another kind of openness. Companies like Amazon now offer their back end transaction processing services over the web through the Elastic Cloud Computing service. Utilizing Amazon's Elastic Cloud service gives companies access to world class IT processes, and saves them the cost and headaches of developing and maintaining such an infrastructure. Amazon also clearly benefits, both from the additional revenue that comes from opening its infrastructure to others, and also from sharing its infrastructure costs with a larger base of volume. So Amazon's internal costs go down, even as its revenues go up.

Conclusion

This volume clearly establishes the growing importance of services – and services innovation – in an advanced economy. We can learn much about innovating services from the product management literature. Yet important departures from the world of products are necessary in order to grasp the challenges inherent in advancing services businesses.

We have focused in this chapter on five such departures. The role of complexity, though often daunting in complex products, is even more challenging when intangible services are being discussed. The roles of codified and tacit knowledge become greater, and the tradeoff of standardization vs. customization becomes even more fundamental.

A second departure is the role of dynamics, and how services innovation is likely to differ over the technology or product life cycle. The early stages of the life cycle tend to advantage systems sellers, while the later stages shift advantage toward systems integrators. Relatedly, the concepts of modularity and systems integration also support this shift, as external participants and their offerings overwhelm the capabilities of even the most well-resources systems sellers.

Openness figures prominently in services innovation as well. And this openness plays two different roles. One role involves leveraging economies of scope to enable one stop shopping for customers. The other role exploits economies of scale to achieve very high volume, reliability and availability at very low cost. Openness here requires either allying with others who have such capabilities, or building the capabilities yourself and inviting others to share the utilization of those resources.

As a result of these four departures, a fifth departure emerges in organizational structure. Innovative service organizations must be mindful of the underlying systems knowledge required to identify, access, and leverage the wealth of external knowledge surrounding them. They must avoid the Not Invented Here syndrome that neglects the external as they develop the internal. And they would do well to consider both the customer facing side of their business and the back end transactional side of their business, in order to achieve both economies of scale and scope in their markets.

References

Abernathy, W.J. and Utterback, J.M. (1978). Patterns of Industrial Innovation, *Technology Review*, Vol. 80, No. 7, 40-47.

Baldwin, C.Y. and Clark, K.B. (2000). *Design Rules: The Power of Modularity*, The MIT Press: Cambridge, Mass.

Barras, R. (1986). Towards a theory of innovation in services', *Research Policy*, 15, 161-173.

Basole, R.C. and Rouse, W.B. (2008). Complexity of service value networks: Conceptualization and empirical investigation. *IBM Systems Journal 47*(1).

Bessant, J. and Davies, A. (2007). Managing Service Innovation, DTI Occasional Paper, No. 9, *Innovation in Services*, 65-94.

Brusoni, S., Prencipe, A., and Pavitt, K. (2001). Knowledge specialization and the boundaries of the firm: why do firms know more than they make?, *Administrative Science Quarterly*, Vol. 46, 597-621.

Chesbrough, H. (2005). Toward a science of services. *Harvard Business Review*, 83, 16-17.

Chesbrough, H. and Spohrer, J. (2006). A research manifesto for services science. *Communications of the ACM. 49(7)*. July. 35-40.

Chesbrough, H.W. (2003). *Open Innovation: The New Imperative for Creating and Profiting from Technology*, Harvard Business School Press, Boston, Mass.

Chesbrough, H.W. (2006). Open Business Models: How to Thrive in the New Innovation Landscape, Harvard Business School Press, Boston, Mass.

Chesbrough and Kusunoki (2001). The Modularity Trap: Innovation, Technology Phase-Shifts and the Resulting Limits of Virtual Organizations, in Ikujiro Nonaka and David Teece, *Managing Industrial Knowledge*, Sage Publications, 2001

Cusumano, M.A. and Gawer, A. (2002). The elements of platform leadership, *MIT Sloan Management Review*, Spring 2002, 51-58.

Cusumano, M. and Suarez, F.F. (2007). Product, Process, and Service: A New Industry Lifecycle Model, http://web.mit.edu/sis07/www/cusumano.pdf

Davies, A. (2004). Moving base into high-value integrated solutions: a value stream approach, *Industrial and Corporate Change*, Vol. 13, No. 5, 727-756.

Davies, A., Brady, T. and Hobday, M. (2006). Charting a path toward integrated solutions, *MIT Sloan Management Review*, Spring 2006, 39-48.

Davies, A., Brady, T. and Hobday, M. (2007). 'Organizing for solutions: systems seller vs systems integrator', *Industrial Marketing Management*, Special Issue 'Project marketing and marketing solutions', 36: 183-193.

Drucker, P. (1991). The New Productivity Challenge. *Harvard Business Review*, November-December 1991 69-79.

Galbraith, J. R. (2002a), Organizing to Deliver Solutions. *Organizational Dynamics*, 31/2, 194-207.

Galbraith, J. R. (2002b). *Designing Organizations: An Executive Guide to Strategy, Structure, and Process*, San Francisco: Jossey-Bass, Wiley.

Gawer, A. and M. A. Cusumano (2002). *Platform Leadership: How Intel, Microsoft and Cisco Drive Industry Innovation*, Boston: Harvard Business School Press.

Gerstner, L. V. (2002). *Who Said Elephants Can't Dance? Inside IBM's Historic Turnaround.* London: Harper Collins Publishers.

Hanniford, W.J. (1976). 'Systems selling: problems and benefits for buyers and sellers', *Industrial Marketing Management*, (5), 139-145.

Hax, A. C. and Wilde, D. L. (1999). The Delta Model: Adaptive Management for a Changing World. *Sloan Management Review*, Winter: 11-28.

Hayes, R.H., and Wheelwright, S.C. (1984). *Restoring our Competitive Edge: Competing through Manufacturing*, John Wiley & Sons: New York.

Heskett, J. L., Jones, T. O., Loveman, G. O., Sasser, W. E., Schlesinger, L. A. (1994). Putting the service profit chain to work. *Harvard Business Review*, 72, 164-174.

Hobday, M., Prencipe, A. and Davies, A. (2003). 'Introduction' , in A. Prencipe, A. Davies and M. Hobday (eds.), *The Business of Systems Integration*, Oxford: Oxford University Press, 1-12.

Hobday, M., Davies, A. and Prencipe, A. (2005). Systems Integration: A Core Capability of the Modern Corporation, *Industrial and Corporate Change*, Vol. 14, 1109-1143.

Horn P. (2005). The New Discipline of Services Science. *BusinessWeek*, January 21, 2005.

IfM and IBM (2007). *Succeeding through Service Innovation: A Discussion Paper.* Cambridge, United Kingdom: University of Cambridge Institute for Manufacturing. ISBN: 978-1-902546-59-8.

Lampel, J., and Mintzberg, H. (1996). 'Customizing Customization', *Sloan Management Review*, Vol. 38, No. 1, 21-30.

Levitt, T. (1976). The Industrialization of Service, *Harvard Business Review*, Vol. 54, No. 5, 63-74.

Levitt, T. (1983). 'After the sale is over...' *Harvard Business Review* **61** 87-93.

Lusch, R.F., Vargo S.L., and Wessels, G. (2008). Toward a conceptual foundation for service science: Contributions from service-dominant logic. *IBM Systems Journal: Service Science, Management, and Engineering, 47*(1), 5-14.

Marsh, P. (2007). Back on a roll in the bearings business, *Financial Times*, 6 February 2007.

Mattson. L-G. (1973). Systems selling as a strategy on industrial markets, *Industrial Marketing Management*, Vol. 3: 107-120.

Normann, R. (2001). *Reframing Business: When the Map Changes the Landscape.* Wiley, Chichester, New Sussex

Normann, R. & Ramirez, R. (1993). From value chain to value constellation: Designing interactive strategy. *Harvard Business Review, 71*, 65-77.

Quinn, J. B., Baruch, J. J., and Paquette, P.C. (1987). Technology in Services. *Scientific American. 257*(2). December.

Quinn, J. B. (1992). *Intelligent Enterprise: A Knowledge and Service Based Paradigm for Industry.* New York: The Free Press.

Pine, II, B.J., & Gilmore, J.H. (1999). *The Experience Economy: Work is Theatre & Every Business a Stage*, Boston, MA: Harvard Business School Press.

Prahalad, C. K. and Ramaswamy, V. (2000). 'Co-opting Customer Competence'. *Harvard Business Review*, January-February: 79-87.

Prencipe, A., Davies, A. and Hobday, M. (2003). (ed.) *The Business of Systems Integration*, (2003). Oxford: Oxford University Press.

Schmenner, R. W. (1986). How Can Services Businesses Survive and Prosper?. *Sloan Management Review*, Spring 1986, 27 (3) 21-32.

Slywotzky, A. J. (1996). *Value Migration: How to Think Several Moves Ahead of the Competition.* Boston, MA: Harvard Business School Press.

Slywotzky, A. and Morrison, D. J. (1998). *The Profit Zone: How Strategic Business Design Will Lead You to Tomorrow's Profits.* Chichester: John Wiley & Sons.

Utterback, J.M. (1994). *Mastering the Dynamics of Innovation: How Companies Can Seize Opportunities in the Face of Technological Change*, Harvard Business School Press: Boston, Mass.

Vargo, S. L. & Lusch, R. F. (2004). Evolving to a new dominant logic for marketing. *Journal of Marketing, 68*, 1-17.

Voss, C.A. (2003). Rethinking paradigms of service – service in a virtual Environment, *International Journal of Operations and Production Management*, Vol. 23, No. 1, 88-104.

Wise, R. and Baumgartner, P. (1999). Go Downstream: The New Profit Imperative in Manufacturing. *Harvard Business Review*, September-October: 133-41.

Womack, J. P. and Jones, D. T. (2005). *Lean Solutions: How Companies and Customers Can Create Value and Wealth Together.* Free Press. New York, NY.

What Effects Do Legal Rules Have on Service Innovation?

Pamela Samuelson

School of Law

University of California, Berkeley

Intellectual property, contract, and tort laws likely have some effects on levels of innovation in service sectors of the economy. Legal rules that are too strong or too strict may discourage investment in service innovation; yet, rules that are too weak or too loose may result in suboptimal investments in sound innovation. Intellectual property protections have traditionally been quite strong in   protecting innovation in manufacturing sectors, but much less so in service sectors. Services have, for example, traditionally been unpatentable because they were perceived to be non-technological. Whether digital information services, such as web services, should be patentable is currently unsettled and highly controversial. Contract and tort rules are currently quite strict as to manufactured goods, but less so as to services. The emergence of digital information services raises questions about whether existing contract and tort rules governing goods or services should be applied to them, or whether some new legal rules are needed to promote innovation in digital information services and social welfare more generally.

Introduction

The first decade of the twenty-first century has witnessed phenomenal growth in the digital information services sector of the global services economy (Triplett and Bosworth 2004). This includes technology-enabled self-service systems, such as ATMs, online shopping, and online reservation systems, installation, customization, and maintenance of software systems, and computational or machine-to-machine services, such as those that drive supply chains or operate business systems (Cohen 2007).

Relatively little is known, however, about how much research and development (R&D) investment is necessary to promote socially optimal levels of innovation in digital information services. Nor is it clear what role legal rules, such as intellectual property (IP), contract, or tort liability rules, are playing or are likely to play

P.P. Maglio et al. (eds.), *Handbook of Service Science*, Service Science: Research and Innovations in the Service Economy, DOI 10.1007/978-1-4419-1628-0_26,
© Springer Science+Business Media, LLC 2010

in encouraging or discouraging innovation or investments in innovation in digital information services.[1]

This chapter will consider whether the legal frameworks that promoted economic growth and innovation in the manufacturing era, whose heyday was in the nineteenth and twentieth centuries, are appropriate for the emerging digital information services sector. Should innovative digital information services, for example, be as patentable as mechanical innovations have been? Should the answer to this question depend on how "technological" the service innovation is? Should contract and tort liability rules that have historically protected consumers from defective products be extended to protect consumers when firms provide defective digital information services? To what extent will contract and tort rules foster or impede desirable levels of innovation in digital information services?

IP rules have long been recognized as providing important incentives to invest in innovation by establishing ownership rights in innovations and giving innovators the right to exclude unlicensed persons from commercially significant uses of them. But incentives to innovate are also deeply affected by contract and tort rules that establish who has responsibility for defective products or services. Too much liability is likely to dampen incentives to invest in innovation, but too little may lead to under-investments in safe products and services.

During the nineteenth and twentieth centuries, the law created a relatively sharp distinction between "goods" (i.e., manufactured products) and "services," and this distinction continues to be very important in IP law as well as in contract and tort law. Digital information services are, in a sense, hybrid subject matters, with some characteristics of goods and some of services. Because of this, there is some uncertainty about how IP, contract, and tort rules will evolve to regulate this relatively new technologically intensive service sector.

IP Rules Affecting Goods and Services

IP laws have generally played a much more important role in promoting innovation in the manufacture of goods than in the provision of services. There are historical as well as economic and policy reasons for this. It is as yet unclear how IP law will evolve to regulate digital information services and whether there will be more innovation in such services with or without IP protection.

---

[1] This article will focus on U.S. law because it is the law that the author knows best, but she believes that the legal principles articulated in the essay are generally applicable in other jurisdictions, particularly those in the developed world.

The Traditional Role of IP in Manufacturing Sectors

IP laws have been important in fostering high levels of investment in innovation in manufacturing industries. Manufacturing technologies are often expensive to develop and commercialize; once developed and marketed, however, the innovations they embody are often cheap and easy to copy, especially when products sold in the marketplace bear the know-how required to make them on the face of the product. A new or improved product feature, for example, may be readily apparent from inspection of the goods or easily discerned through reverse engineering.

In the absence of IP protection, competitors will be free to copy the innovations with impunity, which may undermine the ability of the innovator to recoup its R&D investments and have sufficient resources to invest in future innovations. Copyist-competitors will not have had to pay for the R&D required to produce the innovation, which allows them to capture sales that the innovator might otherwise have made by selling an identical or near-identical product at a lower price. IP laws address this problem by giving innovators a period of exclusive rights during which they can stop competitors from making market-destructive appropriations of their innovations. Innovators typically recoup R&D investments by being the only firm in the market that can lawfully sell products embodying the innovation or by licensing their IP rights to other firms.

Patent laws protect novel and inventive machines, manufactures, compositions of matter, and technological processes. To qualify for patent protection, firms have to apply to national patent offices and have their applications scrutinized by government examiners who must determine whether or not the claimed invention satisfies patent standards. Patent applicants must disclose what the innovation is, how it differs from the prior art, and how to instantiate it in sufficient detail so that someone skilled in the art could read the patent (a document issued by the government after a patent examiner is satisfied that the standards of patentability have been met) and implement the innovation from what he or she learned thereby. In exchange for this disclosure, the patentee will be able to exclude other people from making, using, or selling the invention for up to twenty years. Many widely used technologies are covered by patents.

Trade secrecy laws are also widely used to protect manufacturing innovations. Chemical formulas, blueprints, molds, tools for making products, and design details that cannot be easily reverse-engineered are examples of commercially significant manufacturing innovations that are often capable of being maintained as trade secrets. Firms sometimes chose to keep innovations secret instead of seeking patents because trade secrecy is less costly and avoids patent disclosure requirements. However, some commercially significant innovations may be kept as trade secrets because they are ineligible for patent protection (as when the innovation is too modest a technical advance to qualify as an invention).

Copyrights and trademarks are also very important forms of protection for many manufactured products. Copyright protection attaches automatically by operation of law to original works of authorship. Among other things, it protects authors and publishers of books, photographers, sound recording companies, and makers of DVD movies against unauthorized copying of copyrighted works embodied in the goods they sell. Trademarks provide additional protection to manufacturers of goods because other firms cannot use in commerce the same or confusingly similar words or symbols that signify the origin of these particular goods. IBM for computers, Ford Motor Co. for cars, Xerox for photocopiers are among the many strong trademarks that protect manufacturers from unfair competition by those who might, in the absence of trademark protection, try to free-ride on the good will associated with the trademark owner's products.

The Traditional Role of IP in Service Sectors

IP laws have played a much less significant role in service sectors of the economy. This is not to say that IP laws have played no role at all. Many service providers (say, chefs at fancy restaurants or financial analysts) keep key innovations (e.g., recipe ingredients or algorithms) secret, and many rely heavily on trademarks (e.g., the Merrill Lynch bull for financial services or the McDonalds golden arches for fast food). But neither patent nor copyright protection has generally been available for service innovations.

Because services are not "machines," "manufactures," or "compositions of matter,"[2] they have generally been considered ineligible for patent protection. Although services can generally be described as methods of accomplishing some task, there was, until relatively recently, a longstanding consensus among judges and patent professionals that only technological processes are eligible for patent protection (Pollack 2002). Services have generally been viewed as non-technological in nature. Indeed, so novel is the conception of services as having technological dimensions that a recent paper entitled "Technology Infusion of Service Encounters" became an instant classic with hundreds of citations (Bitner et al. 2000).

Services have also generally been unprotectable by copyright law. Many innovative services (e.g., original ways of providing banking, consulting, automobile repair, hair styling, or lawyering services) are simply not "expressive" in a copyright sense (that is, they aren't creative expressions of artistic or literary ideas), and so fail on subject matter grounds under copyright law.[3] Yet, the inher-

---

[2] 35 U.S.C. sec. 101 (setting forth these categories of patentable subject matter).

[3] See 17 U.S.C. sec. 102(a) (copyright protection extends to original works of authorship), 102(b) (excluding methods and processes from the scope of copyright protection). If, however, one develops a computer program to carry out specific services, the program is eligible for copyright protection because the program itself is considered a "literary work" under U.S. and other national copyright laws.

ent intangibility of services has often caused service providers to proffer tangible artifacts to signal the delivery or co-creation of a particular service (such as a diploma to certify that a particular service customer has completed a certain service experience) (Bitner et al. 2008).

Even when a service is expressive in a copyright sense (that is, when it expresses artistic and literary sentiments, as in a lecture or dramatic performance), it may not qualify for protection under the copyright laws of the U.S. and some other countries because these laws often require a work of authorship (e.g., a song, a dramatic play, or a dance) to be "fixed" in some tangible medium of expression (e.g., written down, captured on tape, or painted on some surface) to be eligible for protection.[4] In essence, this fixation requirement transforms "the work" from an intangible entity or service into a manufactured object. Once the fixed (i.e., manufactured) copy exists, copyright may be implicated by the service of rendering the work, for example, by public performances of a play or a song. Copyright law thus regulates competition in the provision of some kinds of services, although this is rare.

Why Is the Role of IP So Different in Manufacturing and Service Sectors?

There are several reasons why service providers have relied so much less on IP protection than manufacturing industries. For one thing, service innovation has typically not required substantial up-front investments—no engineering teams, no R&D labs, no expensive equipment, and no clinical trials—that undergird the perceived need for IP protection for manufacturing innovations. Without high up-front costs to recoup, there is simply less need for IP protection for service innovations. A departure from this traditional model can be found in a recent decision by the German government to fund a first-of-its-kind service R&D lab to promote the development of service engineering techniques to improve service design (Spath et al. 2008). The ServLab, as it is known, will use virtual reality techniques to simulate physical service landscapes and enable more robust evaluation of service concepts before deployment.

In addition, service innovations may be more difficult to copy than manufacturing innovations. Many service innovators have unique characteristics (e.g., special training or experience that others cannot easily acquire) that make their services more attractive than those of would-be competitors. Service innovators may also enjoy lead-time and reputational advantages over their competitors that

---

[4] 17 U.S.C. sec. 101 (defining "fixation"), 102(a) (requiring fixation). In some countries, however, a live performance of music or dance—that is, the service of providing them—do qualify for copyright protection.

obviates the need for IP protection. Service innovators may have less for need of IP protection because their innovations may lie in the application of expertise to a particular problem at hand (e.g., the doctor's skill at surgery, the hair stylist's creation of just the right cut for the person before her), rather than the repetition of identical items, which is characteristic of manufacturing. Service innovators may also excel at co-producing value with their customers (Lusch et al. 2008). Artifacts generated from service encounters, such as diplomas or restaurant receipts, may be easily duplicated, but these are easily distinguished from the service encounters themselves. Moreover, some types of services do not depend on IP because their providers have other means of recouping their investments. Lawyers, for example, may charge a retainer fee and handsome sums by the hour for their services.

Professional values may diminish the desirability of IP rights for some kinds of innovative service providers. Teachers, librarians, social workers, and child-care professionals may be as creative in their work as engineers or poets, but the social and professional values of their fields make it less likely that that they will be relying on IP protections as a means of compensation.

Social norms within professional communities have sometimes even led to exemptions from IP protections. After one doctor sued another doctor for infringing his patent on a novel surgical technique, the American Medical Association and the overwhelming majority of its members persuaded Congress to amend patent law to exempt doctors from patent infringement liability for treating their patients.[5]   Congress has also created exemptions from copyright liability for some types of services (e.g., classroom performance of dramatic plays in the course of teaching at nonprofit educational institutions).[6]

How Should IP Rules Apply to Digital Information Services?

For more than fifty years, IP practitioners and scholars have heatedly debated whether patent or copyright protection should be available to digital information services. Much of this debate focused on how computer software should be protected (Samuelson 1984, 1990).

The debate over software protection was especially intense during the 1960's and 1970's during which the prevailing view was one of skepticism. The Patent and Trademark Office (PTO) regarded software innovations, such as algorithms and data structures, as unpatentable because they were typically intellectual (or "mental") processes that could be carried out by hand calculations as well as by computer. In a landmark decision, Gottschalk v. Benson, in 1972, the U.S. Supreme Court rejected on subject matter grounds Benson's claims for patent pro-

---

[5] 35 U.S.C. sec. 287.
[6] 17 U.S.C. sec. 110(5).

tection for a method of transforming binary coded decimals to pure binary form. [7] The Court suggested, although it did not so rule, that to be patentable, a process had to transform matter from one physical state to another.

Although the Copyright Office decided to accept registration of computer programs in the mid-1960's, it did so under its "rule of doubt" (which, in effect, said "here's your registration certificate, but we're not really convinced programs are copyrightable"). The Office doubted that copyright could protect machine-executable code because this code did not just convey information about the steps required to perform a particular task or service, but actually did the work or carried out the service. Copyright protection is generally not available for machine designs or mechanical processes (Samuelson 1984).

Although programs did not fit neatly into either the patent or copyright regimes, they were clearly expensive to develop and cheap to copy, so some IP protection for them seemed appropriate. After a brief flirtation with the idea of a "sui generis" (of its own kind) form of legal protection for software (Samuelson 1984), a consensus emerged during the 1980's that computer programs in machine-executable form should be protected by copyright law. The debate then shifted to whether the scope of copyright protection should be "thick" or "thin" (Samuelson, 2007). From the mid-1980's to the mid-1990's, some software companies sued others for copying the "structure, sequence, and organization" (then known as "SSO") of programs and program "look and feel."[8]

Concurrent with this copyright controversy was a debate on the patent side about the implications of the Supreme Court's 1981 decision in Diamond v. Diehr.[9] Diehr applied for a patent on a rubber-curing process, one step of which involved a computer program. The PTO rejected the claim because the only novel element of the process was the computer program, which it regarded as unpatentable subject matter. By a 5-4 majority, the Court ruled that Diehr had claimed a patentable process. Many commentators initially thought *Diehr* did not make software itself patentable because Diehr's process was the sort that transformed matter from one physical state to another (O'Rourke 2006).

By the mid-1990's, the copyright controversy had died down, as courts recognized that the predominantly functional nature of programs meant that copyright protection in them was necessarily "thin."[10] That is, copyright protection is available for program code and expressive aspects of user interfaces, such as videogame graphics, but not for functional designs, such as "SSO" or the "look and feel" of program operations. Perceptions among software developers that

---

[7] Gottschalk v. Benson, 409 U.S 63 (1972).

[8] The two major "SSO" and "look and feel" software cases were: Whelan   Associates, Inc. v. Jaslow Dental Lab., Inc., 797 F.2d 1222 (3d Cir. 1986)(copying of file and data structures and manner of operation of some subroutines); Lotus v. Paperback, 740 F. Supp. 37 (D. Mass. 1990) (copying of command hierarchy and feel of spreadsheet program).

[9] 450 U.S. 175 (1981).

[10] The main case is Computer Assoc. Int'l, Inc. v. Altai, Inc., 982 F.2d 693 (2d Cir. 1992) (Samuelson, 2007).

copyright provided relatively little protection for program innovations seems to have spurred a surge in patent applications (Lerner and Zhu 2005). By the mid-1990's, many patents were issuing for software innovations, as the appellate court that oversees appeals in patent cases, known as the Court of Appeals for the Federal Circuit, developed an ever more expansive view of *Diehr* and of patentable subject matter.

The apogee of judicial endorsement of broad conceptions of patent subject matter came in 1998 in the Federal Circuit's decision in State Street Bank & Trust Co. v. Signature Financial Group, Inc., which ruled that methods of doing business, such as a hub and spoke design for organizing financial services, constituted patentable subject matter.[11] The court viewed "everything under the sun made by man" as patentable subject matter as long as it produced a "useful, concrete, and tangible result."[12]

The *State Street Bank* decision led to a surge in applications for and issuance of a business method patents, including patents covering auction methods, e-commerce techniques, banking and financial service methods, legal processes, and methods of diagnosing human health problems based on levels of a certain chemical in a patient's blood stream.[13] Metabolite, for example, obtained a patent that it claimed was infringed whenever a doctor made the connection between elevated levels of homocysteine in a patient's blood and vitamin deficiencies associated with heart disease. Metabolite sued Lab Corp. for contributory patent infringement because it provided the results of unpatented blood tests to doctors who infringed the patent when diagnosing the patient's health condition. The U.S. Supreme Court decided to accept Lab Corp.'s petition to review the adverse ruling against it before the Federal Circuit to consider whether the patent claimed a discovery of a natural phenomenon (which is not patentable subject matter).[14]

Although the Court ultimately changed its mind about hearing this case, three Justices dissented and asserted that Metabolite's patent was invalid for claiming a monopoly in a basic scientific discovery.[15] The dissenters regarded scientific principles and natural phenomena as unpatentable not because these discoveries are not useful or costly to develop, but because "sometimes too much patent protection can impede rather than 'promote the Progress of Science and useful Arts,' the constitutional objective of patent and copyright protection."[16] Patent law has traditionally "treated fundamental scientific principles as 'part of the storehouse of knowledge' and manifestations of laws of nature as 'free to all men and reserved

---

[11] 149 F.3d 1368 (Fed. Cir. 1998).

[12] Id. at 1373.

[13] See, e.g., In re Bilski, 545 F.3d 943, 1001-03 (Fed. Cir. 2008)(Mayer dissent, giving examples of non-technological inventions that had been patented after *State Street Bank*).

[14] See Lab Corp. of Am. v. Metabolite, Inc., 548 U.S. 124 (2006) (Breyer, J., dissenting from dismissal of Lab Corp.'s appeal).

[15] "In my view, claim 13 is invalid no matter how narrowly one reasonably interprets [the discovery of a natural phenomenon] doctrine." Id. at 135.

[16] Id. at 126-27.

exclusively to none.'"[17] In response to Metabolite's claim that its patent was consistent with the Federal Circuit's *State Street Bank* decision because it produced a "useful, concrete, and tangible result," the dissenters pointed out that the Court had never endorsed this test for patentability, and it was, moreover, inconsistent with Supreme Court precedents.

In a different case decided that same year, Justice Kennedy criticized business method patents for their "potential vagueness and suspect validity" in eBay, Inc. v. MercExchange, L.L.C. [18] The Court in *eBay* overturned the Federal Circuit's ruling that injunctions should virtually always issue in patent infringement cases. And during oral argument in another case that same year, which involved a software patent, several Justices questioned whether software was patentable, even though that was not the issue that the Court had granted the appeal to hear.

It did not take a genius to realize that the Supreme Court was signaling to the Federal Circuit that it was dissatisfied with that court's test for patentable subject matter and unless this court narrowed its conception of patentable subject matter, the Court would take an appeal in appropriate case soon, overturn the Federal Circuit's ruling, and articulate an alternative standard that the PTO should follow. The PTO quickly picked up on this signal and started rejecting patent claims on subject matter grounds.

Bernard Bilski was one of the disappointed applicants who appealed the PTO's denial of his business method claim to the Federal Circuit. Bilski argued that his claim for a method of hedging risks of fluctuation in prices of energy commodities was patentable subject matter under the *State Street Bank* decision because it yielded a "useful, concrete, and tangible result." In an unusual move, the Federal Circuit heard Bilski's appeal en banc (that is, with all twelve judges presiding, rather than in a three judge panel, as is the usual practice). A majority of the judges who heard Bilski's appeal ruled that his method was unpatentable because it didn't satisfy Supreme Court standards under which a process is only patentable if "(1) it is tied to a particular machine or apparatus, or (2) it transforms a particular article into a different state or thing."[19]

At least three Federal Circuit judges would have gone further and ruled that business methods and services per se are unpatentable.[20] Judge Mayer viewed Bilski as claiming a business method patent, but "[a]ffording patent protection to

---

[17] Id. at 127-28, quoting Funk Bros. Seed Co. v. Kalo Inoculant Co., 333 U.S. 127, 130 (1948).

[18] 548 U.S. 388 (2006).

[19] In re Bilski, 545 F.3d 943, 954 (Fed. Cir. 2008).

[20] Id. at 966-76 (Dyk, J., Linn, J. concurring), at 998-1011 (Mayer, J. opinion). Mayer's opinion is characterized as a dissent, id. at 998, but he agreed with the majority that Bilski's method was unpatentable. However, he dissented from endorsing the machine/transformation test for patentability endorsed by the majority. Judge Rader similarly agreed that Bilski's method was unpatentable as an abstract idea, but disagreed with the machine/transformation test announced in the majority opinion. Id. at 1011-15. Only one of the judges would have upheld the patentability of Bilski's method and continued to endorse the *State Street Bank* test. Id. at 976-98 (Newman, J. dissenting).

business methods lacks constitutional and statutory support, serves to hinder rather than promote innovation, and usurps that which rightfully belongs in the public domain."[21] In his view, the *State Street Bank* decision had wrongly "jettisoned" the long-standing prohibition against patenting method of doing business.[22] Only technological inventions are patentable under the U.S. Constitution and patent law, and business methods do not qualify "because they are not directed to any technological or scientific innovation."[23] Since *Bilski*, the PTO has continued to reject claims for non-technological methods and even for many software innovations on the grounds that they do not claim patentable subject matter. The Federal Circuit has also affirmed some other PTO denials of business method, software and other non-technological claims on subject matter grounds. Notwithstanding the Federal Circuit's ruling in *Bilski*, the U.S. Supreme Court has granted Bilski's petition for review of the Federal Circuit's decision. Chances are quite high that the Court will rule that Bilski's method is unpatentable, but it may articulate a different test for patentable subject matter than the Federal Circuit articulated in its *Bilski* decision.

The pendulum of patentability has thus swung away from the broad *State Street Bank* conception and back toward more restrictive conceptions. It remains to be seen which, if any, digital information services will be patentable after the Court decides *Bilski*.

It is fair to observe that the doctrinal debates in which the courts and commentators have been engaged concerning the patentability of business methods and services do not directly address a key underlying question: are patents on services in general, or digital information services in particular, needed to promote adequate levels of investment in innovation? In *State Street Bank,* the Federal Circuit expressed confidence that patents on business methods were desirable in order to promote innovation, but it had no empirical basis on which to base this claim. The Supreme Court's recent skepticism about business method and other non-technological patents assumes that such patents are likely to impede rather than promote innovation, but the Justices have no direct evidence of this either. In *Bilski*, the Federal Circuit repudiated its earlier *State Street Bank* decision, but this was largely driven by its perception that the Supreme Court would reverse it soon unless the Federal Circuit adopted a more restrictive interpretation of patent subject matter.

There is disagreement among academic commentators about whether patents on business methods and software are desirable to promote innovation in these sectors of the economy (Mann 2005; Samuelson 1994). A recent survey of high technology entrepreneurs, including software and e-commerce firms, indicates that about two-thirds of them do not own patents and have not applied for them by

---

[21] Id. at 998.

[22] Id. at 1000.

[23] Id. at 1000-01. Judge Mayer cited numerous cases as rejecting patent claims for business methods (i.e., services). Id. at 1001-03.

comparison with more than eighty percent of other high tech firms that either have patents or have applied for them (Samuelson & Graham 2010). Even the software and e-commerce firms that do have patents regard these patents as having little value as a source of competitive advantage. Yet some software and Internet firms consider patents to have value as insurance against lawsuits or as an asset to aid financing (Mann 2005).

There does seem to be considerable innovation in the digital information ser- vices sector today. Web services are proliferating, and service providers are in- creasingly using technology back-end innovations to improve front-end experi- ences with customers (Glushko and Tabas 2009). Whether there would be more innovation if there was stronger IP protection for digital information services is a good question, but an unanswerable one. But consider these observations. First, some digital information service providers probably do not need patent protection. Firms like Salesforce.com, for example, that provide software as a service can keep the "sweet sauce" of their service innovations inside the firm. To the extent digital information services are customized for clients, patents are probably also not needed. Second, firms whose digital information services are widely marketed in a form that is vulnerable to cheap copying are those for whom patents are most likely to be important for recoupment of investments. Third, many factors, includ- ing first mover advantages, network effects, and reputation enhancement, allow innovative digital information service providers to develop competitive advan- tages in the marketplace (Graham et al. 2009). Fourth, to the extent some service- innovation patents have issued in the *State Street Bank* decade (1998-2008), they are probably invalid unless they meet the new test for patentability the Supreme Court announces in *Bilski*. Fifth, IP protection may play a smaller role in promot- ing innovation and investment in innovation in the services sector of the economy than some IP professionals assume.

Liability Rules for Defective Products and Services

The roles of contract and tort rules in promoting or impeding investments in innovation are less obvious than the role of IP protection, but they are nonetheless significant (Alces 1999). If contractual warranty rules and tort negligence rules are too strict—for example, by imposing unlimited liability for any losses that cus- tomers or other persons might suffer as a result of a defect in the product—firms may decide it is too risky to invest in making these products or too risky to intro- duce innovative new features to a stable and non-defective product.[24] Yet, if liability rules are very loose and there is little risk of being held responsible for de- fects, firms may not invest as much as would be socially optimal in refining new

---

[24] This is why some states have adopted "caps" (e.g., no more than $5 million) on punitive dam- age awards for torts such as negligent design of products.

designs so that they are safe or otherwise sound. The proper policy goal is to find a middle ground in which the rules are strict enough to induce investment in innovations with few defects, yet loose or limited enough to allow firms to take some risks when innovating.

This section explains how contract and tort liability rules evolved in respect of goods and services in the nineteenth and twentieth centuries. There are some important historical reasons why goods have been subject to stricter contract and tort liability rules than services. There is some uncertainty and debate about how strict contract and tort liability rules should be as to digital information services. Although there is as yet no certain answer to the question whether they should be treated more like manufactured goods or more like traditional services, digital information service providers would be well-advised to be careful in how they contract with customers to limit their liability for defects that might affect the customers and exercise reasonable care in implementing services that, if defective, could harm the providers' customers.

Evolution of Contract and Tort Rules as to Goods

Until the mid-twentieth century, contract warranty rules were generally quite manufacturer-friendly because they substantially limited firms' exposure for harms caused by defective products (Gomulkiewicz et al. 2008). A manufacturer of goods could generally not be held liable for a defective product unless it had expressly warranted that its product would achieve some performance goal that it was later proven not to achieve (e.g., "I guarantee this car will go 150 mph"). A manufacturer could also insulate itself from liability by selling its goods through intermediaries (e.g., wholesalers and retailers) because old-fashioned contract law only extended protection to those who were "in privity" (that is, those who bought the goods directly from the manufacturer).

Even when manufacturers expressly warranted their products, contract law substantially limited the manufacturer's liability for defects. Breach of an express warranty allowed the customer to be compensated for the difference between the price the buyer actually paid for the goods (say, $1000) and the value of the goods actually received ($50 less because of the defect). Customers could not recover damages from the manufacturer for any lost productivity that may have been a consequence of the defective goods unless the customers had specially negotiated with the manufacturer to get consequential damages for breach of warranty.

Tort rules were similarly manufacturer-friendly until the mid-twentieth century (White 1980; Owen 2007). A defective product might cause physical injury to a person or to property, but liability for negligence depended on whether the firm being sued had failed to live up to a duty of care to the customer. As long as the manufacturer could show it had exercised some care in its design of the product, it would generally be free from liability. Buyers were also supposed to exercise care in inspecting the goods or otherwise investigating the manufacturer's reputation.   Tort privity rules often limited manufacturer liability for defective goods, for if the manufacturer did not sell directly to the end users, it would not be "in privity" with them, and hence owed them no duty of care.   Nor did manufacturers generally owe a duty of care to outsiders (e.g., a passenger injured in the owner's car) up until the second half of the twentieth century.

Manufacturers of goods thus had relatively little reason to worry that an injured customer would be able to hold it liable for injuries sustained as a result of defective products.   Consumer protection laws were rare until the mid-twentieth century, and mass media coverage was sufficiently limited in scope that firms had little reason to worry about bad publicity arising from harms caused by its   defective products.

By the mid-twentieth century, however, both contract and tort rules changed significantly.   "Privity" rules eroded, as courts recognized that direct sales between manufacturers and their customers were increasingly rare.   If the wholesale and retail outlets through which customers bought defective goods had made no changes to the products, but simply resold them to customers, judges were persuaded that it was fair to hold manufacturers responsible for harms that resulted from, for example, defective brakes in a car that caused a crash that severely injured the customer and his family.   It also made little sense to allow manufacturers to insulate themselves from liability simply by selling through intermediaries or to require end-users to sue retailers, who would then sue wholesalers, who would then sue the manufacturers for defects that caused injury.   Increasingly, courts also recognized that manufacturers were in a better position to manage the risk of defective products, either through more careful designs or through insurance, and so imposing a burden on them to avoid defects was socially desirable.

Probably the most significant mid-twentieth century contract law development was the widespread adoption in the 1960's of the Uniform Commercial Code (UCC) by state legislatures.   Article 2 of the UCC sets forth contract rules that regulate sales of goods.   Sec. 2-313 of Article 2, for instance, provides that "any affirmation of fact or promise made by the seller to the buyer which relates to the goods and becomes part of the basis of the bargain creates an express warranty that the goods shall conform to the affirmation or promise."   Descriptions of the goods, samples, and models of the goods were likewise deemed express warranties about the product's characteristics insofar as buyers relied upon them in contracting with the sellers.   It was thus unnecessary to use formal words such as "warrant" or "guarantee" to create an express warranty.

Even more significant were the implied warranty provisions of Article 2.   Sec. 2-314 provides that merchants who sell goods to the public impliedly warrant that the goods are of fair and average quality for goods of that kind and that they are fit for ordinary purposes for which such goods are used.   Moreover, when a seller has reason to know that a prospective buyer is relying on its expertise when purchasing goods for a particular purpose, Sec. 2-315 imposes on the transaction an implied warranty of fitness for a particular purpose.

While these provisions increase the potential liability of a manufacturer for defective goods, Sec. 2-316 gives sellers an opportunity to disclaim the implied warranties through use of expressions such as "as is" or "with all faults." Sellers also have the right under Article 2 to limit their liability for breach of warranty through proper contractual language, such as liquidated damages provisions (e.g., buyer agrees that remedies for breach will be limited to $100). Yet, Article 2 protects consumer interests by providing that if sellers limit their liability for breach of warranty so substantially as to cause the contract to fail of its essential purposes in protecting buyer as well as seller interests, the contractual limits will be ignored and all of the remedies that Article 2 normally provides for breach will apply.

The goal of Article 2 was to develop a balanced rule set from which buyers and sellers could know what default rules were, and to the extent they wished to deviate from them, they were free to do so, as long as the negotiated terms were consistent with general good faith obligations. Article 2 thus allows parties to manage their risks by how they configure their contracts.

The most significant mid-twentieth century development affecting manufacturers of goods in tort law was the widespread adoption by states of a strict liability in tort rule for makers of defective products that caused physical injury to persons or property (Owen 2007). No longer was liability dependent on whether a firm had exercised due care in designing its products; rather, manufacturers were held strictly liable for physical injuries caused by these defects. As with the stricter contract warranty rules, the strict liability in tort rules were regarded as important ways to induce manufacturers to invest in designing safe products, as they are in the best position to ensure product designs are safe. They are also better positioned than consumers to insure against injuries from defective products.

Contract and Tort Rules as to Services

Contract and tort rules affecting the provision of services are far less strict than comparable rules as to the provision of goods. There is, for example, no equivalent to Article 2 warranty rules for services. Warranties play little role in regulating services in part because it is more difficult to determine what baseline to use, as service providers do not typically make the kinds of objective statements about their services to customers akin to those that manufacturers routinely make about their products.

A hairdresser may promise her customer a stylish cut. A lawyer may promise her client that the will she drew up will achieve his objectives. An accountant may promise to file accurate tax returns. And a surgeon may promise to cut out a patient's tonsils or appendix. But none of these promises is really anything more than a promise to perform the service in a competent manner. Competence is then at the core of tort or contract rules for assessing liability for providing defective services (Geistfeld 2008). Customer satisfaction with services often depends on context; a hair cut may be experienced as stylish in part because of the smart salon in which the service is delivered. A client's satisfaction with professional services may likewise depend in part on the handsome office in which it is delivered, which may contribute to the client confidence in the professional.

From the standpoint of the law, a hair stylist, lawyer, accountant, surgeon or comparable service provider has a duty of care toward his or her customers only to perform the required service in a competent manner. Failure to live up to this duty of care that causes injury—a hair dresser's inadvertent gouging of her customer with scissors, a lawyer's failure to know of a certain state law inheritance rule, an accountant's mistake in calculating tax liability, a surgeon's neglect in leaving a sponge in the patient's wound—will result in liability for negligence.

There is also considerable variability among service providers and often no one standard way to provide a service. Indeed, until the emergence of automated self-service and computational services, whose inputs and outputs are standardized by design, variability in service delivery was perceived to be inevitable, and even desirable. Service providers often strived to "empower" their front-line employees to adapt services to each customer (Lashley 1995; Frei 2006). However, the variability of services contributes to difficulties in assessing service competence. Whether a particular haircut is stylish, for instance, may be a matter of taste. A particular lawyer may have interpreted a legal rule differently than another lawyer would have, but that doesn't necessarily mean the former interpretation is incompetent. An accountant may have taken an aggressive view of his client's eligibility for a deduction, but the fact that another accountant would have done otherwise does not necessarily make the aggressive accountant incompetent. Surgeons have to make difficult judgment calls quite frequently, and it may difficult to second-guess whether an alternative treatment, for instance, would have been successful.

Instead of product warranties akin to those provided by manufacturers of goods, service providers tend to promise customers a refund, discount, or future free service if they are not satisfied and sometimes an unconditional satisfaction guarantee (Hart 1988). Service satisfaction is often subjective, based on a gap between what the customer expected and then experienced with the service (Parasuraman et al. 1985). The exact same service may, in fact, be experienced differently by different customers. Consider the first class seat on an airplane with which one customer might be highly satisfied because she got an upgrade, while the customer sitting next to her might think of the same service as a disappointment compared with the private jet in which he was used to traveling.

Licensing of service providers is one common societal mechanism for ensuring a certain baseline of service quality. Hair stylists, lawyers, accountants, and surgeons are, for example, typically licensed by state authorities based on a demonstration that their training qualifies them for a license that is necessary to be a professional in their fields and/or by standardized examinations to demonstrate minimum levels of professional competence.

Reputation also plays a very important role in assuring certain levels of quality in the provision of services. Hotels, for instance, often seek to attract repeat customers by providing high quality service to frequent visitors. Bloomberg and Reuters, among others, have attained excellent reputations for providing high quality information services, and their competitive advantage over other firms depends on maintaining this quality. A BMW-endorsed motorcycle repair service is also more likely to draw customers than one that is not so endorsed, unless, of course, the latter attains a reputation for quality service that exceeds that provided by BMW-endorsed services. Service innovation often enhances the reputation of service innovators, and innovative firms may be able to recoup costs of these innovations by maintaining or extending their client bases based on reputational advantages derived from their innovations.

What Contract and Tort Rules Should Apply to Digital Information Services?

There is as yet some uncertainty about whether digital information services are or should be subject to the same kinds of contract and tort rules that have for decades governed the manufacture and sales of goods, those that govern the provision of services, or some yet-to-be-determined contract and tort rules. Two quick rules of thumb would predict, first, that the more deeply technological a digital information service is, the more likely it is the courts will use goods-like contract and tort rules, and second, the closer the service approximates or is adjunct to human-to-human services, the more likely it is that courts will apply contract and tort rules that have traditionally governed services. Yet, there is some reason to be optimistic that courts will, over time, develop rules that recognize digital information services as in need of some rules that are specially tailored to them.

The first digital information service to pose such questions was computer software. From the early 1980's, developers of software argued strenuously that computer programs are significantly different than manufactured goods—for example, because every program has "bugs" and so inevitably has defects that would be problematic under Article 2 and strict-liability-in-tort rules—and hence, they should be governed by relaxed contract and tort rules (Gomulkiewicz et al. 2008). Because the American Law Institute had already agreed to relax some rules for leases of goods by adopting Article 2A to govern them, software developers lobbied for a new Article 2B to govern licensing of computer programs.

For more than ten years, a drafting committee worked on a proposed law, which by the 1990's had expanded in scope as a model law to regulate all transactions involving computer information, which seemingly covers digital information services.[25] By 1998, proposed Article 2B had become quite controversial, in part because its rules were perceived to be too favorable to developers and inadequately protective of consumer interests. This, among other things, led to ALI's withdrawal as a sponsor of the project, and the reconstitution of the law as the Uniform Computer Information Transaction Act (UCITA).[26] UCITA was adopted in two states in the first year after its promulgation, but its drafters' ambition that it would become a uniform law for all such transactions was thwarted.

Notwithstanding the software developer arguments for somewhat looser contract rules, UCITA incorporated express and implied merchantability warranty rules that are substantially similar to Article 2 warranty rules.[27] UCITA applied looser rules, however, to warranties as to informational content. Merchants of computer information who collect, compile, process, provide, or transmit informational content warrant to their licensees only "that there is no inaccuracy in the informational content caused by the merchant's failure to perform with reasonable care."[28] No such warranty was created, however, if the informational content was published or if the person transmitting the information acted merely as a conduit of the information or provided no more than editorial services.[29] An information provider who had been paid for time and effort to supply information impliedly warranted under UCITA—unless adequately disclaimed—only "that the information will not fail to achieve the licensee's particular purpose as a result of the licensor's lack of reasonable effort."[30] Note that both of these warranties are essentially built on tort principles of due care and reasonable efforts, not the stricter contract rules that apply to defective goods.

One reason that UCITA did not fare well in the legislative arena was that it was over-ambitious in scope. It started out to be a law to regulate the licensing of software, but then morphed into a law that would regulate transactions of all kinds as to all kinds of computer information. Some groups that would have been affected by the law, such as the financial services and entertainment industries, asked to be excluded from its scope, but as different sectors asked for exclusions, UCITA lost the mantle of being a well-drafted comprehensive law and started to look like the product of special interest lobbying, which indeed it was becoming.[31]

In 2004, the ALI began a new project, more modest in scope, which aimed to articulate principles of software contracts. These principles should be useful to judges in applying contract law to software. Insofar as digital information services are software-implemented, the ALI principles are likely to apply to them

---

[25] Drafts and supporting materials on proposed Article 2B can be found at
http://www.law.upenn.edu/bll/archives/ulc/ulc.htm

[26] The full text of UCITA can be found at
http://www.law.upenn.edu/bll/archives/ulc/ucita/ucita200.htm.

[27] UCITA, secs. 402, 403.

[28] Id., sec. 404(a).

[29] Id., sec. 404(b).

[30] Id., sec. 405(a).

[31] UCITA, sec. 103(d)(list of exclusions).

(American Law Institute 2008). These principles adopt Article 2-like express and implied merchantability warranties, but create a new implied warranty that the software contains no material hidden defect of which the developer was aware at the time it transferred the software to its customers.[32]

The development of these principles signals a new receptivity among lawyers to the idea that the current economic environment is more complicated than the bifurcation of "goods" vs. "services" vis-à-vis contract and tort rules that prevailed in the twentieth century. Digital information services are often hybrids, with some technology elements and some service elements. Some digital information services are clearly more like traditional services than they are like traditional goods. This is especially true as to services that are customized for particular customers or that provide back-end support for services provided to individuals, such as hotel service databases or online reservation systems. Machine-to-machine web   services or other embedded software-implemented services, such as avionics support, are more like goods.

One policy option is to treat the more service-intensive digital information services the way services have been treated, and the more technologically-intensive services like goods have been treated. Another policy option is to recognize that digital information services deserve recognition as sui generis (of its own kind) phenomena to which contract and tort rules need to be adapted, rather than trying to fit them into pre-existing bins.

Conclusion

This chapter has provided an overview of some legal rules affecting innovations in important sectors of the economy. Intellectual property protections have often been very important to development of innovative technologies. Without such protections, the risks have seemed high that investments in innovation would be less than is socially optimal. Services have rarely been protected by patent or copyright laws, although some back-end activities of service providers could be maintained as trade secrets and trademarks have been important to denote quality in service provision. While 1998-2008 was a decade in which patents began to issue for innovations in services, more recent developments have called into question the patentability of service innovations. There is, in any event, a dearth of empirical data to support either extending or denying patent protection to service innovation.

This chapter has also explained that contract and tort rules have evolved over time to provide protections to victims who suffer losses as a result of defective products. The law has been much stricter about defective products, particularly those that cause physical injury to persons or property, than about defective ser-

---

[32] Id., sec. 3.05.

vices, in part because it is generally easier to detect when a product is defective than when a service is. It remains to be seen whether the law will evolve new types of contract and tort rules to be applied to digital information services or whether courts will continue to apply either "goods" or "services" rules, depending on whether the digital information service is more like one or the other. At this point, it does not appear that liability risks are so severe that innovative designers of digital information services are under-investing in innovation, nor are the rules so weak that digital information services are seriously defective. So perhaps the right policy balance for contract and tort rules has been or soon will be found.

References

Alces, P. (1999). W(h)ither warranty: the b(l)oom of products liability theory in cases of deficient software design, *California Law Review*, 87(1): 269-304.

American Law Institute (2008). *Principles of the Law of Software Contracts*, Tentative Draft, No. 1.

Bitner, M.J., Ostrom, A., and Morgan, F. (2008). Service Blueprinting: A Practical Technique for Service Innovation. *California Management Review*, 50(3): 66-94.

Bittner, M.J., Brown, S., and Meuter, M. (2000). Technology infusion in service encounters, *Journal of the Academy of Marketing Science*, 28(1): 139-49.

Cohen, S. (2007). Ontology and taxonomy of services in a service-oriented architecture, *Microsoft Architecture Journal*, April 2007.

Frei, Frances X. (2006). Breaking the trade-off between efficiency and service. *Harvard Business Review*, 84(11): 93-101.

Geistfeld, M. A. (2008). *Essentials of Tort Law*, Aspen Publishers, New York.

Glushko, R.J. & Tabas, L. (2009). Designing service systems by bridging the "front stage" and "back stage," *Information Systems and E-Business Management*, 7 (in press).

Gomulkiewicz, R., Nguyen, X.T., Conway-Jones, D. (2008). *Licensing Intellectual Property: Law and Applications*, Aspen Publishers, New York.

Graham, S.J., Merges, R.P., Samuelson, P., and Sichelman, T. (in press). High Tech Entrepreneurs and the Patent System: Results of the 2008 Berkeley Survey. *Berkeley Technology Law Journal*.

Hart, C.W.L. (1988). The power of unconditional service guarantees. *Harvard Business Review*, 66(4): 54-62.

Lashley, C. (1995). Toward an understanding of employee empowerment in hospitality services. *International Journal of Contemporary Hospital Management*, 7(1): 27-32.

Lerner, J. and Zhu, F. (2005). What is the impact of software patent shifts?: evidence from Lotus v. Borland, *Nat'l Bureau of Economic Research Working Paper No. 11168*.

Lusch, R.F., Vargo, S.L. and Wessels, G. (2008). Toward a conceptual foundation for service science: contributions from service-dominant logic. *IBM Systems Journal: Service Science, Management, and Engineering*, 7: 20-41.

Mann, R. (2005). Do Patents Facilitate Financing in the Software Industry? *Texas Law Review*, 83(4): 961-986.

O'Rourke, M. (2006). The story of Diamond v. Diehr: toward patenting software, in Jane C. Ginsburg and Rochelle Cooper Dreyfuss (eds.), *Intellectual Property Stories*, Foundation Press, New York.

Owen, D.G. (2007). The evolution of products liability law, *Review of Litigation*, 26: 955-989.

Parasuraman, A., Zeithaml, V., and Berry, L.L. (1985). A conceptual model of service quality and its implications for further research. *Journal of Marketing*, 49(4): 41-50.

Pollack, M. (2002). The multiple unconstitutionality of business method patents, *Rutgers Computer & Technology Law Journal*, 28(1): 61-120.

Samuelson, P. (1990). Benson revisited: the case against patent protection for algorithms and other computer program-related inventions, *Emory Law Journal*, 39(4): 1025-1154.

Samuelson, P. (1984). CONTU revisited: the case against copyright protection for computer programs in machine-readable form, *Duke Law Journal*, 1984(4): 663-769.

Samuelson, P. and Graham, S. (2010). Software entrepreneurs and the patent system: Some results of the Berkeley Patent Survey, work in progress

Samuelson, P. (2007). Why Copyright Excludes Systems and Processes From the Scope of Its Protection, *Texas Law Review*, 85(7): 1921-1977.

Spath, D., Ganz, W., Meiren, T., and Bienzeisler, B. (2008). Service Engineering—A Transdisciplinary Approach in Service Research, in Bernd Stauss, Kai Engelman, Anja Kremer, and Achim Lund (eds.), *Services Science Fundamentals, Challenges and Future Developments*, 41-53. Springer, Berlin Heidelberg New York.

Triplett, J.E. and Bosworth, B.P. (2004). *Productivity in the U.S. Services Sector: New Sources of Economic Growth*, Brookings Institution Press, Washington D.C.

White, G.E. (2003). *Tort Law in America: An Intellectual History*, Oxford University Press, New York.

Part 7
Future

The Future of Service Is Long Overdue

Evert Gummesson

Stockholm University School of Business, Sweden

How can the future be overdue; it isn't there yet? Or is it? The chapter lays bare select issues concerning service systems and an emerging service science. What happens now in service should have happened long ago. But why complain now that things start picking up? I do it to emphasize that we need to unfold mental blindfolds and be less conservative, ritualistic and bureaucratic. We need to see things in a productive light and a contemporary context and to act accordingly.

The chapter offers a travel account from service management to service science. The itinerary includes scheduled stops in areas where I am particularly engaged: the service sector as witchcraft rather than science; the urgency to include complexity, context and change in scientific models and university education; the usefulness of case study research and network theory in handling complexity; the broadening of the service encounter to a general approach of the co-creation of value; and it ends with a summary.

What are we waiting for? The future? No need; we are already deep into it.

From Service Management to Service Science

Everybody keeps telling me that everything is developing faster and faster and faster. Genetic engineering and information technology are frequently cited to "prove" this. "Developing" has the connotation of "good", meaning that everything is improving faster and faster and faster. It's time that somebody says that it is not – with some exceptions. Many things may be changing faster and faster and faster but not getting better and better and better, just getting different.

When this is written, times are far less normal than normal. A financial meltdown hit the world in 2008, showing that financial systems, market systems, health care systems, legal systems, energy systems, political systems, and social systems lack in efficiency, direction and human considerations. In other words: they don't deliver the service we want.

We need to be more open-minded, innovative and entrepreneurial in academic research and education as well as in business and government practice. We have to

P.P. Maglio et al. (eds.), *Handbook of Service Science*, Service Science: Research and Innovations in the Service Economy, DOI 10.1007/978-1-4419-1628-0_27,
© Springer Science+Business Media, LLC 2010

be down to earth and engage in what creates value in life, with consideration of all stakeholders in society: customers (the 55+, too, and not just the 55-), suppliers, citizens, employees, shareholders, and others.

There are far too many fools and crooks in science, business and politics. There are also "jay customers", those who cross the street at the wrong place and in general spoil the co-creation of service (Lovelock and Wirtz 2007, p. 250). It is not all darkness and nightmares, though. There are great people who do great things. There is sustainable business and public action in many areas and there is a lot of will to set things right in service research, education and practice. In a constructive but realistic spirit: Service systems have a great potential for improvements.

Service research took off in the 1970s and had its heydays in the 1980s mainly because a backlog of extant knowledge had to be documented, conceptualized and disseminated. The growth of publications, conferences and courses was fast but I felt mounting frustration with the academic contributions. Some ideas were so heavily promoted through "top journals" that other contributions were held back. I do not entirely blame the authors and the journals; the readers could equally well be blamed for mainstreamism and lack of integrity and reflection. It was co-creation but not necessarily of value. We still suffer from this; most service marketing textbooks are still carrying a backpack of 1980s mythology.

Research and much of practice in service marketing has not been characterized by a service-dominant logic but by a "survey-dominant logic" focused on various indicators and scales of customer satisfaction. This logic is based on limiting assumptions, simplifications, statistical conjecture, numbers, decimals, averages, distributions, probabilities, and indices offering pseudo-precision of fragments but little synthesis and contributions to theory. The "survey-dominant logic" became popular because of its alleged scientific qualities. There is also convenience; surveys fit academic course formats, journal review processes, and tenure systems for professors. Surveys can provide specific data to research in certain instances and be useful in consulting assignments but the contributions to general knowledge have been limited. Generally valid knowledge could more effectively be extracted from systematic case study research and the researchers' experiences as consumers, citizens and employees.

I wrote a book chapter which was also published in a journal; it won the best article of the year award (Gummesson 1991). It was not an academic top journal but a practitioner journal and therefore rarely quoted by academics. There I claimed that "…all organizations produce and sell both goods and services but in varying proportions and that the customer is buying utility and need satisfaction, not goods and services as such." This was not the first time I said this and others had said it as well. Wyckham et al. said it in 1975 but nobody really took notice. I further claimed that computer software quality was a juvenile delinquent. It still is, and that is one reason for service science to offer a fresh approach to service systems development.

I have emphasized this because there is snobbism and ritualism in academic research and publishing which severely slows down progress and distorts priorities. We can't afford that. And why should we?

In 1993 Fisk et al. concluded that service research was now walking erect after having crawled out (pre-1980) and scurried about (1980-1985). It was an informed account which not only considered US research but also international contributions. It seemed logical in its contemporary context.

What led to what is hard to tell but service research and business-to-business marketing (B2B) showed growing interest in *relationships, networks* and *interaction*. This opened a new door to the secret service chambers and broadened our view. It offered a partly parallel track to the ongoing service management research. I found it compelling and focused my research in the relationship direction.

Through personal experience we have an intuitive idea about what private and commercial relationships are. When relationships involve more than two people or organizations, complex patterns quickly emerge and we get networks of relationships. What happens in relationships is called interaction. Relationship marketing, CRM (customer relationship management) and one-to-one marketing are the best known approaches that came out of it.

I define relationship marketing as follows (Gummesson 2008a): "Relationship marketing is interaction in networks of relationships." This definition is broader and more generic than other definitions with the purpose of catching the essence of marketing, its DNA. In the same source I define CRM in this way (Gummesson 2008a): "CRM is the values and strategies of relationship marketing – with emphasis on the dyadic customer-supplier relationship – turned into practical application and dependent both on human action and information technology." Although CRM is too often associated with computer software, I am very "pushy" about CRM being a "tech & touch" issue. There is the expression high tech/high touch (Naisbitt 1982) but I am prone to see a two by two matrix as more valid, adding high tech/low touch, low tech/high touch and low tech/low touch. These combinations will be exemplified later in the chapter. For further on relationship marketing and CRM and their link to service, see Storbacka and Lehtinen (2001); Payne and Frow (2005); Grönroos (2007a, 2007b); Mele (2007); and Quero (2007).

In the real world the two-party supplier-customer relationship, the dyad, is inadequate as we live in complex systems. This view is acknowledged in service-dominant (S-D) logic and its Premise No. 9 (Vargo and Lusch 2008) saying that "... the context of value creation is networks of networks (resource integrators)." I have used the concept of one-to-one marketing to contrast the network complexity by defining the expression many-to-many marketing (Gummesson 2009): "Many-to-many marketing describes, analyzes and utilizes the network properties of marketing." For recent exposés of network approaches, see Kohlbacher (2007) and Wilkinson (2008).

The Nordic School, which is an informal community of researchers, educators, consultants and practitioners from Northern Europe, has made itself known through contributions to service and relationship marketing and management (Fisk et al. 2000; Grönroos 2006). So far relationships and interaction have been its prime target, but now it is time to take the next step to networks, many-to-many.

In revising my book *Total Relationship Marketing* for a third edition (Gummesson 2008a), I made an effort to integrate S-D logic and an emerging service science with my approach. The book addresses relationship marketing in a more holistic way than is common. Instead of just discussing one straightforward customer-supplier relationship, its core embraces thirty relationships, the 30Rs. They are a combination of relationships between parties and properties of relationships, which I have found exist in business practice and theory. This is an antecedent to a more focused many-to-many network theory. For a brief discourse of how marketing is adapting to the new developments, see Ballantyne and Varey (2008).

A Man on the Moon Is Fine but Now It's Time to Put Service on Earth!

In the 1960s space race between the USA and the Soviet Union President Kennedy defined a clear goal: *Put a man on the moon!* A grand vision was necessary to make things happen; incremental technological progress did not have enough momentum, direction, and resources. As we know, the goal was fulfilled and in 1969 Neil Armstrong put his left foot down on the moon and declared: "That's one small step for man, one giant leap for mankind." Despite walking erect in the 1990s, service has not yet become rocket science. It's therefore time that somebody with presidential-like power and charisma sets the goal and gives the order: *Put service on earth!* It's high time to take a giant service leap for mankind.

Although not phrased in this way, in 2004 a vision emerged from two directions, one from academe with the *Journal of Marketing* as the power and charisma platform, and one from industry, with the power and charisma of IBM. Two service babies were born in two different families: S-D logic and service science.

Other chapters of this book lay out the content of service science and S-D logic, but allow me to establish a few statements that form my personal "forward-to-basics" vantage point. Service science is a long term program to build a solid base for a future IBM as a provider of better service systems and for the improvement of systems in society in general. It addressed schools of technology and their research and education and found that service was not on the agenda despite the service sector being considered the driver of economic growth. It was in business schools, though. S-D logic made a synthesis of the viable parts of service research that had been on the agenda since the late 1970s at business schools. Contributions were found under the labels of service management, services marketing, service quality, and service operations.

The parents of the two babies found a common playground and the babies became buddies. S-D logic is now the philosophy and overriding theory; the service science program is an instrument for implementation (Maglio and Spohrer 2008; Spohrer and Maglio 2009). But a third baby representing methodology is necessary. I have concluded that two basic research approaches are superior in helping us understand a complex reality and take action. These are network theory and case study research. They will be referred to throughout the chapter.

In the midst of an ongoing change, it is hard to discern and predict if it is just a temporary, cyclical change or whether the tipping point, the quantum leap, the discontinuity and the paradigm shift are taking over the stage. Experts did not predict the sudden scrapping of the Soviet Iron Curtain and the Berlin Wall in the late 1980s. In 2007 few experts sensed the gathering financial storm that showed its ugly face in the fall of 2008. Local Thai elephants and snakes with no college education understood that the tsunami was coming and fled to the mountain tops. At the same time Western tourists, many with a college degree, ran down from the mountains to take pictures of the "great wave" with their cellphones. How clever are we really? Low tech/high touch won over high tech/low touch. So what is useful knowledge that creates value and what is not?

The Service Sector: A Category of the Past Cannot Guide Us into the Future

S-D logic and service science liberate us from the historical, supplier-centric goods/services divide and we can concentrate on the value of the output. On the supply side value is a financial concept; value-added is calculated as cost-added and value-in-exchange refers to price. On the customer side, value means value-in-use, service (see further Ravald 2008).

To make research and practice manageable we put phenomena with similar properties into categories. These categories had better be good and they have to change with the times or they become mental terrorists. The description of economies first brought up farming and subdivided it into fishing, hunting, forestry, and so on. Then came mines and gradually manufacturing. In the 19th century and the first half of the 20th century, the two major economic sectors were agriculture and industry. What did not fit in there was dumped in a bin with miscellaneous content called residuals, invisibles or intangibles, much like all types of waste were mixed in the same garbage can before sorting became common. The garbage can was later named the service sector.

Services were analyzed at great length by Adam Smith (1723-1790) and probably by others before him. They were declared non-productive by Karl Marx and communism, and capitalist economies more or less pretended they did not exist (see further Delaunay and Gadrey 1992). Services did not become part of management and marketing studies and raise a critical mass of researchers until the late 1970s. How differently service and services are perceived is shown in Edvardsson et al. (2005).

But times change and in the Western world the service bin now contains 80 to 90 per cent of all employees and 100 per cent of all new jobs. When everything is dumped in one category it does not discriminates any more. Especially so when a category is fuzzy, sloppily defined and made up of diverse phenomena, and when manufactured goods, agricultural produce and what we call services through historical convention constitute inseparable combinations of what people buy. The official economic categories of today look more like the ruins of old cities. They are great for historians and archeologists and tourists come and take pictures and buy ice-cream and T-shirts. How come politicians and professors fall for this? As long as they stick to the intersubjectively approved mythology, they seem to be safe. Some of the more common myths which are currently offered in almost every textbook and service course include:

- Services are intangible, heterogeneous, inseparable and perishable. This has been shown not to be well-grounded; see Lovelock and Gummesson (2004), Vargo and Lusch (2004) and Gummesson (2007a).
- Service quality is difficult whereas goods quality is easy. This is built on the obsolete idea that goods are manufactured in standardized components by easily controlled machines whereas services are handmade by erratic human beings. Close to this is the equally obsolete claim that manufacturing requires heavy investment whereas services do not.
- Services marketing and goods marketing are two different things. Not any more; it's all marketing of value propositions.
- Scales are presented that range from pure goods to pure service. They may sound compelling but it is not obvious how this can be turned into strategies and action. One "continuum" puts clothing on the pure goods side and a visit to your shrink on the pure service side. However, clothing is surrounded by service, not least through retailing, fashion shows and the magic of branding; and the remedy against psychic disorders is to a large extent the psychiatrist's prescription of manufactured pills.
- The service sector is growing and the manufacturing and agricultural sectors are shrinking. Then consider that we
  - never had so much goods and so much product waste;
  - never had so much food and were never so overweight – but at the same time undernourished; and
  - lack basic service: health care for everyone, affordable elder care, good schools, working legal systems, and so on.

The special case of a service sector is now the universal case – still treated in the bulk of literature and education as a special case. Consider this analysis of new jobs and the interdependence between goods and services and the manufacturing and service sectors:

In the early 2000s the housing boom in the US created a million new jobs subdivided between construction, building supplies, real estate and mortgage brokers, furniture and appliance manufacturing and distribution, home-supply stores, architects and interior designers. Simultaneously the information technology bust lay off even more people. New jobs also came from health care service, but few from producers of pharmaceuticals and none from the medical equipment and supplies industry. Between 2001 and 2006 US health care added 1.7 million new jobs subdivided between private and government hospitals, physicians' offices, nursing facilities, health insurers, and diagnostic labs. The rest of the private service sector added none. The government sector (except hospitals) added 700,000 jobs of which over half a million were in education. (Based on Mandel 2006)

These dramatic changes in the economic sub-sectors are not visible in aggregated statistics. To say that the service sector contributed all the new jobs is meaningless as changes up and down were caused by a few of its sub-sectors.

My proposition is that we scrap the "service sector" and instead "call a spade a spade" as the old saying goes. We can talk about restaurants, today classified as services although their core consists of agricultural goods and manufacturing in factories and the restaurant kitchen. We can then talk about different types of restaurants and we can add the neighboring cases where, for example, your lunch can be picked up on the shelf in a supermarket and be eaten on a bench in the park. We can talk about health care but not in general; there is too much diversity and little commonality between many of its numerous pieces.

Complexity, Context and Change – Three Cs in Need of Case Study Research and Network Theory

An overriding issue for social sciences today should be the understanding of complex systems and their human, social, technological and environmental dimensions. We need to apply methods and techniques that support this understanding. I have only found two that can be used in social sciences and handle real world complexity and scientific requirements: *case study research* and *network theory*. I have found them the most advanced, comprehensive, and useful tools for addressing the new concept of service. This chapter does not go into detail of the two approaches, their philosophies and techniques but examples of applications will be given. For a discussion and comparison, see Gummesson (2007b).

The noun complexity stems from the Latin *complexus* meaning "network" accompanied by the verb *complecti* meaning "to twine together". The word "system" is derived from the Greek *systema*, meaning "a whole composed of many parts". "Context" comes from Latin *contexere*, "to join together".

These words and several others, like "ecology" and "holism", obviously belong to the same family. I will use the word system in its generic and general sense, for example "service system", but let networks through network theory and case study research be the basis for analysis and discussion.

Services (pre S-D logic) are described as activities, processes or chains. This is very well but for one aspect. It does not recognize the enormous complexity and non-linearity; life does not consist of a few well-defined factors that can be arranged in a straight sequence. Service (in the S-D logic format) is neither an activity, nor a process, nor a chain – it consists of value-creating networks.

What is a complex system? Complex systems may be mistaken for mundane and taken for granted when they work well and we find that unskilled employees can operate them. We may not realize that these "simple" people tacitly get lots of activities and things together and that they are adaptable to the situation. Even the simplest systems, like getting a ticket to the subway, have elements of complexity, especially so for the co-creating customer and before he or she has learnt the system:

> I stepped down into the Milan (Italy) Metropolitana subway one summer evening to travel to a meeting with a friend. The departing station was called Centrale and I had been instructed to take the green line a few stops to Moscova. Piece of cake. But first I had to buy a ticket in a machine. I had travelled the Milan subway for the first time two years before. When I then looked lost a gentleman in a Prada suit (or was it Gucci?) carrying a smart briefcase and buying a ticket realized my predicament and showed me how to do it. I had tried to read the instructions in Italian, a language I don't know but thought I might be able to decipher enough to get a ticket. Vain hope. This time I started out with self-confidence: "Metropolitana, here I come!" But no; the ticketing system had changed. I did not get through and a young student, from Albania it turned out, showed me. What the instruction did not tell was that you had to press one of the buttons not just once but twice. I got my ticket. Next time, if they don't change the system, it may be simple now that I know its logic and idiosyncrasies. Does it matter to the Milanese people? Perhaps not, but Milan has millions of visitors each year. It's the industrial hub of Northern Italy, it's a fashion capital, and La Scala is the world most famous opera.

A ticket machine is low touch with elements of high tech and low tech. It was probably time-consuming, messy and costly to get the decision to go automatic and to design, build and install the machines. They replaced hundreds, perhaps thousands of people which probably met with trade union resistance and meant organizational and cultural change. It required new roles in co-creation. It required new software to make the new service system work. Change will continue to occur, triggered by technology, new systems ideas, political disputes about fair fares, and so on.

The subway case shows that even simple service is complex. As a young hitchhiker in postwar Germany I learnt the old saying "Why make it simple when it can be made so beautifully complicated." It was a joke about ivory tower academics and their lofty language and theories. For pragmatic scientists and dedicated practitioners it should be the other way around, to find the soul of a service and turn a complex function into something which is manageable for users. Complexity and simplicity go hand-in-hand; they are yin and yang.

A ticket machine offers a quick way of paying. Still it turns out to be difficult to design its plastic, tin, paper, instructions, and digits and make them work harmoniously together. Ticketing is a necessary overture to the real opera, the subway transport system. The complexity of getting all trains and rails and platforms and wires together and working in interaction with thousands of passengers every minute is mind-boggling.

We now turn to health care. Its service has enormous impact on our lives and well-being. Health care can be straightforward and effective but medical knowledge is limited. Despite the fact that health care is a most obvious case of co-creation of service, it is still approached as if doctors do something to patients and patients get well, doctors being operant resources and customers being operated on, thus being passive resources. Sometimes health care functions well, even achieves "miracles" like a heart transplant after which the patient can live a good life, let be within some restrictions. Health care is the number one headache for many governments and citizens around the world. There is no painkiller even if the reorganization pill, the more money pill, the more research pill, the more doctors pill, the more equipment pill, and the smoother logistics pill are continually being prescribed. In Europe the cost of health care is 7-10 percent of the GNP; in the US 16 percent (Kotler et al. 2008, p. 49). Health care is not a coherent and reliable service system although some of its subsystems and components may work well. More realistically the health care system is a deficient, problem-ridden pseudo system.

Doctors and nurses and other health care staff are bunched together with fast food restaurant burger flippers, lawyers, subway cleaners, opera singers, and marine soldiers into a supra category called the service sector. It is blatantly meaningless. Even its subsector "health care" is a monstrosity. It is huge and diverse, anything from prescribing a painkiller to eight hour trauma surgery after a traffic accident with recurrent need for treatment and perhaps lifelong suffering. There are thousands of service systems within the health care span. Here is a case to exemplify its complexity and network dimensions:

82 year old Anna has 23 diagnosed and age-related disorders including chronic fatigue, pain, memory loss, and reduced eyesight and hearing. She is not the odd case. With people living longer follows more health problems and the senior citizens already use up the major share of hospital resources. Anna has been through 11 different therapies encompassing 41 components. During one year she was exposed to 7 types of therapies performed by 55 specialists. From 5 doctors she has been prescribed 9 types of medication to be consumed daily, and 2 to be used on demand. She goes to massage and physical exercise, and twice a week a social assistant comes to her home to help. The assistants typically stay short periods on their job and others fill in when the regular assistant has a cold or is on vacation. It is impossible for Anna to establish a personal and trusting relationship with any of them, the very service that may be of most value to her. She is also dependent on social insurance people – who also come and go. During a year she is perhaps in contact with 70 different health care representatives plus tens of others like ambulance and taxi drivers, receptionists, and pharmacists, say, 100 in all. Anna has no family but neighbors and friends sometimes give her a hand.

To get 23 disorders, 9+2 pills and 100 people together to co-create some kind of value and service requires advanced project and network management. To become such a manager you need 1. training; 2. practice; 3. ability to keep many balls in the air; and 4. excellent health and tons of energy. Anna hasn't got any of it. What kind of service, service system and value does this represent? To be blunt: the service system is a bureaucratic and professional disaster. Yet it is representative of present-day eldercare service systems.

One consolation is that Anna lives in a country, Sweden, where health care is a citizen's right and is essentially free. Who would be able to pay for it all anyway, year after year, except perhaps Bill Gates and Warren Buffet. In Sweden health is still primarily a domain for doctors and nurses but increasingly for politicians, administrators and financiers; lawyers and insurance companies have not [yet] taken charge. (Based on Akner 2004)

To understand Anna's need for service and how to co-create value-in-use we have to describe and analyze her complex situation with empathy and in great detail. Case study research and network theory can do that; surveys can not. All service appears in the context of service systems. The two cases – the subway ticketing service and the health care service – show very different contexts and different degrees of complexity. In Anna's context the varying standard of the professionals' skills, their personalities and mood swings come in, too, and the nodes and links of Anna's network keep changing, not all the time but some of the time.

Co-Creation of Value: The Service Encounter Expanded

In its orthodox version in service management and marketing, the service encounter refers to face-to-face interaction between a service provider's front line personnel and a customer. It builds on the notion that services are produced, delivered and consumed during this interaction. This is, however, a special case, but it is erroneously treated as the general case. I have previously described the service encounter in the broadened context of the supplier-customer interaction; customers interacting between themselves (customer-to-customer, C2C) during a service delivery; interaction with the servicescape and its physical objects; and interaction with the overriding service system. The service system further includes internal encounters between the frontline, back office and management, as well as encounters with the environment of society in general, its infrastructure, and the market competition.

S-D logic has broadened the service encounter to all aspects of co-creation of value and all aspects of value propositions, and so has service science. It is necessary to understand that co-creation is not just interaction in a service encounter. In designing value propositions the following questions therefore must be answered:

- Who are the customers and who are the suppliers?
- What do suppliers do best?
- What do customers do best?
- What do third parties do best?
- What should be one-party (individual) action?
- What should be two-party (dyadic) interaction?
- What should be multiparty (network) interaction?
- What should be C2C interaction?

- What should be face-to-face interaction, ear-to-ear interaction, email interaction, Internet interaction, cellphone text messaging, and interaction with automatic machines?
- What do human beings do best?
- What does technology do best?
- Is there a no-man's land where service is neglected?

In the new service logic the customer and supplier roles have merged, although they perform different tasks. The following categories of suppliers are found in the market:

- business enterprises
- governments on a national, regional and local level and increasingly on a mega, supra-national level, such as the EU
- NGOs and voluntary organizations which arise where the first two have failed, or act as supplementary to them.

In B2B, the suppliers are also customers; it is both a value-in-exchange and a value-in-use situation, better described as value-in-context (Vargo et al. 2008). In B2C we find

- consumers
- citizens

They are traditionally referred to as end-users. In many-to-many the roles have broadened from a single individual consumer to social networks of family, friends, neighbors, and others. Being citizen goes beyond the commercial consumer role; a citizen has certain rights and should primarily be served by the government sector. In the new logic with co-creation as a foundational premise, consumers and citizens are also suppliers through value-in-use and can take initiatives. The traditional acronym B2C had better be supplemented by C2B, or be replaced by B2C/C2B.

The following case illustrates many of the co-creation dimensions discussed above. It stresses ideas of S-D logic and service science systems but also those of a network and case approach. Here is "The Cold Case":

> On a Friday night our freezer went dead. A crisis was in the making. We discovered it by coincidence; the freezer did not tell us, its service quietly expired. There was no alarm. Why not, Electrolux? I would have liked a voice to say: "Hi, my name is Hans and I am the CEO of Electrolux. I'm sorry to inform you that your freezer has given up. If you look on the bright side of life, your freezer has served you impeccably for 25 years and 134 days, far longer than can be expected. I am sure you would like to buy a new one quickly. To do so, look at our product line on www.electrolux.se. To make sure you don't miss this alert, I will also send this as an email and a text message on your cellphone." This is what CRM systems are about, isn't it? Or wouldn't it work in practice? There was no co-creation effort on the supplier side at this critical stage.

What do you do? You can leave it and let the insurance cover as much as possible. Still you need to get the freezer out of the house before its content starts smelling, which would be Saturday afternoon. Considering the age of the freezer, repairing it was no option. It seemed better to save the food, especially as much of it was home-made from natural ingredients and could not be replaced in the supermarket. But the salvage had to occur within the next few hours.

We squeezed some of the food into our smaller freezer and then explored other sources of assistance, starting with the closest neighbors. Dagmar, the old lady living across the street, took some. We walked over to two more neighbors, a family of four who had an extra freezer in their garage, and to Gunnar and Ingrid two houses away. Still there was food left. Some of the other houses in the immediate neighborhood were dark and in some we did not feel that our relationship to the people was intimate enough to ask for this kind of help. I phoned our daughter in the city and drove for 15 minutes to her home.

This was of course an unexpected and annoying situation. There was no script but immediate action was called for. We could not handle the situation by ourselves and social skills and the cooperation of others had to be activated. It embraced 10 people in a family, friends and neighbors network. Their nodes and links formed a temporary service system with my wife and me as the hub and project managers. So far, it's all happening on the customer and citizen side and there is not yet a supplier in sight. It's C2C interaction for the co-creation of value.

B2C, or rather C2B interaction commenced on Saturday morning. My wife went on the Internet to find the type of freezer we needed and a retailer who could deliver it. Electrolux had one in its product line that seemed adequate, and it could be viewed and read about on its website. After comparing value propositions we placed our order. The comparison encompassed the manufacturers' product specifications in a number of dimensions and the retailers' price including transport, installation, and removal of the old freezer.

"Electrolux delivers to us on Wednesdays," the retailer declared. "We can deliver next Thursday." We had now merged two networks, the C2C social network of family and neighbors, and a commercial retailer and manufacturer network on the supplier side; B2C/C2B interaction was brought in. We had to ask our C2C network to keep the food until Thursday. As "network captains" we spent time on the delivery and we were forced to do so. Basically it was aggravating but it also had a sunny side with friendly people helping each other.

Checking the physical quality of the freezer was not possible although the service literature is full of statements like "the customer can easily assess the quality of physical goods because they are tangible but not services because they are intangible." It claims that this is a difference between goods and services. It is not. You can only check if the specification is met by the physical product as to certain apparent variables such as size. Only in hindsight did we know the quality of the previous freezer.

On Wednesday the retailer phoned and said that Electrolux could not deliver this week so it would have to wait until Thursday next week. The delivery time has now doubled to two weeks. New contact with the neighbors and our daughter. The transport firm arrived on Thursday and became the third member of our B2C/C2B network. They took the old freezer from the basement and brought in the new one. It was heavy work carrying the freezer downstairs and through narrow doorways. When they unwrapped the freezer we found three big holes in its front. They had to wrap it again. "See you next Thursday," they said. Next Thursday the transport firm came back and finally plugged it in. Three weeks had passed. We began to recover our food, starting on the Friday. But Gunnar and Ingrid had left for their country house to be back on Tuesday, and Dagmar was gone until Sunday night. Before all the food was back in place, about four weeks had passed since the old "servant" gave up. (Based on Gummesson 2008b)

During the Cold Case experience – some in marketing claim that *experiences* are what we *really* buy – we had initiated C2C, B2C/C2B, and B2B networks. It is obvious that each of these networks is contextually conceived but they are interdependent in the moulding of the value proposition and its actualization (Gummesson and Polese 2009). We started out with our social network and then activated a commercial network, first many-headed but then reduced to three-headed during the search process: Electrolux, the retailer and the transport firm. The complete network is shown in Figure 1.

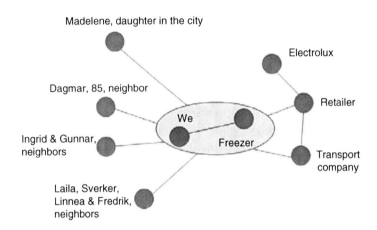

Figure 1. The Cold Case network (from Gummesson 2008b, used with permission).

However, complexity does not end here. Each node is embedded in yet other networks. In principle, networks are scale-free, meaning that they are infinite unless restrictions are imposed on them. Therefore a truer image of many-to-many networks is shown in Figure 2 where the nodes are indicated as networks on a deeper level. We do not live in one single system at a time; we constantly interact in networks of networks which consist of numerous systems. Some of these function well most of the time; some are erratic and become stressful to the user; and some seem to have malfunctioning as its mission and no improvements can be discerned over the last decades. Even if the description and analysis of the Cold Case does not penetrate the deeper layers of networks it is far more realistic then what is shown in the service, relationship marketing and CRM literature, not to talk about the mainstream marketing management and consumer behavior literature. To add to the high tech aspect, even the freezer is a node in a larger network, the electricity grid. It connects electricity suppliers from increasingly more places; the molecules must speak many languages to each other. We are repeatedly told that we are globally connected, even that we live in a global village. With the new information technology this has become part of our everyday lives. We do not live in a simple world; it's becoming increasingly complex. We are part of a systemic whole, but yet service systems are fragmented and many are better characterized by *holes* than by *wholes*.

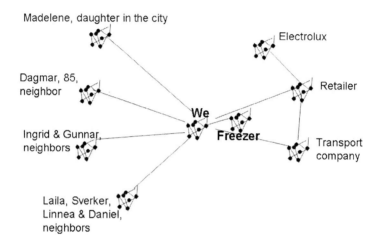

Figure 2. The Cold Case network expanded. (from Gummesson 2008b, used with permission).

What was the value proposition, who did what in the co-creation process, how efficient was the service system and for whom was it meant to be efficient? What was demanded of the customer in the value-in-use process? The proposition consisted of goods, services, information, knowledge, software and what have you. It was C2C, C2B/B2C, and B2B. It merged the manufacturing and service sectors (as defined in conventional economic analysis). It built a temporary network from a more permanent network and initiated interaction, many-to-many. It requires balanced centricity; each member of the network should get something out of it – the commercial side money, the social side investment in continued good relations and the possibility to get help when needed. It shows complexity, context and change.

From Service Management to Service Science: Last Words – For Now

A selection of service issues have been treated in this chapter. Here is a condensation of the chapter's main messages:

- Despite all the courses and conferences for academics and practitioners, in business enterprises as well as in government organizations, it is not easy to deduce whether service in general has improved or not. There are specific cases of improvement, yes. There are organizations which have used common sense and empathy with customers to provide excellent service. Others have learnt from service management and quality management to deploy such viable strategies as continuous improvements and management commitment. Yet others have ignored the lessons and have failed. But the complexity of service is often titanic and with globalization and larger systems complexity is growing. My general conclusion is that there is urgent need for enhancing the quality of service systems and make them truly value-creating. Service science is needed to achieve this goal.
- *Goods, services* and *the service sector* are ill-defined categories. One reason is that they represent fuzzy phenomena; another that tradition and inertia block necessary changes. Mock classifications of our economies have to be weeded out as they mislead decision-making and action. We have to be direct and talk about hotels, management consultants, aircraft engines, professional football, pizzas, and their variations and address them in specific terms.
- In line with *S-D logic, service* is used as the outcome of something of value. A supplier has a *value proposition* but *value actualization* takes place during the customer's usage and consumption process. Suppliers and customers are *co-creators of value*. The understanding of the customer's active involvement in value-creation is growing. Service marketing and management, S-D logic, relational approaches to marketing, developments on the Internet, and increased understanding of C2C interaction all provide heavyweight empirical and conceptual evidence for *re-casting supplier and customer roles*.
- What we have learnt about the *service encounter* is not limited to services in the traditional sense but is applicable to all value propositions and service systems. Service science as an academic discipline should provide both *general and specific strategies*. We should note similarities and learn from them but equally note differences and address each situation on its own terms with consideration of the specific context. A specific configuration of strategies has to be designed to each unique situation. Sometimes a situation is uniquely unique and sometimes marginally unique, but it is not differences between goods and ser-

vices that determine the uniqueness. Intangibility, heterogeneity, inseparability and perishability – constantly used to create a goods versus services pseudo-world – are just a few of a multitude of properties to characterize a value proposition. They do not and never did separate services from goods in any meaningful way.

- *Relationships, networks* and *interaction* are key concepts that emerged in relationship marketing, CRM, one-to-one marketing, many-to-many marketing and B2B marketing. They grasp the essence of life – life is a network of relationships in which we interact – and are thus universal. To be of practical use in service systems and value creation, they have to be adapted to specific management and systems applications.
- *Complexity* is a key dimension together with *context* and *change* and these three Cs have to be addressed in service science. *Network theory* together with *case study research* offer the most constructive mindset and manageable techniques for approaching complexity. *Many-to-many* is a concept for merging network theory and marketing reality. The "survey-dominant logic" of service research has to be abandoned in favor of in depth network cases where the three Cs are addressed.
- It adds to the complexity that customer live in *a network of value propositions*. A value proposition is most often approached in science as a stand-alone, for example hotel service. But customers do not ask for the service from one proposition after another in a neat sequence. They live in a web of service where different services systems are used in individual combinations. A network of service systems is active at a certain moment, and other service systems are stand-by.
- With expanding *technology*, especially information technology, and the prevailing idea that high tech and integrated systems are more productive than people, attention to the *tech/touch balance* becomes progressively critical. We need to be realistic and accept that low and high touch should live in symbiosis with low and high tech in optimal combinations.
- Customer-centricity is advocated in marketing but cannot be the sole focus in a service and network context. Nor can shareholder value or employee satisfaction stand out as the guiding stars for an organization. A realistic alternative is to leave *one-party centricity* for *balanced centricity*, a stakeholder and network approach where the interests of multiple parties are mediated.
- Although we have not yet got it conceptually and consistently together, I am prepared to say that *a paradigm shift* is taking place in management that needs to be reflected in research priorities, textbooks and education at a faster pace than today. All the talk about everything going so fast has not yet affected service research and education. Service science and S-D logic were presented in 2004 and have had an unprecedented breakthrough in research but they are often not noted and much less integrated with current knowledge even in recent text-

books on marketing and service. Network theory has been around in B2B research and in many-to-many marketing for even longer and are also little noted.

Even if these are my last words they are not my "famous last words"; they are for now only. In 2009 several sources claim that we are at the brink of a bottomless pit into which Western market economies will soon fall. We get this from financial analysts and think tanks but equally from the Maya scriptures, Vedic philosophers, Red Indian cultures, aborigines and others who we have learnt to label primitive. We may currently be at the bottom of a longer and deeper recession than we have seen in modern times and swing ourselves back to the top. Whatever the future will be, should we survive we will not come out the same; we may even wake up in a new world order.

Irrespective of outcome, it is my conviction that in both scenarios we will be better off with a more advanced service science and superior service systems.

References

Akner, G. (2004). *Multisjuklighet hos äldre.* Malmö, Sweden: Liber.

Ballantyne, D. and Varey, R.J. (2008). The service-dominant logic and the future. *Journal of the Academy of Marketing Science,* 36 (1), 11-14.

Delaunay, J.-C. and Gadrey, J. (1992). *Services in EconomicThought,* Boston, MA: Kluwer.

Edvardsson, B., Gustafsson, A. and Roos, I. (2005). Service portraits in service research: a critical review. *International Journal of Service Industry Management,* 16 (1), 107-121.

Fisk, R. P., Brown, S. W. and Bitner, M. J. (1993). Tracking the Evolution of the Services Marketing Literature. *Journal of Retailing,* 69 (Spring), 61-103.

Fisk, R. P., Grove, S.J. and John, J., eds. (2000). *Services Marketing Self-Portraits.* Chicago, IL: American Marketing Association.

Grönroos, C. (2006). On defining marketing: finding a new roadmap for marketing. *Marketing Theory,* 6, (4), 395-417.

Grönroos, C. (2007a). *Service Management and Marketing: Customer Management in Service Competition.* Chichester, UK: Wiley (3rd edition).

Grönroos, C. (2007b). *In Search of a New Logic for Marketing.* Chichester, UK: Wiley.

Gummesson, E. (1991). Service Quality – A Holistic View. *The Journal of the Quality Insurance Institute,* July, 41-50.

Gummesson, E. (2007a). Exit *Services* Marketing – Enter *Service* Marketing. *Journal of Customer Behaviour,* 6 (2),113-141.

Gummesson, E. (2007b). Case study research and network theory: Birds of a feather. *Qualitative Research in Organizations and Management,* 2 (3), 226-248.

Gummesson, E. (2008a). *Total Relationship Marketing.* Oxford: Elsevier/Butterworth-Heinemann (3rd edition).

Gummesson, E. (2008b). Quality, service-dominant logic and many-to-many marketing. *The TQM Journal,* 20 (2),143-153.

Gummesson, E. (2009). *Marketing As Networks: The Birth of Many-to-Many Marketing,* Publishing House Djursholm, Stockholm.

Gummesson, E. and Polese, F. (2009). B2B is not an island. *Journal of Business and Industrial Marketing,* 24 (5-6), in press.

Kohlbacher, F. (2007). *International Marketing in the Network Economy.* Houndmills, UK: Palgrave/Macmillan,.

Kotler, P., Shalowitz, J. and Stevens, R. J. (2008). *Strategic Marketing for Health Care Organizations.* San Francisco, CA: Jossey-Bass.

Lovelock, C. and Gummesson, E. (2004). Whither Services Marketing? In Search of a Paradigm and Fresh Perspectives. *Journal of Service Research,* 7 (1), 20-41.

Lovelock, C. and Wirtz, J. (2007). *Services Marketing: People, Technology, Strategy.* Upper Saddle River, NJ: Pearson/Prentice Hall, (6th edition).

Maglio, P.P. and Spohrer, J., (2008). Fundamentals of service science. *Journal of the Academy of Marketing Science,* 36 (1),18-20.

Mandel, M. (2006), What's Really Propping Up The Economy. *Business Week,* September 25, 54-62.

Mele, C. (2007). The synergetic relationship between TQM and marketing in creating customer value. *Managing Service Quality,* 17 (3), 240-258.

Naisbitt, J. (1982), *Megatrends.* New York, NY: Warner Books.

Payne, A. and Frow, P. (2005). A Strategic Framework for Customer Relationship Management. *Journal of Marketing,* 69 (October), 167–176.

Quero, M. J. (2007). Relationship marketing and services marketing: Two convergent perspectives for value creation in the cultural sector. Empirical evidence on performing arts consumers in Spain. *International Review on Public and Non Profit Marketing,* 4 (1-2) (December), 101-115.

Ravald, A. (2008). *Hur uppkommer värde för kunden?* Helsinki, Finland: Hanken School of Economics.

Spohrer, J. and Maglio, P. P. (2009). Service Science: Toward a Smarter Planet. In Service Engineering, ed. Karwowski & Salvendy. Wiley: New York, NY.

Storbacka, K. and Lehtinen, J. R. (2001). *Customer Relationship Management.* Singapore: McGraw-Hill.

Vargo, S.L. and Lusch, R.F. (2004). The Four Service Marketing Myths: Remnants of a Goods-Based, Manufacturing Model. *Journal of Service Research,* 6(6), May, 324-35.

Vargo, S.L. and Lusch, R.F. (2008), Service-dominant logic: continuing the evolution. *Journal of the Academy of Marketing Science,* 36 (1), 1-10.

Vargo, S.L., Maglio, P.P. and Archpru Akaka, M. (2008). On value and value co-creation: A service systems and service logic perspective. *European Management Journal,* 26, pp. 145-152.

Wilkinson, I. (2008). *Business Relating Business.* Cheltenham, UK: Edward Elgar.

Wyckham, R. G., Fitzroy, P. T. and Mandry, G. D. (1975). Marketing of Services. *European Journal of Marketing,* 9 (1), 59-67.

The Evolution and Future of Service

Building and Broadening a Multidisciplinary Field

Raymond P. Fisk

Texas State University - San Marcos

Stephen J. Grove

Clemson University

This chapter describes the evolution of the service field over two eras that encompass its emergence, growth and eventual broadening into a multidisciplinary field. The first era, described with the metaphor of biological evolution, encompasses the development of the service marketing field across three stages: Crawling Out, Scurrying About, and Walking Erect. The second era witnessed the rapid expansion of the service field beyond service marketing. This era, described with the metaphor of social evolution, progresses through three additional stages: Making Tools, Creating Language, and Building Community. We expand on Building Community as the future of the service field with discussion of the state of Service Science, Management, and Engineering (SSME), the idea of adding service arts, the need to serve customers, and memes for building the service community. We envision a service field that is customer-centered, multidisciplinary and collaborative.

Introduction

This chapter is an historical account of the development of the service field and includes speculation about the field's future. The concepts of biological and social evolution are used for this history of the service field. Evolution is the time-honored scientific explanation for how life forms change over time. Hence, evolution provides a powerful metaphor for telling the story of the service field because services are by, for and about human beings.

P.P. Maglio et al. (eds.), *Handbook of Service Science*, Service Science: Research and Innovations in the Service Economy, DOI 10.1007/978-1-4419-1628-0_28,
© Springer Science+Business Media, LLC 2010

Over the years, various disciplines have taken inspiration from biological evolution as a means to frame their concepts. As described by the sociologist, Jonathan Turner:

> "It was in the 19th century that biological discoveries were to alter significantly the social and intellectual climate of the times…And most important, conceptions of evolution, culminating in the theories of Wallace and Darwin, were stimulating great intellectual and social controversy. Since it was in this social and intellectual milieu that sociology as a self-conscious discipline was born, it is not surprising that conceptions of social order were influenced by a preoccupation with biology." (Turner 1978, p. 20).

More recently, in a 2003 TED Conference talk titled "How Science is Like Democracy", physicist Lee Smolin stated, "Our concepts of society have paralleled our understanding of space and time"(Smolin 2003). He proposed three parallel stages: 1) the hierarchical universe; 2) the Newtonian "liberal" universe; and 3) the relational/pluralistic universe of today. Smolin notes that in the third stage "the universe is nothing but an ever evolving network of relationships." If the sciences of sociology and physics can each be portrayed as the evolution of relationships, then we think evolutionary concepts and metaphors can help explain the past, present and future of the service field. Relationships are at the heart of services, too.

Service in Human History

Prior to telling the story of the service field, a brief retrospective is needed on the centuries of human history before the emergence of the service field. Humans have walked the earth for approximately 250,000 years. Service activities of many types have been essential aspects of the evolution of human culture and civilization–certainly long before 20th century scholars directed attention to the service economy. Services are performed for people, which means that service activities are embedded in the five social institutions that sociologists describe as fundamental to human civilization: family, education, government, economy, and religion (Poponoe 1980). Most classifications of service entities would describe education, government, and religion as services (Fisk, Grove and John 2008). Additionally, despite the fact that the economy includes agriculture and manufacturing, such instrumental services as finance, transportation, and communication were vital to the growth of human civilization. Finally, in addition to being the essential biological and social unit of human culture, the family is also the fundamental service unit. Services involve human relationships and interactions, the underpinnings of which are learned within the context of the family institution. In sum, the services performed within the five fundamental social institutions were essential to the evolution of human culture and civilization.

Service Science or Service Knowledge?

This handbook concerns "service science." Both words originate in Latin (Merriam-Webster 2003). The Latin root of service is "servus," which means "slave, servant or serf," while the Latin root of science is "scientia," which means "knowledge." In the ancient Latin, then, "servus scientia" would mean slave knowledge. The etymology of these two words has taken remarkably different paths over the centuries. The term "service" has evolved from referring to people in subservient roles to broadly referring to activities performed for others. (For some people, the word service may still possess a negative connotation that undermines their willingness to learn more about the service economy). Meanwhile, the term "science" evolved from meaning knowledge in general to meaning specific kinds of knowledge that are discovered through rigorous methods of inquiry.

Many people who use the term "service science" today seem to employ "service" in its most modern meaning and "science" in its ancient meaning. Moreover, for many new participants in the service field, the term "service science" has become the shorthand name for the entire service field. While it may be somewhat controversial, we strongly disagree with this idea. It is inaccurate and paradoxically nonscientific to label the entire service field as "service science." Instead, we suggest that the nomenclature in the service field should be similar in logic to the scientific nomenclature used in biology. The genus-species classification system allows flexibility across the vast range of life forms. With this logic, the word "service" should be considered the genus, which permits a large number of genus-species labels. The species become science, management, engineering, etc. In short, the service field should adopt a nomenclature that allows for and encourages flexible classification of service knowledge.

The word "science" may one day return to its original meaning of "knowledge," but to avoid confusion and to be more precise, our chapter employs the phrase "service knowledge" instead of "service science" when we refer to the whole of service knowledge. This chapter utilizes the phrases service science, service management, service engineering and service arts in more specific ways as subsets of service knowledge.

Early Thinking About the Role of Service and Customers

Business scholars first began tracking the economic impact of service activities during the 20th century as the economic data showed that services accounted for more than 50% of gross domestic product. Colin Clark (1957) was the first economist to document the impact of service activities on gross domestic product. Service activities didn't show up strongly in economic data until the 20th century because only monetary exchanges were being monitored and many services performed in families, education, government and religion were not being measured.

Many 20th century business scholars were not very supportive of the emerging service economy. It was sometimes described as a "Disney economy" or a "McDonald's economy," which was meant to suggest that the service economy was nonessential. Other critics suggested that the service economy was a low skill, low wage economy. Fortunately, not all business scholars were so antagonistic. One of the most prescient marketing scholars regarding the service economy was George Fisk (1967) who wrote:

> "At the present moment mankind seems poised for another leap, this time into the service revolution, in which machines will replace mind power in the production of ideas and services, just as in the industrial revolution the use of machines replaced muscle power."

When Fisk wrote this comment in 1967, he could not have envisioned the shrinkage of computing and communications technology into the powerful handheld service tools of today. Nevertheless, his description captures how technology has transformed the service economy.

The marketing discipline arose in the 20th century (Bartels 1976; Sheth and Gardner 1984) and one of its defining aspects as an applied business discipline is its central focus on customers. Peter Drucker, one of the most influential business scholars of the 20th century, was a strong proponent of this customer orientation. For example, his classic book *The Practice of Management* (1954) stated that "There is only one valid definition of business purpose: *to create a customer*." (p. 37, italics in the original). Similarly, a famous marketing scholar, Ted Levitt (1960) argued in his classic "Marketing Myopia" article that businesses risk failure if they are product-oriented instead of customer-oriented. Arguably, the customer focus of marketing was an essential enabling condition for the early emergence of service research in the marketing discipline.

Plan of Procedure

This chapter examines how the academic study of service phenomena has evolved from its origins in service marketing and management to its expansion to engineering, science and the arts. Two developmental eras in the evolution of the service field are described using evolutionary metaphors. In the first era, the metaphor of biological evolution is used to describe the development of the service marketing literature across three stages labeled Crawling Out, Scurrying About, and Walking Erect. In the second era, the metaphor of social evolution is used to describe the rapid expansion of the service field beyond its roots in service marketing and management. These three stages are labeled: Making Tools, Creating Language, and Building Community. The building community section describes our perspective on the future of the service field. That section discusses the state of Service Science, Management, and Engineering (SSME), the idea of adding service arts, the need to serve customers, and memes for building the service community: service activism and electronic networks. We foresee a customer-centered, multidisciplinary, and collaborative service field.

The First Era: Service Marketing

Fisk, Brown and Bitner (1993) employed the metaphor of biological evolution to describe the emergence and development of the service marketing field across three stages: Crawling Out, Scurrying About, and Walking Erect. Figure 1 portrays these three stages. The *Crawling Out* stage (Pre 1980) is akin to the first amphibians crawling out of the primordial swamp. In this stage, the early service scholars created the service marketing field and defended its right to exist. The *Scurrying About* stage (1980 to 1985) reflects the frantic activity characteristic of our primate ancestors. In this stage, a rapidly growing and enthusiastic community of scholars quickly expanded upon the basic structure of service marketing. The *Walking Erect* stage (1986 to 1992) resembles the evolutionary transition from a primate scurrying about on four feet to early humans walking on two feet. In this period, the service marketing field achieved a measure of legitimacy within the marketing discipline and beyond. The following summary is based on the Fisk, Brown and Bitner (1993) article.

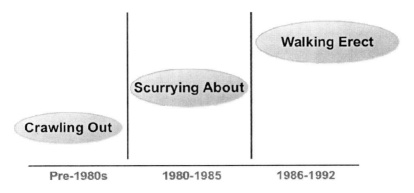

Figure 1. Evolution of the Service Marketing Field

Crawling Out (Pre 1980)

The *Crawling Out* stage began when a few marketing scholars scattered worldwide started studying service marketing topics. These early service scholars took significant risks. Most were in the early stages of their academic career. Few publication outlets were receptive to service marketing topics, but these scholars persevered nonetheless. The majority of the literature in the Crawling Out Stage was conceptual in nature. A landmark *Journal of Marketing* article by Lynn Shostack (1977), bank executive at Citibank, altered the future of the service marketing field. Shostack argued that the academic marketing discipline was myopic by failing to offer useful guidance for marketing managers in the service sector. Shostack's observations became a rallying cry that inspired many early service marketing scholars and helped prompt the field's rapid growth. The *Crawling Out* stage culminated in a fierce debate within the marketing discipline over the question, "Is service marketing really different?" At the heart of the debate was the question of whether service marketing should exist as a distinct subfield within the marketing discipline.

Scurrying About (1980-1985)

In the *Scurrying About* stage, a thriving colony of service scholars emerged. This period saw the appearance of numerous service conferences, articles, dissertations, and several books. The American Marketing Association convened its first service marketing conferences during this period, which provided the first contact for scholars and business people from North America and Europe who shared a passion for service research. These early conferences enabled the formation of a service research community. Also, during this period the first service marketing textbook was published by Christopher Lovelock (1984), which further legitimated the field of study and increased the number of students learning about service marketing. Four influential conceptual articles (Lovelock 1983; Parasuraman, Zeithaml, and Berry 1985; Solomon et. al. 1985; Zeithaml, Parasuraman, and Berry 1985) appeared in this period and were published in the *Journal of Marketing,* which is arguably the premier journal in the marketing discipline. Another notable event was the creation by Stephen Brown at Arizona State University of the first academic research center devoted to service research, which is now known as the Center for Service Leadership.

Walking Erect (1986-1992)

In the *Walking Erect* stage, the service marketing field achieved a respected position within the marketing discipline. The quantity of service conferences, articles, dissertations, and books dedicated to the study of service marketing phenomena continued to grow rapidly. This included numerous conferences and symposia in North America and Europe. Research during this period became more empirical and more multidisciplinary. Perhaps the most notable quantitative study from this period was the SERVQUAL scale (Parasuraman, Zeithaml and Berry 1988). It was the first significant attempt to create a measurement scale in service and provided the first tool to measure service quality. SERVQUAL inspired a wave of new measurement-focused research.

Before examining the second era of service evolution, it is worth pondering why marketing was one of the first disciplines to examine, articulate and research service phenomena. As suggested earlier, the marketing field is, by nature and necessity, customer-centered. Hence, marketing managers and marketing academics were quick to observe the many service failures, as well as successes, experienced by customers as the service economy expanded. Further, it is noteworthy that marketing managers and academics in North America and Europe were studying these problems nearly simultaneously.

The Second Era: The Emergence of a Multidisciplinary Field

Remarkable changes have occurred in the service field since Fisk, Brown and Bitner (1993) documented the first era. To capture the changes in the second era, an evolutionary metaphorical approach is continued, but the nature of the metaphor is shifted from biological to social evolution. While biological evolution depicts changes in life forms, social evolution depicts changes in human culture. In simple evolutionary terms, the metaphor is shifted from genes to memes. The term "meme" was introduced by Richard Dawkins (1976) to reflect a "unit of imitation" (p. 206). Memes comprise cultural information that is learned and transmitted across generations. Examination of the concept of memes continues (Aunger 2002; Blackmore 1999; Bloom 2000; Brodie 2004; Distin 2005). Based on the memes concept, the stages of social evolution–and hence the diffusion of memes–are not discrete stages like those of biological evolution. Instead, each social evolution stage is cumulative as cultures evolve.

After service marketing became an established subfield within the marketing discipline, the creation and sharing of service memes emerged as the next era in the development of the field. Recent changes in service marketing represent memes that diffused across the marketing discipline. More importantly, these memes are key elements in the emergence of a much broader, multidisciplinary service field.

The social evolution of the broader service field can be described in three stages: *Making Tools, Creating Language, Building Community*. These labels were created with the help of service scholars, Stephen W. Brown and Mary Jo Bitner. Figure 2 portrays these stages. In the *Making Tools* stage, many technological tools were developed that advanced the sophistication of the service field. In the *Creating Language* stage, the terminology associated with service marketing and service management began to diffuse widely and new language creators emerged. In the *Building Community* stage, social structures are emerging to support the work of service researchers–academics and practitioners alike–from diverse backgrounds and perspectives.

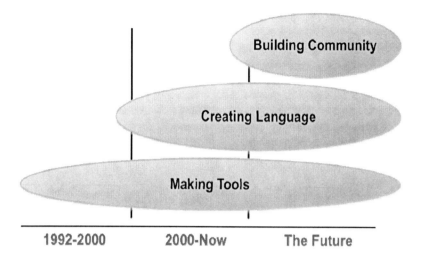

Figure 2. Recent Stages of Service Evolution

Making Tools

In the *Making Tools* stage, rapid technological improvements made it possible for most service industries to improve the sophistication of the service they provide to customers. Prominent among these new technologies is the Internet and many web-based services. Also, technological advances enabled numerous self-service technologies that facilitate the customer-organization interface. Researchers began studying technology readiness in service (Parasuraman 2000) and the role of self-service technologies in the development and maintenance of customer-firm relationships (Meuter et al. 2000). In addition, during this stage many new tools raised the level of sophistication of research regarding service customers and organizations (e.g., Rust, Zahorik, and Keiningham 1995). These include numerous measurement scales and data analysis techniques.

Successful service memes continue to emerge and endure. The *Making Tools* stage helped lay the foundation for the development of the broader service field. The infusion of new service researchers from various backgrounds and their tool making skills will greatly enhance the field.

Creating Language

In the *Creating Language* stage, a technical service language is emerging to communicate and share knowledge across the community of service scholars and managers. Many of the technical words, phrases and concepts that originated in service marketing (which were previously isolated there) became commonplace within the marketing discipline. These terms include service encounters, service quality, service theater, service experience, servicescapes, service blueprint and service recovery. Gradually, service terms are becoming the language of marketing in general as well as diffusing across diverse disciplines. Perhaps the best evidence for this transformation is the service-dominant logic introduced by Vargo and Lusch (2004). In a landmark *Journal of Marketing* article, they argued that service, rather than physical goods, is fundamental to all economic exchange.

As service research continues its rapid expansion, the *Creating Language* stage is evolving rapidly. IBM has contributed significantly to the new service language with its SSME initiative. Languages develop as more and more people who share a common vocabulary speak to each other. The service language that is emerging from the broad community of new participants will reflect a wide range of disciplines and perspectives. The challenge is to create a common language that improves communication across the developing service research community. Gorman, Groves, and Shrager (2004), propose the use of creoles (simplified common languages) that allow specialists from different areas to communicate with each other.

The Future of the Service Field: Building Community

In the *Building Community* stage, we envision the future of the service field. As the study of service phenomena has broadened from its early origins in marketing and management to include more areas of inquiry, the service field continues to expand rapidly. The huge increase in the number of participants in the service field and the diversity of their training creates both opportunity and peril as the boundaries of contributing disciplines and the domain of service itself are questioned. In short, the broader service field is approaching a critical juncture.

Throughout history, academic disciplines have played essential roles in creating and diffusing knowledge. Each discipline tends to claim exclusive ownership and be very protective of the knowledge created within its field. A presumption of intellectual property rights prevails. Often, academic disciplines seem to treat the boundaries of their knowledge in the same manner that nations treat their borders. In disciplines or nations, fierce disputes may occur with respect to their borders. Academic disciplines also have a tendency to become isolated from each other. This territorial phenomenon is sometimes described by the metaphor of "silos" of knowledge.

The boundaries and isolation of disciplines are impediments to innovation and progress. To assure optimum development of the service field, knowledge should be communicated and shared across any disciplines interested in service. To facilitate such a goal, "trading zones" that span discipline boundaries and share expertise should be established (Gorman, Groves, and Shrager (2004). Efforts to deliberately blur the borders that separate disciplines are desirable. One such effort is found in Campbell's (1969) "fish-scale" metaphor for all knowledge. Campbell argued that the content of disciplines should overlap like scales on a fish. Sharing and cooperation across disciplines makes it possible to build a research community that generates knowledge and serves the needs of customers before serving the interests of specific disciplines. The major problems facing our species are larger than any one discipline and require transdisciplinary solutions (Klein et al. 2001).

This section examines the state of Service Science, Management, and Engineering (SSME), proposes adding Service Arts to this set of key service disciplines, argues that serving customers should be the unifying purpose of all service disciplines, and offers two memes for building the service community.

Service Science, Management, and Engineering (SSME)

Under the leadership of Jim Spohrer, IBM has taken a major role in building the service community through its Service Science, Management and Engineering (SSME) initiative. The SSME initiative seeks to broaden the perspectives and tools available to understand the complexity of service phenomena. Among the activities sponsored by IBM are conferences, workshops, books, and a large collection of electronic materials available via the web.

In the 20th century, IBM led the efforts to create the academic field of computer science. The development of computer science did not draw from as many diverse areas as those now forming the foundation of the service field. Hence, the emerging service field will evolve in a much more multidisciplinary manner. As previously noted, service marketing and service management were among the first parts of the service field to develop long before those in the sciences or engineering were exploring service issues. As the service field expands beyond its roots in marketing and management, scholars in service engineering and service science will need to embrace the perspective that the purpose of any service is to serve customer needs. In the following sub-sections, three areas of SSME: service science, service management and service engineering are examined.

Service Science

While many others (Chesbrough and Spohrer 2006; Glushko 2008; Hefley and Murphy 2008; Larson 2008; Lusch, Vargo, and Wessels 2008; Maglio and Spohrer 2008; Spohrer and Maglio 2008; Stauss et al. 2007) are writing about service science, this chapter takes a more historical approach. As noted in the introduction, services are performed for people and services have been part of human history from the beginning. Hence, any discussion of service science should start with the earliest sciences that were applied to human beings, the social sciences.

The social sciences include such fields as anthropology, economics, psychology, and sociology. In many ways, applying science to human beings would be easier if we were not human beings ourselves. Humans are subject to biases and prejudices that often distort our observational abilities. Scientists studying human beings often have difficulty objectively separating themselves from their scientific work (Miller 1972; Rosenthal 1967).

None of the early social sciences focused their attention directly on service phenomena. In an ideal world of science, the social sciences would have been the first to chronicle and to categorize service phenomena. The data were everywhere, yet the significance of service activities was not recognized. Narrower perspectives on human phenomena seemingly distracted the various social sciences. For instance, the field of anthropology focused for decades on primitive cultures and only recently turned its attention to modern cultures. The field of economics based many of its early theories on the "rational man" assumption. This assumption simplified economic theories, but lost the subtleties of human behavior. The field of psychology devoted much of its early work to abnormal psychology and ignored topics such as consumer psychology until relatively recently. The field of sociology neglected noncommercial aspects of human behavior until the recent past. In short, service activities were not perceived as important—a bias that was perhaps embedded in the original Latin meaning of "servus."

The field of computer science was spawned by the first generation of 20th century computing technology. As evidenced by its name, computer science focused on computers and not on the human beings who created them or used them. However as the field evolved, more and more attention has been given to the human-to-computer interface. Hence, computer science is included in this section because it too should become part of service science.

What should service science be? As a new scientific field, service science should be human-centered. Further, it needs to focus on the customers being served, not just the service organization, its employees, or its technology. This requires a synthesis of the existing social sciences in such areas as the economics of, the anthropology of, the psychology of, and the sociology of *serving customers,* as well as the development of computer science as a field that focuses on how computers serve customer needs.

Service Management

The label service management is used here to encompass the business disciplines that concern managing service organizations. This includes general management (including operations and human resource management), marketing, accounting, and finance. Economics is also included because it is considered the foundational field of business disciplines. While service marketing and service management were the very first service-oriented fields and became significant academic subfields within their respective disciplines, several other business disciplines have not devoted much attention to service. Accounting, economics, and finance have mostly overlooked the implications of the modern service economy. For much of their history, accounting, economics, and finance shared the archaic (and nonscientific) assumption that human beings act rationally. By contrast, as the most people-based business fields, marketing and management never completely adopted the "rational man" logic. Early researchers in the two fields observed that human behavior was much more complex.

In recent years, the fields of accounting, economics and finance are progressing toward a broader understanding of human behavior. Behavioral research has taken root in the accounting (Riahi-Belkaoui 2001), economics (Allison 1983; Ariely 2008), and finance (Goldberg and von Nitzsch 2001) fields. The concept of "bounded rationality" has become part of the logic of these fields. Clearly, to avoid the unintended shortcomings of accounting, economic, or financial systems that are poorly attuned to the human psyche and human behavior, a greater appreciation of human complexity is needed. As these essential business fields embrace the breadth of human complexity, they are likely to address the problems they have neglected or overlooked in the service economy.

Service Engineering

Engineering is often described as "applied science," a description that emphasizes the importance of applied knowledge to the engineering field. Engineering has tended to focus on the engineering of physical entities, such as chemical engineering, mechanical engineering, or electrical engineering. As such, the field of engineering has historic links to the agricultural and industrial eras. Further, engineering has a focus similar to the focus associated with the field of computer science—a focus on physical things rather than people. Engineering is done for people, but engineering training and practice tends to center on technology rather than people's needs. This issue was recently addressed in a call to action by engineering scholars Grasso and Martinelli (2007) when they argued "In this evolving world, a new kind of engineer is needed, one who can think broadly across disciplines and consider the human dimensions that are at the heart of every design challenge." (p. B8).

Service engineering is a rather unorthodox idea to traditional engineers, so the challenge for the engineering field is to fully embrace service engineering. Engineering subfields like human factors engineering, industrial engineering, process engineering, and software engineering are likely to become even more important as serving human needs becomes the focus of service engineering.

Service Arts

At the 2007 AMA Frontiers in Service Research Conference, the case was made that the service field should include an additional service area—the service arts (Fisk et al. 2007). The arts encompass many subfields such as architecture, dance, design, drawing, film, language, literature, music, opera, painting, photography, poetry, sculpture, and theater. While there are many ways to categorize the arts, one that is particularly relevant for services is a distinction between transitory and fixed arts (Wilson 2001). The *transitory* arts involve moment-to-moment shifts in impressions and stimuli. They are known as the performing arts. The *fixed arts* involve finished products that are tangible and unchangeable once they leave the artist' hands. These are known as the visual arts and literature. Nevertheless, both transitory and fixed art forms focus upon and reflect an understanding of the human experience, and represent an important source of valuable insights for framing and delivering service excellence. Hence, a wide spectrum of arts topics and scholars should be included in developing a comprehensive service discipline.

What can the arts contribute to the emerging SSME initiative? Like the arts, service delivery systems are concerned with creating a desired customer experience and connecting with customers emotionally (Haeckel, Carbone and Berry 2003; Wilburn 2007). Hence, the arts offer direction for designing and implementing the organization-customer interface. There are four significant reasons to consider the arts as a source for ideas in developing the burgeoning service domain.

First, the arts are concerned with aesthetics and beauty. Aesthetics and beauty are essential to planning and implementing service systems that appeal to human beings (Postrel 2004). Inputs from both the visual arts and performing arts can enrich the aesthetics associated with the design and delivery of various services, whether those services are offered in bricks and mortar settings or cyberspace.

Second, the arts spring from and are strongly focused on creativity. Creativity is a multi-faceted phenomenon necessary to generate and apply new ideas or concepts. As an associated theme, innovation and originality are some of the most revered human qualities. Modern research demonstrates that arts training can increase an individual's creativity (Pink 2005, Robinson 2001) and that "musical training and involvement in music enlarges various parts of the brain" (Sacks 2007) leading to creativeness. These outcomes and the arts related processes that lead to them have significant implication for enhancing service workers' and managers' performance in such areas as organization-customer interaction, servicescape design, or service process improvement.

Third, the arts have the capacity to stir human emotions and deliver such positive emotions as joy, contentment, surprise, or excitement (Richins 1997) to the human experience. Emotions are central to people's life experience and are a powerful feature of service encounters (Haeckel, Carbone and Berry 2003). Hence, accentuating the positive emotional character of the service setting– whether it is a bricks and mortar setting or an "e-servicescape" (Hopkins, Grove and Raymond 2005)–and investing in the service employees' emotional capital (Thompson 1998) are desirable pursuits. To that end, principles and practices found among the visual and performing arts should be studied by service organizations for insights regarding creating emotional response.

A fourth reason why the arts should be included is that the arts involve learned skills that draw upon centuries of rich history for inspiration and guidance. While the application of skill is a basic aspect of any human endeavor, the arts are characterized by the diligent and careful acquisition of expertise that is necessary for their creative expression. That expertise culminates in a communication form that affects the audience's experience. Since services are concerned with creating customer experiences, services should look to the arts for valuable skills that can be applied in service organizations.

These four reasons help distinguish the arts from science, management and engineering and serve as a source of new concepts and tools for the emerging service field. In fairness to IBM's role in service knowledge, we should note that more recent versions of IBM articles and presentations refer to SSMED, for Service Science, Engineering, Management and Design (Spohrer and Kwan 2007). Design is part of what are often called applied arts, so this is the first inclusion of any arts-related area. We agree that design should be included in the service field, but we think that many other arts have much to offer, too.

Serving Customers

During an IBM SSME conference in Palisades, New York, marketing scholar Roland Rust (2006) argued that a broadened view of service knowledge was needed that includes a customer and revenue focus. Rust proposed a "big tent" metaphor to capture the idea that the service field should be expansive enough to include a customer and revenue focus and many others. At the 2007 AMA Frontiers in Service Research conference, we argued that adopting Rust's big tent metaphor requires erecting five "tent poles" to support the canopy of service knowledge and described the various activities that should be found under the canopy's coverage (Epworth et al. 2007).

In response to IBM's SSME initiative and incorporating our arguments for the arts, we envision four side poles that support the "big tent" of service and contribute to a broad perspective on service knowledge. The four side poles are four large academic disciplines–arts, science, management and engineering that offer different perspectives on service. Ultimately, the four side poles provide input and direction for serving customers. The first side pole represents service arts, which includes the performing arts (e.g., theater and music), visual arts (video and painting), architecture, and design. A second side pole embodies service science, which incorporates psychology, sociology, anthropology, ergonomics, systems science, and computer science. The third side pole comprises service management, which includes marketing, operations, human resources and finance. The fourth and last side pole pertains to service engineering, which involves industrial engineering, process engineering, software engineering, and ergonomics. Each of the side poles may include other areas that are related to each pole's general thrust, so rather than being exclusionary in nature, they embrace various subfields. In addition to the four side poles, there is a larger fifth pole at the center of the tent, which we label "serving customers." Labeling the center pole as "serving customers" is based on the logic that attending to customer needs and wants should be the principal concern of any service field. Essentially, the fifth pole serves to unify the various service subfields in the pursuit of serving customers. The relationship among the five tent poles is represented in Figure 3.

Each of the four sets of academic disciplines creates knowledge that has relevance for serving customers. In simplistic terms, the arts disciplines generate insights for creating service performance, the science disciplines provide the means to objectively understand service delivery systems, the management disciplines supply direction for delivering services, and the engineering disciplines offer guidance for designing services. In each case, serving the customer should be the focus of knowledge development for any service field.

The logic for linking all of these academic disciplines to the need to serve customers is rooted in the marketing concept. Focusing on customers is required for long-term organizational success (Kohli and Jaworski 1990). Organizations often lose sight of the customer as an individual and begin describing customers in dehumanizing terms such as market segments, target markets or assets. Such organizational behavior undervalues and demeans customers (Grove, John and Fisk 2006). After all, customers are the source of the revenue that fuels organizations. The phrase "serving customers" emphasizes the first step of customer co-creation of value. A central reason for the existence of the marketing field is the necessity of initiating customer exchanges. In short, someone has to start the process of co-creation. Organizations that initiate carefully orchestrated efforts to serve customer needs are more likely to achieve stable customer co-creation of value.

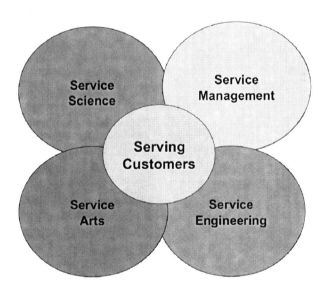

Figure 3. A Unified Service Perspective

Memes for Building the Service Community

The service community should develop an eclectic marketplace of ideas representing the widest range of diversity. As seen in the early history of the social sciences, human beings tend to adopt orthodoxies of traditional thought, which can delay the growth of knowledge. The physicist Lee Smolin (2003) argued that science should be like a democracy. He also argued that democracies should embrace respect and rebellion. Respect for traditional knowledge is essential, but the spirit of rebellion is necessary to find new knowledge.

Two memes are offered for building the service community. Service activism is a human-to-human meme that asks those participating in the service community to actively contribute to building and caring for the community. Electronic networks are human-to-computer-to-human memes. Such networks offer computer-aided expansion of human potential, which will be essential to support and connect a community that spans the diverse disciplines of service knowledge and participants dispersed across the entire planet.

Service Activism

Activism is required to build a pluralistic and inclusive service field. As part of IBM's SSME initiative, Jim Spohrer has popularized the notion that T-shaped people–people who are trained deeply within their core service field, but have basic knowledge and communications skills across diverse service areas–are needed to foster the service growth that companies like IBM are pursuing. We extend this metaphor to the third stage of social evolution in the service field: *Building Community*. Anyone can make a "t-shape" by extending both arms outward horizontally. Metaphorically, T-shaped service scholars extend their hands toward other T-shaped scholars, inviting collaboration and sharing of service knowledge.

Scholars who are already "T-shaped" should seek out T-shaped collaborations in areas far removed from their original training. A set of six social networking dyads are the first step to collaborative possibilities: science and management; science and engineering; science and arts; management and engineering, management and arts; engineering and arts. There are many more complicated collaboration possibilities by linking three or more service knowledge areas. In addition to general collaboration, many more specific collaborative pairings are needed. As one example, Ray Fisk (service marketing), João Falcão e Cunha (software engineering) and Lia Patrício (service engineering) have collaborated over several years to study interdisciplinary ways of improving the human-to-computer interface for electronic services (Patrício, Fisk, and Cunha 2003, 2008). Another example of collaboration the partnership between ServLab and Vitamin T. ServLab is a service simulator is at the Fraunhofer Institute for Work, Economy, and Organization. Vitamin T is a business theater company (Vitamin T 2008). Together they are creating more realistic simulations of service environments and service performance.

The emerging international service community should adopt the same ethos that helped the service marketing community grow so quickly. The service marketing community began as a very friendly field, which encouraged and welcomed new people from diverse areas of endeavor and from different parts of the world. This open networking approach accelerated the growth and reach of service marketing. To build an even larger service field, perhaps an "Adoption Program" is needed. Those in older service fields (such as marketing and management) should "adopt" the new service engineers, scientists, and artists. Such adoption will require initiating contact, exchanging ideas, and finding opportunities to collaborate on service research projects, as well as teaching those from the newer service fields about the importance of a customer-centered service culture in driving revenue growth.

Academic centers for the study of service and professional associations dedicated to the dissemination of service knowledge are becoming widespread. The growing networks of scholars and practitioners that participate in these centers and associations provide a glimpse of what is possible. Such organizations will play essential roles in fostering a larger service community of T-shaped scholars and collaborations.

Electronic Networks

Group collaboration has received considerable attention, which is illustrated by a recent book titled *The Global Brain* (Nambisan and Sawhney 2007). For the broader service field, a collaborative approach is needed that is interdisciplinary, multidisciplinary, and transdisciplinary. This will require active recruiting of new participants from more service businesses, more academic fields and more parts of the world. To be truly successful, in the spirit of co-creation, such collaborations should include customers, too.

Building a broad-based service community will also require adopting electronic networking tools that reach academe, businesses and customers. Several Internet tools have recently been developed that facilitate social networking. These tools include Facebook, MySpace and Twitter. Similar electronic networking tools are needed to facilitate full spectrum collaboration in the service field between academe, businesses, and customers. Few social networking sites focus on business purposes. The best-known service is LinkedIn with 41 million members. "LinkedIn is an interconnected network of experienced professionals from around the world, representing 170 industries and 200 countries." (Linkedin.com 2009). The Service Research and Innovation Community (2009) (http://forums.thesrii.org/srii) is forming in the service field and is an electronic outgrowth of the Service Research and Innovation Initiative, which was started by IBM, Oracle, The Technology Professionals Service Organization, and the Service & Support Professionals Association. As described on their web site:

It's the place where a community of service-based "seekers" and "solvers" come together to collaborate with the common goal of driving increased levels of innovation into a growing globally dominated services economy. SRIC is an online community that will enable Industry, Government and Academia to share information, connect with peers and collaborate around service research and innovation ideas and best practices. (http://thesrii.org/community.asp)

Electronic networks enable systems for pooling and archiving knowledge. Various forms of electronic knowledge collaboration are emerging. Wikipedia is a collaborative encyclopedia where "There are more than 75,000 active contributors working on more than 13,000,000 articles in more than 260 languages." (Wikipedia.com 2009). A related venture for scholarly manuscripts is arXiv.org (2008), which provides open access to more than 500,000 e-prints in physics, mathematics, computer science, quantitative biology and statistics. The broader service field needs its own open access knowledge archiving project. A structure is needed like the *Encyclopedia of Life* (2008), which attempts to "organize and make available via the Internet virtually all information about life present on Earth. At its heart lies a series of Web sites—one for each of the approximately 1.8 million known species." Such an effort could be labeled *The Encyclopedia of Service* and begin with sections for service science, service management, service engineering, and service arts.

Conclusion

In this chapter, we described the evolution of the service field from its beginnings to the present and speculated about its future. The service field has passed through two eras. In the first era, service evolution was described relying on a biological evolution metaphor: genes. The service field evolved in this era through the three stages of Crawling Out, Scurrying About and Walking Erect. In the second era, the present and future stages of service evolution were detailed using a social evolution metaphor: memes. This period has seen the field develop through three stages: Making Tools, Creating Language, and Building Community, with the last stage currently evolving.

As the service field continues to evolve, we should build a service community that supports a multidisciplinary, collaborative community of scholars, business leaders and customers. With the big tent metaphor, we described a wide canopy of service knowledge from diverse disciplines that include service science, service management, service engineering and service arts. To develop the service field as a collaborative community, T-shaped people– including those from the arts—are needed who can communicate via a common service language that bridges the many areas of service inquiry. T-shaped people such as these can replace the traditional isolated silos of service knowledge with interconnected networks of service understanding.

   While this multidisciplinary transformation occurs, a focus on serving customers should be adopted and maintained across the contributing service disciplines.
The emerging service field is not likely to prosper if service marketing and management are the only contributing areas that are customer-centered. The purpose
of any service is to serve customer needs. After all, without customers there is no
service to perform!

References

Allison, James (1983), *Behavioral Economics*. New York: Praeger Publishers.
Ariely, Dan (2008), *Predictably Irrational: The Hidden Forces that Shape Our Decisions*. New
   York: Harper.
ArXiv.org (2008), http://arxiv.org/, Accessed on December 3, 2008.
Aunger, Robert (2002), *The Electric Meme: A New Theory of How We Think*. New York, NY:
   The Free Press.
Bartels, Robert (1976), *The History of Marketing Thought* (2nd ed.). Columbus, Ohio: Grid, Inc.
Blackmore, Susan (1999), *The Meme Machine*. Oxford, UK: Oxford University Press.
Bloom, Howard K. (2000), *Global Brain: The Evolution of Mass Mind from the Big Bang to the
   21st Century*. New York: John Wiley & Sons, Inc.
Brodie, Richard (2004), *Virus of the Mind: The New Science of the Meme*. Seattle, Washington:
   Integral Press.
Campbell, Donald T. (1969), "Ethnocentrism of Disciplines and the Fish-Scale Model of Omnis-
   cience," in *Interdisciplinary Relationships in the Social Sciences*, Muzafer and Carolyn W.
   Sherif Sherif, ed. Chicago: Aldine.
Chesbrough, Henry and Jim Spohrer (2006), "A Research Manifesto for Services Science,"
   Communications of the ACM, 49 (7), 35-40.
Clark, Colin (1957), *Conditions of Economic Progress* (Third ed.). New York: MacMillan.
Dawkins, Richard (1976), *The Selfish Gene*. New York: Oxford University Press, Inc.
Epworth, Roger, Raymond P. Fisk, Stephen J. Grove and Michael J. Dorsch (2007), "Pitching a
   Big Tent for Service Knowledge: Arguments for a Pluralistic Approach," Presented at the
   2007 AMA Frontiers in Service Conference, San Francisco, California.
Distin, Kate (2005), *The Selfish Meme: A Critical Reassessment*. New York: Cambridge Univer-
   sity Press.
Drucker, Peter (1954), *The Practice of Management*. New York: Harper & Brothers Publishers.
Encyclopedia of Life (2008), http://www.eol.org/, Accessed on December 15, 2008.
Fisk, George (1967), *Marketing Systems: An Introductory Analysis*. New York: Harper & Row.
Fisk, Raymond P., Stephen W. Brown and Mary Jo Bitner (1993), "Tracking The Evolution of
   the Service Marketing Literature," *Journal of Retailing*, 69 (Spring), 61-103.
Fisk, Raymond P. Stephen J. Grove, Aidan Daly, and Walter Ganz (2007), "Service Arts: Broa-
   dening the Services Field," Presented at the *2007 AMA Frontiers in Service Conference*, San
   Francisco, California.
Fisk, Raymond, Stephen J. Grove, and Joby John (2008), *Interactive Services Marketing* (3rd
   ed.). Boston: Houghton Mifflin.
Glushko, Robert J. (2008), "Designing a Service Science Discipline with Discipline," *IBM Sys-
   tems Journal*, 47 (1), 15-27.
Goldberg, Joachim and Rüiger von Nitzsch (2001), *Behavioral Finance* (Adrianna Morris,
   Trans.). Chichester, England: John Wiley & Sons, Ltd.

Gorman, Michael E., James F. Groves, and Jeff Shrager (2004), 'Societal Dimensions of Nanotechnology as a Trading Zone: Results from a Pilot Project," in *Discovering the Nanoscale*, D. Baird, A. Nordmann and J. Schummer, eds. Amsterdam: IOS Press.

Grasso, Domenico and David Martinelli (2007), "Holistic Engineering," *The Chronicle of Higher Education*, March 16, B8-B9.

Grove, Stephen J., Joby John and Raymond P. Fisk (2006), "Back to the Future: Putting the People Back in Marketing," in *Does Marketing Need Reform?*, Jagdish N. Sheth and Rajendra S. Sisodia, eds., New York, NY: M. E. Sharpe, 306-311.

Haeckel, Stephan H., Lewis P. Carbone and Leonard L. Berry (2003), "How to Lead the Customer Experience," *Marketing Management*, Vol. 12 (1), 18-23.

Hefley, Bill and Wendy Murphy Ed. (2008), *Service Science, Management and Engineering: Education for the 21st Century*. New York: Springer.

Hopkins, Christopher, Stephen J. Grove and Mary Anne Raymond (2005), "Retailing in Cyberspace: The Impact of E-servicescape Design, Involvement and Familiarity   on   Customer Response," *Proceedings of the Society for Marketing Advances*, W. K. Kehoe and L. K. Whitten, eds. Charlottesville, VA: University of Virginia.

Klein, Julie Thompson, Walter Grossenbacher-Mansuy, Rudolf Häberli, Alain Bill, Roland W. Scholz, and Myrtha Welti Ed. (2001), *Transdisciplinarity: Joint Problem Solving among Science, Technology, and Society*. Basel, Switzerland: Birkhäuser Verlag.

Kohli, Ajay K. and Bernard J. Jaworski (1990), "Market Orientation: The Construct, Research Propositions, and Managerial Implications," *Journal of Marketing*, Vol. 54 (April), 1-18.

Larson, R. C. (2008), "Service Science: At the Intersection of Management, Social, and Engineering Sciences," *IBM Systems Journal*, 47 (1), 41-51.

Lusch, Robert F., Stephen L. Vargo, and Gunter Wessels (2008), "Toward a Conceptual Foundation for Service Science: Contributions from Service-Dominant Logic," *IBM Systems Journal*, 47 (1), 5-14.

Levitt, Theodore (1960), "Marketing Myopia," *Harvard Business Review*, 38 (July-Aug), 45-56.

Linkedin.com (2009), http://www.linkedin.com. Accessed on June 2, 2009.

Lovelock, C. H. (1983), "Classifying Services to Gain Strategic Marketing Insights," *Journal of Marketing*, 47 (3), 9-20.

Lovelock, Christopher (1984), *Services Marketing: Text, Cases and Readings*. Englewood Cliffs, New Jersey: Prentice-Hall, Inc.

Maglio, Paul P. and Jim Spohrer (2008), "Fundamentals of Service Science," *Journal Academy of Marketing Science*, 36 (1), 18-20.

Matravers, Derek (1998), *Art and Emotion*, New York, NY: Oxford Press.

Merriam-Webster (2003) in Merriam-Webster's Collegiate Dictionary. Eleventh ed. Springfield, MA: Merriam-Webster, Incorporated.

Meuter, Matthew L., Amy L. Ostrom, Robert I. Roundtree, and Mary Jo Bitner (2000), "Self-service Technologies: Understanding Customer Satisfaction with Technology-Based Service Encounters," Journal of Marketing, 64 (3), 50-64.

Miller, Arthur G. Ed. (1972), *The Social Psychology of Psychological Research*. New York: The Free Press.

Nambisan, Satish and Mohanbir Sawhney (2007*)*, *The Global Brain: Your Roadmap for Innovating Faster and Smarter in a Networked World*, Upper Saddle River, NJ: Wharton School Publishing.

Parasuraman, A. (2000), "Technology Readiness Index (TRI): A Multiple-Item Scale to Measure Readiness to Embrace New Technologies," *Journal of Service Research*, 2 (4), 307-320.

Parasuraman, A., Zeithaml, Valarie A., and Berry, Leonard L. (1985), "A Conceptual Model of Service Quality and Its Implications for Future Research," *Journal of Marketing*, 49 (Fall), 41-50.

Parasuraman, A., Zeithaml, Valarie A., and Berry, Leonard L. (1988), "SERVQUAL: A Multiple-item Scale for Measuring Consumer Perceptions of Service Quality," *Journal of Retailing*, 64 (Spring), 12-37.

Patrício, Lia, Raymond P. Fisk, and João Falcão E Cunha (2003), "Improving Satisfaction with Bank Service Offerings: Measuring the Contribution of New Delivery Channels," *Managing Service Quality*, 13 (6), 471-82.

Patrício, Lia, Raymond P. Fisk, and João Falcão e Cunha (2008), "Designing Multi-Interface Service Experiences: the Service Experience Blueprint," *Journal of Service Research*, 10 (4), 318-34.

Pink, Daniel (2005), *A Whole New Mind: Why Right-Brainers Will Rule the Future*. New York: Riverhead Books.

Popenoe, David (1980), *Sociology*. 4th ed., Englewood Cliffs, NJ: Prentice-Hall, Inc.

Postrel, Virginia (2004), *The Substance of Style: How the Rise of Aesthetic Value Is Remaking Commerce, Culture & Consciousness*. New York: Perennial.

Riahi-Belkaoui, Ahmed (2001), *Behavioral Management Accounting*. Westport, Connecticut: Quorum Books.

Richins, Marsha L. (1997), "Measuring Emotions in the Consumption Experience," *Journal of Consumer Research*, 24 (September), 127-146.

Robinson, Ken (2001), Out of Our Minds: Learning to Be Creative. Chichester, UK: Capstone.

Rosenthal, Robert (1967), "Unintended Communication of Interpersonal Expectations," *The American Scientist*, 10 (8), 24-26.

Rust, Roland T. (2006), "SSME—Let's Not Forget About Customers and Revenue," Presented at the *IBM SSME Conference*, New York, New York.

Rust, Roland T., Anthony J. Zahorik, and Timothy L. Keiningham (1995), "Return on Quality (ROQ): Making Service Quality Financially Accountable," *Journal of Marketing*, 59 (2), 58-70.

Sacks, Oliver (2007), *Musicophilia: Tales of Music and the Brain*. New York: Alfred A. Knopf.

Service Research & Innovation Community (2009), http://forums.thesrii.org/srii. Accessed on June 2, 2009.

Sheth, Jagdish N. and David M. Gardner (1984), "History of Marketing Thought: An Update," in *Marketing Theory: Distinguished Contributions*, Stephen W. Brown and Raymond P. Fisk, ed. New York: John Wiley & Sons, Inc.

Shostack, G. Lynn (1977), "Breaking Free from Product Marketing," *Journal of Marketing*, 41 (April), 73–80.

Smolin, Lee (2003), "How Science is Like Democracy," Presented at TED Conference, February, Monterey, California.

Solomon, Michae R., Surprenant, Carol, Czepiel, John A., and Gutman, Evelyn G. (1985), "A Role Theory Perspective on Dyadic Interactions: The Service Encounter," *Journal of Marketing*, 49 (Winter), 99-111.

Spohrer, Jim and Stephen K. Kwan (2008), "Service Science, Management, Engineering and Design (SSMED): Outline and References," in *The Future of Services: Trends and Perspectives*, Dieter and Walter Ganz Spath, ed. Munich, Germany: Hanser.

Spohrer, Jim and Paul P. Maglio (2008), "The Emergence of Service Science: Toward Systematic Service Innovations to Accelerate Co-Creation of Value," *Production and Operations Management*, 17 (3), 238-46.

Stauss, Bernd, Kai Engelmann, Anja Kremer, and Achim Luhn Eds. (2007), *Services Science: Fundamentals, Challenges and Future Developments*. New York: Springer.

Thompson, Kevin (1998), *Emotional Capital*, Oxford, UK: Capstone Publishing.

Turner, Jonathan H. (1978), *The Structure of Sociological Theory* (Revised Edition). Homewood, Illinois: The Dorsey Press.

Vargo, Stephen L. and Robert F. Lusch (2004), "Evolving to a New Dominant Logic for Marketing," *Journal of Marketing*, 68 (January), 1-17.

Vitamin T (2008), http://www.vitamint4change.de. Accessed on November 22, 2008.

Wikipedia .com (2009), http://www.wikipedia.com. Accessed on June 2, 2009.

Wilburn, Morris (2007), *Managing the Customer Experience*, American Society for Quality, Milwaukee, WI: Quality Press.

Wilson, Edwin (2001), *The Theater Experience*, Eighth Edition, New York, NY: McGraw-Hill.

Zeithaml, Valarie A., Parasuraman, A., and Berry, Leonard L. (1985), "Problems and Strategies in Services Marketing," *Journal of Marketing*, 49 (Spring), 33-46.

Trading Zones, Normative Scenarios, and Service Science

Michael E. Gorman

University of Virginia

This chapter will consider how service science could transform socio-technical systems in beneficial ways. The term socio-technical system is used in the science and technology studies (STS) literature to refer to the way in which technological and human activity are tightly coupled (M. E. Gorman, 2008). Beneficial here refers both to improvements in quality of life and to increasing revenue for services—complementary objectives, because adding social value is one way of creating sources of revenue.

The way to jump-start such a process of transformation, and ensure that it is beneficial for multiple stakeholders, is to construct a normative scenario, a concept introduced in Gibson and Scherer's classic account of the systems method (Gibson, Scherer, & Gibson, 2007). Normative scenario refers to a desired future state that stakeholders can imagine themselves in. Different stakeholders often have different normative scenarios, and means for reconciling these differences will be discussed under the section on trading zones, below. The descriptive scenario is the current state of affairs and it, too, must be specified in appropriate detail. From the perspective of the descriptive scenario, change seems impossible; therefore, the best use of the method is to begin with a normative scenario, creating momentum and a sense of urgency.

IT as collaborator: Example of a Normative Scenario

In 1960, J.C. Licklider proposed symbiosis between human beings and computers as a normative goal, in which the computer becomes "a colleague whose competence supplements your own" (Waldrop, 2001)p. 176. Let me offer a normative scenario that is only a step in this direction, one that could probably be accomplished with existing technology. My laptop and Blackberry and other devices might be combined into an intelligent IT system whose intelligence complements my own:

P.P. Maglio et al. (eds.), *Handbook of Service Science*, Service Science: Research and Innovations in the Service Economy, DOI 10.1007/978-1-4419-1628-0_29,
© Springer Science+Business Media, LLC 2010

- Find information in dialogue with me, and in contact with other people's expert assistants, databases, etc.
- Take care of references intelligently, noting what format they have to go in and making it so.
- Highlight and help resolve schedule conflicts.
- Serve as a travel consultant and guide when I am on the road, getting maps and providing translation for the kind of simple phrases every traveler needs.
- Free me from worrying about the back-end of the IT I am using, paying attention to the operating system, the University system, security issues and how specific software interacts with all of these. I would like to have a front-end intelligent assistant handling all of these details and alerting me only when I had to intervene.[1]

Back-end capabilities would include the ability for such an IT collaborator to answer natural language questions, drawing on a vast array of data. Steps in this direction are being taken by the Wolfram project (http://www.wolframalpha.com/) and by the Watson project at IBM (http://www.research.ibm.com/deepqa/). The normative scenario for Watson is the ability to play Jeopardy. From a computational standpoint, this is a significant and difficult goal. But it should be linked to a normative scenario that imagines the way in which this new technology will transform the system of which it is a part.

Creating a normative scenario forces consideration of why questions. In my personal, immediate case, it forces me to consider how I want to work, and why. In the societal case, it asks us all to consider whether these new technologies will produce a better world, and for whom? These questions are traditionally seen as the province of ethics, but they also fulfill one of the goals of service science: creating new markets (Rust & Chung, 2006).

Current state of my IT: example of a descriptive scenario

I am sitting at a desk working with what Arnold Pacey called halfway technologies (Pacey, 1989) . I am logged into a laptop that is connected to the internet; my courses are on-line, I can communicate around the world, I can access too much information on almost any topic. But all of this works less than half as well as it should:

---

[1] For more on front and back end services and the interaction between them, see Glushko and Tabas, "Bridging the "Front Stage" and "Back Stage" in Service System Design", available on-line (http://repositories.cdlib.org/ischool/2007-013/).

- I have to sit and type in order to use the laptop. Sitting is one of the worst things one can do for the human body. The mouse and trackpad cause injuries like carpel tunnel.
- The computer itself is a kind of partly-disabled idiot savant. It does have a phenomenal memory for data and information, but periodically it blanks completely and loses all of its information.
- I now have to spend almost half of each day dealing with IT back-end issues like security, compatibility and connections among peripherals which cuts way down on productivity.
- I get constant e-mails asking me to do or respond to things, and I have to put some of them off—which means they disappear in my in-box (like the original deadline for this chapter). A frequent conversation-starter is, "Did you get my e-mail?" My cognitive system is over-whelmed by the number of the contacts and the expectation that I am multi-tasking and can respond immediately. Here the beauty of the internet—the constant connectedness—comes into conflict with my own cognitive and social capabilities.
- I have used two different awkward, kludgy reference citation pro-grams that make errors and still leave me too much of the work.
- Much of what I now do would have been handled in a social system where I had help from service providers like secretaries and travel agents. These providers still exist, but their roles are constrained to the point where I am my own administrative assistant and travel agent—and I would fire me, if I could!

In other words, what I have now is a cluster of artifacts loosely coupled into a system that involves continuous cognitive repair: I have to work every day to inte-grate my cognitive functions with the information systems in which I am embed-ded.

What I want is a service: a system that learns from and works with me seam-lessly, compensating for my (many) shortcomings. The advantages of these half-way technologies outweigh the disadvantages—at least for someone like me, who rarely had the use of an office assistant. Building the competencies of such assis-tants into IT would transform halfway technologies into intelligent assistants. Adding modeling, literature search, mathematical analysis and other discovery-related capabilities would create an intelligent collaborator if they were all synched into a system that would turn me into even more of a distributed and shared cognitive system.

Many of these functions will be carried out by human beings who could be lo-cated anywhere on the globe. The old question would have been what parts of these functions depend on IT, and which depend on humans. The new question is whether this IT/human distinction matters, given the way that what we now call IT will be integrated with what we now consider human as nano, bio, info and cogni-tive technologies converge (Spohrer & Engelbart, 2004; Spohrer, McDavid, Maglio, & Cortada, 2006).

Capabilities for developing multi-stakeholder normative and descriptive scenarios

In the examples above, I deliberately used my own experiences to illustrate normative and descriptive scenarios. One way to satisfy such concerns is a variety of personalized digital/human services, adaptable to the user's needs. But in order for service science to transform socio-technical systems in beneficial ways, consultations with multiple stakeholders will have to occur. I can imagine what kind of collaborative system I want. But what about other users? What about the people who have to maintain the back-end of such systems? Would my imagined scenario scale globally, or does it simply reflect my own cultural values and personal preferences? Co-evolving service systems that facilitate collaboration obviously requires consultation with multiple stakeholders.

Trading zones

Stakeholders with different values, perspectives and practices can exchange knowledge and make compromises via trading zones. Peter Galison studied the development of radar and particle accelerators and found that different expertise communities had to develop trading zones to work together (Galison, 1997). Scientists, engineers and military leaders came to the problem of radar with radically different assumptions on how it ought to be solved. During the development of radar, the military often tried to get the MIT laboratory to simply develop devices according to their specifications—in other words, to conform to the military's normative scenario.   The eminent physicist I.I. Rabi responded by telling Navy officers to "bring back your man who understands radar, you bring your man who understands the Navy, who understands aircraft, you bring your man who understands tactics, then we'll talk about your needs" (Conant, 2002) (256) Rabi transformed the military top-down decision model into a trading zone, where multiple expertises would have to share knowledge and resources in order to co-evolve a new technology. The service scientist will need to facilitate such trading zones between different disciplines and stakeholders to co-evolve solutions to emerging problems and opportunities.

According to Galison, trading zones require a common language to get around disciplinary barriers to collaboration--first a jargon, then a pidgin, and finally a full-scale creole.[2] A creole is a hybrid of two or more languages that is then taught

---

[2] The philosopher-of-science Thomas Kuhn recognized the importance of working towards at least a common jargon when crossing these kinds of disciplinary and practice boundaries: "what the participants in a communication breakdown can do is recognize each other as members of different language communities and then become translators. Taking the differences between their own intra- and inter-group discourse as itself a subject for study, they can first attempt to discover the terms and locutions that, used unproblematically within each community, are nevertheless foci of trouble for inter-group discussions." (Kuhn, 1962) p. 202.

to another generation; eventually, a new language can emerge from a creole. This kind of common language will also be essential to integrate the multiple fields involved in service science, especially if it is to become an interdisciplinary enterprise.

Interactional expertise

Another way of facilitating trading zones is for one of the members—in this case, the service scientist—to be able to understand enough of the different perspectives and expertises in a trading zone to facilitate a serious conversation (Collins, Evans, & Gorman, 2007). This kind of expertise is referred to as interactional because the key is the ability to interact with someone from another disciplinary community in their own language. The interactional expert can 'talk the walk' of another discipline—can understand enough about the assumptions and practices of another discipline to make intelligent suggestions about research strategy without being able to 'walk the walk', i.e., do the actual research. Harry Collins was able to do this with the community of gravitational wave physicists (Collins, 2004).

In effect, the interactional expert can serve as a kind of trade agent, facilitating exchanges across disciplinary and stakeholder communities. But being a good trade agent requires skills other than shared expertise. Interactional expertise is similar to T-shaped expertise. IBM at one point characterized technical knowledge as the vertical bar and business knowledge as the horizontal, indicating that the T-shaped concept is more amorphous than interactional expertise (Glushko, 2008). In the case of an interactional 'trade agent', the tall 'leg' of the T is depth in one area of expertise and the shorter cross-bar on top indicates the ability to interact with those from at least one other expertise community, plus the kinds of business 'soft skills' that are necessary to facilitate exchanges. "SSME qualifications, which we see as critical to developing adaptive innovators with a service mindset and service innovation skills, should include interactional skills across the main disciplines of service science. Interactional skills enable proficiency in the concepts and vocabulary for framing problems and discussing potential solutions across disciplines."[3]

Let us apply trading zones and interactional expertise to one of my normative scenarios for education.

---

[3] See "Succeeding through service innovation: Developing a service perspective on economic growth and prosperity", Cambridge Service Science, Management and Engineering Symposium, Cambridge University, July 14-15, 2007 (www.ifrm.eng.cam.ac.uk/ssme). p. 12.

Immersion and serious games

As a professor, my goal is to become a designer of educational environments, where I provide scaffolding for students, who feel like they are learning on their own. My normative scenario still includes lectures, readings and discussion but as part of an environment that allows students to put ideas into practice. Just as Licklider outlined a normative scenario for collaborative computing in the sixties, so George Leonard also outlined one for educational design (Leonard, 1968) involving experiences reminiscent of a Star Trek holo-suite. The goal of this 'holo-suite' experience was to allow students to experience different local environments—perhaps a village in another part of the world, where they could engage with a different culture in a different eco-system.

A related method is to create immersive, game-like environments where students make strategic decisions, individually and/or collectively, that relate to themes of the class. In a fourth-year engineering course, I teach students about civilizations and sustainability by using Jared Diamond's book on why some civilizations collapsed and others managed to sustain themselves (Diamond, 2005). To complement the reading, I would like to design a version of the Civilization IV game that would include variables discussed by Diamond—like realistic resource constraints, the way in which civilizations spread invasive species, and collective global impacts like the rise in greenhouse gases.

One of the options available to a civilization outstripping its resources is to shift to a service-dominant logic, in which resources and goods are means to providing services. "Service-dominant logic shifts the primary focus from what we call operand resources—tangible, static resources that require other, more dynamic resources to act on them to be useful – to operant resources– dynamic resources that can act on other resources, both operand and operant, to create value through service provision. Importantly, static operand resources are usually finite and depletable, while dynamic operant resources are not only non-depletable in most cases—but also replenishable, replicable, and capable of creating additional, new operant resources. This shift has important implications for issues of social wellbeing and resource sustainability in a true global economy" (Lusch, Vargo, & Malter, 2006) p. 267. One response a society can make to imminent shortages in static resources is to focus on operant resources, on being an indispensable global service provider. This operant transformation should be an option in a Civ IV simulation of sustainable civilization management practices.

In a simulation designed specifically to teach client-producer relations, students or practitioners could be put into the role of service scientists working with real clients, an AI simulation of clients and/or other student teams in environments like Second Life. Systems-level interactions could be built in, including environmental and policy constraints—which might involve other groups of students playing roles similar to Congress or the EPA.

Not all service providers and recipients would agree with my normative scenario. For example, some students might not learn as well in an immersive game environment, or at least would need more scaffolding before they were ready to experience such an environment, and more time reflecting on lessons learned and transferring to other environments. Trading zones facilitated by service scientists involving teachers, administrators, students and gamers could begin by co-constructing a normative scenario.

Transition scenarios

Once participants in a trading zone have agreed on a normative scenario, the service scientist can help them back-cast from the normative to the descriptive, figuring out how to transition from here to there. It is important to have participants regard the normative as so urgent, in terms of its importance, that they will overcome all the usual objections that arise when participants look at change from the perspective of the descriptive scenario. Standard operating procedures have great momentum and are often entrenched in, and defended by, the bureaucracy—to make changes, participants have to be able to visualize a different way of operating, one that they are willing to buy into.

The normative scenario also guards against change for its own sake. It requires that participants negotiate and endorse a vision of how things could be, not simply make trial and error changes that are simply disruptive. Members of the trading zone should be encourage to develop metrics, or indicators, of progress towards their goals—and also to iterate on the goal itself as new possibilities emerge. The normative scenario is dynamic, which means that one is always in transition towards something better.

The service scientist as agent of transition—and transformation

Service scientists will have to create and manage trading zones, developing appropriate interactional expertise. What makes service into a science is the willingness to do empirical research on how to create and manage these trading zones. Adaptive management of this sort will not only apply to the development of normative and transition scenarios, but also to the processes used by the service scientist to create trading zones. One approach would involve adapting critical incident techniques (Zsambok & Klein, 1997) to the study of trading zones formed by clients and providers. In a typical critical incident interview, an expert is asked to tell a story about a crisis situation that required unusual skill and judgment to navigate (Klein, 1999). This method could be used to shed light on critical situations where major differences in mental models, methods and/or language had to be resolved in a trading zone; it could also be used to identify critical stages in the development of a creole, and breakthroughs that result from the collaboration.

The major weakness of interviews of this sort is that human memory is reconstructive, so informants may engage unwittingly in hindsight bias. As a corrective, critical incident interviews would have to be supplemented with observation of meetings where disciplines have to coordinate and with relevant data from blogs and diaries.

Service scientists could be trained to keep diaries of the sort advocated by Jeff Shrager, a cognitive scientist who developed a diary method to track his acquisition of skills in molecular biology (Shrager, 2005). The service scientist could:

1. Record his acquisition of interactional expertise,
2. Take notes on her or his interactions with the group, on his visits to the laboratory and on his efforts to help supervise the students.
3. Develop a problem-behavior graph that shows both the actual trajectory of the trading zone and also possible paths that were not taken.

Problem-behavior graphs are used by cognitive scientists to turn protocols of individual problem-solving sessions into branching-tree diagrams that reflected different states in the problem-solving process, the operators or activities used to change the states, and progress towards the goal (Ericsson & Simon, 1984). This method has been used to graph Alexander Graham Bell's progress towards both a telephone patent and a working device (Gorman, 1997), and implemented computationally to track Michael Faraday's path towards his discoveries (Gooding & Addis, 1993).

As service scientists co-evolve new technologies, normative scenarios will be transformed by higher expectations generated by successes. Each new disruptive, unexpected socio-technical solution will transform expectations.

Another source of transformation will be the interaction between multiple service systems. Teachers do not exist in isolation from the rest of society, nor do other user groups who are eager to improve their situations—for example, women in the developing world who want to obtain finance and reach markets around the world, and also see their children have access to the best possible education. Like healthcare, education is a complex adaptive system (Rouse, 2008)

When values differences prevent a normative scenario

The contradictions and misunderstandings among normative scenarios increases when one goes beyond a single vocation, or industry, or culture, or user group. Here one runs into cultural and values issues. Service scientists will have to manage trading zones that include these kinds of values difference. To accomplish this goal, they will have to facilitate moral imagination (Johnson, 1993). The models on which we base much of our ethical reasoning are often implicit and can become confused with reality for those who hold them. Moral imagination begins with the recognition that these realities, these truths, are views. Once I know that I have a view, I can listen to yours without immediately dismissing it, and we now have the potential to learn from one another. But if I think I see reality, and you only have a view, then there is no possibility of deep communication. Applied to educational technology, moral imagination would require service scientists in a trading zone to bracket their own notions of what the client needs and be able to listen to alternate views. But listening is not the same as agreeing. As service science becomes a field with its own expertise, the service scientist will be able to help the client form better problem definitions and show the client the likely consequences of decisions. Here the trading zone will be immensely helpful, because the client will be confronted with different views of the expected benefits of a new solution. It requires skill to get these different expectations articulated in ways that all can understand.

One promising technology is the Decision Theater at Arizona State University (http://dt.asu.edu/), where participants in a trading zone can visualize their assumptions about (say) the future of Phoenix in a room with 3-D imaging capabilities. Participants could be put into these normative scenarios in Second Life or an Open Sim environment build especially for that purpose.

The end result might not be agreement; instead, stakeholders might favor unique future scenarios that maximize their freedom to be different. Here the end result could be a diversity of service solutions, co-evolved with the different constituencies. However, optimizing service solutions for separate stakeholders could be dysfunctional at the systems level.

Constant iteration and improvement is built into the Gibson-Scherer method, and also into service science. These iterations have to consider not just the constraints of local sub-systems like a particular company and its customers, but also the impact of interaction effects with larger, more complex systems. For example, the normative scenarios for users and education I sketched above did not explicitly consider environmental impacts like the effect on energy consumption. One of the reasons I like bringing speakers in virtually is the savings on fuel (and travel costs), but I have never calculated the energy costs of running the back-end hardware that makes the IT possible. These sorts of energy calculations will be an important part of the analysis of service systems.

There are also potential intangible costs of virtual trading zones. To what extent do trades depend on the traditional hand-shake, or hug, or meal to seal the deal? Will more compelling computational simulations and worlds decrease student interests in maintaining the actual environment on which these virtual worlds depend?

The service scientist cannot dictate values or the outcome, but can facilitate a process by which clients see how achieving their individual goals might lead to systems-level interactions that threaten to undermine their own normative scenario by (say) crashing the ecosystem on which it depends. Ultimately, service systems need to be resilient (Folke, Hahn, Olsson, & Norberg, 2005) because even the most prescient systems engineer cannot anticipate the consequences of all systems-level interactions.[4] The service scientist can facilitate resilience by making agility a goal (Rouse, 2008).

---

[4] Taleb argues that instead of trying to predict, we should be prepared to be surprised (Taleb, 2007). In a resilient system, failure of a component sub-system does not crash the whole, because system components are not tightly coupled (Perrow, 1984).

Service science is itself made up of trading zones among multiple service providers from a very wide variety of disciplines (IfM & IBM, 2008). One result of such trading zones can be the formation of a creole and of a shared interactional expertise that leads to a new discipline. Service scientists are already discussing what that discipline ought to look like, and prominent universities have service science curricula (Hidaka, 2006). These individual curricular experiments should be linked in a trading zone, where practitioners share not only their courses and methods but also their normative visions.[5]

References

Collins, H., Evans, R., & Gorman, M. (2007). Trading zones and interactional expertise. *Studies in History and Philosophy of Science, 38*(4), 657-666.

Collins, H. M. (2004). *Gravity's shadow : The search for gravitational waves.* Chicago: University of Chicago Press.

Conant, J. (2002). *Tuxedo park: A wall street tycoon and the secret palace of science that changed the course of world war II.* New York: Simon & Schuster.

Diamond, J. M. (2005). *Collapse : How societies choose to fail or succeed.* New York: Viking.

Ericsson, K. A., & Simon, H. A. (1984). *Protocol analysis : Verbal reports as data.* Cambridge, Mass.: MIT Press.

Folke, C., Hahn, T., Olsson, P., & Norberg, J. (2005). Adaptive governance of social-ecological systems. *Annual Review of Environmental Resources, 30,* 441-473.

Galison, P. (1997). *Image & logic: A material culture of microphysics.* Chicago: The University of Chicago Press.

Gibson, J. E., Scherer, W. T., & Gibson, W. E. (2007). *How to do systems analysis.* Indianapolis: Wiley.

Glushko, R. J. (2008). Designing a service science discipline with discipline. *IBM Systems Journal, 47*(1), 15-28.

Gooding, D. C., & Addis, T. R. (1993). *Modelling faraday's experiments with visual functional programming 1: Models, methods and examples*

Gorman, M. E. (1997). Mind in the world: Cognition and practice in the invention of the telephone. *Social Studies of Science, 27 Number 4,* 583-624.

Gorman, M. E. (2008). Service science, management and engineering: A way of managing sociotechnical systems. In W. E. Hefley, & W. Murphy (Eds.), *Service science, management and engineering: Education for the 21st century* (pp. 77-82). New York: Springer.

Hidaka, K. (2006). Trends in services sciences in Japan and abroad. *Quarterly Review, 19*(4), 39.

IfM, & IBM. (2008). Succeeding through service innovation: A service perspective for education, research, business and government. *University of Cambridge Institute for Manufacturing, Cambridge,*

Johnson, M. (1993). *Moral imagination.* Chicago: University of Chicago Press.

Klein, G. (1999). *Sources of power: How people make decisions.* Cambridge, MA: MIT Press.

Kuhn, T. S. (1962). *The Structure of scientific revolutions.* Chicago: The University of Chicago Press.

Leonard, G. B. (1968). *Education and ecstasy.* New York: Delacorte Press.

---

[5] To an extent, this already goes on informally at meetings like Frontiers in Service, but these efforts could be accelerated by having a workshop similar to the one that produced the Cambridge Manifesto.

Lusch, R. F., Vargo, S. L., & Malter, A. J. (2006). Marketing as service-exchange:: Taking a leadership role in global marketing management. *Organizational Dynamics, 35*(3), 264-278.

Pacey, A. (1989). *The culture of technology.* Cambridge, MA: MIT Press.

Perrow, C. (1984). *Normal accidents.* New York: Basic Books.

Rouse, W. B. (2008). Health care as a complex adaptive system: Implications for design and management. *BRIDGE-WASHINGTON-NATIONAL ACADEMY OF ENGINEERING-, 38*(1), 17.

Rust, R. T., & Chung, T. S. (2006). Marketing models of service and relationships. *Marketing Science, 25*(6), 560-580.

Shrager, J. (2005). Diary of an insane cell mechanic. In M. E. Gorman, R. D. Tweney, D. C. Gooding & A. Kincannon (Eds.), *Scientific and technological thinking* (pp. 119-136). Mahwah, NJ: Lawrence Erlbaum Associates.

Spohrer, J. C., & Engelbart, D. C. (2004). Converging technologies for enhancing human performance: Science and business perspectives. In M. C. Roco, & C. D. Montemagno (Eds.), *The coevolution of human potential and converging technologies* (pp. 50-82). New York: The New York Academy of Sciences.

Spohrer, J. C., McDavid, D., Maglio, P. P., & Cortada, J. W. (2006). NBIC convergence and technology-business coevolution: Towards a services science to increase productivity capacity. In B. Bainbridge, & M. C. Roco (Eds.), *Managing nano-bio-info-cogno innovations: Converging technologies in society* (pp. 227-253). Dordrecht, The Netherlands: Springer.

Taleb, N. (2007). *The black swan : The impact of the highly improbable* (1st ed.). New York: Random House.

Waldrop, M. M. (2001). *The dream machine : J. C. licklider and the revolution that made computing personal.* New York: Viking.

Zsambok, C., & Klein, G. (1997). *Naturalistic decision making.* Mahwah, N.J.: Lawrence Erlbaum Associates.

The Cambridge-IBM SSME White Paper Revisited

James C. Spohrer

Global University Programs, IBM, San Jose, California, USA

Mike Gregory

Institute for Manufacturing
University of Cambridge, Cambridge, UK

Guangjie Ren

Institute for Manufacturing
University of Cambridge, Cambridge, UK

In July 2007, IBM and Cambridge University's Institute for Manufacturing (IfM), in conjunction with BAE Systems, convened a group of leading academics and senior industrialists in a two-day symposium to address the critical questions facing the emerging field of Service Science, Management and Engineering (SSME). The meeting, together with a consultation process involving over a hundred international respondents, created a white paper for universities, businesses and governments globally (IfM and IBM 2008). The report called for (1) the advancement of SSME as a distinct subject of research and education through intensive collaboration across disciplines, and (2) the creation of national Service Innovation Roadmaps (SIR) to double investment in service research and education worldwide by 2015. Since the white paper was released, exciting progress has taken place; many universities have started SSME courses while various governments released SIR reports (see Appendices I and II for lists of such initiatives). In the remainder of this chapter, we provide an updated summary of the white paper and revisit its original recommendations for SSME stakeholders.

Acknowledgments: Thanks to Cambridge University's Institute for Manufacturing (IfM), IBM, BAE Systems, and US NSF grant IIS-0527770 for support. We especially thank the symposium participants, correspondents, and respondents for their efforts; a complete list of over one hundred names can be found in Appendix II and Appendix III of the original white paper (IfM and IBM 2008). The diverse backgrounds of this multicultural and multidisciplinary group produced remarkable commonality of view as to how we can move the field forward, as well as points of ongoing debate (see in the original white paper, Appendix VIII: On-going debate)

P.P. Maglio et al. (eds.), *Handbook of Service Science*, Service Science: Research and Innovations in the Service Economy, DOI 10.1007/978-1-4419-1628-0_30,
© Springer Science+Business Media, LLC 2010

Executive Summary

Innovation, a term applied almost exclusively to technologies in the past, is increasingly used in relation to services (Miles 2003). *Service systems[1]*, which form a growing proportion of the world economy, are dynamic configurations of *people, technologies, organisations* and *shared information*, creating and delivering value to customers, providers and other *stakeholders* (Spohrer *et al.* 2007). Thanks to globalisation, demographic changes and technology developments, today's service systems have been driven to an unprecedented level of scale, complexity and interdependence. The rising significance of service and the accelerated rate of change mean that *service innovation* is now a major challenge to practitioners in business and government as well as to academics in education and research (Chesbrough and Spohrer 2006).

In response, *Service Science, Management and Engineering (SSME)*, or in short *Service Science*, is emerging as a distinct field aimed at improving our knowledge of service systems (IBM 2005). Its vision is to discover the underlying logic of complex service systems and to establish a common language and shared frameworks for service innovation. To this end, we can no longer afford to work in unconnected silos; instead, an *interdisciplinary* approach has to be adopted. And to encourage knowledge and skill development, governments and businesses should double the investment in service research and education.

Developing Service Science is no easy task. Drawing upon the expertise and experience of leading academics and senior practitioners, this article provides a starting point to raise awareness and establish benchmark. More specifically, it makes the following interrelated recommendations:

For education: Enable graduates from various disciplines to become *T-shaped professionals* or *adaptive innovators*; promote SSME education programmes and qualifications; develop a modular template-based SSME curriculum in higher education and extend to other levels of education; explore new teaching methods for SSME education.

For research: Develop an interdisciplinary and intercultural approach to service research; build bridges between disciplines through grand research challenges; establish *service system* and *value proposition* as foundational concepts; work with practitioners to create data sets to understand the nature and behaviour of service systems; create modelling and simulation tools for service systems.

For business: Establish employment policies and career paths for T-shaped professionals; review existing approaches to service innovation and provide grand challenges for service systems research; provide funding for service systems research; develop appropriate organisational arrangements to enhance industry-academic collaboration; work with stakeholders to include sustainability measures.

---

[1] Words in *italics* are defined in the glossary.

For government: Promote service innovation and provide funding for SSME education and research; demonstrate the value of Service Science to government agencies; develop relevant measurements and reliable data on knowledge-intensive service activities; make public service systems more comprehensive and citizen-responsive; encourage public hearings, workshops and briefings with other stakeholders to develop service innovation roadmaps.

Service Science is still in its infancy; but we are confident that, by adopting these recommendations, we can accelerate its development and benefit from service innovations in the future (e.g. a smarter planet).

The structure of this chapter follows the diagram below.

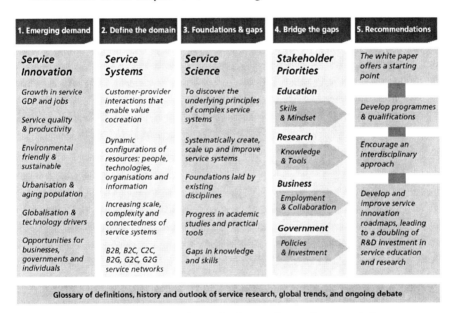

Figure 1. Succeeding through service innovation: a framework for progress.

Introduction

Growing demand for service innovation

While service growth[2] is broadly recognised across industries, our understanding of *service systems* remains rudimentary. Today's service systems are increasingly dispersed yet inter-connected, and their effectiveness, efficiency and sustainability matter to billions of people. Besides economic factors, service systems are complicated by our values in social, ecological and political dimensions.

Thanks to the application of science, management and engineering to the improvement of agriculture and manufacturing, remarkable products, from disease resistant crops to automobiles and personal computers, can be produced flexibly and efficiently and are widely available (Cohen & Zysman 1988). As a result, more time and more resources are used to search for, obtain, install, maintain, upgrade and dispose of products than production itself (Womack & Jones 2005). This trend offers a wealth of opportunities for *service innovation* – both incremental and radical.

To start with, service innovation can improve customer-provider interactions and enhance organisations' capabilities to create value with stakeholders. It often takes the form of better self-services, eliminating waiting and allowing 24/7 access via modern devices such as mobile phones, web browsers and kiosks. The benefits of service innovation can also be extended into government programmes, such as health care and education. For families and individuals, service innovation is needed to improve the quality of life and deal with important issues such as aging populations. In the virtual world, new service models, such as Amazon and Google, are changing our behaviour in decision making and in many other areas.

New skills and knowledge required

The rising demand for service innovation has huge implications for skills and the knowledge base that underpins them (NAE 2007). People are needed who can understand and marshal diverse global resources. Quite often, these resources are accessed using advanced information and communication technologies (ICT) and novel business models. The people with such skills are known as *adaptive innovators* – those who identify and realise a continuous stream of innovation in service

---

[2] By service growth we mean both the growth of the service sector in the economy as traditionally measured by statistics, as well as the growth of service activities in agriculture and manufacturing sectors (Vargo and Lusch 2004).

systems (Council on Competitiveness 2008). The demand for service innovation does not mean that the need for science, management and engineering in agriculture and manufacturing has gone away. But as the scope of innovation continues to move beyond products, we must prepare ourselves with the right skills and knowledge (BHEW 2008).

Service Science: an emerging field

The prominence of service in modern economies has gradually driven scholars to service-related studies. While research into service can be traced to as early as the 1940s, significant development was seen in the late 1970s when service research was broken free from product-centric concepts and theories (Fisk *et al.* 1993). The field of Service Science, Management and Engineering (SSME)[3] now covers a wide range of subjects, including *service economics, service marketing, service operations, service management, service engineering, service computing, service human resources management, service sourcing, service design,* and many others. Nevertheless, a more integrated approach is needed if real progress is to be made.

Key concepts and world view

There are four key concepts in Service Science: *service system* (entity), *value proposition* (interaction), *adaptive innovator* (individual trait), and *Service Science, Management and Engineering (SSME) graduates* (education focus). These concepts provide a service perspective on the traditional concepts: factory (entity), trade (interaction), problem solver (individual trait), and *Science, Technology, Engineering and Mathematics (STEM) graduates* (education focus). Based on the four concepts, the changing landscape of business and society can be viewed as a large global ecosystem, consisting of service system entities that are interacting via *value propositions* to co-create value (Anderson *et al.* 2007). Individuals with suitable traits fill roles in complex service systems, which in turn fill roles in even more complex service networks. When challenges and opportunities arise, individuals may want to change, improve or create service systems. With such a world view, adaptive innovators will benefit from their SSME knowledge and skills (Spohrer and Maglio 2009).

---

[3] Considering the integral role of design and the arts in customer experience, SSME could be logically extended to SSMED or SSMEA (Service Science, Management, Engineering and Design/Arts). In recent publications (Spohrer & Kwan 2008; Spohrer & Maglio 2009), the term SSMED has been used along with a discussion of ten basic concepts: ecology, entities, interactions (networks), outcomes (ISPAR), value-proposition-based interactions, governance-mechanisms-based interactions, stakeholders, measures, resources, and access rights.

Clarifying the rationale and defining the domain

What is a service system?

A service system is a dynamic configuration of resources (people, technology, organisations and shared information). Primary interactions take place at the interface between the provider and the customer, each with their own constellation of resources. Moreover, with the advent of ICT, interactions among customers and those among suppliers have also become prevalent. The interactions create a complex system whose behaviour is difficult to explain and predict. As a convenient illustration, the present global financial crisis started with subprime mortgage loans in the US, but has quickly rippled around the world and put most economies into a downturn.

Why are we interested in service systems?

We live in a world where it is a daily experience to interact with various service systems such as banking, communications, transport and health care. We all suffer frustrations (or worse) when service quality is poor and we all pay more when productivity is low. Yet this business-to-consumer (B2C) or government-to-consumer (G2C) view of service systems is just the tip of the iceberg. Although invisible to most consumers and citizens, service systems in business-to-business (B2B), business-to-government (B2G) and government-to-business (G2B) environments are also experiencing enormous change and growth.

In 2006, for the first time in human history, worldwide service jobs (42%) outnumbered jobs in agriculture (36.1%) and manufacturing (21.9%) (ILO 2007). If we consider service activities in manufacturing, even the latest figures are an understatement. However, although service sector accounts for over two thirds of GDP and jobs in many developed economies, investment in services represents less than one third of total R&D spending (RTI international 2005). This mismatch hinders our ability to address service challenges.

Businesses, competing in a global economy, are familiar with many of the issues and challenges that need to be addressed. Service performance relies on both *front-stage* and *back-stage* components (Teboul 2006). The 'front stage' is about provider-customer interactions: how can customer satisfaction be ensured in the presence of multiple customer touch points and various channels of contact? The 'back stage' is about operational efficiency: how can productivity be improved through skilled employees, advanced technology, streamlined processes and robust global sourcing relationships? More than anything else, businesses want to know: how can an extended *service network* be managed in a seamlessly integrated manner (Allee 2002; Nambisan & Sawhney 2007)? Service businesses are not alone in asking the questions; manufacturers are keen to understand the same issues as they embark on a *servicisation* journey (Ren 2009).

Similarly, government agencies and non-profit organisations feel the compelling need to provide better service to the public (Collins 2006). Commercial competition is replaced by demands for transparency, fairness, and accountability. For households, there is a growing recognition of the need to seek better education, health care and financial planning. And environmental concerns are high on everyone's agenda. The constellations of resources around individuals, families, non-profit organisations, government agencies, and businesses generate an enormous number of service interactions to be studied, designed, engineered and managed.

What is the vision for Service Science?

Our ability to address the practical challenges relies on our understanding of service systems. Unlike the IT industry, however, there is no *Moore's Law* roadmap for the service domain to guide organisations on what investments to make in order to see predictable performance improvements. As a result, we have poor knowledge about: (1) how to invest in service systems to sustainably improve key performance indicators (e.g. revenue, margin, growth, customer satisfaction, productivity, innovation, quality of life, social responsibility, environmental sustainability, and regulatory compliance), and (2) how to develop new service offerings, together with creative value propositions and improved business models.

The vision of Service Science, therefore, is to discover the underlying principles of complex service systems (and the value propositions that interconnect them into service networks). It should provide the structure and rigour for building a coherent body of knowledge to support ongoing innovation in service systems. To this end, it must provide answers to the following questions:

- What are the architectures of service systems?
- How is hierarchical complexity and diversity built up from simpler elements?
- How might we best understand the origins, lifecycles and sustainability of service systems?
- How can service systems be optimised to interact and co-create value?
- Why do interactions within and between service systems lead to particular outcomes?

For each question, we have pieces of the answer today, spread across many disciplines, but not yet a unified whole. Thus, Service Science provides motivation, methods and skills for integration, optimisation and sustainability, equipping adaptive innovators with knowledge and tools for service innovation.

Who are the stakeholders of Service Science?

The stakeholders of Service Science include both individuals and organisations dependent on complex service systems. Businesses want to improve their service revenues and profit margins. Non-profit organisations want to deliver desired service offerings sustainably. National and local governments want to create a high-skilled workforce and develop infrastructures to improve the competitiveness and quality of life of their citizens. These stakeholders all need the knowledge and skills for service innovation, though they sometimes work at cross purposes (Reich 2007). Knowledge workers (academics and professionals alike) across a wide range of disciplines and professions are also important stakeholders. Indeed, the system of disciplines and professions has to evolve if it is to remain relevant to the changing landscape of service systems (Abbot 1988).

Why now?

Global trends, such as demographic shift, technology advancements and global sourcing, challenge us to create new ways of doing things. As we become more and more technology-enabled, globally integrated (interconnected), many new challenges and opportunities emerge.   Physics, chemistry, biology, cognitive science, and computer science are some of the sciences that have enabled the development of today's service system ecology. Service Science has the potential to be as important in the future as these earlier sciences have proven in the past (Spohrer & Maglio 2009). However, modern tools of Service Science, such as a computer-aided design for service system simulation, will require significant investment.

Recognising the foundations and identifying the gaps

What foundations have been laid by existing theories?

The resources used to form service systems offer a useful starting point for developing Service Science. They can be divided into four clusters:

- Whole businesses and organisations: Studied primarily by schools of management (marketing, operations management, operations research and management sciences, supply chain management, innovation management)
- Technology: Studied primarily by schools of science and engineering (industrial engineering, computer science, statistical control theory)
- People: Studied primarily by schools of social sciences and humanities (economics, cognitive science, political science, design, humanities and arts)
- Shared information: Studied primarily by schools of information (communications, management information systems, document engineering, process modelling, simulation)

The white paper (IfM and IBM 2008) provided a list of 35 disciplines, from Architecture to Total Quality Management, and related each of them to the four types of resources above. Since then, a number of publications have provided further explanation of the relationship between disciplines and resource types (Spohrer and Kwan 2009; Spohrer & Maglio 2009).

Discovering fundamental building blocks of service systems and the way they can be combined to form our current service system ecology is well underway. Pioneering attempts to develop a normative view on how service systems can be described and their behaviours explained, include the Customer Contact model (Chase 1978), the Service Quality GAPS model (Parasuraman 1985), Service-Dominant Logic (Vargo and Lusch 2004), Unified Theory of Service (Sampson 2001), Service as Leasing (Lovelock and Gummesson 2004), and Work System Method (Alter 2006), to name but a few. These form initial efforts at resource classification schemes, along with associated access rights, service level agreements, standards and protocols, safeguarding mechanisms, intellectual property and failure recovery methods. They also provide foundational views from multiple stakeholder perspectives (customer, provider, authority, competitor, criminal, victim, etc.) on associated measures of service system performance (quality, productivity, compliance, sustainability, etc.).

Meanwhile, tools, methods and data sets for practical use are emerging (e.g. IBM's Component Business Modelling approach and toolkit) (Sanz *et al.* 2006). The use of service-oriented architectures (SOA) for describing information technology 'services' that support work and business practices is on the rise and has gained widespread acceptance. And more broadly, there have been new developments to model industrial evolution, which has generated interest among historical economists and organisation theorists (Beinhocker 2006).

Where is the knowledge gap?

Still, despite significant progress, achieving the vision of Service Science is perhaps a decade or more away. For one thing, there are still challenges within individual disciplines. For example, operations research and industrial engineering often model people waiting in queues, but the model fails to recognise people as emotional and psychological beings that can learn and adapt over time (e.g. Mansfield 1981). Computer science and information science often model information system architectures on the basis of well-understood environmental variations, but governance mechanisms that allow information systems to respond proactively to strategy changes and predictable technological advances are less understood.

In a similar vein, economics and business strategy need to accommodate predictable innovations (e.g. Christensen *et al.* 2004). Service management and operations need to create a better knowledge of service system scaling and lifecycle (Normann 2001). Law and political science need to build a better comprehension of social innovation and the way that legislation can improve service system productivity (March 1991). Complex systems engineering should provide more specific insights into the robustness of service systems (Sterman 2000). Last but not least, integration across all these disciplines and areas of study remains the ultimate challenge.

The current situation stems from the tradition that academic institutions are structured along disciplines and sub-disciplines (or areas of study). As shown in Figure 2, academic silos encourage deeper understanding of a specialised subject. The expectation from institutions and funding bodies is that academics conduct research and provide courses within their disciplines. Although often addressing similar matters, each discipline or department usually has a presumed set of interests, paradigms and methodologies. Over time, academics see interdisciplinary research as being highly risky and potentially career-damaging.

Figure 2. The gaps between academic disciplines.

As a result, service research is often imbalanced; studies tend to focus on either customers from a marketing perspective or providers from an operations perspective. This is reflected, and indeed reinforced, by top journals, which tend to be highly specialised. For instance, less than 20 percent of the papers in operations management journals focus on service topics while research on operations has a similar profile in service journals (Johnston 2007). Moreover, disciplines also tend to focus on specific sectors; marketing tends to be concerned with business-to-consumer and operations with business-to-business (Johnston 2005). Gradually, a gap has emerged between academic output and practical interest.

Where is the skill gap?

Similarly, the supply of people with the right skills is increasingly inadequate. The role of education in the 20th century was in a large part to prepare students for jobs. Universities have been rewarded for creating people with specialised knowledge. The increasing complexity of service systems, however, requires an extended role of education in the 21st century – universities must prepare people to be adaptive innovators (NAE 2007).

Adaptive innovators are still taught in their home disciplines. In parallel, however, they also develop the ability to think and act across multiple disciplines. They can build consensus across functional silos and work in inter-inter-organisational and inter-cultural environments. They can communicate with specialists who may not have the same background. They embrace a service mindset, which is supported by intellectual, psychological and social capital components. They are driven by an integrative 'service logic' rather than the competing logics associated with individual functions or units. These adaptive innovators are in short supply as the service economy grows (Council on Competitiveness 2008).

Working together to bridge the gaps

What are the possible approaches to addressing the gaps?

The gaps in knowledge and skills needed to deal with complex service systems indicate that we need to reassess our approach to research and education. Figure 3 shows three possible routes to address the gaps. To some people, Service Science is seen as a *multidisciplinary* 'superset' embracing all appropriate, but as yet not agreed, disciplines and functions. To others, Service Science is seen as a multidisciplinary 'subset' embracing select elements of the major disciplines and functions. Finally, Service Science can be seen as an *interdisciplinary* activity which attempts to create an appropriate set of new knowledge to bridge and integrate various areas based on *transdisciplinary* and *crossdisciplinary* collaboration.

In this document, we advocate the interdisciplinary approach. Since many barriers to integration are well established, attempts to remove them would not only require considerable effort but deflect attention from purposeful bridging activities. Therefore, one way to overcome the barriers is to accept their existence and build bridges over them. This approach will lead to

"curricula, training, and research programs that are designed to teach individuals to apply scientific, engineering, and management disciplines that integrate elements of computer science, operations research, industrial engineering, business strategy, management sciences, and social and legal sciences, in order to encourage innovation in how organisations create value for customers and stakeholders that could not be achieved through such disciplines working in isolation" (US Congress HR 2272, 2007).

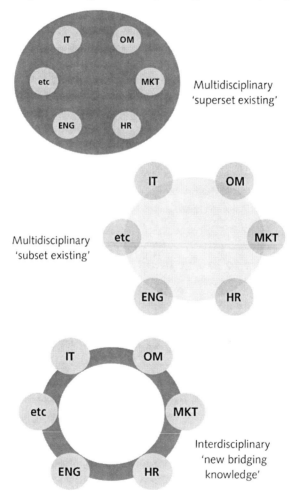

Figure 3. Three perspectives of service science.

Adam Smith (1776) laid the foundations of modern economics with his exploration of the division of labour (specialists) and its role in creating the wealth of nations. Today specialisation alone is not the answer to increasing value creation capacity of nations. To grow the wealth of nations sustainably, we must become far more systematic. We need both specialization and integration to create, improve and sustain service systems.

Where are the opportunities to address the knowledge gap?

Interdisciplinary activities are not new (e.g. Derry *et al.* 2005). In fact, they are practiced in many universities, often in close cooperation with industries. Opportunities exist at all levels to address the barriers between disciplines.

Individual level: Leaders in academia, business and government are well positioned to highlight the value of interdisciplinary work and to reduce the risks associated with moving outside a specialism or discipline. The potential of service science to improve society, not just business, can attract diverse people to the field.

Project level: Interdisciplinary interactions happen at a project level. Exemplary service system improvement projects (e.g., design the X of the future, given societal constraints Y) in the form of case studies can stimulate more cooperative behaviours with common purpose across disciplines or functions.

Business interactions: Business opportunities are often best explored via interdisciplinary and cross-functional teams. Businesses can supply engaging challenges and hard data for academic research to reach robust and practical conclusions (e.g., design the X of the future, given business reality Y).

Academic journals: Leading journals in the field of service research are extremely influential in setting the tone and agenda of academic research. They are uniquely placed to encourage interdisciplinary studies. Major specialised journals should be encouraged to initiate special issues on interdisciplinary topics. One of the tools that can be used is web-based communication (e.g., http://www.sersci.com/ServiceScience/).

Funding agencies: Except in certain areas of physics and mathematics, little is known about the methods needed to create integrated yet parsimonious theories that span multiple areas. Besides discipline-specific studies, funding should also be provided to support interdisciplinary service research through mechanisms such as dual appointments and shared rewards.

Where are the opportunities to address the skill gap?

Discipline-based education remains a vital role of modern universities. Yet in order to close the skill gap and create more adaptive innovators, universities should offer students the opportunity to gain qualifications in the interdisciplinary requirements of SSME. Such qualifications help equip graduates with key concepts and essential vocabulary to discuss the design and improvement of service systems with peers from other disciplines. Industry refers to these people as T-shaped professionals, who are deep problem solvers in their home discipline but at the same time are also capable of interacting with and understanding specialists from a wide range of disciplines and functional areas (Leonard-Barton 1995).

Widely recognised SSME programmes would help ensure the availability of a large population of T-shaped professionals (from many home disciplines) with the ability to collaborate to create service innovations. Graduates with SSME qualifications, including improvement projects across industries and performance measures, would be well prepared to 'hit the ground running' and make significant contributions when joining a service innovation project (Spohrer & Kwan 2009).

Interdisciplinary course development requires significant effort to develop because different faculty members might find it hard to work together sustainably over time. Educational innovations are vulnerable because they are often reliant on the efforts of one or two people. Interdisciplinary programmes are even harder to organise, and more expensive to initiate and maintain, than conventional ones. Rapid progress in the design and delivery of these programmes would require support and resources from business and government.

Recommendations

Even though the service sector contributes over two thirds of GDP and employment in developed economies, investment in services accounts for less than one third of total R&D expenditure (RTI 2005). To address this imbalance, we urge the development of more national Service Innovation Roadmaps (SIR)[4], leading to a doubling of service R&D investment by 2015. Public Private Research Partnership (PPRP) programmes should be encouraged to support the improvement of service systems, e.g. to create a smarter planet. The following recommendations are offered as a starting point for a more inclusive conversation of all stakeholders as nations formulate and update their SIR reports:

---

[4] For an example of an innovation roadmap, see Appendix VII Example of innovation roadmap, in the original white paper (IfM and IBM 2008), as well as Appendix II of this chapter.

Recommendations for education

Enable graduates of disciplines to become T-shaped professionals, adaptive innovators with a service mindset.

All students and employees, who wish to, should have the opportunity to learn about Service Science and develop themselves into T-shaped professionals. This can be achieved by adding an SSME specialisation to an existing discipline. As adaptive innovators, they will have a good background in the fundamentals of service innovation. With a service mindset, they can work effectively in project teams across disciplines, functions, and cultural silos. As research creates a truly integrated theory of service systems, students of Service Science will become system thinkers prepared to succeed in a 21st century service-driven globally integrated economy.

Promote SSME education programmes in conjunction with industry recruitment of SSME qualified graduates.

SSME qualifications should include interactional skills across the main disciplines of Service Science. Such skills enable proficiency in the concepts and vocabulary for framing problems and discussing potential solutions across disciplines (Collins & Kusch, 1999). The main disciplines of Service Science include service economics, service marketing, service operations, service management, service quality (especially customer satisfaction), service strategy, service engineering, service human resource management (especially in a professional service firm), service computing, service supply chain (especially eSourcing), service design, service productivity, and service measurement.

Develop a modular template-based SSME curriculum in higher education at all levels of education.

SSME qualifications should employ a template-based curriculum model and specify modules that can be switched in and out across different faculty and courses. Practical or industry capstone projects are essential for students to develop a service mindset and to acquire the ability to solve problems cross-functionally in real-time. Capstone projects prepare students to understand service systems in action. The design and provisioning of such projects should ideally involve student teams with members from different areas, including business, government, and different universities (cultures). Attention should also be given to primary and secondary education. The design of Service Science laboratory space would enable multidisciplinary project teams to work together with collaborators in remote locations (ideally, via tele-presence technology). Projects should encourage links between real world, virtual world, and simulated world service systems.

Explore new teaching methods for SSME education across industries.

SSME qualifications should be accessible through a range of channels, including on-line eLearning and virtual worlds. They should offer access to cases, simulations, and lab activities in major sectors of the modern economy, including the public sectors (government and security, healthcare and education, environment and recreation), commercial sectors (retail and franchise, hospitality and entertainment), information sectors (financial and banking, consulting and professional, media and internet), and infrastructure sectors (transportation and communications, utilities and construction, manufacturing and mining).

Recommendations for research

Develop an inclusive interdisciplinary and intercultural approach to service research.

Many of the pioneering service research journals and conferences have made this a stated priority. However, much more needs to be done to measure and reward efforts that increase the actual amount of interdisciplinary and intercultural work in this emerging field.

Build bridges between disciplines through grand research challenges.

A good architecture helps to reduce a complex problem to separable components. However, when decomposition is not fully effective or has enormous complexity associated with it, a deeper foundational understanding is often needed. Researchers from multiple disciplines should look for opportunities to bridge between disciplines, especially in the context of grand research challenges that span multiple disciplines.

Establish service system (entity) and value proposition (interaction) as foundational concepts.

Every science must clearly define its boundaries in terms of the entities that it studies and the relevant interactions between those entities. Service systems and value propositions represent a starting point for Service Science.

Work with practitioners to create data sets to better understand the nature and behaviour of service systems.

Much real world data about service systems often has a proprietary nature and security concerns associated with it. The confidential feature of the data may require novel methods of archiving and releasing. Unlike many other subjects, service science researchers must focus their efforts on establishing appropriate legal, social, and economic conventions around data sharing for specific purposes.

Create modelling and simulations tools for the complete service systems ecology.

Perhaps more than any other subjects, advancement in Service Science depends on models and simulations of alternative service systems designs, where local optimisation may not lead to global optimisation (Ricketts 2007). When data are not readily available, service practitioners need simulation and computer-aided design (CAD) tools to support their decision-making processes.

Recommendations for business

Establish employment policies and career paths for T-shaped professionals.

Businesses should define career paths for T-shape professionals and indicate their preference for SSME qualifications in recruitment. This would demonstrate the demand for academic programmes and encourage the formation of interdisciplinary Service Science communities.

Review existing approaches to service innovation and provide grand challenges for service systems research.

Understanding, modelling and measuring service activities that take place in business today is already underway; for example, activity-based costing and service-oriented architecture. Despite promising progress, surprisingly little is known about (a) how to make optimal investment for service innovation (Ricketts 2007), (b) how to scale up margins as service revenues increase (Spohrer et al. 2007), (c) how to systematically reduce the complexity of service systems, and (d) how to devise measurement systems that can be used internally and shared externally to protect privacy and preserve competitive advantage (Spitzer 2007). These issues and others are potential grand challenges.

__Provide funding for service systems research.__

Businesses should provide resources for service systems research, through regional Public Private Research Partnerships (PPRP), with a focus on smart water systems or smart transportation systems, that create win-win-win's for local government agencies, businesses, and universities. Businesses can also fund industry Special Interest Group (SIG) initiatives via global organisations such as the Service Research and Innovation Initiative (SRII). Benchmarks on the current level of service research investment are a starting point.

__Develop appropriate organisational arrangements to enhance industry-academic collaboration.__

Businesses can also encourage employees to participate in SSME relevant SIG membership organizations, conferences and to support academic SSME programmes with the latest projects and case studies. Tools, methods and data sets are an ideal focus for business-academic collaborations.

__Include sustainability measures and create actionable service innovation roadmaps.__

As sustainability becomes an increasingly urgent global concern, businesses should take the opportunity to expand the definition of stakeholder value. Roadmaps for service innovation should include updated performance measures and better balance efficiency, effectiveness, and sustainability.

Recommendations for government

__Promote service innovation for all parts of the economy and fund SSME education and research.__

History repeatedly shows that focused research and development efforts can advance science and build a body of knowledge with long-term practical benefits. The separate discipline areas of service research have developed to a point that an integrated theory is within reach. National funding for university-based research in Service Science is critical and has far-reaching benefits for economy and society. Benchmarks on the current level of service research investment are a starting point.

Demonstrate the value of Service Science on national projects that create a smarter planet.

Improvements in government service systems, which employ over 20% of the populations in some nations, would lead to a ripple effect through the rest of the economy. Smarter transportation systems, water management systems, health care systems, education systems, energy systems, and green jobs initiatives create tools, methods, and data sets and can stimulate Public Private Research Partnerships (PPRP).

Develop relevant measurements and reliable data on knowledge-intensive service activities across sectors to underpin leading practice for service innovation.

Measuring service activities across sectors of the economy to better understand service quality, productivity, regulatory compliance, and sustainable innovation is an important starting point. More funding is needed for nationally directed data collection about multiple aspects of the service economy, including employment, skills and career paths, exports, investment, pricing, and IT-enabled activities, among others (Innovate America 2004).

Make government service systems more comprehensive and citizen-responsive.

Government service systems are especially in need of comprehensive review by engaging citizens. Transforming from a provider-centric to a citizen-centric perspective is a good first step (Clarke et al. 2007).

Encourage public hearings, workshops to develop national service innovation roadmaps (SIR) reports.

Continuous improvement of service systems requires an investment roadmap to focus and align academic, industry, and government stakeholders. Investment is needed in three categories: run, transform, and innovate (March 1991). Priority should be given to investment, legislative and policy initiatives that can systematically support the growth of the knowledge economy (knowledge creation) and the service economy (knowledge application to create value); both are needed in an innovation economy (Bell 1973).

In conclusion, we applaud the nations, universities, and businesses acting on these recommendations to advance SSME-related education and research and establish and revise SIR reports to guide ongoing investment in service innovation.

References

Abbot, Andrew (1988) The System of Professions: An Essay on the Division of Expert Labor. University of Chicago Press. Chicago, IL.

Allee, Verna (2002) The Future of Knowledge: Increasing Prosperity through Value Networks. Butterworth-Heinemann.

Alter, S. (2006). The Work System Method: Connecting People, Processes, and IT for Business Results. Larkspur, CA: Work System Press.

Anderson, J.C., N. Kumar, and J. A. Narus (2007) Value Merchants: Demonstrating and Documenting Superior Value in Business Markets. Harvard Business School Press. Cambridge, MA.

Beinhocker, Eric D. (2006) The Origin of Wealth: Evolution, Complexity, and the Radical Remaking of Economics. Harvard Business School Press. Cambridge, MA.

Bell, Daniel (1973) The Coming of the Post-Industrial Society: A Venture in Social Forecasting. Basic. New York, NY.

Board on Higher Education and Workforce (BHEW) (2008) Science Professionals: Master's Education for a Competitive World. Committee on Enhancing the Master's Degree in the Natural Sciences. The National Academies Press. Washington, DC.

Chase, R. B. (1981). The customer contact approach to services: theoretical bases and practical extensions. Operations Research, 29(4): 698-706.

Chesbrough, H. and J. Spohrer (2006) A research manifesto for services science. Communications of the ACM. 49(7). July. 35-40.

Christensen, C., S. D. Anthony and E. A. Roth. (2004). Seeing What's Next: Using Theories of Innovation to Predict Industry Change. Boston: Harvard Business School Press.

Clarke, J., J. E. Newman, N. Smith, E. Vidler and L. Westmarland. (2007). Creating Citizen-Consumers: Changing Publics and Changing Public Services. London: Sage.

Cohen, S. S. and J. Zysman (1988) Manufacturing Matters: The Myth of the Post-Industrial Economy. Basic, New York.

Collins, H. and M. Kusch (1999) The Shape of Actions: What Humans and Machines Can Do. MIT Press. Cambridge, MA. (See also: http://en.wikipedia.org/wiki/Interactional_expertise).

Collins, J. (2006). Good to Great and the Social Sector. London: Random House.

Council on Competitiveness. (2008). Thrive: The Skills Imperative, Washington D.C.: Council on Competitiveness.

Derry, S. J., C. D. Schunn and M. A. Gernsbacher. (2005). Interdisciplinary Collaboration: An Emerging Cognitive Science. London: Psychology Press.

Fisk, R. P., S. W. Brown, and M. J. Bitner. (1993). Tracking the Evolution of the Service Marketing Literature, Journal of Retailing, 69 (1):61-103.

IBM (2005). Services Sciences: A new academic discipline? Available at http://almaden.ibm.com/asr/SSME/facsummit.pdf

IfM and IBM. (2008). Succeeding through Service Innovation: A Service Perspective for Education, Research, Business and Government. Cambridge, United Kingdom: University of Cambridge Institute for Manufacturing. ISBN: 978-1-902546-65-0

Innovate America (2004) Report of the National Innovation Initiative, December.

International Labour Organisation (ILO). (2007). Key Indicators of the Labour Market (KILM), 5th edition.

International Labour Organization (ILO). (2008). Global Employment Trends 2008. Available at http://www.ilocarib.org.tt/portal/images/stories/contenido/pdf/LabourMarketInformation/get08.pdf

Johnston, R. (2005). Service operations management: from the roots up. International Journal of Operations and Production Management, 25 (12), 1298-1308.

Johnston, R. (2007). The internal barriers to service quality: reviving TQM. POMS Service College Conference, London, UK, 12–13 July 2007.

Leonard-Barton, D. (1995). Wellsprings of Knowledge: Building and Sustaining the Sources of Innovation. Boston: Harvard Business School Press.

Lovelock, C., & Gummesson, E. (2004). Whither services marketing? In search of a new paradigm and fresh perspectives. Journal of Service Research, 7(1): 20-41.

Mansfield, J. W. (1981). Human factors of queuing: a library circulation model, Journal of Academic Librarianship, 6(6): 342-4.

March, J.G. (1991) Exploration and exploitation in organizational learning. Organizational Science. 2(1).71-87.

Miles, I. (2003). Services Innovation: coming of age in the knowledge-based economy. In B. Dankbaar (Ed.), *Innovation Management in the Knowledge Economy* (pp. 59-82). London: Imperial College Press.

National Academy of Engineering. (2007). Rising Above the Gathering Storm: Energizing and Employing America for a Brighter Economic Future. Washington D.C.: National Academies Press.

Nambisan, S. and M. Sawhney (2007) The Global Brain: Your Roadmap for Innovating Faster and Smarter in a Networked World. Wharton School Publishing.

Normann, R. (2001) Reframing Business: When the Map Changes the Landscape. Wiley, Chichester, New Sussex.

Parasuraman A., V. A. Zeithaml, and L. L. Berry. (1985). A conceptual model of service quality and its implications for future research. Journal of Marketing, 49(4): 41-50.

Reich, Robert (2007) Supercapitalism: The Transformation of Business, Democracy, and Everyday Life. Knopf. New York, NY.

Ren, Guang-Jie (2009) Service Business Development in Manufacturing Companies: Classification, Characteristics and Implications. Doctoral Dissertation. University of Cambridge, Cambridge, United Kingdom.

Ricketts, J.A. (2007) Reaching the Goal: How Managers Improve a Services Business Using Goldratt's Theory of Constraints. IBM Press. New York, NY.

RTI international. (2005). Measuring Service-Sector Research and Development. RTI Project Number 08236.002.004

Sampson, S. (2001). Understanding Service Businesses: Applying Principles of Unified Services Theory, New York: John Wiley and Sons.

Sanz, J. L., N. Nayak, and V. Becker (2006). Business Services as a New Operational Model for Enterprises and Ecosystems. The 8th IEEE International Conference on E-Commerce Technology and The 3rd IEEE International Conference on Enterprise Computing, E-Commerce, and E-Services (CEC/EEE'06), 2006.

Smith, A. (1776). An Inquiry into the Nature and Causes of the Wealth of Nations. London: Methuen & Co.

Spitzer, Dean R. (2007) Transforming Performance Measurement: Rethinking the Way We Measure and Drive Organizational Success. AMACOM.

Spohrer, J. & Kwan, S. K. (2009). Service Science, Management, Engineering, and Design (SSMED): An Emerging Discipline - Outline & References. Int. J. of Information Systems in the Service Sector, 1(3).

Spohrer, J. & Maglio, P.P. (2009). Service science: Toward a smarter planet. W. Karwowski & G. Salvendy (Eds.), Introduction to service engineering.

Spohrer, J, Maglio, P.P., Bailey, J., Gruhl, D. (2007). Steps towards a science of service systems. IEEE Computer, 40(1), pp. 71-77.

Sterman, John D. (2000) Business Dynamics: Systems Thinking and Modeling for a Complex World. Irwin McGraw-Hill. Boston, MA.

Teboul, J. (2006) Service Is Front Stage: Positioning Services for Value Advantage. INSEAD Business Press, Palgrave MacMillan.

Vargo, S. L. and R. F. Lusch. (2004) Evolving to a New Dominant Logic for Marketing. Journal of Marketing, 68, 1-17.

Womack, J. P. and Jones, D. T. (2005) Lean Solutions: How Companies and Customers Can Create Value and Wealth Together. Free Press. New York, NY.

Glossary

Adaptive innovators: People who are entrepreneurial and capable of systems thinking in the many project roles they may fill during their professional life. In contrast to the specialised problem solvers of the 20th century, who are sometimes called 'I-shaped' professionals for their knowledge depth, adaptive innovators of the 21st century are still grounded in their home disciplines but have strong communication skills across areas of business, technology and social sciences. Hence, they are sometimes called T-shaped professionals.

Back-stage service activities: Activities that do not involve direct interaction with the customer, for example, back office operations of a retail bank or marking of student coursework by a teacher. Information processing is a common back-stage service activity.

Crossdisciplinary: The teaching of one discipline from another disciplinary perspective (e.g., physics for poets). The knowledge of one discipline is used as a lens through which another discipline is studied.

Customer service system: A service system from the viewpoint of a customer or consumer. A customer service system searches provider value propositions looking for win-win value-cocreation opportunities. For example, a task the customer currently does (self service) may be outsourced to a provider, a problem the customer does not have the knowledge, capability, or authority to solve may be outsourced to a provider, or the customer may learn of a novel service offered by a provider that they desire (demand innovation).

Goods-dominant logic: Goods-dominant logic is the traditional economic world view, which considers services (plural) and products as two distinct value-creating mechanisms.

Front-stage service activity: Activities that involve direct interaction with a customer, for example, a doctor talking to and examining a patient or a teacher lecturing to a class of students. Customer communication is a common front-stage service activity.

Interactional Skills: Also known as complex communications skills, the ability to communicate across knowledge domains or disciplinary boundaries, without necessarily possessing deep contributory expertise. Contributory expertise allows experts or specialists to extend the knowledge in a discipline.

Interdisciplinary: The creation of new knowledge that bridges, connects, or integrates two or more disciplines (e.g., biophysics).

Moore's Law: In 1965, Intel co-founder Gordon Moore forecasted that the number of transistors on a chip will double about every two years. The prediction, popularly known as Moore's Law, has proved to hold for more than 40 years.

Multidisciplinary: Relating to two or more existing, separate disciplines (e.g., physics and biology). The knowledge of individual disciplines is viewed as separate and additive to each other.

Organisations: From a service system perspective, an organisation is an accessible non-physical resource that has the ability to establish formal contractual relationships as well as informal promissory relationships. Organisations themselves are either formal (legal entities that can contract and own property) or informal service systems. Organisations that are formal service systems include businesses and government agencies. Organisations that are informal service systems include open source communities, temporary project teams and working groups.

People: From a service system perspective, people are legal entities that have knowledge, capabilities, authority and can create contracts (formal value propositions) and promises (informal value propositions) with other service systems. People can own property (such as technology and shared information). People exist in modern society as roleholders (see Stakeholder) in many service systems. People are complex and adaptive, with the ability to learn and change their knowledge and capabilities over time. People have unique life cycles and life spans. People are resources that can be accessed in creating value propositions. They are also the atomic type of service systems, capable of configuring resources and creating value via interactions with other service systems.

Provider service system: A service system from the viewpoint of a provider (see Stakeholder). A provider service system aims to meet the customer's needs better than competing alternatives consistently and profitably (in business context) or sustainably (in non-business context). Provider service systems seek deep knowledge of customer service systems (their own service activities, their unsolved problems, and their aspirations) to improve existing, and create new, value propositions.

Service or service activity:

(1) Archaic: Referring to economic residual; any economic exchange or production process that does not result in a physical product transfer or output; non-productive labour.

(2) Modern: The application of competences (knowledge, skills and resources) by one entity for the benefit of another entity in a non-coercive (mutually agreed and mutually beneficial) manner.

(3) Modern: Value-cocreation interactions (typically with well-defined customer-provider entities as parties who initiate, directly or indirectly, front-stage and back-stage activities in anticipation of value-cocreation results).

(4) Modern: An economic activity offered by one party to another, most commonly employing time-based performances to bring about desired transformation results in recipients themselves or in objects or other assets for which purchasers are responsible. In exchange for their money, time and effort, service customers expect to obtain value from the access to goods, labour, professional skills, facilities, networks and systems; but they do not normally take ownership of any of the physical elements involved.

Many typologies of service exist: external customer (market-based) and internal customer service; direct and indirect customer and provider interactions; automated, IT-reliant and non-automated service; customised, semi-customised and non-customised service; personal and impersonal service; repetitive and non-repetitive service; long-term and short-term service; service with varying degrees of self-service responsibilities.

Service computing: The use of information technology (IT) to support customer-provider interactions. Topics include web services, e-commerce, service-oriented architectures (SOA), self-service technologies (SST), software as a service (SaaS) and IT Infrastructure Library (ITIL).

Service design: The application of design methods and tools to the creation of new service systems and service activities with special emphasis on perceptions of quality, satisfaction and experience.

Service-dominant logic: The service-dominant logic advocates that service (singular) involves value-cocreation interactions as service systems create, propose and realise value propositions. The interactions may include things, actions, information and other resources. Value propositions are built on the notion of asset sharing, information sharing, work sharing (actions), risk sharing as well as other types of sharing that can create value in customer-provider interactions. Service Science embraces the world view of the service-dominant logic.

Service economics: The definition and measurement of service activities in an economy. Typical measures include productivity, quality, regulatory compliance and innovation.

Service engineering: The application of technologies, methodologies and tools to the development of new service offerings and the improvement of service systems.

Service experience and service outcome: The customer's perceptions of the process and result of a service interaction or relationship. The perceptions are based in large part on customer expectations and hence there is always a subjective as well as objective component to the customers' evaluation of the process and result. Expectations may inflate over time, resulting in degradation of service experience even when objective measures have not changed. Exceptional recovery from a service failure has been shown, under certain conditions for repeated service, to lead to greater customer lifetime value for a provider.

Service human resources management: The application of human resource management to service activities. This term is rejected by many social scientists and those who do not believe it is appropriate to talk about people as resources. The term human relations management is sometimes seen as a more appropriate alternative. Many service firms have the motto to treat employees like they treat valued customers.

Service innovation: A combination of technology innovation, business model innovation, social-organisational innovation and demand innovation with the objective to improve existing service systems (incremental innovation), create new value propositions (offerings) or create new service systems (radical innovation). Often radical service innovation will create a large population of new customers (public education – students; patent system – inventors; money markets – small investors). Service innovation can also result from novel combinations of existing service elements.

Examples of service innovation include: On-line tax returns, e-commerce, helpdesk outsourcing, music download, loyalty programs, home medical test kits, mobile phones, money market funds, ATMs and ticket kiosks, bar code, credit cards, binding arbitration, franchise chains, instalment payment plans, leasing, patent system, public education and compound interest saving accounts.

Service management: The application and extension of management methods and tools to service systems and service activities, including capacity-and-demand management that integrates insights from service operations (supply capacity) and service marketing (customer demand).

Service marketing: The study of value-creating customer-provider interactions, outcomes and relationships. It uses and extends the tools and methods of marketing. It is gradually replacing 'services marketing', with the emphasis on the outcome of all economic activity being service (or value) whether the service/value comes from things ('goods') or activities ('services').

The notion of service marketing is supported by relationship marketing and customer relationship management, both primarily focused on the two-party relationship between customer and provider, and the new concept of many-to-many marketing (a network and stakeholder perspective).

This discipline places special emphasis on quality and customer satisfaction, demand forecasting, market segmentation and pricing, customer life-time value, and the design of sustainable value propositions.

Service mindset: An orientation geared towards the innovation of customer-provider interactions (service systems and value propositions), combined with interactional skills to enable teamwork across academic disciplines and business functions. It is one of the characteristics of adaptive innovators.

Service operations: The study of value-creating (work) processes, which include customer-input as a key component. It uses and extends the tools and methods of operations research, industrial engineering, management science, operations management, human resource management, lean methods, six sigma quality methods, logistics and supply chain management.

Service networks: Also known as service system networks. As service systems connect to other service systems, they form networks of relationships, which may have one or more associated value propositions. Social network analysis (people as service systems) and value network analysis (businesses as service systems) are tools that can be used to analyze service networks for robustness, sustainability, and other properties.

Service Science: An umbrella term for the emerging discipline of Service Science, Management and Engineering (see SSME below), it is named as a symbol of rigour in pursuing the truth. Service Science is the study of service systems and value propositions. It is the integration of many service research areas and service disciplines, such as service economics, service marketing, service operations, service management, service quality (especially customer satisfaction), service strategy, service engineering, service human resource management (especially in a professional service firm), service computing, service supply chain (especially eSourcing), service design, service productivity, and service measurement.

Service sourcing: The make-versus-buy decision for service activities, including the study of outsourcing, contracts, service level agreements, and business-to-business on-line markets.

Service system: Service systems are dynamic configurations of resources (people, technology, organisations and shared information) that can create and deliver service while balancing risk-taking and value-cocreation. The dynamics are in part due to the ongoing adjustments and negotiations that occur in all systems involving people. People are the ultimate arbiters of value and risk in service systems (in part because people are legal entities with rights and responsibilities).

Service systems are complex adaptive systems. They are also a type of 'system of systems', containing internal smaller service systems as well as being contained in a larger service system (see Stakeholder). They typically interact with other service systems via value propositions, which may form stable relationships in extended value chains or service networks (see Service networks).

Formal service systems are legal entities that can create legally binding contracts with other service systems. Informal service systems cannot create contracts, though individual people within them may be able to do so.

Servicisation: A process whereby manufacturers moves from product-led towards a service-oriented business model. For example, instead of selling jet engines, manufacturers develop service offerings in which customers are charged for propulsion usage.

Shared information: From a service systems perspective, an accessible conceptual resource that does not have the ability to establish formal contractual relationships. It includes language, laws, measures, methods, process descriptions, standards, and others. It can be codified and turned into explicit information. If people can talk about it and name it, then from a communication perspective, it is a type of shared information.

Stakeholders: Stakeholders include participants in service systems and others who are indirectly affected. Stakeholders who are 'named participants' are also known as roleholders, who can be people or other service systems that fill named roles in service systems.

The two main roles in any service system are customer and provider. To create successful value propositions, it is also important to consider authority and competitor roles. Examples of roleholders are employees and customers in businesses, politicians and citizens in nations, teachers and students in schools, doctors and patients in hospitals, and parents and children in families.

SSME: Service Science, Management and Engineering (SSME), or in short Service Science, is an emerging field. It includes curricula, training, and research programs that are designed to teach individuals to apply scientific, engineering, management and design disciplines that integrate elements of computer science, operations research, industrial engineering, business strategy, management sciences, social and legal sciences, and others in order to encourage innovation in how organisations create value for customers and stakeholders that could not be achieved through such disciplines working in isolation.

STEM: The Science, Technology, Engineering and Mathematics (STEM) fields are widely considered to be the driving force behind a modern society. The STEM workforce is viewed by many governments, academic and business organisations as the key to a nation's innovation capacity and long-term competitiveness.

Systems and systems world view: Systems are dynamic configurations of entities (elements or components) that interact over time and result in outcomes (internal changes to entities and external changes to regions of the system and the system as a whole). The study of physical, chemical, biological, computational, cognitive, economic, legal, social, political, service or any other type of systems, typically begins with a statement of the entities, interactions and outcomes of interest. Reductionist science attempts to discover more fundamental building blocks out of which the entities of the system are composed (new architectures), often with the goal of finding simpler or more parsimonious explanations of observed variety.

In complex adaptive systems, entities have life spans and the types of entities change over time in ways that are difficult to predict. Service Science studies the evolution of entities known as service systems, which interact via value propositions and result (normatively) in value-cocreation outcomes. Understanding the evolution may shed light on the shifts from social to economic, political to legal, and cognitive to computational systems. The shift seems to depend heavily on an increasing amount of shared information to solve motivation and coordination problems.

T-shaped professionals: Those who are deep problem solvers with expert thinking skills in their home discipline but also have complex communication skills to interact with specialists from a wide range of disciplines and functional areas (see also Adaptive Innovators).

Technology: From a service systems perspective, technology is an accessible physical resource that does not have the ability to establish formal contractual relationships. It includes any human-made physical artefact or portion of the environment accessible to service system stakeholders. Technology (physical) and shared information (codified conceptual) are two important types of properties that service systems can own and provide access rights to others in value exchanges.

Transdisciplinary: Transcending, or extending beyond the knowledge of any existing disciplines. For example, symbolic reasoning and general systems theory are considered to be applicable to all disciplines and hence labelled as transdisciplinary knowledge.

Value proposition: A specific package of benefits and solutions that a service system intends to offer and deliver to others. Division of labour is at the root of many value propositions. By traditional economic and marketing definitions, value propositions may be confined to either products (things) or services (activities). However, the modern meaning of service is value-cocreation that involves both products and services.

Value proposition emphasizes key points of difference in comparison to competing alternatives. They may be rejected because a potential customer does not trust the provider's capabilities or believes the proposal violates a law or policy. They may also be rejected in favour of self service, a competitor's proposal, or other options. Designing, proposing, negotiating, realising (actualising), and resolving disputes around value propositions are an integral part of the formation and improvement of service systems.

Appendix I: University initiatives

The following list provides some examples of SSME-related university initiatives. In April 2009, there were 250 universities in 50 countries with related work.

Table 1. Illustrative list of service science related efforts at universities

University	SSME initiatives
Arizona State University (USA)	Center for Services Leadership
Bahcesehir University (Turkey) and Northeastern University (USA)	Information Technologies Service Management
Carnegie Mellon University (USA)	IT Services Qualification Center
Howe School of Technology Management (USA)	Service Management tracks, Master of Science in Information Systems
Karlstad University (Sweden)	Master Programme with a Profile in Service Science
Masaryk University (Czech)	SSME Master Degree in the Faculty of Informatics
Michigan Technological University (USA)	Service Systems Engineering courses for undergraduate studies
National Tsing Hua University (Taiwan)	Institute of Service Science
North Carolina State University (USA)	Service Engineering concentration, MS in Computer Networking; Service Management and Consulting concentration, MBA
Ohio State University (USA)	Initiative for Managing Services, Fisher College of Business
Peking University (China)	Department of Service Science and Engineering
Politecnico di Milano (Italy)	Service Engineering and Technologies Master Program
San Jose State University (USA)	SSME Undergraduate and MBA concentration
Swiss Institute of Service Science (Switzerland)	Zurich University of Applied Sciences, University of Applied Sciences Western Switzerland and University of Applied Sciences North-West Switzerland
University of Cambridge	Service and Support Engineering Programme
University of Manchester (UK)	SSMEnetUK
University of Porto (Portugal)	Master in Services Engineering and Management
University of Alberta (USA)	Service Systems Research Group
University of California at Berkeley (USA)	Information and Service Design Program
University of California at Merced (USA)	Minor in Service Science and Management
University of California at Santa Cruz (USA)	Knowledge Services and Enterprise Management
University of Maryland (USA)	Center for Excellence in Service
University of Pennsylvania (USA)	Fishman-Davidson Center for Service and Operations Management
University of Sydney (Australia)	IT Professional Services course
University of Tokyo (Japan)	Service Innovation Working Group

Appendix II: Service innovation roadmaps

The following list provides a selection of national service innovation roadmap (SIR) reports. These reports are intended to focus and align stakeholders, benchmark existing and guide further service innovation investments, report progress and challenges, and increasingly provide the foundation for Public Private Research Partnership (PPRP) programmes to create improved service systems for a smarter planet.

Table 2. Illustrative list of service innovation roadmaps by nation

Nation	Service Innovation Roadmap title	Year
Finland	Serve - Innovative Services Programme, Tekes	2006
USA	Service Enterprise Systems Program, National Science Foundation	2006
USA	Study of Service Science, The National Competitiveness Investment Act	2007
UK	Supporting innovation in services	2008
Netherlands	Service innovation and ICT: vision and ambition	2008
Ireland	Catching the Wave: A Service Strategy for Ireland	2008
Australia	Science and Technology-Led Innovation in Services for Australian Industries	2008
Korea	Measures to Vitalize R&D in Service Industry	2009

Service Science, Management, and Engineering (SSME) in Japan

Kazuyoshi Hidaka

IBM Tokyo Research Laboratory, Yokohama, Japan

This paper reports the latest academic and government activities relating to Service Innovation and Service Science, Management, Engineering (SSME) in Japan. Universities, government institutes, and government officials are looking for new ideas to cultivate economic growth, especially following the financial crisis that began in late 2008. Service innovation makes an excellent place to look for these new ideas, and SSME, as a new academic initiative for giving fundamentals for service innovation, may make an excellent basis for service innovation.

Introduction

After Service Science, Management, and Engineering (SSME) was introduced into Japan in 2005, there has been growing interest about this new academic initiative there (Hidaka, 2006), as the Japanese look for new economic drivers. There is some sense that SSME might provide the basis for new economic growth.

Service activities in Japan's economy are growing in terms of gross domestic product (Figure 1) and workforce (Figure 2). These economic trends are accelerated by the development of service industries and the growth of services in manufacturing. However, the labor productivity growth rate of Japanese services is much lower than that of other countries, although Japanese manufacturing is higher than that of other countries (Table 1). This is regarded as a very serious problem for Japan's economy, and new government policies are aimed at improving labor productivity for services (Ministry of Economy, Trade, and Industry, 2007)

P.P. Maglio et al. (eds.), *Handbook of Service Science*, Service Science: Research and Innovations in the Service Economy, DOI 10.1007/978-1-4419-1628-0_31,
© Springer Science+Business Media, LLC 2010

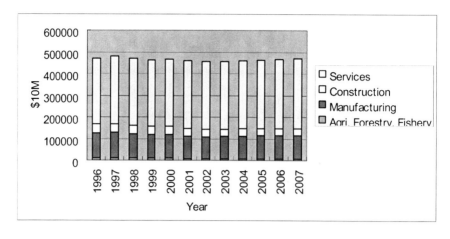

Figure 1. Japan's gross domestic product by economic activity;
data from Cabinet Office, Government of Japan (2009)

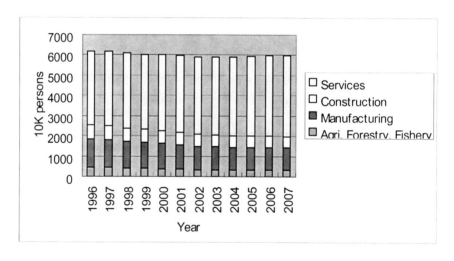

Figure 2. Japan's workforce by economic activity;
data from Cabinet Office, Government of Japan (2009)

Table 1. Labor productivity growth rate (1995 to 2003);
data from Ministry of Trade, Economy, and Industry (2007)

	US	UK	Germany	Japan
Manufacturing	3.3%	2.0%	1.7%	4.1%
Services	2.3%	1.3%	0.9%	0.8%

As Drucker (1993) claimed, the tension between those in knowledge-intensive business jobs with high-labor productivity and those in service jobs with low-labor productivity will be the basis of a new social structure in the era of post capitalist society. Japan may have already come to this post-capitalist in terms of social labor structure.

I think SSME can be used to solve some of the social and business problems in a post-capitalist knowledge society. There are two parts to this: (1) a science for better services, which will provide the knowledge and methodology to improve the existing services by applying scientific and engineering approaches; and (2) a science for new services, which will provide innovative ways to create new service businesses by developing processes for new value co-creation.

The research areas of both science for better services and science for new services include:

- develop methods and tools for evaluating service innovation
- develop methods and tools for quantitative evaluation of service value
- model and optimize service value
- visualize and formalize service knowledge
- develop technologies to improve service productivity
- models and method for pricing services
- define metrics and measure the productivity of services
- test the service
- manage the risk of service projects
- analyze the performance of service organizations
- integrate knowledge in different domains for service innovation

Japanese and foreigners alike recognize the many advances Japan has made in hospitality services, such as the excellent services at Japanese hotels (Ryokan) and restaurants. These excellent service practices create intangible "high value" through highly labor-based services, service workers' beliefs in their jobs, synthesis of business and culture, and sustainable service systems with low-impact on the environment. Therefore, in Japan, SSME may aim to provide answers to the questions such as, "how we can articulate the intangible values of these excellent Japanese service practice?", and "how we can make ourselves globally competitive through Japanese hospitality?"

SSME at Japanese Universities

Fostering Service Innovators

In 2007 and 2008, Ministry of Education, Culture, Sports, Science and Technology (MEXT) in Japan started programs to develop university curricula that foster the development of service innovators. Thirteen Japanese universities were funded by this program and are now working to develop SSME education. These programs will eventually share the education materials with other universities. (see http://www.mext.go.jp/a_menu/koutou/service/index.htm).   Following is a short description of each of these university programs.

Tohoku University

The goal of the program is to foster Service Innovation "Managers" who can evaluate the productivity of services at the level of sector and practitioner, create new services, and maintain service quality. To achieve the goal, they will develop a new educational program by integrating mathematical science, engineering, economics, and management science, and also will develop the project to measure, evaluate, and improve service productivity.

University of Tsukuba

In the master's program of Business Administration and Public Policy, the University of Tsukuba will establish interdisciplinary educational program in the Science of Services to realize customer-focused business innovation. They will also develop an integrated educational database for service innovation, which will be used to foster the high skill service practitioner. Finally, they will develop an education program to be offered by other universities and enterprises.

Tokyo Institute of Technology

To maximize the societal value of Science and Technology efficiently, the Tokyo Institute of Technology will foster service innovators who can create the societal service value by designing, evaluating, and innovating services based on science and technology. They will develop a multidisciplinary liberal arts programs for the twenty-first century for graduate students.

Bunri University of Hospitality

The Seibu Bunri University of Technology will develop a packaged educational program following the case method. They will focus on fostering middle managers in the service practice by developing the skill of analysis, decision, and imagination.

Meiji University

To develop a curriculum for fostering service innovators, Meiji University classified service innovations into 2 layers. The first layer is a logical process layer toward standardization, and the second layer is a deviation management layer which manages exceptions and tacit knowledge toward individualization. For the first layer, they will provide integrated knowledge based on management science, theory of services management, information theory, and behavioral science; and for the second, science for tacit knowledge.

Kyoto University, Graduate School of Management

To foster creation of a "service creative class" that can lead the high quality service society, Kyoto University, Graduate School of Management will develop an educational program for management of service-value creation based on anthropology and information technology.

Kyoto University, Graduate School of Pharmaceutical Science

Kyoto University Graduate School of Pharmaceutical Science will develop a course for innovators to lead medical services for this new era, including home care and self-medication.

Shiga University, Department of Economics

Shiga University will develop a service innovation education course at the undergraduate level, aiming to teach basic knowledge of service science to develop creative minds and foster the capacity of evaluating innovation value.

Kobe University, Research Institute of Economics and Business Administration

Kobe University aims to formalize and categorize service innovation, and are developing video contents based on the case method to teach introduction to service innovation. They will also collaborate with businesses to gain insight in service value creation.

Japan Advanced Institute of Science and Technology (JAIST)

JAIST will start a new "Management of Service" course for business people, adding to the current "Management of Technology" course, as a common program in the graduate schools of Knowledge Science and Information Science. They will develop programs that cover all aspects of service innovation based on approaches from technology, human science, social science, and economics. (see http://www.jaist.ac.jp/mos/)

Keio University

Keio University will develop an internship program with IBM Business Consulting Services to foster services leaders in the area of knowledge-based professional business services.

Waseda University

Waseda University will develop a "Financial Market Simulator" using the results of financial engineering. They will also develop an education course using this simulator to foster service leaders for the global financial market.

Kansai University

Kansai University will develop an education program to foster business consultants who have can do analytics of business processes based on the skills from mathematical science and data mining.

Service Innovation Research Initiative, Division of University Corporate Relations, University of Tokyo

Recently, a study group, named Service Innovation Research Initiative, Division of University Corporate Relations, University of Tokyo, finalized its study on service innovation, and issued the final proposal and study report (University of Tokyo, 2009). The members of this initiative were professors from different academic domains, including information science and technology, engineering, humanities, and sociology, and business and technology leaders from leading Japanese IT companies.

The scope of this initiative was innovation in services that relate tightly to information technology. The group recognized the significance of creating a science of service, and proposed establishing the "Informatical Foundations of Services", a set of fundamental knowledge and methodologies common to general information-based service systems. This Informatical Foundation will provide a set of tools enabling the solution of the problems service providers have in improving their end-user services. The research areas that significantly relate to service innovation include (a) understanding human psychology and behavior, (b) handling large amounts of data, (c) overcoming the complexity of systems, (d) dealing with evolution/variation, and (e) consensus formation/system design .

SSME by Ministry of Economy, Trade, and Industry Japan (METI)

Grand Strategy by Ministry of Economy, Trade, and Industry Japan (METI)

In 2006, Ministry of Economy, Trade, and Industry Japan (METI) issued the Grand Strategy of Economic Growth in Japan for the next 10 years (Ministry of Economy, Trade, and Industry, 2006). In this strategy, the Ministry was aiming to continue 2.2 % economic growth in GDP. To realize this growth rate, they suggested that Japan's strategic focus be (a) enhancing the global competitiveness, (b) improving productivity of services using Information Technology, (c) vitalizing local economy and small and medium business, (d) developing new market through transforming the government system, and (e) investing in social infrastructure. After the global financial crisis in 2008, Japanese economic growth rate is now far below the target (Cabinet Office Government of Japan, 2009). So now the expectations for service innovation are even higher. To realize this strategy,

METI leads the research and development programs to promote service innovations.

Center for Services Research, National Institute of Advanced Industrial Science and Technology (AIST)

In 2008, National Institute of Advanced Industrial Science and Technology (AIST) established the Center for Services Research, especially focusing on service engineering. This group aims to realize service innovation for service providers (improving productivity) and service consumers (adding service value) by developing engineering approaches for services. They are trying to develop methodologies and tools for service engineering by (a) observing the behavior of providers and consumers in the service interactions (not in the laboratory), (b) analyzing the data, (c) making the model, (d) designing the system, (e) applying the system to actual service interactions, and f) running the loop from (a) - (e) (see http://unit.aist.go.jp/cfsr/ci/indexj.html)

IBM Japan

IBM Japan leads many efforts across Japan's SSME Universities, and runs an seminar series for university professors to promote Service Science, Management, and Engineering in Japan by through lectures from professors and business leaders in service research. (IBM Japan, 2009)

References

Cabinet Office, Government of Japan (2009). *Annual Report on National Accounts*. Available at http://www.esri.cao.go.jp/jp/sna/h19-kaku/21annual-report-j.html

Cabinet Office, Government of Japan (2009, Jun). *Quarterly Estimates of GDP*: Jan. - Mar. 2009 . Available at http://www.esri.cao.go.jp/jp/sna/qe091-2/main1.pdf

Drucker, P. F. (1993). *Post Capitalist Society*. New York: HarperCollins.

Hidaka, K. (2006). Trends in Services Sciences in Japan and Abroad, *Science & Technology Trends Quarterly Review* No.19, pp. 35 – 47, National Institute of Science and Technology Policy, Ministry of Education, April 2006.

IBM   Japan   (2009).   SSME   University,   Available   at   http://www-06.ibm.com/software/jp/academic/skills/ssme/ssme2009.html

Ministry of Economy, Trade, and Industry (2007). *Towards Innovation and Productivity Improvement in Service Industries*. Commerce and Information Bureau, Service Unit, Japanese Ministry   of   Economy,   Trade,   and   Industry,   April   2007.   Available   at http://www.meti.go.jp/english/report/downloadfiles/0707ServiceIndustries.pdf.

Ministry of Economy, Trade, and Industry (2006). *New Economic Growth Strategy of Japan.* Available at http://www.meti.go.jp/policy/economic_oganization/s_senryaku.html

University of Tokyo (2009). *Towards the Establishment of an Informatical Foundation of Services to Realize Innovation,* Service Innovation Research Initiative, Division of University Corporate Relations, University of Tokyo. Available at http://www.ducr.u-tokyo.ac.jp/service-innovation/pdf/090331teigen-en.pdf

Innovation and Skills

Future Service Science Education

Linda Macaulay

Centre for Service Research
Manchester Business School
The University of Manchester

Claire Moxham

Centre for Service Research
Manchester Business School
The University of Manchester

Barbara Jones

Manchester Institute of Innovation Research
Manchester Business School
The University of Manchester

Ian Miles

Manchester Institute of Innovation Research
Manchester Business School
The University of Manchester

Maglio and Spohrer (2008) state that a work force that is capable of adaptation and problem solving requires people with capability and unique skills across many areas. While this cannot be disputed, it is clear that we still lack understanding of key skill areas within the service economy and of the relationship between skills requirements and education provision. This chapter describes the range and diversity of service and presents a forecast of the demand for higher level skills and knowledge. It examines education provision in terms of context, content and constructs and discusses the challenge for higher education in meeting the demands of a complex service economy.

P.P. Maglio et al. (eds.), *Handbook of Service Science*, Service Science: Research and Innovations in the Service Economy, DOI 10.1007/978-1-4419-1628-0_32,
© Springer Science+Business Media, LLC 2010

Introduction

Contemporary societies are widely described as service economies and the service sectors comprise the bulk of employment and value-added in most OECD (Organization for Economic Co-operation and Development) countries. Service occupations have risen to the fore across all sectors of the economy, and many firms in manufacturing and elsewhere take their "product services" (advice, after sales and services complementary to the material product) very seriously. Numerous manufacturers see such service activities and products as having displaced the focus on their traditional material product (Spring and Araujo, 2009). The perspective that "service" is the ultimate objective of economic activity has reoriented a great deal of management philosophy. This transformation – the new "service dominant logic" (Vargo and Lusch, 2004) challenges many established approaches and practices. It opens up topics requiring new knowledge, and highlights where existing knowledge should be coordinated and communicated more consistently and more widely via education and training.

The challenge for higher education is to develop a new 'service science' discipline (Horn, 2005) and to design curricula that meet the need of a future service economy. The task is complex, as it requires universities to consider not only future skills requirements but also combinations of skills in a range of future scenarios for work organization.

There are examples of service science programs emerging but many are based on single discipline thinking e.g. service marketing, while others are incremental development of existing programs. It is argued here that more attention should be paid to the design of curriculum to meet the complex needs of the service economy. Service science is inherently multidisciplinary but at the same time service firms need people with in-depth specialist knowledge and with a range of skill profiles. Not all firms have the same requirements, for example, knowledge intensive services, technical services, professional services and business related creative services all provide very different contexts for service education.

The changing nature of work organization presents further challenges for educators; increasing numbers of people working in services develop their skills through innovative project work where work processes are being constantly redesigned. Service activity is increasingly conducted through networks and project-based work with individuals and teams operating across organizational and national boundaries. The challenge for education is to design a curriculum that engenders qualities of flexibility, creativity, innovation and problem-solving, (Maglio and Spohrer, 2008), together with the ability to participate in multiple project teams.

Earlier work conducted at the University of Cambridge (IfM and IBM, 2007) discussed three possible approaches to developing service science as a discipline:

1. 'super' multi-disciplinary – embracing all appropriate, but yet not agreed, disciplines and functions
2. multi-disciplinary – embracing elements of the major disciplines and functions
3. Inter-disciplinary – attempting to unite various areas based on collaboration between disciplines.

This chapter contributes to the discussion on Service Science as a discipline by highlighting the future needs of European service industries and contributes to curriculum by linking future needs to educational constructs.

The chapter is in three parts, the first part describes the diversity of service, the different ways in which services can be generated and the range of service activities. Traditional definitions of service occupations are used to present an analysis of the current level of graduate employment across sectors. However traditional definitions of skills are based on the more technical elements of a job and the level of training required and are no longer adequate for the future service economy. Part two presents a forecast of the demand for higher level skills and knowledge, discusses a number of scenarios for future organization of work and classification of more complex skills profiles appropriate to the needs of the future economy. Part three discuss the challenge for higher education in responding to these needs and in making service science curriculum relevant and worthy of investment for both individual and company.

The Diversity of Service

Services can be generated and supplied in different ways. Much traditional service management is analysis concerned with human-to-human services, where the service interaction is largely between the client and a human service supplier. Human to human service systems inevitably involve more than just this interaction of two individuals – their architecture also involves a "servicescape" of dedicated buildings and physical infrastructure, or support by material tools (such as surgical, teaching, restaurant, and transport equipment). Increasingly service suppliers have moved to formats that link humans with IT systems. In these human-IT formats, people interact with and acquire services from workstations, websites and other IT agents and interfaces – whether or not human beings are involved at some point in approving, packing, dispatching, or delivering the core service. IT systems interact in IT system-to-IT system frameworks famously in "robot trading" in financial services, more familiarly in, for example, search engines automatically updating newsfeeds or other information requests, auction software automating eBay bidding, and so on. It is too simplistic to think that the movement is always from human-to-human to IT-IT services. Innovation often supports trends in this direction, but there are counter forces (for example, where "high-touch" is valued more than "high-tech") – and innovation can also produce new human-to-human services.

Services are very diverse, and across and within specific services sectors we find considerable variation in the types of service rendered and the means of service production. Within industries (in all sectors) we typically see a mix of the different sorts of service activities, organized into systems of production, regardless of whether the main final product is a good or service. While there are numerous ways of 'classifying services – producer/consumer/public services, for example, or "knowledge-intensive" versus "other" services (an approach currently popular with OECD and CEC analysts) – the efforts of statisticians to categorize services sectors provide a very useful starting point. The current industrial classification systems, such as the European Statistical Classification of Economic Activities (NACE), provide much richer accounts of service industries than did earlier frameworks such as the International System of Industrial Classification (ISIC). The highest-level categorization in NACE identifies nine "sections":

1. G: Wholesale and retail trade ("trade services"); plus repair of motor vehicles, motorcycles and personal and household goods.
2. H: Hotels and restaurants (often identified as HORECA – hotels, restaurants, catering).
3. I: Transport, storage and communication.
4. J: Financial intermediation.
5. K: Real estate, renting and business activities. (Often J and K are collapsed together for statistical analysis into the FIRE group. Note that the highly important Knowledge-Intensive Business Services – KIBS - are located here within "business activities")
6. L: Public administration and defence; compulsory social security.
7. M: Education
8. N: Health and social work.
9. Other community, social and personal service activities. (This includes many creative and cultural activities, some of which are KIBS.)

These industries are grouped together, despite being so diverse, because they originally fell into a "residual" sector. They are what was left over, once the statisticians in the mid-twentieth century had classified the sectors that they saw as the main wealth producers. But they do have more in common than not producing raw materials and tangible artifacts in the way that the primary and secondary sectors do. In addition to their common tendency to be concerned with intangible products, to be highly interactive with clients, and so on, we can characterize them in terms of the broad transformations effected. Service activities are typically transforming states, rather than creating raw materials (primary sector) or physical artifacts (secondary sector). Broadly, there are three major entities whose state is transformed by service processes:

1. **Physical artifacts**, that are moved, stored, maintained, manipulated – by services such as freight transport, repair and maintenance, warehousing, etc. The artifacts may be goods, buildings, even parks.
2. **People,** whose state of health, social welfare, and personal appearance is the central concern of some public and most personal services. Some services perform similar transformations for other biological entities, as in veterinary and some environmental services.
3. **Symbols,** where services are engaged in creating, communicating and processing data, providing and interpreting information, generating and reproducing knowledge – finance services process information about property rights, telecommunications services store and move information, consultancy services attempt to impart advice, and so on.

This simple threefold classification can be employed to differentiate between service industries, where we see both striking differences and commonalities in the types of technological innovation that are relevant to broad sets of services. In particular, across the aforementioned nine service sections, we see that IT plays a central role in information processing and in delivering informational services. Of course, this is particularly marked in those services – especially financial services, communications, and knowledge intensive businesses – whose essence is symbol-processing (Miles, 2008). Since all service sectors have information processes within their production processes (e.g. office work of various forms) and many services are at heart about producing and supplying information to end-users, IT-based innovation in and of services has attracted considerable attention in the both IT and service industries. It effectively became a catalyst for the growing efforts to establish a new discipline around service(s).

Much early work on services focused on relatively low-skill physical and personal services, such as hotels, restaurants and catering, where much "service management" and "service quality" work was traditionally located. Two points should be made here. First, the very different types of service involved in these industries as compared to, say, management consultancy or computer services, helps to explain the fragmentation of the service research field. Quite simply, there was often very little perception of common issues that could be fruitfully addressed. More recently we do see approaches to service quality – such as the SERVQUAL (Carman, 1990) assessment instruments – being applied and elaborated in fields such as ecommerce web pages, and we can anticipate further constructive diffusion of methods and concepts in the immediate and longer-term future.

Second, the important variation across services in terms of skills and knowledge is highlighted by these examples. Some services industries are among those characterized by the greatest proportion of low-skill workers in their labor forces.

This was often seen as part of the explanation for low productivity growth in services, and is probably one reason for the disdain with which service work is often regarded. In contrast, some other service industries are the sectors that are most knowledge-intensive in terms of the proportions of graduates in their labour forces, and we see very clear specifications from industrial sources that there is a very real need to access employees with skills in managing professionals and experts spanning a wide range of specialized knowledge bases. More evidence is required as to the nature of the skills required in many new service operations; there are major deficits in our frameworks for documenting skill profiles and capability requirements. Better understanding of skill requirements, and of how these may be managed, is a priority.

We need to recognize the diversity of foci and approaches, in order to constructively bridge and synthesize their contributions. At present work on services is extremely fragmented, with, for instance, more firm-level analysis of new service development being only occasionally taken on board in (typically more industry-level) service innovation studies. In this context it is interesting to note the appraisal that "the importance of service innovation is not matched by the sophistication of new service development practices and methodologies, in contrast with the variety and sophistication of methodologies for new product development. Much of the research about new service development is critical of current practice" (Ginzberg et al. 2007). This implies that the attention being given to service innovation as an important factor in growth and wellbeing (more remote economic analysis) is not matched by the attention given to how such innovation is, and might better be, conducted (more close-up management studies). We have much analysis of what service innovation management is not (rarely R&D and R&D-type management processes, for example), but much less positive evidence of the forms it takes in empirical circumstances. Yet this is central for the understanding of how service systems are evolving.

This pattern of fragmentation is typical across the bodies of literature examining services from the perspective of different disciplines, or exploring specific types of service in isolation. It has probably been reinforced not just by the diversity of service(s), but also by their relatively marginal position in most disciplines and statistics. It has taken a long time for assertions about the need for SSME, or to adopt a "service dominant logic", to gain much of an audience (Hunt, 2004). Indeed, it is possible to see a shift in debate, with service specialists arguing for the distinctiveness of services, and gradually moving toward a position which argues for a synthesis in approaches to service and manufacturing sectors and activities, reflecting in part the tendency for production chains to engage both services and goods, whatever their nominal final products. This is sometimes captured through use of terminology such as "product-service systems" (though since services can be products as well as activities, this is potentially confusing).

Firms of all types produce services for their internal consumption, and often for their customers and collaborators (from after-sales service to research support services). Service can be used to describe the work that one party undertakes for another (or for oneself, in the case of self-service), or the outcome of this work (the customer being transported, entertained, presented with a requested, repaired, stored or otherwise transformed artefact). The term "services" is even more ambiguous, being applied to firms and industries, as well as products and commodities, and activities and occupations. Service and services are thus remarkably diverse in terms of their occupational profiles: some are low skill activities, while others have the highest share of graduate employees of any sectors (see Figure 1: Occupational data from the UK Community Innovation Survey 2006, http://www.dti.gov.uk/iese/ecslist.htm)

Service work exists everywhere, across and in all sectors. Data derived from the UK Community Innovation Survey 2006 shown in Figure 1 gives an illustration of the proportions of graduates, as percentages of total employee numbers, employed within UK firms by Standard Industrial Classification (SIC) codes. The percentages are particularly striking in technology based and professional knowledge intensive business services. This survey (which is based on employers' responses) collects information about product and process innovation as well as organizational and marketing innovation during the three-year period 2004 to 2006 inclusive. Most questions cover new or significantly improved goods or services or the implementation of new or significantly improved processes, logistics or distribution methods.

Traditional definitions of skills that were based on the more technical elements of a job and the level of training required are no longer adequate to cover the full spectrum of the abilities needed to perform new roles. It is therefore apparent that the future "service economy" will require different skills and competencies across a wide range of professions (Miles, 2005). A challenge for educators and trainers is to "unbundle" what the required skills and competences are or will be and to respond with appropriate educational practice.

Forecasting the Demand for Future Skills

A recent study for the European Techno-Economic Policy Support Network (Miles et al 2009) was commissioned to consider the research needed to understand future skills needs in a presumed innovative European Services Sector. The study focused on those service activities that have been knowledge intensive service activities (KISA) in the light of technological innovation. The main objective of the study was to raise questions and map out where research is needed to better understand the future skills requirements in KISA. The concept of KISA is relatively new. Knowledge-Intensive Service Activities (KISA) are defined by the Organization for Economic Co-operation and Development OECD as 'the production and integration of service activities undertaken by firms in manufacturing or service sectors, in combination with manufactured outputs or as stand-alone services'. KISA can be provided by private enterprises or public sector organizations.

Typical examples include: R&D services, management consulting, IT services, human resource management services, legal services such as IP-related issues, accounting and financing services, and marketing services.

The concept of KISA has been introduced in part because of perceived limitations in the widely used construct KIBS – Knowledge-Intensive Business Services. KIBS are firms that specialize in producing services to support the business

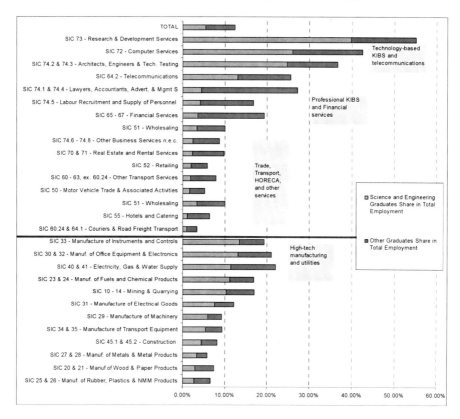

Figure 1. Occupational data from the UK Community Innovation Survey 2006
(from http://www.dti.gov.uk/iese/ecslist.htm)

processes of private firms and public organizations. They fall into three broad categories: i) technical services (computer support, R&D, engineering, industrial product and process design, etc.), ii) professional services (accountancy, legal services, market research), and iii) business-related creative services (advertising in particular, but also elements of architecture and design). The limitation of the KIBS construct is that it deals only with services provided by specialist firms and sold to other organizations and does not consider similar services provided in-house by employees within organizations across the economy. These in-house services are included in the KISA concept. Indeed most, if not all, professional jobs could be thought of as KISA.

Figures 2 and 3 show employment projections by sector and skill levels. They highlight an increasing need for highly skilled graduates in business, other and non-marketed services (e.g. voluntary services).

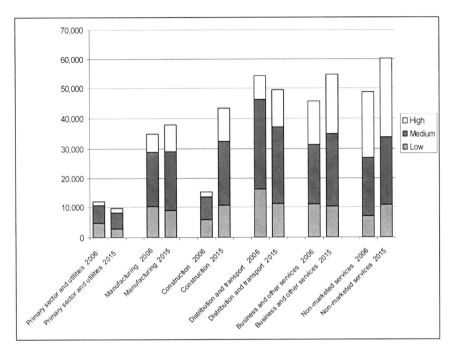

Figure 2. Employment projections by sector and skill levels: Absolute employment numbers and projections, three skill levels high, medium and low. (Elaborated from data in Tables 34a/34b pp 100-103: in, Future Skill needs in Europe Medium term Synthesis Report (2008), CEDEFOP, Luxembourg EC.)

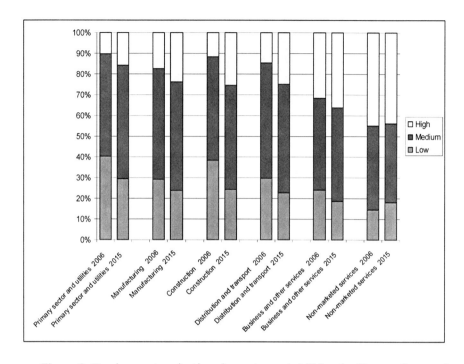

Figure 3. Employment projections by sector and skill levels: Shares of sectoral employment (%), three skill levels high, medium and low. (Elaborated from data in Tables 34a/34b pp 100-103: in, Future Skill needs in Europe Medium term Synthesis Report (2008), CEDEFOP, Luxembourg EC)

In forecasting skill demands the study found that basic modeling of trends in demand for specific professions, or for professional occupations more broadly, is possible. There have been both detailed assessments of quantitative trends in demand for a few professions (mainly ICT-related) and for professional occupations in general. In these cases the main approach has been to simply extrapolate trends or to estimate demand for employees as a consequence of general trends in economic growth and industrial structure. These "independent variables" are conditional on broad patterns of economic development, and recent financial shocks indicate that it is unwise to assume that steady long-term growth is the most probable future. Alternative lines of enquiry could examine changing skill requirements associated with established jobs (e.g. studies of future management skills) or economic sectors (e.g. professions in financial services).

An outcome of the study pointed to a number of drivers that are liable to shape the development of KISA jobs in the future. Broadly, the key drivers can be classified as:

1. The technologies in use for KISA, and the technologies where KISA support is required by clients
2. The organization of the KIBS sector, in terms of the roles of firms (specialization/integration), firm size, and the use of off-shoring
3. Demand for KISA on the part of clients, and client strategies (and management philosophies) in relation to internalization of KISA versus externalization to KIBS, to off-shoring internal KISA and/or using overseas KIBS, and moving into the commercial supply of KISAs to other firms
4. Factors affecting demand such as technological change, regulations, turbulence in markets and levels of economic growth and client firm internationalization
5. The availability and quality of training in KISA skills, modes of provision of training (on-the job and in formal institutions, life-long learning, etc.).

A further interesting outcome of the study concerned KISA in highly innovative service firms. Such firms have teams that produce work patterns, which are not easily formalized or reproducible under different circumstances (however highly specifiable the technical components of the system may be). These innovative service firms have to cope with knowledge spillover as a necessary consequence of the need to develop many aspects of an innovative new system simultaneously. Therefore, any benchmark procedure for evaluating qualifications and skills has to be flexible enough to cover such cases.

It is worth noting that an increasing number of people are employed in services where their skills are developed in and through innovative project work, within which the division of labor is never finalized before work processes are redesigned. The continual change of working practices presents a real challenge for curriculum and training development.

Miles and Jones (2008) identified three scenarios for organization of work associated with services: professional communities, situated clusters and organizational aggregates, each described briefly below.

Scenario 1: Professional Communities: Networking is predominantly organized on a bottom-up basis. Professionals come together to operate as virtual organizations around specific projects. Particular sets of professionals may often collaborate in this way, in changing configurations as projects succeed each other. Collaboration is based on trust, on reasons to believe in each other's competences, track records, originality, etc. Not all players in this scenario would be equal, let alone being single individuals. Some agents would be larger than others; some would act as system integrators, brokers, and clearing houses. But in this scenario, there are many such players, and power is widely dispersed. Professional Communities can be thought of as dynamic networks and can be either local or geographically extended.

Scenario 2: Situated Clusters: In this scenario there is considerable influence from initiatives undertaken by local governments and other regional actors. Such initiatives lower transaction costs, provide common facilities, and perhaps build on subsidies, procurement, and local comparative advantages. The networks make a lot of use of information technology to liaise and communicate, but the KISA professionals are typically familiar with each other on a face-to-face basis, they (mostly) inhabit the same urban area or region. (There may be mechanisms for collaboration across regional partners, especially where there is a common project or value-chain relation between the economies of the two areas.) Situated Clusters are typically 'local' and stable or static over a period of time.

Scenario 3: Organizational Aggregates: Here long-term strategic partnerships, largely constructed by large business organizations (or groups of organizations) are the basis for establishing networks and developing and diffusing common technologies and standards. Various sorts of business relationship are liable to coexist – ownership and spin-offs, joint ventures, collaboration in large projects for common clients (including public funding agencies), etc. The relationships may be mainly "vertically" organized around value chains, though other structures are possible (e.g. the East Asian zaibatsu and chaebol structures which cover many sectors of the economy). The larger players will play an important governance role, for example in making arrangements about intellectual property, about common tools and standards, and so on. Organizational Aggregates are extended networks but are typically stable or static over a period of time.

In conjunction with the three future scenarios that have been outlined, there is also a need to think about competencies – specific combinations of skills. While there are probably infinite combinations of specific skills, several ideal types of skill profile have been identified (Miles and Jones, 2008). Drawing on efforts to classify skills into various groups, research proposes that there are certain specific skills associated with particular KIBS specialism (accountancy, architecture, computing services, etc), and a range of generic skills associated with management of people, projects, inter-organizational and interpersonal relations, communications, and so on. (These are, admittedly, the specialism of some types of management profession – but they are not typically the activities supplied as services by a specialized KIBS firm to its clients). A set of skills profiles is shown as Figure 4:

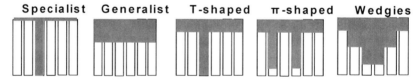

Specialist   Generalist   T-shaped   π-shaped   Wedgies

Figure 4. A Preliminary classification of skill profiles (Miles and Jones 2008).

1. **Specialist**   - this is the classic highly-specialized professional worker, with huge depth of skill in a particular technical domain – this might be law, computer software, architecture, etc. – but with relatively low levels of other skills required of professionals in the organization, such as project management, marketing, interpersonal communication, resource allocation, etc.
2. **Generalist**   - this is perhaps the classic general manager, with a broad range of skills but limited depth in any of them. Such an individual has more than lay knowledge of the specialties that characterize their organization's services, but is also skilled in the range of other activities mentioned above.
3. **T-shaped**   - this category considers emerging skills profiles: the industrialists in the workshop stated that they required people whose deep specialist knowledge was complemented with broader generalist knowledge than that of the specialist – people who could manage and market services as well as master the deep technical specificities.
4. **π-shaped**   - this hypothetical profile implies individuals who have deep knowledge of one or other of the management and other professional areas, in addition to deploying profound technical skills from a specific technical specialty.
5. **Wedgies**   – this profile lies between the Generalist, T-shaped, and pi-shaped categories: it features moderately deep knowledge of several fields, together with more detailed skills in a few, and generalist capabilities as well.

The discussion of profiles effects a helpful clarification of issues around skills and skill combinations, while demonstrating that there is still work required on establishing a framework that can effectively be used across sectors, occupations, and contexts. As skill clusters and the constituents of profiles are constantly being reconfigured by technological and organizational change there is clearly a requirement to avoid treating profiles in too static and rigid a way. In addition to seeing skill profiles and competences at the individual level, it is essential to be able to examine how different skills are put together in workplaces, organizations, groups and teams.

Each scenario also requires specific combinations of skills. Four key skills areas have emerged from recent research as i) generic and specialist skills, ii) managerial and entrepreneurial skills, iii) technical skills: information technology related, iv) technical skills: aspects of professional work other than information technology (Miles et al., 2009). Table 1 maps the skills requirements against the three scenarios identified.

This section has discussed the demand for future skills based on recent European employment projections by sector and by skills; on future scenarios for work organization and on future skills profiles. Forecasting demand is complex and requires further examination, none the less it is clear that there is a requirement for an adaptable, multi-skilled and highly knowledgeable workforce across a range of service sectors. The challenge for Higher Education is to translate that requirement into a coherent discipline and a portfolio of curricula

Table 1. Future Scenarios and Skills Requirements

Skills	Common Features	Scenarios		
		1 Professional Communities	2. Situated Clusters	3. Organizational Aggregates
Generic/Specialist Skills	Demand for some highly skilled professionals with advanced specialized technical skills; but more generally demand for multiskilled professionals (T- & π- shaped, and wedgies) with interpersonal and managerial capacities.	Relatively less demand for highly skilled professionals without generic skills, since key requirements are being able to find and fit into evolving teams.	Likely to vary across regions, with requirements for skills being typically between scenarios 1 and 3.	Relatively more demand for highly skilled professionals without generic skills, since they can be mobilized within larger organizations. Scope for higher division of labor means also more scope for associate professions to support advanced professionals. Multiskilled managers of specialist workers required.
Managerial & Entrepreneurial Skills	Generic skills in great demand reflecting need to bring together many tasks in complex arrangements.	Entrepreneurial skills; interpersonal and especially customer-facing skills important. Teamwork and self-organization vital.	Regions vary, depending on specialisation and quality of local decision-making. In general, closer to scenario 1 than scenario 3.	Ability to work within large organization and complex division of labour important.
Technical Skills: Information Technology-related	Increase demand in all scenarios, especially to extent that economic growth and technology change. If technological change slows down, then some specialist technology-related skills should be less	IT-related skills (including those of users of IT systems) are needed on a wide basis, with capability to work with open standards, and design and integrate systems for one's own work, becoming a premium.	In some regions, IT support provided as a service to clusters on a semi-public service basis; growth in need for user skills may then be diminished.	Slower growth in need for user skills as advanced IT-based support systems diffused within organizational networks (though liable to be learning periods where assimilation of new systems requires more skill than anticipated).

Innovation and Skills 731

	in demand, as these become more part of general competences.			
Technical Skills: Aspects of Professional work other than IT	In all scenarios, increasing demand for advanced professional skills, resulting from challenges and specialized knowledge associated with technical, organizational, and broader socioeconomic change.	Deep knowledge required, but also capacity to combine knowledge from various domains and effect new creative solutions – possibly π-shaped professionals particularly relevant.	In less successful regions, more routine KISA and professional work requirements might dominate; in more successful regions, model might be more similar to scenario 1.	Increased efficiency-led division of labor and in particular introduction of para- and associate professional support to professional workers. Effort to capture specialist knowledge in IT-based support systems.

The Challenge for Higher Education

Education is targeted at the individual with the goal of helping the person to achieve transformation from current levels of knowledge, understanding and capabilities to some future level. The challenge for the educator is to design programmes that meet the needs of the individual as well as the needs of the economy. It is argued here that three major sets of factors should be considered when designing future curriculum (i) the context of the future work settings into which the individual may be placed upon graduation (ii) the content of the material to be taught and the way the material will be delivered that will lead to the individual acquiring appropriate knowledge and skills and (iii) the construct through which learning will occur to enable the individual to move forward from their current level of attainment to the next level.

Context takes account of the future scenarios for work organization and the situations in which service science professionals will operate:

- professionals coming together to operate as virtual organizations around specific projects, within dynamic networks
- professionals working within situated clusters within regions, often within small or medium sized organizations and within networks that are stable over time

- professionals working within long-term strategic partnerships, within large organizations, in extended networks that are typically stable over time.

Each of the scenarios has implications for curriculum design. For example, working in geographically dispersed teams, understanding of inter-organizational working, cultural differences, or knowledge of how networks form and operate.

Particular programs may focus on one scenario to meet the needs of particular groups of individuals, but explicitly addressing the context of future scenarios will help to overcome one of the areas of complexity of service science curriculum design.

The content of the curriculum focuses on the need to design curriculum that meets future knowledge and skills requirements. Glushko (2008) distinguishes between service science as a new discipline or as a new curriculum.

'A discipline is an integrated field of study defined by some level of agreement about what problems are worth studying, how they should be studied, and the criteria by which findings or theories about those problems can be evaluated.' (Glushko, 2008).

Whereas a curriculum is 'a program of study to instil in students some specified body of knowledge or skills' (Glushko, 2008).

Ideally the discipline should come first with major stakeholders agreeing on the body of knowledge, then the curriculum or program of study should follow. In the case of service science there has been a push for curriculum before the key tenets of the discipline have been established or at best they are being defined in tandem.

From the earlier discussion four key areas can be identified:

- The need for multi-skilled individuals with both generic skills and specialist skills.
- The need for people with managerial and entrepreneurial skills, customer facing skills, self organization, team working and interpersonal skills
- the need for people with high levels of both technical skills in IT and profession specific skills
- Service specific knowledge and understanding, for example, of service concepts, methods, systems. Key concepts would include, for example, the service-centered conceptual foundation proposed by Lusch and others (Lusch et al., 2008), service systems as the basic abstraction of service science (Spohrer et al. 2008), service life cycle (Glushko, 2008), and appropriate research methods.

Figure 5 illustrates the service science curriculum content. As discussed in Table 1 the specific requirement for each of these may depend on the scenario and hence curriculum content should be viewed within context.

Educational constructs are internationally understood mechanisms for delivering education to individuals. Key constructs include:

- **Undergraduate** (UG) for developing knowledge and understanding of key principles within in a particular subject
- **Specialist Masters** (MSc) for developing further in-depth understanding within a particular subject area
- **Master of Business Administration** (MBA) for providing a broader understanding of theory and practice within a the business context
- **Executive MBA** for developing further specialist knowledge and understanding linked to specific work practice and requirements
- **Post-experience Masters and Continued Professional Development** Certificates and Diplomas to consolidate and enhance workplace practice and experience
- **Doctoral in Business Administration** (DBA) to conduct in-depth research and discovery within a business context and to contribute to business knowledge
- **Doctor of Philosophy** (PhD) to conduct in-depth research within a specialist subject domain and to contribute original research to that domain.

Each educational construct will typically deliver differing levels of awareness, knowledge, understanding, practical project work, experiential learning, workplace practice and research as shown in Table 2.

These educational constructs can be offered to individuals to help achieve transformation into one or more of the skills profiles identified in Figure 4. Table 3 shows which combinations of constructs will help to deliver the range of profiles

Table 2. Educational constructs and level of awareness, knowledge and understanding

Target market/ Level	UG	Masters	MBA	Exec MBAs	PhD/DBA	Post MSc
Awareness	Yes	Yes	Yes	Yes	Yes	Yes
Knowledge/ understanding	Yes	Yes	Yes	Yes	Yes	Yes
Practical project/experiential learning	Yes	Yes	Yes		Yes	
Workplace practice			Yes	Yes		Yes
Research and innovation					Yes	

Table 3. Relationship between educational construct and skills profiles

Skills profile versus Constructs	New-entrant	Specialist	Generalist	T-shaped	Pi-shaped	Wedgies
Undergraduate	X	X	X	X	X	X
Master	X	X		X	X	X
MBA			X	X	X	X
Executive MBA					X	X
Post-experience Masters		X				
DBA					X	X
Phd		X				

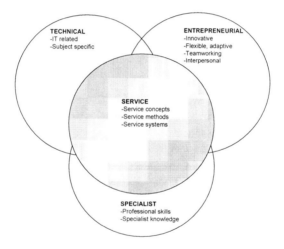

Figure 5. Curriculum Content, adapted from 'A Framework for Service Science Curriculum' 2008, http://www.ssmenetuk.org/docs/ ssme_framework.pdf (BT, HP and IBM, 2007)

One implication of Table 3 is that to achieve the 'T', 'Pi' or 'wedgies' skills profile an individual must have many years of education and experience. Davis (2008) describes business schools today as 'organized by functional departments-such as marketing, finance, and accounting and operations management – with little interaction between them'. This picture is replicated across many university schools leading to 'silo' curriculum and thus an individual must attend courses in a number of separate schools/departments in order to achieve a multidisciplinary skills profile. Despite continued efforts by Maglio et al. (2006) and IfM and IBM (2007) the need for defining the service science discipline and consequent curriculum is still urgent in order to reduce the amount of time taken to transform a traditionally educated individual into a multi-skilled adaptable service scientist.

Conclusions

The findings of the Cambridge workshop still hold true, that: *'The gaps in knowledge and skills needed to deal with complex service systems indicate that we need to reassess our approach to research and education.'* (IfM and IBM, 2008).

This chapter adds to the discussion by exploring some of the complexities associated with future skills identification, highlighting the context specific requirements of the service industry and identifying the skills profiles required by future service organizations.

Understanding the context of service science education would be greatly aided by a higher level of involvement of public and private sector organizations with universities and by greater attention to the outputs of skills forecasting bodies such as the OECD.

Articulating content for university programs depends of the development of the discipline as a whole and should be research led for example through university research centers and the Service, Research and Innovation Community (www.thesrii.org). There is clearly a need for a community of practice for academics and practitioners to co-create and exchange curriculum content such as that being developed through IBM's Academic Initiative in SSME. New educational constructs may need to be explored to speed up the delivery of service science education, for example, through continued professional development in the workplace, through e-learning or through immersive 3D worlds.

Existing systems of vocational training, professional and academic education and accreditation are the results of deeply embedded systems of governance and widely differing structures of society and the economy. It can be argued that the current approach to service science education is itself product led as it is designed from a university perspective using existing educational products such as MBA. What new service-oriented educational constructs can be envisaged that are more relevant to the complex, ever changing service economy?

This chapter identifies the need for demand-led education that provides the skills and knowledge necessary for the future service economy. The challenge for Higher Education is to make service science curriculum relevant and worthwhile for both the individual and the company to invest in.

References

BT, HP and IBM. (2008). A framework for service science curricula. SSMENetUK Curriculum Conference, University of Manchester, UK.
http://www.ssmenetuk.org/docs/ssme_framework.pdf. Accessed 16 June 2009

Carman, J.M. (1990). Consumer perceptions of service quality: An assessment of SERVQUAL dimensions. *Journal of Retailing*, 66(1), 33-55.

Davis, M. M. and Berdrow, I. (2008). Service science: catalyst for change in business school curricula. *IBM Systems Journal, 47(1), 29-39.*

Ginzburg, I., Higgins, A., and Lichtenstein, Y. (2007). Looking for the Locus of Innovation in New Service Development. *Proceedings of the 40th Hawaii International Conference on System Sciences*. Hawaii, USA, IEEE Computer Society, 230-236.

Glushko, R. J. (2008). Designing a service science discipline with discipline. *IBM Systems Journal, 47*(1), 15-27.

Horn   P.   (2005).   The   New   Discipline   of   Services   Science
http://www.u.arizona.edu/~jlzhao/SIRE/Busienssweek%20Jauary%2021%202005%20Servic es%20Science.pdf. Accessed June 16, 2009

Hunt, S. D. (2004). On the Service-Centered Dominant Logic of Marketing. *Journal of Marketing, 68*, 18-27.

IfM and IBM. (2007). Succeeding *through Service Innovation: A Discussion Paper.* Cambridge, United Kingdom: University of Cambridge Institute for Manufacturing. ISBN: 978-1-902546-59-8

Lusch, R.F., Vargo S.L., and Wessels, G. (2008). Toward a conceptual foundation for service science: Contributions from service-dominant logic. *IBM Systems Journal: Service Science, Management, and Engineering, 47*(1), 5-13.

Maglio, P. P. and Spohrer, J. (2008). Fundamentals of Service *Journal of the Academy of Marketing Science* 36, 18-20.

Maglio, P. P., J. Kreulen, S. Srinivasan, and J. Spohrer.(2006). Service systems, service scientists, SSME, and innovation. *Communications of the ACM* 49(7), 81 – 85.

Miles, I., 2008. Patterns of innovation in service industries. *IBM Systems Journal*, 12 (1), 115-120.

Miles, I. and B. Jones. (2008). Innovation in the European service economy - scenarios and implications for skills and knowledge, European Techno-Economic Policy Support Network. http://www.eteps.net/projects.htm. Accessed 16 June, 2009.

Miles, I. (2005). Knowledge intensive business services: prospects and policies, *Foresight,* 7(6), 39-63.

Spohrer, J, P. P. Maglio, J. Bailey, D. Gruhl. (2007). Toward a Science of Service Systems. *Computer*, 40(1), 71-77

Spring, M. and Araujo, L. (2009). Service, services and products: rethinking operations strategy. *International Journal of Operations and Production Management*, 29(5), 444-467.

Vargo, S. L. and R. F. Lusch. (2004a). Evolving to a New Dominant Logic for Marketing. *Journal of Marketing,* 68 (January), 1-17.

Author Index

A

Aarflot, U., 103
Abbot, A., 684, 695
Abe, N., 458
Abernathy, W. J., 584, 586, 599
Abowd, G., 247
Achrol, R., 3, 6, 145, 154
Ackerman, M., 451, 458, 460
Adamic, L., 460
Addis, T. R., 672, 674
Agar, M., 286, 304
Aguilar-Escobar, V. G., 309, 318
Aho, K., 322, 357
Akaka, M. A., 2–4, 8, 133–134, 156,
    165, 172, 174–175, 193, 385, 642
Akner, G., 634, 641
Aksoy, L., 24–25, 27, 29
Alam, I., 566, 568, 570, 576
Alba, R., 451, 458
Alces, P., 613, 621
Alder, K., 421, 434
Alic, J., 166–167, 190
Allee, V., 467, 479, 683, 696
Allison, J., 654, 661
Allmendinger, G., 233, 246
Al-Sabt, M., 248
Alter, S., 169, 171, 177, 179, 188, 482,
    503–504, 685, 696
Altshuler, Y., 460
Alvine, M. J., 100
American Law Institute, 618, 620–621
Amin, A., 553, 556
Amoako-Gyampah, K., 309, 316,
    318–319
Amory, C., 285, 305
AMR, 439, 458
Anderson, E. W., 37, 57
Anderson, H., 285, 304
Anderson, J. C., 168, 188, 360, 367,
    381–382, 390, 413, 565, 576,
    681, 696
Anderson Healy, K., 261, 281
Andreassen, T. W., 25, 29
Ang, J., 190
Anthony, S. D., 379–380, 383

Antonides, G., 218
Apple, 230, 246
Apte, U., 220, 225, 247, 419–420,
    427–429, 434
Araujo, L., 718, 736
Archer, T., 568, 577
ArchiMate Forum, 258, 281
Argote, L., 324, 357
Ariely, D., 171, 189, 565, 577,
    654, 661
Armstrong, A., 226, 247, 628
Arnold, A., 457–458, 666
Arnould, E. J., 203, 217, 383
Arsanjani, A., 190
Arthur, W. B., 467–468, 479
Arundel, A., 520, 522–524, 528, 531
ArXiv.org, 660–661
Ash, R. C., 309, 318
Asubonteng, P., 516, 528
Aunger, R., 649, 661

B

Baars, H., 233, 247
Baba, M. L., 169, 171, 192, 463, 480
Babbar, S., 310, 318
Bacon, R., 86, 89, 100
Bailey, J., 3–4, 7, 20, 29, 59, 103, 156,
    172, 174, 177, 179, 191, 193, 249,
    283, 290, 304, 318, 385, 558, 697,
    736
Bailey, M., 318
Baines, 393, 413
Baldwin, C. Y., 589, 595, 599
Ballantyne, D., 164, 189, 628, 641
Banavar, G., 5, 481
Baran, R., 248
Barash, M. M., 473, 479
Barber, F., 211, 217
Barbera, K., 50, 58–59
Barcet, A., 548, 556
Barney, J., 397, 413
Baron, J., 519, 528
Barras, R., 516, 528, 545, 556, 585,
    599
Bartels, R., 646, 661

Subject Index

Breinigsville, PA USA
06 May 2010
237446BV00004B/2/P

9 781441 916273